PERSPECTIVES

on Contemporary Issues

Readings Across the Disciplines

FOURTH EDITION

Katherine Anne Ackley
University of Wisconsin at Stevens Point

THOMSON
——————————— TM
WADSWORTH

Australia • Canada • Mexico • Singapore • Spain • United Kingdom • United States

For the newlyweds in our family
Robin and Terry
Jon and Laurie

THOMSON
WADSWORTH

Perspectives on Contemporary Issues: Readings Across the Disciplines,
Fourth Edition
Katherine Anne Ackley

Publisher: Michael Rosenberg
Acquisitions Editor: Dickson Musslewhite
Development Editor: Edward Dodd III
Editorial Assistant: Cheryl Forman
Technology Project Manager: Cara Douglass-Graff
Exec. Marketing Manager: Carrie Brandon
Advertising Project Manager: Patrick Rooney
Project Manager, Editorial Production:
  Brett Palana-Shanahan
Manufacturing Supervisor: Marcia Locke

Permissions Editor: Bob Kauser
Production Services and Text Design:
  Hearthside Publishing Services
Photo Manager: Sheri Blaney
Photo Researcher: Jill Engebretson
Cover Designer: Gina Petti
Compositor: ATLIS Graphics & Design
Printer: Malloy Incorporated
Cover Art: Photo of India. © Yann
  Arthus-Bertrand/Altitute

For more information about our products,
contact us at:
Thomson Learning Academic Resource Center
1-800-423-0563
For permission to use material from this text
or product, submit a request online at
http://www.thomsonrights.com
Any additional questions about permissions can be
submitted by e-mail to **thomsonrights@thomson.com**

Library of Congress Control Number: 2005920368

Student Edition: ISBN 1-4130-1068-7

Instructor's Edition: ISBN 1-4130-1854-8

Thomson Higher Education
25 Thomson Place
Boston, MA 02210-1202
USA

Asia (including India)
Thomson Learning
5 Shenton Way
#01-01 UIC Building
Singapore 068808

Australia/New Zealand
Thomson Learning Australia
102 Dodds Street
Southbank, Victoria 3006
Australia

Canada
Thomson Nelson
1120 Birchmount Road
Toronto, Ontario M1K 5G4
Canada

UK/Europe/Middle East/Africa
Thomson Learning
High Holborn House
50-51 Bedford Road
London WC1R 4LR
United Kingdom

Latin America
Thomson Learning
Seneca, 53
Colonia Polanco
11560 Mexico
D.F. Mexico

Spain (including Portugal)
Thomson Parainfo
Calle Magallanes, 25
28015 Madrid, Spain

CONTENTS

Chapter 10   The Arts   290

PART THREE   Social and Behavioral Sciences   319

Chapter 11   Education   321

PREFACE

Perspectives on Contemporary Issues: Readings Across the Disciplines, Fourth Edition, presents an approach to thinking, reading, and writing that views learning as the interconnectedness of ideas and disciplinary perspectives. Contemporary issues engage the students, while the readings provide rich material for both class discussion and writing topics. The essays focus on individual, national, and global issues by authors from a variety of disciplines and professions. Likewise, the writing assignments enhance the skills that students will use, regardless of their majors.

The goals of *Perspectives on Contemporary Issues: Readings Across the Disciplines* are

- to sharpen students' thinking skills by presenting them with a variety of perspectives on current issues;
- to give students practice in both oral and verbal expression, by providing questions for discussion and writing after each selection;
- to provide students with a variety of writing assignments representing the kinds of writing they will be asked to do in courses across the curriculum; and
- to encourage students to view issues and ideas in terms of connections with other people, other disciplines, or other contexts.

The questions for discussion and writing encourage critical thinking by asking students to go well beyond simple recall of the readings and to use higher-order skills such as integration, synthesis, or analysis of what they have read. Most of the questions are suitable for work in small groups, as well as for class discussion.

NEW TO THIS EDITION

New Chapters

There are three new chapters in this edition:

Chapter 4: Writing an Argument. Because so many of the suggestions for writing that accompany the readings ask students to argue, a separate chapter provides detailed guidelines on argumentation as well as sample student and professional papers.

This new chapter represents a significant expansion of discussion of argumentation than in previous editions of the book.

Chapter 17: America Abroad in Political Science.   This new chapter contains readings reflecting or commenting on the perception from abroad of America in a political context.

Chapter 25: The Economic Impact of Outsourcing.   The chapter called "The American Image Abroad" in previous editions has been replaced with a new chapter more directly related to business and economics. This new chapter, "The Economic Impact of Outsourcing," has readings on the effects of outsourcing, both positive and negative.

Photos/Graphics

Responding to Visuals.   Each chapter in Parts Two to Five concludes with a new section entitled *Responding to Visuals,* which features two photographs or images related to the theme of the chapter. The images are accompanied by questions for discussion or suggestions for writing. Because of this new feature, Chapter 1, "Reading Critically," includes a lengthy section on the rhetorical analysis of visuals.

E-Readings Online.   Readings available in InfoTrac® College Edition, the Internet database that Thomson Wadsworth sponsors, are listed in a new section at the end of each major part in Parts Two to Five. For each chapter in the part, students are directed to three or four articles in the database, all on a single topic related to that chapter. Each cluster of readings is followed by questions for discussion and suggested writing topics.

New Readings.   There are 45 new readings, almost all of them published in the early 2000s. Many of the older readings from the third edition have been dropped. Among the new readings are essays that focus on topics of recent interest, such as the death penalty, terrorism and war, bioethical issues, and globalization. In addition, the classic essay "A Modest Proposal" by Jonathan Swift is included in the chapter on poverty and homelessness. A couple of chapters from the previous edition, "Terrorism and War" (chapter 16) and "Digital Technology and the Internet" (chapter 18, previously called "Computers and Cyberspace"), have been updated with all new readings.

Expanded Discussion of Evaluating Internet Sources.   This edition includes more discussion of and guidelines for evaluating Internet sources. Listservs and blogs are included in this expanded section (see chapter 1).

READING SELECTIONS

The reading selections are divided into four sections within the book, representing four broad disciplinary areas: the arts and media studies, the social sciences, the natural sciences, and business and economics. Within each broad division are chapters on specific topics related to the larger subject. Part Two, The Arts, Media Studies, and Popular Culture, contains chapters with readings on music and video games, media violence, advertising, Hollywood films, television, and the visual arts. In Part Three, Social and Behavioral Sciences, the chapters address such matters as education, poverty and homelessness, criminal behavior, gender and sex roles, race and ethnicity, terrorism, and war. In Part Four, Science and Technology, writers from a variety of disciplines explore such subjects as the relationships among science, technology, and society; public-health issues; computers and digital technology; the ethical implications of technology and human genetic experimentation; and science and the imagination. Finally, in Part Five, Business and Economics, the essays address marketing and the American consumer, the work place, the economic impact of outsourcing, and the United States in the global marketplace.

The selections in each chapter encourage students to consider issues from different perspectives because their authors come from a wide range of disciplinary backgrounds and training. Sometimes the writers cross disciplinary lines in their essays. For example, a chemist explores the metaphor of discovery, and a historian extols the virtues of reading. The individual perspectives of the writers may differ markedly from students' own perspectives, thus generating discussion and writing topics.

ACTIVITIES AND ASSIGNMENTS

Following each selection, students have an opportunity to make a *Personal Response* to some aspect of the reading. Each reading is also followed by several *Questions for Class or Small-Group Discussion.* These questions invite students to consider rhetorical strategies of the piece, to think of larger implications, to discuss related issues, or to make connections between the readings and their own experiences. Many of these questions are appropriate for writing topics as well, and many others will prompt students to discover related topics on which to write.

The selections in each chapter are followed by a section called *Perspectives on . . .* , which provides writing topics based on ideas generated by the collected readings in that chapter. These writing assignments are arranged in two categories:

- *Suggested Writing Topics* suitable for synthesis, argumentation, and other modes of writing such as the report, the letter, the personal essay, and the comparison and contrast essay; and
- *Research Topics* suitable for development into research papers.

Finally (as mentioned previously), each chapter in Parts Two through Five concludes with a new section, *Responding to Visuals,* which features two photographs or other visual images. These images relate to the thematic focus of the chapter and are accompanied by questions on rhetorical strategies and other relevant matters.

Given the title of this textbook, a definition of "issues" is in order. An issue is usually taken to mean a topic that is controversial, that prompts differences of opinion, or that can be seen from different perspectives. It often raises questions or requires taking a close look at a problem. While this is not primarily an argument textbook, the inclusion of topics and essays guaranteed to spark controversy is deliberate. Many of the readings will surely prompt students to take opposing positions. Some of the readings are provocative; others may anger students. Such differences of opinion will not only generate lively class discussions, but they will also result in writing opportunities that engage students.

ACKNOWLEDGMENTS

I would like to thank the following reviewers for their helpful suggestions on revisions to the new edition:

Valerie K. Anderson, *York College, The City University of New York*
Bim Angst, *Penn State Schuykill*
M. Susan Bonifer, *Mountain State University*
Robert Brown, *Champlain College*
Charlene Bunnell, *University of Delaware*
Joan Canty, *Columbia College*
Edward Carmien, *Westminster Choir College of Rider University*
Jo Cavins, *North Dakota State University*
N. Bradley Christie, *Erskine College*
Judith Cortelloni, *Lincoln College*
Robert Con Davis-Undiano, *University of Oklahoma*
Stacey Donohue, *Central Oregon Community College*
Clark L Draney, *Idaho State University*
Sarah Duerden, *Arizona State University*
David Elias, *Eastern Kentucky University*
Virginia Fambrough, *Baker University*
James Gifford, *Mohawk Valley Community College*
Keith Hale, *South Texas Community College*
Letitia Harding, *University of the Incarnate Word*
M. Hunter Hayes, *University of Southern Mississippi*
Kathy Henkins, *Mt. San Antonio College*
Hyo-Chang Hong, *Marshall University*
Elizabeth Huston, *Eastfield College*
William T. Hyndman, III, *Rosemont College*
Karen R. Jacobs, *Louisiana Tech University*
Margaret Johnson, *Idaho State University*
Joyce Kessel, *Villa Maria College*

James Kirpatrick, *Central Piedmont Community College*

Mary Kramer, *University of Massachusetts, Lowell*

Linda Lawliss, *College of the Desert*

Jun Liu, *California State University, Los Angeles*

Jeanette Lugo, *Valdosta State University*

Christopher Mattson, *Keene State College*

James McNamara, *Alverno College*

Brett J. Millan, *South Texas Community College*

Deborah Montuori, *Shippensburg University*

Rosemary Moore, *Iowa Western Community College*

Sean Nighbert, *St. Philip's College*

Debbie Ockey, *Fresno City College*

Debbie Olson, *Central Washington University*

Marc Prinz, *Hofstra University*

Louise Rosenberg, *University of Hartford*

Kiki Leigh Rydell, *Montana State University*

Daniel Schenker, *University of Alabama in Huntsville*

Judith Schmitt, *Macon State College*

Marilyn Schultz, *Delta State University*

Allison D. Smith, *Middle Tennessee State University*

Harvey Solganick, *LeTourneau University*

Shannon C. Stewart, *Coastal Carolina University*

Rosalee Stilwell, *Indiana University of Pennsylvania*

Steve Street, *The State University of New York*

William Tashman, *Baruch College, The City University of New York*

Tiffany Trent, *Virginia Polytechnic Institute and State University*

Sandi Ward, *West Virginia University*

Gwen Wilkinson, *University of Texas at San Antonio*

As always, I thank my family for their support: my daughters Heather Schilling and Laurel Yahi and son Jeremy White as well as my sons-in-law Brian Schilling and Gianni Yahi and daughter-in-law Jenni White. My grandchildren Elizabeth and Lucas Schilling, Zack and Celia Yahi, and Che White were a delightful distraction. I dedicate this edition of the book to my step-children Robin Ackley-Fay and her husband Terry Fay and Jon and Laurie Ackley. Both couples were married during the year this book was in production.

I am grateful to my colleagues in the English Department at the University of Wisconsin at Stevens Point. In particular, Tom Bloom and Ann Bloom shared their suggestions on writing an opinion paper, which I have incorporated into the discussion of the research paper, and Don Pattow, former Director of Freshman English, gave me materials on writing across the curriculum. I also want to thank the following students in my English classes who gave permission to use material from their research papers: Erin Anderson, Rita Fleming, Nathan Hayes, Missy Heiman, Linda Kay Jeske, Kari Kolb, Steph Niedermair, Barbara Novak, Shawn Ryan, Jodi Simon, Jennifer Sturm, and Cory L. Vandertie.

Finally, heartfelt gratitude goes to my editor, Edward Dodd III, who was truly a pleasure to work with. He provided wonderful guidance and insightful comments at every stage of the development of the book.

PART ONE

WRITING CRITICALLY AND CONDUCTING RESEARCH

CHAPTER

1

READING CRITICALLY

READING CRITICALLY IN PREPARATION FOR WRITING CRITICALLY

Critical reading does not necessarily mean that you object to what someone has written or that you view it negatively. Rather, it means that you read something carefully, thoughtfully, and thoroughly for two reasons: first, to understand it, and second, to assess it. You read for meaning first because, obviously, you must understand what you read before it can be examined. Once you develop a clear understanding of a piece of writing, you have a solid basis for moving beyond comprehension to evaluation.

Reading critically involves examining an author's ideas and the evidence the author has supplied in support of those ideas. It means that you try to recognize the difference between reasonable, logical assertions and those that are unreasonable or lack credibility. It requires you to distinguish between fact and opinion, to sort out the evidence an author cites, and to evaluate that evidence in terms of its relevance, accuracy, and importance. Thus, reading critically means that you actively engage in what you read, that you analyze it, and that you evaluate it. Learning to be a critical reader also helps to make you a better writer. If you pay attention to the ways in which professional writers and scholars use language, structure their essays, and develop their ideas, you will learn some valuable lessons for your own writing.

The following guidelines are not ironclad rules for reading critically, but they are useful suggestions to help you get the most from your reading. These reading guidelines will also be very helpful for any kind of writing required in your college courses, especially the one for which you are using this textbook. If you read the assigned selections carefully, you will very likely be fully prepared to write on one of the topics that end each chapter. Certainly, reading critically is a necessity for any of the varieties of writing discussed in the remaining chapters in part 1: summary, critique, argument, synthesis, and research paper.

Read the Title.   Before you read, consider the title. A title often not only reveals the subject of the piece, but it can also tell you something about the way in which the subject will be treated. It may reflect the tone of the piece and sometimes indicates the author's position on the subject. A number of essays in this textbook have revealing titles. For instance, the title "Don't Ignore the Arts" in chapter 10 clearly indicates that its author, Harold M. Williams, thinks highly of the arts. You cannot tell from the title alone the context of his plea, but you can expect an argument or a plea for the inclusion of arts in whatever that context is. Similarly, the title "Stop Blaming Kids and TV" in chapter 9 indicates that the subject will be young people and television viewing and that the author believes they are being unfairly blamed for something—though what that is will not be clear until you read the essay. Sometimes authors ask questions in their titles, as in "TV Violence: Does It Cause Real-Life Mayhem?" (chapter 9). As readers, we assume that the author of that essay, Susan R. Lamson, answers the question she poses in her title. There is no indication in that title, however, of how she answers it.

Find Out About the Author.   If information about the author is provided, read it. Knowing who the author is, what his or her publications are, and what his or her profession is, for example, gives you an idea of the authority from which the author writes. In magazines, journals, and collections of essays, such as those you will use in many of your college courses, the headnote often tells you about the author. The headnote is the information located between the title and the beginning of the essay, usually highlighted or set off from the body of the essay itself. Here is the headnote for George Henderson's "Race in America" (chapter 15):

> George Henderson is Director of Advanced Studies and former Dean of the College of Liberal Arts at the University of Oklahoma, where he is also a professor of human relations, education, and sociology. Henderson has served as a race-relations consultant to many national and international organizations. He is author of more than 70 articles and 29 books, including *Cultural Diversity in the Workplace* (1994); *Social Work Interventions: Helping People of Color* (1994); *Migrants, Immigrants and Slaves* (1995); *Human Relations Issues in Management* (1996); *Our Souls to Keep: Black/White Relations in America* (1999), and *Ethnicity and Substance Abuse* (2002). He also co-edited, with Grace Xuequin Ma, *Rethink Ethnicity and Health Care: A Sociocultural Perspective* (1999). This essay appeared in a special issue on race in America in the Spring 2000 issue of *National Forum.*

The information in the first sentence about his professional appointments as director of an academic program and former university dean and, perhaps more importantly, his academic areas as a professor indicate his qualification to write as a professional on a subject related to his academic background. The next sentence, about his service as a race-relations consultant, provides further evidence of his qualifications to write on racial issues. Finally, the titles of his books reveal that he has the experience to write with some authority on the subject of race in America.

Determine the Purpose.   Good writers have clear purposes in mind as they plan and draft their writing. Most nonfiction writing falls into the categories of persuasive, expository, and expressive writing. These forms of writing are used to achieve different goals, and they adopt different strategies for achieving those goals. In persuasive writing, the emphasis is on the reader: The writer's purpose is to convince the reader of the validity of his or her position on an issue and sometimes even to move the reader to action. In expository writing, the goal is to inform or present an objective explanation. The emphasis is on ideas, events, or objects themselves, not on how the writer feels about them. Much of the writing in college textbooks is expository, as are newspaper, magazine, and professional-journal articles, and nonfiction books. Expository writing can take many forms, including cause–effect analysis, comparison/contrast, definition, and classification. Expressive writing emphasizes the writer's feelings and subjective view of the world. The writer's focus is on personal feelings about, or attitude toward, the subject. A journal or diary includes expressive writing. Persuasive, expository, and expressive writing often overlap, but usually a writer has one main purpose. From the opening paragraphs of a written work, you should be able to determine its general purpose or aim. A clearly implied or stated purpose helps the writer to shape the writing, and it helps the reader to understand and evaluate the work.

Try to Determine the Intended Audience.   Writers make assumptions about the people they are writing for, and these assumptions influence the tone they use; the evidence they select; the way in which they organize and develop their writing; and even their sentence structure, word choices, and diction level. Knowing whom the writer is addressing helps you to understand the writer's point of view and to explain the choices the writer has made in writing the piece. In writing for college courses, students usually assume a general audience of people like themselves who are reasonably intelligent and interested in what they have to say. However, professional writers or scholars often write for specific audiences, depending on the publications in which their writing appears. Writers want to know if their audiences will be sympathetic or opposed to their positions. Knowing the likely positions of readers helps the writer to make decisions about what tone to use and what details to include.

Knowing whether an audience is familiar with a subject or whether the audience is specialized or general also governs what kind of evidence to offer and how much to include. Where the writing is published gives you a good idea of who the audience is. Take, for instance, the essays by Susan R. Lamson and Mike Males in chapter 9. You know from the headnote that accompanies "TV Violence: Does It Cause Real-Life Mayhem?" that the piece was first published in *American Hunter*. Readers of *American Hunter* very likely would support those who blame the high rate of violent crime in America on television violence, rather than on the ready availability of guns in America. When you combine the knowledge of who Susan R. Lamson is writing for with the information that she is director of federal affairs for the National Rifle Association, you can guess that she will answer "yes" to the question she poses in her title. Similarly, knowing that Mike Males' essay, "Stop Blaming Kids and TV," was first published in *The Progressive,* it is fair to assume that readers of the magazine share the magazine's mission, which is, according to its website (http://www.progressive.org), to be "a journalistic voice for peace and social justice at home and abroad." Males probably anticipated an audience that is likely to be liberal in its political, social, and philosophical views.

Locate the Thesis Statement or Main Idea.   The thesis states the main idea of the entire essay. Sometimes it is embodied in a single sentence—the thesis statement—and sometimes it is stated in several sentences. If the main idea is not explicitly stated, it should be clearly implied. The thesis statement answers the question, What is the main point of this essay? Whether the thesis is explicit or implicit, it is a necessary component of a clearly written work. A thesis helps the writer to focus the writing and guides the organization and development of key ideas. It also helps to provide direction to the reader and assists in the reader's understanding of the piece.

Locate Key Ideas and Supporting Evidence or Details.   For this step in your critical reading, you should underline or highlight the major points of the essay. One important tool for an active, critical reader is a pen or pencil. As you read, underline, star, or in some way highlight major points of development. Look for topic sentences of paragraphs. The thesis statement answers the question, What is this essay about? In the same way, the topic sentence answers the question, What is this paragraph about? If a topic sentence is not clearly stated, it should be clearly implied.

Make Marginal Notes as You Read.   In the margins, write your response to a passage or make note of words, phrases, or entire passages you think are important to the piece. Make notes about the evidence or details that support major points. If you have a question about something the author says, write it in the margin for later consideration. If you are not sure of the meaning of a word, circle it and look it up in a dictionary after you have finished reading. Finally, if you are struck by the beauty, logic, or peculiarity of a passage, note marginal comments on that as well.

Summarize What You Have Read.   This is the point at which you test your understanding of what you have read. Go back now and look at your underlinings and notations. Then try to state in your own words what the writing is about and the main points the writer made. If you can accurately summarize a piece of writing, then you probably have a good idea of its meaning. Summarizing also helps you to recall the piece later, perhaps in class or in small-group discussions. Incidentally, summarizing is also a good strategy for your own study habits. After reading an assignment for any of your courses, try to write or tell someone a summary of your reading. If you cannot express in your own words the major ideas of what you have just read, it should be reread.

Evaluate What You Have Read.   When you are sure that you understand what you have read and can summarize it objectively, you are ready to respond. You can evaluate something in a number of ways, depending on its purpose. First, consider whether the author achieves the stated or implied purpose and whether the thesis or main idea is thoroughly explained, developed, or argued. Has the writer supplied enough details, examples, or other evidence? If you are evaluating an argument or persuasion essay, is the evidence convincing to you? Does the piece make a logical and reasonable argument? Are you persuaded to the writer's position? What questions do you have about any of the writer's assertions? Do you wish to challenge her or him on any

GUIDELINES FOR READING CRITICALLY

- Consider what the title tells you about the essay.
- Try to learn something about the author.
- Determine the purpose of the writing.
- Determine the audience for whom the piece was written.
- Locate the thesis statement or main idea.
- Locate key ideas and supporting evidence or details.
- Make marginal notes as you read, including not only a summary of key ideas but also your questions about the content.
- Summarize what you have read.
- Evaluate what you have read.

points? If the purpose of the essay is to describe, has the writer conveyed to you the essence of the subject with appropriately vivid language? For any piece of writing, you can assess how well-written it is. Is it organized? Is the writing clear to you? Does the introduction give you enough information to get you easily into the essay, and does the conclusion leave you satisfied that the writer has accomplished the purpose for the essay? In chapter 3, Writing a Critique, you will find a more detailed discussion of how to evaluate a passage or entire essay.

ORGANIZING AND DEVELOPING IDEAS

It is helpful in both your own writing and in evaluating the writing of others to be familiar with common kinds of writing and the strategies writers use for organizing and developing their ideas. If you understand what strategies are available to a writer and what elements make those strategies work, you can better evaluate how well a selection is written. Writers use many different **strategies or rhetorical methods** to organize and develop their ideas, depending on their purposes and their audience. Whether they pursue persuasive, expository, or expressive purposes, writers must be focused and clear if they want to engage their readers. They can achieve clarity or coherence with good organization and logical development of ideas. Writers seldom use any one method exclusively, or even think about any particular pattern or mode of development. Instead, they first decide what their purpose for writing is, and then they use whatever combination of patterns best achieves that purpose.

In your college courses, you will often be given written assignments. No matter what the course, whether it is art history, communications, paper science, anthropology, or business, the instructor may require a paper on a subject relevant to the course. Furthermore, students are very likely to encounter essay questions on exams, for instructors in courses across the curriculum seem to agree that one of the best tests of understanding is to ask students to write in some detail on quizzes or exams about important course material. Whether it is biology or English, students may be asked to argue a position on a controversial issue. An art professor may ask students to write a description of a painting, or a math professor may test understanding by asking students to explain in writing how to solve a problem. Whatever a writer's purpose, some fairly standard models can help to organize written work. But remember: seldom will a writer use just one of these rhetorical modes in isolation; they are almost always used in combinations of two or more. The important consideration is how a writer can organize and develop the material for the best effect, that best suits the purpose of the assignment.

Argument/Persuasion.   Argument is a mode of persuasion in which the goal is either to convince readers of the validity of the writer's position (argument) or move readers to accept the author's view and even act on it (persuasion). In argument, writers set forth an assertion (often called a *proposition*) about a debatable topic and offer proof intended to convince readers that the assertion is a valid or true one. In persuasion, a writer goes a step further and offers a course of action, with the ultimate goal of making readers take action. The supporting evidence or proof must be so convincing that readers cannot help but agree with the validity of the author's position. The reasoning process must be so logical that readers inevitably draw the same conclusions that the author does from the evidence.

Many of the readings in this textbook are arguments, including some that are paired because their authors hold differing viewpoints on an issue. For instance, in chapter 4, Alfie Kohn in "The Dangerous Myth of Grade Inflation" disagrees completely with Harvey C. Mansfield's argument in "Grade Inflation: It's Time to Face the Facts." Other pairs of readings expressing differing viewpoints on the same subject are Susan R. Lamson's "TV Violence: Does It Cause Real-Life Mayhem?" and Mike Males' "Stop Blaming Kids and TV" (chapter 9), and James D. Watson's "All for the Good" and Ian Wilmut's "Dolly's False Legacy" (chapter 20). You will find readings whose primary purpose is argument or persuasion located throughout the textbook. For a fuller discussion of argumentation, see chapter 4.

Cause–Effect Analysis.   A writer who wants to explain why something happened or show what happened as a result of something—or perhaps both—is doing cause and effect analysis. This type of analysis is used frequently in news broadcasts and magazine and newspaper articles to explain phenomena, such as the chain of events that led to a particular action, the effects of a particular event or crisis, or both causes and effects of a specific situation. Cause and effect analysis is also used frequently to argue. A writer might use the strategy of causal analysis in arguing that offering sex education in schools or making contraceptives readily available to high-school students would be more effective in reducing the number of teenage pregnancies than prohibiting explicit sex scenes on prime time television. The writer would have to sort out possible causes to explain the high rate of teenage pregnancies, determine which likely are most responsible and which are contributing factors, and then conjecture likely results if the recommendation were followed.

Most of the argumentative essays cited in the previous section use causal analysis to develop their argument. Indeed, any argument on the effects of an activity—viewing television, playing video games, listening to violent music—of necessity is a causal analsyis. Sissela Bok undertakes a causal analysis in her look at opposing sides on the issue of media violence in "Aggression: The Impact of Media Violence" (chapter 8). For a slightly different approach, Andrew Solomon in "The Closing of the American Book" (chapter 11) attributes a variety of effects to a non-activity: he believes that not reading is a direct cause of crises in national health, national politics, and national education.

Comparison/Contrast.   Another strategy for developing ideas is to show similarities and differences between two elements. Comparison and contrast can be useful in an argument piece in which the writer supports one of two possible choices and needs to explain reasons for that choice. In an expository essay—that is, one with the purpose of explaining something—comparison and contrast can be useful to demonstrate a thorough understanding of the subject. Comparing or contrasting usually promotes one of two purposes: to show each of two subjects distinctly by considering both side by side, or to evaluate or judge two things. An analogy is a useful kind of comparison when seeking to explain a complicated or unfamiliar subject by showing its similarities to a less-complicated or more familiar subject. An example of a writer using comparison/contrast to make a point is Joshua Foer, whose essay "Enter Right, Exit Left" in chapter 2 compares the political attitudes of his graduating class in 2004 to what they were when they began as college freshmen in 2000.

Classification/Division.   Classification is sorting information and ideas into categories or groups; division is breaking information, ideas, or concepts into parts in order to better understand them. A writer may use classification to explain how a particular class of people, things, or ideas can be separated into groups and labeled according to common characteristics that distinguish them from other groups. A writer may use division to make a large, complex subject easier to understand by dividing it into smaller, more manageable parts. Thus, Murray Weidenbaum in "Dispelling the Myths about the Global Economy" (chapter 26) looks at the negative connotations of "globalization" by identifying ten different components of that negative image and examining each one in terms of why he feels it is false.

Definition.   Writers often need to define as they inform or argue. Definition is the process of making clear a precise meaning or significance. In definition, a writer conveys the essential characteristics of something by distinguishing it from all other things in its class. You are familiar with dictionary definitions of words. Writers employ a similar technique to clarify or to explain, but usually in more detail than dictionaries give. In addition to providing brief definitions of terms, a writer may provide an extended definition—that is, take the meaning of a word beyond its dictionary definition or beyond the limits of a simple definition. An extended definition may go for a paragraph or two or even for the length of an entire essay. A writer using abstract terms or concepts unfamiliar to an audience will find the extended definition a useful tool. In her highly personal essay on living in poverty as a child, Melanie Scheller defines both the condition of poverty and the emotion of shame in "On the Meaning of Plumbing and Poverty" (chapter 12).

Exemplification.   Examples and illustrations are crucial to writing, no matter what the primary purpose. Without examples, writing stays at the general or abstract level and leaves readers only vaguely understanding what the writer means. Examples make meaning clear and help make writing more interesting, livelier, and more engaging than in an essay without details. Examples may be brief and numerous or extended and limited in number, and they may take the form of narratives. Most of the readings in this textbook contain examples of one kind or another. Much of Jean Kilbourne's "Advertising's Influence on Media Content" in chapter 8 consists of examples that both illustrate and argue her thesis. It would be difficult to find an effective piece of writing that does not use examples of some sort.

Narration.   Narration is the re-creation of an experience for a specific purpose. It may be a brief anecdote, a story, or a case history. Writers use narration for a variety of purposes: to explain, to illustrate a particular point, to report information, to entertain, or to persuade. Often a narrative is only one part of a written work, but occasionally it may be the entire means of development. Journalists are accustomed to asking themselves a series of questions when they write their stories to ensure they give complete narratives: What happened? To whom did it happen? When did it happen? Where did it happen? Why did it happen? How did it happen—that is, under what circumstances or in what way did it happen? Narration is often combined with description. In the process of defining what poverty and shame meant to her, Melanie Scheller uses narration in "On the Meaning of Plumbing and Poverty" (chapter 12).

Description.   Description depicts in words a person, place, or thing by appealing to the senses—that is, by evoking through words certain sights, smells, sounds, or tactile sensations. Description is an almost indispensable part of writing; it is certainly inextricably linked with narration. As with narration and all other kinds of writing, description has a purpose. The purpose of description may be objective: to convey information without bias—or it may be subjective: to express feelings, impressions, or attitudes about a person, place, or thing. We can see how a writer combines description and narration in Jane Smiley's "You Can Never Have Too Many" (chapter 14).

Keep in mind that these various rhetorical methods—ways of organizing and developing ideas—are almost never used in isolation. Seldom will you find a piece of writing that does not combine two or more of these strategies, and they are all equally useful depending on your purpose for writing, the audience you are writing to, and the context you are writing in. For instance, in addition to narration and description, Jane Smiley, in the essay just mentioned, also uses exemplification and comparison/contrast as she examines the effects of Barbie dolls on her daughters' development. You will notice as you read the essays in this textbook that all of the writers employ a variety of strategies to achieve their purpose.

ILLUSTRATION: READING CRITICALLY

A demonstration of how a reader might apply the guidelines for critical reading follows the essay "What's in a Name? More than You Think" by Joe Saltzman. Read the essay first, noticing words and passages that are underlined and addressed in the marginal comments. After you have read the essay, write a response to the personal response question before you read the discussion. Then read the discussion and prepare for class or small-group discussion of the questions. For class, take into consideration the ways in which your own critical reading might differ from the comments following "What's in a Name?" Would you add anything? What other words or passages would you underline or highlight? What other marginal comments would you make?

WHAT'S IN A NAME?
MORE THAN YOU THINK

Joe Saltzman

Academic and professional credentials.

Joe Saltzman is Associate Mass Media Editor of USA Today; *associate dean and professor of journalism, University of Southern California Annenberg School for Communication, Los Angeles; and director of the Image of the Journalist in Popular Culture, a project of the Norman Lear Center. He is author of* Frank Capra and the Image of the Journalist in American Film. *This piece first appeared in the July 2003 issue of* USA Today Magazine.

His subject.

His thesis— note word choice.

Re-states thesis.

Television coverage of the Iraqi war and postwar illustrates once again how American television news is obsessed with show business terminology that at the very least is poor journalism and at its worst corrupts and ignores a basic rule of journalism: fairness and accuracy in all reporting.

    With the government's public relations arm pushing hard, phrases to describe the war and postwar stories moved from a fair account of what was going on to an oppressive vocabulary that gave a spin to the coverage. Colorful phrases, sometimes patriotic, sometimes just plain wrong, gave much of the TV news coverage a convenient anti-Iraqi/pro-American stance. Some examples:

1st example:
"Operation Iraqi
Freedom"—
sounds noble
and heroic.

"Operation Iraqi Freedom" was used constantly by Fox and MSNBC as a banner for summing up the coverage of the war in the Middle East. Few would dispute that "Operation Iraqi Freedom" sounded noble and gave a heroic and honorable reason for going to war as opposed to the accurate and more evenhanded "The War in Iraq" or "The Iraqi Conflict." Fighting for a country's freedom brings images of the American and French revolutions, of World War II soldiers fighting against Hitler and the Japanese, and of friendly, grateful citizens waving American flags to greet soldiers who had liberated their country. These images neatly fit with a title like "Operation Iraqi Freedom." "The War in Iraq" conjures up destruction and death. It is one thing for the Administration to use favorable phrases to win support for its policies, quite another for the American media to use such phrases in trying to describe what is going on in a Middle East war.

2nd example:
"coalition
forces"—says
there was no
coalition, just
American
soldiers.

4   "Coalition forces" sounds as if a worldwide coalition of military force is being used to fight the war. It's certainly the Bush-approved term for the American and British forces fighting in Iraq. News organizations, however, shouldn't use phrases that do not adequately describe the situation. It was American soldiers in Baghdad, not coalition forces, but most of the news media used the phrase "coalition forces" throughout the coverage of the war.

3rd example:
"weapons
of mass
destruction"—
sound
fearsome.

Going into a foreign country to get rid of "weapons of mass destruction" makes sense. As *Time* magazine put it, "they sound so much more fearsome than chemical or biological weapons. A few papers, like *The New York Times*, have been careful to use 'unconventional weapons' or other terms instead."

Restates main
point.

If you were trying to figure out whether the war in Iraq was justified, see which sentence would convince you: "Operation Iraqi Freedom was underway as coalition forces went into Iraq to discover and destroy weapons of mass destruction"; or "The war in Iraq was underway as American and British forces went into Iraq to discover and destroy unconventional weapons." "Collateral damage" doesn't sound as horrific as civilian casualties or, even more accurately, civilians who were wounded, maimed, or killed by American bombs and ground fire.

4th example:
"collateral
damage"—
softens the
reality.

Reaffirms his
position: using
catchphrases is
demeaning.

Certain phrases make a difference in our perception of what goes on in our world. Catchphrases that make unpopular events less difficult to accept should not be a part of daily news media coverage. It demeans both the journalist and the viewer.

8   Many watching the television war coverage were impressed with the pictures sent back by "embedded" journalists traveling

with various military units in the field. And many of the images
and reports were spectacular, but at what cost? No one would
deny that reporters embedded with individual units would be
partial to the people around them saving their lives. No one
would deny that this kind of coverage simply gives the viewer a
glimpse at specific moments in war. No embedded reporter has
the chance or the ability to interview the other side during a
battle. In many ways, this coverage, while unique in the history
of war reporting, gave an even more-distorted view of what was
going on in the field than battle reports issued by reporters
safely away from the sounds and sights of immediate warfare.

None of this is to say that we shouldn't have reports from
embedded reporters. It is one more attempt to figure out what
is going on during wartime. It must be put into proper perspective, however. The British broadcasters and the Middle East
press did an effective job in showing other sides of the war, other
sides that were either not reported by the American news media or given short shrift next to the action-packed, myopic reports from embedded correspondents in the field.

Perhaps even more damaging was the news media's attempt
to "censor" unpleasant sights and sounds from the battlefield because they were worried about offending American sensibilities.
The most-grievous example was the failure of U.S. news media
to show the footage of the American prisoners of war when the
entire world was watching what was happening to them. Moreover, other pictures of wounded Iraqi civilians were also missing
in much of the American news media coverage. Many viewers
turned to other sources for news of the war—newspapers, magazines, the Internet, the BBC, and cable stations showing some
of the foreign coverage.

The TV news media never should assume the role of a parent deciding what images and sounds the American people
should be allowed to see. While it is true that pictures of
wounded Iraqi civilians and abused POWs do not give viewers
an accurate and complete picture of the war by themselves, they
would have been an important addition to the embedded war
coverage of bullets and sand-clouded battles. One wonders
what the news media would have shown, however, if an embedded reporter was suddenly blown to bits on camera.

12   War is always brutal and the images always horrible and
hard to watch. If the American TV news media want to cover
modern warfare, they will have to do far more than give us fancy
showbiz titles and only the sounds and images that they deem
suitable for G-rated TV news.

DISCUSSION OF "WHAT'S IN A NAME? MORE THAN YOU THINK"

The Title.   The title tells readers the subject of the article—names and their conno-tations—but not what kinds of names. The title does suggest that the author is going to be critical of whatever sort of naming he discusses in the paper (names mean "more than you think").

The Author.   The information in the headnote suggests that the author seems well qualified to write critically of news reporting. He is a mass media editor of a major news magazine and a professor of journalism. He is active in his discipline, having published a book on the image of journalists in film.

The Audience.   The headnote also says that "What's in a Name? More than You Think" was first published in *USA Today Magazine,* a publication for a general audi-ence of urban readers who like to get the essentials of news stories quickly. Saltzman likely assumed an audience of educated readers who want analyses of important na-tional and international developments but who do not necessarily have the time to read lengthy articles on those topics. Saltzman therefore writes in a style appropriate to newspapers and news magazines—that is, he avoids informal language such as slang or colloquialisms as well as specialized terms or difficult vocabulary. He uses words and terms that would be familiar to an audience of readers who keep up on America's involvement in Iraq. His word choice and sentence structure are appropri-ate for educated adults who take an interest in the news.

Purpose and Main Idea.   Saltzman states his subject and main idea in his first sen-tence: he believes that television coverage of the Iraqi war and postwar is unfair and inaccurate. He elaborates in the second paragraph by suggesting that TV reporters gave in to pressure from the government and adopted "an oppressive vocabulary" to give "spin" to their coverage of the war. We know from the headnote that Saltzman was writing not long after the American War against Iraq and during its aftermath, so his use of present tense is appropriate for reporting what was going on at the time he wrote his piece. He uses language that makes his view of such reporting quite clear when he accuses television news of being "obsessed with show business terminology," which "corrupts and ignores" the basic rule of journalism to be fair and accurate in its reporting. It is clear from those opening paragraphs that his purpose is to argue that American television news reporters have been unfair, inaccurate, and demeaning in their reporting of the war in Iraq and its aftermath.

Key Ideas and Supporting Evidence.   Saltzman primarily uses **exemplification** to develop his **argument.** In paragraphs 3–6, he gives examples of the phrases that he finds offensive in American television news reporting, along with his explanation of why their use is very bad journalism. He believes that the phrase "Operation Iraqi Freedom," with its associations of patriotism and nobility, is appropriate for the Ad-ministration but not for reporters, who are supposed to remain neutral and unbiased.

His preferred phrase would be "The War in Iraq." Next he cites the phrase "coalition forces," which suggests a worldwide joining of military forces, when, he asserts, it was only American soldiers who were fighting in Baghdad. He goes on to "weapons of mass destruction," which suggests something quite fearsome, as opposed to a more neutral phrase like "unconventional weapons." His last example is "collateral damage," which downplays or helps soften the reality that the phrase refers to "civilian casualties" or "civilians who were wounded, maimed, or killed by American bombs and ground fire" (paragraph 6).

After arguing that the language of American television news reporters is unfair and biased, he goes on to discuss the images that were broadcast on television. He believes that using "'embedded' journalists" gave a very narrow, distorted view of the battlefield and that viewers did not get a proper perspective of what was going on in the war. His last example is the "even more damaging" attempts by the media to "'censor' unpleasant sights and sounds from the battlefield" because they did not want to offend "American sensibilities." His point about both embedded journalists and attempts to withhold disturbing images is that reporters give a narrow and distorted perspective of what was happening during the war and what has been going on after it. He argues for a broader picture of the realities of war. Saltzman concludes by asserting that if American television news media want to cover modern warfare, they must drop the "fancy showbiz titles" and stop "censoring" images they believe Americans would find disturbing.

Summary.   In "What's in a Name? More than You Think," Joe Saltzman argues that American television news reporters violate the basic rules of reporting by using language and making choices that give an unfair, inaccurate, and distorted view of the war in Iraq and its aftermath. His gives a number of examples of language to make his point. He cites the phrase "Operation Iraqi Freedom," which stirs up patriotic feelings, more appropriately the business of the government's public relations people than reporters. Saltzman then asserts that "coalition forces" is a misleading and inaccurate phrase because there were only American soldiers in Baghdad, not an alliance of many forces from around the world. His remaining two examples are "weapons of mass destruction," with its connotations of terror, and "collateral damage," which softens the reality of what the term actually denotes. From language, Saltzman moves to the images that were broadcast on television. The use of embedded reporters to cover the war was not a bad idea, he says, but it narrowed the view of the war rather than helped present a broad perspective of what was going on. Worse, he argues, was the decision not to show images of the abuses of prisoners of war and wounded Iraqi citizens. Such a failure amounts to censorship. He concludes by reasserting his major point that American television journalists failed in their coverage of the war in Iraq and the period after the war, and he suggests that they change their ways if they want to report modern warfare accurately and fairly.

Evaluation.   Saltzman's essay is organized sensibly and logically written in clear, straightforward prose. His use of specific examples and his reasons why they are inappropriate make a convincing case for his argument that American television journalists were inaccurate and unfair in their reporting of the Iraq war. The repetition of "no one would deny" in paragraph 8 lends emphasis to the point he is making about the limited perspective of embedded reporters. Furthermore, the disclaimer in the first sentence of paragraph 9 is his concession, in a way, to readers who may think that he is being overly critical of embedded reporters, and it leads to his repeating—and emphasizing—his opinion. Despite Saltzman's excellent use of examples to support and develop his central idea, he does not go into real depth in his analysis of any of them. It is quite possible that space limitations imposed by the magazine kept him from a fuller discussion. The fact that many of his paragraphs are short—one or two sentences in several cases—may reflect his training in journalism: the physical space of newspaper and in some cases magazine columns requires shorter paragraphs.

Saltzman is an accomplished writer who is not afraid to express opinions that may not be popular with the general public, and these opinions raise questions that bear further exploration and thought. His assertion that American television news reporting of war should give a broader picture, showing if possible the perspective of the enemy and the effects of war on the people we are fighting, is fair. On the other hand, is it the place of the press to be critical of the Administration or to challenge the decisions of its country's leaders in time of war? Is it not important to keep up morale on the home front as well as on the battlefield? What is gained by a press hostile to or even subversive of its government in a time when patriotism and public support of its military are crucial to the war effort? These are tough questions that both the press and its critics have been struggling with, and Saltzman's essay is a good starting place for an open discussion of the issues he raises.

RHETORICAL ANALYSIS OF VISUALS

Rhetorical considerations apply to visual images as well as to written forms of communication. "Analysis" as a process involves taking something that is whole and complex and breaking it into its individual components to better understand it. Thus, a rhetorical analysis is a close examination of not just what a work says but, just as importantly, how it says it. Whether you are critiquing an essay in a book or periodical, a visual art form, or an Internet website, questions of audience, tone, purpose, organization, content, and meaning apply. With visuals, as with written works, you must consider perspective or point of view, context, and connotation. Connotation—the emotional associations of a thing—is perhaps even more important when viewing visuals than in reading words. Just as words have associations that go beyond or add layers of meaning to what they denote ("the dictionary definition"), images have powerful associations. Images often have the ability to express things—emotions, nuances, insights—in a way that words often cannot. They can reveal what is difficult to put into words by conveying impressions or depicting in sharp detail what it would take a great many words to describe or explain, including subtleties of meaning that emerge only after thoughtful consideration and careful perusal of the image. Visuals also have the potential to argue a viewpoint or persuade an audience; their authors use strategies to present a viewpoint or make a statement that is similar to those used by authors of written text.

We see images daily in a variety of forms—in photographs, drawings, paintings, pictures, brochures, advertisements, CD album covers, posters, and Internet web pages, and of course on television and in film. Most of these images go unexamined because we see so many images in our lives that we simply would not have time to analyze them all. But when we find it useful to consider an image closely, how do we analyze it? What can we say about it? How can we express in words what an image means or implies? The answer to these questions is that analyzing images critically requires skills that are quite similar to those for analyzing a piece of writing critically. Just as writers select details and organize essays to make specific points, so, too, do artists shooting a scene or painting a picture select details and arrange them in order to convey specific ideas or impressions. Writers and artists alike make judgments that in turn shape how readers or viewers perceive their work.

Analyzing visuals involves doing a close "reading" of the image and asking a series of questions about it. In looking critically at a visual image, you want to consider many aspects of it: What do you see when you first look at it? How do you respond initially? What details does the image highlight? What else is included and what might have been excluded? How does the positioning of various elements of the image emphasize its meaning? The following list of questions will help you analyze the visual images that are located throughout the textbook in each of the chapters of parts 2–5. The answers you get when you ask these questions can give you a greater understanding of the images you are scrutinizing. Most of the visual images reproduced in this textbook are photographs or paintings, so the first set of questions is designed to help you in your analysis of them. However, the questions can easily be adapted to other kinds of images, such as advertisements, newspaper page layouts, and Internet web pages. Furthermore, television, film, music videos, and documentaries also convey messages through images that can be analyzed rhetorically in much the same way as the other forms of visual communication can be. For more on the power of images to shape opinions about and affect memories of certain events, see Charles Paul Freund's "Flag-Draped Memories" in chapter 16.

Questions to Ask About a Visual Image:

- What is your overall immediate impression of the image? First impressions often linger even after rethinking one's initial response, so what strikes you immediately about an image is particularly important.
- What detail first catches your attention? After noting your immediate overall response, consider what detail or details first attract you. Is it the prominence, size, or positioning of the subject? Is it the colors or absence of them? Is it the size, the physical space it occupies? More than likely, the artist wanted you to notice that detail first, and very likely, it is an integral part of the "message" or "statement" the image makes.
- What details emerge after you have studied the image for a while? Do you detect any pattern in the arrangement of details? If so, how does the arrangement of details function to convey the overall impression?
- How does the arrangement of objects or people in the picture help draw your attention to the central image, the one you are initially drawn to? Are some

things placed prominently in the center or made larger than others? If so, what is the effect of that arrangement? How does the background function in relation to what is placed in the foreground?

- If the image is in color, how does the artist use color? Are the colors selected to represent certain emotions, moods, or other qualities? If it is in black and white, what use does the artist make of the absence of color? Does the artist use degrees of shading and brightness? If so, to what effect?
- From what perspective is the artist viewing the subject? Is it close to or far away from the subject? Is the subject viewed straight-on or from the side? Why do you think the artist selected this particular perspective? How might a shift in perspective alter the view of the subject, not just physically but on the level of meaning as well?
- What emotions does the image evoke in you? Why? Which details of the image convey the strongest emotion?
- Has anything important been left out of the image? What might have been included, and why do you think it was left out?
- What is happening in the picture? Does it tell a story or give a single impression?
- What does the picture tell you about its subject? How does it convey that message?
- If there are people in the image, what can you tell about them? What details tell you those things? Is it the way they are dressed? Their physical appearance? What they are doing?
- Does the picture raise any questions? What would you like to ask about the image, the activity, or the people in it? How would you find the answers to your questions?

EXERCISE

Ask the questions for analyzing visuals listed above as you study the following photograph. Then, selecting the details you believe are important, write an analysis of the photograph. Begin your analysis with an introductory paragraph that includes a thesis statement or a statement of the main idea of the photograph. This thesis should reflect your understanding of what the photograph means to you—its message, its story, what it suggests symbolically, or whatever ultimately you decide about the photograph. The rest of the paper should draw on details from your answers to the questions as you explain or support your thesis statement.

Here are some questions specific to this photograph that you might want to think about as you work through the questions listed above: Besides showing the tattoo, what effect is achieved by taking the picture from behind the man? What does the tattoo suggest to you about the man? Does the earring in his left ear add anything to your image of him? Can you tell the race or ethnicity of the man and, if so, does that detail add a layer of meaning or implication to the picture? Does the man's stance—the way he is standing, the shape of his shoulders, the position of his arms—tell you anything about what he is thinking or what he is about to do? Is the man anticipating a challenge? Is he preparing to climb the dune? Does it make a difference that this is a sand dune and not a mountain or some other challenge? What do you anticipate happening if the man tries to climb the dune? Do the clouds represent anything? Why is the sunlight hidden by the clouds? Is the sun trying to break through the clouds, or are the clouds preventing the sun from shining?

Tattooed man looking at sand dune.
© Herb Watson/CORBIS

Questions to Ask About an Advertisement.   Advertising is a powerful and pervasive force in our world. Ads have the ability to affect how we think, act, and even feel about ourselves and others. Ads can shape, reflect, or distort both individual perceptions and social values, and they do so by employing some of the classic strategies of argument and persuasion: they have a proposition, they know their audience, they make appeals, they use comparisons and examples, and they particularly want to persuade us to action. In addition to the questions to ask about visual images, the following questions will help you analyze both print and non-print advertisements:

- What is the message of the advertisement? What does it say to potential buyers of the product? That is, what is its argument?
- Who is the intended audience? How can you tell?
- What strategies does the ad use to convey its message? What appeals—to logic, to emotion, to ethics, or to shared values—does it use? Does it rely primarily on one appeal only or does it combine them? How do the specific details convey that message?
- How does the text—the actual words used—convey the message of the advertisement? How are words arranged or placed in the ad and why are they placed that way? If a non-print ad, how are the voice-overs or dialogue used to convey the message?
- How would you describe the style and tone of the advertisement? How do they help convey the message or sell the product?

EXERCISE

1. Select a print advertisement for analysis. Ask the questions noted above and write an analysis based on your notes in which you assess the effectiveness of the ad in achieving its purpose. Attach the advertisement with your analysis when you hand it in to your instructor.
2. Select two advertisements for the same kind of product (for instance, clothing, tooth paste, or laundry detergents). Apply the questions noted above and choose the one that you think is more effective at selling or promoting the product. Formulate a thesis sentence that states your preference and use details from your scrutiny of both of them to support that statement.

Questions to Ask About a Newspaper Page.   Newspapers can shape reader response in the choices they make about the layout of text and photographs. While we like to think that newspapers are unbiased in their reporting of news items, reading just two different newspapers on the same subject reveals that the choices a newspaper makes about a news item have a huge influence on the impressions it leaves on readers. Just the visual effect of a page layout alone tells us many things. Where an article or picture is located on a page, what page it appears on, and where on the page it is located all represent a judgment on the part of the paper about the importance of the image or article and cannot help but shape how readers respond to it. Consider the following list about photographs and news articles when looking at a newspaper page:

- Where in the paper is the article or photograph placed? Front-page placement indicates that the newspaper considers it more important as a news item than placement on the inside pages.

- How are photographs and news articles positioned on the page? Items that are placed high on the page or in the center of the page are likely to draw the attention more readily than those placed low or off center.
- How large are the photographs or the headlines? Visually, larger photographs or headlines are likely to draw attention and interest quicker than small ones.
- Are photographs in color or black and white? Choosing to run a picture in color indicates a value judgment that the paper has made about the interest or newsworthiness of the image.

EXERCISE

1. Select a newspaper page for analysis. Front pages are particularly important in newspapers for attracting reader attention, so perhaps you will want to analyze the front page of the newspaper. Ask the questions listed above and write an analysis based on the answers to your questions. What article(s) does the newspaper think more important than others? How are photographs used on the page? Attach the page with your analysis when you hand it in to your instructor.
2. Select two different newspapers covering the same news story and compare their treatment of the story. How do the two newspapers compare and contrast in their handling of the story? Is one more effective than the other in reporting it? Formulate a thesis that reflects your ultimate judgment of the two papers' treatment of the news story and support that thesis with details gathered from your comparison of the two.

RHETORICAL ANALYSIS OF WEBSITES

The Internet provides a seemingly endless variety of sites to visit for every taste and interest. Web pages can function rhetorically to influence visitors to the site in much the same way as other forms of discourse. The very way in which the web page is constructed can work to produce a desired effect, especially if the constructor of the site wishes to persuade an audience, sway opinion, or impose a particular point of view. A rhetorical analysis looks at the ways a site achieves its stated or implied purpose. Because websites vary considerably in their reliability and currency, you will find additional information about evaluating them in chapter 6. Many of the same questions one asks when evaluating a website apply when doing a rhetorical analysis of it. What follows are some of the components of a web page and questions to ask about it as you analyze its rhetorical effectiveness.

Questions to Ask About a Website:

- **Domain.** What is the URL (Uniform Record Locator) of the site? The domain—the logical or geographical location of the site on the Internet, indicated by the very last part of the URL—tells you something about the site. Domains differ according to the entity sponsoring them: *edu* for educational institutions, *gov* for government agencies, *com* or *net* for commercial or personal enterprises, *org* for organizations. These broad categories give you the first piece of information about the site. Within the categories, there are countless subcategories.

- **Author.** Who created the web page? Is it an individual, an organization, a government agency, an educational institution, or a corporation? Does the text at the site give you information about the author? If not, why do you think that information is not provided? Does the site tell you how to contact the author?
- **Audience.** What audience does the web page target? How can you tell? Is the intended audience stated or implied? Does it make assumptions about values, beliefs, age, sex, race, national origin, education, or socio-economic background its target audience?
- **Purpose.** Does the web page want to inform, entertain, sell, argue a position, or persuade people to change their minds or to take action? If it has more than one purpose, what combination of purposes does it have? Is the implied purpose the same as the stated purpose? Does the text state one purpose, while word choice, graphics, and page layout suggest or imply another? For instance, a political candidate's website might state that it has no intention of bringing up an opponent's past wrongdoings, while the very fact of stating that there are past wrongdoings to bring up casts doubt on the character of the opponent.
- **Text.** What rhetorical appeals does the written text of the website make? Does it appeal to logic or reason? Does it appeal to emotions? If emotions, which ones does it appeal to—pity, fear, joy, anger, sympathy?
- **Content.** Does the website cover the topic thoroughly? Does it use language that you understand? Does it offer links and if so, how many links? Are the links still active? What is the quality of the links?
- **Background color.** How does the background color choice affect the mood and tone of the page? Is it a vibrant color or a sober one? Does it intrude on the text or enhance it?
- **Page layout.** Is there space between items on the page or are things cramped together? How does the use of space on the page affect your overall impression of the page and your ability to read it?
- **Loading and positioning of items.** What gets loaded first when you go to the web page? Where is that material positioned? What is loaded later or positioned low on the page? Sometimes certain components of a web page are purposely programmed to load first in order to further emphasize the purpose of the site.
- **Graphics.** Are graphics on the web page static or active? Is the print used for the text large, small, or a mix of both? If a mix, what does larger print emphasize that smaller print doesn't? What font is used? Are bold print, italics, or underlining used, and if so to what effect? Is there a banner? What purpose does the banner serve?

- **Photographs or drawings.** If photographs or other images are used, what is their function? Do they illustrate or help explain something, give information, or serve to decorate the page?
- **Lighting and contrast.** Does the web page make use of contrasts of light and dark? If so, what is the effect of those contrasts?

Forums on the Web: Listservs and Blogs

In addition to websites that people go to for information, entertainment, or news, the Internet also has available a number of forums for people to participate in, such as chat rooms, newsgroups, discussion lists (listservs), and blogs. While most web sites are fairly dynamic in that they are (or should be) regularly updated, forums typically change at least daily and sometimes multiple times a day. Two very popular forums are **listservs** and **blogs.** Listservs have been around for many years, but blogs are a relatively new phenomenon. Both are capable of influencing people's views or the way they think about the topics for discussion at the sites, but blogs in particular have gotten a great deal of attention for their potential to actually bring about changes. Blogs are able to effect change because of the high degree of involvement that they have generated among visitors to their sites. Another distinguishing characteristic of listservs and blogs is that people are invited to participate in an ongoing, ever-changing discussion. People who become members of listservs or who visit blog sites have an opportunity to be not just passive readers but also active writers.

Listservs.   Listservs are e-mail based discussion groups linked to specific topics. Listservs function as forums for the exchange of ideas, where members can debate, discuss, post news items, seek or give advice, and share in a community of people who have in common their interest in the topic of the listserv. Although listservs have official websites where people can subscribe, read the guidelines for posting, and locate archived postings, among other things, the real activity takes place through e-mail. Members can elect to receive messages either individually as they are posted or in digests that are sent daily or whenever a specific number of messages have posted. Members are usually required to follow certain rules or guidelines, primarily those related to conduct and appropriate content, and often the listserv has a moderator who monitors the content of messages to make sure that posts do not violate those rules. Listservs typically archive messages by date, subject of message, and/or author, and these archives can be viewed by nonmembers as well as members. They vary widely in membership numbers, from just a few people to thousands. For instance, a listserv devoted to British novelist Barbara Pym has a small membership of around 100, and posts to the site are occasional and few. On the other hand, DorothyL, a discussion and idea list for lovers of the mystery genre, has almost 3,000 subscribers and 50 to 100 postings each day. Since listservs attract people with at least the subject of the listserv in common, they can create a strong sense of community among subscribers. While listservs are good for reading what many people have to say on various subjects related to the primary topic of the discussion group, postings are in general unedited and may not be completely reliable. On the other hand, a posting that seems wrong-headed or erroneous is likely to be corrected or at least commented on by other members of the group.

Blogs.   The term "blog" (**web log**) is a relatively new word to describe an activity that people had been doing long before the term was coined: maintaining a website where they record personal thoughts and provide links to other sites. Many of them are essentially personal pages that bloggers (owners of the sites) update daily. They provide a forum for the bloggers themselves to argue, explain, comment on, vent frustrations, air opinions, or just gossip, while visitors to the site can express their own opinions or make observations. Membership is not required; anyone can read and respond to anyone's blog. In addition to online journals, blogs can be news summaries, collections of bits and pieces from other websites, and valuable resources for instant access to the latest news. Thus blogs have been described as a cross between an online diary and a cybermagazine, but one of the key characteristics of the most successful or popular blogs is that they are constantly updated. While just a few years ago there were only a small number of blogs, today there are millions of them. Many blogs are run by professionals like educators, reporters, researchers, scientists, and political candidates, with visits to the sites numbering in the thousands and in a few cases millions, but the vast majority are run by individuals who see them as chatty, stream-of-consciousness journals and whose readership is very limited.

A few blogs have attracted so many readers that they have achieved the kind of readership that large newspapers enjoy. Because of the sheer number of readers and their ability to communicate instantly with other bloggers around the world, a few blogs have been responsible for bringing to light events or issues that mainstream media have ignored. For instance, bloggers were largely responsible for revealing that reporter Dan Rather relied on false information about President George W. Bush's National Guard service to document a news story in 2004 because they analyzed the typescript used in the memos featured in the story. Blogs with the most impact on public affairs appear to be those with large numbers of daily visitors, and they tend to have the most influence in politics. One of the oldest blogs is DrudgeReport, which records 8 to 10 million visits daily and provides many links to a wide variety of news sources. For instance, it has links to the front pages of most of the major newspapers in the world, links to all the wire services, links to the opinion columns of perhaps a hundred columnists who are read in newspapers around the United States, links to constant updates on America's involvement in foreign countries, and many more features that make it an excellent site for keeping up on what is being said, thought, and done around the world. Many other respected sites attract millions of visits daily or weekly.

Blogs have certain common features, including making it convenient for people to post or respond to the blog owner, posting messages in reverse chronological order for others to read, and providing links to other blogs and websites. However, blogs differ greatly in the quality and reliability of the information at the site. Blogs by definition are logs or journals and as such are often unedited, not very well thought out musings on a variety of topics. Be very careful when choosing blogs to follow and even more careful in accepting as truth what you read on a blog. You can apply the same questions to blogs that you would use for analyzing other websites rhetorically, but keep in mind the special nature of blogs and how their unrestricted, constantly changing content is very likely slanted or biased to fit the viewpoint of the blogger.

EXERCISE

1. Locate two websites on the same topic and compare and contrast their rhetorical effectiveness by applying the guidelines listed above. After deciding which one you think is more effective, write an analysis in which your thesis states which site you prefer. Use details from your perusal of both of them as proof or evidence to support your thesis statement.

2. Locate two listservs on topics that interest you and read a few days' worth of posts. How do they compare and contrast? What is your impression of the sense of community among its members? What sorts of posts do people send? Do they stay on topic? Do the listservs have moderators? If you were going to join a listserv, which one would you prefer?

3. Locate several blogs on a topic that interests you—baseball, water skiing, crime prevention, politics, a hobby, your major—and assess their rhetorical effectiveness, using the guidelines discussed above.

2

WRITING A SUMMARY

Students often must write both informal exercises and formal papers based on readings in their textbooks. In writing assignments for the course using this textbook, for instance, you will find frequent use for information or ideas discussed in the readings. For formal writing assignments, you may be instructed to choose among the writing topics that end each chapter in parts 2–5, or you may be asked to suggest your own topic for a paper on a reading or readings. You may choose to argue in favor of or against a position another author takes; you may use information from one or more of the readings to write an essay suggested by a particular chapter; you may decide to compare and contrast two or more essays in a chapter or explain various perspectives on an issue. At some point, you may want to use some of the readings from this or another textbook in combination with other print and Internet resources in a research paper.

This and the next three chapters introduce several specific types of assignments and provide guidelines for writing them. This chapter focuses on the summary, chapter 3 on writing a critique, chapter 4 on writing an argument, and chapter 5 on writing a synthesis with documentation. In all of these assignments, you may be called on to paraphrase, quote, and document material on which you are writing. The guidelines for paraphrasing, quoting, and documenting sources are explained in chapter 5. All illustrations of handling source material follow MLA (Modern Language Association) documentation style. (*Note:* If your instructor prefers that you use APA style or gives you a choice of styles, guidelines for APA documentation style appear in chapter 6.)

WRITING A SUMMARY

Summarizing produces an objective restatement of a written passage in your own words in a much shorter version than the original. The purpose of a summary is to highlight both the central idea or ideas and the major points of a work. A summary does not attempt to restate the entire reading. You might summarize an entire book in the space of a paragraph or perhaps even a sentence, although you will not do full justice to a lengthy work that way. Many reasons call for summarizing. Your instructor may ask you to write a summary of an essay, or a passage from one, to gauge your understanding. Such an assignment may be informal, something that you write in class as a quiz or an ungraded journal entry, or you may be assigned a formal summary, a longer piece that you write out of class in detail and with care. Many kinds of writing include summaries as part of the development of their main ideas. For instance, if you are asked to report on an individual or group research project for a science class, you will probably summarize your purpose, methodology, data, and conclusions. If you write an argumentative paper, you may need to summarize either opposing viewpoints or your own supporting evidence. A research paper often includes summaries of information from source materials, and the research process itself necessitates summarizing portions of what you read. Reviews of books or articles almost always include summaries of the works under discussion, and essay questions on an examination often require summaries of information or data. Across the curriculum, no matter what course you are taking, you will probably be asked to summarize.

Summaries serve useful purposes. Professors summarize as they lecture in order to convey information in a condensed way when a detailed review would take far too much time. Textbook chapters often present summaries of chapter contents as part of chapter introductions (as in parts 2–5 of this textbook). In this textbook, some of the questions for small-group and class discussion following the readings ask you to summarize major points or portions of readings, in order to facilitate your understanding of the text. That process, in turn, enhances the quality of your classroom experience and develops your abilities to follow the discussion intelligently and to make useful contributions to the discussion yourself. Your instructor may ask you to write a summary of a piece you have read as a formal assignment. Summarizing is also an excellent strategy to enhance your own study habits. After reading an assignment for any of your courses, try to write a summary of the reading. If you cannot put into your own words the major ideas of what you have just read, you may need to go back and reread the material.

Outside the classroom and the academic environment, summaries routinely give brief introductions, overviews, and conclusions of subjects at hand. In business, industry, law, medicine, scientific research, government, or any other field, both managers and workers often need quick summaries to familiarize themselves with the high points or essence of information. Knowing how to summarize accurately is a skill that you will find useful in both your academic writing and in your profession or job.

A Summary Is Not a Substitute for Analysis.
Do not mistakenly assume that putting another person's words into your own words is an analysis. Instead, a summary is a brief, concise, objective restatement of the important elements of a piece of writing of any length, from a paragraph to an entire book. A summary may be brief, as in a one-paragraph abstract that precedes a report or long paper and gives a very short overview of it, or it may be several paragraphs or even pages in length, depending on the length of the writing or writings being summarized. You may summarize

as an informal exercise for your own purposes or as a formal assignment that you hand in to your instructor for evaluation.

Abstract.   An abstract, like all summaries, is a condensed, objective restatement of the essential points of a text. Its distinguishing characteristic is its brevity. Abstracts are usually quite short, perhaps 100 to 200 words, whereas summaries may be much longer, depending on the length of what is being summarized. As with all summaries, an abstract helps readers determine quickly if an article or book will be of interest or use. It can also serve as a brief guide to the key points before reading an article or as an aid in recalling the contents of the piece after reading it. Below is an example of an abstract of Henry Jenkins' "Art Form for the Digital Age" (chapter 7). This abstract provides a broad overview of Jenkins' article, including his major points and conclusions. In his essay, he discusses or develops each of these components at length, providing examples and supporting evidence where necessary. You can see how an abstract, like summaries of other lengths, is useful for getting a quick overview of a report or essay.

Formal and Informal Summaries.   Informal summaries are primarily for personal use and are usually not handed in for evaluation by an instructor. Formal summaries are those that others will read and are sometimes graded assignments. In either case, the process for writing a summary is virtually the same. For an example of an informal summary that would help a student prepare for a class discussion or recall key elements of an article, see the summary of Joe Saltzman's "What's in a Name? More than you Think," located in the discussion that follows that reading in chapter 1. An example of a formal summary follows Joshua Foer's "Enter Right, Exit Left," later in this chapter. The summaries of both Saltzman's and Foer's articles underscore the need for a close, critical reading of the text to fairly represent what a writer says.

The trick in summarizing accurately is knowing what is important, and therefore must be included, and what is secondary, and therefore should be omitted. Here you

ART FORM FOR THE DIGITAL AGE
Henry Jenkins

Abstract

The cultural impact of video games is underrated, despite their widespread use. They have been described as a waste of time and money, and experts warn that games are teaching children to kill. Computer games are nevertheless an emerging form of popular art and should be recognized as such. They have evolved from being primitive ball-bouncers to sophisticated participatory tales with cinema–quality graphics. Games also influence contemporary cinema, whose history can be compared to that of video games. Gilbert Seldes was one of the first academics to treat film as an art form. Games have the potential to follow the same path as cinema, but they need innovation, creativity, and intelligence to make them richer and more emotionally engaging than they are now.

see the usefulness of the guidelines for critical reading. When you read critically, you identify the main idea or thesis of the selection, and you highlight or in some way mark major points. A summary must include the main idea of what you are summarizing, and it should include major points, and only major points. Thus, if you learn to read critically, you can write a summary.

Although the process is the same for both an assignment that you will hand in to your instructor and a summary for your own use, a formal summary requires the kind of care that you give to longer writing assignments. Begin by carefully reading the work. Make a mental note of its thesis or main idea but do not write anything in the margins yet. If you try to highlight for a summary on your first reading, you might end up underlining or noting too many things. Wait until you have read the entire selection through once before writing anything. After your first reading, write in your own words the thesis or central idea as you understand it. Then go back to the article, locate the thesis or main idea, underline it, and compare it with the sentence you wrote. If your sentence differs from the sentence(s) you underlined, rephrase your own sentence. Next, read the article again, this time looking for major points of development or illustration of the thesis. As you reread, make marginal notes and underline, circle, or in some way mark the key supporting points or major ideas in the development of the thesis. After you have finished reading, look at your notes and state in one sentence, in your own words, the thesis and each major point. Do not

GUIDELINES FOR WRITING A SUMMARY

- On your first reading, mentally note the thesis or central idea of the work or passage you are summarizing without writing anything down.
- After your first reading, write down your understanding of the thesis, locate the thesis in the work, underline it, check what you have written against it, and adjust your own sentence if necessary.
- Now reread the work, noting key points, either in the margin, by highlighting, or on a separate piece of paper.
- When you have finished your second reading, once again write in your own words a one-sentence summary of the thesis or central idea. Use the author's name and title of the reading in that sentence.
- Write in your own words a one-sentence summary of each major point the author has used to develop, illustrate, or support the thesis or central idea. State only essential details related to each major point.
- Do not include minor points unless you believe their omission would give an unfair representation of what you are summarizing.
- Where appropriate, write in your own words a one-sentence summary of any conclusion from the piece.
- Keep your summary short, succinct, and focused on the central idea and major points of the piece you are summarizing.
- Edit for grammar, punctuation, and spelling before handing in your assignment.

include details or minor supporting evidence unless leaving them out would misrepresent or unfairly represent what you are summarizing. If the writing you are summarizing comes to any important conclusions, note them as well in one sentence in your own words. If you are still unclear about which are major and which are minor points, give the piece another reading. The more you read it, the better you understand its purpose, method of development, and major points.

Now you are ready to write your summary. In your opening sentence, state the author's full name, the title of the work, and the thesis or main idea. Write in complete sentences, whether your summary is 100 words or 500 words long. Use the author's last name when referring to what he or she says in the article or when quoting the author directly. Do not use the exact words of the author unless you use quotation marks around those words. The summary must use your own wording. Use direct quotations sparingly, and only for a significant word, phrase, or sentence, and make sure that anything you put in quotation marks uses the exact wording of the article. Use present tense to describe or explain what the author has written ("Foer explains" or "Foer concludes"). Provide clear transitions from point to point, just as you would in a longer assignment, and write in clear, coherent language. Edit what you have written before turning it in to your instructor.

ILLUSTRATION: MAKING MARGINAL NOTES AND SUMMARIZING

Joshua Foer's "Enter Right, Exit Left" is reprinted here, along with examples of the kinds of marginal notes a student might make after a first reading of the essay when preparing to write a formal summary of an essay. The notes highlight the central idea and major points of the selection, so that when the student is ready to write a summary, he or she will already have marked the important points to include. Following the essay, the chapter presents questions for discussion, writing topics suggested by Foer's piece, and a sample summary of the essay.

ENTER RIGHT, EXIT LEFT

Joshua Foer

Joshua Foer was a senior at Yale University and about to graduate when he wrote this piece for the May 23, 2004, issue of the New York Times.

Thirty-eight years ago, John Kerry delivered a graduation speech on behalf of his Yale class that was sharply critical of the conflict in Vietnam. In many ways, his words that day set the tone for the radicalism that would define the Yale campus for generations to come.

Opening paragraphs contrast his parents' generation with his own.

Thesis: His generations' attitudes have changed as world has changed.

9/11 was his generation's first national trauma, whereas his parents' generation had experienced many traumas.

His generation supported Iraqi war.

Class of 2004 had faith in government.

4

For my parents' generation, which went to school in the 1960's and 70's, college was often a radicalizing experience. For the Yale class of 2004—which I graduate with tomorrow—it has been the opposite. The world has changed significantly since we entered college four years ago; over that time, our attitudes have changed, too.

On 9/11, we were barely a week into our sophomore year. Because the terrorist attacks were the first national trauma my generation experienced, I believe they had a more profound effect on our still malleable political psyches than they had on our parents and grandparents, who had lived through national traumas before.

What do I base this on? Consider this: One of the most under-reported statistics about the war in Iraq is my generation's overwhelming support for it—not just in its early stages but well into last year. While the conventional wisdom holds that young Americans tend to be more liberal than older Americans, that wasn't the case this time. According to a CNN/USA Today/Gallup poll taken in October [2003], a majority of 18 to 29-year-olds thought the war worthwhile, the same percentage as in the population at large. The same survey found that President Bush had a 9 percent higher approval rating among people under 30 than he did among older respondents.

Of my 11 junior-year suite-mates, a racially and geographically diverse group of Democrats, only three opposed the war in Iraq. Across the Yale campus, similar sentiments reigned. During our junior year, when the national debate over Iraq was at its height, one of the most visible student political organizations on campus was the Yale College Students for Democracy, a group of hawkish liberals and neo-conservatives who supported the war. The biggest campus-wide "Support Our Troops" rally was at least as well attended as any antiwar protest.

Certainly the 9/11 attacks left a deep imprint on our political conscience, but my generation was probably predisposed to these more hawkish views long before the planes crashed into the Twin Towers and the Pentagon.

The class of 2004 grew up at a time when it was easy to have faith in the goodness of our government. Vietnam, Watergate and even Iran-contra were not a part of our direct political memory. For my generation, abuse of power meant sexual indiscretions in the Oval Office—not shifting rationales for war. While President Bush's claims about weapons of mass destruction and links between Iraq and Al Qaeda may have revived memories of the Gulf of Tonkin for some of our parents, my generation wasn't inclined toward incredulousness. After all, according to that same poll, 50 percent of those surveyed under 30 said they trusted government to do the right thing; for Americans older than us, that number was 36 percent.

Believed   8
America was a force for the good.

Many of us in the class of 2004 grew up in the 1990's believing that America was a force for good in the world. We became conscious of international affairs at a time when the American military was intervening to stop genocide in the Balkans, fighting to distribute food to starving people in Somalia, and protecting democracy in Haiti. Even if these ventures weren't always successful, they were at least apparently selfless. Many of us reached the conclusion that the United States was wrong not when it intervened in the affairs of others, but when it sat on its hands, as it did in the case of Rwanda. It was only natural that we would apply that same logic to Iraq.

Now young people are re-thinking their trust in the government: disillusioned by inaccurate claims about weapons of mass destruction and prisoner abuse in Iraq.

But that logic may not hold. As conditions in Iraq have grown more chaotic, many of us who supported the war are re-evaluating our positions. Over the last year, we've been forced to relearn the lessons of our parents' generation, and it has been a deeply disillusioning experience. The revelation that our government exaggerated claims about weapons of mass destruction has taught us that you can't always trust authority. The photos of Abu Ghraib and flag-draped coffins have taught us the cost of our untempered idealism about spreading our values.

Young people's support for the Administration and the war is not as strong as it once was.

According to a poll released last month by the Harvard University Institute of Politics, college students are no longer more supportive of President Bush than the population at large, and their support for the war has dropped sharply from 65 percent a year ago to 49 percent last month. But the most notable change, which suggests just how deeply young people have been affected by recent events, is that the percentage of students who describe themselves as liberal has increased significantly over the last year—from 36 percent to 44 percent.

Still an open question whether today's generation of young people will remain liberal or return to being more conservative than their parents' generation.

Do these numbers indicate a profound rethinking of our political orientation or are they just a blip? It's possible, I guess, that my generation will remain liberal on social issues (like gay marriage) and conservative when it comes to foreign affairs and national security. It's even possible that we will be the first generation in a long time to be more conservative than our parents. I imagine, though, that we'll have to wait until our 10th reunion to find out.

PERSONAL RESPONSE

Where do you position yourself politically? Do you find yourself more or less radical, more or less conservative, than your parents' generation?

QUESTIONS FOR CLASS OR SMALL-GROUP DISCUSSION

1. Analyze the rhetorical effectiveness of Foer's essay. How well does the title reflect the content? What organizing principle does Foer use? What supporting proof or examples does he use to develop or explain his thesis?

2. Discuss the events that Foer says have had the most impact on his generation and their effects on young people's political views by considering what effect they have had on you. Would you name other events that have had an equal or greater impact than those he cites?

3. Foer says that it is possible that his generation "will be the first generation in a long time to be more conservative than [their] parents" (paragraph 9). What is your viewpoint on that statement? Do you find your friends and classmates to be conservative on some issues and liberal on others?

4. Foer comments on that his generation grew up "believing that America was a force for good in the world" (paragraph 8). To what degree did/do you share that view of America? Has your opinion of America's involvement in international affairs changed in any way by developments in recent years?

WRITING TOPICS

1. Using Foer's essay as a starting point, explain what social or political event has had the most influence on your life. Argue for its importance as a key influence by explaining the event's impact on you personally and how you believe it has affected society in general.

2. Explain the degree to which you feel optimistic about either your personal future or the future of your country, and why.

SUMMARY OF JOSHUA FOER'S "ENTER RIGHT, EXIT LEFT"

In his essay "Enter Right, Exit Left," Joshua Foer explains the change from conservative to liberal in the attitude of many of his generation of undergraduate college students toward the American government and its foreign policies. Many in his generation were more conservative politically than their parents, he says, because they grew up believing in the goodness of the American government and its position as a positive world force. Many in his generation supported the Administration and the war in Iraq. However, revelations about the absence of proof that there were weapons of mass destruction in Iraq and the prisoner abuse in Abu Ghraib have led to a drop in their support of the Administration, a drop in their support for the war, and an increase in the number declaring themselves liberal. Foer concludes by stating that it remains to be seen whether those shifts are temporary or permanent.

EXERCISE

Read Roger Ebert's "Stern Belongs on Radio Just as Much as Rush" below and then summarize it, following the guidelines for writing a summary outlined previously. Your instructor will tell you whether you are to hand in your summary. Prepare for class discussion by considering your responses to the questions that follow the essay.

STERN BELONGS ON RADIO JUST AS MUCH AS RUSH

ROGER EBERT

Film critic for the Chicago Sun Times *since 1967, Ebert was the first-ever recipient of a Pulitzer Prize for film criticism (in 1975) and is perhaps best known for his TV work opposite critic-colleague Gene Siskel on "Siskel and Ebert" and PBS's "At the Movies." He is the author of fifteen books on the cinema, including* A Kiss is Still a Kiss *(1984), and he has also written screenplays, most notably for Russ Meyer's cult classic,* Beyond The Valley of the Dolls *(1970). He currently co-hosts "Ebert & Roeper at the Movies," a syndicated weekly series of film criticism. This piece was published in the April 16, 2004, issue of the* Chicago Sun-Times.

Like millions of Americans, I listen to Howard Stern on the radio in the mornings. I think he is smart, quick and funny. Sometimes he is "offensive," but to be quite frank, I am not "offended," because what he says falls within the realm of words and subjects that, as an adult, I have long been familiar with even without the tutelage of Stern.

Unlike millions of Americans, I do not listen to Rush Limbaugh on the radio. One reason for that is that I am usually at the movies when he's on the air—an alternative I urge on his listeners. Limbaugh does offend me when I monitor him, because he has cheapened political discourse in this country with his canned slogans and cheap shots. Once you call a feminist a "feminazi," what else is there to say about feminism?

Of course you may disagree with me and prefer Limbaugh. I may disagree with you and prefer Stern. *That is our right as Americans.* What offends me is that the right wing, secure in its own right to offend, now wants to punish Stern to the point where he may be forced off the air.

4   The big difference, of course, is that Stern's offenses usually have to do with sex and language, while Limbaugh's have to do with politics. Stern offends the puritan right, which doesn't seem to respect the American tradition of freedom of expression.

You don't have to listen to Stern. Exercising the same freedom, I am Limbaugh-free. And please don't tell me that Stern must be fined and driven off the radio because he uses the "public airwaves." If they are public, then his listeners are the public, and we want to listen to him on our airwaves. The public airwaves cannot be held hostage to a small segment that wants to decide what the rest of us can hear—especially now that President Bush supports consolidating more and more media outlets into a few rich hands.

But what if a child should tune in? Call me old-fashioned, but I believe it is the responsibility of parents to control their children's media input. The entire nation cannot be held hostage so that everything on the radio is suitable for 9-year-olds. Nor do I know of any children who want to listen to Stern, anyway; they prefer music.

It is a belief of mine about the movies, that what makes them good or bad isn't what they're about, but how they're about them. The point is not the subject but the form and purpose of its expression. A listener to Stern will find that he expresses humanistic values, that he opposes hypocrisy, that he talks honestly about what a great many Americans do indeed think and say and do. A Limbaugh listener, on the other hand, might not have guessed from campaigns to throw the book at drug addicts that he was addicted to drugs and required an employee to buy them on the street.

8   But listen carefully. I support Limbaugh's right to be on the radio. I feel it is fully equal to Stern's. I find it strange that so many Americans describe themselves as patriotic when their values are anti-democratic and totalitarian. We are all familiar with Voltaire's great cry: "I may disagree with what you say, but I shall defend, to the death, your right to say it." Ideas like his helped form the emerging American republic. Today, the Federal Communications Commission operates under an alternative slogan: "Since a minority that is very important to this administration disagrees with what you say, shut up."

PERSONAL RESPONSE

When you have time and the opportunity, do you listen to either Rush Limbaugh or Howard Stern (or both) on the radio? If yes, explain why, and if not, explain why not.

QUESTIONS FOR CLASS OR SMALL-GROUP DISCUSSION

1. Keeping in mind that this appeared as a newspaper column and therefore limited the number of words that Ebert could write, analyze Ebert's success at making a case for the position he takes on media censorship.

2. What is the rhetorical effect of the italicized sentence in paragraph 3? Does it help strengthen his point? Is Ebert's repetition of the phrase "cannot be held hostage" in paragraphs 5 and 6 effective? Explain why or why not.

3. Are you satisfied with Ebert's response to his own question in paragraph 6: "But what if a child should tune in?" How would you respond to that question in the context of this argument?

4. What is your response to Ebert's final paragraph? Do you agree with him that Howard Stern and Rush Limbaugh have an equal right to be on the radio? How effective do you find his use of the Voltaire quotation?

3

WRITING A CRITIQUE

THE CONNECTION BETWEEN READING CRITICALLY AND WRITING A CRITIQUE

Recall the guidelines for reading critically outlined in chapter 1 (page 7): The final step is to evaluate what you have read. A critique is the written form of an evaluation of a passage or an entire work. Reading critically is the biggest aid to writing a critique; applying the guidelines for reading critically is a crucial part of preparing to write a critique. You will need to understand not only the purpose of the piece and its central idea but also the main points the writer makes. Reading critically enriches your understanding of a work and its components, enabling you to focus your critique. So the first step in writing a critique is to read critically and, in the process, to determine your opinion of the piece. Apply the guidelines detailed in chapter 1, but especially look for the thesis and purpose of the writing, who the likely intended audience is, key ideas or supporting evidence for the thesis, the author's use of language, how well the piece is organized, and how successfully the piece has achieved its stated or implied goal. You may need to read the piece several times before you are clear on your own viewpoint and therefore prepared to write.

WRITING A CRITIQUE

When you write a critique, your goal is to make a formal analysis of and response to a piece of writing, whether a selected passage or an entire essay. Your purpose encompasses both explaining and evaluating a piece of writing. In general, a written critique includes these components: (1) an introduction; (2) an objective, concise summary of the work or passage; (3) an objective analysis of the author's presentation; (4) a subjective response detailing your opinion of the author's views; and (5) a conclusion. *A critique differs from a summary, which is an objective restatement in your own words of the original material. When you summarize, you leave out your personal or subjective viewpoint. In a critique, you begin objectively but then add your own subjective response to the work.*

A Note on Verb Tense.   Whenever you write about or refer to another person's work, use the present tense: "Robert Sollod **argues** . . ." or "Sollod **asserts** that. . . ." Use the past tense only to refer to something that happened before the time span of the essay: "Sollod **says** that this omission is not a new development, recalling that his own undergraduate career over thirty years earlier **lacked** any real information on religion and spirituality."

Determining your Position.   To convince an audience that your analysis and response are reasonable or valid, you must convey your views confidently. Thus, before you even begin writing your critique, you must have a clear idea of your own viewpoint on the work. A firm conviction of your own position will help persuade an audience that your critique is sensible and fair. How do you arrive at your position? You do so by carefully reading and rereading the piece you are to critique, by thinking seriously about what the piece says and how it says it, and by assessing how persuaded you are as a reader by what the author has said. This stage in the writing process is crucial for helping you formulate and make concrete the points you want to make in the formal assignment.

As with other kinds of writing, any number of tools for generating writing ideas can be used to help you arrive at your position when writing a critique. The following suggestions are no doubt familiar to you from other writing classes, but here they are worded specifically for discovering your response to a piece of writing that you are to critique.

Free Writing.   As soon as you have read or reread the work, write for 10 minutes on any impressions of any aspect of the piece that occur to you. Write down everything that comes to mind, no matter how jumbled. When your time is up, select a phrase or word that seems important to your purpose, no matter how vaguely, and write a sentence with the phrase or word in it. Put that sentence at the top of another blank piece of paper and repeat the process of writing for 10 minutes without thinking very deeply or long about what you are writing. If you do this several times, you should end up with a fairly good idea of the position you want to take in the analysis/assessment part of your paper.

Listing.   Another way to discover your viewpoint is to simply list terms or phrases describing your response to the piece you are critiquing. Then study your list and group related ideas together. Do you see a pattern? Does one dominant viewpoint emerge from these groupings? If so, write a statement reflecting that pattern or viewpoint. That should give you a sense of your position when it comes to writing your assessment of and response to the work.

Asking Questions.   Asking questions is a very useful tool for generating ideas, perhaps most useful when thinking about and drafting your response to a piece of writing. See the discussion on analysis in the next page or so for a number of useful questions to ask when assessing the success of a writer's argument, language, evidence, and logic. These questions will help you arrive at your overall response to the work and discover your own position in relation to that of the writer whose work you are critiquing. However, because the response section of a critique expresses your personal, subjective reaction to the work, you will want to ask additional questions:

- Do you agree with the writer's position on the subject? Why or why not?
- What reasons can you give for supporting or disagreeing with the writer?
- Are you convinced by the writer's logic, evidence, and language? Why or why not?
- If you are not convinced, can you give other evidence to counter the arguments or evidence of the writer?

You do not need to go into great detail in the response section of your paper, but you do need to explain your reasons for your response. Give careful thought, then, to not only what you think of the piece of writing but also why you think that way. What specific elements of the work influence your reaction to the work? As with free writing and listing, write your questions and answers. Review what you have written and consider whether you have left anything unasked or unanswered.

When you are satisfied with your pre-writing activities and feel that you have generated enough ideas to write your critique confidently, you are ready to write your first draft. As with all writing assignments, you will likely write several drafts of a paper before you reach the final version. The following section lists the components of a formal critique and gives directions for writing each of those components.

Introduction.   The first paragraph of your critique should name the author and title of the work that you are critiquing. Do not neglect this information, as it immediately tells readers the subject of your critique. Then give a very brief overview of the piece in two to four sentences. Your intent in the introduction is not to summarize the piece but to tell readers its purpose. Generally, stating the thesis or central idea of the piece along with a highlight or two and/or its major conclusion(s) will be enough to convey its essence and provide background for the rest of your paper. Finally, your introduction should state your own thesis. In one sentence, indicate your assessment of the passage or work that you examined. Your thesis statement should be worded to reveal your position to readers before they begin reading the body of your paper.

Summary.   The first section in the body of your critique should offer an objective summary of the piece. This summary states the original author's purpose and includes key ideas and major points. Where appropriate, include direct quotations that are particularly important to the development of the piece. Do not write anything evaluative or subjective at this point. Your purpose here is to give a fair and accurate summary of the intent and main points of the work you are analyzing.

Analysis.   Once you have summarized the work by stating its purpose and key points, begin to analyze the work. Your goal is to examine how well the author has achieved the purpose and consider the validity or significance of the author's information. Do not try to look at every point the author makes; rather, limit your focus to several important aspects of the piece. Remain as objective as possible in this section, saving your personal opinion of the author's position for the response section of your critique. Different purposes for writing—persuasive, expository, and expressive—require application of different criteria to judge a writer's success in achieving the intended purpose. In general, however, certain considerations help in the assessment of any piece of writing. Questions about validity, accuracy, significance, and fairness help you to evaluate any author's success or failure.

Assessing Persuasive Writing.   Recall that in chapter 1, argumentive writing is defined as a mode of persuasion in which the goal is either to convince readers of the validity of the writer's position (argument) or to move readers to accept the author's view and perhaps even act on it (persuasion). This means that the writer must supply evidence or proof to support his or her position in such a way as to convince readers that the position is valid, whether they agree with the position or not. If the purpose is to persuade, the supporting evidence or proof must be so convincing that readers adopt the position themselves. Chapter 4 is devoted to a full discussion of writing an argument, so you may want to look at the section on structuring an argument (page 58). In any event, when assessing the success of another writer's argument, you should gauge how well that writer has used the standard strategies for argumentation. Furthermore, pay attention to the writer's use of language. Finally, assess the validity of the argument by examining the evidence the writer presents to support his position and the logic of his conclusions.

Examining a Writer's Language.   In particular, make sure that the writer defines any words or terms that may be unclear, abstract, or ambiguous. Ask yourself if the writer's language seems intended to intimidate or confuse readers or if the writer attempts to manipulate readers by relying on emotionally loaded words. Does the writer make sarcastic remarks or personal attacks? Ultimately, examine a writer's evidence, to evaluate credibility and fairness. Good writers do not rely on manipulative language, unclear terms, or loaded or sarcastic words to achieve their purposes.

Examining a Writer's Evidence.   A writer should support any generalizations or claims with ample, relevant evidence. As a critical reader, consider the value or significance of that evidence. Evidence may be supplied in the form of statistics, facts, examples, or appeals to authorities. Keep in mind that statistics can be manipulated to conform to the needs of the person using them, so make sure that they are based on a large and representative sample, that the method of gathering the statistics yields accurate results, and that the statistics come from reliable sources. Look closely at statements of facts, as well; they should give accurate, complete, and trustworthy information. Examples are specific instances or illustrations that reveal a whole type, and they should give believable, relevant, reliable, and representative support for an author's thesis. Finally, authorities are people who have the training or experience needed to make trustworthy and reliable observations on matters relating to their areas of expertise. In completing a critique, make sure, as far as possible, that the piece under study appeals to believable and credible authorities.

Judging a Writer's Logic. Argumentative or persuasive writing must portray a logical, reasonable, and accurate reasoning process supplemented by relevant, sensible supporting proofs. You will be in a good position to evaluate a writer's reasoning process if you are mindful of any pitfalls that undermine the success of the argument. Evaluating the writer's logic is part of the process of critiquing a work. *For a fuller discussion and more examples of common flaws or fallacies, see the section on assessing evidence in chapter 4.* The following list is a summary of some of these flaws in logic that you should look for when writing your critique:

- **Hasty or faulty generalization.** The drawing of a broad conclusion on the basis of very little evidence. Example: Assuming that all rock musicians use hard drugs before performances because of the highly publicized behavior of one or two musicians is an example of faulty generalization.

- **Oversimplification.** Offering a solution or an explanation that is too simple for the problem or issue being argued. This fault in logic overlooks the complexity of an issue. Example: Arguing that the crime rate will go down if we just outlaw handguns overlooks such important considerations as crimes committed with weapons other than handguns and the likely probability that the criminal underworld would continue to have access to guns, illegal or not.

- **Stereotyping.** A form of generalization or oversimplification in which an entire group is narrowly labeled or perceived on the basis of a few in the group. Example: Arguing that women are not suited for combat because women are weaker than men is a stereotype based on the fact that the average woman is weaker than the average man. Not all women are weaker than men.

- **False analogy.** Falsely claiming that, because something resembles something else in one way, it resembles it in all ways. Example: Arguing that anti-abortionists cannot favor the death penalty because they view abortion as murder is a false analogy.

- *Non sequitur.* Drawing inferences or conclusions that do not follow logically from available evidence. Example: Reminding a child who will not eat her food of all the starving children in the world is a line of reasoning that does not follow: if the child eats her food, will that lessen the starvation of other children? If the child does not eat the food, can the food itself somehow aid those starving children?

- *Ad hominem* **arguments.** Attacking the character of the arguer rather than the argument itself. Example: Arguing that because someone has been in prison, you shouldn't believe anything she says.

- **Circular reasoning or begging the question.** Making a claim that simply rephrases another claim in other words. It assumes as proof the very claim it is meant to support. Example: A parent replying "because I said so" when a child asks why he must do something.

- **Emotionally charged language.** Relying on language guaranteed to appeal to their audiences on an emotional rather than an intellectual level. Example: Invoking images of dirty homeless children in rags living on dangerous streets and eating scraps of garbage when arguing for increased funds for child services is an appeal to the emotions. This appeal is all right to use sparingly, but it becomes a fault in logic when the argument is based entirely on such language.

- **Either/or reasoning.** Admitting only two sides to an issue and asserting that the writer's is the only possible correct one. Example: Arguing that if you do not support your country's involvement in war as I do, you are not patriotic. The implication is that "either you are for your country or you are against it and the right way is my way."
- **Red herring.** Diverting the audience's attention from the main issue at hand to an irrelevant issue. Example: Calling attention to the suffering of a victim's family when arguing for the death penalty shifts focus away from the relevant reasons for capital punishment.
- *Post hoc, ergo propter hoc* **reasoning.** Assuming that something happened simply because it followed something else without evidence of a causal relationship. Example: Arguing that an airline is faulty because of flight delays at an airport assumes that the airline caused the delays, when a more important factor might be weather conditions that prevented airplanes from flying.

Response.   In this part of your critique, express your own position relative to that of the writer of the piece and give reasons why you believe as you do. You may find yourself in total agreement or absolutely opposed to the author's position, or you may

---

WRITING A CRITIQUE: PREPARATION AND EVALUATION

First, read the text critically by
- determining the main point, the chief purpose, and the intended audience;
- identifying arguments that support or develop the main point;
- locating evidence used to support the arguments; and
- determining any underlying biases or unexamined assumptions.

Then evaluate the text by asking
- Has the author clearly stated or implied a thesis, main idea, or position?
- Has the author written to a clearly identifiable audience?
- What rhetorical strategies in the development and organization of the essay does the writer use? Is the development appropriate to the purpose? Is the essay logically and clearly organized?
- If the writing is an argument, does the author use verifiable facts or convincing evidence? If the essay seeks to explain, define, describe, or accomplish some other purpose, has the writer supplied enough details to clearly achieve the stated or implied purpose?
- Are language and word choice accurate, imaginative, correct, and/or appropriate?
- Does the text leave any unanswered questions?

GUIDELINES FOR WRITING A CRITIQUE

- Begin with an introduction. The introduction familiarizes readers with the work under discussion, provides a context for the piece, and states your thesis.
- Summarize main points. The summary tells readers what major points the writer makes to support her position.
- Analyze how well the writer has achieved her purpose. The analysis tells readers what aspects of the work you have examined, depending on the kind of writing you are considering. In general, assess the overall presentation of evidence, judging its validity, accuracy, significance, and fairness.
- Explain your response to the piece. The response section tells readers your personal viewpoint by explaining the extent to which you agree or disagree with the author.
- Conclude with your observations of the overall effectiveness of the piece and your personal views on the subject. The conclusion summarizes for readers the results of your analysis and your overall judgment of the piece.

place yourself somewhere in between. You may agree with some points the author makes but disagree with others. No matter what position you take, you must state your viewpoint clearly and provide reasons for your position. These reasons may be closely linked to your assessment of key elements of the paper, as laid out in your assessment section, or they may spring from ideas that you generated in your prewriting activities.

Conclusion. The final paragraph of your critique should reiterate in several sentences your overall assessment of the piece, the conclusions you have drawn from your analysis, and your personal response to the work. This section is not the place to introduce new material; rather, it is an opportunity to provide an overall summary of your paper. You want your readers to feel that you have given them a thorough and thoughtful analysis of the work under consideration, and that you have brought your comments to a satisfying close.

EXERCISE

Read Robert N. Sollod's "The Hollow Curriculum" and the sample critique that follows. Prepare for class discussion by answering the questions for response and discussion after the essay and considering how your response to the piece compares to that of the student writer Kari Kolb.

THE HOLLOW CURRICULUM

ROBERT N. SOLLOD

Robert N. Sollod is a professor of clinical psychology at Cleveland State University. He is author of many articles on spirituality, psychology, and related topics, and was a member of the Task Force on Religious Issues in Graduate Education and Training for the American Psychological Association when he wrote this essay for the March 18, 1992, issue of The Chronicle of Higher Education, *a professional publication for faculty, staff, and administrators in colleges and universities.*

The past decade in academe has seen widespread controversy over curricular reform. We have explored many of the deeply rooted, core assumptions that have guided past decisions about which subjects should be emphasized in the curriculum and how they should be approached. Yet I have found myself repeatedly disappointed by the lack of significant discussion concerning the place of religion and spirituality in colleges' curricula and in the lives of educated persons.

I do not mean to suggest that universities should indoctrinate students with specific viewpoints or approaches to life; that is not their proper function. But American universities now largely ignore religion and spirituality, rather than considering what aspects of religious and spiritual teachings should enter the curriculum and how those subjects should be taught. The curricula that most undergraduates study do little to rectify the fact that many Americans are ignorant of religious and spiritual teachings, of their significance in the history of this and other civilizations, and of their significance in contemporary society. Omitting this major facet of human experience and thought contributes to a continuing shallowness and imbalance in much of university life today.

Let us take the current discussions of multiculturalism as one example. It is hardly arguable that an educated person should approach life with knowledge of several cultures or patterns of experience. Appreciation and understanding of human diversity are worthy educational ideals. Should such an appreciation exclude the religious and spiritually based concepts of reality that are the backbone upon which entire cultures have been based?

4 Multiculturalism that does not include appreciation of the deepest visions of reality reminds me of the travelogues that I saw in the cinema as a child—full of details of quaint and somewhat mysterious behavior that evoked some superficial empathy but no real, in-depth understanding. Implicit in a multicultural approach that ignores spiritual factors is a kind of critical and patronizing attitude. It assumes that we can understand and evaluate the experiences of other cultures without comprehension of their deepest beliefs.

Incomprehensibly, traditionalists who oppose adding multicultural content to the curriculum also ignore the religious and theological bases of the Western civilization that they seek to defend. Today's advocates of Western traditionalism focus, for the most part, on conveying a type of rationalism that is only a single strain in

Western thought. Their approach does not demonstrate sufficient awareness of the contributions of Western religions and spirituality to philosophy and literature, to moral and legal codes, to the development of governmental and political institutions, and to the mores of our society.

Nor is the lack of attention to religion and spirituality new. I recall taking undergraduate philosophy classes in the 1960s in which Plato and Socrates were taught without reference to the fact that they were contemplative mystics who believed in immortality and reincarnation. Everything that I learned in my formal undergraduate education about Christianity came through studying a little Thomas Aquinas in a philosophy course, and even there we focused more on the logical sequence of his arguments than on the fundamentals of the Christian doctrine that he espoused. I recall that Dostoyevsky was presented as an existentialist with hardly a nod given to the fervent Christian beliefs so clearly apparent in his writings. I even recall my professors referring to their Christian colleagues, somewhat disparagingly, as "Christers." I learned about mystical and spiritual interpretations of Shakespeare's sonnets and plays many years after taking college English courses.

We can see the significance of omitting teaching about religion and spirituality in the discipline of psychology and, in particular, in my own field of clinical psychology. I am a member of the Task Force on Religious Issues in Graduate Education and Training in Division 36 of the American Psychological Association, a panel chaired by Edward Shafranske of Pepperdine University. In this work, I have discovered that graduate programs generally do not require students to learn anything about the role of religion in people's lives.

8   Almost no courses are available to teach psychologists how to deal with the religious values or concerns expressed by their clients. Nor are such courses required or generally available at the undergraduate level for psychology majors. Allusions to religion and spirituality often are completely missing in textbooks on introductory psychology, personality theory, concepts of psychotherapy, and developmental psychology.

Recent attempts to add a multicultural perspective to clinical training almost completely ignore the role of religion and spirituality as core elements of many racial, ethnic, and national identities. Prayer is widely practiced, yet poorly understood and rarely studied by psychologists. When presented, religious ideas are usually found in case histories of patients manifesting severe psychopathology.

Yet spiritual and mystical experiences are not unusual in our culture. And research has shown that religion is an important factor in the lives of many Americans; some studies have suggested that a client's religious identification may affect the psychotherapeutic relationship, as well as the course and outcome of therapy. Some patterns of religious commitment have been found to be associated with high levels of mental health and ego strength. A small number of psychologists are beginning to actively challenge the field's inertia and indifference by researching and writing on topics related to religion and spirituality. Their efforts have not as yet, however, markedly affected the climate or curricula in most psychology departments.

Is it any wonder that religion for the typical psychotherapist is a mysterious and taboo topic? It should not be surprising that therapists are not equipped even to ask the appropriate questions regarding a person's religious or spiritual life—much less deal with psychological aspects of spiritual crises.

12   Or consider the field of political science. Our scholars and policy makers have been unable to predict or understand the major social and political movements that produced upheavals around the world during the last decade. That is at least partly because many significant events–the remarkable rise of Islamic fundamentalism, the victory of Afghanistan over the Soviet Union, the unanticipated velvet revolutions in Eastern Europe and in the Soviet Union, and the continuing conflicts in Cyprus, Israel, Lebanon, Northern Ireland, Pakistan, Sri Lanka, Tibet, and Yugoslavia—can hardly be appreciated without a deep understanding of the religious views of those involved. The tender wisdom of our contemporary political scientists cannot seem to comprehend the deep spirituality inherent in many of today's important social movements.

Far from being an anachronism, religious conviction has proved to be a more potent contemporary force than most, if not all, secular ideologies. Too often, however, people with strong religious sentiments are simply dismissed as "zealots" or "fanatics"—whether they be Jewish settlers on the West Bank, Iranian demonstrators, Russian Baptists, Shiite leaders, antiabortion activists, or evangelical Christians.

Most sadly, the continuing neglect of spirituality and religion by colleges and universities also results in a kind of segregation of the life of the spirit from the life of the mind in American culture. This situation is far from the ideals of Thoreau, Emerson, or William James. Spirituality in our society too often represents a retreat from the world of intellectual discourse, and spiritual pursuits are often cloaked in a reflexive anti-intellectualism, which mirrors the view in academe of spirituality as an irrational cultural residue. Students with spiritual interests and concerns learn that the university will not validate or feed their interests. They learn either to suppress their spiritual life or to split their spiritual life apart from their formal education.

Much has been written about the loss of ethics, a sense of decency, moderation, and fair play in American society. I would submit that much of this loss is a result of the increasing ignorance, in circles of presumably educated people, of religious and spiritual world views. It is difficult to imagine, for example, how ethical issues can be intelligently approached and discussed or how wise ethical decisions can be reached without either knowledge or reference to those religious and spiritual principles that underlie our legal system and moral codes.

16   Our colleges and universities should reclaim one of their earliest purposes—to educate and inform students concerning the spiritual and religious underpinnings of thought and society. To the extent that such education is lacking, our colleges and universities are presenting a narrow and fragmented view of human experience.

Both core curricula and more advanced courses in the humanities and social sciences should be evaluated for their coverage of religious topics. Active leadership at the university, college, and departmental levels is needed to encourage and carry out needed additions and changes in course content. Campus organizations should develop forums and committees to examine the issue, exchange information, and develop specific proposals.

National debate and discussion about the best way to educate students concerning religion and spirituality are long overdue.

PERSONAL RESPONSE

Describe the degree to which you are spiritual or religious. How important is religion in your life?

QUESTIONS FOR CLASS OR SMALL-GROUP DISCUSSION

1. Sollod gives examples of how an understanding of religion and spirituality would help someone trained in his field, psychology, and how it would help political scientists. In what other disciplines or fields do you think such training would be important? Explain how it would enhance the understanding of people trained in those fields.

2. Discuss whether you agree with Sollod that religion and spirituality have a place in the college curriculum.

3. Sollod calls for campus organizations to develop forums and committees to examine the place of religion and spirituality on the college campus and to develop specific proposals on the issue (paragraph 18). Conduct your own class forum or create a class committee to consider the issues that Sollod raises. Where do people learn about spirituality? How do you think a person could benefit from learning about religion and spirituality in college courses?

ILLUSTRATION: CRITIQUE

Kolb 1

Kari Kolb

English 150

September 20, 2005

A Critique of "The Hollow Curriculum"

In his essay "The Hollow Curriculum," Robert Sollod addresses the controversial subject of religion in the public school system, particularly at the college level. Sollod believes that by failing to acknowledge religious histories and teachings, universities contribute to the declining morality of

Kolb 2

society. He recommends an evaluation of course offerings in terms of ways in which courses on religion or spirituality can be integrated into higher education curriculum. Such a project would involve not only university faculty and administrators but also American citizens nationwide. While it may be true that recent years have seen a moral or ethical decline in the general public, Sollod's assertion that this decline is due to religious ignorance is not only unfounded but also untrue.

Sollod begins his piece by exploring the lack of religious and spiritual emphasis in the national curriculum and in the lives of college alumni. After explaining the religious background of America's history, he goes on to look at other cultures as well. Noting that much of multicultural appreciation depends on understanding others' cultures, Sollod points out that many other civilizations have built the foundation of their culture upon religious and spiritual beliefs. He does not endorse one particular faith; rather, he suggests that all-inclusive religious studies would enrich the careers and lives of college students. Sollod continues by warning that a lack of religious studies has resulted in "the loss of ethics, a sense of decency, moderation, and fair play in American society" (45). His proposed solution includes a curriculum assessment of current course offerings in religion and spirituality, active leadership of faculty and administrators across the university to initiate curriculum change, and the involvement of students in the form of debates and committees (45).

Kolb 3

Sollod has a solid sense of his audience, made up primarily of faculty and staff in higher education. By implication, what he proposes is of interest to students as well. Sollod draws readers into his argument with a series of questions and then offers information in a simple yet authoritative manner. He provides detailed examples, explaining how religious understanding would enhance all areas of study, ranging from the broad fields of political science and psychology to the ideas of Shakespeare and Socrates. This wide-ranging analysis enables Sollod to reach his large and somewhat diverse audience. He bases much of his reasoning upon the idea that "religious and spiritually based concepts . . . are the backbone upon which entire cultures have been based" (43).

Sollod's valid argument is made even more credible when he extends it to include familiar examples, such as conflicts in the former Soviet Union, Ireland, and the Middle East. At times, Sollod relies on emotional appeals, seen most often in his occasional use of loaded words and phrases such as "continuing shallowness and imbalance" (43) and "mysterious and taboo" (44). In general, though, he makes a fair and logical argument, and he concludes with a rational solution to what he sees as a serious problem.

I agree with Sollod when he states that the college curriculum would be greatly enhanced by the addition of courses in religion and spirituality or the incorporation of such material in traditional

Kolb 4

courses. Such courses would provide a solid grounding
for most professions and promote a greater cultural
understanding in general. I do believe, however, that
Sollod exaggerates in his statement that the loss of
ethics in American society is "a result of the
increasing ignorance, in circles of presumably
educated people, of religious and spiritual world
views" (45). Here, Sollod makes an inaccurate
generalization, with no evidence or clear reasoning
to back up his stance. On the contrary, statistics
show that in the past thirty years, religion has not
only sustained itself, but it has also diversified.
According to a recent survey, "Some 375 ethnic or
multiethnic religious groups have already formed in
the United States in the last three decades.
Sociologists of religion believe the numbers will
only increase in the coming years" (Beckman). These
religious groups are not only the creations of
immigrants, but they also reflect America's growing
diversity. In fact, as Joanne Beckman of Duke
University explains, almost half of the baby boomer
generation has dropped out of their traditional
churches and are "just as willing to sample Eastern
religions, New Age spiritualism, or quasi-religious
self-help groups. . . . [F]or [these] seekers,
spirituality is a means of individual expression,
self-discovery, inner healing, and personal growth."
Although the deterioration of moral values is a
frustrating problem in our society, it cannot, as
Sollod suggests, be attributed entirely to a lack of
religious appreciation and diversity.

Kolb 5

"The Hollow Curriculum" endorses a controversial proposal that has prompted much deliberation: the addition of, or increase in, religious and spiritual studies in our national curriculum. Although Sollod does well in arguing his position on the subject, he assumes, without proof, that much of university life is shallow and that university curricula is unbalanced. Further, he makes a hasty generalization when he places the blame of America's ethical undoing on the lack of "knowledge or reference to those religious and spiritual principles that underline our legal system and moral codes" (45). In this generalization, he neglects to recognize the growing religious and spiritual diversity of the American people. This omission weakens the foundation of his argument—that an increase in religious studies will benefit all areas of life—by overlooking evidence showing that, despite an increase in spiritual awareness, the loss of ethics remains a problem in our society. Sollod thus undermines his own position and leaves his readers, though inspired by his zeal, understandably skeptical.

Works Cited

Beckman, Joanne. "Religion in Post-World War II in
    America." *Divining America*. October 2000. Duke
    U. 17 Sept. 2004. <http://uni52v.unity.ncsu.
    edu:8080/tserve/twenty/tkeyinfo/trelww2.htm>.

Sollod, Robert. "The Hollow Curriculum." *Perspectives
    on Contemporary Issues: Readings Across the
    Curriculum*, 4th ed. Ed. Katherine Anne Ackley.
    Boston, MA: Thomson Wadsworth, 2006. 43-45.

WHO NEEDS COLLEGE?

LINDA LEE

Linda Lee is an editor and writer for the New York Times. *An article she wrote for the Education Life supplement of that publication in 1998, called "What's the Rush? Why College Can Wait," was the basis for her book* Success Without College: Why Your Child May Not Have to Go to College Right Now—And May Not Ever Have to Go *(2000). In addition to contributing to the* Times, *Lee is the author of several books. This brief essay, which touches on some of the ideas explained in her book, appeared in the "Full Circle" column of the June 12, 2001, issue of* Family Circle.

Do you, like me, have a child who is smart but never paid attention in class? Now it's high school graduation time. Other parents are talking Stanford this and State U. that. Your own child has gotten into a pretty good college. The question is: Is he ready? Should he go at all?

In this country two-thirds of high school graduates go on to college. In some middle-class suburbs, that number reaches 90 percent. So why do so many feel the need to go?

America is obsessed with college. It has the second-highest number of graduates worldwide, after (not Great Britain, not Japan, not Germany) Australia. Even so, only 27 percent of Americans have a bachelor's degree or higher. That leaves an awful lot who succeed without college, or at least without a degree. Many read books, think seriously about life and have well-paying jobs. Some want to start businesses. Others want to be electricians or wilderness guides or makeup artists. Not everyone needs a higher education.

4   What about the statistics showing that college graduates make more money? First, until the computer industry came along, all the highest-paying jobs *required* a college degree: doctor, lawyer, engineer. Second, on average, the brightest and hardest-working kids in school go to college. So is it a surprise that they go on to make more money? And those studies almost always pit kids with degrees against those with just high school. An awful lot have additional training, but they are not included. Ponder for a moment: Who makes more, a plumber or a philosophy major?

These are tough words. I certainly wouldn't have listened to them five years ago when my son was graduating from high school. He had been smart enough to get into the Bronx High School of Science in New York and did well on his SATs. But I know now that he did not belong in college, at least not straight out of high school.

But he went, because all his friends were going, because it sounded like fun, because he could drink beer and hang out. He did not go to study philosophy. Nor did he feel it incumbent to go to class or complete courses. Meanwhile I was paying $1,000 a week for this pleasure cruise.

Eventually I asked myself, "Is he getting $1,000 a week's worth of education?" Heck no. That's when I began wondering why everyone needs to go to college. (My hair colorist makes $300,000 a year without a degree.) What about the famous people who don't have one, like Bill Gates (dropped out of Harvard) and Walter Cronkite (who left the University of Texas to begin a career in journalism)?

8   So I told my son (in a kind way) that his college career was over for now, but he could reapply to the Bank of Mom in two years if he wanted to go back. Meanwhile, I said, get a job.

If college is so wonderful, how come so many kids "stop out"? (That's the new terminology.) One study showed only 26 percent of those who began four-year colleges had earned a degree in six years. And what about the kids who finish, then can't find work? Of course, education is worth a great deal more than just employment. But most kids today view college as a way to get a good job.

I know, I know. What else is there to do? Won't he miss the "college experience?" First off, there are thousands of things for kids to do. And yes, he will miss the college experience, which may include binge drinking, reckless driving and sleeping in on class days. He can have the same experience in the Marine Corps, minus the sleeping in, and be paid good money for it and learn a trade and discipline.

If my son had gone straight through college, he would be a graduate by now. A number of his friends are, and those who were savvy enough to go into computers at an Ivy League school walked into $50,000-a-year jobs. But that's not everyone. An awful lot became teachers making half that. And some still don't know what they want to do.

12   They may, like my son, end up taking whatever jobs they can get. Over the last two years, he's done roofing, delivered UPS packages and fixed broken toilets. His phone was turned off a few times, and he began to pay attention to details, like the price of a gallon of gasoline.

But a year ago he began working at a telecommunications company. He loves his work, and over the last year, he's gotten a raise and a year-end bonus. He tells me now he plans to stay there and become a manager.

So, just about on schedule, my son has had his own graduation day. And although I won't be able to take a picture of him in cap and gown, I couldn't be any more proud. He grew up, as most kids do. And he did it, for the most part, in spite of college.

PERSONAL RESPONSE

Respond to the questions posed by Lee in her first paragraph. Are you ready for college? Should you go at all? What would you do if you were not in college?

QUESTIONS FOR CLASS OR SMALL-GROUP DISCUSSION

1. Lee states in paragraph 3 that "not everyone needs a higher education." Do you agree with her? Discuss your response to her statement.

2. In paragraph 5, Lee says that her son "did not belong in college, at least not straight out of high school." Explore the implications of that statement by considering the advantages and disadvantages of postponing entry into college after high-school graduation.

3. Summarize Lee's "case against college." What is her strongest argument? How do you respond to that point?

4. What is your reaction to Lee's characterization of "the college experience" in paragraph 10? Is it true of your own experience in college? Would you describe the college experience differently? If so, how would you describe it?

CHAPTER

4

WRITING AN ARGUMENT

Argumentation is a reasoning process that seeks to provide evidence or proof that a proposition is valid or true. An argument sets forth a claim and presents a coherent, organized set of reasons why that claim is reasonable. A typical way of viewing argumentation is to see it in terms of *premises* and a *conclusion*. The conclusion is the statement being argued for, and the premises are the statements of proof. When you make a statement about something that you believe is logical or right and then offer reasons why you believe that way in order to convince someone, you are making an argument. An argument may have several goals or purposes, either singly or in combination, such as to show relationships between things (causal argument), to explain or define something (definition argument), to evaluate something or support a position on it (evaluative argument), or to sway an audience to take action on something (persuasive argument). In actuality, much of the writing you do in college is a form of argument. Argumentation is a useful tool for developing critical thinking because doing it well requires close analysis of our own ideas as well as those of others.

NARROWING YOUR FOCUS AND DISCOVERING YOUR POSITION

All arguments begin with a position, claim, or proposition that is debatable and that has opposing viewpoints. Statements of fact are not debatable; abstract generalizations are too vague. If your position is not debatable, there is no argument. Furthermore, in an argument, your goal is to convince those opposed to your position that yours is valid or true. You might even want to persuade your audience to abandon their position and adopt yours. Your first step, then, is to select a controversial subject or issue that you have a strong interest in. That begins the process that will ultimately lead you to the position you want to take on it.

One way to approach this step in the process of writing an argument is to ask questions about a controversial or debatable subject or issue. Should bilingual education be offered in public schools? Should the Electoral College be abolished? Is Affirmative Action a fair policy? Should marijuana be legalized? Should gay couples be allowed to marry? While such questions seldom have absolutely right or wrong answers, it is useful to frame your position by saying (or implying), "Yes, bilingual education should be offered in public schools," or, "No, Affirmative Action is not a fair policy." But making up your mind about how you feel about an issue is only the beginning. You must also convince others that your position is logical, reasonable, or valid. You do that by providing strong evidence or reasons to support your position and by anticipating and addressing the arguments of those who do not agree with you.

A good starting point for discovering a topic to argue is to make a list of controversial issues currently in the news or being discussed and debated publicly or among your friends or family. *Remember that this is only a starting point.* These general topics are far too broad for a short paper, but they give you a beginning from which to start narrowing your focus. From your list, select the subjects that interest you most or that you feel strongly about and develop a series of questions that you might ask about them. This process of considering a variety of views when contemplating a topic you would like to argue helps you solidify your position.

Examples.

1. Suppose you are interested in the subject of downloading music from the Internet, currently illegal but still being done all over the world. Should those who download music from the Internet be charged with a crime? Should those who wish to download music from the Internet have to pay for that service? People will disagree on how these questions should be answered; thus, they are legitimate subjects for argumentation. Suppose you believe that, no, downloading music from the Internet should not be regarded as a criminal act. What other questions does that position lead to, then? Should downloading music be free and open to anyone who wants to do it? If so, what is the fairest way to treat artists whose music is being downloaded from the Internet? Do they not have the right to profit from the use of their music?

2. Consider the suggestion that the grading system at the college level be abolished. You might wonder: Should the grading system be abolished? Why should the grading system be abolished? Why should the grading system not be abolished? What would replace the grading system were it abolished? How would abolishing the grading system affect students and instructors? Would it change the dynamics of the learning process?

The following list of potentially controversial subjects may give you an idea of the kinds of general topics that can be narrowed for an argumentative paper. To this list, add others that appeal to you as potential topics for an argument. Then, select those subjects that you have the strongest interest in or hold opinions about and, taking each in turn, spend some time writing down questions that come to mind about that subject, issues related to it that you are aware of, and/or what your preliminary position on the subject is: What do you think should be done? Why do you believe it should it be done? Which is the best solution to the problem?

At this stage, you are simply **brainstorming** or **free writing** to see what you know about certain self-selected subjects that you would be comfortable with developing into an argument paper. When you have finished, examine the results of your brainstorming session and narrow your list to the one or two that you have the most to say about or feel most strongly about. Brainstorm further on those issues by framing questions about the subject or trying to identify the problem associated with it. Keep in mind that you not only want to find an issue or issues that you have a strong interest in, but you also must consider the implications of the position you take on that issue. How will you convince your audience that your position is reasonable or logical? How can you best defend your position? How can you best meet the arguments of those opposed to you?

You are looking for a topic that poses a question or problem you believe you know the answer or solution to. This is your position. Once you know your position, you are

---

POSSIBLE SUBJECTS FOR ARGUMENTATION

Abtinence-only education	Eliminating the grading system	The Patriot Act
Advertising images		Pay inequity
Affirmative Action	Embryo or stem-cell research	Poverty
AIDS treatment or prevention	English Only movement	Publishing images of war
Animal rights	The Environment	Racial profiling
Arts funding	Euthanasia and assisted suicide	Reparations for slavery
Bilingual education		Same-sex marriages
Binge drinking	Gender issues	School prayer
Capital punishment	Genetic engineering	Space exploration
Censorship	Global warming	Steroids and athletes
Civil rights	Gun control/Gun rights	Sweatshops
Downloading music from the Internet	Homelessness	Terrorism in America
Drugs and drug abuse	Human cloning	Tobacco use
	Human rights	Violence in film
Drunk driving punishment	Immigration	Violence in rock lyrics
Eating disorders	Legalization of marijuana	Violence in schools
Electoral College	Nuclear proliferation	Violence on television
	Outsourcing	Workplace discrimination

NARROWING YOUR FOCUS AND DISCOVERING YOUR POSITION

- Make a list of controversial or arguable subjects about which you have an opinion or are strongly interested in.
- Ask questions about each subject from as many angles as you can think of.
- Keep narrowing your focus as often as possible.
- Write down ideas that occur to you as you ask your questions.
- Select one or two topics that seem most promising to you.
- Repeat the brainstorming process by asking more questions and writing more thoughts as they occur. At this stage you are working toward a defensible position on a fairly narrow topic.
- Consider how you might defend your position, how you would counter arguments against it, and what evidence you might need.
- Select the topic that emerges as your strongest and begin the process of thinking about, researching, and writing your paper on that narrow topic.

ready to commit time to thinking about and researching the best evidence or proof to support your position.

Example.   Erin was intrigued by an essay she read on advertising images of women, so she began the process of discovering her position by thinking about the very general subject "advertising images." Her questions, answers, and ideas look rambling but

ADVERTISING IMAGES

Do advertising images affect behavior? Very likely, or advertisers wouldn't put so much money into advertising.

Isn't it the purpose of an ad to influence behavior?

So what if they do affect behavior? What's the harm?

Such power might influence behavior the wrong way.

What is the wrong way? Affects self esteem. Makes people feel inadequate. Reduces women to objects.

What about men? Ads affect them too.

Some ads set up unrealistic images of men and women. Young or old, male or female.

Present false images of relationships between men and women. Ads focus a lot on sex and on attacking people's vulnerabilities.

Who bears responsibility? Advertisers. They need to consider the effects of their ads. What should they do? Modify images that attack and weaken self esteem.

Topic: advertisers' responsibility for their ads. (Use Kilbourne's essay on harmful images and O'Toole's defense of advertising.)

ultimately led her to her topic. Her paper appears on page 74 in the section on sample student papers.

STRUCTURING AN ARGUMENT

Formal argumentation has its roots in ancient Greek and Roman rhetoric. Its essential parts are based on their classical counterparts: introduction *(exordium)*, statement of the case *(narratio)*, thesis or position statement *(proposition)*, refutation of opposing arguments *(refutatio)*, development of the argument *(confirmatio)*, and conclusion *(peroration)*. Effective arguments follow this pattern, or variations of it.

Introduction.   The opening of your argument lays the groundwork for the rest of the paper by establishing the tone you will take, providing any clarification or preliminary information necessary, and/or giving a statement of your own qualifications for asserting a position on the topic.

Statement of the Case.   As clearly as possible, provide a rationale or need for the argument. You might provide a context for the argument, give relevant background material, or explain why you believe as you do. For example, you might explain that the position is worth upholding or endorsing because it has some bearing on the lives of readers or the common good of a community or society, or you might indicate the degree to which a particular issue or policy is controversial.

Proposition.   The proposition is an assertion or claim about the issue. The proposition corresponds to a thesis statement in other kinds of writing and should be stated clearly near the beginning of the essay. You must make your position clear very early in the argument and then devote the rest of your paper to providing evidence, details, or facts to "prove" that your position is a logical or reasonable one. The strength of your argument will come from the evidence or other details that you select to support your position.

Refutation of Opposing Arguments.   This is the stage of the process in which you present your evidence or proof to persuade your audience of the validity of your position. In the rhetoric of classical argument, this stage is called **invention** and involves determining what arguments will be most effective for supporting your proposition. Nor is it enough to find facts or evidence that argue your own position; you must also realize that those opposed to your position will have their own facts or evidence. You must try to project what you think others may say or even try to put yourself into their position. One of the chief strengths of a good argument is its ability to counter evidence produced by the opposing side. In fact, you must imagine more than one opposing side; what possible positions can others take? Rarely is an issue represented by just two equal and opposing arguments. Often it is represented by multiple viewpoints. Thus you must anticipate what the other possible positions on your subject may be. The preparatory step of anticipating or imagining the opposing position(s)

STRUCTURE OF AN ARGUMENT

- **Introduction**—Familiarizes audience with subject, provides background, and establishes tone.
- **Statement of the case**—Provides rationale or need for the argument.
- **Proposition**—Asserts a position or claim that will be supported, demonstrated, or proved in the course of the paper.
- **Refutation of opposing arguments**—Mentions and counters potential evidence or objections of opposing arguments.
- **Development of your argument**—Offers convincing, creditable, evidence in support of proposition.
- **Conclusion**—Brings paper to a satisfactory end.

---

will be a huge help in developing your own argument. What do you think will be the strategy of those opposed to your position? How can you best address that opposition and counter it with your own logical reasoning?

Development of Your Argument.   The argument will be most effective if it is organized with the least-convincing or least-important point first, building to its strongest point. This pattern lends emphasis to the most-important points and engages readers in the unfolding process of the argument as the writer moves through increasingly compelling proofs. A successful argument also gives evidence of some sort for every important point. Evidence may include statistics, observations or testimony of experts, personal narratives, or other supporting proof. A writer needs to convince readers by taking them from some initial position on an issue to the writer's position, which readers will share if the argument succeeds. The only way to do this is to provide evidence that convinces readers that the position is a right or valid one.

Conclusion.   In the closing paragraph(s) of your paper, you have a final opportunity to convince your audience that the evidence you have presented in the body of your paper successfully demonstrates why your proposition is valid. You may want to summarize your strongest arguments or restate your position. You may want to suggest action, solutions, or resolutions to the conflict. This final part of your paper must leave your audience with a feeling that you have presented them with all the essential information they need to know to make an intelligent assessment of your success at defending your position and possibly persuading them to believe as you do.

STRATEGIES FOR ARGUING EFFECTIVELY

While the previous section outlines the essential structure of an argument, the following comments will also help you write an effective argument.

Know Your Audience.   A consideration of who your audience is will help you anticipate the arguments of those opposed to you. Many instructors tell their students to imagine an audience who disagrees with your position. After all, there really is no argument if you address an audience of people who believe exactly as you do. Knowing your audience will help you figure out what strategies you must use to make your position convincing. Imagine that you are addressing an audience who is either indifferent to or opposed to your position. This will help direct the shape of your argument because such an audience will require solid evidence or persuasive illustrations to sway its opinion.

Establish an Appropriate Tone.   **Tone** refers to the writer's attitude toward his or her subject. As a writer of argument, you want your audience to take you seriously, to weigh what you have to say in defense of your position, and, ideally, to not only agree that your reasoning is sound but also to agree with your position. Therefore, try to keep your tone sincere, engaging, and balanced. You do not want to take a hostile, sarcastic, or antagonistic tone because then you risk alienating your audience. If you are too light, flippant, or humorous, your audience might believe you to be insincere or not truly interested in your topic.

Follow a Logical Line of Reasoning.   Formal argumentation typically follows one of two common lines of reasoning, **deductive** and **inductive** reasoning. In *deductive* reasoning, you move from a general principle, or shared premise, to a conclusion about a specific instance. Premises are assumptions that people share, and the conclusion will be implied in the premises or assumptions. The traditional form of deductive reasoning is the **syllogism,** which has two premises and a conclusion. The premises are often referred to as *major* and *minor,* with the major premise being the general truth and the minor premise a specific instance. The classic syllogism, offered by Aristotle (384–322 BCE), a Greek mathematician and logician, is the following:

> **Major premise:** All men are mortal.
> **Minor premise:** Socrates is a man.
> **Conclusion:** Socrates is mortal.

This simple example of syllogism indicates the basic formula: A is B. C is B. Therefore A is C. Arguments are described as valid when the premises lead logically to the conclusion. If they do not, the argument is invalid. Similarly, an argument is said to be sound if the argument is valid and leads to the conclusion; it is unsound if the argument is valid but does not lead to the conclusion or if the conclusion is valid but the argument is not. Here is another example:

> **Major premise:** Drinking while drunk is illegal.
> **Minor premise:** Joe was drunk when he drove home from the party.
> **Conclusion:** Joe committed a crime.

In contrast, *inductive* reasoning moves from a number of specific instances to a general principle. Rather than begin with a shared assumption or generalization, you must provide sufficient data or evidence that the generalization is warranted. Your intent is to show the general pattern by presenting relevant specific instances as evidence. To avoid being accused of over-generalizing or making a hasty generalization, you must provide enough data, examples, or specific instances to ensure that your audience is satisfied with your conclusion. In contrast to deductive reasoning, which rests on certainties (shared or commonly acknowledged truths), inductive reasoning relies on probability (the likelihood that something is true). Example:

> **Observation one:** Students entering the classroom have wet hair and damp clothes.
> **Observation two:** Students typically come from outside the building to class.
> **Conclusion:** It must be raining outside.

With induction, you must be very careful that your data do indeed warrant your conclusion. For instance, consider the following example of **hasty generalization:**

> **Observation one:** The daily high temperatures for the last several days have been unusually high.
> **Observation two:** I don't remember its ever being this hot during the summer.
> **Conclusion:** We must be experiencing global warming.

Obviously there is not enough evidence in either of the observations to establish that global warming accounts for the recent high temperatures.

While formal argumentation is useful when arguing in abstract or ideal disciplines, such as mathematics, it is less effective in complex, real-world situations—that is, the kinds of arguments in which you are likely to be engaged. Aristotle himself realized that syllogistic reasoning, which deals in absolutes, was not suited to all arguments and that many arguments depended on an informal logic of probabilities or uncertainties. His study of this system of reasoning was known as *rhetoric,* which he defined as "the faculty of discovering in any particular case all of the available means of persuasion." Formal syllogistic logic typically leads to one correct and incontrovertible conclusion, while informal or rhetorical logic allows for probable or possible conclusions. As in syllogistic logic, the reasoning process must be rational and practical. One highly effective model of informal argumentation, or practical reasoning, is that described by Stephen Toulmin, a 20th-century philosopher, mathematician, and physicist.

The Toulmin Model of Reasoning.

The Toulmin Model of Reasoning.   Toulmin defined argumentation as a process or logical progression from **data** or **grounds** (evidence or reasons that support a claim), to the **claim** (the proposition, a debatable or controversial assertion, drawn from the data or grounds) based on the **warrant** (the underlying assumption). The *claim* is the point your paper is making, your thesis or arguable position statement. *Data* or *grounds* constitute your proof and demonstrate how you know the claim is true or the basis of your claim. *Warrants* are the underlying assumptions or inferences that are taken for granted and that connect the claim to the data. They are typically unstated or implied and can be based on any of several types of appeals: logic, ethics, emotion, and/or shared values.

This view of argumentation as a logical progression has similarities to formal argumentation but does not rely on inductive or deductive reasoning that leads inevitably to one true conclusion. Rather, it relies on establishing the relationship between data and the claim by offering evidence that supports the warrant and leads to the best possible, the most probable, or the most likely conclusion. In such reasoning, the argument often attempts to defuse opposing arguments with the use of **qualifiers** such as *some, many, most, usually, probably, possibly, might,* or *could.* Qualifiers indicate awareness that the claim is not absolute but reasonable in the specific instance. This step reveals how sure you are of your claim.

The argument should also recognize any **conditions of rebuttal**—that is, exceptions to the rule. Rebuttals address potential opposing arguments, usually by showing flaws in logic or weakness of supporting evidence. An argument will also, if necessary, make **concessions** or acknowledgments that certain opposing arguments cannot be refuted. The act of acknowledging limitations or exceptions to your own argument actually strengthens your argument. It indicates your commitment to your position despite its flaws, or suggests that, even flawed, your position is stronger than the positions of those opposed to it. Often **backing**—additional justification or support for the warrant—is supplied as a secondary argument to justify the warrant. To succeed, an argument following the Toulmin model depends heavily on the strength of its warrants or assumptions, which in turn means having a full awareness of any exceptions, qualifications, or possible reservations.

Use Appeals Effectively.   Aristotle maintained that effective persuasion is achieved by a balanced use of three appeals to an audience: *logos* (logic), *ethos* (ethics), and *pathos* (emotion, related to the words pathetic, sympathy, and empathy). Other appeals may be used, such as shared values. In the Toulmin method, appeals support warrants. Thus, an argument will call upon recognized authority or establish the

---

SUMMARY OF THE TOULMIN MODEL

Data or **grounds**—Evidence or facts that support the claim. This is your proof and demonstrates how you know the claim is true or what the basis of your claim is.

Claim—The arguable or controversial assertion. This is the point the paper is making.

Warrant—The underlying assumptions or inferences that are taken for granted and that connect the claim to the data. The warrant is typically unstated or implied and can be based on any of several types of appeals: logic, ethics, emotion, and/or shared values.

Qualifiers—Words such as *some, many,* and *probably* that indicate awareness that the claim is not absolute but reasonable in the specific instance. This step reveals how sure you are of your claim.

Conditions of rebuttals—Addressing potential opposing arguments, usually by showing flaws in logic or weakness of supporting evidence. This step may include making concessions and acknowledging limitations or exceptions to your own argument.

Backing—Additional justification or support for the warrant.

Concession—Acknowledging validity of opposing argument(s).

credibility of a source (ethics); it will use sound reasoning or apply inductive or deductive reasoning (logic). A good argument will even make an appeal to the emotions of its audience, in moderation. Finally, an argument may want to appeal to the audience on the basis of shared values, such as human dignity, free speech, fairness, and the like.

Assess the Evidence.   Reading critically is important in argumentation. You can build your own argument by trying to keep an open mind when analyzing the arguments of those opposed to your position as you read in search of evidence to support your position. What questions should you ask when analyzing the positions of those opposed to you? Consider the following: What is the author's purpose? How well does he or she achieve that purpose? What evidence does the writer give in support of that purpose? How does the author know the evidence is true? What is the argument based on? Has the writer omitted or ignored important evidence? Does the author's argument lead to a logical conclusion? Sometimes something that seems to be logical or reasonable turns out to be false. Are you convinced of the credibility of the author's sources? What sort of language does the writer use? Is it clear and fair? Does the writer use words that are heavily charged or "loaded" and therefore likely to play on emotions rather than appeal to reason? Does the writer make any of the common fallacies (errors of reasoning) associated with attempts to be logical and fair? (See the following common fallacies.)

Common Rhetorical Fallacies

Part of your strategy in writing a good argument is to evaluate your own reasoning process as well as that of other writers, especially those whose works you may use in support of your own argument. Look for these **common flaws** or **fallacies** in your own writing or in that of any writing you analyze:

- **Hasty generalization.** A writer makes a hasty generalization if she draws a broad conclusion on the basis of very little evidence. Such a writer probably has not explored enough evidence and has jumped too quickly to conclusions. **Examples:** Assuming that all politicians are corrupt because of the bad behavior of one is an example of making a hasty generalization. Condemning all films with violent content because of one film that has received widespread criticism for its graphic violence is another example.
- **Oversimplification.** In oversimplification, the arguer offers a solution that is too simple for the problem or issue being argued. **Example:** For instance, arguing that the problem of homelessness could be solved by giving jobs to homeless people overlooks the complexity of the issue. Such a suggestion does not take into account such matters as drug or alcohol dependency that sometimes accompanies life on the streets or a range of other problems faced by people who have lost their homes and learned to live outdoors.
- **Stereotyping.** Another form of generalization is stereotyping—that is, falsely applying the traits of a few individuals to their entire group or falsely drawing a conclusion about a group on the basis of the behavior or actions of a few in

that group. Stereotyping is also oversimplification because it ignores the complexity of humans by reducing them to a few narrow characteristics. Stereotyping produces a false image or impression of a large number of people who have a certain thing in common—most frequently race, ethnicity, gender, or sexual preference—but also such widely differing things as occupation, hair color, speech habits, or educational level. **Example:** Any assertion about an entire group of people on the basis of a few in that group is stereotyping.

- **False analogy.** A writer may falsely claim that, because something resembles something else in one way, it resembles it in all ways. This warning does not deny that analogy has a place in argument. It can be an extremely useful technique by emphasizing a comparison that furthers an argument, especially for a difficult point. Explaining a difficult concept in terms of a simpler, more familiar one can give helpful support to readers. However, make sure that the analogy is true and holds up under close scrutiny. **Example:** A controversial analogy that is sometimes used is the comparison of America's internment of American citizens of Japanese descent during World War II to Hitler's concentration camps. On some levels the comparison is justified: people in the U.S. internment camps were held against their will in confined areas guarded by armed soldiers, they often lost all of their property, and some were even killed in the camps. On the other hand, they were not starved to death, exterminated, or used as subjects of medical experiments. The analogy is useful for making a point about the unfair treatment of American citizens during wartime, but many would argue that the analogy breaks down on some very important points.

- *Non sequitur.* This Latin term, meaning "does not follow," refers to inferences or conclusions that do not follow logically from available evidence. Non sequiturs also occur when a person making an argument suddenly shifts course and brings up an entirely new point. **Example:** The following demonstrates a *non sequitur:* "My friend Joan broke her arm during a gymnastics team practice after school. After-school activities are dangerous and should be banned."

- *Ad hominem* **arguments.** This Latin term means "against the man" or "toward the person" and applies to arguments that attack the character of the arguer rather than the argument itself. *Ad hominem* arguments often occur in politics, for instance, when opponents of a candidate refer to personal characteristics or aspects of the candidate's private life as evidence of her or his unsuitability to hold office. **Example:** Arguing that a candidate would not make a good senator because she is a single parent or that a candidate would not be effective as mayor because he is homosexual ignores the more important questions of qualifications for the office, the candidate's stand on issues relevant to the position, the candidate's experience in political office, and similar substantive considerations.

- **Circular reasoning or begging the question.** This error makes a claim that simply rephrases another claim in other words. It assumes as proof the very claim it is meant to support. **Example:** This sort of logic occurs in statements such as "We do it because that's the way we've always done it," which assumes the validity of a particular way of doing things without questioning or examining its importance or relevance.

- **Emotionally charged language.** Writers may rely on language guaranteed to appeal to their audiences on an emotional level rather than an intellectual level. Writers do not have to avoid appeals to the emotions entirely, but they should limit their use of such appeals. Arguments on ethical or moral issues such as abortion or capital punishment lend themselves to emotional appeals, but arguments on just about any subject may be charged with emotion. This fallacy can appeal to any number of emotions, such as fear, pity, hatred, sympathy, or compassion. Emotionally charged language also includes **loaded words,** those whose meanings or emotional associations vary from person to person or group to group, and **slanted words,** those whose connotations (suggestive meaning as opposed to actual meaning) are selected for their emotional association. **Examples:** Abstract words are usually loaded, such as democracy, freedom, justice, or loyalty. Words may be slanted to convey a good association, such as those used in advertisements—cool, refreshing, or smooth—or to convey a bad association—sweltering, noisy, or stuffy. In argumentative writing, loaded or slanted language becomes problematic when it is used to deceive or manipulate.
- **Either/or reasoning.** If a writer admits only two sides to an issue and asserts that his is the only possible correct one, the writer has probably not given full thought to the subject or is unaware of the complexity of the issue. Most arguable topics are probably complex, and few are limited to either one or another right viewpoint. Be wary of a writer who argues that there is only one valid position to take on an issue.
- **Red herring.** A red herring diverts the audience's attention from the main issue at hand to an irrelevant issue. Writers of mystery fiction often use red herrings to distract readers from identifying the stories' criminals. That is part of the fun of reading a mystery. But an argumentative writer who tries to use red herrings probably does not have enough relevant supporting evidence or does not recognize the irrelevance of the evidence. **Example:** Arguing against the death penalty on the grounds that innocent people have been executed avoids the issue of why the death penalty is wrong. Citing the execution of innocent people is a red herring.
- *Post hoc, ergo propter hoc* **reasoning.** This Latin term means "after this, therefore because of this." It applies to reasoning that assumes that Y happened to X simply because it came after X. **Example:** Accusing a rock group of causing the suicide of a fan because the fan listened to the group's music just before committing suicide is an example of such reasoning. Although the music might be a small factor, other factors are more likely to account for the suicide, such as a failed love relationship, feelings of low self-worth, or personal despair for a variety of reasons.

Anticipate the Arguments of the Opposition.   As mentioned above, one key aspect of argumentation is refuting arguments of those who hold opposing opinions.

How do you anticipate what those opposed to your position believe? Perhaps you are already familiar with opposing positions from your own observations or discussions with others, but a good step in your preparation is to look for written articles that express an opinion or position that you do not share. Read the articles, determine the authors' position, and note the evidence they produce to support their positions. How can you refute them? What evidence of your own contradicts them and supports your own position? Sometimes students find themselves being convinced by the arguments of others and find themselves switching positions. Do not worry if that happens to you. In fact, it will probably aid you in your own argument because you are already familiar with the reasoning of that position and can use the new evidence that persuaded you to find fault with your old position.

Make Concessions.   Sometimes it is necessary to concede a point to the opposition—that is, to acknowledge that the opposition has made a reasonable assertion. Making a concession or two is inevitable in arguments of complex issues. Conceding to the opposition is actually a good strategy as long as you follow such a concession with even stronger evidence that your position is the reasonable one. You agree that the opposition makes a good point, but you follow that agreement with an even more persuasive point.

STRATEGIES FOR CONSTRUCTING A CONVINCING ARGUMENT

- **Know your audience.** This helps you know what evidence you need to make your argument convincing.
- **Establish appropriate tone.** Your attitude toward your subject is important in making you argument convincing. Using the appropriate tone strengthens your argument.
- **Follow a logical line of reasoning.** Whether formal or informal, inductive or deductive, or some other method recommended by your instructor, your argument must be reasonable and sound.
- **Use appeals effectively.** Appeals to logic, ethics, emotions, or shared values all help develop your argument. Be cautious when appealing to emotions; such appeals are all right in small measure but your main appeals should be to logic and/or ethics.
- **Assess the evidence.** Examine carefully the evidence you use for your argument. Weak or flawed evidence weakens your own argument.
- **Look for flaws in your own and others' reasoning process.** Avoid fallacies or errors in reasoning in your own writing and examine the arguments of others for such flaws.
- **Anticipate the arguments of those opposed to you.** Anticipating and countering others' arguments strengthens your own position.
- **Make concessions where necessary.** Acknowledging truths in the arguments of others reveals that you are aware of those truths but are still committed to your own position. Follow such concessions with your own even stronger evidence, proof, or support.

SAMPLE STUDENT PAPERS

In the following pages you will find two student papers demonstrating effective argumentation. The first one is annotated with marginal comments on the student's strategies. The second is presented without comment as an exercise for classroom use or your own study.

In her introductory women's studies and sociology classes, Rita became interested in the status of women in the work force. She learned about federal legislation that made it illegal to discriminate in the workplace on the basis of sex, among other things. She also knew that when her mother and grandmother were growing up, the women's movement had done much to address inequities in women's lives. So she was surprised by some of the facts that she learned in her classes about women's work force participation and earnings. On the other hand, Rita had often heard people comment that women have now achieved equity, even arguing that there was no longer job discrimination or discrepancies between what men and women earn for the same work. Furthermore, several class-action sex-discrimination lawsuits brought by female employees against large corporations had been in the news recently, with the corporations hotly denying any form of sex discrimination. Therefore, when her English instructor assigned an argumentative paper using source materials, Rita decided to research this controversial subject.

Rita's question was, have women really achieved equality in the work place? Her reading in this area led her to the conclusion that, no, despite everything that has been done to make women equal to men in employment, they have not yet achieved that goal. Although she found that there are differences in not only earnings but also rates of promotion and representation at higher, managerial ranks, she decided to focus her paper on just the issue of the wage gap. The proposition she formulated for her paper is the following: Despite decades of struggling for women's equality in the workplace, the wage gap between men and women remains unacceptably wide.

Fleming 1

Rita Fleming

English 102-2

April 19, 2005

Women in the Workforce: Are They Really Equal?

Nearly seventy-one million American women, over half of those over the age of 16, are in the civilian labor force, and over half of those women work full time, year round. Many people have the perception

Fleming 2

Rita begins with background information and establishes importance of issue by appealing to the common good. Her proposition states clearly what her position is.

that women's large presence in the workforce in combination with federal laws that prohibit job discrimination means that women enjoy equality with men in the workplace. However, recent class-action sex-discrimination suits brought by women workers against large corporations suggest that millions of women feel discriminated against in the workplace. Furthermore, a look at labor statistics compiled by the federal government, such as those from the U.S. Census Bureau, reveals that women on average are still paid significantly less than men. Despite decades of struggling for women's equality in the workplace, the wage gap between men and women remains unacceptably wide.

Rita acknowledges the opposition, makes concessions, and reaffirms her position.

Some argue that workplace inequity has disappeared as a result of federal legislation that makes discrimination in employment illegal. It is true that efforts to correct disparities between men's and women's wages have a long history. Executive Orders have been legislated to fight discrimination in employment, beginning in 1961 with President John F. Kennedy's Executive Order 10925 creating a President's Committee on Equal Employment Opportunity prohibiting discrimination on the basis of sex, race, religious belief, or national origin. The Equal Pay Act of 1963 prohibits paying women less than men working in the same establishment and performing the same jobs, and Title VII of the 1964 Civil Rights Act prohibits job discrimination on the basis of not only race, color, religion, and national origin but also sex. It is also true that when the Equal Pay Act was signed, women working full-time,

Fleming 3

year round made only 59 cents on average for every
dollar a man made and that the figure had increased to
77 cents by 2002 ("Evidence" 11). Yes, women have
made gains over the past forty years, but is 77 cents
for every dollar a man makes acceptable? If women are
truly equal to men in this society, why are their
average earnings not equal?

Rita offers explanations for the inequity by citing data supporting her position.

There are many reasons for this inequity. One
reason is that most women work in service and
clerical jobs, including such occupations as
secretaries, teachers, cashiers, and nurses. For
instance, in 2001, 93% of registered nurses and 82.5%
of elementary school teachers were women ("101
Facts"). In 1999, 97.3% of preschool and kindergarten
teachers as well as dental assistants were female,
and 96.7% of secretaries were ("Evidence" 11). Women
also tend to work at jobs that pay less than the jobs
that men typically work at. Eitzen and Zinn point out
that, as the economy shifted in recent times from
being manufacturing-based to being more service-
oriented, a dual labor market emerged. In a dual
labor market, there are two main types of jobs,
primary and secondary. Primary jobs are usually
stable, full-time jobs with high wages, good benefits,
and the opportunity to move up the promotion ladder,
whereas secondary jobs are the opposite. Secondary
occupations are unstable, normally part time, with
few benefits and little opportunity for advancement
(218). Unfortunately, large corporations have been
eliminating many primary jobs and creating new,
secondary jobs to take their places, and it is mostly
women who are hired to fill these secondary positions.

Fleming 4

Continues to explain, backing assertions with supporting proof.

The term "occupational segregation" is used to describe the phenomenon of women workers being clustered in secondary or low-paying jobs (Andersen and Collins 238). This segregation is particularly startling when you consider such statistics as the following: "Since 1980, women have taken 80 percent of the new jobs created in the economy, but the overall degree of gender segregation has not changed much since 1900" (Andersen and Collins 236). Fully 60% of women workers are in clerical and service occupations, while only 30% are managers and professionals ("USA" 68). In the very few occupations where the median earnings for women are at least 95% of those for men, only one—meeting and convention planners—employs a higher percentage of female workers than male ("Evidence" 13). Women are simply not crossing over into traditionally male-dominated occupations at a very high rate. This does not mean that women do not have opportunities or are not educated. It could mean, however, that the workplace is still plagued by old, outdated stereotypes about gender-based occupations.

As she offers more reason to account for the wage gap, Rita reinforces her position that the gap is unacceptable.

Another explanation for the wage gap is that women earn less because of the differences in years of experience on the job. Collectively, women earn less because they haven't worked as many years as men have in certain professions (Robinson 183-84). Women often drop out of the job market to have their families, for instance, while men stay at their jobs when they have families. Yet another reason for the wage gap, offered by Borgna Brunner, is that older women may be working largely in jobs that are "still

Fleming 5

subject to the attitudes and conditions of the past."
Brunner points out: "In contrast, the rates for young
women coming of age in the 1990s reflect women's
social and legal advances. In 1997, for example,
women under 25 working full-time earned 92.1% of
men's salaries compared to older women (25-54), who
earned 74.4% of what men made." This is great news
for young women but a dismal reality for the
significantly large number of working women who fall
into the 25-54 age group.

Rita ends with strongest argument, that the wage gap cannot be explained by the usual means.

Reasons to account for the persistence of a wage
gap are many, but <u>sometimes there is no explanation
at all.</u> Analysts have tried to determine why, as the
U.S. Census Bureau figures for 1999 reveal, "Men earn
more than women at each education level," taking into
account all year-round, full-time workers over age 25
("Big Payoff" 4). Surprisingly, the wage gap is
greater than one might expect at the professional
level: female professionals (doctors, lawyers,
dentists) make substantially less than what male
professionals make. Female physicians and surgeons
aged 35-54, for instance, earned 69% of what male
physicians and surgeons made ("Evidence" 21). How can
such a wage gap be explained? The reality is,
according to the *Women's International Network News*,
"Between one-third and one-half of the wage
difference between men and women cannot be explained
by differences in experience, education, or other
legitimate qualifications" ("USA" 68). Even the U. S.
Census Bureau concludes: "There is a substantial gap
in median earnings between men and women that is
unexplained, even after controlling for work

Fleming 6

experience . . . education, and occupation"
("Evidence" 21). Given this statement, it is likely
that the most unfair reason of all to explain why
women are paid less than men for the same or equal
work is simply discrimination. This situation is
intolerable.

Rita suggests actions to address the problem she has substantiated in her paper.

What can be done to correct the wage
differential between men's and women's earnings? Laws
have failed to produce ideal results, but they have
done much to further women's chances in the workplace
and they give women legal recourse when they feel
that discrimination has taken place. Therefore,
better vigilance and stricter enforcement of existing
laws should help in the battle for equal wages. Young
women should be encouraged to train for primary jobs,
while those who work in secondary jobs should lobby
their legislators or form support groups to work for
better wages and benefits. Working women can join or
support the efforts of such organizations as 9to5,
the National Association of Working Women. Women's
position in the workforce has gradually improved over
time, but given the statistics revealing gross
differences between their wages and those of men,
much remains to be done.

*Rita follows
MLA style
guidelines for
documenting
sources.*

Fleming 7

Works Cited

Andersen, Margaret L., and Patricia Hill Collins, ed.
     Race, Class and Gender: An Anthology. 3rd ed.
     Belmont, CA: Wadsworth Publishing Company, 1998.

"The Big Payoff: Educational Attainment and Synthetic
     Estimates of Work-Life Earnings." U. S. Census
     Bureau. July 2002. 15 April 2005
     <http://www.census.gov/prod/2002pubs/
     p23-210.pdf>.

Brunner, Borgna. "The Wage Gap: A History of Pay
     Inequity and the Equal Pay Act." March 2005.
     Infoplease. 14 April 2005 <http://www.
     infoplease.com/spt/equalpayact1.html>.

Eitzen, Stanley D., and Maxine Baca Zinn. Social
     Problems. 7th ed. Needham Heights, MA: Allyn and
     Bacon, 1997.

"Evidence from Census 2000 about Earnings by Detailed
     Occupation for Men and Women." U.S. Census
     Bureau. May 2004. 15 April 2005
     <http://www.census.gov/prod/2004pubs/censr-
     15.pdf>.

"101 Facts on the Status of Working Women." January
     2003. Business and Professional Women. 12 April
     2005 <http://bpwusa.org/content/
     PressRoom/101Facts/101Facts.html>.

Robinson, Derek. "Differences in Occupational
     Earnings by Sex." Women, Gender, and Work. Ed.
     Martha Fetherolf Loutfi. Geneva: International
     Labor Office, 2001.

"USA: The Facts about Wage Discrimination and Equal
     Pay." Women's International Network News 25.1
     (Winter 1999): 68.

EXERCISE

Read the student paper that follows and evaluate its success as an argument. How well is the essay structured? What strategies does Erin use for developing her argument? Are you convinced that her position is valid or reasonable?

Anderson 1

Erin D. Anderson

English 150-2

October 24, 2005

Ads and Attitudes:

Advertisers' Responsibility for the Images They Produce

Flipping through the latest issue of a popular fashion magazine, a high-school freshman encounters in-your-face color advertisements on literally every second or third page, displaying pop superstars in their favorite brand of makeup and models flaunting their Barbie-doll physiques in the latest styles. At the same time, a middle-aged housewife changes the channel from a commercial about super-mom to an infomercial claiming that she, too, can have great abs if she calls now. Both the impact of advertising on culture and the accountability required of those publicizing the messages reflected in advertisements are the topics of much debate. Although the overall purpose of advertising is to promote and sell a product to the population in order to make a profit, advertisers must also take responsibility for the powerful images that their advertisements portray and the sometimes-unattainable standards that they endorse.

Anderson 2

In addition to creating a market for products, advertisements have the unparalleled power to define what is popular and accepted in a society, therefore creating images in the minds of those who are subjected to the advertisements. Advertisers seek to create a universal ideal about the world behind the products, thus developing a correlation between the product and the new and better world. In splashing their ads with image after image of stunning blondes with swarms of men at their beck and call, advertisers imply that a female consumer can attain this fantasy if she can pass this silent test of physical attractiveness (with help from the advertised product, of course). They hope that through appeals to the internal desires of people to be or have what is popular, the consumers will rush out and buy their products or risk not living up to society's standard. Although this tactic may lead to increased sales for the advertiser, which is what he/she has set out to do, it raises questions as to the appropriateness of an advertising strategy that can so seriously distort a person's view of himself or herself.

Jean Kilbourne reflects on this ability of ads to "sell values, images, and concepts of success and worth, love and sexuality, popularity and normalcy" in her essay entitled "Beauty and the Beast of Advertising" (8). She contends that when magazine ads, television commercials, and other means of advertising continue to reinforce the same types of images, stereotypes result, and these stereotypes can have negative effects on consumers (9). One detrimental stereotype that Kilbourne traces back to advertising is the view of women as sex objects. She sees that women are constantly confronted with images of outward perfection and are taught that if they are not the thin, long-legged, forever radiant beauties of these idealistic ads, their "desirability and lovability" suffer (9). This leads not only to feelings of dissatisfaction and shame, but also to more serious problems such as eating disorders or obsession over weight. Although Kilbourne's essay focuses on the images in advertising that negatively affect females, males in society can also be influenced by advertisements. One must merely think of all the ads he/she has seen in his or her lifetime showing a rugged cowboy without a care in the world pushing a certain brand of deodorant or cigarettes in order to understand the scope of these images.

In light of the tremendous power of advertisements, one is compelled to conclude that something must be done to monitor the images entering our society via ads; thus, the responsibility of the advertisers themselves comes into question. John O'Toole, president of the American Association of Advertising Agencies, defines the purpose and scope of advertising and defends the methods advertisers use to sell products in his aptly titled piece "What Advertising Isn't." O'Toole contends that advertising is "salesmanship [. . .] functioning in the paid space and time of mass media" (292). He points out that advertising, unlike other forms of communication, is not meant to cover all sides of the story; instead, it presents products in their most

Anderson 4

favorable light (294). He also asserts that in order to get a full understanding about a product and its benefits, one should look to all relevant sources, including unbiased reports in newspapers or magazines and opinions of others (293).

Another argument employed by O'Toole in support of advertisers is that ads simply reflect the values of society (293). One of these societal values includes the consumers' desire to see themselves in the place of these flawless images on billboards and in magazines. However, the near impossibility of attaining this standard even further causes self-image problems. It is evident that there are additional elements at work that factor into the values and expectations of a culture, such as other media forms, family influences, job and peer pressures. Moreover, each person is responsible for the way he or she interprets advertisements, and he or she must recognize attempts to alter a belief and refuse to allow this to happen.

Although I do agree that ads are not the sole cause of the self-image problem, constant subjection to such unrealistic concepts of beauty, success, and popularity in advertising can contribute to an already vulnerable sense of self. For this reason, it is the responsibility of advertisers to realize this vulnerability and modify the images they are presenting to the masses in such a way as to begin displaying a representative image of today's women and men. This shift would cause more of America to relate to the people being shown and would be a welcome respite from the artificiality in many of today's advertisements.

Anderson 5

Advertising, an undeniable force in contemporary American society, not only markets products themselves but also creates a sense of what one should have, look like, and/or be. The extraordinary power of advertising to influence self-concept leads one to question the responsibility of advertisers to convey fair images. Only after advertisers modify their strategies to accommodate the physical realities of today's population, thereby further connecting with their audience, can advertising images really reach their optimum effectiveness for society as a whole.

Works Cited

Kilbourne, Jean. "Beauty and the Beast of Advertising." <u>Media&Values</u> Winter 1989: 8-10.

O'Toole, John. "What Advertising Isn't." <u>Perspectives on Contemporary Issues: Readings Across the Disciplines,</u> 3rd ed. Ed. Katherine Anne Ackley. Boston: Thomson/Heinle, 2003. 292-297.

ILLUSTRATION: OPPOSING ARGUMENTS

EXERCISE

Read the two essays that follow and then compare them in terms of their authors' success at writing a convincing argument, keeping in mind the guidelines for successful argumentation outlined above. What strategies do the writers use to advance their arguments? Is either of the essays more logical or convincing than the other, or are they equally persuasive?

GRADE INFLATION: IT'S TIME TO FACE THE FACTS
HARVEY C. MANSFIELD

Harvey C. Mansfield, William R. Kenan, Jr. Professor of Government,
teaches political philosophy at Harvard University. His books include
Taming the Prince: The Ambivalence of Modern Executive Power
(1989), America's Constitutional Soul (1991), Machiavelli's Virtue
(1996), and translations of Machiavelli's The Prince *(1998) and of*
Tocqueville's Democracy in America *(2000). His current research is a*
book on manliness. This essay appeared in the April 6, 2001, issue of the
Chronicle of Higher Education, *a professional publication for faculty,*
staff, and administrators in colleges and universities.

This term I decided to experiment with the grading of my political-philosophy course at Harvard. I am giving each student two grades: one for the registrar and the public record, and the other in private. The official grades will conform with Harvard's inflated distribution, in which one-fourth of all grades given to undergraduates are now A's, and another fourth are A-'s. The private grades, from the course assistants and me, will be less flattering. Those grades will give students a realistic, useful assessment of how well they did and where they stand in relation to others.

A longtime critic of grade inflation, I have seen my grades dragged gradually higher over the years, while still trailing the rising average. I could not ignore the pressure to meet student expectations that other faculty members have created and maintained, but I did not want just to go along silently. The two-grade device is a way to show my contempt for the present system, yet not punish students who take my course. My intent was to get attention and to provoke some new thinking

I certainly got attention. I was pleased at the degree of interest from around the country, both in the news media and from the general public. The grades that faculty members now give—not only at Harvard but at many other elite universities—deserve to be a scandal.

4   People often criticize elementary and secondary schools for demanding too little of students. In the past presidential race, both candidates spoke frequently of the need to raise standards. But at Harvard, the supposed pinnacle of American education, professors are quite satisfied to bestow outlandishly high grades upon students. We even think those grades reflect well on us; they show how popular we are with bright students. And so we are quite satisfied with ourselves, too.

There is something inappropriate—almost sick—in the spectacle of mature adults showering young people with unbelievable praise. We are flattering our students in our eagerness to get their good opinion. That our students are promising makes it worse, for promise made complacent is easily spoilt. What's more, professors who give easy grades gain just a fleeting popularity, salted with disdain. In later life, students will forget those professors; they will remember the ones who posed a challenge.

In a healthy university, it would not be necessary to say what is wrong with grade inflation. But once the evil becomes routine, people can no longer see it for what it is.

Even though educators should instinctively understand why grade inflation is a problem, one has to be explicit about it.

Grade inflation compresses all grades at the top, making it difficult to discriminate the best from the very good, the very good from the good, the good from the mediocre. Surely a teacher wants to mark the few best students with a grade that distinguishes them from all the rest in the top quarter, but at Harvard that's not possible. Some of my colleagues say that all you have to do to interpret inflated grades is to recalibrate them in your mind so that a B+ equals a C, and so forth. But the compression at the top of the scale does not permit the gradation that you need to rate students accurately.

8   Moreover, everyone knows that C is an average grade, whereas a B+ is next to the top. Mere recalibration does not address the real problem: the raising of grades way beyond what students deserve.

At Harvard, we have lost the notion of an average student. By that I mean a Harvard average, not a comparison with the high-school average that enabled our students to be admitted here. When bright students take a step up and find themselves with other bright students, they should face a new, higher standard of excellence.

The loss of the notion of average shows that professors today do not begin with their own criteria for the performance of students in their courses. Professors do not say to themselves, "This is what I can require; anything above that enters into excellence." No. With an eye to student course evaluations and confounded by the realization that they have somehow lost authority, professors begin from what they think students expect. American colleges used to set their own expectations. Now, increasingly, they react to student expectations—even though, by contrast to stormy times in the past, students are very respectful.

Thus another evil of grade inflation is the loss of faculty morale that it reveals. It signifies that professors care less about their teaching. Anyone who cares a lot about something—for example, a baseball fan—is very critical in making judgments about it. Far from the opposite of caring, being critical is the very consequence of caring. It is difficult for students to work hard, or for the professor to get them to work hard, when they know that their chances of getting an A or A- are 50-50. Students today are still motivated to get good grades, but if they do not wish to work hard toward that end, they can always maneuver and bargain.

12   Some say Harvard students are better these days and deserve higher grades. But if they are in some measures better, the proper response is to raise our standards and demand more of our students. Cars are better-made now than they used to be. So when buying a car, would you be satisfied with one that was as good as they used to be?

Besides, the evidence clearly undermines that argument. The Harvard University Extension School, taught mostly by Harvard faculty members, has about the same grading distribution as Harvard College, although exact figures on grades are difficult to come by. The school holds evening classes open to the public—a mix of Ph.D.'s, college dropouts, and high-school students—and is not reserved for the super-smart of America's youth. Yet the Harvard professors who teach those admirable, self-improving souls cannot restrain their own—well, it's not generosity, because high grades cost professors nothing.

Another point calls into question the claim that students are smarter now: Grades in humanities courses are notably higher than those in the social sciences, and both are higher than grades in the natural sciences. Yet would anyone say that Harvard's best students are in the humanities and its worst in the natural sciences? In fact, science students regularly do better in nonscience courses than nonscience students do in science courses.

16   How did we get into this mess? Perhaps I should be asking how we should get out of it. But to answer that question, one needs to appreciate the strength of feeling behind grade inflation.

Grade inflation has resulted from the emphasis in American education on the notion of self-esteem. According to that therapeutic notion, the purpose of education is to make students feel capable and empowered. So to grade them, or to grade them strictly, is cruel and dehumanizing. Grading creates stress. It encourages competition rather than harmony. It is judgmental.

A child-development professor recently expressed the spirit of such self-esteem with rare clarity: "As soon as you get into some of the more complicated things, kids may experience failure. They may feel like they're stupid." This spirit is as rampant in higher education as it is in elementary and secondary schools. At colleges, self-esteem often goes hand in hand with multiculturalism or sensitivity to people of diverse races and ethnicities—meaning that professors must avoid offending the identities (still another name for self-esteem) of victimized groups.

I know what that means. It means that despite all the talk about free speech at Harvard, you had better watch what you say. And how you grade.

20   When I was interviewed by *The Boston Globe* about my two-grade policy, one cause of grade inflation that I cited provoked a fiercely defensive reaction from the administrators at Harvard. I said that when grade inflation got started, in the late 60's and early 70's, white professors, imbibing the spirit of affirmative action, stopped giving low or average grades to black students and, to justify or conceal it, stopped giving those grades to white students as well. Of course, I also mentioned faculty sympathy with student protesters against the Vietnam War, but it was my talking about white professors that proved quite intolerable to the Harvard administration.

A dean called my remark "groundless and false," "irresponsible," and "divisive." He accused me of having no evidence, though providing none himself. Then President Neil L. Rudenstine weighed in, responding to a demand from the Black Students Association that my statement be censured. Rudenstine, while defending free debate, stated ex cathedra that nothing he had seen, read, or heard would allow him to agree with my point. He, too, offered no evidence.

Because I have no access to the figures, I have to rely on what I saw and heard at the time. Although it is not so now, it was then utterly commonplace for white professors to overgrade black students. Any professor who did not overgrade black students either felt the impulse to do so or saw others doing it. From that, I inferred a motive for overgrading white students, too.

Of course, it is better to have facts and figures when one speaks, but I am not going to be silenced by people who have them but refuse to make them available. I've been on the Harvard faculty since 1962, and in that time I can't remember any other professor being honored with an official, factually unsupported "tain't so" like this. Somehow it didn't convince me that I was wrong.

24   Despite the obvious connection between self-esteem and affirmative action, some might think that I went off on a tangent from the problem of grade inflation. To me, however, my experience suggests that I got closer to the problem, not farther from it, and that I learned something about American education today. From top to bottom, we need to put our standards first.

     I used to believe that that is what Harvard stands for. I still think it can recover.

     Remedies for grade inflation are not beyond our ingenuity. What we need above all is to muster the determination to act. Our leaders need to lead.

PERSONAL RESPONSE

Describe your experience with or observation of grade inflation, either in college or during your high-school education. Do you think it is as serious a problem as Mansfield seems to think it is?

QUESTIONS FOR CLASS OR SMALL-GROUP DISCUSSION

1. What assumptions does Mansfield make about high grades at Harvard?
2. Mansfield identifies several reasons why he finds grade inflation objectionable. What are those reasons and what do you think of his explanations of them?
3. Where does Mansfield address those opposed to his position? Do you think he adequately addresses those objections?
4. Where does Mansfield use emotionally-charged language? Do you think his use of such language is effective?
5. Mansfield admits that he has no facts because he is denied access to student records at his university. On what evidence does he base his conclusions, then? How persuasive do you find that evidence?

THE DANGEROUS MYTH OF GRADE INFLATION
ALFIE KOHN

Alfie Kohn writes and speaks widely on human behavior, education, and parenting. His nine books include No Contest: The Case Against Competition *(1986),* Punished by Rewards *(1993),* The Schools Our Children Deserve *(1999),* The Case Against Standardized Testing *(2000), and* What Does it Mean to be Well Educated? And More Essays on Standards, Grading, and Other Follies *(2004). This essay first appeared in the November 8, 2002, issue of the*

Chronicle of Higher Education. *For more information, please see* <*www.alfiekohn.org*>.

Grade inflation got started . . . in the late '60s and early '70s. . . . The grades that faculty members now give . . . deserve to be a scandal.
                                    —Professor Harvey Mansfield, Harvard University, 2001

Grades A and B are sometimes given too readily—Grade A for work of no very high merit, and Grade B for work not far above mediocrity. . . . One of the chief obstacles to raising the standards of the degree is the readiness with which insincere students gain passable grades by sham work.
    —Report of the Committee on Raising the Standard, Harvard University, 1894

Complaints about grade inflation have been around for a very long time. Every so often a fresh flurry of publicity pushes the issue to the foreground again, the latest example being a series of articles in *The Boston Globe* last year that disclosed—in a tone normally reserved for the discovery of entrenched corruption in state government—that a lot of students at Harvard were receiving A's and being graduated with honors.

The fact that people were offering the same complaints more than a century ago puts the latest bout of harrumphing in perspective, not unlike those quotations about the disgraceful values of the younger generation that turn out to be hundreds of years old. The long history of indignation also pretty well derails any attempts to place the blame for higher grades on a residue of bleeding-heart liberal professors hired in the '60s. (Unless, of course, there was a similar countercultural phenomenon in the 1860s.)

Yet on campuses across America today, academe's usual requirements for supporting data and reasoned analysis have been suspended for some reason where this issue is concerned. It is largely accepted on faith that grade inflation—an upward shift in students' grade-point averages without a similar rise in achievement—exists, and that it is a bad thing. Meanwhile, the truly substantive issues surrounding grades and motivation have been obscured or ignored.

4   The fact is that it is hard to substantiate even the simple claim that grades have been rising. Depending on the time period we're talking about, that claim may well be false. In their book *When Hope and Fear Collide* (Jossey-Bass, 1998), Arthur Levine and Jeanette Cureton tell us that more undergraduates in 1993 reported receiving A's (and fewer reported receiving grades of C or below) compared with their counterparts in 1969 and 1976 surveys. Unfortunately, self-reports are notoriously unreliable, and the numbers become even more dubious when only a self-selected, and possibly unrepresentative, segment bothers to return the questionnaires. (One out of three failed to do so in 1993; no information is offered about the return rates in the earlier surveys.)

To get a more accurate picture of whether grades have changed over the years, one needs to look at official student transcripts. Clifford Adelman, a senior research analyst with the U.S. Department of Education, did just that, reviewing transcripts from more than 3,000 institutions and reporting his results in 1995. His finding:

"Contrary to the widespread lamentations, grades actually declined slightly in the last two decades." Moreover, a report released just this year by the National Center for Education Statistics revealed that fully 33.5 percent of American undergraduates had a grade-point average of C or below in 1999-2000, a number that ought to quiet "all the furor over grade inflation," according to a spokesperson for the Association of American Colleges and Universities. (A review of other research suggests a comparable lack of support for claims of grade inflation at the high-school level.)

[Addendum 2004: A subsequent analysis by Adelman, which reviewed college transcripts from students who were graduated from high school in 1972, 1982, and 1992, confirmed that there was no significant or linear increase in average grades over that period. The average GPA for those three cohorts was 2.70, 2.66, and 2.74, respectively. The proportion of A's and B's received by students: 58.5 percent in the '70s, 58.9 percent in the '80s, and 58.0 percent in the '90s. Even when Adelman looked at "highly selective" institutions, he again found very little change in average GPA over the decades.]

However, even where grades *are* higher now as compared with then, that does not constitute proof that they are inflated. The burden rests with critics to demonstrate that those higher grades are undeserved, and one can cite any number of alternative explanations. Maybe students are turning in better assignments. Maybe instructors used to be too stingy with their marks and have become more reasonable. Maybe the concept of assessment itself has evolved, so that today it is more a means for allowing students to demonstrate what they know rather than for sorting them or "catching them out." (The real question, then, is why we spent so many years trying to make good students look bad.) Maybe students aren't forced to take as many courses outside their primary areas of interest in which they didn't fare as well. Maybe struggling students are now able to withdraw from a course before a poor grade appears on their transcripts. (Say what you will about that practice, it challenges the hypothesis that the grades students receive in the courses they complete are inflated.)

8   The bottom line: No one has ever demonstrated that students today get A's for the same work that used to receive B's or C's. We simply do not have the data to support such a claim.

Consider the most recent, determined effort by a serious source to prove that grades are inflated: "Evaluation and the Academy: Are We Doing the Right Thing?" a report released this year by the American Academy of Arts and Sciences. Its senior author is Henry Rosovsky, formerly Harvard's dean of the faculty. The first argument offered in support of the proposition that students couldn't possibly deserve higher grades is that SAT scores have dropped during the same period that grades are supposed to have risen. But this is a patently inapt comparison, if only because the SAT is deeply flawed. It has never been much good even at predicting grades during the freshman year in college, to say nothing of more important academic outcomes. A four-year analysis of almost 78,000 University of California students, published last year by the UC president's office, found that the test predicted only 13.3 percent of variation in freshman grades, a figure roughly consistent with hundreds of previous studies. (I outlined numerous other problems with the test in "Two Cheers for an End to the SAT," *The Chronicle,* March 9, 2001.)

Even if one believes that the SAT is a valid and valuable exam, however, the claim that scores are dropping is a poor basis for the assertion that grades are too high. First, it is difficult to argue that a standardized test taken in high school and grades for college course work are measuring the same thing. Second, changes in aggregate SAT scores mostly reflect the proportion of the eligible population that has chosen to take the test. The American Academy's report states that average SAT scores dropped slightly from 1969 to 1993. But over that period, the pool of test takers grew from about one-third to more than two-fifths of high-school graduates—an addition of more than 200,000 students.

Third, a decline in overall SAT scores is hardly the right benchmark against which to measure the grades earned at Harvard or other elite institutions. Every bit of evidence I could find—including a review of the SAT scores of entering students at Harvard over the past two decades, at the nation's most selective colleges over three and even four decades, and at all private colleges since 1985—uniformly confirms a virtually linear rise in both verbal and math scores, even after correcting for the renorming of the test in the mid-1990s. To cite just one example, the latest edition of "Trends in College Admissions" reports that the average verbal-SAT score of students enrolled in all private colleges rose from 543 in 1985 to 558 in 1999. Thus, those who regard SAT results as a basis for comparison should *expect* to see higher grades now rather than assume that they are inflated.

12   The other two arguments made by the authors of the American Academy's report rely on a similar sleight of hand. They note that more college students are now forced to take remedial courses, but offer no reason to think that this is especially true of the relevant student population—namely, those at the most selective colleges who are now receiving A's instead of B's.

[Addendum: Adelman's newer data challenge the premise that there has been any increase. In fact, "the proportion of all students who took at least one remedial course [in college] dropped from 51 percent in the [high school] class of 1982 to 42 percent in the class of 1992."]

Finally, they report that more states are adding high-school graduation tests and even standardized exams for admission to public universities. Yet that trend can be explained by political factors and offers no evidence of an objective decline in students' proficiency. For instance, scores on the National Assessment of Educational Progress, known as "the nation's report card" on elementary and secondary schooling, have shown very little change over the past couple of decades, and most of the change that has occurred has been for the better. As David Berliner and Bruce Biddle put it in their tellingly titled book *The Manufactured Crisis* (Addison-Wesley, 1995), the data demonstrate that "today's students are at least as well informed as students in previous generations." The latest round of public-school bashing—and concomitant reliance on high-stakes testing—began with the Reagan administration's "Nation at Risk" report, featuring claims now widely viewed by researchers as exaggerated and misleading.

Beyond the absence of good evidence, the debate over grade inflation brings up knotty epistemological problems. To say that grades are not merely rising but inflated—and that they are consequently "less accurate" now, as the American

Academy's report puts it—is to postulate the existence of an objectively correct evaluation of what a student (or an essay) deserves, the true grade that ought to be uncovered and honestly reported. It would be an understatement to say that this reflects a simplistic and outdated view of knowledge and of learning.

16   In fact, what is most remarkable is how rarely learning even figures into the discussion. The dominant disciplinary sensibility in commentaries on this topic is not that of education—an exploration of pedagogy or assessment—but rather of economics. That is clear from the very term "grade inflation," which is, of course, just a metaphor. Our understanding is necessarily limited if we confine ourselves to the vocabulary of inputs and outputs, incentives, resource distribution, and compensation.

Suppose, for the sake of the argument, we assumed the very worst—not only that students are getting better grades than did their counterparts of an earlier generation, but that the grades are too high. What does that mean, and why does it upset some people so?

To understand grade inflation in its proper context, we must acknowledge a truth that is rarely named: The crusade against it is led by conservative individuals and organizations who regard it as analogous—or even related—to such favorite whipping boys as multicultural education, the alleged radicalism of academe, "political correctness" (a label that permits the denigration of anything one doesn't like without having to offer a reasoned objection), and too much concern about students' self-esteem. Mainstream media outlets and college administrators have allowed themselves to be put on the defensive by accusations about grade inflation, as can be witnessed when deans at Harvard plead nolo contendere and dutifully tighten their grading policies.

What are the critics assuming about the nature of students' motivation to learn, about the purpose of evaluation and of education itself? (It is surely revealing when someone reserves time and energy to complain bitterly about how many students are getting A's—as opposed to expressing concern about, say, how many students have been trained to think that the point of going to school is to get A's.)

20   "In a healthy university, it would not be necessary to say what is wrong with grade inflation," Harvey Mansfield asserted in an opinion article last year (*The Chronicle,* April 6, 2001). That, to put it gently, is a novel view of health. It seems reasonable to expect those making an argument to be prepared to defend it, and also valuable to bring their hidden premises to light. Here are the assumptions that seem to underlie the grave warnings about grade inflation:

The Professor's Job Is to Sort Students for Employers or Graduate Schools. Some are disturbed by grade inflation—or, more accurately, grade compression—because it then becomes harder to spread out students on a continuum, ranking them against one another for the benefit of postcollege constituencies. One professor asks, by way of analogy, "Why would anyone subscribe to *Consumers Digest* if every blender were rated a 'best buy'?"

But how appropriate is such a marketplace analogy? Is the professor's job to rate students like blenders for the convenience of corporations, or to offer feedback that will help students learn more skillfully and enthusiastically? (Notice, moreover, that even consumer magazines don't grade on a curve. They report the happy news if it turns out that every blender meets a reasonable set of performance criteria.)

Furthermore, the student-as-appliance approach assumes that grades provide useful information to those postcollege constituencies. Yet growing evidence—most recently in the fields of medicine and law, as cited in publications like *The Journal of the American Medical Association* and the *American Educational Research Journal*—suggests that grades and test scores do not in fact predict career success, or much of anything beyond subsequent grades and test scores.

24 *Students Should Be Set Against One Another in a Race for Artificially Scarce Rewards.* "The essence of grading is exclusiveness," Mansfield said in one interview. Students "should have to compete with each other," he said in another.

In other words, even when no graduate-school admissions committee pushes for students to be sorted, they ought to be sorted anyway, with grades reflecting relative standing rather than absolute accomplishment. In effect, this means that the game should be rigged so that no matter how well students do, only a few can get A's. The question guiding evaluation in such a classroom is not "How well are they learning?" but "Who's beating whom?" The ultimate purpose of good colleges, this view holds, is not to maximize success, but to ensure that there will always be losers.

A bell curve may sometimes—but only sometimes—describe the range of knowledge in a roomful of students at the beginning of a course. When it's over, though, any responsible educator hopes that the results would skew drastically to the right, meaning that most students learned what they hadn't known before. Thus, in their important study, *Making Sense of College Grades* (Jossey-Bass, 1986), Ohmer Milton, Howard Pollio, and James Eison write, "It is not a symbol of rigor to have grades fall into a 'normal' distribution; rather, it is a symbol of failure—failure to teach well, failure to test well, and failure to have any influence at all on the intellectual lives of students." Making sure that students are continually re-sorted, with excellence turned into an artificially scarce commodity, is almost perverse.

What does relative success signal about student performance in any case? The number of peers that a student has bested tells us little about how much she knows and is able to do. Moreover, such grading policies may create a competitive climate that is counterproductive for winners and losers alike, to the extent that it discourages a free exchange of ideas and a sense of community that's conducive to exploration.

28 *Harder Is Better (or Higher Grades Mean Lower Standards).* Compounding the tendency to confuse excellence with victory is a tendency to confuse quality with difficulty—as evidenced in the accountability fad that has elementary and secondary education in its grip just now, with relentless talk of "rigor" and "raising the bar." The same confusion shows up in higher education when professors pride themselves not on the intellectual depth and value of their classes but merely on how much reading they assign, how hard their tests are, how rarely they award good grades, and so on. "You're going to have to *work* in here!" they announce, with more than a hint of machismo and self-congratulation.

Some people might defend that posture on the grounds that students will perform better if A's are harder to come by. In fact, the evidence on this question is decidedly mixed. Stringent grading sometimes has been shown to boost short-term retention as measured by multiple-choice exams—never to improve understanding or promote interest in learning. The most recent analysis, released in 2000 by Julian R. Betts and Jeff Grogger, professors of economics at the University of California at San Diego and at Los Angeles, respectively, found that tougher grading was initially correlated with higher test scores. But the long-term effects were negligible—with the exception of minority students, for whom the effects were negative.

It appears that something more than an empirical hypothesis is behind the "harder is better" credo, particularly when it is set up as a painfully false dichotomy: Those easy-grading professors are too lazy to care, or too worried about how students will evaluate them, or overly concerned about their students' self-esteem, whereas we are the last defenders of what used to matter in the good old days. High standards! Intellectual honesty! No free lunch!

The American Academy's report laments an absence of "candor" about this issue. Let us be candid, then. Those who grumble about undeserved grades sometimes exude a cranky impatience with—or even contempt for—the late adolescents and young adults who sit in their classrooms. Many people teaching in higher education, after all, see themselves primarily as researchers and regard teaching as an occupational hazard, something they're not very good at, were never trained for, and would rather avoid. It would be interesting to examine the correlation between one's view of teaching (or of students) and the intensity of one's feelings about grade inflation. Someone also might want to examine the personality profiles of those who become infuriated over the possibility that someone, somewhere, got an A without having earned it.

32   ***Grades Motivate.*** With the exception of orthodox behaviorists, psychologists have come to realize that people can exhibit qualitatively different kinds of motivation: intrinsic, in which the task itself is seen as valuable, and extrinsic, in which the task is just a means to the end of gaining a reward or escaping a punishment. The two are not only distinct but often inversely related. Scores of studies have demonstrated, for example, that the more people are rewarded, the more they come to lose interest in whatever had to be done in order to get the reward. (That conclusion is essentially reaffirmed by the latest major meta-analysis on the topic: a review of 128 studies, published in 1999 by Edward L. Deci, Richard Koestner, and Richard Ryan.)

Those unfamiliar with that basic distinction, let alone the supporting research, may be forgiven for pondering how to "motivate" students, then concluding that grades are often a good way of doing so, and consequently worrying about the impact of inflated grades. But the reality is that it doesn't matter how motivated students are; what matters is *how* students are motivated. A focus on grades creates, or at least perpetuates, an extrinsic orientation that is likely to undermine the love of learning we are presumably seeking to promote.

Three robust findings emerge from the empirical literature on the subject: Students who are given grades, or for whom grades are made particularly salient, tend to display less interest in what they are doing, fare worse on meaningful measures of learning, and avoid more challenging tasks when given the opportunity—as compared with those in a nongraded comparison group. College instructors cannot help noticing, and presumably being disturbed by, such consequences, but they may lapse into blaming students ("grade grubbers") rather than understanding the systemic sources of the problem. A focus on whether too many students are getting A's suggests a tacit endorsement of grades that predictably produces just such a mind-set in students.

These fundamental questions are almost completely absent from discussions of grade inflation. The American Academy's report takes exactly one sentence—with no citations—to dismiss the argument that "lowering the anxiety over grades leads to better learning," ignoring the fact that much more is involved than anxiety. It is a matter of why a student learns, not only how much stress he feels. Nor is the point just that low grades hurt some students' feelings, but that grades, per se, hurt all students' engagement with learning. The meaningful contrast is not between an A and a B or C, but between an extrinsic and an intrinsic focus.

36   Precisely because that is true, a reconsideration of grade inflation leads us to explore alternatives to our (often unreflective) use of grades. Narrative comments and other ways by which faculty members can communicate their evaluations can be far more informative than letter or number grades, and much less destructive. Indeed, some colleges—for example, Hampshire, Evergreen State, Alverno, and New College of Florida—have eliminated grades entirely, as a critical step toward *raising* intellectual standards. Even the American Academy's report acknowledges that "relatively undifferentiated course grading has been a traditional practice in many graduate schools for a very long time." Has that policy produced lower quality teaching and learning? Quite the contrary: Many people say they didn't begin to explore ideas deeply and passionately until graduate school began and the importance of grades diminished significantly.

If the continued use of grades rests on nothing more than tradition ("We've always done it that way"), a faulty understanding of motivation, or excessive deference to graduate-school admissions committees, then it may be time to balance those factors against the demonstrated harms of getting students to chase A's. Ohmer Milton and his colleagues discovered—and others have confirmed—that a "grade orientation" and a "learning orientation" on the part of students tend to be inversely related. That raises the disturbing possibility that some colleges are institutions of higher learning in name only, because the paramount question for students is not "What does this mean?" but "Do we have to know this?"

A grade-oriented student body is an invitation for the administration and faculty to ask hard questions: What unexamined assumptions keep traditional grading in place? What forms of assessment might be less destructive? How can professors minimize the salience of grades in their classrooms, so long as grades must still be given? And: If the artificial inducement of grades disappeared, what sort of teaching strategies might elicit authentic interest in a course?

To engage in this sort of inquiry, to observe real classrooms, and to review the relevant research is to arrive at one overriding conclusion: The real threat to excellence isn't grade inflation at all; it's grades.

PERSONAL RESPONSE

Kohn suggests that the grading system creates the wrong incentive in students, that they focus on getting good grades at the expense of learning for the sake of learning. In your experience, is he correct on that point? Do you and/or your classmates worry more about what grade you will make in a course than what you are actually learning in the course?

QUESTIONS FOR CLASS OR SMALL-GROUP DISCUSSION

1. What strategies for effective argumentation does Kohn use? For instance, what use does he make of data? How successfully does he establish credibility? Does he use a logical line of reasoning to develop his argument?

2. Kohn states: "Meanwhile, the truly substantive issues surrounding grades and motivation have been obscured or ignored" (paragraph 4). What does he think are those issues?

3. Where does Kohn acknowledge those opposed to his position? Does he make any concessions to them?

4. Locate and comment on the hidden assumptions that Kohn says are implicit in the arguments of those who warn about grade inflation. How well do you think he addresses each of those assumptions? Where do you agree or disagree with him?

5. What do you think of Kohn's suggestion that narrative comments replace grades (paragraph 35)? What other means of evaluating student learning might effectively replace grades?

Additional examples of argumentation are located throughout the textbook. Here is a list of arguments, by chapter:

Chapter 2
Roger Ebert's "Stern Belongs on the Radio Just as Much as Rush"

Chapter 3
Robert N. Sollod's "The Hollow Curriculum"

Chapter 7
Henry Jenkins' "Art Form for the Digital Age"

Chapter 8
Jean Kilbourn's "Advertising's Influence on Media Content"

Chapter 9
John H. McWhorter's "Up from hip-hop"
Susan R. Lamson's "TV Violence: Does It Cause Real-Life Mayhem?"
Mike Males' "Stop Blaming Kids and TV"

CHAPTER

5

SYNTHESIZING MATERIAL AND DOCUMENTING SOURCES USING MLA STYLE

WRITING A SYNTHESIS

A synthesis draws conclusions from, makes observations on, or shows connections between two or more sources. In writing a synthesis, you attempt to make sense of the ideas of two or more sources by extracting information that is relevant to your purpose. The ability to synthesize is an important skill, for people are continuously bombarded with a dizzying variety of information and opinions that need sorting out and assessment. To understand your own thinking on a subject, it is always useful to know what others have to say about it. You can see the importance of reading and thinking critically when synthesizing the ideas of others. The sources for a synthesis may be essays, books, editorials, lectures, movies, group discussions, or any of the myriad forms of communication that inform academic and personal lives. At minimum, you will be required in a synthesis to reflect on the ideas of two writers or other sources, assess them, make connections between them, and arrive at your own conclusions on the basis of your analysis. Often you will work with more than two sources; certainly you will do so in a research paper.

Your purpose for writing a synthesis will be determined by the nature of your assignment, although syntheses are most commonly used to either explain or argue. Perhaps you want to explain how something works or show the causes or effects of a particular event. You may argue a particular point, using the arguments of others as supporting evidence or as subjects for disagreement in your own argument. You may want to compare or contrast the positions of other writers for the purpose of stating your own opinion on the subject. When you write a research paper, you most certainly must synthesize the ideas and words of others. Whether your research paper is a report or an argument, you must sort through and make sense of what your sources say. Sometimes you will want to read many sources to find out what a number of people have to say about a particular subject in order to discover your own position on it.

Synthesis, then, involves not only understanding what others have to say on a given subject but also making connections between them, analyzing their arguments or examples, and/or drawing conclusions from them. These are processes you routinely employ in both your everyday life and in your courses whenever you consider the words, ideas, or opinions of two or more people or writers on a topic. Beginning with chapter 7, each chapter in parts 2–5 ends with a list of suggestions for writing. Many of the topics require that you synthesize material in the readings in that chapter. These topics ask you to argue, to compare and contrast, to explore reasons, to explain something, to describe, or to report on something, using at least two of the essays in the chapter.

In all cases, no matter what your purpose for writing the synthesis, you will need to state your own central idea or thesis early in your paper. In preparation for writing your essay, you will complete a very helpful step if you locate the central idea or thesis of each of the works under analysis and summarize their main points. The summary is itself a kind of synthesis, in that you locate the key ideas in an essay, state them in

---

GUIDELINES FOR WRITING A SYNTHESIS

- **Determine your purpose for writing by asking yourself what you want to do in your essay.** Without a clear purpose, your synthesis will be a loosely organized, incoherent jumble of words. Although your purpose is often governed by the way in which the assignment is worded, make sure you understand exactly what you intend to do.

- **Consider how best to accomplish your purpose.** Will you argue, explain, compare and contrast, illustrate, show causes and effects, describe, or narrate? How will you use your sources to accomplish your purpose?

- **Read each source carefully and understand its central purpose and major points.** If you are unclear about the meaning of an essay, reread it carefully, noting passages that give you trouble. Discuss these passages with a classmate or with your instructor if you still lack a clear understanding.

- **Write a one-sentence statement of the central idea or thesis and a brief summary of each source you will use in your paper.** This process will help clarify your understanding of your sources and assist you in formulating your own central idea. These statements or summaries can then be incorporated appropriately into your synthesis.

- **Write a one-sentence statement of your own thesis or central purpose for writing the synthesis.** This statement should be a complete sentence, usually in the first paragraph of your essay. The thesis statement helps you focus your thoughts as you plan your essay by limiting the nature and scope of what you intend to accomplish. It also is a crucial aid to your readers, because it is essentially a succinct summary of what you intend to do.

- **Develop or illustrate your thesis by incorporating the ideas of your sources into the body of your paper, either by paraphrasing or directly quoting.** Part of your purpose in writing a synthesis is to demonstrate familiarity with your sources and to draw on them in your own essay. This goal requires that you make reference to key ideas of the sources.

- **Document your sources.** Keep in mind the guidelines for documenting all borrowed material.

your own words, and then put the ideas back together again in a shortened form. This process helps you understand what the authors believe and why they believe it. Furthermore, your own readers benefit from a summary of the central idea or chief points of the articles you are assessing. As you write your essay, you will not only be explaining your own view, opinion, or position, but you also will be using the ideas or words of the authors whose works you are synthesizing. These will have to be documented, using the appropriate formatting for documenting sources illustrated in this chapter.

ILLUSTRATION: SYNTHESIS

Following is an example of a student paper that synthesizes material from several sources located in this textbook. The marginal comments call attention to various strategies of writing an effective synthesis. Note that a "Works Cited" list appears at the end. The works-cited page gives full bibliographic information for each source. Notice that works are listed alphabetically and that each citation conforms in punctuation and spacing to the MLA style of documentation (chapter 6). A discussion of paraphrasing and quoting follows the sample paper. For more on formatting of the works cited list, see chapter 6.

Hayes 1

Nate Hayes

English 102-2

December 1, 2005

Hello, Dolly

The opening paragraph introduces readers to the controversial issue that is the subject of the paper.

Little Bo Peep has lost her sheep, but now she can clone a whole new flock! When Dr. Ian Wilmut and his team successfully cloned Dolly the sheep, the world was mystified, amazed, and scared. Immediately, members of the shocked public began to imagine worst-case scenarios of reincarnated Hitlers and Dahmers. The medical field, however, relished the possibilities of cloning in curing patients with debilitating or terminal illnesses. The controversy over human cloning is part of the larger debate about the potential capabilities of scientists to alter or

Hayes 2

enhance the biological makeup of humans. This debate

over how far "homo sapiens [should] be allowed to go"

has grown increasingly heated with developments such

as the successful cloning of sheep (Pethokoukis 559).

To many people, human cloning makes sense as the next

major breakthrough in medical science, but until the

troubling issues associated with the procedure are

resolved, human cloning must not be allowed to

happen.

Scientists, politicians, and the general public

all have mixed feelings about the developments in

medical science. Even people like Ian Wilmut, the

Scottish embryologist whose team of researchers was

responsible for cloning Dolly, and James D. Watson,

Nobel-Prize-winning co-discoverer of the double helix

configuration of DNA, hold different views on the

issue. Despite his previous work on cloning, Wilmut

is very cautious, especially about whole-being

cloning. He raises a number of questions about the

wisdom of carrying on full speed with cloning

research, suggesting: "Even if the technique were

perfected, however, we must ask ourselves what

practical value whole-being cloning might have"

(564). On the other hand, Watson urges: "You should

never put off doing something useful for fear of evil

that may never arise" (563). Although he does not

directly address the issue of cloning in his article

"All for the Good," Watson touches on the subject

when he states his strong support of research on

germ-line genetic manipulations in pursuit of what he

calls "'superpersons'" or "gene-bettered children"

(563). The controversy has divided people and spurred

Nate's thesis is a straightforward declarative sentence that makes his position on the subject clear.

Nate briefly indicates the views of two scientists holding differing opinions on the subject of the paper.

Only page numbers are given in the citation because the author's name is mentioned in the text. Note that last names only are used because Nate has already given their full names.

Hayes 3

ongoing discussions—or arguments—about the extent to
which human genetic makeup should be modified or
amended.

The populations that might benefit most if human
cloning were to become a reality are infertile
couples, homosexual couples, or single people wanting
children. In commenting on this possible use for
cloning, Wilmut suggests that having an identical
version of yourself or someone you love would be
unsettling and difficult to handle emotionally (565).
Cloning has even been suggested as a possibility for
grieving parents to replace—or bring back to life—a
child who has died tragically or violently by using
cells to clone a new, identical person. On this
point, Wilmut wonders how the cloned child would feel
when he learns that he exists to replace another
child.

Wilmut's cautious approach to the issue of
cloning is sensible. Many potential problems
associated with human cloning need close examination.
For instance, it is commonly believed that an infant
would be exactly the same as the parent it is cloned
from. This cannot be true. The infant would look the
same, of course, but mentally and emotionally he or
she would be an entirely new person. This new child
would have feelings, thoughts, and experiences
completely different from those of the person he or
she was cloned from. The same would be true in the
case of cloning a child that had died. Even were the
parents to attempt replicating an environment
identical to that of the original child, it would be
an impossible task. Furthermore, a clone would surely

Nate continues to draw on Wilmut's comments because Nate shares his viewpoint.

Nate expresses his own views on the points that Wilmut raises in opposition to human cloning.

Hayes 4

have problems with individuality. How could a carbon copy of another human being feel unique? Cloning thus poses the risk of serious psychological harm.

An alternative to cloning a whole person is to clone an entity for making spare human parts. The idea is that a brainless clone might be produced that could supply crucial body parts, such as a heart, a liver, kidneys, and eyes. However, this possibility still lies in the realm of science fiction. No one has figured out how to do such a thing in the first place, let alone suggest ways to deal with all the potential problems of dealing with such a creature. Such a step is obviously not the best use of human cloning.

A potentially beneficial use of genetic manipulation lies in stem cell research. Stem cells are those that have not yet specialized. Scientists believe that such cells could be isolated and grown into healthy tissue that could then be used in humans to cure just about any ailment known to humans. Research in this area holds far more promise than research into cloning whole humans, although this research has its detractors and critics also. As James Pethokoukis reports, "[G]enetic engineering might be able to alter mankind in some astounding ways," and such potential has many people worried (560).

There are just far too many unanswered questions, and who knows how many remain unasked? It is not easy to anticipate all the possible ramifications for mankind of human cloning. The bottom line is that ethical, psychological, social, and religion questions need to be explored, discussed,

Nate mentions an alternative use of cloning but rejects that as well.

Nate suggests a possible alternative to human cloning, stem-cell research, but notes that it is controversial as well.

Author's full name is given because this is the first mention of his name in the text of the paper, even though it is mentioned parenthetically in paragraph 1.

Nate's conclusion rephrases and emphasizes his thesis statement.

```
                                            Hayes 5
and resolved before research in genetic engineering
that aims to create new life or significantly alter
existing life can be allowed to continue.
                    Works Cited
Ackley, Katherine Anne, ed. Perspectives on
      Contemporary Issues: Reading across the
      Disciplines, 4th ed. Boston: Thomson Wadsworth,
      2006.
Pethokoukis, James. "Our Biotech Bodies, Ourselves."
      Ackley 559-561.
Watson, James D. "All for the Good." Ackley 561-563.
Wilmut, Ian. "Dolly's False Legacy." Ackley 564-566.
```

In-Text Citations, Paraphrasing, and Quoting

No matter what your purpose or pattern of development, if you draw on the writing of someone else, you must be fair to the author of the material you borrow. If you paraphrase an author's words or, occasionally, quote them exactly as they appear in the original text, you must cite your source. In any case, when you are using the ideas or words of another, you must give credit to your source. In academic writing, credit is given by naming the author of the borrowed material, its title, the place and date of publication, and the page number or numbers where the information is located.

The rest of this chapter introduces some basic skills needed to incorporate the words and ideas of others into your own written work. It begins with a discussion of documenting sources, goes on to provide guidelines and examples for paraphrasing and quoting, illustrates some useful tools for handling source material and integrating source materials, and ends with directions for documenting sources from collections of essays, such as this textbook. The guidelines in this chapter follow MLA (Modern Language Association) documentation style. (*Note:* If your instructor prefers that you use APA style or gives you a choice of styles, guidelines for APA documentation style appear in chapter 6.) MLA style is used primarily in the humanities disciplines, such as English and philosophy, whereas other disciplines have their own guidelines. If you learn the skills necessary for paraphrasing, quoting, and documenting the material located in this textbook, you will be prepared to incorporate library and Internet resources, as well as other materials, into long, complex research papers. For more discussion of MLA style, with sample works-cited entries for a broad range of both print and nonprint sources, including the Internet, see chapter 6.

IN-TEXT CITATIONS USING MLA STYLE

The MLA style of documentation requires that you give a brief reference to the source of any borrowed material in a parenthetical note that follows the material. This parenthetical note contains only the last name of the authority and the page number or numbers on which the material appears or only the page number or numbers if you mention the author's name in the text.

The parenthetical citation is placed within the sentence, after the quotation or paraphrase, and before the period. If punctuation appears at the end of the words you are quoting, ignore a comma, period, or semicolon but include a question mark or exclamation mark. In all cases, the period for your sentence follows the parenthetical citation.

The name or title that appears in the parenthetical citation in your text corresponds to an entry in the Works Cited page at the end of your paper. This entry contains complete bibliographic information about the work you reference, including the full name of the author, the complete title, the place of publication, and the date of publication.

Treat World Wide Web sources as you do printed works. Because many web sources do not have page numbers, omit page numbers. Some authorities recommend naming the title of Internet source material in the text and placing the author's name in the parentheses, or repeating the author's name in the parentheses, even if it is used in the text.

Illustration: In-text Citations. The following examples show formats for citing sources in the text of your paper. The "works cited" format for many of the references illustrated here can be found in the section "Creating a Works Cited Page" in chapter 6.

- **Book or article with one author.** Name the author followed by the page number:

  (Sollod 15)

GUIDELINES FOR DOCUMENTING SOURCES

- Provide a citation every time you paraphrase or quote directly from a source.
- Give the citation in parentheses following the quotation or paraphrase.
- In the parentheses, give the author's last name and the page number or numbers from which you took the words or ideas. Do not put any punctuation between the author's last name and the page number.
- If you name the author as you introduce the words or ideas, the parentheses will include only the page number or numbers.
- At the end of your paper, provide an alphabetical list of the authors you quoted or paraphrased and give complete bibliographic information, including not only author and title but also where you found the material. This element is the "Works Cited" page.

- **Book or article with two or three authors.** Name authors followed by the page number:

  (Barrett and Rowe 78)   (Fletcher, Miller, and Caplan 78)
- **Book or article with more than three authors.** Name just the first author followed by "et al." (Latin for "and others") and then the page number:

  (Smith et al. 29)

Note: Reproduce the names in the order in which they appear on the title page. If they are not listed alphabetically, do not change their order.

- **Article or other publication with no author named.** Give a short title followed by the page number:

  ("Teaching" 10)

Note: If you cite two anonymous articles beginning with the same word, use the full title of each to distinguish one from the other.

("Classrooms without Walls" 45) ("Classrooms in the 21st Century" 96)

- **Two works by the same author.** Give the author's name followed by a comma, a short title and the page number:

  (Heilbrun, *Hamlet's Mother* 123) (Heilbrun, *Writing a Woman's Life* 35)
- **Works by people with the same last name.** If your list of cited works has works by authors with the same last name, include the first name of the author in the parenthetical citation and then the page number or numbers.

  (Gregory Smith 16)

PARAPHRASING

Paraphrasing is similar to summarizing in that you restate in your own words something someone else has written, but a paraphrase restates everything in the passage rather than highlighting just the key points. Summaries give useful presentations of

---

GUIDELINES FOR PARAPHRASING

- Restate in your own words the important ideas or essence of a passage.
- Do not repeat more than two or three exact words of any part of the original, unless you enclose them in quotation marks.
- If you must repeat a phrase, clause, or sentence exactly as it appears in the original, put quotation marks around those words.
- Keep the paraphrase about the same length as the original source.
- Give the source of the paraphrased information either in your text or in parentheses immediately after the paraphrase.
- Try to paraphrase rather than quote as often as possible, saving direct quotations for truly remarkable language, startling or unusual information, or otherwise original or crucial wording.

the major points or ideas of long passages or entire works, whereas paraphrases are most useful in clarifying or emphasizing the main points of short passages.

To paraphrase, express the ideas of the author in your own words, being careful not to use phrases or key words of the original. Paraphrases are sometimes as long as the original passages, though often they are slightly shorter. The purpose of paraphrasing is to convey the essence of a sentence or passage in an accurate, fair manner and without the distraction of quotation marks. If your paraphrase repeats the exact words of the original, then you are quoting, and you must put quotation marks around those words. A paper will be more interesting and more readable if you paraphrase more often than you quote. Think of your own response when you read something that contains quotations. Perhaps, like many readers, you will read with interest a paraphrase or short quotation, but you may skip over or skim quickly long passages set off by quotation marks. Readers generally are more interested in the ideas of the author than in his skill at quoting other authors.

Illustration: Paraphrasing.   This section provides examples of paraphrases using selected passages from the sources indicated.

1. **Source:** Graff, Gerald. *Beyond the Culture Wars: How Teaching the Conflicts Can Revitalize American Education.* New York: W. W. Norton, 1992.

   > **Original** (page 118): But the most familiar representation of the sentimental image of the course as a scene of conflict-free community is the one presented on untold numbers of college catalog covers: A small, intimate class is sprawled informally on the gently sloping campus greensward, shady trees overhead and ivy-covered buildings in the background. Ringed in a casual semicircle, the students gaze with rapt attention at a teacher who is reading aloud from a small book—a volume of poetry, we inevitably assume, probably Keats or Dickinson or Whitman. The classroom, in these images, is a garden occupying a redemptive space inside the bureaucratic and professional machine.
   >
   > **Paraphrase:** Gerald Graff notes that many colleges project a common sentimental image of campus life as an idyllic community set among ivy-covered buildings and characterized by small classes, attentive students, and poetry-reading instructors. The classroom becomes a haven from conflict and stress (118).

COMMENT

Even when you put material into your own words, you must cite the source and give a page number where the paraphrased material is located.

COMMENT

When it is clear that you are paraphrasing from the same source in two or more consecutive sentences *and* you have named the author or source in the first sentence, you need give only one parenthetical citation at the end of the series of sentences.

2. **Source:** Dahl, Ronald. "Burned Out and Bored." *Newsweek* 15 Dec. 1997: 8.

> **Original** (page 8): What really worries me is the intensity of the stimulation. I watch my eleven-year-old daughter's face as she absorbs the powerful onslaught of arousing visuals and gory special effects. Although my son is prohibited from playing violent video games, I have seen some of his third-grade friends at an arcade inflicting blood-splattering, dismembering blows upon on-screen opponents in distressingly realistic games. . . . Why do children immersed in this much excitement seem starved for more? That was, I realized, the point.
>
> **Paraphrase:** Dahl believes that the over-stimulation of today's youth has resulted in a generation with a previously unprecedented threshold for excitement. It takes increasingly more violent, more shocking, and more thrilling events to stimulate young people (8).

3. **Source:** Watkins, Wes. "English Should Be America's Official Language." *Washington Window* 20 Feb. 1998. 5 Dec. 2002 <www.house.gov/watkins/wwenglsh.html>.

> **Original:** This assimilation has always included the adoption of English as the common means of communication. Unfortunately, our government now sends mixed signals which contribute to linguistic division in our country. This division of the United States into separate language groups contributes to racial and ethnic conflicts. Designating English as the official language will halt this harmful process.
>
> **Paraphrase:** According to Congressman Wes Watkins, who favors making English America's official language, when the government supports the choice of people to speak their native language, it helps create racial tension. Watkins believes that making English America's official language would ease that tension (Watkins).

COMMENT

For Internet or other electronic sources without pagination, many instructors recommend that you repeat the author's name in parentheses after all paraphrases and direct quotations, even if the name is already included in the text.

QUOTING

When you want to include the words of another writer, but it is not appropriate to either paraphrase or summarize, you will want to quote. Quoting requires that you repeat the exact words of another, placing quotation marks before and after the material being quoted. A crucial guideline requires that you copy the words exactly as they appear in the original text. To omit words or approximate the original within quotation marks is sloppy or careless handling of your source material.

Be selective in the material you choose to quote directly, however. You should usually paraphrase the words of another, restating them in your own language, rather than relying on exactly copying the words. How do you know when to quote rather than paraphrase? You should quote only words, phrases, or sentences that are particularly striking or that must be reproduced exactly because you cannot convey them in your own words without weakening their effect or changing their intent. Quote passages or parts of passages that are original, dramatically worded, or in some way essential to your paper. Otherwise, rely on paraphrasing to refer to the ideas of others. In either case, document your source by identifying the original source and the location of your information within that source.

Illustration: Quoting.   This section provides examples of quotations using selected passages from Gerald Graff's "Ships in the Night." The source for all examples in this section is the following:

> *Source:* Graff, Gerald. *Beyond the Culture Wars: How Teaching the Conflicts Can Revitalize American Education.* New York: W. W. Norton, 1992.

> 1. **Original** (page 106): To some of us these days, the moral of these stories would be that students have become cynical relativists who care less about convictions than about grades and careers.
>
>   **Quotation:** Gerald Graff suggests that "students have become cynical relativists who care less about convictions than about grades and careers" (106).

GUIDELINES FOR QUOTING

- Be selective: Quote directly only words, phrases, or sentences that are particularly striking and whose beauty, originality, or drama would be lost in a paraphrase.
- Quote directly passages that are so succinct that paraphrasing them would be more complicated or take more words than a direct quotation would require.
- Enclose the exact words you are quoting between quotation marks.
- Do not change one word of the original unless you indicate with brackets, ellipses, or other conventions that you have done so.
- Provide the source of your quoted material either in your text or in parentheses following the material.

COMMENTS

- Place double quotation marks before and after words taken directly from the original.
- When the quoted material is an integral part of your sentence, especially when preceded by the word "that," do not capitalize the first letter of the first word.
- Where possible, name the author whose ideas or words you are quoting or paraphrasing.
- In parentheses after the quotation, give the page number in the source where the quotation is located (hence the phrase "parenthetical citation"). This example contains only the page number because the author's name is mentioned in the text. If the text had not given the author's name, it would be included in the parenthetical citation.

2. **Original** (page 118): The more fundamental question we should be asking in most cases is not how *much time* teachers are spending in the classroom but *under what conditions.*

   Quotation: Gerald Graff believes that "[t]he more fundamental question [. . .] is not *how much* time teachers are spending in the classroom but *under what conditions*" (118).

3. **Original** (page 109): Among the factors that make academic culture more confusing today than in the past is not only that there is more controversy but that there is even controversy about what can legitimately be considered controversial. Traditionalists are often angry that there should even be a debate over the canon, while revisionists are often angry that there should even be a debate over "political correctness," or the relevance of ideology and politics to their subjects.

   Quotation: In discussing the factors that confuse people about college curricula today, Gerald Graff notes: "Traditionalists are often angry that there should even be a debate over the canon, while revisionists are often angry that there should even be a debate over 'political correctness' [. . .]" (109).

COMMENTS

- When a quotation preceded by *that* forms an integral part of your sentence, do not capitalize the first word in the quotation, even when it is capitalized in the original. In this example, because the *t* in *the* is capitalized in the original, the bracket around the lower-cased *t* in the quotation indicates that the letter has been changed. Use the ellipsis (three spaced periods) to indicate the omission of text from the original.
- If some text is italicized in the original, you must italicize it in your quotation.
- Use brackets around ellipsis points to indicate that they are your addition.

> ### COMMENTS
>
> - If your direct quotation is preceded by introductory text and a colon or comma, capitalize the first letter of the first word of the quotation.
> - If you quote something that appears in quotation marks in the original source, use single marks within the double quotes.
> - If your quotation appears to be a complete sentence but the actual sentence you quote continues in the original, you must use the ellipsis at the end of your quotation to indicate that.
> - If an ellipsis comes at the end of a quotation, the closing quotation mark follows the third period, with no space between the period and quotation mark. The parenthetical citation follows as usual.

Combination of Paraphrase and Direct Quotation. The following example illustrates how one can combine paraphrasing and quoting for a balanced handling of source material.

4. **Original** (page 118): But the most familiar representation of the sentimental image of the course as a scene of conflict-free community is the one presented on untold numbers of college catalog covers: A small, intimate class is sprawled informally on the gently sloping campus greensward, shady trees overhead and ivy-covered buildings in the background. Ringed in a casual semicircle, the students gaze with rapt attention at a teacher who is reading aloud from a small book—a volume of poetry, we inevitably assume, probably Keats or Dickinson or Whitman. The classroom, in these images, is a garden occupying a redemptive space inside the bureaucratic and professional *machine.*

   Paraphrase and Quotation: Gerald Graff thinks that colleges project an image different from the realities of academic life. College catalog covers, he says, foster "the sentimental image of the course as a scene of conflict-free community" when they portray students sitting outside on a sunny day, mesmerized by the instructor who stands before them, reading someone's words of insight or wisdom. According to him, the classroom becomes "a garden occupying a redemptive space inside the bureaucratic and professional machine" (118).

Here are two more examples of correctly handled direct quotations:

5. Jack Santino in "Rock and Roll as Music; Rock and Roll as Culture" maintains that "[s]uch things as suicide, drugs, sex, and violence *are* teenage concerns" and that, "while artists have a responsibility not to glamorize them, that does not mean these themes should not be explored" (196).

COMMENTS

• Notice the difference between examples 5 and 6. The first integrates the quoted material into the sentence with the word *that,* so the first words in each of the quoted passages do not require a capital first letter. In the second example, the quotation is introduced and set off as a separate sentence, so the first word after the quotation mark begins with a capital letter.

6. In "Rock and Roll as Music; Rock and Roll as Culture," Jack Santino observes: "Furthermore, such things as suicide, drugs, sex, and violence *are* teenage concerns. While artists have a responsibility not to glamorize them, that does not mean these themes should not be explored" (196).

INTEGRATING SOURCE MATERIALS INTO YOUR PAPER

When quoting or paraphrasing material, pay special attention to your treatment of source materials. Authors have developed many ways of skillfully integrating the words and ideas of other people with their own words. Your paper should not read as if you simply cut out the words of someone else and pasted them in your paper. You can achieve smooth integration of source materials into your text if you keep the following suggestions in mind:

• **Mention the cited author's name in the text of your paper to signal the beginning of a paraphrase or quotation.** The first time you mention the name, give both first and last names. After the first mention, give only the last name:

Robert Sollod points out in "The Hollow Curriculum" that colleges would not think of excluding courses on multiculturalism from today's curriculum, given the importance of "appreciation and understanding of human diversity." **Sollod** asks: "Should such an appreciation exclude the religious and spiritually based concepts of reality that are the backbone upon which entire cultures have been based?" (A60).

CAUTION

Never incorporate a quotation without in some way introducing or commenting on it. A quotation that is not introduced or followed by some concluding comment, referred to as a "bald" or "dropped" quotation, detracts from the smooth flow of your paper.

- **Mention the source if no author is named.** This practice gives credit to the source while providing an introduction to the borrowed material:

  > A *U.S. News & World Report* **article** notes that, although no genes determine what occupation one will go into, groups of genes produce certain tendencies—risk-taking, for instance—that might predispose one to select a particular kind of work ("How Genes Shape Personality" 64).

- **Give citations for all borrowed material.** State the authority's name, use quotation marks as appropriate, give the source and page number in a parenthetical citation, give some sort of general information, and/or use a pronoun to refer to the authority mentioned in the previous sentence. *Do not rely on one parenthetical citation at the end of several sentences or an entire paragraph:*

  > **Regna Lee Wood** has also researched the use of phonics in teaching children to read. **She** believes that the horrible failure of our schools began years ago. Wood notes that "it all began in 1929 and 1930 when hundreds of primary teachers, guided by college reading professors, stopped teaching beginners to read by "matching sounds with letters that spell sounds" (52). **She** adds that since 1950, when most reading teachers switched to teaching children to sight words rather than sound them by syllable, "fifty million children with poor sight memories have reached the fourth grade still unable to read" (52).

- **Vary introductory phrases and clauses.** Avoid excessive reliance on such standard introductory clauses as "Smith says," or "Jones writes." For instance, vary your verbs and/or provide explanatory information about sources, as in the following examples:

  > Jerry Baker notes the following:
  > Professor Xavier argues this point convincingly:
  > According to Dr. Carroll, chief of staff at a major health center:
  > As Marcia Smith points out,

- **The first mention of an authority in your text (as opposed to the parenthetical citation) should include the author's first name as well as last name.** The second and subsequent references should give the last name only (never the first name alone).

  > **First use of author's name in your paper: Susan Jaspers** correctly observes that . . .
  > **Second and subsequent mentions of that author: Jaspers** contends elsewhere that . . .

- **Combine quotations and paraphrases.** A combination provides a smoother style than quoting directly all of the time:

  > Arthur Levine's 1993 survey of college students reveals that today's generation of young people differs from those he surveyed in 1979. Levine discovered that today's college students "are living through a period of profound

demographic, economic, global, and technological change." Since these students of the 90s see themselves living in a "deeply troubled nation," they have only guarded optimism about the future (32–33).

- **For long quotations (more than four typed lines), set the quoted material off from the text (referred to as a block quotation).** Write your introduction to the quotation, generally followed by a colon. Then begin a new line indented ten spaces from the left margin, and type the quotation, double spaced as usual.
- **Do not add quotation marks for block quotations indented and set off from the text.** If quotation marks appear in the original, use double quotation marks, not single. If you quote a single paragraph or part of one, do not indent the first line any more than the rest of the quotation.
- **For block quotations, place the parenthetical citation after the final punctuation of the quotation.** See the following example of a block quotation:

  > In her article exploring the kind of workforce required by a high-tech economy, Joanne Jacobs suggests that many of today's high school graduates lack crucial skills necessary for jobs in the rapidly growing technical and computer industries. For instance, a number of corporations agreed on the following prerequisites for telecommunications jobs:
  >
  > - Technical reading skills (familiarity with circuit diagrams, online documentation, and specialized reference materials).
  > - Advanced mathematical skills (understanding of binary, octal, and hexadecimal number systems as well as mathematical logic systems).
  > - Design knowledge (ability to use computer-aided design to produce drawings) (39–40).

USING ELLIPSIS POINTS, BRACKETS, SINGLE QUOTATION MARKS, AND "QTD. IN"

This section offers some additional guidelines on the mechanics of handling source materials and incorporating them into your paper.

Ellipsis Points

- **If you want to omit original words, phrases, or sentences from your quotation of source material, use ellipsis points to indicate the omission.** Ellipsis points consist of three spaced periods, with spaces before, between, and after the periods. In quotations, ellipses are most frequently used within sentences, almost never at the beginning, but sometimes at the end. In every case, the quoted material must form a grammatically complete sentence, either by itself or in combination with your own words.

MLA style calls for the use of brackets around ellipsis points to distinguish between your ellipses and the spaced periods that sometimes occur in works. In that case, leave a space before the second and third periods but no space before the first or after the third. Use an ellipsis mark to indicate that you have left words out of an otherwise direct quotation:

> **Original:** The momentous occurrences of an era—from war and economics to politics and inventions—give meaning to lives of the individuals who live through them.
>
> **Quotation with ellipses in the middle:** Arthur Levine argues, "The momentous occurrences of an era [. . .] give meaning to lives of the individuals who live through them" (26).

Use ellipsis marks at the end of a quotation only if you have dropped some words from the end of the final sentence quoted. In that case, include four periods. When the ellipsis coincides with the end of your own sentence, leave a space before the first bracket, and immediately follow the last bracket with the sentence period and the closing quotation mark.

> **Quotation with ellipses at the end:** You know the old saying, "Eat, drink, and be merry [. . .]."

If a parenthetical reference follows the ellipsis at the end of your sentence, leave a space before the first bracket, and immediately follow the last bracket with the closing quotation mark, a space, the parenthetical reference, and the sentence period.

> According to recent studies, "Statistics show that Chinese women's status has improved [. . .]" (*Chinese Women* 46).

- **Ellipsis points are not necessary** if you are quoting a fragment of a sentence, that is, a few words or a subordinate clause, because context will clearly indicate the omission of some of the original sentence.

> Sociobiologists add that social and nurturing experiences can "intensify, diminish, or modify" personality traits (Wood and Wood 272).

Brackets

- **The *MLA Handbook for Writers of Research Papers*, 6th ed., says that "[u]nless indicated in brackets or parentheses . . . , changes must not be made in the spelling, capitalization, or interior punctuation of the source" (3.7.1).** Although you should look for ways to integrate source material into your text that avoid overuse of brackets, the following guidelines apply when changing source material is unavoidable.
- **If you want to change a word or phrase to conform to your own sentence or add words to make your sentence grammatically correct, use brackets to indicate the change.** The brackets enclose only the changed portion of the original.

Original: They were additional casualties of our time of plague, demoralized reminders that although this country holds only two percent of the world's population, it consumes 65 percent of the world's supply of hard drugs.

Quotation: According to Pete Hamill in his essay "Crack and the Box," America "holds only two percent of the world's population, [yet] it consumes 65 percent of the world's supply of hard drugs" (267).

Original: In a miasma of Walt Disney images, Bambi burning, and Snow White asleep, the most memorable is "Cinderella."

Quotation: Louise Bernikow recalls spending Saturday afternoons at the theatre when she was growing up "[i]n a miasma of Walt Disney images, [. . .] the most memorable [of which] is 'Cinderella' " (17).

Note: This example illustrates the use not only of brackets but also of ellipsis points and single and double quotation marks.

- **Use brackets if you add some explanatory information or editorial comment, or use them to indicate that you have changed the capitalization in the quoted material.**

  Original: Marriage is another dying institution [. . .]. "If we live together," the attitude goes, "why should I commit myself? Why should I assume responsibility?"

  Quotation: Even the perspective toward marriage carries the attitude, " '[W]hy should I commit myself? Why should I assume responsibility?' " (Barrett and Rowe 346).

  Original: Then, magically, the fairy godmother appears. She comes from nowhere, summoned, we suppose, by Cinderella's wishes.

  Quotation: Louise Bernikow points out that "[s]he [the fairy godmother] comes from nowhere, summoned [. . .] by Cinderella's wishes" (19).

- **The Latin word *sic* (meaning "thus") in brackets indicates that an error occurs in the original source of a passage you are quoting.** Because you are not at liberty to change words when quoting word for word, reproduce the error but use [*sic*] to indicate that the error is not yours.

  Original: Thrills have less to do with speed then changes in speed.

  Quotation: Dahl makes this observation: "Thrills have less to do with speed then [*sic*] changes in speed" (18).

Single Quotation Marks

- **If you quote text that itself appears in quotation marks in the original, use single marks within the double that enclose your own quotation.**

  Original: This set me pondering the obvious question: "How can it be so hard for kids to find something to do when there's never been such a range of stimulating entertainment available to them?"

Quotation: Dahl is led to ask this question: " 'How can it be so hard for kids to find something to do when there's never been such a range of stimulating entertainment available to them?' " (18–19).

- **Occasionally you will have to quote something that is already a quotation within a quotation,** where the original contains single quotation marks within double quotes. In that case, use double quotation marks within single within double:

    Original: In my interviews with the chief witness, he swears he heard Smith say: " 'It wasn't me! I didn't do it!' "

    Quotation: Johnson records an interview with a chief witness in the case. Smith is said to have proclaimed, " ' "It wasn't me! I didn't do it!" ' " (23).

Qtd. in

- **If you quote or paraphrase material that is already quoted, use the abbreviation "qtd." with the word "in."** Use "qtd. in" whenever you quote or paraphrase the published account of someone else's words or ideas. The works cited list will include not the original source of the material you quoted or paraphrased but rather the indirect source, the one where you found the material. You will likely be using the single quotation marks within the double because you are quoting what someone else has quoted.

    Original: Printed in bold letters at the entrance of the show is a startling claim by Degas' fellow painter Auguste Renoir: "If Degas had died at 50, he would have been remembered as an excellent painter, no more; it is after his 50th year that his work broadened out and that he really becomes Degas."

    Quotation: Impressionist painter Auguste Renoir observed of Degas: " 'If Degas had died at 50, he would have been remembered as an excellent

---

GUIDELINES FOR INTEGRATING SOURCE MATERIALS INTO YOUR PAPER

- Avoid "bald" or "dropped" quotations by introducing all direct quotations.
- Use the author's name, where appropriate, to signal the beginning of a paraphrase or quotation.
- Cite sources for all borrowed material.
- Name a source, if the article does not list an author's name.
- Vary the way you introduce source material.
- Try combining direct quotations and paraphrases in the same sentence.
- Become familiar with appropriate uses of ellipsis points, brackets, single quotation marks, and "qtd. in."

painter, no more; it is after his 50th year that his work broadened out and that he really becomes Degas'" (qtd. in Benfey).

Original: Teen suicide is nearly four times more common today than it was a few decades ago, says Dr. Janice Grossman, a suicide expert.

Quotation: According to Dr. Janice Grossman, an expert on suicide, "Teen suicide is nearly four times more common today than it was a few decades ago" (qtd. in Arenofsky).

DOCUMENTING SOURCES IN A COLLECTION OF ESSAYS

You have been reading about and looking at examples of one important component of source documentation: in-text citations. The other component is the alphabetical list, appearing at the end of your paper, of all the works you quoted from or paraphrased. This is the list of works cited. Each entry in the list begins with the author's name, last name first, followed by the title of the article, book, or other source and information about its place and date of publication. The author's name (or title of the work, if it is published anonymously) in the text's parenthetical citation refers to one item in this list at the end of the paper.

You will find more discussion of documenting sources in chapter 6, but the brief treatment here gives useful guidelines for short papers using materials reprinted in a collection of essays, such as this textbook. Although the examples in this section illustrate how to document materials reprinted in the third edition of this textbook, the guidelines apply to any collection of essays. Because *Perspectives on Contemporary Issues* is a collection of other people's works, not the editor's, you will probably not have occasion to use the words or ideas of Ackley herself. However, because you are not reading the essays in their original source, you must indicate that you have read them in her book.

You may prefer an acceptable alternative to constructing a separate page of works cited. Cite bibliographic information about the source parenthetically in your text, just as you do for author and page numbers. If you are writing about one of the readings from this book, or even two or three of them, your instructor may prefer that you provide information that would otherwise appear on a "Works Cited" page in parenthetical citations.

A fairly simple difference distinguishes a formal "Works Cited" page from parenthetical citations of full publication details: The former is more appropriate when the sources are not the focus or subject of the paper but rather provide supporting or illustrative material, as in a synthesis or research paper. The latter is more appropriate when the source is the focus of the paper, its main subject, as in a summary or critique. See the example at the end of this chapter.

Citing One Source.   Suppose your paper quotes or paraphrases a statement from Robert Hughes's essay "Behold the Stone Age." After you write either the exact words of Hughes or your paraphrase of his words, put a parenthesis, then give his last name and the page number where you read the words *with no punctuation between them,* and then close the parenthesis: (Hughes 161). Do not write the word page or pages nor insert a comma between the author's name and the number of the page. If Hughes's piece is the only one you use in your paper, write "Work Cited" at the end of your paper and enter complete bibliographic information for the Hughes article:

```
                          Work Cited

    Hughes, Robert. "Behold the Stone Age." Perspectives

        on Contemporary Issues: Readings across the

        Disciplines, 4th ed. Ed. Katherine Anne Ackley.

        Boston, MA: Thomson Wadsworth, 2006. 295-299.
```

Citing Two or More Sources.   If you draw material from two or more essays from Ackley (or from any collection of essays), you do not need to repeat the full information for the collection with the citation for each essay. Instead, list the collection by the editor's name, giving full bibliographic information. Then list separately each article you use by author and title, but after each essay title, give only the collection editor's name and the inclusive page numbers of the essay. You may, if you wish, follow the model for citing one source.

For example, suppose in a paper on the "Arts" chapter of this textbook (chapter 10), you use information or words from the Hughes article, Harold M. Williams's "Don't Ignore the Arts," and Michael Chabon's "Solitude and the Fortresses of Youth." Here is how your "Works Cited" page might look:

```
                         Works Cited

    Ackley, Katherine Anne, ed. Perspectives on

        Contemporary Issues: Reading across the

        Disciplines, 4th ed. Boston, MA: Thomson

        Wadsworth, 2006.
```

Chabon, Michael. "Solitude and the Fortresses of
Youth." Ackley 292-295.

Hughes, Robert. "Behold the Stone Age." Ackley
295-299.

Williams, Harold M. "Don't Ignore the Arts." Ackley
299-304.

You may also do your "Works Cited" page this way:

Works Cited

Chabon, Michael. "Solitude and the Fortresses of
Youth." *Perspectives on Contemporary Issues:
Readings across the Disciplines*, 4th ed. Ed.
Katherine Anne Ackley. Boston, MA: Thomson
Wadsworth, 2006. 292-295.

Hughes, Robert. "Behold the Stone Age." *Perspectives
on Contemporary Issues: Readings across the
Disciplines*, 4th ed. Ed. Katherine Anne Ackley.
Boston, MA: Thomson Wadsworth, 2006. 295-299.

Katherine Anne Ackley. Boston, MA: Heinle, 2003.
182-186.

Williams, Harold M. "Don't Ignore the Arts."
*Perspectives on Contemporary Issues: Readings
across the Disciplines*, 4th ed. Ed. Katherine
Anne Ackley. Boston, MA: Thomson Wadsworth,
2006. 299-304.

Parenthetical Documentation of Source Material.   When a single reading is the primary focus of your paper (or it concentrates on two or three readings)—that is, the paper deals with limited primary sources, as opposed to secondary source materials that provide illustration or supporting evidence—you can provide full bibliographic information parenthetically the first time you mention each source. Then you do not have to construct a separate Works Cited page. This technique may be convenient when your paper focuses on just one work; for instance, if you were to write a formal summary or critique of one reading or a paper on one or two works of literature. At the first mention of the source, provide full publication information in a parenthetical citation:

> According to Robert Hughes in "Behold the Stone Age"
> (in Katherine Anne Ackley, ed., *Perspectives on Contemporary Issues: Reading across the Disciplines*, 4th ed. [Boston, MA: Thomson Wadsworth, 2006] 295-299), early cave paintings suggest something significant about the importance of art for humans.

Notice that the author's name and the title of the work are mentioned in the text of the paper and not in the parenthetical citation. Brackets indicate parentheses within parentheses. After this first documentation of full publication information, parenthetical citations will give only author and page number or just page number.

ILLUSTRATION: SYNTHESIS WITH IN-TEXT CITATIONS USING MLA STYLE

The sample student paper in the first part of this chapter is one model of a synthesis that incorporates paraphrases and quotations from several sources, all from the 4th edition of this textbook. Following is another model, using sources from the 3rd edition of this textbook.

Novak 1

Barbara Novak

English 150

September 24, 2005

The Shock-Proof Generation

Arthur Levine, an education faculty member at
Harvard, firmly believes that "every college
generation is defined by the social events of its age"
(26). To confirm his belief Levine questioned
university students about "what social or political
events most influenced their generation" (26). The
Great Depression influenced those who grew up after
World War I. Those born after World War II were
affected by the assassination of John F. Kennedy.
Students surveyed in 1979 rallied around Vietnam and
Watergate. Those questioned in 1993 remembered the
explosion of the Challenger. What modern political or
social events will the youth of today be influenced
by?

Psychiatric professor Ronald Dahl might suggest
that the events that have the greatest impact on
today's youth will be more stunning and dramatic than
ever. While observing his own young children and
their friends, Professor Dahl could not help but
notice that despite "ever-greater stimulation, their
young faces were looking disappointed and bored"
(19). Dahl believes that the over-stimulation of
today's youth has resulted in a generation with a
previously unprecedented threshold for excitement.
Consequently, it takes increasingly shocking,
violent, or thrilling events to stimulate young
people. Consistent with their insatiable appetite for
excitement, the upcoming generation, described by

Dahl as "burned out and bored," will be influenced by political and social events that are more violent, thrilling, or fast-paced than those remembered by previous generations.

The widely publicized tragedy at Columbine High School is one example of a political and social event shocking enough to influence the current generation of young Americans. Two high school students, Eric Harris and Dylan Klebold, entered their own school on April 20, 1999, and executed a carefully planned rampage of terror. Fifteen members of the school community were killed before the young men took their own lives (Pellegrini). The violence carried out that day by Harris and Klebold reached a climactic point high enough to actually have a shocking effect on modern over-stimulated youth. Therefore, the calamity that occurred at Columbine High School will be an occurrence indicated by most of today's youth as an event that defines their generation.

Dahl writes: "What really worries me is the intensity of the stimulation. I watch my eleven-year-old daughter's face as she absorbs the powerful onslaught of arousing visuals and gory special effects in movies" (19). Over-exposure to such violence, whether in video games, television, movies, or music lyrics, leads to de-sensitization of the viewer. Prior to, as well as after, the events in Littleton there were numerous school shootings; however, the impact of these paled in comparison to that of Columbine. If an increase in exposure to violence creates youth who are increasingly tolerant of violence, it can be inferred that the power of the

Novak 3

events at Columbine was greater than that of other school shootings because it was phenomenally more violent. If Dahl's beliefs regarding today's youth are correct, the social and political events that define this generation will become increasingly violent simply because it will take more violence to obtain a reaction.

Dahl also poses the following question: "Why do [small] children immersed in this much excitement seem starved for more? That was, I realized, the point. I discovered during my own reckless adolescence that what creates exhilaration is not going fast, but going faster [. . .]. Thrills have less to do with speed than changes in speed" (19). The unthinkable actions carried out by Eric Harris and Dylan Klebold were attempts to create exhilaration by changing the speed of a normal day at Columbine High School. Unfortunately, Harris and Klebold were raised in a world of "ever-greater stimulation" (Dahl 19). Therefore, the efforts necessary to create exhilaration were nearly as enormous as the impact of the shooting.

Recognizing the tragedy at Columbine High School as an event that will define a generation allows it to be examined as an indicator of the problems that exist within that age group. The future of our nation lies upon the shoulders of the young. It is crucial to be aware of the immense effects of the violent and negative images that bombard this group on a daily basis. Realizing the over-stimulation that is occurring among young Americans will help not only to prevent another tragedy like Columbine, but it will

Novak 4

also ensure that the next generation will have the ability to successfully handle the problems of the future.

Works Cited

Ackley, Katherine, ed. *Perspectives on Contemporary Issues: Readings Across the Disciplines*, 3rd ed. Boston: Heinle, 2003.

Dahl, Ronald. "Burned Out and Bored." Ackley 18-20.

Levine, Arthur. "The Making of a Generation." Ackley 26-33.

Pellegrini, Frank. "Colorado Shootings: Now, the Aftermath." *Time* 21 Apr. 99. 20 Sept. 01. <http://www.time.com/time/daily/0,2960,23427,00. html>.

CHAPTER

6

WRITING A RESEARCH PAPER USING MLA STYLE

No matter what course you write a research paper for, your goal is the same: to skill-fully support a carefully formulated thesis with documented evidence. Writing such a paper can seem both overwhelming and exciting, especially if you have never written one before. This chapter presents a brief overview of the key steps in discovering a topic, researching it, and writing a paper incorporating the sources you have used. Keep in mind the discussion in chapter 5 on paraphrasing, quoting, and documenting sources. A research paper is likely to be much longer than a writing assignment generated from readings in this book, but otherwise little difference separates the processes of using materials from this textbook and using materials from other sources in terms of accuracy and fairness to your sources.

DEFINING YOUR PURPOSE

Your instructor will tell you whether your purpose in the research paper is to argue, explain, analyze, or come to some conclusion about something. Many instructors prefer that students write argumentative papers. In that case, you will make a judgment about your topic on the basis of what you find in your research. You will begin your research with an idea of what your position is, then research your subject extensively, arrive at an informed opinion, and finally defend that position by presenting evidence that seems valid (that is, logical and convincing) to you. If you want to go a step further and convince your audience to adopt your position or to act on suggestions you propose, then your purpose is persuasion. In addition to proving the validity of your own position, you must also present some opposing arguments. Obviously you cannot present every aspect and every position of an issue, but you must demonstrate that you are aware of the major viewpoints on your subject and that the position you have taken is a reasonable one. Ignoring an opposing opinion is a major fault in argumentation, because it suggests that you have not explored enough aspects of the topic to warrant the position you are taking. The subjects for argumentative papers are virtually unlimited, but they often include controversial issues, such as those addressed in this textbook, topics with widely varying opinions.

On the other hand, some instructors direct students to explain or analyze something in their research papers. An informative paper does not necessarily address a controversial subject. If you are to write an explanatory paper, you will gather information about your topic and present it in such a way that your reader fully understands it. You will explain, describe, illustrate, or narrate something in full detail, such as what a black hole is, how photosynthesis works, the circumstances surrounding a historical event, significant events in the life of a famous person, and the like.

Audience.   Whether your instructor tells you what audience to write for or leaves the selection of an audience up to you, having a clear sense of your audience will direct your research and help you write your paper. If you are writing an argument, the most useful audience to address is one that is opposed to your position or, at best, uncertain about where they stand on the issue. A good argument seeks to persuade or convince an audience, so anticipating readers who are not already convinced will help sharpen your argument. If your purpose is to explain, illustrate, or analyze, your audience is likely to be informed in general about the particular subject of your paper but not in great depth. Unless instructed otherwise, assume an intelligent audience of non-specialists who are interested in learning more about the topic of your paper. Imagining this audience will keep you from having to define or explain every term or concept and give you room for interesting, informative, and/or intriguing material about the topic.

Thesis Statement.   No matter what your purpose, you will have one central idea, most often articulated early in the paper in the form of a single thesis statement. You will take a position on your topic and defend or illustrate it convincingly with evidence from your source materials. Because the argumentative paper is a common research assignment, much of the discussion in this chapter will be about selecting an appropriate topic on which to base an argument.

ASKING QUESTIONS AND DISCOVERING A TOPIC

Once you know your purpose and audience, the next step in writing a research paper is to find a subject you will be comfortable working with for many weeks and then narrow it to a specific topic. Some instructors assign topics, but most leave the choice to students. The freedom to choose your own research paper topic can be intimidating because so much depends on selecting the right topic. You want a topic that not only holds your interest but that also offers you an opportunity to investigate it in depth.

The process of discovering what you will write about involves first determining the broad subject you are particularly interested in pursuing. Once you have settled on the subject, you will need to narrow it to one specific aspect of that subject. For many research paper assignments, that topic will have to be arguable, one that requires you to investigate both sides and arrive at and defend your own position. This position will be worded in the form of a hypothesis or thesis, stated most often as a declarative statement but sometimes as a question. Discovering your final topic takes time, so do some serious thinking about this important step as soon as the paper is assigned. You will be reshaping, narrowing, and refining your topic for much of the research process, so you do not want to switch subjects halfway through.

Asking Questions.   One of the best ways to approach the research project is to ask questions about a subject that interests you and that seems worth investigating. As you read through the suggestions for discovering a topic that follow, from brainstorming to generating topics from controversy, think in terms of questions that you might ask about the initial subjects you come up with. Try to think in terms of questions that can be answered in a research paper as opposed to a short essay. As you narrow your field of potential topics, look for those about which you can ask questions whose answers are neither too broad nor too narrow. You want the topic that you ultimately select to be challenging enough that your paper will be interesting to you as well as to your audience. Avoid topics about which questions are unanswerable or highly speculative. Your goal in the research process will be to arrive at an answer, insofar as that is possible, to your question.

Here are examples of questions that would be appropriate to ask when trying to generate ideas for a research paper:

- Should the Electoral College be abolished?
- Should grades be abolished?
- Does America need an official language?
- Should research into human cloning continue?
- Do advertising images of women set up impossible standards of femininity?
- Is hormone replacement therapy a safe choice for women?
- Which plays a more prominent role in determining behavior, genes or environment?
- What role does phonics education play in the teaching of reading?
- How dangerous is secondhand smoke?
- Was King Arthur a real person?
- What is the best strategy for combating terrorism?

Brainstorming.   As you consider various suggestions for generating a research paper topic, you can apply a useful technique for discovery that you have probably used before in your writing classes. Most students are familiar with **brainstorming** or **free writing,** which involves simply writing without stopping, putting on paper everything that occurs to you as you think about your subject. To brainstorm or free write, spend five or ten minutes listing on a blank sheet of paper all of the subjects you are interested in without stopping to think too hard about what you are doing. Then select one or more of the subjects on your list and brainstorm for another five to ten minutes in order to find out what you already know about your subject.

Generating a Topic from Personal Interest.   One way to find a topic for your research paper is to begin with subjects you already know well, are interested in, or think you would like to improve your knowledge of. Begin by writing down such things as hobbies, sports, issues in your major, contemporary social issues, or topics in classes you are taking. Consider topics that attracted your interest in high school or in previous college classes, any reading you have already done on subjects that appeal to you, or the kinds of things that capture your attention when you watch television news, read news magazines or newspapers, or select nonfiction books for leisure-time reading.

Narrowing Your Subject to a Specific Topic.   Most research paper assignments are short enough that you simply must narrow your focus to avoid a too shallow or too hopelessly general treatment of your topic. Keep in mind the distinction between **subject** and **topic:** Subject is the general area under investigation, whereas topic is the narrow aspect of that subject that you are investigating. For example, Jack the Ripper is a subject, but entire books have been written on the notorious 1888 murders in the Whitechapel area of London. A suitable topic on the subject would be to explore the controversy surrounding the alleged links of the Duke of Clarence with the murders, taking a position in favor of the theory most plausible to you.

One way to get a sense of how a general topic can be narrowed is to look at the table of contents of a book on a subject that interests you. Notice the chapter headings, which are themselves subtopics of the broad subject. Chapters themselves are often further subdivided. You want to find a topic that is narrow enough that you can fully explore it without leaving unanswered questions, yet broad enough that you can say enough about it in a reasonably long paper.

To narrow your subject to a topic, take a general subject and go through the brainstorming process again, this time listing everything that comes to mind about that particular subject. What subtopics does your subject have? What questions can you ask about your general subject? How might you narrow your focus on that subject? Ultimately, you want to generate an idea that gives focus to your preliminary library search.

Generating Topics from Personal Opinions.   Virtually any topic can be turned into an argument, but opinions are always subject to debate. So one way to generate a research paper topic is to begin with your own strongly held opinions.

Caution: Avoid a topic that is based entirely on opinion. Evaluative statements are especially good for argumentative papers, because they are likely to have differing opinions. Once you say that something is the best, the most significant, the most important, or the greatest, for instance, you have put yourself in the position of defending that statement. You will have to establish your criteria for making your judgment and defend your choice against what others might think. Here are some ideas for this particular approach:

- The most influential person in the twentieth century (or in America, in the world, in a particular field such as education, government, politics, arts, entertainment, or the like)
- The most significant battle in the Civil War (or World War I, World War II, the Korean War, the Vietnam War, the Gulf War)
- The greatest basketball (or football, tennis, soccer, baseball) player (either now playing or of all time)
- The greatest or worst president
- The best movie, book, or album of all time
- The business or industry with the greatest impact on American life in the last decade (or last 20 years, last 50 years, or century)

Because your conclusion on any of these or similar topics is your opinion, you need to establish criteria for your conclusion, clearly describe the process you used to make it, and explain the logical basis for that process.

Generating Topics from Commonly Held Opinions.   Another possibility for a research paper topic is to take a commonly held opinion (though not necessarily one that you share), especially one based on stereotyped assumptions about a group or class of people, and explore the validity of that belief. Your goal is to determine whether the commonly held opinion is a valid, partially valid, or invalid position. Even if you cannot arrive at a definitive evaluation of the validity of the statement, you can still present the evidence you find and explain why your research does not reach a conclusion. Here are examples of commonly held beliefs:

- Watching violence on television produces violent behavior
- People who were abused as children often grow up to be abusers themselves
- Men naturally perform mechanical tasks better than women do
- Women naturally perform better at nurturing children than men do
- Young people do not have much hope for a bright future
- Women are more emotional than men
- People stay on welfare because they are too lazy to work
- Homosexuals could become "straight" if they wanted to
- Homeless people could get off the streets if they really tried

When determining the validity of a commonly held opinion or belief, your research focuses on gathering evidence without bias. Although you may want to interview people about their opinions on a particular belief, the basis of your conclusion must rest on clearly reliable evidence.

Generating Topics from Controversy.   Yet another way to discover a topic you find intriguing enough to commit many hours of time to is to think of controversial issues that always generate heated debate. These topics may be frequently discussed in newspapers, news magazines, and on television news programs and talk shows. They may be issues on which candidates for public office, from local county board members to state and federal officials, are pressed to take stands. Here are some examples of controversial statements:

- Affirmative action laws are unfair to white males and should be repealed
- Media coverage of celebrity trials should be banned
- Birth parents should always have a legal right to take back children they have given up for adoption
- Children whose parents are on welfare should be placed in state-run orphanages
- Women should be barred from participating in combat duty
- Graphic violence in the movies (or in video games or MTV videos) poses a serious threat to the nation's moral values
- The federal government should stop funding projects in the arts and the humanities
- The federal government should provide unlimited funds to support research to find a cure for AIDS
- Children who commit murder should be tried as adults no matter what their age

FORMING A PRELIMINARY THESIS

When you believe that you have narrowed your topic sufficiently, you are ready to form your preliminary thesis. This is the position that you believe you want to take on your topic, based on your early thinking about and narrowing down of a subject. Your preliminary or working thesis can be in the form of either a question or a statement. In much the same way as your final thesis gives direction and focus to your paper, your preliminary thesis gives you direction and focus in the research process. As you review potential sources and read about your topic, you may find yourself changing your preliminary thesis for any number of reasons. Perhaps your topic is too narrow or too new and you simply cannot find enough sources with which to write a fair and balanced research paper. Or you may discover that your topic is too broad to cover in a research paper and that you need to narrow your focus even more. A common reason for changing a preliminary thesis is that, once you actually start reading sources, you discover that you want to change your initial position. You may discover that you were wrong in your assumption or opinion about your topic and that you are persuaded to change your position. Part of the pleasure in researching a topic is discovering new ideas or information, so it makes sense that your early views on your topic may shift as you learn more about it. More than likely, your final thesis will differ in some way from your preliminary thesis.

DEVELOPING A WORKING BIBLIOGRAPHY

With your preliminary thesis in mind, you are ready to start the actual research process. First, you need to locate potential sources. A working bibliography is a list of the sources you **might** use in your research paper, those that look particularly promising during a preliminary search. At this point, you will not have had time to read or even carefully skim all potential sources, let alone imagine how they fit together to support your hypothesis. Your goal is to find the sources that bear most directly on your topic and select from them the most useful ones to read carefully, taking notes as you read. One obvious place to start looking for sources is the library; another source is the Internet.

For the working bibliography, some instructors require that you prepare a separate bibliography card for each source with promise. Others suggest that you simply make a list of titles and locations of potential sources and wait until you have looked at them more closely before filling out bibliography cards. If you use your computer to locate sources, you can make a list of potentially useful sources in a special file. Your instructor may have a preference, but most allow students to use the methods that best suit them.

GUIDELINES FOR DEVELOPING A WORKING BIBLIOGRAPHY

- List sources that sound promising for your research, recording titles and locations as you discover them.
- If the source is a library book, record the title, author, and call number.
- If the source is an article from your library, write the title of the piece, the name of its author, the title of the magazine or journal where it appears, the date of the issue, and the inclusive pages numbers. You will need all this information to find the article.
- For other sources in the library, such as videotapes, audiotapes, government documents, or pamphlets, write down as much information as you can find to help locate them. Write the location of any source, such as a special collection, government document, stack, periodical, and so on.
- For an Internet site, record the URL (Uniform Resource Locator), the name of the site, the name of its creator or author, if available, and the date the site was created, if available. If you use the source in your paper, you will add the date that you accessed the material in the works cited entry, so include that as well.
- You may want to retrieve the full text files of Internet sites that seem promising as you discover them to ensure their availability when you are ready to begin reading and taking notes.

USING THE LIBRARY

Your library has a good number of valuable resources to help you in your search for materials on your research topic. While the Internet has made searching for reference materials easy and quick, libraries house books, periodicals, and other materials that you can hold, leaf through, check out, and read. Furthermore, many libraries have special collections on specific subjects and offer databases that are inaccessible from the Internet. Increasingly libraries are working to connect their own digital resources stored in databases to Internet search engines. In the meantime, do not overlook the potential for excellent sources available on your own campus or through your university library's online catalog. Your library may have print copies of sources that you cannot find on the Internet.

Online Catalog.   Begin your library search for sources on your general subject or topic (if you have sufficiently narrowed your focus) by reviewing the **online catalog** for titles of potential sources. The catalog cross-references sources by name of author, by title, and by subject matter. In this searching stage, you probably will not know titles of works or authors, so you will begin by looking under subject headings for titles that sound relevant to your research subject. The catalog gives titles of books, audio-visual materials, and government documents housed in the library. Jot down the titles and call numbers of materials that look promising and then locate them. One advantage of using your library is that you can physically examine a book, flip through its table of contents, check its index, read the author's credentials, and skim some of the text. If it seems to suit your purpose, you can check it out and take it home with you.

Computer Databases.   Many libraries provide access to computer databases or CD-ROMs that list books and periodical articles related to particular subject areas. You can search these resources by subject, author, title, or keywords. Generally, such a listing provides the full name of the author, the title, and complete bibliographic information (publisher and year for books; title of magazine or journal, month and year of issue, and page numbers for articles). Often, computer services provide abstracts of articles and sometimes entire texts that you can download and print out or send for via mail or fax for a fee.

Indexes.   In addition to books and other materials listed in the catalog of the library, you should look into both general and specialized indexes for additional titles of sources. These resources are usually located in the reference room. Here are titles of some **general indexes:**

- *Bibliographic Index* lists by subject bibliographies that appear in books, pamphlets, and periodical articles.
- *Biography Index* lists articles and books on important people; it also lists the people included in the index by profession or occupation.
- *Essay and General Literature Index* focuses on material in the social sciences and humanities, organized according to author, subject, and title. It lists periodical articles, individual essays, and book chapters on particular subjects.

- *Monthly Catalog of United States Government Publications* indexes all government-generated materials.
- *General Science Index* is arranged by subject and lists articles in general science periodicals.
- *Periodical Abstracts* provides abstracts of articles from over 1,600 periodicals, covering the humanities, social sciences, general science, and general interest. It is updated monthly and is available in electronic format.
- *Reader's Guide to Periodical Literature* is a standard reference tool for locating articles in popular magazines. Organized by both subject and author, it provides titles of articles, authors, names of publications, and dates of publication. It publishes supplements every two weeks, so you can find very recent articles. It is also available in electronic format.

Specialized indexes list articles on particular subjects or areas that appear in professional journals, written by and published for specialists in those areas. Indexes cover specific areas of interest in the humanities, fine arts, social sciences, and natural and applied sciences. A look at just a few of the titles of specialized indexes gives you an idea of the resources available in your library's reference room:

- *Art Index* collects titles of articles on archaeology, art history, architecture, and the fine arts.
- *Biological Abstracts* gives brief summaries of articles on biology and biomedicine.
- *Business Index* is a good source for current material on business topics.
- *The Directory of Online Databases* provides a current listing of databases in all fields.
- *Historical Abstracts* contains abstracts of articles on world history.
- *Humanities Index* lists titles of periodical articles on a broad range of topics in the social sciences and humanities.
- *MLA International Bibliography of Books and Articles on the Modern Languages and Literatures* provides titles of articles on languages and literature, arranged by nationality and literary period.
- *Philosopher's Guide to Sources, Research Tools, Professional Life, and Related Fields* is useful for all sorts of information on philosophical topics.
- *Psychological Abstracts* presents abstracts of articles and books in all areas of the social sciences.
- *Political Science: A Guide to Reference and Information Sources* cites current sources on a range of topics in political science.

USING ELECTRONIC SOURCES

Although you do not want to miss the pleasure of going to the library for sources for your research paper, the Internet can be another valuable tool in your search for potential sources. Most colleges and universities make computers readily available to their students, so even if you do not own a computer, you will likely have access to one in your campus library or computing services center. While it cannot replace the library, the Internet does offer resources that a library does not. The same could be said of the library, of course. A fair conclusion notes that each offers excellent but different kinds of materials for the researcher.

Locating Material on the Internet.   To find Internet materials, you can use any of a number of equally good search engines available on the web. Search engines collect many sites in their databanks; they return sites that match the keywords you type to begin your search. Search engines get their information in one of two major ways, either crawler-based technology or human-powered directories, but increasingly they use a combination of both. Crawler-based search engines gather their information automatically by "crawling" or sending "spiders" out to the web, searching the contents of other systems and creating a database of the results. Human-powered directories depend on humans for the listings you get in response to a search; they manually approve material for inclusion in a database. You can find more about these terms and others related to the Internet by going to http://www.Webopedia.com, an online dictionary and search engine for definitions of computer and Internet terms.

Search Engines.   Be very careful when searching for sources on the Internet, keeping in mind the guidelines in Chapter 1 on evaluating Internet sources. Begin by choosing your search engine from among the best known or most used; they are likely to be the most reliable. Commercially-backed search engines are usually well maintained and frequently upgraded, thus ensuring reliable results. The following search engines are well known, quite reliable, and likely to give you the results you seek in your search:

- **Google (http://www.google.com),** which daily gives millions of people around the world access to billions of documents, is the search engine used most by people searching for information on the web. Using crawler-based technology, Google has many features that make it attractive to users. Besides providing links to web pages containing the key words of your search, the top of the search box on Google's home page offers links to images, discussion groups, news sites, shopping (Froogle), and its many other web features such as catalogs, web directories, and special searches. Google offers many web tools, including "Blogger," which lets you create your own blog and links you to other blogs, a translation tool, and Google's toolbar.
- **Yahoo (http://www.yahoo.com)** is the web's oldest directory, having been established in 1994. It is easy to search and suitable for both experienced and novice Internet users. In addition to links to websites, you can use the tabs above the search box on its home page to find, among other things, groups, Yellow page listings, and shopping sites. Yahoo used to use human editors to organize websites into categories but in 2002 shifted to crawler-based listings, getting most of its sites from Google. In 2004 it created its own search technology.
- **Ask Jeeves (http://www.askjeeves.com).** This site became very popular in the late 1990s because it allowed you to search by asking a question and

getting an answer to the question. Although it was once human-powered, to-day it depends on crawler-based technology. You can ask Jeeves to search the web, pictures, news, or products.

Other search engines that will give you satisfactory results and can therefore be very useful in your search include the following:

- **Teoma (http://www.teoma.com)**, owned by Ask Jeeves, is a web crawler that has a smaller index size than Google or Yahoo but is still reliable and quite popular.
- **Hotbot (http://www.hotbot.com)** gets its information from other search engines but cannot blend the results, which are listed according to which search engine is used.
- **Alta Vista (http://www.altavista.com)** at one time had the largest index in the industry, but attempts to change its nature caused it to fall behind the larger Google and Yahoo. Alta Vista is still a good, reliable source of information and, in addition to the usual links like news, images, and shopping, lets you find MP3/Audio, Video, and human category results.
- **Infotrac College Edition (http://www.infotrac-college.com)** provides a searchable database of some 15 million periodical articles from over 5,000 journals, newspapers, and magazines covering the last twenty years. It is a rich resource of readings on just about any topic you are interested in searching. Infotrac College is a subscription service that requires a passcode to access the database.
- **LookSmart (http://www.looksmart.com)** is a human-compiled directory of websites. Its best feature is likely its index of articles, which provides access to the contents of thousands of periodicals. You can search by subject, author, or title in your choice of all periodicals, certain categories of periodicals, or a specific periodical.
- **Lycos (http://www.lycos.com)**, like Yahoo, was established in 1994 and is therefore one of the oldest search engines on the web. It provides both human-powered results from LookSmart for some queries, usually the most popular, and crawler-based results for others.
- **Excite (http://www.excite.com)** provides a full-text index of some 50 million web pages, lets you search from over 60,000 reviewed sites, and rates each site it lists.
- **Search.com (http://www.search.com)** is a collection of tools designed to find all kinds of information, from World Wide Web sites to phone numbers to movies to stock quotes. It searches Google, Ask Jeeves, LookSmart, and dozens of other search engines to give you a broad range of responses to your queries.

Using Other Sources.   Do not overlook other excellent sources of information, such as interviews, taped television shows, and government publications. For example, if you research the human genome project, you will likely find a number of books, periodical articles, and government documents on the subject. A search of the

World Wide Web will turn up hundreds of thousands of site matches. You could easily become overwhelmed by the mass of materials available on your subject. Your task is to select the sources that seem most relevant to your project and to narrow your research topic as quickly as possible to avoid wasting time gathering materials you ultimately cannot use. To clarify and focus your own approach to the subject, you may want to interview a biology professor for information about the scientific aspects of the project and a philosophy professor for an opinion on its ethical implications. In addition to such interviews, you may use material from a lecture, a television documentary, a film, or your own survey.

CREATING A PRELIMINARY BIBLIOGRAPHY

Once you compile a list of sources to investigate, start locating and evaluating them. If you discover that you cannot use a source, cross it off your list or discard the card on which your source information was noted. When you find a source that definitely looks promising for your research topic, either make a bibliography card or record in a computer file for that source. Make sure you record all pertinent bibliographic information about your source, preferably in the form in which it will appear on your Works Cited page. The section in this chapter entitled "Documenting Sources" lists appropriate formats for various kinds of sources. Note the following sample work-cited formats for some common types of sources:

Book with One Author

> Best, Judith A. The Choice of the People?: Debating
>
>   the Electoral College. Lanham, MD: Rowman &
>
>   Littlefield, 1996.

Journal Article with One Author

> Weaver, Constance. "Weighing the Claims about Phonics
>
>   First." Education Digest 56 (April 1991): 19-22.

Journal Article with Two Authors

Fabes, Richard A., and Jeremiah Strouse. "Formal
versus Informal Sources on Sex Education:
Competing Forces in the Sexual Socialization of
Adolescents." <u>Adolescence</u> 20 (1985): 250-61.

Journal Article with No Author Named

USA: The Facts about Wage Discrimination and Equal
Pay." <u>Women's International Network News</u> 25.1
(Winter 1999): 68.

Newspaper Article with Author Named

Warrick, Pamela. "Questions of Life and Death." <u>The
Los Angeles Times</u> 4 Aug. 1991: E1+.

Magazine Article with Author Named

Moody, Howard. "Sacred Rite or Civil Right?" <u>The
Nation</u> 5 July 2004: 28.

Magazine Article with No Author Named

"Another Challenge to Coffee's Safety." <u>Science News</u>
    20 October 1990: 253.

Chapter from a Collection of Essays

Smiley, Jane. "You Can Never Have Too Many." <u>The</u>
    <u>Barbie Chronicles: A Living Doll Turns Forty.</u>
    Ed. Yona Zeldis McDonough. New York:
    Touchstone/Simon and Schuster, Inc., 1999.
    189-192.

Government Document

United States. Cong. House. Committee on Armed
    Services. <u>Women in the Military: Hearing before</u>
    <u>the Military Personnel and Compensation</u>
    <u>Subcommittee.</u> 101st Cong., 2nd sess. 20
    Mar.1990: 14-56.

Internet Website

```
Americans Have Long Questioned Electoral College."
     Gallup Poll Releases. 16 Nov 2000. 29 Nov. 2000
     <http://www.gallup.com/poll/releases/pr001116.
     asp>.
```

Using a Computer for a Preliminary Bibliography.   If you store bibliographic information about your sources in a computer file and follow the formatting guidelines for the Works Cited page, you will save time later in the process when you put your paper in its final form. Record information in the proper format and alphabetize your list, placing new items in the appropriate alphabetical position. Then, when you need to assemble the Works Cited page, just move the list to the file where you store your paper (or keep the list in the same file). Here is how a list of the works on the previous sample bibliography cards would look in a computer file:

```
"Americans Have Long Questioned Electoral College."
     Gallup Poll Releases. 16 Nov 2000. 29 Nov. 2000
     <http://www.gallup.com/poll/releases/pr001116.
     asp>.
"Another Challenge to Coffee's Safety." Science News
     20 Oct. 1990: 253.
Best, Judith A. The Choice of the People?: Debating
     the Electoral College. Lanham, MD: Rowman &
     Littlefield, 1996.
Fabes, Richard A., and Jeremiah Strouse. "Formal
     versus Informal Sources on Sex Education:
     Competing Forces in the Sexual Socialization of
     Adolescents." Adolescence 20 (1985): 250-61.
```

Moody, Howard. "Sacred Rite or Civil Right?" *The Nation* 5 July 2004: 28.

Smiley, Jane. "You Can Never Have Too Many." *The Barbie Chronicles: A Living Doll Turns Forty.* Ed. Yona Zeldis McDonough. New York: Touchstone/Simon and Schuster, Inc., 1999. 189-192.

United States. Cong. House. Committee on Armed Services. <u>Women in the Military: Hearing before the Military Personnel and Compensation Subcommittee.</u> 101st Cong., 2nd sess. 20 Mar. 1990: 14-56.

"USA: The Facts about Wage Discrimination and Equal Pay." <u>Women's International Network News</u> 25.1 (Winter 1999): 68.

Warrick, Pamela. "Questions of Life and Death." <u>Los Angeles Times</u> 4 Aug. 1991: E1+.

Weaver, Constance. "Weighing the Claims about Phonics First." <u>Education Digest</u> 56 (April 1991): 19-22.

EVALUATING PRINT SOURCES

Before you begin taking notes from any source, carefully assess its reliability. Ideally, your research should rely on unbiased, current, well-documented sources written by people with the authority to discuss the subject. However, you are likely to find a great number of sources that are written from particular perspectives that are out of date or incomplete, that are written by people with no authority whatsoever, or that do not document their own sources. Part of your job as a researcher is to try to discover these aspects of your sources, to reject those that are completely unreliable, and to use with caution sources about which you lack complete confidence. While you may never know for sure how much to trust a particular source, you can check certain things to help in your assessment.

Check for Bias.   Try to find out if the author, publication, organization, or person being interviewed is known to give fair coverage. People, organizations, and publications often promote particular perspectives, which you should recognize and take into account. You need not reject sources outright if you know they take particular positions on subjects, especially controversial issues. However, your own paper should be as unbiased as possible, which requires acknowledgment of the known biases of your sources.

Check the Date of Publication.   In general, an increasingly recent publication or update of a website provides an increasingly reliable source. For many subjects, current information is crucial to accurate analysis. If you are researching issues such as global warming, morality at high governmental levels, or controversial treatments for AIDS victims, for instance, you need the most recent available information. However, if you are examining a historical matter, such as the question of Richard III's guilt in his two young cousins' deaths or whether King Arthur of Britain is an entirely mythical figure, you can rely in part on older materials. You still want to look for the latest theories, information, or opinions on any subject you research, though.

Check the Author's Credentials.   Find out if the author has sufficient education, experience, or expertise to write or speak about your subject. You can do this in a number of ways. Any book usually gives information about an author, from a sentence or two to several paragraphs, either on the dust jacket or at the beginning or end of the book. This information reveals the author's professional status, other books the author has published, and similar information that helps to establish her authority. You can also look up the author in sources like *Contemporary Authors, Current Biography,* and *Who's Who.* Other checks on an author's reliability might review what professionals in other sources say about her or to note how often her name shows up on reference lists or bibliographies on your subject.

Check the Reliability of Your Source.   In evaluating a book, determine whether the publishing house is a respectable one. For a magazine, find out if it is published by a particular interest group. Evaluation of a book could include reading some representative reviews to see how it was received when first published. Both the *Book Review Digest* and *Book Review Index* will help you locate reviews.

Check the Thoroughness of Research and Documentation of Sources.   If your source purports to be scholarly, well-informed, or otherwise reliable, check to see how the evidence was gathered. Determine whether the source reports original research or other people's work and what facts or data support its conclusions. Look for references either at the ends of chapters or in a separate section at the end of a book. Almost all journal articles and scholarly books document sources, whereas few magazine articles and personal accounts do. Also, consider how statistics and other data are used. Statistics are notoriously easy to manipulate, so check how the author uses them and confirm his fair interpretation.

EVALUATING INTERNET SOURCES

As with print sources, you must take care to evaluate any material you locate on the Internet before you use it in your paper. The Internet may pose more difficulty, because its resources may offer fewer clues than a book or journal article might give. However, searching the Internet will turn up many useful sources, such as scholarly projects, reference databases, text files of books, articles in periodicals, and professional sites. You must use your judgment when selecting sources for your research paper. Remember that anyone with some knowledge of the Internet can create a website, so be very cautious about accepting the authority of anything you find on the Internet. In general, personal sites are probably not as reliable as professional sites and those of scholarly projects. Reference databases can be extremely useful tools for locating source materials.

You must apply the same sort of skills that you bring to critical reading when looking at an Internet website, particularly when searching for materials for a class assignment. You must ask a number of questions about the site before accepting and using materials that you locate on the Internet. Some key areas to consider are the authority or credentials of the person or persons responsible for the site, the scope, accuracy, timeliness, and nature of the information at the site, and the presentation of the information at the site. Here is a list of questions that will help you evaluate Internet websites:

- **What can you tell about the site from its URL (Uniform Record Locator)?** Websites exist for a variety of purposes, including the following: to sell a product, to advocate a position, to influence readers, and to inform. They may be sponsored by individuals for personal reasons, by professionals to impart information, by corporations to sell products, by agencies or groups to influence opinion or advocate a specific position. Knowing what domain the abbreviation at the end of the URL represents can give you your first clue about a website's purpose. The domain is the system for indicating the logical or geographical location of a web page from the Internet. Outside the United States, domains indicate country, such as ca (Canada), uk (United Kingdom), or au (Australia). In the United States, the following are common domains:
  - **Educational** websites exist to provide information about educational institutions, including elementary, secondary, and university levels. Their Internet address ends in **.edu**.
  - **Government** websites provide information about governmental departments, agencies, and policies at all levels of government, including city, county, state, and federal governments. Their Internet address ends in **.gov**.
  - **Organizational** websites advocate the viewpoint of particular groups. The URL for an organizational website typically ends in **.org**.
  - **Commercial** websites aim to sell products or services. Their URL usually ends in **.com**.
  - **Military** websites provide information about the military. Their Internet address ends in **.mil**.

- **News** websites exist to provide information about current events. Their Internet address usually ends in **.com**.
- **Personal** websites are constructed by individuals about themselves. The address or personal sites end in various ways, probably most typically **.com**.
- **Entertainment** websites exist to amuse, entertain, and provide information about the entertainment industry. Their Internet address usually ends in **.com**.
- **Internet service provider** websites exist to provide information about companies and services related to the Internet. Their website address ends in **.net**.
- **What do you know about the author of the site?** Is the author of the website qualified to give information on the subject? Does the site give information about the author's qualifications? Are the author's credentials, such as academic affiliation, professional association, or publications, easily verified? Since anyone can create a webpage, you want to determine whether the author of the website you are looking at is qualified to give the information you are seeking.
- **Is the material on the website presented objectively, or do biases or prejudices reveal themselves?** The language used may be a clue, but probably the best way to discover a particular bias is to look at a great many sites (and other sources) on the same topic. When you understand the complexity of your topic and the variety of viewpoints on it, you should be able to determine whether a site is objective or subjective.
- **Is the information reliable?** Can you verify it? How does it compare with information you have learned from other sources? How well does the website compare with other sites on the same topic? Does the site offer unique information or does it repeat information that you can find at other sites?
- **How thoroughly does the website cover its topic?** Does it provide links to other sites for additional information? Does the site have links to related topics, and do those links work?
- **How accurate is the information?** This may be difficult to assess when you first begin your research, but the more you read about your topic and examine a variety of sources, the better able you will be to evaluate information accuracy.
- **When was the website last updated?** Is the information at the site current?
- **What is your impression of the visual effect of the site?** Are the graphics helpful or distracting, clear or confusing? Are words spelled correctly? Is the page organized well?

ILLUSTRATION: SEEKING PROMISING WEBSITES

Suppose, for example, that Shawn Ryan is interested in finding information on the Internet for his paper on King Arthur. When he first enters the keywords "Arthurian legend," a search engine returns almost 80,000 matches. Obviously, he cannot look at every match, but he can begin his search by scrolling through the first page of matches, picking a site that sounds promising, and going to that site. The list shows several entries that appear to be newsgroups or personal sites, whereas two will take him to the sites of a scholarly society and a scholarly project associated with a university. Because he is looking for sources for a research paper, as opposed to satisfying general curiosity, Shawn prefers the scholarly sites.

Both of the scholarly sites provide enormously useful information. The entry labeled "Arthurian websites" takes him to the home page of the North American branch of the International Arthurian Society, whose journal, *Arthuriana,* Shawn can read on the web. Furthermore, the site offers manuscripts, reviews, and scholarly essays, including the titles of over two hundred sources listed under the heading "Nonfiction and Research." In addition, the site offers links to other Arthurian sites.

As with print sources, Shawn has to judge the trustworthiness and reliability of an Internet source on the basis of who created the site, the credentials of the authorities, and the kind of information it gives. For instance, he particularly likes the information available at the website for the Camelot Project at the University of Rochester. Shawn determines that this site is a reliable source for several reasons. According to its home page, the Camelot Project aims to create a database of Arthurian texts, bibliographies, and other information. This goal tells Shawn that the site is not devoted to one person's opinions or to an informal collection of materials. Rather, it has a legitimate, scholarly aim, making it a valuable source of relevant materials for his paper. The Camelot Project itself is sponsored by the University of Rochester and the Robbins Library, associations that assure a certain level of reliability and scholarly appropriateness. Finally, the material at the site is continually updated, the most recent change occurring just one month before Shawn visited the site. Thus, Shawn has found a source that he is confident he can trust and that is sure to lead him to other reliable sources.

QUESTIONS TO ASK WHEN EVALUATING SOURCES

- Is the publication or site known to be fair, or does it have a bias or slant?
- Does the source seem one sided, or does it try to cover all perspectives on an issue?
- Is the information current or outdated?
- Does the authority have respectable credentials?
- How reliable is the source?
- How thoroughly does the source cover its subject?
- Does the source offer adequate documentation for its information?
- If the source relies on research data, how was evidence gathered? Are statistics used fairly, or are they misrepresented?

TAKING NOTES

When you find an article, book, pamphlet, website, or other source you believe will be important or informative in your research, take notes from that source. There are several kinds of notes that you will take:

Summary.   A summary produces an objective restatement of a written passage in your own words. A summary is much shorter than the original work. Since its purpose is to highlight the central idea or ideas and major points of a work, make summary notes to record general ideas or main points of a large piece of writing, perhaps several pages, a chapter, or an entire article.

Paraphrase.   A paraphrase is a restatement of the words of someone else in your own words. Use paraphrasing when you want to use another writer's ideas but not the exact words, or to explain difficult material more clearly. Your own version of someone else's words must be almost entirely your own words. When incorporating paraphrased material into your research paper, you must be clear about when the paraphrased material begins and ends.

Direct Quotation.   A direct quotation is a record of the exact words of someone else. You will want to quote directly when the words are unique, colorful, or so well stated that you cannot fairly or accurately paraphrase them. Use direct quotations when you do not want to misrepresent what an author says or when the author makes a statement that you wish to stress or comment on. You may want to quote directly in order to analyze or discuss a particular passage. Use direct quotations sparingly and integrate them smoothly into your paper. Too many direct quotations in your paper will interrupt the flow of your own words.

ILLUSTRATION: SUMMARIZING, PARAPHRASING, AND QUOTING

Chapter 5 has detailed directions and summary guidelines for both paraphrasing source material and quoting directly. Chapter 5 also discusses some common tools for handling source material: ellipsis points, brackets, single quotation marks, and "Qtd. In." Sample research papers located later in this chapter also give examples of the correct handling of source material. Here is another illustration that shows how to handle source material based on this opening paragraph from Ian Wilmut's "Dolly's False Legacy," located in chapter 20:

> Overlooked in the arguments about the mortality of artificially reproducing life is the fact that, at present, cloning is a very inefficient procedure. The incidence of death among fetuses and offspring produced by cloning is much higher than it is through natural reproduction—roughly 10 times as high as normal before birth and three times as high after birth in our studies at Roslin. Distressing enough for those

working with animals, these failure rates surely render unthinkable the notion of applying such treatment to humans.

In the following passage from Nate Hayes' research paper, "A Positive Alternative to Cloning" (see sample pages at the end of this chapter), he combines summary, paraphrase, and direct quotation. Nate begins by summarizing and then paraphrases and quotes from the introductory paragraph:

> One big question has to do with the high failure rate of cloning. Despite having been responsible for the first cloned mammal, Dr. Wilmut is very conservative in his views of the wisdom of carrying on full speed with cloning research because of its unreliability. In "Dolly's False Legacy," he identifies some of the likely problems a cloned human might have. For instance, Wilmut warns of the inefficiency of cloning, noting the high death rate in fetuses and live births when cloning is used in animal tests. This fact leads him to suggest that "these failure rates surely render unthinkable the notion of applying such treatment to humans" (564).

Nate first identifies the author and title of his source and summarizes a key point of Wilmut's essay. Then he paraphrases the reference to death rates in animals produced by cloning versus those produced naturally. Finally, Nate quotes directly a passage that he believes is forcefully worded.

Recording Source and Page Numbers.

Note-taking is crucial to the success of your paper. You must take accurate and careful notes, reproducing an author's words exactly as they appear if you quote, completely restating the author's words if you paraphrase, and accurately capturing the essence of the material if you summarize. In any case, you will give a citation in your paper, so *you must record the source and page number for any notes.*

Caution: When taking notes, some students are tempted to write every detail as it appears in the original, thinking that they will paraphrase the material at some later time. They must then spend valuable time later rephrasing material when they should be concentrating on writing their papers, or else they take the easier route and use the direct quotations. The result may be a paper that is too full of direct quotations and lacking in effective paraphrases. Remember that you should quote directly only language that is particularly well expressed or material that you do not feel you can adequately restate in your own words. Your final paper should have far more paraphrases than direct quotations.

Note Cards.

Where you record your notes does not matter, as long as you develop an efficient system. The important consideration is the accuracy and fairness of your notes. Traditionally, researchers have been told to use 4×6 cards, because they are large enough to record ideas, summaries, quotations, or major points. When the note-taking part of the research ends, the researcher can shuffle the cards about, arranging them in the order that makes sense for the research paper. Many people like the note-card system and work well with this system.

GUIDELINES FOR TAKING NOTES

- **Write both the author's last name and the page number from which the information is taken.** That is all the information you need, as long as you have a bibliography card or file for the source that lists complete bibliographic information.
- **Place a subject heading at the top of each card or note in a computer file.** This labeling system will help you sort and arrange your cards when you write your paper.
- **Record only one idea or several small, related ones in each note.** This practice will help you to organize your notes when you begin writing.
- **Place quotation marks before and after the material taken directly from a source.** Don't rely on memory to determine whether words are identical to the original or paraphrased.
- **Use notes to summarize.** A note may refer to an entire passage, an article, or a book without giving specific details. Make a note to remind you that the information is a summary.
- **Use notes to record original ideas that occur to you while you are reading.** Make sure you identify your own ideas.

Word Processor. If you work better with a word processor, then by all means use one. A word processor can be very helpful for organizing and sorting notes. Most programs allow you to arrange your notes in numerical order. However, make sure to develop a filing system for your notes. If your program lets you create folders, you can keep your notes from different sources under specific headings, each with its own subheadings. Place the subject heading at the beginning of your notes, and put the page number at the end. Make sure that your notes clearly identify sources for all information.

AVOIDING PLAGIARISM

Giving proper credit to your sources is a crucial component of the research process. It is also one of the trickiest aspects of the process, because it requires absolute accuracy in note-taking. Many students have been disheartened by low grades on papers that took weeks to prepare, because they were careless or inaccurate in handling and documenting source materials.

Simply defined, **plagiarism** is borrowing another person's words without giving proper credit. The worst form of plagiarism is deliberately using the words or important ideas of someone else without giving any credit to that source. Handing in a paper someone else has written or copying someone else's paper and pretending it is yours are the most blatant and inexcusable forms of plagiarism, crimes that on some campuses carry penalties like automatic failure in the course or even immediate expulsion from school. Most student plagiarism is not deliberate, but rather results from carelessness either in the research process, when notes are taken, or in the writing process, when notes are incorporated into the student's own text. Even this unintentional plagiarism can result in a failing grade, however, especially if it appears repeatedly in a paper.

Keep the following standards in mind when you take notes on your source materials and when you write your research paper:

- **You commit plagiarism if you use the exact words or ideas of another writer without putting quotation marks around the words or citing a source.** The reader of your paper assumes that words without quotation marks or a source citation are your own words. To use the words of another without proper documentation suggests that you are trying to pass the words off as your own without giving credit to the writer.

- **You commit plagiarism if you use the exact words of another writer without putting quotation marks around those words, even if the paper cites the source of the material.** Readers assume that words followed by a parenthetical citation are paraphrased from the original—that is, that they are your own words and that the general idea was expressed by the author of the source material.

- **You commit plagiarism if you paraphrase by changing only a few words of the original or by using the identical sentence structure of the original, with or without a source.** Again, readers assume that words without quotation marks followed by a parenthetical citation are your own words, not those of someone else. In a paraphrase, the *idea* is that of another; the *words* are your own.

- **You inaccurately handle source material when you use quotation marks around words that are not exactly as they appear in the original.** Readers assume that all words within quotation marks are identical to the original.

GUIDELINES FOR AVOIDING PLAGIARISM

- **For direct quotations, write the words exactly as they appear in the original.** Put quotation marks before and after the words. Do not change anything.

- **For paraphrased material, restate the original thought in your own words, using your own writing style.** Do not use the exact sentence pattern of the original, and do not simply rearrange words. You have to retain the central idea of the paraphrased material, but do so in your own words.

- **When using borrowed material in your paper, whether direct quotations or paraphrases, acknowledge the source by naming the author or work as you introduce the material.** Doing so not only tells your reader that you are using borrowed material but also often provides a clear transition from your own words and ideas to the borrowed material that illustrates or expands on your ideas.

- **Provide an in-text citation for any borrowed material.** Give the author's last name if it is not mentioned in the text of the paper, followed by page number(s). If the source material is anonymous, use a shortened version of the title in place of a name.

- **Assemble all sources cited in your paper in an alphabetical list at the end of the paper.** This is your list of works cited, containing only those works actually used in the paper.

Obviously, accuracy and fairness in note-taking are essential standards. Great care must be taken when you read your source materials and again when you transfer your notes to your final paper.

ILLUSTRATION: PLAGIARISM, INACCURATE DOCUMENTATION, AND CORRECT HANDLING OF SOURCE MATERIAL

The passage that follows is from page 8 of Jean Kilbourne's "Beauty and the Beast of Advertising." Complete bibliographic information follows, as it would appear on a bibliography card or list and on the Works Cited page of a research paper:

```
Kilbourne, Jean. "Beauty and the Beast of

    Advertising." Media&Values Winter 1989: 8-10.
```

Note that the title of the magazine is correct as written, with the ampersand (&) instead of "and" and with no spaces between the words. Here is the passage:

"You're a Halston woman from the very beginning," the advertisement proclaims. The model stares provocatively at the viewer, her long blonde hair waving around her face, her bare chest partially covered by two curved bottles that give the illusion of breasts and cleavage.

The average American is accustomed to blue-eyed blondes seductively touting a variety of products. In this case, however, the blonde is about five years old.

Advertising is an over $130 billion a year industry and affects all of us throughout our lives. We are each exposed to over 1,500 ads a day, constituting perhaps the most powerful educational force in society. The average adult will spend 11.2 years of his/her life watching television commercials. But the ads sell a great deal more than products. They sell values, images, and concepts of success and worth, love and sexuality, popularity and normalcy. They tell us who we are and who we should be. Sometimes they sell addictions.

Now look at each of these sentences from a hypothetical research paper using information from the Kilbourne article. The commentary that follows identifies plagiarism, inaccurate handling of the original, or correct handling of source material:

1. Advertising is an over $130 billion a year industry and affects us throughout our lives.
   [This is **plagiarism:** Quotation marks are needed around words identical to the original and a source must be cited.]

2. We are each exposed to over 1,500 ads a day (Kilbourne 8).
   [This is **plagiarism:** Quotation marks are needed around words taken directly from the original.]

3. The average American is used to blue-eyed blondes seductively selling a variety of things (Kilbourne 8).
   [This is **plagiarism:** Original words are changed only slightly and the original sentence structure is retained.]

4. Kilbourne's analysis of advertising begins with the following quotation from a popular advertisement: "You're a Halston woman from the very beginning" (8).
   [This is **inaccurate documentation:** Single quotation marks are needed within the double marks to indicate that quotation marks are in the original.]

5. In her analysis of the ways in which advertising uses women's bodies to sell products, Jean Kilbourne argues that ads sell much more than just products. Ads "sell values, images, and concepts of success and worth" (8).
   [This is **correct:** The text acknowledges the author and the general idea of the article is adequately summarized. Quotation marks enclose material taken directly from the original.]

Students are sometimes frustrated by these guidelines governing note-taking and plagiarism, arguing that virtually everything in the final paper will be in quotation marks or followed by citations. But keep in mind that your final paper is a synthesis of information you have discovered in your research with your own thoughts on your topic, thoughts that naturally undergo modification, expansion, and/or revision as you read and think about your topic. Probably half of the paper will be your own words. These words will usually include all of the introductory and concluding paragraphs, all topic sentences and transitional sentences within and between paragraphs, and all introductions to direct quotations. Furthermore, you need give no citation for statements of general or common knowledge, such as facts about well-known historical or current events. If you keep running across the same information in all of your sources, you can assume it is general knowledge.

HANDLING SOURCE MATERIAL

Handling source material fairly, accurately, and smoothly is one of your main tasks in writing a successful research paper. More than likely your instructor will evaluate your research project not only on how successfully you argue, explain, examine, or illustrate your topic but also on how skillfully you handle source materials. This means that you must take great care not only when you take notes but also when you transfer those notes into your paper. Always keep in mind—as you are taking notes, when drafting your paper, and when writing its final version—that you must acknowledge the source for all borrowed material. Any information that you take from a source must be properly attributed to its author or, if no author, to its title. At the same time, you must not simply drop material into your text but be mindful of providing smooth

GUIDELINES FOR HANDLING SOURCE MATERIAL

- **Introduce or provide a context for quoted material.** "Bald" or "dropped" quotations occur when you fail to integrate quotations smoothly into your text. The abrupt dropping of a quotation disrupts the flow of your text.

- **Name your authority or, when no author is named, use title of the source.** Provide this information either in the text itself or in the parenthetical citation. Rely on standard phrases such as "one writer claims," "according to one expert," and the like to introduce quotations or paraphrases.

- **Use both first and last names of author at the first mention in your text.** After that, use just last name. Always use last name only in parenthetical citations (unless you have sources by two authors with the same last name).

- **Acknowledge source material when you first begin paraphrasing.** Make sure you give some kind of signal to your reader when you begin paraphrasing borrowed material. This is particularly important if you paraphrase more than one sentence from a source. Otherwise, your reader will not know how far back the citation applies.

- **Quote sparingly.** Quote directly only those passages that are vividly or memorably phrased, so that you could not do justice to them by rewording them; that require exact wording for accuracy; or that need the authority of your source to lend credibility to what you are saying.

- **Intermingle source material with our own words.** Avoid a "cut-and-paste" approach to the research process. Remember that source materials serve primarily to support your generalizations. Never run two quotations together without some comment or transitional remark from you.

- **Make sure that direct quotations are exact.** Do not change words unless you use brackets or ellipses to indicate changes. Otherwise, be exact. For instance, if your source says "$2 million," do not write "two million dollars."

- **Make sure that paraphrases are truly your own words.** Do not inadvertently commit plagiarism by failing to paraphrase fairly.

integration of your source material into your own text. After all, the text is your work: the thesis of paper, the overall organization and development, transitions from point to point, general observations, and the conclusions are all yours. Your source materials serve to support, illustrate, develop, or exemplify your own words. This means that the source material must not interrupt the flow of your words or call attention to themselves. They are an important and integral part of your own paper.

DOCUMENTING SOURCES

Follow the Appropriate Style Guidelines.   The examples of documentation and sample research papers that appear in this chapter all follow MLA (Modern Language Association) documentation style. That style governs because this textbook is often used in English courses, and English is located within the discipline of the

---

SUMMARY OF DIFFERENCES AMONG DOCUMENTATION STYLES

- **MLA:** Used by writers in the many areas of the humanities (English, foreign languages, history, and philosophy); requires parenthetical in-text citations of author and page number that refer to an alphabetical list of works cited at the end of the paper.
- **APA:** Used by writers in the behavioral and social sciences (education, psychology, and sociology); requires parenthetical in-text citations of author and date of publication that refer to an alphabetical list of references at the end of the paper.
- **CBE:** Used by writers in technical fields and the sciences (engineering, biology, physics, geography, chemistry, computer science, and mathematics); requires either a name–year format or a citation-sequence format. The name–year format places the author's last name and the year of publication in parentheses, referring to an alphabetical list of references at the end of the paper.
- **Chicago:** Used by some areas of the humanities, notably history, art, music, and theatre; requires a superscript number (e.g., [1]) for each citation, all of which are numbered sequentially throughout the paper; no number is repeated. Numbers correspond either to footnotes at the bottoms of pages or a list of notes at the end of the paper.

    The first note gives complete information about the source, with shortened information for each subsequent reference to that source. A bibliography follows the notes, giving the same information, except for the page number, as in the first citation of each source. The information is also punctuated and arranged differently from the note copy.

---

humanities. However, your instructor may permit you to choose the style appropriate to the major field you intend to study. A section later in this chapter provides guidelines for writing a research paper using APA (American Psychological Association) style. That style is probably as commonly used as MLA in undergraduate course papers. In addition to MLA and APA, other frequently used documentation styles are CBE (Council of Biology Editors) and Chicago. Following this summary of the chief differences among those four styles, the chapter lists stylebooks that give additional guidelines.

Style Guides.   To find full details on a particular documentation style, consult the following style guides:

MLA
Gibaldi, Joseph. *MLA Handbook for Writers of Research Papers.* 6th ed. New York: MLA, 2003.

APA
American Psychological Association. *Publication Manual of the American Psychological Association.* 5th ed. Washington: APA, 2001.

CBE
CBE Style Manual Committee. *Scientific Style and Format: The CBE Manual for Authors, Editors, and Publishers.* 7th ed. Chicago: Council of Science Editors, 2005.

CHICAGO

The Chicago Manual of Style. 15th ed. Chicago: U of Chicago P, 2003.

Turabian Kate L. *A Manual for Writers of Term Papers, Theses, and Dissertations.* 6th ed. Rev. John Grossman and Alice Bennet. Chicago: U of Chicago P, 1996.

Internet Citation Guides.   Many research resources are available on the Internet, including guides for citing such sources. Your university librarian may have created a website where you will find the names and URLs (Uniform Resource Locators) of sites that give directions for citing electronic sources. Keep in mind that Internet sites constantly change. URLs that were correct when this book was published may no longer be correct, or the sites may have ceased functioning. However, the ease of changing and updating Internet sites means that they may have more current information than print guides offer. If you doubt the reliability and currency of a website, consult with your instructor about the advisability of using the site. Here are a few reliable sites:

Columbia Guide to Online Style (site provides models of both MLA and APA formatting): <http://www.columbia.edu/cu/cup/cgos/idx_basic.html>

Using Modern Language Association (MLA) Format, Purdue University's Online Writing Lab. Provides links to APA guidelines, too: <http://owl.english.purdue.edu/handouts/research/r_mla.html>

MLA and APA Citation, University of Delaware's Writing Center: <http://www.english.udel.edu/wc/resource/grammarresource.html>.

Style Sheet for Citing Resources (Print & Electronic). UC-Berkeley Library. Provides examples and rules for MLA, APA, Chicago, and Turabian: <http://www.lib.berkeley.edu/TeachingLib/Guides/Internet/Style.html>.

Cómo citar recursos electronic by Assumpció Estivill and Cristobal Urbana, Spanish-language guide to citing electronic sources: <http://www.ub.es/biblio/citae-e.html>.

How to Cite Electronic Sources, Library of Congress. Explains how to cite media available online, such as films, music, maps, photographs, and texts: <http://lcweb2.loc.gov/ammem/ndlpedu/start/cite/index.html>

MLA Style, Modern Language Association of America. Includes list of frequently asked questions about MLA style: <http://www.mla.org/main_stl.html>.

CITING SOURCES IN THE TEXT

Recall from the discussion in chapter 5 on documenting sources with in-text citations and the discussion in this chapter on taking notes that a crucial task of the researcher is to identify accurately sources for all borrowed material. This section expands the discussion from chapter 5 with illustrations of treatments for several types of sources.

It also includes guidelines for creating a list of works cited that incorporates a variety of sources, including electronic sources. These examples follow MLA guidelines as they appear in Joseph Gibaldi's *MLA Handbook for Writers of Research Papers,* 6th edition (New York: MLA, 2003).

In-Text Citations.   Remember that you must name your source for any borrowed material. The parenthetical citation must give enough information to identify the source by directing your reader to the alphabetized list of works cited at the end of your paper. The citation should also give the page number or numbers, if available, on which the material appears.

Author-Page Format.   MLA guidelines call for the author-page format when acknowledging borrowed material in the text of your paper. You must name the author (or source, if no author is named) and give a page number or numbers where the borrowed material appears in the source. The author's name or title you give in your text directs readers to the correct entry in the Works Cited list, so the reference must correspond to its entry on that list. Here are some examples:

Book or Article with One Author.   Author's last name and page number, without punctuation.
    (Sollod 15)

Book or Article with Two or Three Authors.   Both or all three authors' last names followed by the page number.
    (Barrett and Rowe 78)   (Fletcher, Miller, and Caplan 78)

Note: Reproduce the names in the order in which they appear on the title page. If they are not listed alphabetically, do not change their order.

Book or Article with More than Three Authors.   First author's last name followed by et al. and then page number.
    (Smith et al. 29)

Article or Other Publication with No Author Named.   Short title followed by page number.
    ("Teaching" 10)

Note: When citing any source in a parenthetical reference in your text that appears on your Works Cited list, use the full title if short or a shortened version. When using a shortened version, begin with the word by which the source is alphabetized. If you cite two anonymous articles beginning with the same word, use the full title of each to distinguish one from the other.
    ("Classrooms without Walls" 45)   ("Classrooms in the 21st Century" 96)

Two Works by the Same Author.   Author's name followed by a comma, a short title, and the page number.
    (Heilbrun, *Hamlet's Mother* 123)   (Heilbrun, *Writing a Woman's Life* 35)

Works by People with the Same Last Name.   First and last names of author and page number.
   (Gregory Smith 16)

Example: Consider this example of an in-text citation from Erin Anderson's research paper located at the end of this chapter. Erin uses the following source:

> Longley, Lawrence D., and Neal R. Peirce. The Electoral College Primer 2000. New Haven, CT: Yale UP, 1999.

When Erin quotes from that source in her paper, this is how she documents it:

> In The Electoral College Primer 2000, Lawrence D. Longley and Neal R. Peirce explain their opposition to the electoral college system. They assert that in an "advanced democratic nation, where . . . popular choice is the most deeply ingrained of government principles," a voting system where popular votes don't necessarily mean electoral votes is "irrational" (132).

For her second and subsequent references to this source, she does the following:

> Longley and Peirce also explain the "faithless elector" issue. The Constitution nowhere requires the chosen electors to vote for the winner of the popular vote. However, in the history of the Electoral College, only nine votes of the over 20,000 cast have been known to go " 'against instructions' " (113).

Exceptions to Author-Page Format.   Many papers must accommodate some exceptions to the basic author-page parenthetical citation. For instance, for non-print sources such as an Internet website, a lecture, a telephone conversation, a television documentary, or a recording, name the source in parentheses after the material without giving a page number.

Citing an Entire Work.   You may want to refer to an entire work rather than just part of it. In that case, name the work and the author in the text of your paper, without a parenthetical citation:

> Sir Arthur Conan Doyle's Hound of the Baskervilles features Watson to a much greater degree than do the earlier Holmes stories.

Citing Volume and Page Number of a Multivolume Work.   If you refer to material from more than one volume of a multivolume work, state the volume number, followed by a colon, and then the page number. Do not use the words or abbreviations for *volume* or *page*. The two numbers separated by a colon explicitly indicate volume and page. Your Works Cited entry will state the number of volumes in the work.

> Edgar Johnson's critical biography of Charles Dickens concludes with a rousing tribute to the author's creative imagination: "[T]he world he [Dickens] created shines with undying life, and the hearts of men still vibrate to his indignant anger, his love, his tears, his glorious laughter, and his triumphant faith in the dignity of man" (2: 1158).

Works Cited Entry.

> Johnson, Edgar. <u>Charles Dickens: His Tragedy and Triumph.</u> 2 vols. New York: Simon, 1952.

If you draw material from just one volume of a multivolume work, your Works Cited entry states which volume, and your in-text citation gives only the page number:

> The works of Charles Dickens fervently proclaim "his triumphant faith in the dignity of man" (1158).

Works Cited Entry.

> Johnson, Edgar. <u>Charles Dickens: His Tragedy and Triumph.</u> Vol. 2. New York: Simon, 1952.

Citing a Work by a Corporate Author or Government Agency.

Cite the author's or agency's name followed by a page reference, just as you would for a book or periodical article. However, if the title of the corporate author is long, put it in the body of the text to avoid an extensive parenthetical reference:

> Testifying before a subcommittee of the U.S. House Committee on Public Works and Transportation, a representative of the Environmental Protection Agency argued that pollution from second-hand smoke within buildings is a widespread and dangerous threat (173–174).

Citing Internet Sources.

According to the MLA online guidelines, works on the World Wide Web are cited just like printed works when citing sources in your text. A special consideration with web documents is that they generally do not have fixed page numbers or any kind of section numbering. If your source lacks numbering, MLA says that you have to omit numbers from your parenthetical references. In that case, in your parenthetical citation, give the author's last name, if known (Plonsky), or the title if the original gives no author's name ("Psychology with Style"). If an author incorporates page numbers, section numbers, or paragraph numbers, you may cite the relevant numbers. Give the appropriate abbreviation before the numbers: (Plonsky, pars. 5–6). (*Pars.* is the abbreviation for *paragraphs.*) For a document on the World Wide Web, the page numbers of a printout should normally not be cited, because the pagination may vary in different printouts.

Remember that the purpose of the parenthetical citation is to indicate the location of the quotation or paraphrase in the referenced work and to point to the referenced work in the list of works cited. Whatever entry begins the reference in the Works Cited list (i.e., author's last name or title of work), that same entry should also appear in the parenthetical reference. A citation for an Internet source should reference the site in the body of the text, if possible, rather than including parenthetical information. For example, here is Erin's Internet source:

> Geraghty, Jim. "Do Elections Need New Rules?" <u>Policy.com News and Events: Daily Briefing.</u> 22 Nov. 2000. 29 Nov. 2000 <http://www.policy.com/news/dbrief/dbriefarc834.asp>.

GUIDELINES FOR IN-TEXT CITATION

- Name the source for all borrowed material, including both direct quotations and paraphrases, either in your text or in parentheses following the borrowed material.
- Give the citation in parentheses at the end of the sentence containing the quotation or paraphrase.
- In the parentheses, state the author's last name and the page number or numbers from which you took the words or ideas, with no punctuation between the name and the page number.
- For smooth transition to borrowed material, name the author or source as you introduce the words or ideas. In that case, the parentheses will include only the page number or numbers.
- At the first mention of an author in your text, use the author's full name. Thereafter, use the last name only.
- When citing Internet sources that have no page numbers, use the author's last name in parentheses. If you mention the author's name in your text, it is helpful to repeat it in the parenthetical citation as well, to indicate where the borrowed material ends.
- Create a "Works Cited" page at the end of your paper that lists all sources quoted or paraphrased in the paper. Do not include any works that you consulted but did not directly use in your paper.

In her paper, she documents the source this way:

> Former First Lady Hillary Clinton has given her support for the abolition of the Electoral College; in fact, she is reported to have said that she would "be willing to co-sponsor a measure to abolish the Electoral College" (Geraghty).

Note: *When mentioning the name of an author for a World Wide Web source in the text rather than in the parenthetical citation, it is sometimes difficult to tell when borrowed material ends, especially when paraphrasing. Some instructors recommend that students repeat the author's name in the parenthetical citation, even when it is mentioned in the text. The same holds true when citing a source that has no author, just a title.*

CREATING A *WORKS CITED* PAGE USING MLA STYLE

The Works Cited page of a research report lists in alphabetical order all the sources you cite in your paper. It comes at the end of your paper, beginning on a separate page. Include an entry for every work quoted from, paraphrased, summarized, or otherwise alluded to in your paper. *Do not include on your list of works cited any sources you read but did not use in the paper.* You may want to include a list of useful works that informed your understanding of the topic but that you did not quote or paraphrase from in your final paper; to do so, create a separate page entitled "Works Consulted"

GENERAL GUIDELINES FOR CREATING A *WORKS CITED* LIST

- Begin your list of cited works on a new page after the conclusion of your paper.
- Center the title "Works Cited" one inch from the top of the page.
- Continue the page numbers of the text, with a separate number for each of the Works Cited pages.
- Begin the first line of each entry flush with the left margin. Indent the second and subsequent lines within each entry five spaces.
- Begin with the author's last name, followed by a comma and then the first name. For a source with two or more authors, invert only the first name. List the other name or names in normal order.
- Underline (italicize) the titles of books, journals, magazines, and newspapers. Do not use quotation marks. [**Note:** MLA guidelines recommend underlining instead of italics because printers are not uniform in the way they reproduce italics. Underlining has therefore become a convention that is understood to represent italics. However, if your instructor approves, and if your printer clearly distinguishes italics from regular print, you may use italics for the titles of books and journals.]
- Double-space within and between all entries.
- Place a period at the end of each entire entry.

using the same format as for the Works Cited page. Place the Works Consulted page last in your paper.

The remainder of this section gives guidelines for creating works-cited entries for books, periodicals, and electronic sources, supplemented by models for miscellaneous types of entries. The numbers on this list correspond to the numbered illustrations in each section (books, periodicals, electronic sources, miscellaneous) in the following pages:

Print Sources

1. Book with a single author
2. Article in a collection
3. Collection or anthology
4. Book with two or more authors
5. Two works by the same author
6. Reprint of a book
7. Preface, foreword, introduction, or afterword to a book
8. Edition of a book
9. Multivolume work
10. Article in a journal with continuous pagination
11. Article in a journal with separate pagination

12. Article in a weekly or biweekly magazine
13. Article in a monthly or bimonthly magazine
14. Article in a quarterly magazine
15. Magazine article with no author
16. Newspaper article
17. Periodical article that does not appear on consecutive pages

Creating a Works Cited List for Electronic Sources

18. Scholarly project
19. Professional site
20. Article in a reference database
21. Online article

Online Sources of Full-text Articles

22. Article with author named, scholarly journal
23. Article in magazine
24. Article with no author named
25. Article in magazine from personally subscribed service

Miscellaneous Electronic Sources

26. Personal site
27. Posting to a discussion group
28. E-mail message
29. Government document

Works Cited Formats for Sources Other than Books, Periodicals, and Electronic Sources

30. Congressional record
31. Government publication
32. Lecture
33. Letter
34. Personal interview
35. Reprint of an article provided by an information service
36. Telephone interview
37. Pamphlet
38. Television or radio program

39. Sound recording

40. Article in a reference book

Books in a Works Cited List.   Citations for books have several main parts: author's name, title of book, and publication information, including place of publication, publisher, and date the book was published. Often a book has more than one author or an editor, and often books are collections of a number of essays with individual authors. The following section provides guidelines for documenting the most common kinds of books that you are likely to come across in your research.

1. BOOK WITH A SINGLE AUTHOR

> Author's name. <u>Title of Book.</u> Place of publication. City: Publisher, date of publication.
> Leonardi, Susan J. <u>Dangerous by Degrees: Women at Oxford and the Somerville College Novelists.</u> New Brunswick: Rutgers UP, 1989.

2. ARTICLE IN A COLLECTION

Name the author, the title of the article, the title of the collection, the editor or coeditors of the collection, publication information, and the **inclusive page numbers** of the entire article. Follow this format:

> Author's name. "Title of Article." <u>Title of Collection.</u> The abbreviation "Ed." Editor's name in normal order. Place of publication: Name of

GUIDELINES FOR CREATING A WORKS CITED LIST FOR BOOKS

- **Begin with the author's last name, followed by a comma, and then the first name, followed by a period.** For a source with two or more authors, invert the first author's name with a comma before and after the first name, then write the word *and* and put the other author's name in normal order.
- **Underline the title of the book.**
- **State the place of publication, the publisher, and the date the book was published:** Place: Publisher, date.
- **Separate each item in an entry by a period:** Author. Title. Publication information and date. Note that each period is followed by two spaces. MLA guidelines acknowledge that most editors require material that is going to be printed to use only one space after a concluding punctuation mark but state that there is nothing wrong with using two unless your instructor requests that you do otherwise.
- **For essays in collections, begin by listing the author of the essay, then the title within quotation marks, the book it appears in, the editor's name, and publication information for the book.** Put the inclusive page numbers of the essay at the end of the entry.
- **Shorten publishers' names and drop such words as *Inc., Co.,* and *Press.*** Abbreviate *University* and *Press* for university presses, as "U of Wisconsin P" for University of Wisconsin Press or "Oxford UP" for Oxford University Press.

> publisher, date of publication. Inclusive page numbers on which the article appears.
>
> Rose-Bond, Sherry, and Scott Bond. "Sherlockiana." <u>Encyclopedia Mysteriosa: A Comprehensive Guide to the Art of Detection in Print, Film, Radio, and Television.</u> Ed. William L. DeAndrea. New York: Prentice, 1994. 327-330.

If the edition has two or more editors, use the abbreviation "Eds." followed by both editors' names:

Spacks, Patricia Meyer. "Sisters." <u>Fetter'd or Free?: British Women Novelists, 1670–1815.</u> Eds. Mary Anne Schofield and Cecilia Macheski. Athens, OH: Ohio UP, 1986. 136-151.

3. COLLECTION OR ANTHOLOGY

Use this format when you cite the ideas of the editor(s) or when you refer to the entire collection. Name the editor, followed by the abbreviation "ed." Treat the rest of the entry as you would for a book.

> Editor's name, ed. <u>Title of Collection.</u> Place of publication: Publisher, date of publication.
>
> Salwak, Dale, ed. <u>The Life and Work of Barbara Pym.</u> Iowa City: U of Iowa P, 1987.

For two or more editors, list the first editor's name in inverted order, followed by a comma, the word *and*, and the second editor's name in normal order.

> Schofield, Mary Anne, and Cecilia Macheski, eds. <u>Fetter'd or Free?: British Women Novelists, 1670–1815.</u> Athens, OH: Ohio UP, 1986.

4. BOOK WITH TWO OR MORE AUTHORS

List the names of the authors in the same order as they are listed on the title page, even if they are not in alphabetical order.

> First author's name in inverted order, and second author's name in normal order. <u>Name of Book.</u> Place of publication: Publisher, date of publication.
>
> Gilbert, Sandra M., and Susan Gubar. <u>The Madwoman in the Attic: The Woman Writer and the Nineteenth-Century Literary Imagination.</u> New Haven: Yale UP, 1979.

5. TWO WORKS BY THE SAME AUTHOR

List the books in alphabetical order by title. For the second and subsequent books by the same author, type three hyphens followed by a period in place of the name.

> Heilbrun, Carolyn. <u>Hamlet's Mother and Other Women.</u> New York: Ballantine, 1990.
>
> ---. <u>Writing a Woman's Life.</u> New York: Ballantine, 1988.

6. REPRINT OF A BOOK

Follow the same format as for books, but add the date of the first publication after the title.

> Author's name. <u>Title of Book.</u> First date of publication. Place of publication of this edition: Publisher, date of publication.
> Symons, Julian. <u>Bloody Murder: From the Detective Story to the Crime Novel: A History.</u> 1972. 1985. London: Pan Macmillan, 1992.

If a different publisher produced earlier editions, you have the option of naming the place of publication and publisher for the other editions as well as for the current one.

> Symons, Julian. <u>Bloody Murder: From the Detective Story to the Crime Novel: A History.</u> London: Faber, 1972. London: Viking, 1985. London: Pan Macmillan, 1992.

7. PREFACE, FOREWORD, INTRODUCTION, OR AFTERWORD TO A BOOK

If you use material *only* from the preface, foreword, introduction, or afterword of a book, your Works Cited entry begins with the name of the person who wrote the selection you use, not necessarily with the author of the book (though sometimes they are the same person). You will need to indicate what part of the book you cite (preface, foreword, introduction, or afterword), then name the book and author and give complete bibliographic information. Finally, give the inclusive page numbers of the preface, foreword, introduction, or afterword. Follow this model:

> Author of introduction. Introduction. <u>Title of Book.</u> By author's name in normal order. Place of publication: Publisher, date of publication. Inclusive page numbers on which the introduction appears.
> Green, Richard Lancelyn. Introduction. <u>The Adventures of Sherlock Holmes.</u> By Arthur Conan Doyle. 1892. Oxford: Oxford UP, 1993. xi-xxxv.

8. EDITION OF A BOOK

Use this format for a book prepared for publication by someone other than the author if you refer primarily to the text itself:

> Doyle, Arthur Conan. <u>The Adventures of Sherlock Holmes.</u> Ed. Richard Lancelyn Green. Oxford: Oxford UP, 1994.

If you refer primarily to the work of the editor, for instance, material from the introduction or notes to the text, begin with the editor's name:

> Green, Richard Lancelyn, ed. <u>The Adventures of Sherlock Holmes.</u> By Arthur Conan Doyle. 1892 Oxford: Oxford UP, 1993.

9. MULTIVOLUME WORK

If you draw material from two or more volumes of a work, cite the total number of volumes in the entire work. When you refer to the work in the text of your paper, your parenthetical reference gives the volume number and page number.

> Johnson, Edgar. <u>Charles Dickens: His Tragedy and Triumph.</u> 2 vols. New
> York: Simon, 1952.

If you refer to only one volume of a multivolume work, state the number of that volume in the works-cited entry. Your parenthetical in-text citation supplies page number only, not volume and page.

> Johnson, Edgar. <u>Charles Dickens: His Tragedy and Triumph.</u> Vol. 2. New
> York: Simon, 1952.

Periodicals in a Works Cited List.　　Periodicals are magazines or journals that are published frequently and at fixed intervals. Distinguish between journals and magazines by considering audience, subject matter, and frequency of publication. Journals are fairly specialized, are usually written for people in a specific profession, are more technical and research-oriented than magazines, and generally appear much less frequently than magazines, perhaps bimonthly or four times a year. Magazines, on the other hand, are intended for general audiences, are not heavily research-oriented, and usually appear in monthly or even weekly editions. As with books, Works Cited entries for periodicals have three main divisions: the author's name, the title of the article, and publication information, including the name of the periodical, the date the article was published, and the inclusive page numbers the article appears on.

GUIDELINES FOR CREATING WORKS CITED ENTRIES FOR PERIODICALS

- Place the author's name first, in inverted order, followed by a period.
- If the article is published anonymously, begin the entry with the title. For placing the entries in alphabetical order on the list, ignore *The, A, And,* and numbers at the beginnings of titles.
- State the title of the article, enclosing it in quotation marks, ending with a period.
- State the name of the periodical, underlined, followed by no punctuation.
- Follow periodical title with the date of publication. For publications with a specific day and month named, use this format: day month year. For journals, include volume number and issue number, if given, and enclose the date in parentheses. Abbreviate the names of all months except May, June, and July.
- Follow the date with a colon and the inclusive page numbers of the article.
- Do not use the abbreviations *p.* or *pp.* for pages.
- Separate the main parts of the entry with periods followed by two spaces.

10. ARTICLE IN A JOURNAL WITH CONTINUOUS PAGINATION
Use this format for journals that continue pagination throughout the year.

> Author's name. "Title of Article." <u>Name of Periodical</u> volume number
> (date): inclusive page numbers of article.
> Groff, Patrick. "The Maturing of Phonics Instruction." <u>Education Digest</u>
> 52 (Mar. 1991): 402-408.

11. ARTICLE IN A JOURNAL WITH SEPARATE PAGINATION
Use this format for journals that begin each issue with page 1. Give the issue number as well as the volume number.

> Author's name. "Title of Article." <u>Name of Periodical</u> volume number.
> issue number (date): inclusive page numbers of article.
> Annan, Kofi. "Development Without Borders." <u>Harvard International</u>
> <u>Review</u> 23.2 (Summer 2001): 84.

12. ARTICLE IN A WEEKLY OR BIWEEKLY MAGAZINE

> Author's name. "Title of Article." <u>Name of Magazine</u> complete date,
> beginning with the day and abbreviating the month, page number(s).
> Bazell, Robert. "Sins and Twins." <u>New Republic</u> 21 Dec. 1987: 17-18.

13. ARTICLE IN A MONTHLY OR BIMONTHLY MAGAZINE

> Author's name. "Title of Article." <u>Name of Magazine</u> date, including
> month and year: page number(s).
> Bowden, Mark. "The Lessons of Abu Ghraib." <u>The Atlantic Monthly</u>
> July-Aug. 2004: 33-36.

14. ARTICLE IN A QUARTERLY MAGAZINE

> Fletcher, John C., Franklin G. Miller, and Arthur L. Caplan. "Facing Up
> to Bioethical Decisions." <u>Issues in Science and Technology</u> Fall 1994:
> 75-80.

15. MAGAZINE ARTICLE WITH NO AUTHOR

> "Teaching for Millions." Success Oct. 1992: 10.

16. NEWSPAPER ARTICLE
Supply the following, in this order:

a) author's name, if known;

b) article title;

c) name of the newspaper, underlined;

d) city where the newspaper is published, if not included in its name, in brackets after the name;

e) the date, beginning with the day, abbreviating the month, and the year, followed by a colon;

f) page number(s) where the article appears. If the newspaper has more than one section and each section is paginated separately, give both section and page number. If you gather material from a special edition of the newspaper, indicate that fact, as well.

> Kingsolver, Barbara. "A Pure, High Note of Anguish." <u>Los Angeles Times</u> 23 Sept. 2001: M1.

17. Periodical article that does not appear on consecutive pages
Give only the first page number followed by a plus sign:

> Nye, Joseph S. Jr. "The Decline of America's Soft Power." <u>Foreign Affairs</u> May-June 2004: 16+.

Creating a Works Cited List for Electronic Sources.   As with other types of sources you cite in your research paper, your Works Cited entries for electronic sources should provide enough information that your reader can locate them. These sources pose a particular problem that books, periodicals, and other print media do not: They change frequently, with updates, moves to new sites, or even removal from the Internet. References to electronic works require slightly more and certainly different information than print sources require. Supply as much of the following information as is available, in this order:

a) author's name;
b) title of the work;
c) title of the site;
d) date the site was created or updated or the date of the posting;
e) if a posting, name of the listserv, newsgroup, or forum;
f) date that you accessed the material; and
g) URL (Uniform Resource Locator) of the site.

See the guidelines that follow for additional details. Keep in mind that electronic sources are not uniform in the amount of information they provide. A site may not incorporate page numbers, an author's name, reference markers such as paragraph or page breaks, or other conventional print references. You can supply only the information that is available at any particular site. Use common sense: Include as much information as you have available to you.

18. Scholarly Project

> <u>Virtual London: Monuments and Dust.</u> Co-directors Michael Levenson, David Trotter, and Anthony Wohl. 4 Sept. 2004. U of Virginia. 12 Nov. 2004 <http://www.iath.virginia.edu/mhc>.

19. Professional Site

> <u>The Camelot Project.</u> Ed. Alan Lupack and Barbara Tepa Lupack. 3 Sept. 2004. U of Rochester. 4 Dec. 2004 <http://www.lib.rochester.edu/camelot/cphome.stm>.

GUIDELINES FOR CREATING A WORKS CITED LIST FOR ELECTRONIC SOURCES

- State the title of the work, following conventional punctuation rules. For instance, use quotation marks for titles of poems, articles, or other short works within a scholarly project. Do the same for the title of a posting, that is, the information in the subject line. (Indicate that the source is an online posting.) If you cite a book, underline the title.
- Name the author, editor, or compiler, if known, last name first. Use the abbreviation "ed." following the name of an editor.
- State the title of the scholarly project, database, periodical, or professional or personal site, underlined. If the site gives no title, give a description of the site (e.g., Home page) but do not underline it or enclose it in quotation marks.
- Name the editor of the scholarly project or database, if the site gives the information.
- Supply any identifying information, such as version, volume, or issue number.
- Give the date the electronic publication was created or the date of its latest update. If you are citing a posting to a newsgroup, discussion group, or forum, give the date of the posting.
- For a posting to a discussion list or forum, give the name of the list or forum.
- If pages are numbered, give the number range or total number of pages.
- Supply the name of any institution or organization sponsoring or associated with the site.
- State the date when you accessed the source.
- Give the electronic address or URL of the service (not the URL of the article) in angle brackets.
- Place a period at the end of the entry.

20. Article in a Reference Database

"Susan Brownell Anthony." The Columbia Encyclopedia, 6th ed. Columbia UP. 2003. Online. 12 Apr. 2005 <http://www.bartleby.com/65/>.

21. Online Article

Benfey, Christopher. "Better Late than Ever." Slate 18 Dec. 1996. 28 Nov. 2004 <http://slate.msn.com/Art/96-12-18/Art.asp>.

Online Sources of Full-text Articles

Examples 22 to 25 illustrate citations from online services offering full-text articles, such as EBSCO, InfoTrac, Proquest, and Periodicals Abstract. The format remains essentially the same as for other electronic sources:

a) Name of author (if given);

b) title of article;

c) title of journal or magazine; volume and issue number if a journal;

d) date of publication;

e) page number(s) if given or *n. pag* (for no pagination);

f) name of the service, such as EBSCO, Infotrac, or Proquest;

g) name of the library or library system and the city and state (if necessary) where it is located;

h) date that you read the material; and

i) URL of the site, if you know it, or simply end with the date of access.

22. Article with Author Named, Scholarly Journal

> Taylor, Susan Lee. "Music Piracy: Differences in the Ethical Perceptions of Business Majors and Music Business Majors." Journal of Education for Business 79.5 (May-June 2004): 306+. Infotrac. 14 Nov 2004 <http://Infotrac-college.thomsonlearning.com>.

23. Article in Magazine

> Murphy, Victoria. "The Enemy Strikes Back." Forbes 24 Nov. 2003: 218. Lexis-Nexis. 6 April 2005 <http://wweb.lexis-nexis.com/>.

24. Article with no Author Named

> "Yelling 'Fire.' " *New Republic* 3 April 2000: 9. EBSCO. University Lib. Stevens Point, WI. 6 April 2005 <http://uwsp.edu/library>.

25. Article in Magazine from Personally Subscribed Service
If you access an article through a service that you subscribe to, such as America Online, give the information as usual, followed by the name of the service, the date you accessed it, and the keyword you used to retrieve the source.

> Kalb, Claudia. "The Life in a Cell; Stem-cell Researchers Find Fresh Hope for Curing Deadly Diseases--Along with New Controversies." Newsweek International 28 June 2004: 50. America Online. 12 October 2004. Keyword: Stem-cell research.

Miscellaneous Electronic Sources

26. Personal Site

> Taylor, Andrew. Home page. 21 Sept. 2005 <http://www.thenet.co.uk/~hickafric/ataylor1.html>.

27. Posting to a Discussion Group

> Walton, Hilary. "New Pym Biography." Online posting. 2 Feb. 2004. Pym-1. 3 Feb. 2005 <pym-1@onelist.com>.

28. E-mail Message

> Konrad, Lucas. "Antique Fire Trucks." E-mail to author. 11 Nov. 2005.

29. Government Document

> Bureau of Labor Statistics. U.S. Dept. of Labor. <u>Occupational Outlook Handbook, 2004-05 Edition.</u> Medical Transcriptionists. Online. 18 Sept. 2005 <http://www.bls.gov/oco/ocos271.htm>.

Works Cited Formats for Sources Other than Books, Periodicals, and Electronic Sources

30. Congressional Record

> United States. Senate. <u>Transportation Systems for Alaskan Natural Gas.</u> 95th Cong., 1st sess. S-2411. Washington: GPO, 1977.
>
> United States. House. Committee on Public Works and Transportation. Subcommittee on Public Buildings and Grounds. To Prohibit Smoking in Federal Buildings. 103rd Cong., 1st sess. H. R. 881. Washington: GPO, 1993.

31. Government Publication

> United States. Dept. of Justice. <u>A Guide to Disability Rights.</u> Washington, DC: DOJ, May 2002.

32. Lecture

> Schilling, Brian. "The Role of First Responders in Medical Emergencies." Lecture at Whitko High School, 22 Dec. 2005.

33. Letter

> White, Jeremy. Letter to author. 1 Oct. 2005.

34. Personal Interview

> Yahi, Mourad. Personal interview. 10 Nov. 2005.

35. Reprint of an Article Provided by an Information Service

> Koop, C. Everett. "Life and Death and the Handicapped Newborn." <u>Law & Medicine</u> (Summer 1989): 101-113. Medical Science of Social Issues Resources Series. Boca Raton: SIRS, 1989. Art. 50.

36. Telephone Interview

> Yahi, Laurel. Telephone interview. 12 Jan. 2004.

37. Pamphlet

> Tweddle, Dominic. <u>The Coppergate Helmet.</u> York, UK: Cultural Resource Management, 1984.

38. Television or Radio Program

> News program: <u>60 Minutes.</u> ABC. WPTA, Fort Wayne, IN. 12 Dec. 2004.

Series with episode titles: "Lights Out." <u>ER.</u> NBC. WNBC, Atlanta. 23 Sept. 1999.

Radio program: <u>On the Air,</u> WOWO, Fort Wayne, IN. 12 Apr. 2004.

39. Sound Recording

To cite a compact disc, list first the aspect of the recording you want to emphasize: composer, conductor, or performer. Give that name first, then the title of the recording or selection, the manufacturer, and the year of issue (write *n.d.* if no date appears on the package or disc). If you are not using a compact disc, state the medium, such as audiotape or audiocassette. Do not enclose the name of the medium in italics or quotation marks.

Uchida, Mitsuko, pianist. Piano Sonatas D, KV 284, Sonata in B flat, KV 570, and Rondo in D, KV 485. By Wolfgang Amadeus Mozart. Philips, 1986.

40. Article in a Reference Book

Treat an entry in an encyclopedia or dictionary as you would an article in a collection, but do not cite the book's editor. If the article is signed, begin with the author's name, followed by the title of the entry; otherwise, begin with the title. For familiar reference books such as standard encyclopedias and dictionaries that are frequently updated and reissued, you need not give publication information. Just list the edition (if stated) and year of publication.

Watkins, Calvert. "Indo-Europe and the Indo-Europeans." <u>American Heritage Dictionary of the English Language.</u> 3rd ed. 1991.

When citing less familiar books, give full publication information.

Rose-Bond, Sherry, and Scott Bond. "Sherlockiana." <u>Encyclopedia Mysteriosa: A Comprehensive Guide to the Art of Detection in Print, Film, Radio, and Television.</u> Ed. William L. DeAndrea. New York: Prentice, 1994. 327-330.

Sample Works Cited Page.   Here is a sample of an alphabetized list of sources drawn from the examples on the previous pages.

```
                        Works Cited
     Annan, Kofi. "Development Without Borders." Harvard
          International Review 23.2 (Summer 2001): 84.
     Benfey, Christopher. "Better Late than Ever." Slate
          18 Dec. 1996. 28 Nov. 2004
          <http://slate.msn.com/Art/96-12-18/Art.asp>.
```

Bowden, Mark. "The Lessons of Abu Ghraib." The Atlantic Monthly July-Aug. 2004: 33-36.

Kingsolver, Barbara. "A Pure, High Note of Anguish." Los Angeles Times 23 Sept. 2001: M1.

Leonardi, Susan J. Dangerous by Degrees: Women at Oxford and the Somerville College Novelists. New Brunswick: Rutgers UP, 1989.

Murphy, Victoria. "The Enemy Strikes Back." Forbes 24 Nov. 2003: 218. Online. Infotrac. 23 April 2004 <http://Infotrac-college.thomsonlearning.com>.

Nye, Joseph S. Jr. "The Decline of America's Soft Power" Foreign Affairs May-June 2004: 16+.

60 Minutes. ABC. WPTA, Fort Wayne, IN. 12 Dec. 2004.

Spacks, Patricia Meyer. "Sisters." Fetter'd or Free?: British Women Novelists, 1670-1815. Eds. Mary Anne Schofield and Cecilia Macheski. Athens, OH: Ohio UP, 1986. 136-151.

United States. Dept. of Justice. A Guide to Disability Rights. Washington, DC: DOJ, May 2002.

Yahi, Mourad. Personal interview. 10 Nov. 2005.

WRITING A RESEARCH PAPER

In general, writing a research paper is not so different from writing any other kind of paper. You will have an introduction, though it is likely to be longer than in other writing assignments. You must have a thesis statement or clearly evident central idea. Your paper as a whole and individual paragraphs within it must be organized and fully developed. Sentences must be crafted grammatically and imaginatively, and your language should be idiomatic, colorful, and clear. You must provide transitions between points within paragraphs and from paragraph to paragraph throughout the paper, and you must have a conclusion that brings the paper to a satisfactory finish. Of course a major difference between the research paper and other papers you will write for your college classes is that research papers incorporate the works of others.

The following sections will take you through the process of putting together your final paper. They address the following components of your paper:

- Title page or first page of paper without a separate title page
- Pagination and spacing
- Outline page
- Introductory paragraph and body of the paper
- Works Cited page
- The complete research paper

ILLUSTRATION: SAMPLE PAGES FROM STUDENT RESEARCH PAPERS USING MLA STYLE

Title Page.   Although MLA style does not require a separate title page, some instructors ask for it. If your instructor requires a title page, follow these guidelines:

- Center your title about one-third to halfway down the page.
- Do not underline your title, enclose it in quotation marks, capitalize every letter, or place a period after it.
- Capitalize the first letter of every important word in the title.
- Beneath the title, double-space, type the word *by*, double-space again, and center your own name.
- Drop farther down the page and center your instructor's name, the course name, and the date.

```
                Arthur of Camelot: The Once and Future King

                                    by

                               Shawn Ryan




                             Professor Zackary

                               English 102

                               1 May 2005
```

Pagination and Spacing.   The entire paper should be double-spaced, with each page numbered in the upper right-hand corner, one-half inch from the top and flush with the right margin. MLA style requires that pagination begin with page 1 and recommends that you include your last name before the page number.

First Page of a Research Paper with a Separate Title Page

If your instructor requires a separate title page, follow these guidelines for the first text page of your paper:

- Type your last name and the number 1 in the upper right-hand corner, one-half inch from the top of the page, flush with the right margin.
- Drop down two inches from the top of the page and center your title, exactly as it appears on your title page.
- Do not underline your title, enclose it in quotation marks, capitalize every letter, or place a period after it.
- Capitalize the first letter of every important word in the title.
- Double-space and begin the body of your paper.

```
                                              Ryan 1

              Arthur of Camelot: The Once and Future King

              North and west the wind blew beneath the morning

     sun, over endless miles of rolling grass and far

     scattered thickets . . . [and] Dragonmount, where the

     dragon had died, and with him, some said, the Age of

     Legend--where prophecy said he would be born again.

     (Jordan 13)
```

First Page of a Research Paper without a Separate Title Page

If your instructor does not require a separate title page, follow these guidelines:

- Type the number 1 in the upper right-hand corner, one-half inch from the top of the page, flush with the right margin.
- Place your name, your instructor's name, the course title, and the date in the upper left-hand corner, one inch from the top of the paper and flush with the left margin.
- Double-space between each line.
- Double-space below the date and center your title.

- Do not underline your title, enclose it in quotation marks, capitalize every letter, or place a period after it.
- Capitalize the first letter of every important word in the title.
- Double-space again and begin the body of your paper.

```
Nate Hayes                                          1

Professor White

English 102

15 Nov. 2005

           A Positive Alternative to Cloning

     Since Dr. Ian Wilmut's successful cloning of a

sheep, the debate over how far medical science should

be allowed to go has grown increasingly heated. Some

people are completely opposed to any kind of

experimentation that involves genetic manipulation or

the development of procedures that some consider

should be reserved only for God.
```

Outline Page.   If your instructor requires a formal outline, place it immediately after the title page. Your instructor will tell you how detailed your outline should be, but follow these basic directions in most cases:

- Begin your outline with the thesis statement of your paper.
- Double-space between all lines of the outline.
- Use uppercase roman numerals (I, II, III) for each major division of your outline and capital letters (A, B, C) for each subdivision under each major division.
- If you find it necessary to further subdivide, use arabic numerals (1, 2, 3) under capital letters and lowercase letters (a, b, c) under arabic numerals.
- Do not number the outline page unless it runs to two or more pages. If your outline is two or more pages long, number all pages after the first in lowercase roman numerals (ii, iii, iv), placed in the upper right-hand corner, one-half inch from the top of the page and flush with the right margin.
- End with a statement summarizing your conclusion.

Illustrations.   Here are outline pages from two student papers, the first with a fairly brief outline, the second with more detail.

Outline

Thesis: An examination of some of the research on
Arthurian legend suggests that the evidence supports
the theory that a man like Arthur did exist.

I. The birth of Arthur

    A. The legend

    B. Evidence of Tintagel

II. The places and people most important to Arthur

    A. Camelot

    B. Glastonbury Abbey

    C. Lancelot and Perceval

III. Arthur's impact on society

    A. His image

    B. The difference between the man and the legend

Conclusion: Arthur's existence as a man is
indeterminable, but Arthur's presence in the minds
and hearts of people everywhere gives credence to his
existence as a leader of nations.

Outline

Thesis: Parents, educators, and reading experts
disagree on the issue of whether phonics instruction
is beneficial to beginning readers.

I. Introduction

    A. Rudolph Flesch's observations

    B. National Assessment of Education Progress
       reports

II. Background

    A. Introduction to phonics

    B. Failure of schools to teach reading

    C. Regna Lee Wood

III. Phonics instruction

    A. How phonics works

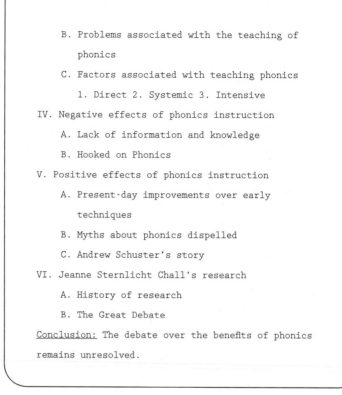

B. Problems associated with the teaching of
   phonics

C. Factors associated with teaching phonics
   1. Direct 2. Systemic 3. Intensive

IV. Negative effects of phonics instruction

   A. Lack of information and knowledge

   B. Hooked on Phonics

V. Positive effects of phonics instruction

   A. Present-day improvements over early
      techniques

   B. Myths about phonics dispelled

   C. Andrew Schuster's story

VI. Jeanne Sternlicht Chall's research

   A. History of research

   B. The Great Debate

Conclusion: The debate over the benefits of phonics
remains unresolved.

Introductory Paragraphs and Body of the Paper.   As for any other kind of writing assignment, begin with an introduction that provides background information that clearly portrays the topic of your paper or the direction your argument will take, or that in some way sets the stage for what follows. State your thesis or central idea early in the paper. If your topic is controversial, explain the nature of the controversy. Once you have introduced your topic sufficiently, begin developing your argument. Here are the opening pages of Nate Hayes' paper, which he expanded from his synthesis paper with his instructor's permission (See "Hello Dolly" in chapter 5).

Nate's introduction provides a context for his topic and states the nature of the controversy over cloning and stem-cell research.

Complete bibliographic information for the Pethokoukis source is given on Nate's Works Cited page.

Nate's thesis states his position: he is opposed to further research on cloning but believes that stem-cell research should continue. Readers can expect to see a development in the rest of the paper of each of these points as well as supporting evidence from various authorities in support of his position.

Hayes 1

A Positive Alternative to Cloning

Since Dr. Ian Wilmut's successful cloning of a sheep, the debate over how far medical science should be allowed to go has grown increasingly heated. A very promising development lies in stem cell research, which could lead to developments that could "alter mankind in some astounding ways" (Pethokoukis 560). Such potential has many people worried about the extent to which human genetic makeup should be modified or amended. Some people are completely opposed to any kind of experimentation that involves genetic manipulation or the development of procedures that some consider should be reserved only for God. Scientists and medical researchers, though, are excited about the potential for previously unimaginable achievements in the prevention and cure of debilitating or fatal diseases. The controversy centers on the questions of how far science should go and who should control the technology. A review of the arguments for and against stem-cell research leads me to conclude that, although there needs to be a long, serious national debate on the subject, scientists should stop short of cloning humans but be allowed to continue their research on stem cells.

What exactly is cloning? According to the National Bioethics Advisory Commission (NBAC), the word "in its most simple and strict sense . . .

Nate provides the acronym for the long name of the advisory commission and then uses it whenever he quotes from the commission again. Nate gives only the page number because he has mentioned the name of the source in his text. The ellipses points (three spaced periods) indicate that he has omitted some words from the original sentence.

Nate is using general knowledge here and does not need to document his statements.

Nate combines a direct quotation and a paraphrase. The parenthetical citation tells the source and the page number on which the quoted and paraphrased material is found.

Paragraph 3 is phrased entirely in Nate's own words. He has done enough reading on his topic to understand some of the questions and to supply his own responses to them. The paragraph consists of general knowledge that Nate has acquired and thus does not require any documentation.

Hayes 2

refers to a precise genetic copy of a molecule, cell, plant, animal or human being" (13). This technique of cloning used by Dr. Wilmut's team to create Dolly is called somatic cell nuclear transplantation. Sex cells contain only one set of 23 chromosomes, whereas body cells house two sets for a total of 46. When the parent's sperm fertilizes the egg, 46 chromosomes establish a human. During nuclear transfer cloning, the fertilization step is skipped because "the nucleus is removed from an egg and replaced with the diploid nucleus of a somatic [body] cell" (NBAC 15). Therefore, there is only one true parent, and the clone will be the exact genetic copy of that parent.

The controversy over cloning involves both ethical and religious issues. Should humans "play God"? What if the process were used to create exact copies of evil people? What potential dreadful side effects might develop in cloned humans? What possible reasons can there be for wanting to clone humans? The suggested uses for cloned humans usually focus on replacing loved ones who have died, particularly young children who have died tragically, either from illness or accident. The idea is that cloning the dead child would in effect replace the child that died. However, that new child would be a real person, with thoughts and feelings unique to him or her. The new child would only look like the dead child and have identical genetic material. He or she would grow up in an entirely different environment, even if the parents attempted to recreate the identical conditions in which the dead child was nurtured. It would simply be impossible to recreate those

Hayes 3

conditions. Furthermore, would the child not be
damaged psychologically if she knew that she was
replacing another child? There are simply too many
unexplored questions associated with cloning.

*Nate does not
need to give a
citation at the
end of the first
sentence in
paragraph 4
because he has
named his
authority, and
his second
sentence clearly
indicates that
he is still
paraphrasing
from that same
authority. The
parenthetical
citation gives
the page
number.*

One big question has to do with the high failure
rate of cloning. Despite having been responsible for
the first cloned mammal, Dr. Wilmut is very
conservative in his views of the wisdom of carrying
on full speed with cloning research because of its
unreliability. In "Dolly's False Legacy," he
identifies some of the likely problems a cloned human
might have. For instance, Wilmut warns of the
inefficiency of cloning, noting the high death rate in
fetuses and live births when cloning is used in
animal tests. This fact leads him to suggest that
"these failure rates surely render unthinkable the
notion of applying such treatment to humans" (564).
Indeed, one of the chief difficulties with cloning is
its high failure rate. Rick Weiss cites one example
of this difficulty in his article "Failure in Monkeys
Hints at Human Cloning Snags": "Despite having tried
135 times, researchers in Oregon have 'utterly
failed' to clone a single monkey" (2). These failures
are particularly significant because of the genetic
similarity between monkeys and humans. The
implications for success in cloning humans is dismal
indeed, much to the delight of those who disapprove
of it.

*Nate introduces
his direct
quotation. The
colon is used
because both
the introductory
statement and
the quotation
are complete
sentences.*

As with human cloning, research on stem cells is
riddled with controversy. Here, though, the
controversy is aimed at research on embryonic stem
cells as opposed to adult stem cell research: "Hailed

The information about James D. Watson establishes his credentials. Nate's combination of both paraphrase and direct quotations serve to smoothly integrate source material into his text.

by some as a cure for deadly disease, derided by others as the destruction of human life, embryonic stem cells are at the center of a heated debate over science, religion and politics around the globe" (Kalb 50). Embryonic stem cells are those that have not yet specialized. Scientists believe that such cells could be isolated and grown into "healthy replacement tissue" that could then be used in humans to cure just about any ailment known to humans (Lemonick 89). The healthy tissue would be surgically implanted into the body, replacing or repairing damaged tissue. Research in this area holds great promises. James D. Watson, Nobel-Prize-winning co-discoverer of the double helix configuration of DNA, is a strong supporter of research on germ-line genetic manipulations in pursuit of what he calls " 'superpersons' " or "gene-bettered children" (563).

This word is in both single and double quotation marks because it is in quotation marks in the original article.

Works Cited Page.   The Works Cited pages for Nate Hayes' research paper on stem-cell research illustrate how to cite some of the most common sources used in undergraduate research papers, including books, essays in a collection, and periodical articles from online full-text sources.

Works Cited

Ackley, Katherine Anne, ed. *Perspectives on Contemporary Issues: Reading across the Disciplines,* 4th ed. Boston: Thomson Wadsworth, 2006.

Hayes 15

Cherfas, Jeremy. <u>Man-Made Life.</u> New York: Pantheon
    Books, 1982.

Kalb, Claudia. "The Life in a Cell; Stem-cell
    Researchers Find Fresh Hope for Curing Deadly
    Diseases—Along with New Controversies." <u>Newsweek</u>
    <u>International</u> 28 June 2004: 50. America Online.
    12 October 2004. Keyword: Stem-cell research.

Lemonick, Michale D. "Tomorrow's Tissue Factor." <u>Time</u>
    11 Jan. 1999: 89. Online. Infotrac. 14 Apr. 2005
    <http://Infotrac-college.thomsonlearning.com>.

Lyon, Jeff. "Playing God: Has Science Gone too Far?"
    Ackley 567-573.

Merzer, Martin. "A Human Clone Won't Be Carbon Copy,
    Experts Say." <u>Houston Chronicle</u> 28 Dec. 1998: 8.
    Online. 14 Oct. 2004. EBSCOhost. University
    Library. Stevens Point, WI
    <http://library.uwsp.edu>.

National Bioethics Advisory Commission (NBAC).
    <u>Cloning Human Beings.</u> Rockville, MD: NBAC, 1997.

Pethokoukis, James. "Our Biotech Bodies, Ourselves."
    Ackley 559-561.

Watson, James D. "All for the Good." Ackley 561-563.

Weiss, Rick. "Failure in Monkeys Hints at Human
    Cloning Snags." <u>The Washington Post</u> 29 Jan.
    1999: A02. Online. 14 Oct. 2004. EBSCOhost.
    University Library. Stevens Point, WI
    <http://library.uwsp.edu>.

---. "Human Embryo Cloned, Korean Researchers Say."
    <u>Denver Post</u> 17 Dec. 1998: A01. 14 Oct. 2004.
    EBSCOhost. University Library. Stevens Point, WI
    <http://library.uwsp.edu>.

Wilmut, Ian. "Dolly's False Legacy." Ackley 564-566.

STUDENT RESEARCH PAPER USING MLA STYLE

Here is an example of a complete student research paper that implements the MLA style guidelines outlined in chapters 5 and 6.

The Electoral College: Time for a Change?

by

Erin D. Anderson

Professor Heather A. Schilling

English 150

April 26, 2005

Anderson 1

The Electoral College: Time for a Change?

The electoral college system, which has been in place for over 200 years, is one of the most widely debated of all governmental policies; in fact, over 850 proposals for its change or abolishment have been offered in Congress (Vile 109). However, only two of these reforms have ever been enacted. Questions are once again being raised concerning whether another alternative would better suit modern America or if reform would do more harm than good. People have many contrasting opinions about the popular direct voting proposal, which would abolish the Electoral College altogether. In light of the year 2000 election, which placed in the White House a candidate who had half a million fewer popular votes than his opponent, should the electoral college be abolished?

The electoral college system has its origins in the Constitutional Convention that took place in Philadelphia in 1787. The Framers themselves were ambivalent when it came to how the President should be elected, which made the process of determining how to choose the President a complicated one. In fact, Pennsylvania delegate James Wilson declared that the presidential selection issue was "'the most difficult of all [. . .]'" of those discussed, one that "'has greatly divided the house, and will also divide people out of doors'" (qtd. in Sayre and Parris 23). Proposals were made for election by Congress, election by the people, and election by state governments (Sayre and Parris 23). However, as the issue remained unsolved and the end of the Convention was nearing, the Brearly Committee on

Anderson 2

Unfinished Parts suggested the electoral college system.

The following very brief summary of this system was adapted from Shlomo Slonim's "Electoral College": Instead of a direct popular election, this system provided for indirect election of the President through a college of electors, in which each state receives a number of electoral votes based on its total number of Senators and Representatives. On the first Tuesday in November of election years, the general population technically casts ballots for the electors that represent their choice for President and Vice President. The electors themselves are individuals "pledged to support a particular candidate's election in the electoral college" (543).

Popular vote totals are used to determine which party slate will become that state's electors. On the Monday following the second Wednesday in December, the electors meet in their respective state capitals and cast their ballots for President and Vice President. A majority of the 538 electoral votes is needed in order to be selected or the matter is put up to vote in the House of Representatives. Under this system, "Popular will is expressed state by state, rather than by a national referendum" (Slonin 543-544). An added feature of the electoral college system is the winner-takes-all unit rule system.

Although the Constitution leaves the choice of how the states' electoral votes are cast up to the states themselves, every state except Maine and Nebraska has chosen over time to award all of a

Anderson 3

state's electoral votes to the winner of the popular vote (Cronin xii).

Michael Glennon proposes in his comprehensive guide to the electoral college that the debate by the Framers of the Constitution about presidential selection was rooted in a disagreement on two essential issues: .rst, the extent and view of democracy to be used in determining the winner, and second, the degree of federalism to be considered (6). These two issues continue to lie at the center of the debate. On one hand are those who desire the abolishment of the electoral college; in their view, direct democracy, where the will of the people is directly translated into policy, is the key principal. On the other hand, those who support the Electoral College as it is believe that federalism is of ultimate importance and that democracy is still supported through the electoral college, but in a different way.

Many people vehemently argue in support of the electoral college system. As explained in William C. Kimberling's <u>The Electoral College,</u> the main arguments center on two requirements that are placed on candidates in order to be chosen President. First, winning a majority in the electoral college means that the candidate has "*sufficient* popular vote to [. . .] govern," even if his/her support is not the majority of the voting population. Secondly, the votes the winner has secured must be "sufficiently *distributed* across the country" (7). According to Kimberling, these two requirements together ensure that whoever is chosen will be able to handle governing the nation (7).

A second strong argument used in support of the Electoral College is that it promotes the important Constitutional concept of federalism. Judith A. Best, distinguished professor of political science at State University of New York at Cortland, refers to federalism as one of the two essential principles of the "constitutional solar system [. . .] around which everything else [. . .] rotates" (65). She believes that this federal principal, based on state-by-state victories and therefore, electoral votes, provides for a better overall assessment of the strengths and weaknesses of the competing candidates than a direct popular vote would because it ensures that the winning candidate has "broad, cross-national support" (67). This requirement of broad support promotes the pulling together of "coalitions of states and regions," rather than the candidate's having support just from specific regions of the country (Kimberling 12).

In response to those who claim that the electoral college is undemocratic, Best points out that "politics and mathematics are two very different disciplines" (18). Those who support abolishing the Electoral College in favor of direct election claim that numbers themselves determine who the President should be. However, Best believes that in a political decision as important as electing a President, the "will of the people" is not necessarily the same as the "will of the majority" (19). She points out that one of the basic principals of the Constitution is majority rule with minority consent; in her view, the Electoral College better provides for the minority.

However, over time many have expressed opposition to the indirect and complex electoral college system. Their main criticism is the possibility of a "minority President," that is, one elected without the majority of the popular vote but with a majority of the electoral votes. Other criticisms leveled against the electoral college system include the "so-called faithless electors," the winner-takes-all unit rule, and the possibility of decreased voter turnout (Kimberling 9). In addition, critics say that the electoral college does not accurately re.ect the national popular will and that rural states are over represented in the current system because each state receives two electoral votes regardless of size plus those attributed to population (Kimberling 9).

In The Electoral College Primer 2000, Lawrence D. Longley and Neal R. Peirce explain their opposition to the electoral college system. They assert that in an "advanced democratic nation, where [. . .] popular choice is the most deeply ingrained of government principles," a voting system where popular votes don't necessarily mean electoral votes is "irrational" (132). In addition, they point out that even if a direct popular vote were to choose a candidate who proved less than ideal in the long run, the candidate would still be the choice of the people (132). Longley and Peirce also explain the "faithless elector" issue. The Constitution nowhere requires the chosen electors to vote for the winner of the popular vote. However, in the history of the Electoral

College, only nine votes of the over 20,000 cast have been known to go "'against instructions'" (113).

Critics of the electoral college system see the 2000 election as a prime example of the minority President criticism. The election of governor George Bush by the electoral college despite Vice President Al Gore's winning the popular vote (50,996,582 to Bush's 50,456,062) is seen by many as a problem. Because of the complicated nature of the electoral college system and what many see as its drawbacks, several reform proposals have been brought to Congress. These proposals generally fall into four categories: the district system, the proportional system, the automatic plan, and the direct popular election. Wisconsin's Role in Electing the President describes the four main Electoral College alternatives. The district system would eliminate the unit rule and provide that two of each state's electoral votes would be determined by popular vote, while the rest would be allocated on a district-by-district basis. The proportional system would divide the state's electoral votes in "direct proportion to the popular vote" of the state. The automatic plan would simply eliminate the role of the actual elector and provide that the electoral votes would automatically be signed to the winner of the popular election. Finally, direct popular election would abolish the Electoral College altogether, instead requiring a "nationwide popular vote," with the winner receiving at least 40% of the votes (Watchke 12).

The direct voting alternative is by far the most popular proposal alternative. However, this alternative has its own set of pros and cons which must be evaluated before making a judgment about which presidential election system should be in place.

Proponents of a direct voting system have several arguments as to why a direct popular vote would be preferable to the electoral college system. They argue that it provide an increased and more direct democracy for the people, an increased authority for the President, and a simpler, one-person-one-vote system that would eliminate the intermediate electoral college in the Presidential selection procedure. In addition, they feel that the electoral college system is out of date because America is faced with a different set of circumstances and challenges than when it was created.

Those in favor of direct election believe this system is the only way to achieve a true democracy. Former First Lady Hillary Clinton has expressed her belief that abolition of the Electoral college is important in a democracy; in fact, she said that she would "be willing to co-sponsor a measure to abolish the electoral college" (Geraghty). Another argument is that a popular vote would give more authority to the President because the vote totals would be a direct communication of the will of the people, rather than an indirect translation that takes electoral votes into account (Sayre and Parris 69). Thirdly, in the words of Yale Law School professor Akhil Amar, the Electoral College is a "brilliant 18th-century device that cleverly solved [. . .]

Anderson 8

18th-century problems." However, he sees that "'[a]s we approach the 21st century, we confront a different cluster of problems, and our constitutional machinery [. . .] does not look so brilliant'" (qtd. in Sung). Finally, those in defense of direct election often cite public opinion surveys that re.ect popular support for abolishment of the Electoral College. One such survey, conducted by the trusted Gallup Organization and released on November 16, 2000, revealed that 61% of Americans would like to see direct popular vote in place of the electoral college system ("Americans Have Long Questioned").

Direct voting also seems to have its drawbacks, however. Its opponents claim that direct election would lead to manipulation in campaigns, jeopardize the two-party system with a multitude of candidates, cause even more runoffs and recounts, and sacrifice the federalist system currently in place.

Curtis Gans, director of the Committee for the Study of the American Electorate, suggests that a direct popular vote system would greatly change the way campaigns are run. With such a system, where the goal is to win over the masses rather than focus on groups of states all around the nation, he believes even more of the election funds would go toward mass television advertising, leading to the "'handing [of the] American presidential campaign to whatever media adviser could outslick the other'" (qtd. in Sung). This, in turn, would lead to increased "'opponent bashing,'" a factor that already has been leading citizens to "'tune out politics'" (qtd. in Sung).

Anderson 9

According to Wallace Sayre and Judith Parris,
direct elections, especially those including a
popular vote runoff provision, would tend to
"encourage a multitude of minor party candidacies"
because, depending on the proposal, these minor party
candidates would not need to win entire states in
order to receive part of the vote (73). They believe,
therefore, that many candidates would tend to run as
"spoilers," with the goal of forcing a runoff. In
order to protect the two-party system, which is an
important basis of American government, they insist
that the electoral college system must stay in place.

Judith Best reflects on the increase in recounts
and runoffs that she feels would follow from a direct
voting system: "If the advocates of direct nonfederal
election stuck with a majority requirement for
victory, nearly every general election would be
turned into a national primary followed by a runoff
election" (57). She believes that with the lifting of
the state division, focusing only on the national
vote, "a recount of every ballot box in the country"
could be necessary, because recounts and challenges
in one state would no longer be limited in scope, but
could demand a national result questioning (57).

Thomas Cronin brings up an important point that
makes one question whether the current system should
be abolished. He argues that while there are some
imperfections in the electoral college system, no one
can be sure of the effects of abandoning it in place
of a direct vote (viii). President John F. Kennedy
himself opposed abolishment, explaining that "'[i]f
it is proposed to change the balance of power of one

of the elements of the [governmental] solar system, it is necessary to consider the others'" (qtd. in Glennon 76). Therefore, because changes would undoubtedly have a holistic effect on the intricate political system, it is necessary to carefully weigh this decision.

After weighing arguments for both the current electoral college system and the direct voting alternative, I tend to agree with Cronin. Although the Electoral College may be complex and does have its imperfections, there is no way of knowing just what other effects and problems may result from its abolishment. Even in light of the 2000 presidential election, in which President George W. Bush did not win the majority of the popular vote, I see the electoral college system as a way to moderate the will of the people in general with the good of the government. I also very much support the argument that the electoral college ensures that the candidate who is victorious has proven that he or she has secured enough voter support to warrant the presidential office. It is very important that the winner has both a sufficient popular vote and a sufficient distribution of votes across the country, a fact that he or she demonstrates by securing enough states' electoral votes to win the election.

However, the current electoral college system could better represent the population in general. Adopting the relatively small change that Maine and Nebraska have made to their system, which selects two electoral votes a popular vote and determines the remainder of the electoral votes by Congressional district, would help to improve the system. This would not be such an extreme change as abolishing the Electoral College altogether, yet it would represent the popular vote more closely because of the district divisions. Thus, the benefits of the current Electoral College would almost entirely remain in place, while those who want the election to more closely reflect the popular will would also be appeased.

The 2000 presidential election was an anomalous one, and the extremely close margins of support, both in the popular vote and the Electoral College count, have caused an increase in discussion about the electoral college system. One even sees divisions among party lines regarding support for or opposition against this system. However, one must note that the conflict in the 2000 election was not completely rooted in the Electoral College itself. Many believe that the recounts and challenges would stillhave taken place even with a system of direct election.

In conclusion, Michael Glennon, author of <u>When No Majority Rules,</u> reflects on the essential dilemma in electing America's President: "Just as Winston Churchill concluded about democracy, the electoral college is probably the worst possible method of choosing the President—except for all the others" (3). Indeed, there is no perfect solution that will satisfy both those desiring voting and those who support the Electoral College. However, weighing both the pros and cons in the arguments over the current system, I believe that the Electoral College should be kept in place, yet modified slightly to better represent the people. Such a compromise would reflect

Anderson 12

what was at the very heart of the Constitution when
it was established over two centuries ago and what
will carry this country and its citizens through the
coming centuries.

Works Cited

"Americans Have Long Questioned Electoral College."
    Gallup Poll Releases. 16 Nov 2000. 29 Nov. 2000
    <http://www.gallup.com/poll/releases/
    pr001116.asp>.

Best, Judith A. The Choice of the People?: Debating
    the Electoral College. Lanham, MD: Rowman &
    Littlefield, 1996.

Cronin, Thomas E. "The Electoral College
    Controversy." Foreword. Best vii-xxv.

Geraghty, Jim. "Do Elections Need New Rules?"
    Policy.com News and Events: Daily Briefing. 22
    Nov. 2000. 29 Nov. 2000
    <http://www.policy.com/news/dbrief/dbriefarc834.
    asp>.

Glennon, Michael J. When No Majority Rules: The
    Electoral College and Presidential Succession.
    Washington, D.C.: Congressional Quarterly, 1992.

Kimberling, William C. The Electoral College.
    Washington, D.C.: National Clearinghouse on
    Election Administration, Federal Election
    Commission, May 1992.

Longley, Lawrence D., and Neal R. Peirce. The
    Electoral College Primer 2000. New Haven, CT:
    Yale UP, 1999.

Anderson 13

Power, Max S. "Logic and Legitimacy: On Understanding
    the Electoral College Controversy." Ed. Donald
    R. Matthews. Perspectives on Presidential
    Selection. Washington, D.C.: Brookings, 1973.
    204-237.

Sayre, Wallace S., and Judith H. Parris. Voting for
    President: The Electoral College and the
    American Political System. Washington, D.C.:
    Brookings, 1972.

Slonim, Shlomo. "Electoral College." Encyclopedia of
    the American Presidency. Eds. Leonard W. Levy
    and Louis Fisher. New York: Simon & Schuster,
    1994. 542-547.

Sung, Ellen. "Time to Reform the Electoral College?"
    Policy.com News and Events: Daily Briefing. 31
    July 2000. 21 Nov. 2000
    <http://www.policy.com/news/dbrief/dbriefarc770.
    asp>.

Vile, John R. "Electoral College Reform."
    Encyclopedia of Constitutional Amendments,
    Proposed Amendments, and Amending Issues,
    1789-1995. Santa Barbara, CA: ABC-CLIO, 1996.
    109-112.

Watchke, Gary. Wisconsin's Role in Electing the
    President. Madison, WI: Wisconsin Legislative
    Reference Bureau, Mar. 2000.

WRITING A RESEARCH PAPER USING APA STYLE

The documentation style of the American Psychological Association (APA), also referred to as the *author–date system*, is used widely in the behavioral and social sciences.
It differs from that of the Modern Language Association (MLA), used primarily in

the humanities, in some significant ways. APA style cites sources in parenthetical notes in the sentences to which they refer, as does MLA style, but the contents of the notes differ. In the APA system, the year of publication is given in the parenthetical note, and page numbers are given only for quotations, not for paraphrases. Finally, sources are listed at the end of the paper on a page called *References* rather than *Works Cited,* and formatting for that page is quite different from formatting in MLA style. This section gives general guidelines for both parenthetical citations and composing a references page using APA style. The guidelines are accompanied by sample pages from a student research paper using APA documentation style. For complete guidelines on APA Style, consult the following book:

> American Psychological Association. *Publication Manual of the American Psychological Association.* 5th ed. Washington: APA, 2001.

For the latest updates on APA Style, go to the official website of the American Psychological Association, located at <http://www.APA.org>.

PARENTHETICAL CITATIONS USING APA STYLE

- For a quotation, include the author's last name, a comma, the year the work was published, another comma, and the page number, preceded by the abbreviation *p.* or *pp.:*

  > Many experts agree that "it is much easier and more comfortable to teach as one learned" (Chall, 1989, p. 21).

- If the source has two authors, name them both, and separate their names with an ampersand (&):

  > President Truman and his advisors were aware that the use of the bomb was no longer required to prevent an invasion of Japan by the Soviets (Alperovitz & Messer, 1991, 1992).

- Omit from the parenthetical citation any information given in the text:

  > Samuel E. Wood and Ellen R. Green Wood (1993a) note that sociobiologists believe that social and nurturing experiences can "intensify, diminish, or modify" personality traits (p. 272).

- If the author's name is given in the text, follow it with the year of publication in parentheses:

  > Nancy Paulu (1988) believes that children who are taught phonics get off to a better start than those who are not taught phonics.

- For works with three to five authors, name all of the authors the first time you refer to the work, but give only the last name of the first author followed by "et al." in subsequent citations. For a work with six or more authors, give only the first author's last name, followed by "et al." for all citations, including the first.

- If the author's name is repeated in the same paragraph, it is not necessary to repeat the year. However, if the author is cited in another paragraph, give the year of the work again.
- For summaries and paraphrases, give author and year but not the page number where the information appears:

    Minnesota scientists have concluded that this data shows that genes are more influential than nurture on most personality traits (Bazell, 1987).

- If the source names no author, cite a short form of the title:

    The twins were both born with musical abilities, but their unique experiences determined whether they acted on this ability ("How Genes Shape Personality," 1987).

Note: The first letter of each word in the short title is capitalized, but in the references list, only the first letter of the first word is capitalized.

- If you use two or more sources by the same author and they were published in the same year, add lowercase letters to refer to their order on the References page:

    Wood and Wood (1993a) observe that . . .
    Other authorities (Wood & Wood, 1993b) agree, pointing out that . . .

- If one of your sources quotes or refers to another, and you want to use the second source in your paper, use the words *cited in,* followed by the source you read and the year the source was published. If you quote directly, give the page number of the source you read on which the quotation appeared:

    Gerald McClearn, a psychologist and twin researcher at Pennsylvania State University, explained personality development realistically when he said: " 'A gene can produce a nudge in one direction or another, but it does not directly control behavior. It doesn't take away a person's free will' " (cited in "How Genes Shape Personality," 1987, p. 62).

- To cite electronic material, indicate the page, chapter, figure, table, or equation at the appropriate point in the text. Give page number(s) for quotations. If the source does not provide page numbers, use paragraph number if available, preceded by the paragraph symbol or the abbreviation *para.* If neither page number or paragraph number is visible, cite the heading and the number of the paragraph so that the reader can locate the material at the website:

    (Merriwether, 2004, p. 27)
    (Johnson, 1999, para. 3)
    (Shaw, 2003, conclusion section, para. 1)

ILLUSTRATION: SAMPLE PAGES FROM A STUDENT RESEARCH PAPER USING APA STYLE

Here are the opening pages of a student research paper illustrating in-text citations using APA style.

In papers written in APA style, provide a shortened version of the title, known as a running head, in the upper right-hand corner of the page along with the page number. If your instructor requires a separate title page, the title page is numbered 1.

Phonics 1

Cory L. Vandertie

Professor Kathy Mitchell

English 102

19 April 2005

The Phonics Controversy

The introductory paragraphs provide background for the research topic.

In recent years, school officials, teachers, and parents have been wrestling with the issue of how best to teach reading, with the controversy often centering on the conflict over the effectiveness of phonics in such instruction. Rudolph Flesch, in his

Cory read about the Flesch book in Groff's book, hence "cited in."

best-selling 1955 book *Why Johnny Can't Read*, was one of the first educators to advocate the use of phonics in reading classes. His book not only brought

Write the author's full name the first time it is mentioned.

national attention to the reading problems of America's children but also endorsed the use of

Although only the first letter of the first word in the title of a work is capitalized in the references list, in your paper you must capitalize as you would other titles.

phonics to overcome those problems (cited in Groff, 1989). Neither the problem of children's inability to read effectively nor the effectiveness of phonics instruction has been satisfactorily addressed in the 50 years since Flesch's book, however. Over a decade ago, Regna Lee Wood (1992) warned about declining literacy rates. In "That's Right--They're Wrong:

Decline in Reading Ability Due to Abandonment of Phonics," she points out that in 1930, only 3 million Americans could not read, but in 1990, 30 to 35 million U.S. citizens could not read and were considered to be truly illiterate. In 2000, the National Assessment of Educational Progress (NAEP) reported that "more than a third (37 percent) of America's fourth grade children (roughly 10 million kids) could not read at even a basic level" and of those 10 million, "up to 40 percent will eventually drop out of high school" (cited in Stephenson, 2002). Statistics such as these have created tension among educators as they debate how to improve reading skills.

The declining literacy rate is an alarming indicator that something must be done differently in our schools. Wood (1998) discovered that 70 percent of U.S. high school students cannot read ninth-grade assignments and that 30 percent of U.S. twelfth-graders cannot read at a fourth-grade level. Educators and parents who are concerned about this dramatic increase in the illiteracy rate and the inability of the majority of students to read at their own grade levels cannot refuse to explore all possible explanations for the failure of our schools to teach reading adequately. One avenue for exploration that may prove fruitful is the phonics controversy. Parents, teachers, and reading experts familiar with phonics all differ sharply in their views, compounding the dilemma of whether phonics instruction should be included in American schools. What role *does* phonics education play in the teaching of reading?

This is a paraphrase, so no page number need be given.

Although there are two works by Regna Lee Wood on Cory's list of references, the date of publication indicates the specific work being cited.

Cory asks a question as his thesis, reflecting the controversy over teaching phonics. He will answer the question in the course of the paper.

Phonics 3

More than 450 years ago, phonics instruction was introduced to help young readers learn more about the relationship between letters and sound (Groff, 1989). Some researchers think that phonics has been used to teach reading since the time of ancient Greeks. Chall (1989) describes the method "as a tool for helping beginners identify words accurately so that they can read texts with comprehension earlier and more efficiently" (p. 4). Groff agrees that phonics instruction can be very useful for the development of children's word recognition skills. The problem is how to convince parents and teachers of the benefits of phonics. Wood (1992) believes that the horrible failure of our schools to teach children to read skillfully began years ago. She writes that "[the failure of schools to teach reading] began in 1929 and 1930 when hundreds of primary teachers, guided by college reading professors, stopped teaching beginners to read by matching sounds with letters that spell sounds" (p. 52).

Phonics is not the entire answer to the question of how best to teach children to read, however. Most reading experts agree that "the most the application of phonics can do is help children produce the approximate pronunciation of words" (Groff, 1989, p. 6). Roberts (1989), writing for Parents magazine, reports that phonics may not help all children learn to pronounce words. He explains that anyone who has a visual or auditory handicap will find it harder to read using phonics. For instance, Roberts points out that a child who has suffered from an ear infection that caused temporary hearing loss at an early age

Give the page number on which a direct quotation appears in the source.

The year of Groff's publication has already been mentioned in this paragraph, so it is not repeated here.

The brackets indicate that Cory has added his own words to the direct quotation.

For a smooth transition and to avoid too many parenthetical interruptions, mention author and source in text whenever you can.

Phonics 4

may find it difficult to learn to read by using phonics
because of missing out on experiencing sound
discrimination.

* * * * *

In conclusion, many experts believe that we have
the ability and the knowledge to educate our
schoolchildren more effectively by using phonics. But
while both traditional and experimental evidence
supports the use of phonics, the debate continues.
Educators who are not familiar with phonics
instruction must be enlightened, perhaps with in-
service workshops from experts on phonics
instruction. Parents, too, may need to be convinced.
Reading experts must be willing to work together to
resolve some of the issues in the phonics debate,
perhaps by putting together a combination of
approaches to the teaching of reading that includes
phonics. The bottom line is that we all must work to
find a solution to the appalling rate of adult
illiteracy in this country and the unsettling
inability of students to read at their own grade
levels. We must find solutions to these problems, or
we risk jeopardizing not only our children's futures
but our own.

APA STYLE REFERENCES LIST

- Bibliographic entries for all works cited in a paper are listed in alphabetical order on a page entitled *References*.
- The first line of each entry in the references list is indented five spaces, and the second and subsequent lines are flush with the left margin.
- Give the last names and only the initials of the first and middle names of authors.

- The year of publication, in parentheses, follows the author's name.
- For a book, capitalize only proper nouns and the first word of the title and subtitle; underline the title.
- If a book is edited, place the abbreviation "Ed." or "Eds." in parentheses after the name(s) of the editor(s).
- If a citation names two or more authors, each name is reversed and an ampersand (&), not the word *and,* is placed before the last name.
- For an article, book chapter title, or title of an essay in a collection, capitalize as for a book title and do not use quotation marks or underlining.
- Capitalize the first letters of all important words in the name of the periodical and underline it.
- Use the abbreviations "p." and "pp." for inclusive page numbers of articles in magazines and journals, except when volume and issue number are given. If volume number is given for a periodical, place it after name of the periodical and underline it. If an issue number is also given, place it in parentheses after the volume number but do not underline it:

> Hamby, A. L. (1991, Spring). An American Democrat: A reevaluation of the personality of Harry S. Truman. <u>Political Science Quarterly, 106,</u> pp. 33-55.
>
> Stephenson, F. (2002, Aug.). The phonics revival. <u>Florida Trend, 45</u> (4), pp. 10-24.

- If two or more works by the same author appear on the references list, put them in chronological order. Repeat the author's name each time, followed by the date in parentheses.
- If you cite two works of one author published in the same year, alphabetize them by title, and give each entry a lowercase letter: (1996a), (1996b).
- Words like "university" and "press" are spelled out, not abbreviated.

```
                                          Phonics 14

                       References
Carbo, M. (1987, February). Reading styles research:

    What works isn't always phonics. Phi Delta

    Kappan, 68, 431-435.

Chall, J. S. (1989). The role of phonics in teaching

    reading. Washington, DC: U.S. Department of

    Education, Office of Educational Research and

    Improvement.
```

Phonics 15

Groff, P. (1977). <u>Phonics: Why and how.</u> Morristown,
    NJ: General Learning.

Groff, P. (1989). <u>Modern phonics instruction.</u>
    Washington, DC: U.S. Department of Education,
    Office of Educational Research and Improvement.

Johnson, D. (1999). Critical issue: Addressing the
    literacy needs of emergent and early readers.
    [Electronic version.] 2 Feb. 2005. North Central
    Regional Educational Laboratory.
    http://www.ncrel.org/sdrs/areas/issues/content/
    cntareas/reading/li100.html.

Roberts, F. (1989, January). Does phonics cure
    reading problems? Parents, p. 49.

Stephenson, F. (2002, Aug.). The phonics revival.
    <u>Florida Trend, 45</u> (4), pp. 10-24.

Weaver, C. (1991, April). Weighing the claims about
    phonics first. <u>Education Digest,</u> pp. 19-22.

Wood, R. L. (1992, September 14). That's right--
    they're wrong: Decline in reading ability due to
    abandonment of phonics. <u>National Review,</u> pp.
    49-52.

Wood, R. L. (1998). <u>Time for a '2 By 1' Core
    Curriculum.</u> Oklahoma City: Oklahoma Council of
    Public Affairs.

PART TWO

THE ARTS, MEDIA STUDIES, AND POPULAR CULTURE

CHAPTER

7

MUSIC AND VIDEO GAMES

People's opinions about what expressive forms can be considered works of art change and evolve over time. Henry Jenkins' "Art Form for the Digital Age," written in 2000 when video games were beginning to get creative in the scope and range of what they offered players, argues that video games are a legitimate art form that must be taken seriously. He writes that they play an important part in "shaping the aesthetic sensibility of the 21st century." As you read what he has to say in defense of his proposition, consider the video games that you and your friends play. Does Jenkins make a compelling case for viewing them as art?

Certainly video games are treated seriously by young people, particularly boys, as John Tierney's "Here Come the Alpha Pups" demonstrates. In the course of his article on the advertising technique of "viral marketing," Tierney comments on the larger issues of whether video games have value and how to account for the fact that they are a "gendered" phenomenon. As you read his essay, consider how you would answer some of his questions: Do video games have any "redeeming social value"? Must they? And how do we account for their wild popularity with boys but girls' almost indifferent attitude toward them? Besides those topics, Tierney's article introduces subjects that are treated in greater length in other chapters in this book, chapter 14 on gender and sex roles, and chapter 23 on marketing and consumerism.

While video games are a very recent development in games—and popular culture—music has been an integral part of humans' lives from their earliest existence. Song and instrumental music have spoken to, soothed, excited, and otherwise influenced humans of virtually all cultures and time periods in a seemingly endless variety of styles, subject matter, and methods of delivery. Each new musician, composer, or singer hopes to create a style uniquely his or her own, often acknowledging the influence of a previous form or artist. Sometimes a wholly new form of musical expression is created, from which generations of musicians and music lovers in turn take their inspiration.

The subject of contemporary music, though, gives rise to sometimes heated debate, especially when rock and roll or alternative music is discussed. Isabelle Leymarie, who wrote "Rock 'n' Revolt" over a decade ago, addresses an issue that is still hotly discussed: the connection between rock and roll music and actual violence. Some people are firmly convinced that certain lyrics of both mainstream and alternative music actually cause violence by promoting and glorifying it. Others argue just as vehemently that such music simply reflects popular culture, rather than influencing it. As you read about the music that she cites as having been banned or stigmatized, think about the music you like. Have you ever been criticized for the kinds of music you like (or perhaps perform)?

Following Leymarie's essay, Cristina Verán in "Rap, Rage and REDvolution" brings up another issue associated with pop music, the racism apparent in certain lyrics. While pointing out that hip-hop music is an empowering voice for Native Americans, she reports on charges of racism against Native Americans in the lyrics of many mainstream rappers. As you read the examples she gives and the responses of Native Americans to actions and lyrics of some hip-hop performers, consider your own view of them. Do you think the criticisms are just, or do you think that critics are over-reacting? Verán's essay has strong relevance to the subject of chapter 15, race and ethnicity.

ART FORM FOR THE DIGITAL AGE

HENRY JENKINS

Henry Jenkins is Director of Comparative Media Studies and Professor of Literature at the Massachusetts Institute of Technology. Among his publications are dozens of periodical articles and nine books, beginning in 1992 with What Made Pistachio Nuts?: Early Sound Comedy and the Vaudeville Aesthetic *and* Textual Poachers: Television Fans and Participatory Culture. *Among his other books are* Classical Hollywood Comedy *(1994), co-edited with Kristine Brunovska Karnick;* From Barbie to Mortal Kombat: Gender and Computer Games *(1998), co-edited with Justine Cassell;* Hop On Pop: The Politics and Pleasures of Popular Culture *(2003), co-edited with Tara McPherson and Jane Shattuc; and* Rethinking Media Change: The Aesthetics of Transition *(2003), co-edited with David Thorburn. This article was first published in the September 2000 issue of* Technology Review.

Video games shape our culture. It's time we took them seriously.

Last year, Americans bought over 215 million computer and video games. That's more than two games per household. The video game industry made almost as much money from gross domestic income as Hollywood. So are video games a massive drain on our income, time and energy? A new form of "cultural pollution," as one U.S. senator described them? The "nightmare before Christmas," in the words of another? Are games teaching our children to kill, as countless op-ed pieces have warned?

No. Computer games are art—a popular art, an emerging art, a largely unrecognized art, but art nevertheless.

4   Over the past 25 years, games have progressed from the primitive two-paddles-and-a-ball Pong to the sophistication of Final Fantasy, a participatory story with cinema-quality graphics that unfolds over nearly 100 hours of play. The computer game has been a killer app for the home PC, increasing consumer demand for vivid graphics, rapid processing, greater memory and better sound. The release this fall of the Sony Playstation 2, coupled with the announcement of next-generation consoles by Nintendo and Microsoft, signals a dramatic increase in the resources available to game designers.

Games increasingly influence contemporary cinema, helping to define the frenetic pace and model the multi-directional plotting of *Run Lola Run*, providing the role-playing metaphor for *Being John Malkovich* and encouraging a fascination with the slippery line between reality and digital illusion in *The Matrix*. At high schools and colleges across the country, students discuss games with the same passions with which earlier generations debated the merits of the New American Cinema. Media studies programs report a growing number of their students want to be game designers rather than filmmakers.

The time has come to take games seriously as an important new popular art shaping the aesthetic sensibility of the 21st century. I will admit that discussing the art of video games conjures up comic images: tuxedo-clad and jewel-bedecked patrons admiring the latest Streetfighter, middle-aged academics pontificating on the impact of Cubism on Tetris, bleeps and zaps disrupting our silent contemplation at the Guggenheim. Such images tell us more about our contemporary notion of art—as arid and stuffy, as the property of an educated and economic elite, as cut off from everyday experience—than they tell us about games.

New York's Whitney Museum found itself at the center of controversy about digital art when it recently included web artists in its prestigious biannual show. Critics didn't believe the computer could adequately express the human spirit. But they're misguided. The computer is simply a tool, one that offers artists new resources and opportunities for reaching the public; it is human creativity that makes art. Still, one can only imagine how the critics would have responded to the idea that something as playful, unpretentious and widely popular as a computer game might be considered art.

8   In 1925, leading literary and arts critic Gilbert Seldes took a radical approach to the aesthetics of popular culture in a treatise titled *The Seven Lively Arts*. Adopting what was then a controversial position, Seldes argued that America's primary contributions to artistic expression had come through emerging forms of popular culture such as jazz, the Broadway musical, the Hollywood cinema and the comic strip. While these arts have gained cultural respectability over the past 75 years, each was disreputable when Seldes staked out his position.

Readers then were skeptical of Seldes' claims about cinema in particular for many of the same reasons that contemporary critics dismiss games—they were suspicious of cinema's commercial motivations and technological origins, concerned about Hollywood's appeals to violence and eroticism, and insistent that cinema had not yet produced works of lasting value. Seldes, on the other hand, argued that cinema's popularity demanded that we reassess its aesthetic qualities.

Cinema and other popular arts were to be celebrated, Seldes said, because they were so deeply imbedded in everyday life, because they were democratic arts embraced by average citizens. Through streamlined styling and syncopated rhythms, they captured the vitality of contemporary urban experience. They took the very machinery of the industrial age, which many felt dehumanizing, and found within it the resources for expressing individual visions, for reasserting basic human needs, desires and fantasies. And these new forms were still open to experimentation and discovery. They were, in Seldes' words, "lively arts."

Games represent a new lively art, one as appropriate for the digital age as those earlier media were for the machine age. They open up new aesthetic experiences and transform the computer screen into a realm of experimentation and innovation that is broadly accessible. And games have been embraced by a public that has otherwise been unimpressed by much of what passes for digital art. Much as the salon arts of the 1920s seemed sterile alongside the vitality and inventiveness of popular culture, contemporary efforts to create interactive narrative through modernist hypertext or avant-garde installation art seem lifeless and pretentious alongside the creativity that game designers bring to their craft.

12   Much of what Seldes told us about the silent cinema seems remarkably apt for thinking about games. Silent cinema, he argued, was an art of expressive movement.

He valued the speed and dynamism of D.W. Griffith's last-minute races to the rescue, the physical grace of Chaplin's pratfalls and the ingenuity of Buster Keaton's engineering feats. Games also depend upon an art of expressive movement, with characters defined through their distinctive ways of propelling themselves through space, and successful products structured around a succession of spectacular stunts and predicaments. Will future generations look back on Lara Croft doing battle with a pack of snarling wolves as the 21st-century equivalent of Lillian Gish making her way across the ice floes in *Way Down East?* The art of silent cinema was also an art of atmospheric design. To watch a silent masterpiece like Fritz Lang's Metropolis is to be drawn into a world where meaning is carried by the placement of shadows, the movement of machinery and the organization of space. If anything, game designers have pushed beyond cinema in terms of developing expressive and fantastic environments that convey a powerful sense of mood, provoke our curiosity and amusement, and motivate us to explore.

Seldes wrote at a moment when cinema was maturing as an expressive medium and filmmakers were striving to enhance the emotional experience of going to the movies—making a move from mere spectacle towards character and consequence. It remains to be seen whether games can make a similar transition. Contemporary games can pump us full of adrenaline, they can make us laugh, but they have not yet provoked us to tears. And many have argued that, since games don't have characters of human complexity or stories that stress the consequences of our actions, they cannot achieve the status of true art. Here, we must be careful not to confuse the current transitional state of an emerging medium with its full potential. As I visit game companies, I see some of the industry's best minds struggling with this question and see strong evidence that the games released over the next few years will bring us closer and closer to the quality of characterization we have come to expect from other forms of popular narrative.

In the March 6 [2000] issue of *Newsweek,* senior editor Jack Kroll argued that audiences will probably never be able to care as deeply about pixels on the computer screen as they care about characters in films: "Moviemakers don't have to simulate human beings; they are right there, to be recorded and orchestrated . . . The top-heavy titillation of Tomb Raider's Lara Croft falls flat next to the face of Sharon Stone. . . ." Yet countless viewers cry when Bambi's mother dies, and World War II veterans can tell you they felt real lust for *Esquire*'s Vargas girls. We have learned to care as much about creatures of pigment as we care about images of real people. Why should pixels be different?

In the end, games may not take the same path as cinema. Game designers will almost certainly develop their own aesthetic principles as they confront the challenge of balancing our competing desires for storytelling and interactivity. It remains to be seen whether games can provide players the freedom they want and still provide an emotionally satisfying and thematically meaningful shape to the experience. Some of the best games—Tetris comes to mind—have nothing to do with storytelling. For all we know, the future art of games may look more like architecture or dance than cinema.

16   Such questions warrant close and passionate engagement not only within the game industry or academia, but also by the press and around the dinner table. Even

Kroll's grumpy dismissal of games has sparked heated discussion and forced designers to refine their own grasp of the medium's distinctive features. Imagine what a
more robust form of criticism could contribute. We need critics who know games the
way Pauline Kael knew movies and who write about them with an equal degree of wit
and wisdom.

When *The Seven Lively Arts* was published, silent cinema was still an experimental form, each work stretching the medium in new directions. Early film critics played
vital functions in documenting innovations and speculating about their potential.
Computer games are in a similar phase. We have not had time to codify what experienced game designers know, and we have certainly not yet established a canon of great
works that might serve as exemplars. There have been real creative accomplishments
in games, but we haven't really sorted out what they are and why they matter.

But games do matter, because they spark the imaginations of our children, taking them on epic quests to strange new worlds. Games matter because our children
no longer have access to real-world play spaces at a time when we've paved over the
vacant lots to make room for more condos and the streets make parents nervous. If
children are going to have opportunities for exploratory play, play that encourages
cognitive development and fosters problem-solving skills, they will do so in the virtual environments of games. Multi-player games create opportunities for leadership,
competition, teamwork and collaboration—for nerdy kids, not just for highschool
football players. Games matter because they form the digital equivalent of the Head
Start program, getting kids excited about what computers can do.

The problem with most contemporary games isn't that they are violent but that
they are banal, formulaic and predictable. Thoughtful criticism can marshal support
for innovation and experimentation in the industry, much as good film criticism helps
focus attention on neglected independent films. Thoughtful criticism could even contribute to our debates about game violence. So far, the censors and culture warriors
have gotten more or less a free ride because we almost take for granted that games are
culturally worthless. We should instead look at games as an emerging art form—one
that does not simply simulate violence but increasingly offers new ways to understand
violence—and talk about how to strike a balance between this form of expression and
social responsibility. Moreover, game criticism may provide a means of holding the
game industry more accountable for its choices. In the wake of the Columbine shootings, game designers are struggling with their ethical responsibilities as never before,
searching for ways of appealing to empowerment fantasies that don't require exploding heads and gushing organs. A serious public discussion of this medium might con-
structively influence these debates, helping identify and evaluate alternatives as they
emerge.

20   As the art of games matures, progress will be driven by the most creative and
forward-thinking minds in the industry, those who know that games can be more
than they have been, those who recognize the potential of reaching a broader public,
of having a greater cultural impact, of generating more diverse and ethically responsible content and of creating richer and more emotionally engaging stories. But without the support of an informed public and the perspective of thoughtful critics, game
developers may never realize that potential.

PERSONAL RESPONSE

Do you find video games aesthetically appealing in any way?

QUESTIONS FOR CLASS OR SMALL-GROUP DISCUSSION

1. Jenkins begins by stating, "Video games shape our culture." How does he support that statement? Do you agree with Jenkins on the importance of video games in "shaping the aesthetic sensibility of the 21st century" (paragraph 7)?

2. In paragraph 5, Jenkins gives examples of video games that illustrate his observation that they have progressed over time from a primitive state to sophistication. What criteria does he use to make that judgment? What examples of currently popular video games can you name that illustrate his point? If you do not believe that they have continued to evolve, give examples that disprove his point.

3. What is Jenkins' argumentative strategy? That is, what is his proposition? What is his supporting evidence? Does he acknowledge opposing viewpoints or make any concessions? Does he urge action? How persuasive do you find the essay?

4. Explain Gilbert Seldes' approach to popular culture (paragraph 9 and following) and assess its applicability to the question of video games as a legitimate art form.

5. In several places, Jenkins states that certain things in the development of video games "remain to be seen" (paragraphs 14 and 16). He also writes in his concluding paragraph of the potential of video games. In your opinion, have video games achieved any of the potential that Jenkins believed they had in 2000? You might first consider whether that is or should be the goal of video games.

HERE COME THE ALPHA PUPS

John Tierney

John Tierney worked first as a newspaper reporter and then in magazine journalism, publishing in such periodicals as the Atlantic Monthly, Discover, Newsweek, Rolling Stone, *and the* Washington Monthly. *In 1990, he joined the* New York Times *and eventually became a staff writer for the* New York Times Magazine. *He now writes the Big City column for the* Times. *"Here Come the Alpha Pups" was first published in the August 5, 2001, issue of the* New York Times Magazine.

Early this year, market researchers headed into playgrounds, skate parks and video arcades throughout Chicago looking for what they called alpha pups. They went up to boys between the ages of 8 and 13 with a question: "Who's the coolest kid you know?" When they got a name, they would look for that kid and put the question to him. The goal was to ascend the hierarchy of coolness, asking the question again and again until someone finally answered "Me." By the end of April, they had found alpha pups in most of the schools in Chicago and made them an offer that sounded too good to be true. Hasbro would pay them $30 to learn a new video game.

One alpha pup was Angel Franco, age 9, whose coolness was certified on his playground in a Mexican-American neighborhood on the South Side. He was invited to an office building near the Loop, where seven other alpha pups were escorted into a conference room; market researchers and executives from Hasbro were behind a one-way mirror. This experiment in viral marketing, as the grown-ups called it, started with a video narrated by a deep male voice.

"They're already here, but we can't see them," the narrator began, explaining that deadly extraterrestrials called Pox had escaped from a laboratory. "Mankind's only hope is to enlist a secret army of the world's most skilled hand-held-game players. Their mission is to use advanced R.F. containment units to create a race of new, more powerful hybrid warriors and test them in battle against these alien infectors." A boy looking like a young Tom Cruise appeared on the screen as the narrator reached a crescendo: "A battle to save Earth is about to begin, and only he can save us. Beware the Pox! Pox is contagious!"

4   Angel and the other alpha pups could not sit still. They kept swiveling their chairs the leader of the training session, a hip, young guy named Nino, introduced himself and explained that they were the first humans chosen to be Pox secret agents: "We chose you because you are the coolest, funniest guys in your school. Raise your hand if you're cool." Every hand shot up, and Nino passed out the Pox units, each a little bigger than a cell phone. He demonstrated how to push the buttons beside the tiny screen to assemble a warrior. Then he revealed the great leap forward in this game: a radio transmitter enabling a player to battle any other player within 30 feet.

"Let's say you're at school, waiting in line, and your friend has one," Nino said. "Turn yours on and put it in Battle mode. You could be in this room, and I could be in that room, and we could battle each other." The alpha pups pumped their fists and shouted.

"Whoa!"

"This game is too wicked!"

8   "This is better than Pokemon!"

"This is the best game ever!"

The adults behind the mirror were psyched too. "Get the name of the kid who said it's the best game ever," one publicist said to another.

Matt Collins, a director of marketing for Hasbro, reminisced about his first encounter with Pox. "It was presented on a storyboard with a simple pitch," he said: "What if there were a game kids could play in two separate cars at a stoplight, and then a third car pulls up, and another kid gets in the game. I've seen a lot of strange concepts at meetings, but never anything like this." Hasbro chose a novel marketing plan. Instead of introducing the game with a national advertising blitz (which won't come until the end of the month), Hasbro decided to start in one place, as if it were an epidemic. The company infected 900 of the 1,400 schools in Chicago. Officially, the game was not supposed to be used at school. Unofficially, everyone knew better. "We're not actually promoting this for use in school," Collins said diplomatically, "but we do want kids talking about it when they're together there."

12   Each alpha pup left the training session with a day pack containing 10 Pox units to be handed out to friends. Angel headed off with his stepfather, Rick Castro, who was dealing with a delicate situation back home. Angel's mother had recently joined a Pentecostal Christian church that frowns on electronic entertainment. She banned the kids from watching television, except for religious programs, and made Angel give away his Nintendo. She was not pleased when Angel was singled out on his playground for the Hasbro experiment.

     Her husband insisted on letting Angel participate. How could they deprive a kid of a chance to earn $30 for playing a video game? Angel's stepfather even tried arguing that Angel might learn something playing the game—not an easy argument to win in any home. Boys' video games are a cultural phenomenon that unites conservatives and liberals, fundamentalists and New Agers. Video battles are considered at best a waste of time, at worst the inspiration for school massacres. Last year, Indianapolis banned anyone under 18 from playing point-and-shoot video games in arcades; this year, the Connecticut Legislature passed similar legislation. Feminists have accused game companies of pandering to boys' worst instincts and ignoring girls' needs. The grand goal among grown-ups has been to get boys and girls who use computers to do something other than kill aliens.

     But there in Chicago, a quarter-century after Space Invaders hit the arcades, the boys were still off by themselves battling squiggly creatures on screens. Hasbro didn't even bother inviting girls to try out Pox. Video games remain largely segregated by sex, generally unaffected by the movement to get boys playing peacefully with girls. Teachers are no longer supposed to tolerate boys who fight and enthuse about weapons—even dodge ball has been banned on many playgrounds—but brutish competition is still the norm on video screens. You could accuse Hasbro of being hopelessly retrograde in ignoring the pleas from child-development experts. You could also wonder if toy makers know something about children that the experts don't.

     The search for the next great toy begins at Hasbro with a brainstorming session in which designers and marketers sit around a table and say repeatedly, "Wouldn't it be cool if. . . ." Pox was conceived at such a session two years ago when someone said, "Wouldn't it be cool if I could build a character and send him out to fight you?" Peter Kullgren, a designer sitting at the table, volunteered to try. The character he settled on was an alien with three distinct parts: head, body, tail. "I wanted it to be a little bit mechanical, a little bit animal," Kullgren recalled. "The mechanical so you can swap body parts, the animal so you can get a little attached to it."

16   Kullgren, a sci-fi buff, came up with the back story about a deadly plague of alien infectors, which turned out to be precisely with the zeitgeist when the mad-cow-disease panic struck. But of course this fear of infection is an old phobia, especially among boys on playgrounds. For centuries, they have been afraid of girls giving them

cooties. The name and the concept of Pox tested well with boys. "Alien infectors sound exciting," a fifth grader said at a focus group in New York City. "Gross but good."

Kullgren devised what's called a king-of-the-hill game, although it also borrows from other genres. You start off by going through a sort of ninja boot camp, a solo exercise in which you maneuver a little stick figure on the screen through a series of passageways and rooms. By finding openings in the walls and battling other stick figures, you graduate to higher levels and amass a collection of heads, bodies and tails. When you're ready to fight a friend, you assemble a warrior and program a "battle sequence." You might start by swinging your warrior's tail at the enemy's head, then using the middle of your body to defend against the counter-thrust from the enemy. The battle becomes an elaborate version of the old playground game of rock-paper-scissors: each body part has particular strengths and weaknesses, so victory requires picking those that work best against the ones chosen by the enemy warrior. Unlike traditional battle games in arcades—known variously as shooters, twitch games or bleed-and-twitch games—Pox depends not on quick reflexes but on the collection of arcana.

Does this do any good for boys? When pressed, Kullgren can imagine a socially redeeming value for his creation. "Pox teaches creative planning," he said. "You'll do better at the game if you think before you act, just as in a job. If you come in for a presentation and you have your facts in order, you won't be tripped up by a question you didn't expect." But the makers of Pox have never pretended to be on an educational mission. It is hard enough just figuring out what kids want to play.

Toy fads are so unpredictable that the big companies spend most of their time promoting safe bets, either proven toys or products tied to TV shows and movies. True breakthroughs are hard to engineer. Wildly successful innovations—Scrabble, Tinkertoys and Legos, Cabbage Patch Kids, Teenage Mutant Ninja Turtles, Rubik's Cube—tend to come from amateurs working on their own. No one expected Pokemon, which started out as a hand-held video game in Japan, to inspire a worldwide mania for collecting cards. Pox's little warriors had obvious parallels with Pokemon's "pocket monsters," but would kids respond?

20   Hasbro's market researchers tried to gauge Pox's appeal by interviewing editors of game magazines about kids' yearnings. They chatted with college students who were hardened veterans of video games. They studied customers browsing in game stores. They described Pox's features to child psychologists. "The psychologists told us the appeal of this game is that it lets kids create a little world that's their own," Kullgren said. "They're at this edge of innocence and adolescence, where they're starting to make decisions for themselves—what to wear, what's cool, what's not cool. Up until now their parents have been doing it. Now they're in control. They're creating characters and making choices that determine the outcome of battles."

The adult theories were tested on focus groups of boys last autumn in New York City and Stamford, Conn. The boys were presented with "positioning statements" summing up the game in different ways, like "the game that you build yourself" or "the ultimate collection" or "the game that you can play secretly anywhere." The big hit was the secrecy. As a fifth grader in Stamford said: "Parents and teachers won't even know we're playing! Only we'll know. That's awesome!" Kids in the focus groups imagined slyly doing battle as they walked around with a Pox unit hidden in the pocket of their cargo pants.

"We originally thought Pox's appeal would be more around the battling and collecting aspects of the game, like Pokemon," said John Chandler, Hasbro's senior vice president for marketing. "What actually appealed the most was the ability to play the game using a stealthy technique. You could put it inside your locker and let it battle whoever was coming down the hall." A kid could savor the joy of a sneak attack against an enemy, and if he lost he wasn't instantly humiliated in public. "There's no pressure," a fourth grader in New York happily told the market researchers. Hasbro executives summed up the appeal of the game with a motto: "Win loudly, lose quietly."

The next question was how to provide the first Pox players with enough enemies to battle. Hasbro hired Target, a Boston-based marketing company, to create a critical mass of players. "Pox is a viral product, so we hit on the idea of viral marketing," said Tom Schneider, Target's president. That meant starting in one city with what marketers call "key influencers," although Schneider used a term inspired by his recent purchase of an English spaniel. "The breeder warned me not to take the alpha dog of the litter because it would run my life," Schneider said. "It seemed to me that was just the kind of kid we were looking for." Teams of field workers in Chicago found 1,600 alpha pups by interviewing kids, teachers and coaches and by administering a five-page questionnaire to parents with questions like, "Does your child like to be the first one to see a movie when it comes out?"

24 By the time Angel Franco sat down in front of the one-way mirror, Schneider and the marketers at Hasbro had watched hundreds of kids learn the game. They knew that Angel and his fellow third graders would shout more than the fifth graders in the next session because fifth graders were too cool to show emotion. The marketers knew precisely when the kids in Angel's group would first shout—when told they could battle someone in another room. "I love the group concept of this game," said Schneider, smiling as he watched the fist-pumping among Angel's group. "It just sounds so cool. You play all day at home, and you get the payoff the next day at school when you go into battle. It will be hard for some of these kids to sleep at night."

When he fell asleep on his first day as a Pox secret agent, Angel was already up to Level 3 of the game. The next morning, he emerged from his home, an apartment above a little grocery and liquor store named La Providencia, carrying four of the units in his day pack. When he reached school and pulled out the packages in the cafeteria, his alpha-pup status was more secure than ever.

"You create your own alien and battle other kids," Angel told his friends as they ripped open the packages. They started creating monsters without glancing at the instructions, the classic male approach to video games and computers: keep punching buttons until something works.

As a test of diligence, Pox proved to be a problem for Angel, because his mother wouldn't let him play as long as his friends did. Within two days of getting the game, some of his friends were up to Level 6, but Angel had reached only Level 5. Sitting in his living room after school, he was trying to catch up, but his mother, Elsa, was not looking pleased. "When are you going to start your homework?" she asked.

28   "I just have to get to the next level," he said. He tried to argue that his electronic quest was just as important as homework. "The game gets you smart. You have to, like, find treasures and figure out a way to open doors to get to the next level. You really do learn something on your own." These seemed to him essential skills for his intended occupation of explorer ("I'll climb mountains and find stuff"), but he realized that the argument didn't go far with his mother. He knew, as researchers say, that video games are a "gendered" phenomenon. "Girls don't like these games," he said, putting down the Pox unit. "They like to play with little babies—yuck!" He grabbed a doll from the floor and absent-mindedly flattened its plastic head between his hands as he talked. "My sisters like to pretend they have babies and live in a house. They use Monopoly money to go shopping. Boys like to play with cool stuff. Boys like aliens. Boys are like, more, I don't know how to say—more mature."

That is not the word used by his sisters. Patty, 10, had spent a couple of hours playing Pox, but she was hardly enthralled. She didn't even know what level she had reached. "I'm not really interested in levels," she said. "I just like to play the game to see how much fun I get." Angel's 15-year-old sister, Jessica, didn't bother trying Pox. Asked to explain Angel's obsession with it, she came up with the same theory as a number of academic researchers: "I've noticed that guys like these games so they can go searching for special places."

Male wanderlust has been documented as early as the womb, where male fetuses move more than females do. At age 1, boys tend to crawl farther away from their mothers and stay away longer, and they are more interested in toys that move, like trains and cars. On playgrounds, boys tend to roam at the edges, while girls tend to stay put at the center. A study in the 1970's found that boys playing after school spent more time outside and covered nearly three times as much ground as girls. For Tom Sawyer, a good day meant fleeing Aunt Polly by hopping over the fence and going off to play war.

Today, though, Tom would probably not be doing much carefree roaming. He would probably be in a city or suburb with his day's activities fully scheduled. Half the day would be spent trying to sit still at a desk. "It's boring when you're in school," Angel said. "The boys got to be calm, but we want to run around and play. The girls like school, because they get to talk to friends. Boys like to talk a little, but we like to play-fight more." The tiny playground at school gives him no chance to run, not that there is much time for it, anyway. Angel doesn't even get a chance to run at recess because his school is one of many that have eliminated recess. After school, Angel goes either to a program at a city recreation center or back home, a two-bedroom apartment for six people without a yard to play in. For this would-be explorer, the closest equivalent to Tom Sawyer's fence-hopping is turning on a video game—if his mother doesn't stop him.

32   Angel's conflict with his mother is a familiar situation to Henry Jenkins, the co-editor of a book of scholarly essays on computer games, "From Barbie to Mortal Kombat." Jenkins, the director of the media studies program at the Massachusetts Institute of Technology, has analyzed the Mom problem. He argues that video games, far from being a corruption of traditional childhood, actually embody the classic boyhood themes celebrated by previous generations and writers like Mark Twain,

Robert Louis Stevenson and Rudyard Kipling. Video games offer boys a chance to explore, fight, master manly skills, make scatological jokes and act out fantasies that would appall their mothers. But whereas boys used to hop the fence and play away from home, today Mom can always look over and see what they're doing on the computer. "Mothers come face to face with the messy process by which Western culture turns boys into men," Jenkins writes. "The games and their content become the focus of open antagonism and the subject of tremendous guilt and anxiety."

Not so long ago, critics used to accuse toy companies of promoting "gender apartheid" among the nation's children because they sold plastic guns and swords to boys and doll houses to girls. The criticism intensified when it was observed that boys were drawn to computers to play violent games, while most girls stuck to their old play routines. Worried about a "digital gender gap," philanthropists and investors poured money into what became known as the girls' game movement. Girls, it became clear, did not share boys' desire to explore "fantasy microworlds" with simple moral codes. "Most girls can't get interested in the lame characters or puzzles in boys' games," said Brenda Laurel, a Silicon Valley veteran whose video-game company interviewed more than 1,000 children. "They don't want to master a skill just to reach a higher level. Mastery for its own sake is not very good social currency for a girl." Laurel designed a game, Rockett's New School, in which the heroine must navigate her way through the first day of eighth grade in a new school. It became one of the more popular girls' games, although sales never rose high enough to keep Laurel's company in business.

It took a more traditional approach to bridge the digital gender gap. The first huge hit in entertainment software for girls was Barbie Fashion Designer, in 1996. Since then, Barbie has been ruling the girls' software charts along with Mary-Kate and Ashley Olsen, the television twins, who lead a computerized trip to the mall. Meanwhile, boys are still battling aliens.

As Angel was working his way through the early levels of boot camp, I sought out a more experienced group of alpha pups: sixth graders who had been playing Pox for more than a week in the Chicago suburb of Lake Zurich. We met at a large shopping mall. My warrior, which I had painstakingly constructed and named NYTMAG, won its first battle, against a kid standing near the central fountain. I headed toward the Disney store with my victory booty—the body parts of the enemy warrior—and put my unit into Battle mode as I approached a kid standing at the entrance. He glanced at his unit in dismay.

36   "I got a virus!" he said, and I eagerly looked down at my unit expecting to see more fruits of victory. Instead, there was a dire message on the screen: "INTRUDER COOOOL." It was the same message on the other kid's screen. The two of us had been infected by the COOOOL warrior, which was now in the process of killing our warriors and transferring the body parts to its owner's unit. But where was COOOOL's owner? There were no other players in sight. Then we heard a cry from above.

"I'm COOOOL!" We looked up to see a kid at the top of the escalator. He had been standing above us, battling invisibly through the floor. "I got your body parts!" he shouted, raising his arms in victory as the escalator bore him down to us at a stately pace. It was not a bad approximation of a Roman general's triumphal procession, except that he had on a T-shirt and the crowd could not see the captured enemies in chains.

This victor, who was 12 and named Michael Cyganek, cheerfully showed us a secret way we could have saved our guys even after COOOOL had won the battle. (This secret turned out to be a surprise even to the game's designer, who was impressed to hear that Michael had found an unintended feature.) We watched an instant replay of the battles, observing which body parts were vulnerable to which attacks by which other body parts. There were thousands of permutations to consider, an exercise that delighted Michael and his friends as they sat around the fountain. Michael was sure that there would soon be a Pox television show, and he was imagining a toy version of the warriors—action figures with interchangeable body parts, maybe, or radio-controlled little robots. Michael had turned down offers of $50 (twice the retail price that would eventually be charged) from classmates desperate to get a game. Kids were playing on the school bus, in the halls, in class.

"Why do you like it?" I asked.

40   "Because it's, like, battling and fighting," Michael said, prompting a chorus of assents from his friends.

"We like violence!"

"It's fun to beat your friends."

They sounded bloodthirsty, but they didn't look at all menacing. I never saw them or any other Pox players in Chicago come to blows. They teased and bickered, and they got frustrated at the defeat of a prized warrior, but I never saw anyone seriously threaten anyone. They played the way Hasbro had predicted—"Win loudly, lose quietly"—and the winners' gloating didn't seem to bother the losers as much as it pleased the winners. I watched only a few dozen players, but my unscientific observations jibed with the results of a classic playground study conducted in 1976 by Janet Lever, a sociologist. The fifth-grade boys she observed often interrupted their games to argue about rules, but the argument never lasted more than seven minutes, and the game always resumed. The girls argued less, but when they did, the game usually ended.

Boys keep the peace through confrontation and competition. Like other young male primates, they learn to get along through rough-and-tumble play. They resolve conflicts with challenges that clearly establish rules and a hierarchy, enabling them to play and work in large groups. Their stoicism enables them to be defeated without losing face, thereby defusing potentially violent situations. Like Robin Hood and Little John, most boys emerge from confrontations as better friends.

44   But what about the boys who played Doom and then killed their classmates at Columbine High School? What about the Mortal Kombat player who shot his classmates in Kentucky? The makers of those games were blamed for the tragedies and sued by the parents of victims. But while this was happening, the news media all but ignored a larger trend that has been evident since those two graphically violent games were introduced—Mortal Kombat in September 1993, Doom four months later. Up until that point, the national rate of youth violence, as measured by arrests of juveniles for homicide, had been rising for nearly a decade. Then the trend promptly reversed.

"Just as violent video games were pouring into American homes on the crest of the personal computer wave, juvenile violence began to plummet," said Lawrence Sherman, a criminologist at the University of Pennsylvania. "Juvenile murder charges dropped by about two-thirds from 1993 to the end of the decade and show no signs of going back up. The rate of violence in schools hasn't increased, either—it just gets more media coverage. If video games are so deadly, why has their widespread use been followed by reductions in murder?"

In an adult's ideal playground, there would be no violent fantasies, no aggression, no hierarchies or cliques, no sexual segregation. By playing with girls, boys would pick up some of their verbal gifts and emotional savvy. Girls would pick up boys' techniques for competing and working in large groups. But in a real playground, most boys and girls don't do that. On my last afternoon in Chicago, I accompanied Angel to a playground near his home, and it was no different from the scene described by social scientists decades ago. The boys were running around in a large group playing dodge ball (still legal in this park); the girls were standing around or using the swings, chatting with one or two friends.

Both sexes were still ignoring grown-ups' advice to play together, and maybe they knew best. Certainly they had been right about computers. Grown-ups' angst over the digital gender gap looks quaintly irrelevant now that teenage girls are addicted to instant messaging and the majority of Internet users in the States are female. Girls had no trouble adapting to computers once the machines did something that interested them. While academics plotted to get boys and girls playing together on computers, the kids seemed to recognize all along that it was a lame idea.

48   Angel played dodge ball for a while, then pulled out his Pox unit to take on another boy. They stood literally head to head, their foreheads touching, as they punched the buttons, oblivious to the shouts of the boys gathering around to watch the alpha pups.

"Man, this is cool."

"I'll battle you, Angel."

"Give it to me!"

52   "You can't even start it."

"I got up to Level 9."

"My brother got to 18."

"I play under the desk in class."

56   "You put Sound Off mode?"

"No sound. The teacher doesn't know."

"Can I try that, Mister?"

The last comment was from a kid who had spotted my Pox unit. He was looking up at me with such desperate eyes that I handed him the game and told him he could keep it. I may never again make someone so happy. As he worked his way through Level 1, it occurred to me that I was now complicit with Hasbro's marketers. Should I feel guilty? Would I want my own son playing Pox under the desk at school?

60   Well, it was probably no worse than shooting spitballs. Pox seemed benign, and maybe it would help him somehow. Maybe the discipline of memorizing all those permutations would prepare him for battles as an adult. I could imagine more constructive and entertaining ways to pass time—Pox was too tedious for a middle-aged

guy like me. But this boy was entranced, just as the makers of Pox had expected, and that seemed justification enough for giving him the game. He and Pox looked very cool together.

PERSONAL RESPONSE

Do you play video games? If you do, what is their appeal? If you do not, explain why.

QUESTIONS FOR CLASS OR SMALL-GROUP DISCUSSION

1. How well do you think Tierney defines the term "alpha pup"? Can you explain what it means in your own words? What strategy does he use for defining what may be unfamiliar concepts or terms throughout the paper, for example, "viral marketing" (paragraph 2) and " 'gender apartheid' " (paragraph 33)?

2. Tierney points out that "conservatives and liberals, fundamentalists and New Agers" find themselves curiously united on the issue of boys' video games (paragraph 13). What do you understand are the complaints of grownups on this issue?

3. In paragraph 18, Tierney asks what good playing video games does for boys. Do you think that video games should have "a socially redeeming value?" What value do video games have, in your opinion?

4. Tierney makes the generalization that girls are not nearly as attached to or engaged by video games as boys are. Do your experiences or observations confirm this generalization? If so, can you explain why it is true?

5. Tierney cites Henry Jenkins (whose article "Art Form for the Digital Age" precedes this one) on the issue of "the Mom problem" (paragraph 32). What do you think of Jenkins' analysis of video games as the embodiment of "classic boyhood themes"?

ROCK 'N' REVOLT

ISABELLE LEYMARIE

Isabelle Leymarie is a Franco-American jazz pianist, dancer, and musicologist who holds a Ph.D. from Columbia University in ethnomusicology. Formerly an assistant professor of African-American Studies at Yale University, she currently resides in Paris. Her study, "Salsa and Migration," appeared in an anthology of writing on Puerto Rico entitled The Commuter Nation *(1992). She has written several books, including* La Salsa et le Latin Jazz *(1993),* Musiques Caraïbes *(Caribbean Music) (1996), and* Cuban Fire: The Saga of Salsa and Latin Jazz *(2003). This essay first appeared in the February 1993 issue of* UNESCO Courier.

Rock, a musical and social phenomenon of unprecedented scope and intensity, raises in acute form the question of the relationship between music and violence. Its history has been fraught with violence. Jim Morrison, leader of The Doors, apostle of sex, alcohol, and LSD, died young, of a heart attack in his bathtub in Paris. Stars Jimi Hendrix and Janis Joplin both died of drug overdoses. Acid rock has become synonymous with punks and English football riots. The fans of Metallica and Guns n' Roses have burned cars, and during a recent concert in Montreal they wrecked a stadium and injured twelve people. The Sex Pistols proclaimed in their song "Anarchy in the UK": "I wanna destroy passers-by, for I wanna be anarchy." John Phillips, a member of The Mamas and The Papas, was reported by musicologist David Tame as claiming that any rock group can whip a crowd into a hysterical frenzy by carefully controlling a sequence of rhythms. In 1967 he went ahead and did just that in Phoenix. When Hell's Angels roughed up spectators during a Rolling Stones concert in California, rocker Mick Jagger remarked that "Something like this happens every time I play that song."

Although physically less conspicuous, violence is also expressed in the lyrics of urban music such as rap (a recent hit by star rapper Ice-T is entitled "Cop Killer") and free jazz ("We are not angry young men, we are enraged!" proclaimed saxophonist Archie Shepp in the late 1960s). Here, violence is palpable in lyrics, song titles, public statements by musicians, and in the music itself: the mega-volumes, "fuzz" effects, and distortions of rock, the hammer beats of rap, the shrieking saxophones and cascading notes of jazz, and the amplified bass of reggae. Violence is also associated with other types of music. In Stanley Kubrick's film *A Clockwork Orange,* the hero, Alex, driven crazy by the sounds of Beethoven, jumps out of a window. In Cuba during the 1920s and 1930s, concerts by rival bands playing the popular music known as *son* degenerated into brawls which had to be broken up by the police.

Violence, in more controlled forms, is present in many musical traditions, old and new: in the wailing of women in the funeral lamentations of Macedonia; in certain Senegalese songs whose lyrics pour out a stream of bitter invective against new wives brought into a household; in the drumbeats of African *griot* storytellers which once stimulated the ardor of warriors and today perform a similar role for the participants in traditional wrestling matches. It is found in martial music, in hunting calls, and in filmed thrillers where it plays a crucial role in setting the mood.

4   Violence is also present in classical music such as Handel's "Saul," Beethoven's *Eroica Symphony,* in operas generally, such as those of Verdi, who once said that he sought to express "passions above all else" and almost all of whose heroines die tragic deaths, in Mahler's *Fourth Symphony,* in Berlioz's *Symphonie Fantastique,* with its dramatic *Dies irae,* and in Stravinsky's *The Rite of Spring,* in which a virgin, sacrificed to the gods, dances herself to death (a riot broke out during the first performance). One could continue the list indefinitely.

An Extraordinary Power

Is it possible, asks musicologist Gilbert Rouget in his book on music and trance, that music may be endowed with a magical power capable of whipping people into the state of madness which the ancient Greeks called *mania?* Or does it have no objective reality? Rouget cites Timotheus of Miletus, who lived in the fourth century B.C. and once said that music "was capable of tempting Alexander away from a banquet to take up arms, and then of luring him back again to his guests with a lilting harmony." Rouget also quotes Boethius, who claimed that the Dorian mode inspired virtue, whereas the Phrygian mode aroused passion and violence, and refers to Aristotle's theory of the ethos of modes, which was similar to that of Boethius. He concludes that music can induce a trance in some cases and calm in others, and that it "derives its power from its integration into a given set of representations."

It is true that in order to grasp the symbolism in a particular type of music it is essential to be familiar with the set of representations into which it is integrated and the context in which it is performed. In the West, for example, the major modes evoke elation and rejoicing and the minor modes inspire melancholy, while in the East other modes such as Arab *maqam* and Indian *ragas* evoke totally different emotional moods. Similarly, drums and trumpets are regarded as martial instruments and flutes are associated with pastoral. All this is bound up with mental associations that are to a large extent culturally determined.

Leibniz spoke of the "anxiety-causing effect" of dissonance, and yet today dissonances, which have become commonplace in contemporary music, have lost much of their disquieting character (even Chopin's mazurkas, when first performed, were criticized for their "dissonance"). Verdi's use of double basses to introduce the final scene of *Othello,* Berlioz's use of percussion instruments in the *Symphonie Fantastique,* and Alfred Hitchcock's use of violins to heighten dramatic tension, are all illustrations of the way in which musical choices are both personal and culturally determined.

8   And yet music, when considered as a group of organized sounds and hence as a purely acoustic phenomenon, is also known to produce certain physiological and psychological effects which have been scientifically documented. Certain rhythms and sound frequencies, for example, can accelerate or slow down the human metabolic rate and even induce hypnosis. John Diamond, a specialist in behavioral physiology, has shown how the relative strength of certain muscles, a function which is easily measurable, varies according to the type of music to which people are listening. Animals and plants are also known to react physically to music. According to studies carried out in India, Russia, and the United States, plants seem to hate "heavy metal" rock music and twist themselves as far away as possible from the offending loudspeaker, while they adore classical violin and will grow even more lushly to the sounds of disco.

Noise engenders violence; it can even drive people to suicide. Some artificial noises, especially those which emanate from continuous-frequency engines, have been found to have a pathological effect on the body's cellular structure, and can sometimes cause cancer, while natural sounds, like those of waves, the warbling of birds, and certain types of classical or African music, can create a sense of wellbeing and even a healing effect by harmonizing with our biorhythms.

In recent years, the practice of music therapy has enjoyed considerable popularity. Members of the Research Group in Pediatric Anaesthesiology at the Hospital for Sick Children in Paris and doctors in many American hospitals have used carefully selected types of music to reduce their patients' dependency on tranquillizers. In *The Burmese Harp* (1956), a fine film by the Japanese director Kon Ichikawa, a soldier-musician saps his comrades' will to fight whenever he plays and sings.

Study of the relationship between music and violence also raises the question of the political aspect of music. In many parts of the world, musicians such as the bards of Nepal, the *griots* or the musicians of Ethiopia are perceived as pariahs or as socially inferior, and are believed to lead dissolute lives and be addicted to drugs and alcohol. Music has often been used as an instrument of domination. In some African societies, *mirliton* reed pipes and other instruments provide a musical accompaniment during the ritual parading of masks, which women and children must not see and which perpetuate male dominance.

12   The French writer Jacques Attali has observed that in Western societies the upper classes have always encouraged artistic creation, but only in order to maintain the established order and legitimize their own authority. In the 1950s, the Dominican dictator Rafael Trujillo y Molina encouraged the practice of the *merengue,* a dance closely related to the samba, but gave orders that the musicians should sing his praises and exiled those who opposed him. In many countries, music has become a form of propaganda or been appropriated by the Church, and judgments about music have been an endorsement of manipulation and intolerance.

Authoritarian colonial regimes arbitrarily associated drums with violence and debauchery, and long banned black music. The "New Age" writer Corinne Hélène claims that jazz and juvenile delinquency go hand in hand. But this baseless claim is fraught with prejudice, for how can the beautiful and expressive phrasing of a Sarah Vaughan or an Ella Fitzgerald be associated with juvenile delinquency? Why should jazz as a whole be connected with this social problem when most young jazz musicians are now graduates of music conservatories and universities and the overwhelming majority of jazz fans are intellectuals? How indeed, when music, for many deprived black and Hispanic adolescents of America's urban ghettos, far from leading to delinquency, is often a lifeline?

In the United States, moral-majority pressure groups have stigmatized some rock records as "obscene," in the hope of getting them withdrawn from the market, but they also tried to ban the Robert Mapplethorpe photo exhibition and other artistic events which did not correspond with their ideals. On the other hand, some kinds of music such as "Muzak," which supposedly increase consumer sales and induce people in restaurants to eat more but are actually a form of audio-brainwashing and noise pollution, are broadcast all day long in shopping centres and other public areas.

Jacques Attali has also remarked that "show business, the star system, and the hit parade are signs of deep-rooted institutional and cultural colonization." In this context music, through a sometimes violent protest against official art and the mechanization of society, becomes a means of fighting authority. "Music exists," adds Jacques Attali, "to help us hear the sound of change. It forces us to invent new categories, to come up with a new momentum capable of rejuvenating a view of society that has become ossified, trapped, moribund." This is partly true of rock and its rebellious anti-establishment stance, and of jazz, rap, and reggae—all musical forms which proclaim their black identity and have rejected old models along with the hypocrisy and inhumanity of materialism. In certain ritualized settings, notably during festivals, subversive songs are often used to express grievances against the establishment.

A Yearning for Harmony

16 Does music engender violence or does it express violence? And if it does express violence, does it, by sublimating violent impulses and dissipating tensions, play a cathartic role and "soothe the savage breast"? Music, for Attali, is the "audible tape of society's vibrations and signs." It is undeniably deeply rooted in the collective psychology: rock, rap, free jazz, and reggae all express the violence of the cultures which have bred them. But people and their environment are inseparable: the pent-up violence in the individual affects society and vice versa. While music reflects the collective *gestalt* of a society, its particular form of expression also reflects the emotions of the musician.

In China, Egypt, India, and ancient Greece, music was believed to possess a certain ethical value and the power to uplift or debase the soul. In ancient China, the imperial government existed in harmony with the twelve celestial tones, and during the Confucian Chin dynasty, certain "virtuous" songs and musical instruments were reputed to temper the harshness of the regime. Classical music is also imbued with spirituality: Mozart's Don Giovanni brings down divine vengeance upon himself by assassinating a nobleman and burns in hell for it. Liszt aspired to compose inspirational works, and although Wagner's *Tetralogy* (the four-opera *Ring* cycle) expresses both the fall of humanity cut adrift from the gods and the distress of the artist faced with the world's misfortunes, Wagner had a deeply moral view of art.

The French sociologist Jean Duvignaud has written that art expresses "nostalgia for a lost form of communication in the shape of a forbidden dream that is continually revived by the irrepressible desire of the human emotional impulse." He goes on to say that a successful work of art "rebuilds behind the self a unity which pieces together the shards of a divided humanity." Now that idealism has been demolished and the philosophy of music has become a thing of the past, while the media (which tend to put the visual image before the musical message) bombard us with vulgar and iconoclastic music, it is more than ever incumbent on musicians and artists in general to adopt an ethical position. The most influential creators of the twentieth century, notably the film-makers whose art is one of our era's most powerful forms of expression—artists such as Kurosawa, Ozu, and Satyajit Ray—have been passionate humanists.

Musical eurhythmics presupposes both inner and outer harmony, peace with oneself and with the universe. Violence, in its latent form, is an intrinsic part of human nature and of the universe generally. But when violence is unleashed and expressed, often in a paroxysm, in music or other art forms, it is a symptom either of social unrest or of inner imbalance or torment, emotional deprivation, and arrested development. And just as the wind can rise from a gentle breeze to a raging hurricane, so music can enchant or destroy us. It is for musicians to create works which enrich life, which contribute to the harmony of humanity, without compromising the quality of their art (some forms of therapeutic music, such as "New Age" music, do not really have any aesthetic value).

20 However, when music achieves perfection, it allows us to catch a glimpse of the divine; it becomes, according to a Buddhist belief, the most refined art, the path to enlightenment. According to the Taoist sage, Zhuangzi, "Music allows man to

remain pure, simple, sincere, and in this way to rediscover his primitive emotions." (A few centuries later, Wagner would also use music to explore primitive forms of expression.) The great violinist Yehudi Menuhin once observed that "music creates order out of chaos." Nietzsche's humorous conclusion was that "Without music, life would be a mistake."

PERSONAL RESPONSE

Describe your favorite kind of music and why it appeals to you. Are you ever criticized for listening to it? What characteristic of this music do you think produces negative or even hostile reactions in some people?

QUESTIONS FOR CLASS OR SMALL-GROUP DISCUSSION

1. Leymarie gives examples of the ways in which certain mental associations with music "are to a large extent culturally determined" (paragraphs 6 and 7). Can you give other examples of the point she makes in this section of her essay?

2. Give examples of musicians or musical groups who have made political statements through their music (paragraphs 11–15), especially those who use music as "a means of fighting authority" (paragraph 15). Discuss the effects, if any, of their music.

3. How would you answer Leymarie's question, "Does music engender violence or does it express violence" (paragraph 16)? Discuss whether you think music creates violent behavior or simply reflects the culture that produces it.

4. Leymarie discusses her subject objectively for the most part, but she offers her own opinions from time to time. Find examples of such subjectivity and consider whether it in any way weakens the essay.

RAP, RAGE AND REDVOLUTION

Cristina Verán

Cristina Verán is a journalist, historian, educator, and United Nations correspondent who has documented global cultural phenomena and socio-political movements extensively. Her work has featured in a wide range of media including Vibe, Ms. Magazine, ColorLines, News From Indian Country, Oneworld, Newsday, The Witness, NPR, *and* The Source, *among many others. "Rap, Rage and REDvolution" was published in* The Village Voice *on April 20th, 2004.*

Conjuring up the charge of cavalries and natives on some futuristic-western warpath, OutKast stormed the 2004 Grammys in February with the brazenness of the former, while bedecked as the latter. Resplendent in neon green Halloween-Hiawatha approximations of Native American regalia—fringe, headbands, and feathers—Andre and Big Boi rose before smoking teepees, prancing proudly through their chart-slaying "Hey Ya!," the chorus of which is itself evocative of powwow singing. Was it some kind of tribute, or did the winners of the Album of the Year Grammy unwittingly channel Al Jolson's "Mammy"?

It's a question many Native Americans have considered, responding promptly to launch boycotts and web petitions voicing their collective displeasure. CBS's brief, lukewarm apology—"if anyone was offended"—brought zero resolution, particularly since OutKast themselves refused even to comment. Two months later, people are still waiting; during an April 1 protest outside the network's Minneapolis affiliate, one person was arrested.

"Janet Jackson's right breast was exposed for three-quarters of a second and both the House and Senate convened hearings immediately, [yet] vulgarisms about Native Americans are prime-time fare . . . and no one does anything," notes Suzan Shown Harjo (Hodulgee Muscogee/Cheyenne), executive director of the Morningstar Institute, in her "Open Letter to Michael Powell, Andre 3000 and Big Boi," first published in *Indian Country Today*.

4   Hip-hop, meanwhile, is speaking to the issue as well. "[It's] currently the most popular music on the reservations," explains Don Kelly, executive director of the Native American Music Awards. Litefoot (Cherokee), NAMA's Male Artist of the Year for 2003, takes up the fight with his new single "What's It Gonna Take": "We only good with feathers on/Don't exist when they're off/I punch the remote/feeling like my whole race is a joke."

Among the masses descending this week upon Albuquerque, New Mexico for the Woodstock-sized Gathering of Nations powwow will be scores of young folks representing the burgeoning Native hip-hop scene on reservations and in urban Indian communities across the continent. They're there not just for fancydancing and fry bread but to catch live sets by headliner Litefoot and other key Native rap artists like Shadowyze (Muscogee Creek/Cherokee) and Tac Tile (San Juan Pueblo/Rosebud Sioux) at the Gathering's Reach the Rez concert, presented by Native Style Entertainment and the nonprofit Association for American Indian Development.

Beyond this forum, from the mouths and mics of other indigenous MCs like Tribal Live and Natay (Navajo), B'Taka & Rollin' Fox (Chiricahua Apache), and New York's own Warriors Blood (from the upstate Akwesasne Mohawk territory) flow universes of verses about life on the rez and on streets from Albuquerque to Tulsa, Minneapolis (home base of the American Indian Movement), even Newark. But rapping about and sampling from their own culture—rather than, say, African Americans'—has hardly earned them props from the mainstream rap world.

Among the handful of American hip-hop performers self-identifying as indigenous who have achieved mainstream recognition, none has been a direct crossover from the Native scene. Two—Taboo of Black Eyed Peas (Shoshone) and Tomahawk Funk (Oglala Lakota) of Funkdoobiest—have been members of non–Indian-specific groups. Still others have come up through largely Latino contexts. Kid Frost's "La Raza" proclaimed, in 1992, "It's in my blood to be an Aztec Warrior/Chicano, and

I'm brown and I'm proud." Myriad West Coast Chicano crews like Aztlán Nation, as well as some East Coast notables—think Tony Touch (Puerto Rican Taino) and battle-rap champ Immortal Technique (of mixed Afro/Indian Peruvian extraction)—have also promoted *indigenismo*.

8   "There is an unwillingness to give Native American artists credit for expressing, really, what hip-hop is supposed to be about: the music and the heritage of the people who present it," says Davey D. Cook, host of Pacifica Radio's *Hard Knock* program and the authoritative hip-hop site DaveyD.com. "If an artist like Litefoot doesn't come out with a song that has a James Brown sample or an 'Apache' bassline, people aren't trying to hear it," he says, appreciating the ironic name of the Incredible Bongo Band's classic breakbeat. Regardless, he's started spinning *REDvolution*, Litefoot's forthcoming, 11th album.

"The way (OutKast) were putting their hands over their mouths with that 'woo woo woo woo' stuff," recalls Lance Gumbs, elected representative of Long Island's Shinnecock Nation. "I couldn't even see them anymore. I just saw white America, that same tired history." The former DJ, who would trek from the rez regularly to attend Grandmaster Flash jams in the Bronx and Harlem during the early '80s, emphasizes, "That these guys are African American made it even more disturbing."

"I can relate to OutKast's irreverent approach in their stage performances because I also use a lot of humor in my own art," says Bently Spang (Northern Cheyenne), whose current Tekcno Pow Wow project melds aspects of hip-hop, techno, and more traditional Native performance. "But in this case, they perpetuated the same stereotypes we're fighting against," he explains, "like the Washington Redskins, the Atlanta Braves' tomahawk chop, the University of Illinois' Chief Illiniwek character."

OutKast's unauthorized inclusion of a sacred traditional Navajo "Beauty Way" song in their performance was, itself, taken as serious offense. "I don't know if Buddhists and Christians find those little Buddha statues and Jesus night-lights I see everywhere offensive," says Raquel Chapa (Ledan Apache/Cherokee/Yaqui), a photographer and collections technician at the National Museum of the American Indian. "[But] Native Americans, for the most part, are more sensitive in terms of our spirituality."

12   Anthony Lee Sr., president of the Navajo Medicine Man Association, made clear to the *Navajo Times* that "it's not for the purpose in promotion of entertainment. . . . [The song] must be kept in the proper respects, not to be taken out of context—especially without consulting the Blessing Way chapters."

"Sinéad O'Connor ripped up a picture of the pope on *Saturday Night Live* and there was an uproar, worldwide," notes Litefoot. "What Andre and company did was the exact equivalent: outrageous, despicable," he says. "We as Native Americans don't have the kind of political power and access that the Catholic Church has, though." For more than 100 years, in fact, Christian churches partnered with the U.S. government to forcibly remove Indian children from their communities for spiritual, cultural, and linguistic "re-education" at boarding-school gulags.

The World Intellectual Property Organization (April 26, in fact, has been declared World Intellectual Property Day) and the United Nations Permanent Forum on Indigenous Issues recognize a collective, perpetual copyright to distinct indige-nous cultural practices—sharply contrasting with U.S. copyright law's temporally limited, individual-rights approach. Atencio López, a legal expert from Panama's Kuna people, defines WIPO's dilemma as "wholesale plundering or pirating of in-digenous knowledge and products without any related benefits [or] concern for the copyright of the peoples affected." Does irreverent, artistic appropriation by pop stars fall into the same, er, canoe?

Black performers who have repped names, accoutrements, and "chants" attribut-able to indigenous peoples of the Americas include Tupac Amaru Shakur, his name thoughtfully bestowed by his then Black Panther mom out of respect for the 16th-century Inca who battled the Spanish conquistadors in what is now Peru. Far less rev-erent have been the feathered headdresses sported by artists from MC Pow Wow of Afrika Bambaataa's Soulsonic Force to hip-hop's quintessential court jesters, Flavor Flav of Public Enemy and Biz Markie, to the late Lisa "Left Eye" Lopes—while in a suede string bikini!—on a 1999 cover of *Honey*. Recently, *Vibe* featured a headdress-donning fashion model of its own.

16   Some song lyrics have been equally questionable. Here's the Sugar Hill Gang, in 1982's "Apache," after shoutouts to General Custer the Indian-killer: "I sting squaws, then I run away/Hi Ho Silver, is what I say." Jay-Z, in "Girls, Girls, Girls," states, "I got this Indian squaw and on the day that I met her/Asked her what tribe she with, red dot or feather." *Squaw,* perhaps unbeknownst to these and such other "s-word"–dropping rappers as Common, Foxy Brown, and Chubb Rock, derives from an Algonquin term for female genitalia, but was adopted by European fur traders to refer to Native women overall.

Biggie's "Navajos creep me/in they teepee" is also, at best, misinformed: Tradi-tional Navajo homes are hogans, not teepees. Boot Camp Click's Buckshot, mean-while, defines his "BDI Thug" alter-ego as derived from "Thugla, who were wiped out with the Native Americans," oblivious to the word's origin not in the history of American Indians but in that of the Indian subcontinent—an ancient cult that en-gaged in murderous ritual rampages to honor Kali, the Hindu goddess of destruction.

"American society . . . should understand that all of those images—from the No-ble Savage to the Bloodthirsty Indian—are based not on our identification but some-one else's definition," cautions Spang, whose work was recently featured in *Only Skin Deep,* the International Center of Photography's exhibition challenging American notions of race and identity.

This country's "Black Indians"—descendants of Africans who were freed or self-liberated during slavery and adopted into tribes like the Seminoles—contributed to the debate last month when *Hard Knock Radio* brought together two such figures: noted Bay Area activist Marcel Diallo and Shaka Zulu of New Orleans, who dons full-feathered "Indian" regalia during annual Mardi Gras festivities. They joined phone-in guests Litefoot and Ernie Paniccioli (Cree), a legendary hip-hop photog-rapher whose recent books include *Who Shot Ya?* and *There's a God on the Mic,* for a two-part dialogue. "[Diallo and Zulu] thought the OutKast performance was pretty cool," reports Davey D.

20   This echoes his experience at P. Diddy's L.A. Grammy Party, in fact. The hosts "stopped the music there just so people could watch OutKast's performance," Davey D recalls. "Everybody clapped and cheered, saying 'Man, that was incredible!' "

Nowhere has the chasm between Native America and black America been expressed more divisively in a hip-hop context than during the "Big Ballers" concert last May at Nassau Coliseum, featuring Ludacris, Busta, and other big names. Lance Gumbs, the show promoter, was excited to include Litefoot on such a bill. The predominantly black crowd, however, voiced its extreme antagonism toward Litefoot—and perhaps all Native Americans—from the start. "As soon as we came out onto that stage," he says, "people began to spit at me, throwing up their middle fingers and screaming racial obscenities."

"Fuck you, prairie n____s!" "Go back to your teepee, red motherfucker!" an angry chorus of woo-woo-wooed boos—all of these were spewed before Litefoot said even one word on the mic. Backed by a flawlessly choreographed stage show comprising Ho-Chunk and Aztec traditional dancers and B-boy legends from the Rock Steady Crew, Litefoot and company walked off the stage in disgust when the third song had hardly begun. The 60,000-strong crowd of tittie-baring, wannabe-blinging, "I'm a ho"-chanting Ludacris fans never even gave this Indian a chance.

"I have never bought into that facile, disingenuous fable that oppressed people cannot be racist," says Paniccioli, who was present at the Coliseum and who has otherwise been warmly embraced by hip-hop's biggest stars and among many sectors of the Black community.

24   "I've extended a sincere invitation to OutKast to join us at the Gathering of Nations," says Litefoot, "and on next year's tour to over 150 reservations." He makes clear that, in any case, an apology is still both desired and expected by Indian country. "This would give Andre 3000 the perfect platform to say what he has to say—to the largest predominantly Native American crowd he would ever be able to gather in person."

Hey ya, OutKast. Are you listening?

PERSONAL RESPONSE

Do you think that OutKast should apologize? Explain your answer.

QUESTIONS FOR CLASS OR SMALL-GROUP DISCUSSION

1. How effective do you find Verán's contrasting the lukewarm or missing apologies to Native Americans over Outkast's appearance at the 2004 Grammys with the public outcry over Janet Jackson's exposure during the 2004 Super Bowl? What is Verán's point? Is it a fair comparison?

2. Explain the title of this essay. How does it reflect the content of the essay?

3. In paragraph 8, Verán quotes Davey D. Cook as saying: " 'There is an unwillingness to give Native American artists credit for expressing, really, what

hip-hop is supposed to be about.' " In your opinion, what is hip-hop "supposed to be about"? Do you agree with what Cooks says it is about?

4. Lance Gumbs makes this remark about Outkast's performance at the 2004 Grammys: " 'That these guys are African American made it even more disturbing' " (paragraph 9). What do you think he means by that statement? Do you agree with him?

5. Assuming that you are familiar with at least one of the musicians or groups that Verán mentions as using racist lyrics, select the one you know best and describe the lyrics in their music. Do you agree that they are racist?

○ PERSPECTIVES ON MUSIC AND VIDEO GAMES ○

Suggested Writing Topics

1. Argue your position on Henry Jenkins's opening statement in "Art Form for the Digital Age" that video games shape our culture and should be taken seriously.

2. Henry Jenkins in "Art Form for the Digital Age writes: "It remains to be seen whether games can provide players the freedom they want and still provide an emotionally satisfying and thematically meaningful shape to the experience" (paragraph 16). Using the example of a specific video game (or more than one, if you like), argue whether you believe that games today have achieved that goal.

3. In paragraph 1 of "Rock 'n' Revolt," Isabelle Leymarie refers to a claim by John Philips "that any rock group can whip a crowd into a hysterical frenzy by carefully controlling a sequence of rhythms." If you have ever seen such a phenomenon, where a crowd became hysterically frenzied, describe what happened and explore why you think music has that kind of control over people's emotions.

4. Argue in support of or against the statement in John Tierney's "Here Come the Alpha Pups" that video games have "a socially redeeming value."

5. Drawing on Cristina Verán's "Rap, Rage and REDvolution," explain your position on the subject of whether Outkast owes Native Americans an apology for their behavior at the 2004 Grammys.

6. Do a detailed analysis of the lyrics of a hip-hop song that you are familiar with.

7. Analyze the lyrics of a song that you believe to be socially responsible or that comments on a current social issue.

8. Analyze your involvement with a video game that you find particularly compelling.

9. Drawing on any of the readings in this chapter, argue in support of or against the statement that music or video games influence violent behavior in individuals.

Research Topics

1. Henry Jenkins in "Art Form for the Digital Age" notes that a leading critic in the 1920s argued that the important contributions to America's artistic expression came from popular culture, especially "jazz, the Broadway musical, the Hollywood cinema and the comic strip" (paragraph 9). Select one of those forms and research its development as a culturally respectable medium. Consider questions like the following: How long did it take for the form to gain legitimacy? What was the nature of early criticism of it? What contributions does the form make to culture? What are the chief characteristics of its evolution from its primitive beginnings to sophistication?

2. In the opening paragraph of "Rock 'n' Revolt," Isabelle Leymarie gives examples of rock musicians and groups whose music and/or lives have been "fraught with violence." Research one, two, or several of the performers or groups that Leymarie names, and argue in support of or against the view that they are violent or that they are menaces to society.

3. Isabelle Leymarie refers to "certain physiological and psychological effects [of music] which have been scientifically documented" ("Rock 'n' Revolt," paragraph 8). Research the phenomenon of the physiological and psychological effects of music. Look not only for information about scientific research on the subject but also for comments or criticisms of people skeptical of such research. Weigh the evidence and arrive at your own opinion on the subject.

4. Research a particular musician, musical group, or entertainer from the 1950s, 1960s, or 1970s. Find out the performer's history, the audience he or she appealed to, what distinguished him or her from others, and what his or her influence seems to have been on popular culture. Formulate your own assessment of the entertainer's significance and make that your thesis or central idea.

5. Research a particular kind of music, such as hip-hop, "grunge," alternative, blues, jazz, or salsa for the purpose of identifying its chief characteristics, the way it differs from and is influenced by other kinds of music, and its artistic merit or social significance. Include opposing viewpoints and argue your own position on its merits or significance.

6. Examine allegations of racism, sexism, and/or homophobia leveled against a particular video game, song, musician, or group and draw your own conclusions about the fairness, appropriateness, and/or accuracy of those allegations.

7. Research the latest studies and opinion pieces on the cultural impact of video games and draw your own conclusions about their importance in shaping culture.

8. Research the history of a popular hand-held video game, including among other things marketing strategy, target audience, responses of users, and longevity of the game.

RESPONDING TO VISUALS

Musicians The Game (left) and 50 Cent (right) perform during the taping of the Vibe Awards in Santa Monica, California, November 15, 2004. Source: Robert Galbraith/Reuters/Landov

1. What do the performers' facial expressions reveal about how they feel about performing?
2. What do the clothes and jewelry of the performers reveal about them? How do the two performers contrast?
3. How does the background function, especially the blurred graffiti on the wall?
4. Vibe awards are presented to outstanding performers in urban music. What impression of urban music might someone who is unfamiliar with it get from this photograph?

RESPONDING TO VISUALS

Youth Express Leader and member, ages 19 and 13, shooting at a Point Blank® video game with red and blue replica 45 caliber plastic pistols in St. Paul, Minnesota. Source: Steve Skjold/Alamy

1. What is the implied message of this photograph? What details of the image contribute to your understanding of that message?
2. What do the looks on the two young men's faces suggest about their enjoyment of the video game?
3. What is the effect of the photographer's perspective? Might a change in perspective alter the implied message of the image?
4. How would the image change were the two young people white or some other ethnic group? Does their age have an effect on your perception of the image?

CHAPTER

8

MEDIA STUDIES

Media studies is a broad subject area that examines the effect of the media on individuals and society. It encompasses all sorts of media—film, television, newspapers, magazines, radio, and the Internet—and looks at the ways that these media influence our opinions, thoughts, behavior, and attitudes. While the subjects of the other chapters in Part Two are also "media," those chapters look at issues relating to specific media; this chapter considers broader issues relating to "the media" as a whole or several kinds of media. Media analysts often serve as watchdogs against threats to freedom of speech and thought. They concern themselves with social issues such as media violence, censorship in the media, biased reporting, discrimination in programming, and the way in which the media shape social and political discourse. They analyze the power of the media and the power behind the media.

A look at the goals and purposes of university media studies programs gives an idea of what is involved in "media studies." Such programs examine the social, cultural, political, ethical, aesthetic, legal, and economic effects of the media and are interested in the variety of contexts in which the media has influence in those areas. They cite in their rationales for their programs the proliferation of media, the interconnectedness of media on a global level, and the pervasiveness of media in our lives. Furthermore, large numbers of groups, agencies, and organizations identify themselves as "media watchers" and many are media activists. You will find both conservative and liberal, extremists and moderates on such a list.

One particular aspect of popular culture that media analysts have long been interested in is violence in the media and its influence on people, especially young people. The first reading in this chapter provides an overview of the issue by one of the most well-known contributors in the debate over the role media violence plays in forming children's characters and values. An excerpt from her book *Mayhem: Violence as Public Entertainment* (1998), Sissela Bok's "Aggression: The Impact of Media Violence" discusses a topic that is often quite volatile. As you read what she has to say, consider your own position on this controversial issue.

Media watchers know that which news stories are reported and how they are reported—what gets emphasized and what gets left out—can shape or destroy someone's reputation or bring an issue to the public's attention. Peter H. Gibbon's "The End of Admiration: The Media and the Loss of Heroes" focuses on the subject of the role that journalists play in building or destroying the reputations of public figures. He suggests that journalists, by encouraging cynicism and celebrity worship, discourage hero worship and idealism. He believes that, with the media's central bias toward bad news, journalists have made it difficult if not impossible for Americans to have heroes. Consider his words carefully as you read his essay. Is he on target with his critique, or does he over-generalize or ignore positive examples to prove his point? Can you supply examples to either support or refute his argument?

Another issue of concern to media analysts is commercial media's dependence on advertising and their need to make a profit. Jean Kilbourne in "Advertising's Influence on Media Content" argues that advertising has a big influence not only on audiences but also on the media itself. She explains two major ways in which that influence is exerted and gives examples to support her allegations. Kilbourne would argue that the power advertisers hold over commercial media produces a biased media. As you read her examples and her analyses of the influence of advertisers on various kinds of media, see if you can think of other examples to either support or refute what she claims.

As Jean Kilbourne and Peter Gibbon illustrate, media analysts are quite interested in whether the media is biased in the way it selects the information it reports. Many people believe the media is biased toward a liberal social and political position. Although many think the media too liberal, others think it too conservative. Indeed, often liberals accuse the media of being too conservative while conservatives accuse it of being too liberal. John Leo and P. J. O'Rourke, who self-identify as conservatives, take up this subject of biased media in their commentaries. Leo in "Liberal Media? I'm Shocked!" is worried that far too many journalists are liberal and thus give privilege to news that represents their own political and social agendas. O'Rourke, who identifies himself as a conservative "a little to the right of Rush Limbaugh," explains in "I Agree with Me" that he has little patience with conservative news programs and books, though he does not think much of liberal media either. Do you listen to any of the programs or have you read any of the books that he mentions?

AGGRESSION: THE IMPACT OF MEDIA VIOLENCE
Sissela Bok

Born in Sweden and educated in Switzerland, France, and the United States, Sissela Bok earned a Ph.D. in philosophy from Harvard University. She has been a professor of philosophy at Brandeis University and is currently a Distinguished Fellow at the Harvard Center for Population and Development Studies. Widely known for her writings on topics in bioethics, applied ethics, biography and autobiography, and public affairs, her books include Lying: Moral Choice in Public and Private Life *(1978),* Secrets: On the Ethics of Concealment and Revelation *(1983),* A Strategy for Peace: Human Values and the Threat of War *(1989),* Alva Myrdal: A Daughter's Memoir *(1991),* Common Values *(1995), and* Mayhem: Violence as Public Entertainment *(1998), from which the following is taken.*

Even if media violence were linked to no other debilitating effects, it would remain at the center of public debate so long as the widespread belief persists that it glamorizes aggressive conduct, removes inhibitions toward such conduct, arouses viewers, and invites imitation. It is only natural that the links of media violence to aggression should be of special concern to families and communities. Whereas increased fear, desensitization, and appetite primarily affect the viewers themselves, aggression directly injures others and represents a more clear-cut violation of standards of behavior. From the point of view of public policy, therefore, curbing aggression has priority over alleviating subtler psychological and moral damage.

Public concern about a possible link between media violence and societal violence has further intensified in the past decade, as violent crime reached a peak in the early 1990s, yet has shown no sign of downturn, even after crime rates began dropping in 1992. Media coverage of violence, far from declining, has escalated since then, devoting ever more attention to celebrity homicides and copycat crimes. The latter, explicitly modeled on videos or films and sometimes carried out with meticulous fidelity to detail, are never more relentlessly covered in the media than when they are committed by children and adolescents. Undocumented claims that violent copycat crimes are mounting in number contribute further to the ominous sense of threat that these crimes generate. Their dramatic nature drains away the public's attention from other, more mundane forms of aggression that are much more commonplace, and from . . . other . . . harmful effects of media violence.

Media analyst Ken Auletta reports that, in 1992, a mother in France sued the head of a state TV channel that carried the American series *MacGyver,* claiming that her son was accidentally injured as a result of having copied MacGyver's recipe for making a bomb. At the time, Auletta predicted that similar lawsuits were bound to become a weapon against media violence in America's litigious culture. By 1996, novelist John Grisham had sparked a debate about director Oliver Stone's film *Natural Born Killers,* which is reputedly linked to more copycat assaults and murders than any other movie to date. Grisham wrote in protest against the film after learning that a friend of his, Bill Savage, had been killed by nineteen-year-old Sarah Edmondson and her boyfriend Benjamin Darras, eighteen: after repeated viewings of Stone's film on video, the two had gone on a killing spree with the film's murderous, gleeful heroes expressly in mind. Characterizing the film as "a horrific movie that glamorized casual mayhem and bloodlust," Grisham proposed legal action:

> Think of a film as a product, something created and brought to market, not too dissimilar from breast implants. Though the law has yet to declare movies to be products, it is only a small step away. If something goes wrong with the product, either by design or defect, and injury ensues, then its makers are held responsible. . . . It will take only one large verdict against the like of Oliver Stone, and his production company, and perhaps the screenwriter, and the studio itself, and then the party will be over. The verdict will come from the heartland, far away from Southern California, in some small courtroom with no cameras. A jury will finally say enough is enough; that the demons placed in Sarah Edmondson's mind were not solely of her own making.

4   As a producer of books made into lucrative movies—themselves hardly devoid of violence—and as a veteran of contract negotiations within the entertainment industry, Grisham may have become accustomed to thinking of films in industry terms as "products." As a seasoned courtroom lawyer, he may have found the analogy

between such products and breast implants useful for invoking product liability to pin personal responsibility on movie producers and directors for the lethal consequences that their work might help unleash.

Oliver Stone retorted that Grisham was drawing "upon the superstition about the magical power of pictures to conjure up the undead spectre of censorship." In dismissing concerns about the "magical power of pictures" as merely superstitious, Stone sidestepped the larger question of responsibility fully as much as Grisham had sidestepped that of causation when he attributed liability to filmmakers for anything that "goes wrong" with their products so that "injury ensues." Because aggression is the most prominent effect associated with media violence in the public's mind, it is natural that it should also remain the primary focus of scholars in the field. The "aggressor effect" has been studied both to identify the short term, immediate impact on viewers after exposure to TV violence, and the long-term influences. . . . There is near-unanimity by now among investigators that exposure to media violence contributes to lowering barriers to aggression among some viewers. This lowering of barriers may be assisted by the failure of empathy that comes with growing desensitization, and intensified to the extent that viewers develop an appetite for violence—something that may lead to still greater desire for violent programs and, in turn, even greater desensitization.

When it comes to viewing violent pornography, levels of aggression toward women have been shown to go up among male subjects who view sexualized violence against women. "In explicit depictions of sexual violence," a report by the American Psychological Association's Commission on Youth and Violence concludes after surveying available research data, "it is the message about violence more than the sexual nature of the materials that appears to affect the attitudes of adolescents about rape and violence toward women." Psychologist Edward Donnerstein and colleagues have shown that if investigators tell subjects that aggression is legitimate, then show them violent pornography, their aggression toward women increases. In slasher films, the speed and ease with which "one's feelings can be transformed from sensuality into viciousness may surprise even those quite conversant with the links between sexual and violent urges."

Viewers who become accustomed to seeing violence as an acceptable, common, attractive way of dealing with problems find it easier to identify with aggressors and to suppress any sense of pity or respect for victims of violence. Media violence has been found to have stronger effects of this kind when carried out by heroic, impressive, or otherwise exciting figures, especially when they are shown as invulnerable and are rewarded or not punished for what they do. The same is true when the violence is shown as justifiable, when viewers identify with the aggressors rather than with their victims, when violence is routinely resorted to, and when the programs have links to how viewers perceive their own environment.

8   While the consensus that such influences exist grows among investigators as research accumulates, there is no consensus whatsoever about the size of the correlations involved. Most investigators agree that it will always be difficult to disentangle the precise effects of exposure to media violence from the many other factors contributing to societal violence. No reputable scholar accepts the view expressed by 21

percent of the American public in 1995, blaming television more than any other factor for teenage violence. Such tentative estimates as have been made suggest that the
media account for between 5 and 15 percent of societal violence. Even these estimates
are rarely specific enough to indicate whether what is at issue is all violent crime, or
such crimes along with bullying and aggression more generally.

One frequently cited investigator proposes a dramatically higher and more specific estimate than others. Psychiatrist Brandon S. Centerwall has concluded from
large-scale epidemiological studies of "white homicide" in the United States, Canada,
and South Africa in the period from 1945 to 1974, that it escalated in these societies
within ten to fifteen years of the introduction of television, and that one can therefore deduce that television has brought a doubling of violent societal crime:

> Of course, there are many factors other than television that influence the amount of
> violent crime. Every violent act is the result of a variety of forces coming together—
> poverty, crime, alcohol and drug abuse, stress—of which childhood TV exposure is
> just one. Nevertheless, the evidence indicates that if hypothetically, television tech-
> nology had never been developed, there would today be 10,000 fewer homicides each
> year in the United States, 70,000 fewer rapes, and 700,000 fewer injurious assaults.
> Violent crime would be half of what it now is.

Centerwall's study, published in 1989, includes controls for such variables as
firearm possession and economic growth. But his conclusions have been criticized for
not taking into account other factors, such as population changes during the time period studied, that might also play a role in changing crime rates. Shifts in policy and
length of prison terms clearly affect these levels as well. By now, the decline in levels
of violent crime in the United States since Centerwall's study was conducted, even
though television viewing did not decline ten to fifteen years before, does not square
with his extrapolations. As for "white homicide" in South Africa under apartheid,
each year brings more severe challenges to official statistics from that period.

Even the lower estimates, however, of around 5 to 10 percent of violence as correlated with television exposure, point to substantial numbers of violent crimes in a
population as large as America's. But if such estimates are to be used in discussions of
policy decisions, more research will be needed to distinguish between the effects of
television in general and those of particular types of violent programming, and to indicate specifically what sorts of images increase the aggressor effect and by what
means; and throughout to be clearer about the nature of the aggressive acts studied.

12   Media representatives naturally request proof of such effects before they are
asked to undertake substantial changes in programming. In considering possible
remedies for a problem, inquiring into the reasons for claims about risks is entirely
appropriate. It is clearly valid to scrutinize the research designs, sampling methods,
and possible biases of studies supporting such claims, and to ask about the reasoning
leading from particular research findings to conclusions. But to ask for some demon-
strable pinpointing of just when and how exposure to media violence affects levels of
aggression sets a dangerously high threshold for establishing risk factors.

We may never be able to trace, retrospectively, the specific set of television programs that contributed to a particular person's aggressive conduct. The same is true

when it comes to the links between tobacco smoking and cancer, between drunk driving and automobile accidents, and many other risk factors presenting public health hazards. Only recently have scientists identified the specific channels through which tobacco generates its carcinogenic effects. Both precise causative mechanisms and documented occurrences in individuals remain elusive. Too often, media representatives formulate their requests in what appear to be strictly polemical terms, raising dismissive questions familiar from debates over the effects of tobacco: "How can anyone definitively pinpoint the link between media violence and acts of real-life violence? If not, how can we know if exposure to media violence constitutes a risk factor in the first place?"

Yet the difficulty in carrying out such pinpointing has not stood in the way of discussing and promoting efforts to curtail cigarette smoking and drunk driving. It is not clear, therefore, why a similar difficulty should block such efforts when it comes to media violence. The perspective of "probabilistic causation" . . . is crucial to public debate about the risk factors in media violence. The television industry has already been persuaded to curtail the glamorization of smoking and drunk driving on its programs, despite the lack of conclusive documentation of the correlation between TV viewing and higher incidence of such conduct. Why should the industry not take analogous precautions with respect to violent programming?

Americans have special reasons to inquire into the causes of societal violence. While we are in no sense uniquely violent, we need to ask about all possible reasons why our levels of violent crime are higher than in all other stable industrialized democracies. Our homicide rate would be higher still if we did not imprison more of our citizens than any society in the world, and if emergency medical care had not improved so greatly in recent decades that a larger proportion of shooting victims survive than in the past. Even so, we have seen an unprecedented rise not only in child and adolescent violence, but in levels of rape, child abuse, domestic violence, and every other form of assault.

16   Although America's homicide rate has declined in the 1990s, the rates for suicide, rape, and murder involving children and adolescents in many regions have too rarely followed suit. For Americans aged 15 to 35 years, homicide is the second leading cause of death, and for young African Americans, 15 to 24 years, it is *the* leading cause of death. In the decade following the mid-1980s, the rate of murder committed by teenagers 14 to 17 more than doubled. The rates of injury suffered by small children are skyrocketing, with the number of seriously injured children nearly quadrupling from 1986 to 1993; and a proportion of these injuries are inflicted by children upon one another. Even homicides by children, once next to unknown, have escalated in recent decades.

America may be the only society on earth to have experienced what has been called an "epidemic of children killing children," which is ravaging some of its communities today. As in any epidemic, it is urgent to ask what it is that makes so many capable of such violence, victimizes so many others, and causes countless more to live in fear. Whatever role the media are found to play in this respect, to be sure, is but part of the problem. Obviously, not even the total elimination of media violence would wipe out the problem of violence in the United States or any other society. The same can be said for the proliferation and easy access to guns, or for poverty, drug addiction, and other risk factors. As Dr. Deborah Prothrow-Stith puts it, "It's not an either or. It's not guns or media or parents or poverty."

We have all witnessed the four effects that I have discussed . . .—fearfulness, numbing, appetite, and aggressive impulses—in the context of many influences apart from the media. Maturing involves learning to resist the dominion that these effects can gain over us; and to strive, instead, for greater resilience, empathy, self control, and respect for self and others. The process of maturation and growth in these respects is never completed for any of us; but it is most easily thwarted in childhood, before it has had chance to take root. Such learning calls for nurturing and education at first; then for increasing autonomy in making personal decisions about how best to confront the realities of violence.

Today, the sights and sounds of violence on the screen affect this learning process from infancy on, in many homes. The television screen is the lens through which most children learn about violence. Through the magnifying power of this lens, their everyday life becomes suffused by images of shootings, family violence, gang warfare, kidnappings, and everything else that contributes to violence in our society. It shapes their experiences long before they have had the opportunity to consent to such shaping or developed the ability to cope adequately with this knowledge. The basic nurturing and protection to prevent the impairment of this ability ought to be the birthright of every child.

PERSONAL RESPONSE

Has this essay in any way changed your views on the question of how media violence affects young people? Select a statement or passage that especially interests you, either positively or negatively, and discuss your response to it.

QUESTIONS FOR CLASS OR SMALL-GROUP DISCUSSION

1. Summarize the viewpoints of both John Grisham and Oliver Stone on the matter of "copycat" killings. What does Bok think that both men sidestep in their arguments? What do you think of Grisham's and Stone's arguments? Do you agree with either one? Do you think that Bok is correct in her comments on their arguments?

2. Explain what you understand Bok to mean by the term " 'aggressor effect' " (paragraph 6). What do investigators have to say about violent pornography and the aggressor effect?

3. What is your response to this statement: "No reputable scholar accepts the view expressed by 21 percent of the American public in 1995, blaming television more than any other factor for teenage violence" (paragraph 9)? What does Bok have to say about the studies conducted by Brandon S. Centerwall?

4. Bok notes the difficulty of showing the precise causal relationships between tobacco smoking and cancer and between drunken driving and automobile

accidents, even though most people seem to accept that smoking causes cancer and that drunk driving is a chief cause of automobile accidents. What do you think of her application of the " 'probabilistic causation' " factor to the matter of media violence? That is, how valid do you find her logic? Are you convinced that even though we cannot precisely pinpoint the direct causes of societal violence, we can still discuss and propose "efforts to curtail" the "risk factors in media violence" (paragraph 15)?

5. What, according to Bok, might be the effects on children of early and ongoing exposure to media violence? Are you persuaded by her argument that research on the causal links between exposure to media violence and violent behavior must continue?

THE END OF ADMIRATION: THE MEDIA AND THE LOSS OF HEROES

PETER H. GIBBON

Peter H. Gibbon is a research associate at Harvard University's Graduate School of Education. He has done extensive research on the educational systems of Japan, China, and Germany and is co-author, with Peter J. Gomes, of A Call to Heroism: Renewing America's Vision of Greatness *(2002), about the disappearance of public heroes in American society. His articles have appeared in magazines such as* Newsweek *and* Time *and in a number of newspapers, including the* New York Times, Los Angeles Times, *the* Philadelphia Inquirer, *and the* Washington Post. *This piece, based on a talk he delivered at a seminar on the history of journalism hosted by Hillsdale College, appeared in the May 1999 issue of* Imprimis.

I travel around the country talking to Americans about the loss of public heroes. I point out that New York City's Hall of Fame for Great Americans attracts only a few thousand visitors each year, while Cleveland's Rock and Roll Hall of Fame draws over one million.

I describe a 25-foot stained glass window in the Cathedral of St. John the Divine—dedicated in the 1920s to four athletes who exemplified good character and sportsmanship—and I offer a quick list of titles of contemporary books on sports: *Shark Attack,* on the short and bitter career of college coaches; *Meat on the Hoof,* about the mercenary world of professional football; *Personal Fouls,* on the mistreatment of college athletes; *The Courts of Babylon,* on the venality of the women's professional tennis circuit; and *Public Heroes, Private Felons,* on college athletes who break the law.

I contrast two westerns: *High Noon,* which won four Academy Awards in 1959, and *Unforgiven,* which was voted "Best Picture" in 1992. The hero of *High Noon,* Will Kane, is a U.S. marshal. The hero of *Unforgiven,* Will Munny, is a reformed killer and alcoholic reduced to pig farming.

4   I mention that our best-selling postage stamps feature Elvis Presley and Marilyn Monroe and that our most popular TV show was, until it left the air recently, *Seinfeld.*

I remind my audiences that Thomas Jefferson is now thought of as the president with the slave mistress and Mozart as the careless genius who liked to talk dirty.

I add that a recent biography of Mother Teresa is titled *The Missionary Position.*

I offer some reasons for the disappearance of public heroes. Athletes have given up on being team players and role models. Popular culture is often irreverent, sometimes deviant. Revisionist historians present an unforgiving, skewed picture of the past. Biographers are increasingly hostile toward their subjects. Social scientists stridently assert that human beings are not autonomous but are conditioned by genes and environment.

8   Hovering in the background are secularism, which suggests that human beings are self-sufficient and do not need God, and modernism—a complex artistic and literary movement that repudiates structure, form, and conventional values.

Finally, in an age of instant communication, in which there is little time for reflection, accuracy, balance or integrity—the media creates the impression that sleaze is everywhere, that nothing is sacred, that no one is noble, and that there are no heroes.

Nothing to Admire

Radio, television, and computers offer news with such speed that newspaper and magazine circulation has plummeted, and readers have smaller vocabularies. I recently wrote an op-ed piece syndicated in several newspapers. My title, "*Nil Admirari,*" which means "nothing to admire," came from the Roman lyric poet Horace. None of the newspapers used the title, and one editor reminded me that newspaper stories are now aimed at a sixth-grade reading level.

In the Age of Information, the image reigns. There are 81 television sets for every 100 Americans. In the typical household, the television is on six hours a day. Television has become our chief source of local and national news, and broadcast journalists have become more prominent and more powerful than columnists. There used to be three channels. Now, there are over one hundred. When we weary of television channels, we can turn to countless radio stations, videotapes, and web pages.

12   This explosion of information means we now have a vast menu of choices that allows us to be transported to many different worlds and provides us with educational opportunities undreamed of thirty years ago. It also means that we spend more time in front of television and computer screens and less time reading to our children. It is no wonder that our children have shorter attention spans and smaller vocabularies.

A Wired World

Along with this vast menu of choices is the absence of gatekeepers. As parents, we need to realize that there are dangers that come with too many choices and too few guides. We need to remind ourselves that their well-being depends not only on nutrition, sunlight, and exercise; on friendship, work, and love; but also on *how they see the world.* Subtly and powerfully, the media helps shape their world view.

The media has a liberal bias, but its *central* bias is toward bad news. Accidents, crimes, conflict, and scandal are interesting. Normality is boring. The prevalence of bad news and the power of the image encourage children—and us—to overestimate the chance of an accident, the risk of disease, the rate of violence, the frequency of marital infidelity. The average policeman, for example, never fires a gun in action, and most Americans are monogamous.

In a wired world with no restraint, the media can misinform us. It can also make us suspicious, fearful, and cynical. It can lead us to lose faith in our nation, repudiate our past, question our leaders, and cease to believe in progress.

16   We know the worst about everyone instantly. Over and over again, we see clips of George Bush vomiting, Dan Quayle misspelling "potato," Gerald Ford tripping. No longer do we want our child to grow up and become president. We harbor dark suspicions about the personal conduct of scoutmasters, priests, and coaches. We think army sergeants harass their subordinates. We have trouble calling any public figure a hero. A wired world becomes a world without heroes, a world of *nil admirari,* with no one to admire.

Americans tell pollsters the country is in moral and spiritual decline. In the midst of peace and prosperity, with equality increasing and health improving, we are sour. With our military powerful and our culture ascendant, pessimism prevails.

Crusaders or Rogues?

Should we blame journalists? It is certainly tempting. Just as we blame teachers for the poor performance of students, so we can blame reporters for the nation's malaise. But just as teachers are not responsible for poverty and disintegrating families, journalists are not responsible for satellites, fiber optic cables, transistors, and microprocessors—the inventions that make possible instant information. Journalists did not cause the sexual revolution. They did not invent celebrity worship or gossip. Nor did they create leaders who misbehave and let us down.

At the same time, in the world of *nil admirari,* journalists are not innocent, and they know it. Roger Rosenblatt, a veteran of the *Washington Post, Time, Life,* and the *New York Times Magazine,* says, "My trade of journalism is sodden these days with practitioners who seem incapable of admiring others or anything." In his memoir, former presidential press secretary and ABC News senior editor Pierre Salinger writes, "No reporter can be famous unless they have brought someone down." And *New Yorker* writer Adam Gopnik comments, "The reporter used to gain status by dining with his subjects; now he gains status by dining on them."

20   Journalists can also be greedy. Eager for money, some reporters accept handsome speaking fees from organizations they are supposed to be covering. Some are dishonest, making up quotations, even inventing stories. No longer content with anonymity, many reporters seek celebrity, roaming the talk shows and becoming masters of the sound bite. They write autobiographies and give interviews to other journalists.

Just as our president is enamored of Hollywood, so are our journalists. Larry King recently spent a full hour interviewing singer Madonna. *Sixty Minutes* devoted much of a show to "bad boy" actor Sean Penn. Actors, supermodels, and musicians are no longer just entertainers. They are treated like philosopher–kings, telling us how to live. In a recent interview, actress Sharon Stone, star of *Basic Instinct,* advises parents to make condoms available to their teenagers.

Aggressive and anxious for ratings, television news shows feature hosts and guests who come armed with hardened opinions. Many are quick to judge and prone to offer easy solutions for complex problems. "Talking heads" argue, yell, interrupt, and rarely make concessions.

But in the world of *nil admirari,* journalists are now reviled more often than revered. In the 1980s, muckraker Steven Brill skewered lawyers. In his new magazine, *Brill's Content,* he lambastes journalists. In *Right in the Old Gazoo,* former Wyoming Senator Alan Simpson accuses journalists of becoming "lazy, complacent, sloppy, self-serving, self-aggrandizing, cynical and arrogant beyond belief." In *Breaking the News,* writer James Fallows comments that while movies once portrayed journalists as crusaders, they are now portrayed as rogues "more loathsome than . . . lawyers, politicians, and business moguls."

24   How much of this is new?

Since the founding of America, reporters have been harsh critics of public figures. George Washington did not like reading in pamphlets that the essence of his education had been "gambling, reveling, horse racing and horse whipping." Thomas Jefferson did not relish the label "effeminate." Abraham Lincoln did not appreciate being portrayed by cartoonists as a baboon.

Throughout our history, reporters have also received harsh criticism. Just after the Civil War, abolitionist Harriet Beecher Stowe claimed the press had become so vicious that no respectable American man would ever again run for president. In 1870, the British critic and poet Matthew Arnold toured America and concluded, "If one were searching for the best means . . . to kill in a whole nation . . . the feeling for what is elevated, one could not do better than take the American newspaper." At the turn of the century, novelist Henry James condemned what he called the "impudence [and] the shamelessness of the newspaper and the interviewer." In the early decades of the 20th century, "yellow journalism," "muckraking," and "debunking" became household words to describe newspaper stories that exaggerated and distorted events to make them more sensational.

Nor is the media's fascination with celebrities new. When silent screen idol Rudolph Valentino and educational reformer Charles William Eliot died within a day of each other in 1926, high-minded Americans complained that the press devoted too many columns to a celebrity and too few to a hero of education. Between 1925 and 1947, millions of Americans listened to Walter Winchell's radio program, *The Lucky Strike Hour* and read his column in the *New York Mirror.* Winchell hung out at the Stork Club, collecting gossip about celebrities and politicians from tipsters. He urged all newspaper offices to post these words on their walls: "Talk of virtue and your readers will become bored. Hint of gossip and you will secure perfect attention."

28   In short, media critics have always called reporters cynical. Reporters have always collected gossip and featured celebrities. And high-minded Americans have always warned that journalists could lower the nation's moral tone.

An Empire of Information

From the outset, thoughtful critics conceded that journalists had an obligation to inform and expose. But those same critics were afraid that reporters would eliminate privacy and slander leaders; that by repeating gossip and emphasizing crime and corruption, newspapers would coarsen citizens; and that journalists would become more influential than ministers, novelists, professors, and politicians. They were right.

Journalists *have* become more powerful than ministers, novelists, professors, and politicians. They preside over an empire of information unimaginable to our ancestors—an empire that reaches small villages in India and can change governments in China; an empire characterized by staggering choice, variety, and technological sophistication.

An empire of information ruled by the modern media *has* eliminated privacy. With recorders and cameras, reporters freely enter dugouts, locker rooms, board rooms, hotel rooms. There are neither secrets nor taboos. Some listen in on private telephone conversations and sift through garbage for incriminating documents.

32   Early critics were also right to worry that journalists could contribute to a decline in taste and judgment, could destroy the feeling for the elevated, could eliminate appetite for the admirable. The empire they have created is slick, quick, hard-hitting, entertaining, and inescapable. It makes us more knowledgeable, but it also leaves us overwhelmed, convinced that the world is a sleazy place, and mistrustful of authority and institutions. It all but extinguishes our belief in heroism.

Hope for the Future

Are there reasons to be hopeful about the future of America and the future of the media? I believe there are. Intent on exposing our faults, we forget what we do well.

America is much better and healthier than the country portrayed in the media and in pessimistic opinion polls. The American people are basically hardworking, idealistic, compassionate, and religious.

American journalism is still biased, but it is slowly becoming more balanced. We have the *Washington Times* as well as the *Washington Post*, *U.S. News & World Report* as well as *Newsweek*, *National Review* as well as the *Nation*, the *Wall Street Journal* as well as the *New York Times*. We have prominent conservative and liberal commentators.

36   In the late 1990s, newspaper and television journalists have become more self-critical. Some recognize the need to become less cynical, less greedy, less celebrity oriented, less combative; and a few recognize the need to report the normal and the good rather than only the sensational and the deviant.

Reporters, editors, and publishers are influential, but they are not all-powerful. In America, the consumer is king. We choose our sources of information just as we purchase cars and potato chips. When CNN interrupted its coverage of the Lorena Bobbitt trial to report on the Chernobyl nuclear disaster, the number of angry callers caused the network's switchboard to crash. Reporters could be more courageous and less concerned with profits, but American citizens could be more high-minded.

In the Age of Information, journalists and citizens face the same challenges. We need to study the past so as not to become arrogant, to remember the good so as not to become cynical, and to recognize America's strengths so as not to dwell on her weaknesses. We need to be honest and realistic without losing our capacity for admiration—and to be able to embrace complexity without losing our faith in the heroic.

PERSONAL RESPONSE

Gibbon states that "we have trouble calling any public figure a hero" (paragraph 16). Are there public figures whom you admire as heroes, and if so, what makes them heroic? If you cannot think of any public hero whom you would regard as a hero, explore reasons why this is so.

QUESTIONS FOR CLASS OR SMALL-GROUP DISCUSSION

1. Assess the effectiveness of the series of contrasts Gibbon makes in the first six paragraphs. Then discuss the explanations he gives to account for them in the next several paragraphs. Do you accept his explanations? Are there any that you would challenge?

2. Gibbon alleges that journalists can be greedy and dishonest, seeking celebrity status for themselves (paragraphs 19 and 20). To what extent do you agree with Gibbon? Can you name journalists who either support or refute his claims?

3. In paragraph 28, Gibbon briefly summarizes both positive and negative views of journalists over time, with emphasis on the negative. He concludes that those who feared the worst "were right." To what extent do you agree with Gibbon that the worst fears of critics of journalists have been realized?

4. To what extent do you agree with Gibbon in this passage from paragraph 31: "The empire they created is slick, quick, hard-hitting, entertaining, and inescapable. It makes us more knowledgeable, but it also leaves us overwhelmed, convinced that the world is a sleazy place, and mistrustful of authority and institutions. It all but extinguishes our belief in heroism"? Do you think he is wrong or unfair in any part of this passage?

ADVERTISING'S INFLUENCE ON MEDIA CONTENT
JEAN KILBOURNE

Jean Kilbourne has lectured for many years on advertising images of women and on alcohol and liquor advertisements. A widely published writer and speaker who has twice been named Lecturer of the Year by the National Association of Campus Activities, she is perhaps best known for her award-winning documentaries on advertising images, Killing Us Softly, Slim Hopes, *and* Pack of Lies. *This piece is an excerpt from chapter 1 of Kilbourne's latest book,* Can't Buy My Love:

How Advertising Changes the Way We Think and Feel *(2000)*
(hard cover title: Deadly Persuasion: Why Women and Girls Must
Fight the Addictive Power of Advertising*). You can find additional
resources and other information at Kilbourne's website: <www.
jeankilbourne.com>.*

Advertising's influence on media content is exerted in two major ways: via the suppression of information that would harm or "offend the sponsor" and via the inclusion of editorial content that is advertiser-friendly, that creates an environment in
which the ads look good. The line between advertising and editorial content is
blurred by "advertorials" (advertising disguised as editorial copy) "product placement"
in television programs and feature films, and the widespread use of "video news
releases," corporate public-relations puff pieces aired by local television stations as
genuine news. Up to 85 percent of the news we get is bought and paid for by corporations eager to gain positive publicity.

Although people have become used to news reporters popping up in commercials and movies (as Joan Lunden and Linda Ellerbee did in television commercials
for Vaseline and Maxwell House coffee, respectively, and as almost everyone at CNN
did in the movie *Contact*), many were shocked in late 1997 when retired newsman
David Brinkley became the pitchman for agribusiness giant Archer Daniels Midland,
a company that has been convicted of price fixing on an international scale.

In 1998 Nike's sponsorship of CBS's Olympic coverage was rewarded when the
correspondents delivered the news wearing jackets emblazoned with Nike's symbolic
swoosh. The president of CBS News vehemently denied that this sponsorship had
anything to do with the thwarting of a follow-up to a hard-hitting investigative piece
on Nike for *48 Hours*. The editor of *The San Francisco Examiner* likewise denied that
Nike's co-sponsorship of their big annual promotion was in any way related to the decision to kill a column by a reporter that was highly critical of Nike.

In 1996 Chrysler Corporation set off a furor by demanding in writing that magazines notify it in advance about "any and all editorial content that encompasses sexual, political, social issues or any editorial that might be construed as provocative or
offensive." According to Chrysler spokesman Mike Aberlich, placing an ad is like
buying a house: "You decide the neighborhood you want to be in." Fear of losing the
lucrative Chrysler account led *Esquire* to kill a long story with a gay theme, already in
page proofs, by accomplished author David Leavitt. Will Blythe, the magazine's literary editor, promptly quit, saying in his letter of resignation that "in effect, we're taking marching orders (albeit, indirectly) from advertisers." Of course, had Blythe not
gone public, the public would never have known what happened. When we don't get
the story, we don't know what we're missing.

In reaction to the Chrysler letter, the American Society of Magazine Editors and
Magazine Publishers of America issued a joint statement in the fall of 1997 calling
for editorial integrity and barring magazines from giving advertisers a preview of stories, photos, or tables of contents for upcoming issues. This is to their credit, of course,
but it won't protect us from similar phenomena occurring: According to an article in
the *Columbia Journalism Review*, in 1997 a major advertiser (unnamed in the article)

warned all three newsweeklies—*Time, Newsweek,* and *U.S. News & World Report*—that it would award all of its advertising to the magazine that portrayed its company's industry in the most favorable light during the upcoming quarter.

More often than not, self-censorship by magazine editors and television producers makes such overt pressure by corporations unnecessary. According to Kurt Andersen, the former editor of *New York* magazine, "Because I worked closely and happily with the publisher at *New York,* I was aware who the big advertisers were. My antennae were turned on, and I read copy thinking, 'Is this going to cause Calvin Klein or Bergdorf big problems.' " No doubt this is what ran through the minds of the CBS executives who canceled Ed Asner's series after two large corporate advertisers—Vidal Sassoon and Kimberly-Clark—withdrew their sponsorship because of Asner's association with Medical Aid for El Salvador.

Sometimes the self-censorship involves an entire industry rather than a specific company or corporation. For example, several radio stations in the Midwest not only refused to play a commercial advocating vegetarianism in which country singer k.d. lang appeared as a spokesperson, but also banned lang's songs from the air. Clearly this kind of thinking has more serious consequences than an occasional editorial omission or favorable mention—it warps a worldview and distorts the editorial content we read and the programs we listen to and watch.

8   Nowhere is this more obvious than in most women's and girls' magazines, where there is a very fine line, if any, between advertising and editorial content. Most of these magazines gladly provide a climate in which ads for diet and beauty products will be looked at with interest, even with desperation. And they suffer consequences from advertisers if they fail to provide such a climate.

Gloria Steinem provides a striking example of this in her article "Sex, Lies & Advertising," in which she discusses an award-winning story on Soviet women that was featured on the cover of the November 1980 issue of *Ms.* In those days, *Ms.,* like every other woman's magazine, depended on advertising. Following that story, *Ms.* lost all hope of ever getting Revlon ads. Why? Because the Soviet women on the cover weren't wearing makeup.

More recently, the editor of *New Woman* magazine in Australia resigned after advertisers complained about the publication's use of a heavyset cover girl, even though letters had poured in from grateful readers. According to *Advertising Age International,* her departure "made clear the influence wielded by advertisers who remain convinced that only thin models spur sales of beauty products." One prevalent form of censorship in the mass media is the almost complete invisibility, the eradication, of real women's faces and bodies.

No wonder women's magazines so often have covers that feature luscious cakes and pies juxtaposed with articles about diets. "85 Ways to Lose Weight," *Woman's Day* tells us—but probably one of them isn't the "10-minute ice cream pie" on the cover. This is an invitation to pathology, fueling the paradoxical obsession with food and weight control that is one of the hallmarks of eating disorders.

12   It can be shocking to look at the front and back covers of magazines. Often there are ironic juxtapositions. A typical woman's magazine has a photo of some rich food on the front cover, a cheesecake covered with luscious cherries or a huge slice of apple

pie with ice cream melting on top. On the back cover, there is usually a cigarette ad, often one implying that smoking will keep women thin. Inside the magazine are recipes, more photos of fattening foods, articles about dieting—and lots of advertising featuring very thin models. There usually also is at least one article about an uncommon disease or trivial health hazard, which can seem very ironic in light of the truly dangerous product being glamorized on the back cover.

In February 1999, *Family Circle* featured on its front cover a luscious photo of "gingham mini-cakes," while promoting articles entitled "New! Lose-Weight, Stay-Young Diet," "Super Foods That Act Like Medicine," and "The Healing Power of Love." On the back cover was an ad for Virginia Slims cigarettes. The same week, *For Women First* featured a chocolate cake on its cover along with one article entitled "Accelerate Fat Loss" and another promising "Breakthrough Cures" for varicose veins, cellulite, PMS, stress, tiredness, and dry skin. On the back cover, an ad for Doral cigarettes said, "Imagine getting more." *The Ladies' Home Journal* that same month offered on its cover "The Best Chocolate Cake You Ever Ate," along with its antidote, "Want to Lose 10 lbs? Re-program Your Body." Concern for their readers' health was reflected in two articles highlighted on the cover, "12 Symptoms You Must Not Ignore" and "De-Stressors for Really Crazy Workdays"—and then undermined by the ad for Basic cigarettes on the back cover (which added to the general confusion by picturing the pack surrounded by chocolate candies).

The diseases and health hazards warned about in the women's magazines are often ridiculous. *Woman's Day* once offered a "Special Report on Deadly Appliances," which warned us about how our appliances, such as toasters, coffeemakers, baby monitors, and nightlights, can suddenly burst into flame. Lest we think this is not a serious problem, the article tells us that in 1993, the last year for which figures were available, 80 people died and 370 were injured by these killer appliances. I don't wish to minimize any death or injury. However, on the back cover of this issue of *Woman's Day* is an advertisement for cigarettes, a product that kills over four hundred thousand people, year in and year out.

The January 1995 issue of *Redbook* warns us on the cover about all sorts of pressing problems from frizzy hair to "erotic accidents" and promotes an article entitled "If Only They'd Caught It Sooner: The Tests Even Healthy Women Need." On the back cover, as always, an ad for Virginia Slims. Needless to say, being set afire from smoking in bed (one of the leading causes of fire deaths) does not make it into the "erotic accidents" article.

An informal survey of popular women's magazines in 1996 found cover stories on some of the following health issues: skin cancer, Pap smears, leukemia, how breast cancer can be fought with a positive attitude, how breast cancer can be held off with aspirin, and the possibility that dry-cleaned clothes can cause cancer. There were cigarette ads on the back covers of all these magazines—and not a single mention inside of lung cancer and heart disease caused by smoking. In spite of increasing coverage of tobacco issues in the late 1990s, the silence in women's magazines has continued, in America and throughout the world. In my own research, I continue to find scanty coverage of smoking dangers, no feature stories on lung cancer or on smoking's role in causing many other cancers and heart disease . . . and hundreds of cigarette ads.

Dr. Holly Atkinson, a health writer for *New Woman* between 1985 and 1990, recalled that she was barred from covering smoking-related issues, and that her editor struck any reference to cigarettes in articles on topics ranging from wrinkles to cancer. When Atkinson confronted the editor, a shouting match ensued. "Holly, who do you think supports this magazine?" demanded the editor. As Helen Gurley Brown, former editor of *Cosmopolitan*, said: "Having come from the advertising world myself, I think, 'Who needs somebody you're paying millions of dollars a year to come back and bite you on the ankle?' "

It is not just women's magazines that tailor their articles to match their ads. The July 1995 issue of *Life* magazine warns us of the dangers our children face, including drugs, and asks, "How can we keep our children safe?" On the back cover is a Marlboro ad. Our children are far more likely to die from tobacco-related diseases than from any other cause, but cigarettes are not mentioned in the article.

Americans rely on the media for our health information. But this information is altered, distorted, even censored on behalf of the advertisers—advertisers for alcohol, cigarettes, junk food, diet products. We get most of our information from people who are likely to be thinking, "Is this going to cause Philip Morris or Anheuser-Busch big problems?" Of course, in recent years there has been front-page coverage of the liability suits against the tobacco industry and much discussion about antismoking legislation. However, there is still very little information about the health consequences of smoking, especially in women's magazines. The Partnership for a Drug-Free America, made up primarily of media companies dependent on advertising, basically refuses to warn children against the dangers of alcohol and tobacco. The government is spending $195 million in 1999 on a national media campaign to dissuade adolescents from using illicit drugs, but not a penny of the appropriated tax dollars is going to warn about the dangers of smoking or drinking.

20   No wonder most people still don't understand that these heavily advertised drugs pose a much greater threat to our young people and kill far more Americans than all illicit drugs combined. Thirty percent of Americans still don't know that smoking shortens life expectancy, and almost 60 percent don't know it causes emphysema. There is still so much ignorance that, when I was invited recently to give a talk on tobacco advertising to students at a progressive private school outside Boston, the person extending the invitation said she was also going to invite someone from the tobacco industry to represent "the other side." I was tempted to ask her if she felt equally compelled to have a batterer on hand during a discussion of domestic violence.

The influence of these huge and powerful corporations on the media leads to a pernicious kind of censorship. The problem is exacerbated by the fact that many of these corporations own and control the media. In 1996 the Seagram Company ran a whiskey ad on an NBC affiliate in Texas, thus breaking the decades-old tradition of liquor ads not being carried on television. Although network television is leery of running liquor ads for fear of offending their beer advertisers, *Advertising Age* reported that Seagram might have a "winning card to play," since the company owns 50 percent of both the USA Network and the Sci-Fi Channel. Although both have a ban on hard-liquor advertising, a top executive for USA Network said, "If Seagram came to us with a hard-liquor ad, we'd have to look at it."

Today, Time Warner, Sony, Viacom, Disney, Bertelsmann, and News Corporation together control most publishing, music, television, film, and theme-park entertainment throughout the developed world. It is estimated that by the end of the millennium these companies will own 90 percent of the world's information, from newspapers to computer software to film to television to popular music. We may be able to change the channel, but we won't be able to change the message.

Almost everywhere we look these days, anywhere in the world, there is a message from one of these conglomerates. An ad in *Advertising Age* shows a huge picture of the earth and the headline, "Do you see the trillion dollar market?" The triumph of democracy is becoming the triumph of consumerism, as the global village is reduced to a "trillion dollar market."

"Why 6,000,000 women who used to carry a little red book now carry a little red lipstick," says an ad for *Allure,* an American beauty magazine, featuring a Chinese woman in a military uniform wearing bright red lipstick. The copy continues, "When nail polish becomes political, and fashion becomes philosophy, *Allure* magazine will be there." In the world of advertising the political is only personal. Six million women carrying a book of political ideas might be a movement, even a revolution. The same women, carrying lipstick, are simply red-lipped consumers. Advertisers are adept at appropriating dissent and rebellion, slickly packaging it, and then selling it right back to us.

Although the conglomerates are transnational, the culture they sell is American. Not the American culture of the past, which exported writers like Ernest Hemingway and Edgar Allan Poe, musical greats like Louis Armstrong and Marian Anderson, plays by Eugene O'Neill and Tennessee Williams, and Broadway musicals like *West Side Story*. These exports celebrated democracy, freedom, and vitality as the American way of life.

Today we export a popular culture that promotes escapism, consumerism, violence, and greed. Half the planet lusts for Cindy Crawford, lines up for blockbuster films like *Die Hard 2* with a minimum of dialogue and a maximum of violence (which travels well, needing no translation), and dances to the monotonous beat of the Backstreet Boys. *Baywatch,* a moronic television series starring Ken and Barbie, has been seen by more people in the world than any other television show in history. And at the heart of all this "entertainment" is advertising. As Simon Anholt, an English consultant specializing in global brand development, said, "The world's most powerful brand is the U.S. This is because it has Hollywood, the world's best advertising agency. For nearly a century, Hollywood has been pumping out two-hour cinema ads for Brand U.S.A., which audiences around the world flock to see." When a group of German advertising agencies placed an ad in *Advertising Age* that said, "Let's make America great again," they left no doubt about what they had in mind. The ad featured cola, jeans, burgers, cigarettes, and alcohol—an advertiser's idea of what makes America great.

Some people might wonder what's wrong with this. On the most obvious level, as multinational chains replace local stores, local products, and local character, we end up in a world in which everything looks the same and everyone is Gapped and Starbucked. Shopping malls kill vibrant downtown centers locally and create a universe of uniformity internationally. Worse, we end up in a world ruled by, in John Maynard

24

Keynes's phrase, the values of the casino. On this deeper level, rampant commercialism undermines our physical and psychological health, our environment, and our civic life and creates a toxic society. Advertising corrupts us and, I will argue, promotes a dissociative state that exploits trauma and can lead to addiction. To add insult to injury, it then co-opts our attempts at resistance and rebellion.

28   Although it is virtually impossible to measure the influence of advertising on a culture, we can learn something by looking at cultures only recently exposed to it. In 1980 the Gwich'in tribe of Alaska got television, and therefore massive advertising, for the first time. Satellite dishes, video games, and VCRs were not far behind. Before this, the Gwich'in lived much the way their ancestors had for a thousand generations. Within ten years, the young members of the tribe were so drawn by television they no longer had time to learn ancient hunting methods, their parents' language, or their oral history. Legends told around campfires could not compete with *Beverly Hills 90210*. Beaded moccasins gave way to Nike sneakers, sled dogs to gas-powered skimobiles, and "tundra tea" to Folger's instant coffee.

Human beings used to be influenced primarily by the stories of our particular tribe or community, not by stories that are mass-produced and market-driven. As George Gerbner, one of the world's most respected researchers on the influence of the media, said, "For the first time in human history, most of the stories about people, life, and values are told not by parents, schools, churches, or others in the community who have something to tell, but by a group of distant conglomerates that have something to sell." The stories that most influence our children these days are the stories told by advertisers.

PERSONAL RESPONSE

What is your initial response to what Kilbourne tells readers that she will argue in the rest of her book: "Advertising corrupts us and, I will argue, promotes a dissociative state that exploits trauma and can lead to addiction. To add insult to injury, it then co-opts our attempts at resistance and rebellion" (paragraph 27)? Are you skeptical or intrigued?

QUESTIONS FOR CLASS OR SMALL-GROUP DISCUSSION

1. What is your opinion on the matter of whether corporations should have the right to review editorial content of publications they advertise in and whether magazines should practice self-censorship? Is it just good business, or is it more than that, as Kilbourne claims? Do you think Kilbourne overreacts when she writes that this practice "warps a worldview and distorts the editorial content we read and the programs we listen to and watch" (paragraph 7)?

2. State in your own words the issues that Kilbourne is most concerned about in her allegations against women's and girls' magazines. To what extent do you agree with her? Although she cites many examples, can you provide others that either support or refute her arguments?

3. Summarize Kilbourne's point about alcohol and tobacco advertising. Is her argument valid? To what extent do you agree with her?

4. Kilbourne alleges that America exports "a popular culture that promotes escapism, consumerism, violence, and greed" (paragraph 26). To what extent do you agree with her? Can you provide examples that either support or refute this view?

5. Without having read the rest of the book that this excerpt comes from *(Can't Buy My Love: How Advertising Changes the Way We Think and Feel),* are you inclined to think that Kilbourne is right in her criticism of advertising, or do you find her argument in this excerpt unconvincing?

LIBERAL MEDIA? I'M SHOCKED!

JOHN LEO

John Leo wrote for Time *magazine and the* New York Times *before joining* U.S. News & World Report *as a columnist and contributing editor in 1988. Leo is a former associate editor of* Commonwealth *magazine, a former book editor of the sociology magazine* Society, *and a former deputy commissioner of New York City's Environmental Protection Administration. He launched the "Press Clips" column in* The Village Voice. *He is author of a book of humor* How the Russians Invented Baseball and Other Essays of Enlightenment *(1989). "Liberal Media? I'm Shocked!" appeared in the June 7, 2004, issue of* U.S. News & World Report.

A new survey by the Pew Research Center says journalists have political and ideological leanings more liberal than those of the general public. Or, as a sensible headline might have put it: "Researchers ferret out the obvious yet again." One amused blogger wrote: "In other news, a second Pew study shows that the Earth is round and that the government's habit of taxing its citizens is likely to continue."

Pew reports that just 7 percent of journalists and news executives call themselves conservative, compared with 33 percent of the general public. The self-identified liberals (34 percent) are five times as common as conservatives in the news business. As you might imagine, this got very little play in the mainstream media. Howard Kurtz did a good job with it at the *Washington Post.* But that was about it. Those who did report or comment on the survey tended to play up the large number of news people (54 percent) who call themselves moderate. Why is it such a big deal to have a newsroom that's only a third liberal? asked Eric Alterman, author of *What Liberal Media?*

I would say that the big deal is that media workers are becoming more liberal at a fairly rapid pace—up from 22 percent nine years ago to 34 percent now, according to Pew. It would be a bigger deal if the hiring of liberals reached the point (as it has in the academic world) where conservatives don't bother to apply for jobs.

Immoderate. In addition, there is debate over what "moderate" means in the survey. My experience is that liberal journalists tend to think of themselves as representing the mainstream, so in these self-identification polls, "moderate" usually translates to "liberal." On the few social questions asked in the survey, most of the moderates sounded fairly liberal. Asked whether homosexuality should be approved of by society, 88 percent of journalists agreed, compared with only 51 percent of Americans. Some 82 percent of the journalists were able to list a news organization that was "especially conservative" (most named Fox News), but an amazing 62 percent could not name any news organization that struck them as "especially liberal." Good grief. Even 60 percent of the Homer Simpson family could probably figure out that the *New York Times* or National Public Radio qualify as liberal.

In response to the survey, some argue that personal social and political views make no difference if a reporter plays the story straight. Well, yes. But nearly half of those polled told Pew that journalists too often let their ideological views color their work. This is a devastating admission, something like an umpire's union reporting that half its membership likes to favor the home team. Even apart from loaded reporting, the selection and framing of news stories have a way of reflecting the opinions of editors. That's why the steady march toward a more liberal newsroom is so puzzling. The news media have to cope with a declining readership and viewership and intense scrutiny of their wayward practices by right-wing outlets and relentlessly critical bloggers. Yet the mainstream media have only those few in-house conservatives who might warn their bosses when news reports are skewing left.

Why does the news business keep hiring more and more people who disagree sharply with the customers, many of whom are already stampeding out the door for a variety of reasons? One explanation is that national journalism is now an elite profession, staffed by people—black and white, female and male—who went to elite colleges and who share the conventional social views of their class. This was not true a generation ago. When I was at the *New York Times,* the leadership was full of people who had gone to the wrong schools and fought their way up with brains and talent. Two desks away from mine was McCandlish Phillips, a born-again Christian who read the Bible during every break, no matter how brief. Phillips was a legendary reporter, rightly treated with awe by the staff, but I doubt he would be hired by most news organizations today. He prayed a lot and had no college degree.

The news business is deeply concerned—I would say obsessed—with diversity, but it has a narrow and cramped view of the word, rarely applying it to background and social attitudes. Tom Rosenstiel, director of the Pew survey, said the fact that "conservatives are not very well represented" is having an effect. He added: "This is something journalists should worry about. Maybe diversity in the newsroom needs to mean more than ethnic and gender diversity." Do tell. A great many thick skulls still must be penetrated by this idea. But eventually it will get through.

PERSONAL RESPONSE

Leo believes that it is a "big deal" that a third of journalists self-identify as politically and socially liberal. Do you think it is a "big deal"?

QUESTIONS FOR CLASS OR SMALL-GROUP DISCUSSION

1. Describe the tone of Leo's opening paragraph and comment on its appropriateness. How is the title a reflection of his tone?

2. What bothers Leo about the findings of the recent survey by the Pew Research Center?

3. Leo asserts that journalists identifying themselves as "moderate" are really "liberal." What is his evidence? Do you agree with him?

4. In paragraph 5, Leo notes that "some argue that personal social and political views make no difference if a reporter plays the story straight." How does he feel about that argument? What is your opinion of it?

I AGREE WITH ME

P. J. O'ROURKE

P. J. O'Rourke was editor-in-chief of the National Lampoon *from 1978 to 1981, when he left to become a freelance writer. He work has been published in many magazines, and he is the author of eleven books:* Republican Party Reptile *(1987),* Modern Manners: An Etiquette Book for Rude People *(1990),* Parliament of Whores *(1991),* Give War A Chance: Eyewitness Accounts of Mankind's Struggle Against Tyranny, Injustice, and Alcohol-free Beer *(1992),* All the Trouble in the World: The Lighter Side of Overpopulation, Famine, Ecological Disaster, Ethnic Hatred, Plague, and Poverty *(1995),* Age and Guile Beat Youth, Innocence, and a Bad Haircut *(1996),* The Bachelor Home Companion: A Practical Guide to Keeping House like a Pig *(1997),* Eat the Rich: A Treatise on Economics *(1999),* Holidays in Hell *(2000),* The CEO of the Sofa *(2002), and* Peace Kills: America's Fun New Imperialism *(2004). "I Agree with Me" was published in the July/August 2004 issue of* The Atlantic Monthly.

Last year, on a long car trip, I was listening to Rush Limbaugh shout. I usually agree with Rush Limbaugh; therefore I usually don't listen to him. I listen to NPR: "World to end—poor and minorities hardest hit." I like to argue with the radio. Of course, if I had kept listening to Limbaugh, whose OxyContin addiction was about to be revealed, I could have argued with him about drugs. I don't think drugs are bad. I used to be a hippie. I think drugs are fun. Now I'm a conservative. I think fun is bad. I would agree all the more with Limbaugh if, after he returned from rehab, he'd shouted (as most Americans ought to), "I'm sorry I had fun! I promise not to have any more!"

Anyway, I couldn't get NPR on the car radio, so I was listening to Rush Limbaugh shout about Wesley Clark, who had just entered the Democratic presidential-primary race. Was Clark a stalking horse for Hillary Clinton?! Was Clark a DNC-sponsored Howard Dean spoiler?! "He's somebody's sock puppet!" Limbaugh bellowed. I agreed; but a thought began to form. Limbaugh wasn't shouting at Clark, who I doubt tunes in to AM talk radio the way I tune in to NPR. And "Shari Lewis and Lamb Chop!" was not a call calculated to lure Democratic voters to the Bush camp. Rush Limbaugh was shouting at me.

Me. I am a little to the right of . . . Why is the Attila comparison used? Fifth-century Hunnish depredations on the Roman Empire were the work of an over-powerful executive pursuing a policy of economic redistribution in an atmosphere of permissive social mores. I am a little to the right of Rush Limbaugh. I'm so conservative that I approve of San Francisco City Hall marriages, adoption by same-sex couples, and New Hampshire's recently ordained Episcopal bishop. Gays want to get married, have children, and go to church. Next they'll be advocating school vouchers, boycotting HBO, and voting Republican.

4   I suppose I should be arguing with my fellow right-wingers about that, and drugs, and many other things. But I won't be. Arguing, in the sense of attempting to convince others, has gone out of fashion with conservatives. The formats of their radio and television programs allow for little measured debate, and to the extent that evidence is marshaled to support conservative ideas, the tone is less trial of Socrates than Johnnie Cochran summation to the O.J. jury. Except the jury—with a clever marketing strategy—has been rigged. I wonder, when was the last time a conservative talk show changed a mind?

This is an argument I have with my father-in-law, an avid fan of such programs. Although again, I don't actually argue, because I usually agree with my father-in-law. Also, he's a retired FBI agent, and at seventy-eight is still a licensed private investigator with a concealed-weapon permit. But I say to him, "What do you get out of these shows? You already agree with everything they say."

"They bring up some good points," he says.

"That you're going to use on whom? Do some of your retired-FBI-agent golf buddies feel shocked by the absence of WMDs in Iraq and want to give Saddam Hussein a mulligan and let him take his tee shot over?"

8   And he looks at me with an FBI-agent look, and I shut up. But the number and popularity of conservative talk shows have grown apace since the Reagan Administration. The effect, as best I can measure it, is nil. In 1988 George Bush won the presidency with 53.4 percent of the popular vote. In 2000 Bush's arguably more conservative son won the presidency with a Supreme Court ruling.

A generation ago there wasn't much conservatism on the airwaves. For the most part it was lonely Bill Buckley moderating *Firing Line.* But from 1964 to 1980 we went from Barry Goldwater's defeat with 38.5 percent of the popular vote to Ronald Reagan's victory with 50.8 percent of the popular vote. Perhaps there was something efficacious in Buckley's—if he'll pardon the word—moderation.

I tried watching *The O'Reilly Factor.* I tried watching Hannity shout about Colmes. I tried listening to conservative talk radio. But my frustration at concurrence would build, mounting from exasperation with like-mindedness to a fury of accord, and I'd hit the OFF button.

I resorted to books. You can slam a book shut in irritation and then go back to the irritant without having to plumb the mysteries of TiVo.

12   My selection method was unscientific. Ann Coulter, on the cover of *Treason*, has the look of a soon-to-be-ex wife who has just finished shouting. And Bill O'Reilly is wearing a loud shirt on the cover of *Who's Looking Out for You?*

Coulter begins her book thus:

> Liberals have a preternatural gift for striking a position on the side of treason. You could be talking about Scrabble and they would instantly leap to the anti-American position. Everyone says liberals love America, too. No they don't. Whenever the nation is under attack, from within or without, liberals side with the enemy.

Now, there's a certain truth in what she says. But it's what's called a "poetic truth." And it's the kind of poetic truth best conveyed late in the evening after six or eight drinks while pounding the bar. I wasn't in a bar. I was in my office. It was the middle of the day. And I was getting a headache.

Who's Looking Out for You? is not as loud as *Treason*. But there's something of the halftime harangue at the team just in the use of the second-person pronoun.

The answer to O'Reilly's title question could be condensed in the following manner: "Nobody, that's who. The fat cats aren't. The bigwigs aren't. The politicos aren't. Nobody's looking out for you except me, and I can't be everywhere. You've got to look out for yourself. How do you do that? You look out for your friends and family. That's how. And they look out for you. And that's the truth, Bud."

16   We've all backed away from this fellow while vigorously nodding our heads in agreement. Often the fellow we were backing away from was our own dad.

O'Reilly casts his net wide in search of a nodding, agreeing audience. He embraces people driving poky economy cars ("not imposing gas mileage standards hurts every single American except those making and driving SUVs") and people with romantic memories of the liberalism of yore ("the gold standard for public service was the tenure of Robert Kennedy as attorney general"). He positions himself as a populist worried about illegal aliens' getting across the border and taking our jobs. (I'm worried about illegal aliens' *not* getting across the border and *leaving* us with jobs, such as mowing the lawn and painting the house.) And O'Reilly reaches out to the young by prefacing each chapter with lyrics from pop music groups that are, as far as I know, very up-to-date, such as Spandau Ballet. But the person that O'Reilly's shouting at is still, basically, me: "If President Hillary becomes a reality, the United States will be a polarized, thief-ridden nanny state . . ."

Does the left have this problem? Do some liberals feel as if they're guarding the net while their teammates make a furious rush at their own goal? NPR seems more whiny than hectoring, except at fundraising time. There's supposed to be a lot of liberal advocacy on TV. I looked for things that debased freedom, promoted license, ridiculed responsibility, and denigrated man and God—but that was *all* of TV. How do you tell the liberal parts from the car ads? Once more I resorted to books.

To answer my question I didn't even have to open Al Franken's *Lies and the Lying Liars Who Tell Them: A Fair and Balanced Look at the Right*. But having done so, I found these chapter headings: "Ann Coulter: Nutcase," "You Know Who I Don't Like? Ann Coulter," and "Bill O'Reilly: Lying Splotchy Bully."

20   Michael Moore's previous book was *Stupid White Men*, titled in a spirit of gentle persuasion unmatched since Martin Luther, that original Antinomian, wrote *Against the Murderous and Thieving Hordes of Peasants*. Moore's new book, *Dude, Where's My Country?*, contains ten chapters of fulminations convincing the convinced. However, Moore does include one chapter on how to argue with a conservative. As if. Approached by someone like Michael Moore, a conservative would drop a quarter in Moore's Starbucks cup and hurriedly walk away. Also, Moore makes this suggestion: "Tell him how dependable conservatives are. When you need something fixed, you call your redneck brother-in-law, don't you?"

    Arguing, in the sense of attempting to convince others, seems to have gone out of fashion with everyone. I'm reduced to arguing with the radio. The distaste for political argument certainly hasn't made politics friendlier—or quieter, given the amount of shouting being done by people who think one thing at people who think the same thing.

    But I believe I know why this shouting is popular. Today's Americans are working harder than ever, trying to balance increasing personal, family, and career demands. We just don't have time to make ourselves obnoxious. We need professional help.

PERSONAL RESPONSE

Do you listen to or view talk shows that reinforce your political or social agenda? Why or why not?

QUESTIONS FOR CLASS OR SMALL-GROUP DISCUSSION

1. What do you understand by the terms "conservative" and "liberal"? What do you think O'Rourke means when he says that he is "so conservative that [he] approve[s] of San Francisco City Hall marriages, adoption by same-sex couples, and New Hampshire's recently ordained Episcopal bishop (paragraph 3)?

2. What is O'Rourke's point about argument in the context of radio and television programs? How does the example of his father-in-law serve to illustrate his point?

3. Describe the television programs, radio programs, and books that O'Rourke mentions. Have you watched, listened to, or read any of them? How do they illustrate or support his main point?

○ PERSPECTIVES ON MEDIA STUDIES ○
Suggested Writing Topics

1. Advertisers contend that they do not create problems but simply reflect the values of society. Explain your position on the subject of how much responsibility advertisers should bear for the images they produce in their advertisements.

2. Define the word "hero" and use a person you admire to illustrate the meaning of the word.

3. With Peter H. Gibbon's "The End of Admiration: The Media and the Loss of Heroes" in mind, argue either in support of or against the statement that America no longer has heroes.

4. Survey a selection of magazines aimed at a specific audience—girls, women, boys, men—in terms of the kind of analysis Jean Kilbourne does in "Advertising's Influence on Media Content." Explain what you find and whether your conclusions agree with or differ from hers.

5. Use examples of well-known advertisements to explore the question of whether advertisers underestimate the intelligence of consumers.

6. With Sissela Bok's "Aggression: The Impact of Media Violence" in mind, write an essay on the subject of the sexual or violent content of any entertainment medium, such as Hollywood film or television programs. How is sex or violence handled? Is there too much? Is it too graphic? How is it portrayed, and what is its relevance to the plot? Are sex and violence linked?

7. Listen to two radio talk shows, one liberal and one conservative, and compare the two. Or, do the same for two television programs or two books. What subjects do they discuss? How do their approaches differ? Do you find yourself persuaded by one over the other? Why?

8. Select a news item in the headlines this week and follow the media's coverage of it, mixing media if possible. For instance, you could track the story as reported on an Internet site, on a national news program, and in a newspaper, or as it is handled by several different Internet sites, television programs, or newspapers. What conclusions can you draw about the media's handling of the story? Do you detect any bias in reporting it?

9. Write a paper in response to the central argument of any of the essays in this chapter.

Research Topics

1. Research the subject of advertising ethics by locating articles and books representing the opinions of both those who are critical of advertisements and those who defend them. Argue your own position on the subject, supporting it with relevant source materials.

2. Research images of a specific group in advertising. For instance, you could focus on images of women, as Jean Kilbourne has done in "Advertising's Influence on Media Content," and locate additional research and opposing viewpoints. Consider, also, the topics of advertising images of men, advertisements that encourage destructive behavior, or advertisements aimed at children.

3. Take as your starting point any of the accusations that Jean Kilbourne makes in "Advertising's Influence on Media Content" about corporate sponsors, self-censorship, alcohol or tobacco advertisements, or conflicting messages

in women's magazines. Locate sources, do some preliminary reading, and narrow your focus on one aspect of the broader topic.

4. Research the question of whether allegations that the media have a liberal bias are true. Is it simply a perception, or can such bias, if it exists, be documented?

5. Select a news story that got a great deal of media coverage and research how it was reported in a variety of media sources. Compare the handling of the news item by the different sources. What conclusions can you draw on whether there is bias in reporting the story?

6. Research any of the issues raised by Sissela Bok's article, perhaps including her book, *Mayhem: Violence as Public Entertainment,* as one of your sources. For instance, you may want to read more about the effects of violent entertainment on children's moral and psychological development, the debate between protecting children and preserving First Amendment rights, or the measures taken by other nations to control media violence without censorship. Formulate your own position on the issue, and support it with references from your source materials.

RESPONDING TO VISUALS

Camel cigarette ad featuring movie star John Wayne, who died of cancer in 1979. Source: S. Blaney/Index Stock Imagery

1. How does the ad make use of the fame of Hollywood film actor John Wayne?
2. In what ways does this advertisement use sex to sell its product?
3. What appeals to authority does the advertisement make?
4. What details of the advertisement do you think are most persuasive?

RESPONDING TO VISUALS

Print advertisement for the North Carolina Film Commission. Source: Loeffler Ketchum Mountjoy for the North Carolina Film Commission

1. What is the point of this advertisement?
2. How does the ad make use of people's perception of big-city violence?
3. Who is the audience for the advertisement? How does the text make it clear who the audience is?
4. Does the ad appeal to audiences other than those it is aimed at?

CHAPTER

9

FILM AND TELEVISION

Makers of Hollywood films, television shows, Broadway productions, and other products of the entertainment industry hope to tap into or even create trends that will have widespread appeal and thus result in huge profits. Because of its high visibility, ready availability, and ease of access to all age groups, the entertainment industry has always been closely scrutinized and subject to attack by its critics. Popular Hollywood films and television programs are particularly prime targets for both criticism and praise. Hollywood watchdogs and film critics pay attention not only to the craft of film production but also to the content of films. Indeed, the current ratings system evolved in response to alarm at the exposure of young viewers to graphic sex and violence, sometimes unwittingly, before such guidelines were in place. In recent years, many people have been sharply critical of films and television programs for what they see as irresponsible depiction of shocking images, excessive violence, and unnecessarily graphic sex. Defenders have been just as heated in their responses.

Television has been the target of suspicion, attack, and ridicule from the time it was invented. At first, people thought "the tube" would never replace the radio, especially when its early live-only broadcasts included inevitable comical errors. Once the problems were resolved and television broadcasting became increasingly sophisticated in both technology and programming, television became a commonplace medium. Television programs now number in the thousands, with not only cable access but also computer-controlled satellite dishes bringing a dizzying array of viewing choices into people's homes. Many families own not only two or three (or more) televisions but also at least both a VCR and a CD player. With the seemingly endless demand for television shows from viewers, network producers and local station managers are always looking for programs that will attract viewers and draw sponsors.

In the first essay in this chapter, John H. McWhorter in "Up from Hip-Hop" looks at both film and theatre for what he sees as changes in their portrayal of black America. Using examples of recent productions in both genres, he surveys shifts in attitude toward blacks in those genres and assesses what he sees as positive steps forward in the fictional representations of blacks. Louise Bernikow, on the other hand, is interested in the portrayal of women's roles. She is critical of a certain type of Hollywood film as well as the fairy tales the films are based on. Her essay, "Cinderella: Saturday Afternoon at the Movies," is a feminist analysis of a specific fairy tale and the Disney movie version that she remembers from her childhood. The essay is a classic example of the kind of critique of popular culture that many writers were making during the 1970s and 1980s. Although the film she refers to was produced years ago, it is still in circulation, and the fairy tale she recalls is very likely familiar to you as well.

One of the oldest debates about television programming has to do with its depiction of violence. The final two essays in this chapter, Susan R. Lamson's "TV Violence: Does It Cause Real-Life Mayhem?" and Mike Males' "Stop Blaming Kids and TV," express opposing opinions on whether television violence causes violent and criminal behavior. Lamson, writing from the perspective of her official position in the National Rifle Association, argues that television violence has enormous influence on children and bears large responsibility for the high U.S. homicide rate, whereas Males argues that television does not cause violent behavior. He offers a vastly different viewpoint on the power of television to affect young people. He cites numerous studies as well as his own personal observations from working with youths to support his firm belief that critics are wrongheaded to blame teens and mass media for problems such as youth violence, excessive teenaged drinking, and increased rates of smoking among teenagers. He argues that there are other, more plausible causes of these problems. Where do you stand on this issue?

UP FROM HIP-HOP

JOHN H. MCWHORTER

John H. McWhorter is Associate Professor of Linguistics at the University of California, Berkeley and is currently a senior fellow of the Manhattan Institute, a think tank whose mission is to develop and disseminate new ideas that foster greater economic choice and individual responsibility. He is the author of The Word on the Street: Fact and Fiction about American English *(1998),* The Missing Spanish Creoles: Recovering the Birth of Plantation Creole Languages *(2000),* Losing the Race: Self-Sabotage in Black America *(2000),* The Power of Babel: A Natural History of Language *(2002),* Authentically Black: Essays for the Black Silent Majority *(2003), and* Defining Creole *(2004). This essay first appeared in* Commentary *in March 2003.*

Last September, America's most popular movie was, briefly, an amusing if rather ordinary film called *Barbershop*. What made the movie notorious were a few lines of dialogue. Eddie, the oldest barber in a shop in a black Chicago neighborhood that has seen better days, grouses: "The problem with us black folks is we gotta stop lying!" He then illustrates his point by means of some salutary truth-telling, exclaiming: "F—k Jesse Jackson!" and "O.J. did it!" Having thus dispatched the black leader who regards himself as the rightful heir to Martin Luther King, Jr., and indicted the canonically innocent O.J. Simpson as a murderer, Eddie closes the movie by observing that King himself was a "ho' " (whore).

As if on cue, Jesse Jackson weighed in with a fury, demanding that MGM delete the offending lines from videotape and DVD editions of the film; Reverend Al Sharpton promptly chimed in. But the movie itself was way ahead of these two increasingly irrelevant weathervanes of black opinion. To most of the characters in Barbershop, Eddie's broadsides are shocking but fair—and howlingly funny. When one customer does take offense at the Jackson comment, Eddie delivers the most quoted line of the film: "If we can't talk straight in the barbershop, then where can we talk straight?"

Meaning: the duty of black Americans is no longer to maintain, at all costs, a retired front in the face of the white establishment, or to adopt a permanently defensive crouch against a mythical "racist" backlash. Nor, to judge by *Barbershop*, is upward striving seen any longer as antithetical to being "really black." In the film, the

shop itself is the usual scruffy dive, but Calvin, the owner and the movie's protagonist, lives in a comfortable home with a poised, intelligent wife. Calvin (played by the
rapper Ice Cube) is thinking of selling the shop and putting the money into a recording studio to provide a better life for the child he and his wife are expecting, but he is
also tempted to keep the shop open as a bastion of community support in a neighborhood where teens so often go wrong. Either way, we have come a long distance
from the New Jack City gangster cycle of black films ten years ago. There, the choice
was usually presented as working for chump change at the post office or raking in the
bucks selling drugs on the street. Half the cast would be dead by the final reel, and
critics were always ready to hail another "authentic" cry of despair from people powerless to save themselves.

4   To be sure, there are signs of a countervailing message even in *Barbershop,* not to
mention elsewhere in black popular culture, and I had better deal with them straight-
away lest I be accused of sugarcoating. For instance: a subplot in the movie pits a well-
spoken, rightward-leaning black barber against the one white barber; the latter has
adopted a hip-hop lingo and wardrobe, flaunts his black girlfriend, and considers
himself "blacker" than black. The movie gives this "white Negro" a pass, the message
being the grand old canard that at heart, "black" is the street.

The same message was crystallized in *8 Mile,* the recent debut film of the white
rapper Eminem. Critics have fallen all over themselves to praise this movie as an eloquent exploration of interracial mixing and "working-class despair," although on both
counts it is ultimately old wine in a new bottle. On the subject of class, *8 Mile* is pure
Hollywood formula: working stiff starts at the bottom (Bunny Rabbit, the character
played by Eminem, is barely hanging on to a factory job while living in a trailer park
with his drunken layabout mother), suffers stinging failure (not only does Bunny
Rabbit choke in a "slam" contest under the withering rhymed insults of the local black
champion, but a new girlfriend cheats on him), the sun inexplicably breaks through
the clouds (Mona wins at Bingo, the factory foreman softens up), and victory arrives
at last when our hero bests the rap slammer in a rematch. Hollywood has been working this routine since before the talkies.

The race message is the same old thing as well—at least once we get past the
novelty of seeing a white boy homing with a black crowd and prefacing every second
sentence with "Yo." Some critics were struck by the fact that nobody in the movie,
white or black, comments negatively when Bunny Rabbit's girlfriend has sex with a
black man. But this, too, is not exactly unheard of, and besides, the filmmaker's point
is rather ambiguous: the girlfriend comes from a different part of town, always
seems to turn up unexpectedly, and is illuminated in a shaft of light that gives her an
otherworldly air—as if black men succumb to white women only in some alternative
reality.

The same ambiguity seems to extend to the Eminem character, who, "black" as
he supposedly is, sleeps exclusively white. Where Bunny Rabbit does demonstrate his
"blackness" is in his poverty, which, conventionally enough, turns out also to be his
trump card. In the final slam contest, he silences his black nemesis by revealing a little
secret: that the poor fellow went to a good school and comes from a middle-class,
two-parent home. Stripped of his "authenticity," the man is left speechless as the
rowdy black audience shouts him off the stage. To be black is to be at the bottom.

8   Many critics were also charmed by the "slam" contests themselves, in which contestants compete by means of loose rhymes set to a beat-box rhythm, mixing self-aggrandizement with ad hominem disparagement. There is indeed a certain knack to the spontaneous rhyming, but the viciousness of the insults is only another gloss on the idea that to be black is to be uncivil and perpetually alienated—itself a consequence, supposedly, of the aforementioned working-class despair. (In one scene, a weary crowd of workers breaks into a spontaneous slam contest while waiting in line at an outdoor food truck.) Must one point out that senseless verbal abuse is by no means an inevitable response to a difficult life? Black people mired much deeper in misery during the Depression created no equivalent to today's rap slamming—"playing the dozens," with its playful insults, was another matter altogether—nor is there any prototype for this sulfurous tone in any African tradition.

On the subject of poetry, as agitprop, I should also mention the Spoken Word movement. It would be oversimplifying to say that Spoken Word is just hip-hop without the instrumental background beat, but hip-hop's cocky cadences, jagged rhythms, verbal prolixity, and alienated message are a foundational element in the mix. In "slam" contests at places like the Nuyorican Cafe in New York, the poets who tend to move audiences the most are the ones channeling a formulaic rage. Spoken Word performances do include tender love poems and non-confrontational prose monologues, but an evening at the Nuyorican when all of the entries were of these latter types would be considered an off night, whereas I doubt anyone would regard a session made up exclusively of spikier offerings as much of a problem.

This past fall, in *Def Poetry Jam,* Spoken Word came to Broadway. The show was produced by the hip-hop mogul Russell Simmons, founder of the Def Jam recording label and impresario of an earlier HBO series along the same lines. It was a rich evening. There was no denying that the nine champions gathered by Simmons were a talented bunch. Spoken Word scansion—where it exists—is on the loose side, and rhyming is optional and often approximate: the guiding impulse is to create dazzling showers of verbiage played against angular rhythms, the dazzle itself being reminiscent of operatic cadenzas. Spoken Word is also a self-consciously demotic art, aimed at the ordinary, listener. But performers clearly craft their work down to the word, and the feats of diction and memorization alone can be stunning.

Yet the adversarial fetish, if one may call it that, makes Spoken Word a narrower art than it might be. At *Def Poetry Jam,* three gimmicks were sure to get a rise out of the audience. One was slipping into black street flavor: a nicely placed funky or allusions to buttocks and vaginas invariably elicited whoops of approval. Another was lacing one's poems with references to Spam, or McDonald's, or other brand names from TV commercials. The third, and most constricting, was the easy reaching for recreational outrage.

12   The Chinese-American poet Beau Sia literally hollered his way through the whole show. I got it—he was playing against the stereotype of Asians as quiet and deferential. But whatever one's color, shouting hinders eloquence. *Def Poetry Jam's* poster depicts all of Sia's fellow performers wearing gentle, reflective expressions, but a more honest version would picture at least seven of the performers in glowering high dudgeon, their reigning theme a contemptuous indictment of the American status quo. *Def Poetry Jam* was, in fact, less a show than a rally. Facing front, proudly

smug, the performers were saying that either you were with them or you were a clueless bigot. The night I attended, I started wondering around the middle of the first act how long the middle-aged white women in the row ahead of me would last; they were gone after intermission.

The ending said it all. Each poet took a turn telling us in a few tart sentences why "I Write America." The endlessly grim Black Ice informed his audience that the United States government had planned the September 11 attacks, and that therefore he just watches America; for this, he got one of the biggest hands of the night. (His sentiment was on a par with Amiri Baraka's notorious lines, delivered at his October debut as New Jersey's poet laureate, "Who knew the World Trade Center was gonna get bombed? / Who told 4,000 Israeli workers at the Twin Towers to stay home that day? / Why did Sharon stay away?") At *Def Poetry Jam,* the lights faded out on all nine performers venting their grievances in one grand cacophony.

Why, then, do I insist that things are looking up? Because, whatever the visceral thrills of continuing to play the underdog, most blacks are well aware that dignity no longer means clinging to the label of victimhood. It means refusing to let obstacles hold them back, especially when the obstacles are so many fewer than those faced by their ancestors. Even at *Def Poetry Jam,* the superficial nature of the black-rage routine made itself clear. Besides Black Ice's 9/11 line, the two other moments that got the biggest audience reaction were (a) when wayward black fathers were admonished to take care of their children and (b) when black men were scolded about drifting into criminality and becoming "just another f—kin' nigger." They, too, came from Black Ice.

In any case, despite the attention paid to rabble-rousers, and despite the sullen ubiquity of hip-hop, there is an ever stronger strain running through black popular culture that insists on bringing things back to earth. A nice example was last fall's Off-Broadway, musical-theater version of *Crowns,* a coffee-table book that celebrates, of all things, the Sunday hats worn by black women to church. In the show, a black high-school girl from Brooklyn is sent to live with her middle-aged relatives in South Carolina after her brother is shot to death on the streets. Finding her new environment dismayingly "unhip," Yolonda soon enough warms to the matchless strength of black women who make the best of a hard life with the aid of a good dose of "hatritude"—the bone-deep pride that, among other things, makes a woman look good in a flashy hat.

16   For *Crowns,* the anti-white, anti-establishment stance is just a pose, and a childish one at that. Indeed; these days, the pose is not even exclusive to blacks but common coin among America's teens and twenty-somethings—if not a defining trait well into middle age, as David Brooks suggests in *Bobos in Paradise.* And just as Brooks's vegetarians and Nader voters fight like the management consultants they are to get their children into top schools and nurse the returns on their mutual funds, black America's embrace of hip-hop is more costume than skin.

One way to measure the true state of affairs is to consider what has not been playing in New York lately. For one thing, no recent film has feted the black criminal. On the contrary, last summer saw two jocular parodies of 1970's blaxploitation films: the minor hit *Undercover Brother* and Beyonce Knowles's portrayal of *Foxxy Cleopatra,* a character in the Austin Powers "threequel." As for *Antwone Fisher,* Denzel Washington's directorial debut, it does feature a sullen young black protagonist who is referred to a psychiatrist for anger management after getting into a scuffle, but despite his tragic upbringing, Antwone turns out to be sufficiently solid and self-directed to work out the issues and go on to a gracious life.

Theater, too, is suggestive for what is absent as much as for what is present. Six years ago, George C. Wolfe's *Bring in da Noise, Bring in da Funk* mobilized music and tap dance to preach the gospel of permanent victimhood. But last fall, at Harlem's Apollo Theater, Wolfe gave us *Harlem Song,* a slick little theme-park-style show celebrating the history of the neighborhood. Wolfe festooned the drama with excerpts from filmed interviews of elderly Harlem residents who, despite the horrors they grew up in, were conspicuously lacking in the "don't-tread-on-me" air of many of their children and grandchildren. In one number, 1920's Harlemites strolled to the smart strut of a vamp, ogling the black celebrities of the day and murmuring "Well, alright, then" with an air of proprietary admiration.

The show only dimly conveyed why Harlem took such a bad turn in the 1960's. Like most people who have lived through gradual societal change, the oldsters in the filmed interviews pointed to symptoms—drugs, riots, the pathologies bred in the housing projects—but missed the cause: the elevation of alienation and rebellion by America's cultural elites, and the social policies that flowed therefrom. But what was noteworthy was that *Harlem Song* did not exploit its musings on the 60's as an occasion for knee-jerk outrage.

20   After all, Wolfe could easily have recycled the angry hip-hop substratum of *Bring in da Noise* as a Big Ending for *Harlem Song,* and ten years ago he probably would have. That is when, in *Jelly's Last Jam,* he fashioned an admittedly brilliant, two-and-a-half hour indictment of Jelly Roll Morton, a creole musician, as much white as black, whose crime was the boast that he had invented jazz; the show's own crime was to have introduced so many people to a genius of jazz in so distorted a fashion. In *Harlem Song,* which was about victory, not victimhood, Wolfe was less interested in this brand of cultural politics. That also meant that the show unfortunately petered out toward the end, but at least the middle-aged white women in the row across from me were in their seats at the final curtain.

What, finally about the once-popular theme of integration? Last fall, in *Far From Heaven,* the director Todd Haynes revisited Douglas Sirk's 1955 *All That Heaven Allows,* a movie in which a suburban housewife falls in love with her gardener, played by Rock Hudson. The issue then was class difference; today, Haynes made the gardener a black man. Where the Rock Hudson character was a lover of poetry, the black gardener turns out to be well-informed about modern art, discoursing casually about Joan Miro.

In the scheme of things, this last was a significant touch. In the 1950's, some white filmmakers made a point of depicting black characters who were as adept as whites in all endeavors. Bill Cosby's erudite undercover agent Scotty on *I Spy,* the 60's television series, sprang from the same impulse. But by the time *I Spy* went off the air in 1968, the days of the Scotties were numbered. As separatist ideology took hold of black America, such characters came to be regarded as so many white wannabes co-opted by The Man. Any white writer who dared to create a black like Scotty—a Rhodes scholar, no less—would have been tarred as a covert racist. What came next was, instead, *Shaft*—"big, bold, black, and bad"—and *The Jeffersons.*

Far From Heaven has not been the only place on the recent pop scene where the integrationist ideal is back. In *Hairspray,* a runaway hit musical set in the year 1962, a Baltimore high-school girl seeks to integrate a dance show on local television. Her otherwise apolitical parents risk imprisonment to help her in her fight, local blacks warmly embrace her cause, and her best friend blithely hooks up with a black man in a display of easy interracial harmony that is decidedly ahistorical for that place and time. The very anachronism is, however, what makes the show relevant to our time. Its message is that integration is where we are headed.

24   At one point in *Hairspray,* three of the black chorus girls appear dressed as the Supremes, ushering in a scene by belting out "Welcome to the 60's." The sequence lasts only about half a minute, but both times I was there, the mostly white audience went crazy; the Motown sound is now imprinted as America's soul food. And when the show climaxes in a rousing dance number, "You Can't Stop the Beat" (of integration, that is)—a number notorious for getting audiences to mime the choreography in their seats—the sentiment no longer feels like the pure fantasy it seemed to represent in 1988 when the film on which Hairspray is based was first released.

Of course, *Hairspray* is a cartoon confection. But in the world of the Broadway theater, at least, integration is not an ideal at all but a living reality, in the sense that it is now perfectly ordinary for black performers to be cast in "white" lead roles with neither producers, reviewers, nor audiences batting an eye. In last fall's revival of the Stephen Sondheim musical *Into the Woods,* Vanessa Williams starred as the witch, a part originated in 1987 by Bernadette Peters. Sheryl Lee Ralph is playing a patrician celebrity in the bonbon *Thoroughly Modern Millie,* set in the lily-white 1920's of John Held, Jr. cartoons. Brian Stokes Mitchell, who has been anointed as Broadway's best baritone, period, is currently starring in a revival of *Man of la Mancha.* And even the revival of *Oklahoma!,* which strives for gritty, realism in its depiction of an Oklahoma frontier town circa 1907, features two black chorus members. Given the actuality of turn-of-the-century Oklahoma, these black performers are in effect playing white people.

The formulaic rage of hip-hop and Spoken Word is not going away any time soon. But it is a mere vaudeville, reflecting the true soul of black America no more than vaudeville reflected white America's a century ago. "If we can't talk straight in the barbershop, then where can we talk straight?" Eddie asks in *Barbershop.* On the evidence of these plays and films, straight talk is extending far beyond the barbershop.

PERSONAL RESPONSE

What current films have you seen that might support or refute McWhorter's statement in paragraph 3 that "we have come a long distance from the New Jack City gangster cycle of black films ten years ago"?

QUESTIONS FOR CLASS OR SMALL-GROUP DISCUSSION

1. In your own words, state McWhorter's thesis or central idea. Are you persuaded that his thesis is valid?

2. McWhorter devotes several paragraphs each to two films, *Barbershop* and *8 Mile,* before going on to discuss Broadway theatre. If you have seen either of those films, discuss how accurately you think McWhorter's analysis of them is. If you have not seen the films, does he make his point about them clear? Do you understand how they illustrate his point?

3. McWhorter mentions a number of New York theatre productions. How well do his examples serve to illustrate his central point?

4. McWhorter refers to "the formulaic rage of hip-hop and Spoken Word" (paragraph 26). What do you understand him to mean by "the formulaic rage" of those forms? To what extent do you agree with him that hip-hop and Spoken Word no longer represent "the true soul of black America"?

CINDERELLA: SATURDAY AFTERNOON AT THE MOVIES

Louise Bernikow

Louise Bernikow's work has centered on women's culture. Her personal essays reflecting on women's psychology, women's friendships, and the ties between women are collected in Among Women *(1980), from which this piece is taken. Her other books include the following:* Let's Have Lunch: Games of Sex and Power *(1981),* Alone in America: The Search for Happiness *(1986),* The Women in Our Lives: Cinderella, Scarlett, Virginia, and Me *(1989),* The American Women's Almanac: An Inspiring and Irreverent Women's History *(1997), and* Bark if You Love Me: A Woman-Meets-Dog Story *(2001).*

No, Cinderella, said the stepmother,
you have no clothes and cannot dance.
That's the way with stepmothers.
    (Anne Sexton, "Cinderella")

Turn and peep, turn and peep,
No blood is in the shoe,
The shoe is not too small for her,
The true bride rides with you.
    (Grimms' Cinderella)

I begin with a memory of movies and mother, a dark theatre and a Saturday afternoon. In a miasma of Walt Disney images, Bambi burning and Snow White asleep, the most memorable is "Cinderella." I carry her story with me for the rest of my life. It is a story about women alone together and they are each other's enemies. This is more powerful as a lesson than the ball, the Prince, or the glass slipper. The echoes of "Cinderella" in other fairy tales, in myth and literature, are about how awful women are to each other. The girl onscreen, as I squirm in my seat, needs to be saved. A man will come and save her. Some day my Prince will come. Women will not save her; they will thwart her. There is a magical fairy godmother who does help her, but this, for me, has no relation to life, for the fairy is not real, and the bad women are. The magical good fairy is a saccharine fluff.

There are two worlds in the Cinderella cartoon, one of women, one of men. The women are close by and hostile, the men distant and glittering. Stepsisters and stepmother are three in one, a female battalion allied against Cinderella. The daughters are just like their mother. All women are alike. Lines of connection, energy fields, attach sisters to mother, leaving Cinderella in exile from the female community at home.

Father is far off. On film, neither he nor the Prince has much character. Father is her only tie, her actual blood tie, but the connection does her no good. Daddy is King in this world; I cannot keep Daddy and King apart in my memory. My own father was as far off, as full of authority, as surrounded by heraldry, the trumpets of fantasy, to me, to my mother. King Daddy.

4   The Prince is rich and handsome. Rich matters more than handsome. The girl among the cinders, dressed in rags, will escape—I am on her side, I want her to escape, get away from the cinders and the awful women—because the Prince will lift her out. The world of the Prince is the world of the ball, music, fine clothes, and good feeling. Were everything to be right at home, were the women to be good to one another and have fun together, it would not be sufficient. The object is the ball, the Prince, the big house, the servants. Class mobility is at stake. Aspiration is being titillated.

To win the Prince, to be saved, requires being pretty. All the women care about this. Being pretty is the ticket, and because Cinderella is pretty, the stepmother and stepsisters want to keep her out of the running. There is no other enterprise. Cinderella does not turn up her nose and hide in a corner reading a book. Being pretty, getting to the ball, winning the Prince is the common ground among the women. What we have in common is what keeps us apart.

Cinderella must be lonely. Why, I wonder, doesn't she have a friend? Why doesn't she go to school? Why doesn't her father tell the awful women to stop? A hurt and lonely girl, with only a prince to provide another kind of feeling. Why doesn't she run away? Why can't the situation be changed? It is as though the house they live in is the only world, there is no other landscape. Women are always in the house, being awful to each other.

Magic. Cinderella has a fairy godmother who likes her and wants her to be happy. She gives the girl beautiful clothes. She doesn't have to instruct Cinderella or give her advice about how to waltz or how to lift her skirt or even give her directions to the palace. Only the clothes and the accoutrements—and a prohibition about coming home at midnight. A powerful woman who wants Cinderella to be pretty and successful in the social world. I know, at whatever age it is that I watch this story unfold, that the mother beside me is not the woman on the screen. Her feelings on such matters are, at best, mixed up. She is not so powerful.

8   I am stirred and confused by the contrast between bad and good women and the way it all seems to revolve around the issue of being pretty. Some women are hostile and thwarting, others enabling and powerful. The stepmother hates Cinderella's prettiness; the fairy godmother adorns it. I look sideways at my mother, trying to decide which kind of woman she is, where she stands on the business of pretty. Often, she braids my hair and settles me into polka dot, parades me before my beaming father. It is good to be pretty. Yet, onscreen, it is bad to be pretty—Cinderella is punished for it. In the enterprise of pretty, other women are your allies and your enemies. They are not disinterested. The heat around the issue of pretty, the urgency and intensity of it, is located among the women, not the men, at whom it is supposedly aimed. Luckily, we move on to the ball and the lost slipper.

This is one of the oldest and most often-told stories, varying significantly from one version to another, one country to another, one period to another. What appears on movie theatre screens or television on Saturday afternoons comes from as far away as China, as long ago as four hundred years. Each teller, each culture along the way, retained some archetypal patterns and transformed others, emphasized some parts of the story, eradicated others. Disney took his version of Cinderella from one written down by a Frenchman named Perrault in the seventeenth century. Perrault's is a "civilized" version, cleaned up, dressed up, and given several pointed "lessons" on top of the original material.

Many of the details about fashionability that we now associate with the story come from Perrault. His has the atmosphere of Coco Chanel's dressing rooms, is modern and glamorous. He concocted a froufrou, aimed at an aristocratic audience and airily decorated with things French. He named one of the sisters Charlotte and set the action in a world of full-length looking glasses and inlaid floors. He invented a couturière called Mademoiselle de Poche to create costumes for the ball, linens and ruffles, velvet suits and headdresses. Disney dropped the French touches.

Perrault's story is set in a world of women with their eyes on men. Even before the King's ball is announced, the stepmother and stepsisters are preoccupied with how they look. They are obsessed with their mirrors, straining to see what men would see. Once the ball is on the horizon, they starve themselves for days so that their shapes shall be, when laced into Mademoiselle de Poche's creations, as extremely slender as those in our own fashion magazines. The ball—and the prospects it implies—intensifies the hostility toward Cinderella. They have been envious. Now, they must keep the pretty girl out of competition. Most of the action of Perrault's story is taken up with the business of the ball.

12   Cinderella is a sniveling, self-pitying girl. Forbidden to go to the ball, she does not object but, instead, dutifully helps her stepsisters adorn themselves. She has no will, initiates no action. Then, magically, the fairy godmother appears. She comes from nowhere, summoned, we suppose, by Cinderella's wishes. Unlike the fairy godmother in other versions of the story, Perrault's and Disney's character has no connection to anything real, has no meaning, except to enable Cinderella to overcome the

opposition of the women in her home, wear beautiful clothes, and get to the ball. Cinderella stammers, unable to say what she wants—for she is passive, suffering, and good, which comes across as relatively unconscious. The fairy divines Cinderella's desire and equips her with pumpkin/coach, mice/horses, rats/coachmen, lizards/footmen, clothes, and dancing shoes. She adds the famous prohibition that Cinderella return by midnight or everything will be undone.

These details of the fairy godmother's magic—the pumpkin, image of All Hallows' Eve; midnight, the witching hour; mice, rats, and lizards originated with Perrault. They are specific reminders of an actual and ancient female magic, witchcraft. Since Perrault wrote his story in the seventeenth century, it is not surprising to find echoes of this magic, which was enormously real to Perrault's audience.

Thousands had been burned at the stake for practicing witchcraft, most of them women. A witch was a woman with enormous power, a woman who might change the natural world. She was "uncivilized" and in opposition to the world of the King, the court, polite society. She had to be controlled. Perrault's story attempts to control the elements of witchcraft just as various kings' governments had, in the not too recent past, controlled what they believed to be an epidemic of witchcraft. Perrault controls female power by trivializing it. The witchcraft in this story is innocent, ridiculous, silly, and playful. It is meant to entertain children.

The prohibition that Cinderella return by midnight is also related to witchcraft. She must avoid the witching hour, with its overtones of sexual abandon. The fairy godmother acts in this capacity in a way that is familiar to mothers and daughters—she controls the girl, warns her against darkness, uses her authority to enforce restraint, prevent excess, particularly excess associated with the ball, the world of men, sexuality.

16 Cinderella's dancing shoes are glass slippers. Perrault mistranslated the fur slipper in the version that came to him, substituting *verre* for *vire* and coming up glass. No pedant came along to correct the mistake, for the glass slipper is immensely appropriate to the story in its modern form and the values it embodies. Call it dainty or fragile, the slipper is quintessentially the stereotype of femininity. I wonder how Cinderella danced in it.

The rags-to-riches moment holds people's imagination long after the details of the story have disappeared. It appeals to everyone's desire for magic, for change that comes without effort, for speedy escape from a bad place—bad feelings. We all want to go to the ball, want life to be full of good feeling and feeling good. But Cinderella's transformation points to a particular and limited kind of good feeling—from ugly to beautiful, raggedy to glamorous. The object of her transformation is not actually pleasure (she does not then walk around her house feeling better) but transportation to the ball with all the right equipment for captivating the Prince.

Transformed, Cinderella goes to the ball, which is the larger world, the kingdom ruled by kings and fathers. The stepmother has no power in that world and does not even appear. This part of the story focuses on men, who are good to Cinderella as forcefully as women have been bad to her. Perrault embellishes Cinderella's appearance in a way that would have been congenial to the French court. In fact, she seems to have gone to the French court. The story is suffused with perfume and "fashionability." The Prince is taken with Cinderella and gives her some candy—"citrons and oranges," according to the text. How French. She, forever good, shares the candy with her stepsisters, who do not, of course, know who she is.

Cinderella has a wonderful time. As readers, hearers, watchers, we have a wonderful time along with her. More than the music and the dancing, the aura of sensual pleasure, everyone's good time comes from the idea that Cinderella is a "knockout." This is exciting. Perrault's word for what happens is that the people are *étonnés,* which means stunned. Cinderella is a showstopper, so "dazzling" that "the King himself, old as he was, could not help watching her." He remarks on this to his Queen, whose reactions we are not told. Being "stunning" is being powerful. This is the way women have impact, the story tells us. This is female power in the world outside the home, in contrast to her former powerlessness, which was within the home, which was another country. This tells me why women spend so much time trying to turn themselves into knockouts—because, in Cinderella and in other stories, it *works.*

20   Presumably, Cinderella's giddiness over her own triumph at the ball makes her forget her godmother's command and almost miss her midnight deadline. Lest we lose the idea that all men adore Cinderella, Perrault adds a courtier at the end of the story, as the search for the missing Cinderella is carried out, and has him, too, say how attractive Cinderella is. She fulfills, then, the masculine idea of what is beautiful in a woman. She is the woman men want women to be.

Cinderella flees at midnight and loses her shoe. Perrault plays this part down, but Disney has a visual festival with the glinting glass slipper on the staircase and the trumpet-accompanied quest to find its owner. Perrault's Prince sends a messenger to find the shoe's owner, which puts the action at some distance, but Disney gives us a prince in all his splendor.

Cinderella is a heroine and in the world of fairy tales what the heroine wins is marriage to the Prince. Like any classic romance, wafted by perfume and fancy clothes, the young girl is lifted from a lowly powerless situation (from loneliness and depression, too) by a powerful man. He has no character, not even a handsome face, but simply represents the things that princes represent, the power of the kingdom.

Opposition to achieving this triumph comes from the women in the house; help comes from daydream and fantasy. The only proper activity for women to engage in is primping. What is expected of them is that they wait "in the right way" to be discovered. Cinderella obeys the rules. Her reward is to be claimed by the Prince. The lesson of Cinderella in these versions is that a girl who knows and keeps her place will be rewarded with male favor.

24   Like a saint, she shows neither anger nor resentment toward the women who treated her so badly. In fact, she takes her stepsisters along to the castle, where she marries each off to a nobleman. Now everyone will be happy. Now there will be no conflict, no envy, no degradation. If each woman has a prince or nobleman, she will be content and the soft humming of satisfaction will fill the air. Women otherwise cannot be alone together.

This is the sort of story that poisoned Madame Bovary's imagination. In Flaubert's novel, a woman married to a country doctor, with aspirations for a larger life, goes to a ball where a princely character pays her some attention. The ball and the Prince, seen by Emma Bovary as possibilities for changing everyday life, haunted her uneasy sleep. The ball was over. Wait as she might for its return, for a second invitation, all she got was a false prince—a lover who did not lift her from the ordinariness of her life—and then despair.

The romance depends on aspiration. The Prince must be able to give the heroine something she cannot get for herself or from other women. He must represent a valuable and scarce commodity, for the women must believe there is only one, not enough to go around, and must set themselves to keeping other women from getting it. In "Cinderella," like other fairy tales and other romances, the world of the Prince represents both actual and psychological riches.

Perrault's Cinderella is the daughter of a gentleman, turned into a peasant within the household. She has been declassed by female interlopers, reduced to the status of servant, for she belongs to her father's class only precariously. One of the ways women exercise their power, the story tells us, is by degrading other women. Cinderella will be saved from her female-inflicted degradation first by another female, the fairy godmother, who puts her on the road to her ultimate salvation. At the end of the story, she is restored to her class position, or, better, raised to an even higher position by the Prince.

28   Her fall from class is represented not only by her tattered clothes, but by the work she is forced to do. She is the household "drudge" and housework is the image of her degradation. Her work has no value in the story; it is the invisible, repetitious labor that keeps things going and makes it possible for the sisters and stepmother to devote themselves to *their* work, which is indolence on the one hand and trying to be beautiful for men on the other. Historically, indolence has been revered as the mark of a lady. What is "feminine" and "ladylike" is far removed from the world of work. Or the world of self-satisfying work. A man prides himself on having a wife who does not work; it increases his value in the eyes of other men; it means he provides well; it enforces conventional bourgeois "masculinity." A lady has long fingernails, neither the typewriter nor the kitchen floor has cracked them. She has porcelain skin; neither the rough outdoors nor perspiration has cracked that. Out of the same set of values comes the famous glass slipper.

The stepmother's class position is as precarious as Cinderella's is. The story does not tell, but we can imagine that whether she was married before to a poorer man or one equally a gentleman, her status and security are now tied to the man she has married and the ones she can arrange for her daughters. History, experience, and literature are full of landless, propertyless women trying to secure marriage to stand as a bulwark against poverty, displacement, and exile, both actual and psychological. The actual situation bears emphasis. The economic reality behind the fairy tale and the competition among the women for the favor of the Prince is a world in which women have no financial lives of their own. They cannot own businesses or inherit property. The kingdom is not theirs. In order to survive, a woman must have a husband. It is in the interest of her daughters' future—and her own—that the stepmother works to prevent competition from Cinderella. She is not evil. Within the confines of her world and the value systems of that world, she is quite nice to her own daughters, only cruel to Cinderella.

Still, the stepmother is an archetypal figure in fairy tales, always a thwarter, often a destroyer of children. Psychologists, and Bruno Bettelheim in particular, have a psychological explanation for this. The "bad" stepmother, Bettelheim points out, usually coexists with the "good" mother, representing two aspects of a real mother as experienced by a child. The stepmother is shaped by the child's unacceptable anger against her own mother. But there are real facts of life at work in these stepmother stories, too, especially as they describe what can happen among women at home. To a man's second wife, the daughter of the first marriage is a constant reminder of the first wife. The second wife is continually confronted with that memory and with the understanding that wives are replaceable, as they frequently and actually were in a world where women died young in childbirth, and men remarried, moved on.

A woman marries a man who has a daughter and comes to his household, where the daughter's strongest connection is to her father; the stepmother's strongest connection is to the husband. The Eternal Triangle appears, husband/father at the center, mediating the relationship, stepmother and daughter as antagonists, competing for the husband/father's attention and whatever he may represent. Anxious, each in her own way and equally displaced, they face each other with enmity. The masculine imagination takes prideful pleasure in the story, placing, as it does, husband/father at center stage, making him King, arbiter of a world of women. . . .

32   I am writing an essay about Cinderella, spending mornings at the typewriter, afternoons in libraries, interpreting information on index cards of various colors and sheets of yellow paper. I discover something bizarre woven in the story as we now know it: that the story took root in ancient China. The remnants of that culture, especially of the ancient practice of foot-binding, are in the story, in the value of the small foot, in the use of the shoe to represent the potential bride. I see, then, the historical truth behind the terrible moment at the end of "Cinderella."

The Prince brings the slipper to the house of Cinderella's father. First one stepsister, then the other attempts to slip her foot into it, but each foot is too large. The first stepsister's toe is too large. The stepmother hands her daughter a knife and says, "Cut off the toe. When you are Queen you won't have to walk anymore." The second stepsister's heel is too large and her mother repeats the gesture and the advice.

Mutilation. Blood in the shoe, blood on the knife, blood on the floor and unbearable pain, borne, covered, masked by the smile. It is too familiar, frightening in its familiarity. The mother tells the daughter to mutilate herself in the interests of winning the Prince. She will not have to walk. Again, indolence enshrined. As mothers, in fact, did in China until the twentieth century—among the upper classes as unquestioned custom and among peasants as great sacrifice and gamble.

It began when the girl was between five and seven years old. The bandages were so tight, the girl might scream. Her mother pulled them tighter and might have tried to soothe her. Tighter. At night, in agony, the girl loosens them. She is punished, her hands tied to a post to prevent unlacing. The bones crack. The pain is constant. Tighter. She cannot walk. Tighter. By her adolescence, the girl has learned to bind her feet herself and the pain has lessened. She has, as a reward, special shoes, embroidered and decorated, for her tiny feet.

36   I translate the actual foot-binding, the ritual interaction of mother and daughter, to metaphor. A black mother straightens her daughter's hair with a hot iron, singeing the scalp, pulling and tugging. The daughter screams. My mother buys me

a girdle when I am fifteen years old because she doesn't like the jiggle. She slaps my face when I begin to menstruate, telling me later that it is an ancient Russian custom and she does not know its origin. I sleep with buttons taped to my cheeks to make dimples and with hard metallic curlers in my hair. Tighter. I hold myself tighter, as my mother has taught me to do.

Is the impulse to cripple a girl peculiar to China between the eleventh and twentieth centuries? The lotus foot was the size of a doll's and the woman could not walk without support. Her foot was four inches long and two inches wide. A doll. A girl-child. Crippled, indolent, and bound. This is what it meant to be beautiful. And desired. This women did and do to each other. Pain in the foot is pain in every part of the body. A mother is about to bind her daughter's feet. She knows the pain in her own memory. She says: "A daughter's pretty legs are achieved through the shedding of tears."

> This women did to each other.
> This women do.
> Or refuse to do.
> . . . .

PERSONAL RESPONSE

Select a film for children that you recall from your childhood and discuss what you remember most about it. Do you think it has the same kinds of messages that Bernikow finds in "Cinderella"?

QUESTIONS FOR CLASS OR SMALL-GROUP DISCUSSION

1. Discuss whether you agree with Bernikow's interpretation that "Cinderella" is chiefly "about how awful women are to each other" (paragraph 1).

2. Discuss whether you think it is true that "rich matters more than handsome" (paragraph 4) for men in today's society, whereas being pretty is most important for women (paragraph 5).

3. Do you agree that females' power resides in their being "stunning" (paragraph 19), whereas other kinds of power in women are feared? Discuss your own perceptions of powerful women: Do you view power in women differently from or the same as the way you see it in men?

4. Bernikow sees a parallel between the stepsisters in "Cinderella" cutting off parts of their feet to win the Prince and the practice of foot-binding in China, and she interprets foot-binding as a metaphor for other interactions between mothers and daughters (paragraphs 36–38). To what extent do you agree with her in this interpretation? Do women today go through painful rituals to make themselves appealing to men? Do men go through painful rituals in order to appeal to women?

5. Can you name any current books or recent Hollywood films that have the same sorts of messages that Bernikow sees in "Cinderella"? What other fairy

tales or children's stories reinforce Bernikow's point about female rivalry and male power? What would happen if you reversed the sex roles in "Cinderella"?

TV VIOLENCE: DOES IT CAUSE REAL-LIFE MAYHEM?

Susan R. Lamson

Susan R. Lamson, former director of national affairs for the National Rifle Association, now directs the Conservation, Wildlife and Natural Resources Institute for Legislative Action, National Rifle Association. At a congressional hearing on television violence in 1993, which she refers to in this article, Lamson explained the position of the National Rifle Association on the role of television violence. She continues to represent the NRA before congressional hearings. In this July 1993 American Hunter *article, Lamson answers the question posed by her title.*

Turn on your TV virtually any time of any day and you can bring a carnival of murder, mayhem, and bloodshed right into your living room. Maybe, like many Americans, you've grown accustomed to it and even expect it. But step back and look at this kaleidoscope of killing through the eyes of a child—and consider what role it's played for America's new generation of ultraviolent killers—and you see what a menace TV violence really is.

Televised mayhem is seen as a leading cause of America's epidemic of violent crime. It was the subject of May 12 hearings before the House Energy and Commerce Committee's Telecommunications and Finance subcommittee and the Senate Judiciary Committee's Constitution subcommittee. I represented NRA at the hearings and was joined by the nation's leading experts on human behavior and psychology to call for an end—or at least a reduction—of the broadcast brutality that's taking such a vicious toll on society.

As Dr. Brandon S. Centerwall, professor of epidemiology at the University of Washington, explained: "The U.S. national homicide rate has doubled since the 1950s. As a member of the Centers for Disease Control violence research team, my task was to determine why. A wide array of possible causes was examined—the 'baby boom' effect, trends in urbanization, economic trends, trends in alcohol abuse, the role of capital punishment, the effects of civil unrest, the availability of firearms, exposure to television."

4   "Over the course of seven years of investigation," Dr. Centerwall continued, "each of these purported causes was tested in a variety of ways to see whether it could be eliminated as a credible contributor to the doubling of rates of violence in the United States. And, one by one, each of them was invalidated, except for television."

If that's frightening to you, consider this: In his landmark 1989 study, Centerwall concluded, "it is estimated that exposure to television is etiologically [causally] related to approximately one-half of the homicides committed in the United States, or approximately 10,000 homicides annually, and to a major proportion—perhaps one half—of rapes, assaults, and other forms of interpersonal violence in the United States."

While not all agree with Centerwall's assessment of the problem's severity, few challenge his claim that Hollywood bloodshed *does* spill out from the screen and into our lives. As the American Psychological Association testified, the cause-and-effect link between TV violence and human aggression has been well-established for nearly twenty years. But until recently the TV networks have been reluctant to change. That's why in 1990 Congress passed the Television Violence Act, that allowed the networks to cooperate and develop programming standards with which they and the public could live.

The problem is, violence sells. Media executives know it and profit from it. More viewers means higher ratings, which add up to more advertising dollars. So, as the National Institute of Mental Health has found, 80 percent of all television programs contain violent acts. But the violence is like a drug: Viewers develop a tolerance for it, so media "pushers" give them steadily more.

8   Typically, prime-time programming has averaged eight to twelve violent acts per hour. A recent study by the Annenberg School of Communications found violence in children's programming at an historic high—thirty-two violent acts per hour. And a recent *TV Guide* study counted 1,845 acts of violence in eighteen hours of viewing time, an average of 100 violent acts per hour, or one every thirty-six seconds.

While adults may see all this TV mayhem as just the latest "action entertainment," children don't get it. Psychologists agree that up to ages three and four, children can't distinguish fact from fantasy on TV. For them, TV is a reflection of the world, and it's not a friendly place. Still, juvenile viewership is high. Children average nearly four hours of TV per day, and in the inner cities that increases to as many as eleven hours. Which means that in many cases, TV is the reality.

And this TV violence "addiction" is taking an increasingly grisly toll. FBI and census data show the homicide arrest rate for seventeen-year-olds more than doubled between 1985 and 1991, and the rate for fifteen- and sixteen-year-olds increased even faster. Psychologists point to several effects of televised mayhem: Children are taught that society is normally violent. They become disproportionately frightened of being victimized and become less likely to help victims of crime. They also grow more aggressive and violent themselves.

Through the Television Violence Act, the major networks have agreed on a set of standards to reduce the level of gratuitous violence in their programs. But so far, there's been little change; network executives promise better for the fall 1993 season.

12   Ironically, this year's congressional hearings on TV violence were in May— "sweeps month,"—when the networks compete for the viewership ratings that determine their advertising profits for the year to come. Some critics are calling May 1993 one of the most violent sweeps months in TV history.

Whereas in years past, entertainment executives flatly refuted the dangers of TV violence, the network heads who testified during the May hearings were more receptive of change—or so they said. Still, their words somehow ring hollow, especially given the brutality of their "sweeps month" programming.

Howard Stringer, president of CBS, Warren Littlefield of NBC, and Thomas S. Murphy of ABC all spoke at the congressional hearings. Stringer talked of his network's "principles," "seriousness," "responsibility," and "careful and extensive discussion"—yet there seems to be no end to the bloodshed. Then, in a *Washington Post* story days later, Stringer blamed firearms: "There are 200 million guns, 66 million handguns in America. That has a lot to do with violence." (Readers will remember that the Washington, DC, affiliate of Stringer's network recently rejected NRA's new commercial on the failings of the criminal justice system. The remarkable excuse given by CBS's affiliate was that the commercial "tends to inflame or incite.") Barring legislation, congressional hearings can't accomplish much without unified grassroots pressure from citizens. Ultimately, your letters, phone calls, and faxes are the best ammunition in the fight to cut televised brutality and thus curb crime and safeguard your Second Amendment rights. When you see examples of pointless, gratuitous violence in your TV programming, write to the network executives and let them know how you feel. The appropriate names and addresses are as follows:

President
ABC TV Entertainment
2040 Avenue of the Stars
Century City, CA 91521

President
CBS Broadcast Group
524 East 57th Street
New York, NY 10019

President
NBC Entertainment
30 Rockefeller Plaza
New York, NY 10112-0002

Better yet, make a note of what products or services are advertised during violent programs, and voice your outrage to the leaders of those companies. You can get the proper names and addresses through your library's reference section. Excellent resources include *Standard & Poor's Register of Corporations, Directors, and Executives,* Dun & Bradstreet's *Million Dollar Directory,* and *Moody's Manuals.*

16   In the end, only you—as a consumer, TV viewer, and voter—can demand an end to the televised violence that's bloodying our society. If all NRA members and gun owners do their part in this fight, we *can* cut into the TV destruction that so gravely threatens both our children and our Bill of Rights.

PERSONAL RESPONSE

Do you agree with Lamson that television depicts entirely too much violence? If so, does such violence bother you? Explain your answer.

QUESTIONS FOR CLASS OR SMALL-GROUP DISCUSSION

1. Lamson asks readers to consider the role that television has played "for America's new generation of ultraviolent killers" (paragraph 1). Discuss whether you think Lamson offers conclusive proof to support her belief in the causal relationship between television violence and real-life violence.

2. Lamson says in paragraph 2 that "televised mayhem is seen as a leading cause of America's epidemic of violent crime." Discuss other causes that may also account for the epidemic of crime.

3. Watch prime-time television for one evening or children's programs for one Saturday morning, and record the number of violent acts you see. Decide beforehand exactly what will be considered a violent act. (For instance, will you include verbal assaults?) If several of your classmates do the same, on different evenings or different channels, you should get a good indication of whether the figures Lamson cites in paragraph 8 are still accurate today. Do a follow-up discussion of your observations.

4. Evaluate the argument Lamson makes here. Do you think her interest in the National Rifle Association in any way influences her argument? Does it influence your evaluation of the argument?

STOP BLAMING KIDS AND TV

MIKE MALES

Mike Males, senior researcher for the Justice Policy Institute and sociology instructor at the University of California, Santa Cruz, is author of several books: The Scapegoat Generation: America's War on Adolescents *(1996),* Framing Youth: Ten Myths About the Next Generation *(1998),* Smoked: Why Joe Camel is Still Smiling *(1999),* Juvenile Injustice: America's "Youth Violence" Hoax *(2000), and* Kids & Guns: How Politicians, Experts and the Press Fabricate Fear of Youth *(2001). This essay first appeared in the October 1997 issue of* The Progressive.

"Children have never been very good at listening to their elders," James Baldwin wrote in *Nobody Knows My Name*. "But they have never failed to imitate them." This basic truth has all but disappeared as the public increasingly treats teenagers as a robot-like population under sway of an exploitative media. White House officials lecture film, music, Internet, fashion, and pop-culture moguls and accuse them of programming kids to smoke, drink, shoot up, have sex, and kill.

So do conservatives, led by William Bennett and Dan Quayle. Professional organizations are also into media-bashing. In its famous report on youth risks, the Carnegie Corporation devoted a full chapter to media influences.

Progressives are no exception. *Mother Jones* claims it has "proof that TV makes kids violent." And the Institute of Alternative Media emphasizes, "the average American child will witness . . . . 200,000 acts of (TV) violence" by the time that child graduates from high school.

4   None of these varied interests note that during the eighteen years between a child's birth and graduation from high school, there will be fifteen million cases of *real* violence in American homes grave enough to require hospital emergency treatment. These assaults will cause ten million serious injuries and 40,000 deaths to children. In October 1996, the Department of Health and Human Services reported 565,000 serious injuries that abusive parents inflicted on children and youths in 1993. The number is up four-fold since 1986.

The Department of Health report disappeared from the news in one day. It elicited virtually no comment from the White House, Republicans, or law-enforcement officials. Nor from Carnegie scholars, whose 150-page study, "Great Transitions: Preparing Adolescents for a New Century," devotes two sentences to household violence. The left press took no particular interest in the story, either.

All sides seem to agree that fictional violence, sex on the screen, Joe Camel, beer-drinking frogs, or naked bodies on the Internet pose a bigger threat to children than do actual beatings, rape, or parental addictions. This, in turn, upholds the Clinton doctrine that youth behavior is the problem, and curbing young people's rights the answer.

Claims that TV causes violence bear little relation to real behavior. Japanese and European kids behold media as graphically brutal as that which appears on American screens, but seventeen-year-olds in those countries commit murder at rates lower than those of American seventy-year-olds.

8   Likewise, youths in different parts of the United States are exposed to the same media but display drastically different violence levels. TV violence does not account for the fact that the murder rate among black teens in Washington, D.C., is twenty-five times higher than that of white teens living a few Metro stops away. It doesn't explain why, nationally, murder doubled among nonwhite and Latino youth over the last decade, but declined among white Anglo teens. Furthermore, contrary to the TV brain-washing theory, Anglo sixteen-year-olds have lower violent-crime rates than black sixty-year-olds, Latino forty-year-olds, and Anglo thirty-year-olds. Men, women, whites, Latino, blacks, Asians, teens, young adults, middle-agers, and senior citizens in Fresno County—California's poorest urban area—display murder and violent-crime rates double those of their counterparts in Ventura County, the state's richest.

Confounding every theory, America's biggest explosion in felony violent crime is not street crime among minorities or teens of any color, but domestic violence among aging, mostly white baby boomers. Should we arm Junior with a V-chip to protect him from Mom and Dad?

In practical terms, media-violence theories are not about kids, but about race and class: If TV accounts for any meaningful fraction of murder levels among poorer, nonwhite youth, why doesn't it have the same effect on white kids? Are minorities inherently programmable?

The newest target is Channel One, legitimately criticized by the Unplug Campaign—a watchdog sponsored by the Center for Commercial-Free Public Education—as a corporate marketing ploy packaged as educational TV. But then the Unplug Campaign gives credence to claims that "commercials control kids" by "harvesting minds," as Roy Fox of the University of Missouri says. These claims imply that teens are uniquely open to media brainwashing.

12   Other misleading claims come from Johns Hopkins University media analyst Mark Crispin Miller. In his critique of Channel One in the May edition of *Extra!*, Miller invoked such hackneyed phrases as the "inevitable rebelliousness of adolescent boys," the "hormones raging," and the "defiant boorish behavior" of "young men." Despite the popularity of these stereotypes, there is no basis in fact for such anti-youth bias.

A 1988 study in the *Journal of Youth and Adolescence* by psychology professors Grayson Holmbeck and John Hill concluded: "Adolescents are *not* in turmoil, *not* deeply disturbed, *not* at the mercy of their impulses, *not* resistant to parental values, and *not* rebellious."

In the November 1992 *Journal of the American Academy of Child and Adolescent Psychiatry*, Northwestern University psychiatry professor Daniel Offer reviewed 150 studies and concluded, in his article "Debunking the Myths of Adolescence," that "the effects of pubertal hormones are neither potent nor pervasive."

If anything, Channel One and other mainstream media reinforce young people's conformity to—not defiance of—adult values. Miller's unsubstantiated claims that student consumerism, bad behaviors, and mental or biological imbalances are compelled by media ads and images could be made with equal force about the behaviors of his own age group. Binge drinking, drug abuse, and violence against children by adults over the age of thirty are rising rapidly.

16   The barrage of sexually seductive liquor ads, fashion images, and anti-youth rhetoric, by conventional logic, must be influencing those hormonally unstable middle-agers.

I worked for a dozen years in youth programs in Montana and California. When problems arose, they usually crossed generations. I saw violent kids with dads or uncles in jail for assault. I saw middle-schoolers molested in childhood by mom's boyfriend. I saw budding teen alcoholics hoisting forty-ouncers alongside forty-year-old sots. I also saw again and again how kids start to smoke. In countless trailers and small apartments dense with blue haze, children roamed the rugs as grownups puffed. Mom and seventh-grade daughter swapped Dorals while bemoaning the evils of men. A junior-high basketball center slept outside before a big game because a dozen elders—from her non-inhaling sixteen-year-old brother to her grandma—were all chain smokers. Two years later, she'd given up and joined the party.

As a rule, teen smoking mimicked adult smoking by gender, race, locale, era, and household. I could discern no pop-culture puppetry. My survey of 400 Los Angeles middle-schoolers for a 1994 *Journal of School Health* article found children of smoking parents three times more likely to smoke by age fifteen than children of nonsmokers. Parents were the most influential but not the only adults kids emulated. Nor did youngsters copy elders slavishly. Youths often picked slightly different habits (like chewing tobacco, or their own brands).

In 1989, the Centers for Disease Control lamented, "75 percent of all teenage smokers come from homes where parents smoke." You don't hear such candor from today's put-politics-first health agencies. Centers for Disease Control tobacco chieftain Michael Eriksen informed me that his agency doesn't make an issue of parental smoking. Nor do anti-smoking groups. Asked Kathy Mulvey, research director of INFACT: "Why make enemies of fifty million adult smokers" when advertising creates the real "appeal of tobacco to youth?"

20   Do ads hook kids on cigarettes? Studies of the effects of the Joe Camel logo show only that a larger fraction of teen smokers than veteran adult smokers choose the Camel brand. When asked, some researchers admit they cannot demonstrate that advertising causes kids to smoke who would not otherwise. And that's the real issue. In fact, surveys found smoking declining among teens (especially the youngest) during Joe's advent from 1985 to 1990.

The University of California's Stanton Glantz, whose exposure of 10,000 tobacco documents enraged the industry, found corporate perfidy far shrewder than camels and cowboys.

"As the tobacco industry knows well," Glantz reported, "kids want to be like adults." An industry marketing document advises: "To reach young smokers, present the cigarette as one of the initiations into adult life . . . the basic symbols of growing up."

The biggest predictor of whether a teen will become a smoker, a drunk, or a druggie is whether or not the child grows up amid adult addicts. Three-fourths of murdered kids are killed by adults. Suicide and murder rates among white teenagers resemble those of white adults, and suicide and murder rates among black teens track those of black adults. And as far as teen pregnancy goes, for minor mothers, four-fifths of the fathers are adults over eighteen, and half are adults over twenty.

24   The inescapable conclusion is this: If you want to change juvenile behavior, change adult behavior. But instead of focusing on adults, almost everyone points a finger at kids—and at the TV culture that supposedly addicts them.

Groups like Mothers Against Drunk Driving charge, for instance, that Budweiser's frogs entice teens to drink. Yet the 1995 National Household Survey found teen alcohol use declining. "Youths aren't buying the cute and flashy beer images," an in-depth *USA Today* survey found. Most teens found the ads amusing, but they did not consume Bud as a result.

By squabbling over frogs, political interests can sidestep the impolitic tragedy that adults over the age of twenty-one cause 90 percent of America's 16,000 alcohol-related traffic deaths every year. Clinton and drug-policy chief Barry McCaffrey ignore federal reports that show a skyrocketing toll of booze and drug-related casualties among adults in their thirties and forties—the age group that is parenting most American teens. But both officials get favorable press attention by blaming alcohol ads and heroin chic for corrupting our kids.

Progressive reformers who insist kids are so malleable that beer frogs and Joe Camel and Ace Ventura push them to evil are not so different from those on the Christian right who claim that *Our Bodies, Ourselves* promotes teen sex and that the group Rage Against the Machine persuades pubescents to roll down Rodeo Drive with a shotgun.

28   America's increasingly marginalized young deserve better than grownup escapism. Millions of children and teenagers face real destitution, drug abuse, and violence in their homes. Yet these profound menaces continue to lurk in the background, even as the frogs, V-chips, and Mighty Morphins take center stage.

PERSONAL RESPONSE

Are you surprised at Males' defense of young people? Have you heard similar arguments before, or is his approach different from what you are used to hearing about television and its influence on young people?

QUESTIONS FOR CLASS OR SMALL-GROUP DISCUSSION

1. Males opens his essay with a quotation from James Baldwin and the following statement: "This basic truth has all but disappeared as the public increasingly treats teenagers as a robot-like population under sway of an exploitative media" (paragraph 1). State the "basic truth" that Males believes the quotation suggests. Then consider what Males seems to mean when he says that teenagers are treated "as a robot-like population." Do you agree with him on that point?

2. Males write: "In practical terms, media-violence theories are not about kids, but about race and class" (paragraph 10). Are you persuaded by the evidence that Males presents to support this assertion? Can you add further proof or offer a counterargument?

3. What is your response to this statement in paragraph 24: "If you want to change juvenile behavior, change adult behavior." Do you agree with Males?

4. How persuaded are you by Males' argument? Do you think that his personal observations strengthen or weaken his argument? What do you think about his use of loaded language and sarcasm? How would you assess the strengths and weaknesses of his argument overall?

○ PERSPECTIVES ON FILM AND TELEVISION ○

Suggested Writing Topics

1. Like advertisers, producers of television shows argue that they do not create problems but simply reflect the values of society. Explain your position on the subject of how much responsibility television producers should bear for the images they produce in their advertisements.

2. Write an analysis of a popular television show. Your analysis can be either positive or negative, depending on your own feelings about the show. You

may criticize a ridiculous, boring, or poorly acted show, for instance, or you may praise a brilliant, hilarious, or wonderfully acted one.

3. Do an analysis of any fairy tale or children's film for its depiction of female and male sex roles. Do you find stereotyped assumptions about masculinity and femininity? In what ways do you think the fairy tale or film reinforces or shapes cultural definitions of masculinity and femininity?

4. Referring to John H. McWhorter's "Up from Hip-Hop" where appropriate, write an essay analyzing any of the films or plays he mentions in terms of their portrayal of Blacks: *Barbershop* (film); *8 Mile* (film); *Def Poetry Jam* (play); *Far From Heaven* (film); *Hairspray* (motion picture or play); *Antwone Fisher* (film); *Bring in da Noise, Bring in da Funk* (play); *Crowns* (play); *Harlem Song* (play); *Jelly's Last Jam* (play). If you have not seen any of these, select a film or play that you have seen.

5. John H. McWhorter comments that "the formulaic rage of hip-hop and Spoken Word is not going away any time soon." Write an essay explaining and giving examples of "the formulaic rage" in hip-hop or Spoken Word.

6. Compare and contrast Susan R. Lamson's argument in "TV Violence: Does It Cause Real-Life Mayhem?" with Mike Males' in "Stop Blaming Kids and TV." State whose argument you agree with more and why.

7. Explore the positive and negative aspects of a particular type of television programming, such as situation comedies, medical dramas, or soap operas.

8. Assess the quality of today's films by using examples of a film or films you have seen recently. Consider, for instance, evaluating the values endorsed by the film(s).

9. Write a position paper on the topic of sexually explicit and graphically violent Hollywood films by selecting one film for close analysis and two or three others to use as examples to support your position.

10. Explore the effects on you, either positive or negative, of a movie or television program that you saw when you were growing up.

11. If you are a fan of reality shows on television, choose one that you particularly like and explain why it appeals to you. If you do not like reality shows, pick one that you particularly dislike and explain why you do not like it.

12. Examine portrayals of any of the following in several television programs: the American family, women, men, a particular ethnic group, or a particular age group.

13. Write a letter to the president of one of the major television networks in which you express your views on the nature and quality of its programming for children.

14. Write a letter to either or both the sponsors and the producer of a television program you find particularly violent, mindless, or vulgar, explaining your complaint and what you would like to see changed.

15. Write a letter to the sponsors or producer of a television program you find intellectually stimulating, educational, or informative, praising the program and pointing out its best features.

Research Topics

1. Select a particular genre of film, such as comedy, western, romance, fantasy, or action, and research observations of various film historians, film critics, and other film commentators about the films in that genre. One approach is to assess the historical development of the genre and its current state. As you do your preliminary reading, look for a controversial issue on which to focus your research. Then draw your own conclusions after you thoroughly research your subject.

2. Select a particular type of television program, such as reality TV, news program, talk show, children's entertainment, drama, or situation comedy and research what critics say about such programming currently and historically. Is there a program that represents the best of the type? The worst of the type?

3. Film or television critics and commentators sometimes use the term "golden age" to refer to a period in the past when a particular type of film or program reached its peak of excellence. Select a medium—film or television—and a genre—comedy, drama, or another of your choice—and research what characterizes "golden age" for the type and which program(s) or film(s) represent the type. If possible, view representative programs or films and include your responses to them in your research paper.

4. Much has been written about certain images in films or on television, such as the portrayal of women, of minorities, and of class issues. Select a particular image or theme to research for its representation in films or on television. Choose a specific period (films/programs from this year or last year, or films/programs from a previous decade, for instance) and narrow your focus as much as possible. This task will become more manageable once you begin searching for sources and discover the nature of articles, books, and other materials on the general subject.

5. Research a recent film that generated much controversy, for instance, *The Passion of the Christ* or *Barbershop*. View the film yourself and read what critics and other authorities on the subject of film have to say about this particular one.

6. Research the development of the Spoken Word movement, its relationship to hip-hop, and the representation or use made of Spoken Word and/or hip-hop in film and/or television.

7. Research the Television Violence Act. Find out what it is and what critics, behaviorists, and media experts say about its potential effectiveness. Then explain your own opinion of the effectiveness of such an act.

8. In 1961, Newton N. Minow coined the term *vast wasteland* for what he saw as television's empty content and anti-intellectualism. Argue either that television remains a vast wasteland or that the phrase is unfair to television. Base your position on research into the views of experts or others who have published opinions on the subject. Include the results of studies or any other relevant data you find.

9. Research any of the subjects relevant to this chapter that are suggested by the titles of books that Mike Males has written: *The Scapegoat Generation: America's War on Adolescents* (1996), *Framing Youth: Ten Myths About the Next Generation* (1998), *Smoked: Why Joe Camel is Still Smiling* (1999), *Juvenile Injustice: America's "Youth Violence" Hoax* (2000), or *Kids & Guns: How Politicians, Experts and the Press Fabricate Fear of Youth* (2001). Refer to one or more of these books in your paper.

RESPONDING TO VISUALS

A still image from director Mel Gibson's film The Passion of the Christ. *Source: Icon Prod./Marquis Films/The Kobal Collection/Antonello, Phillipe*

1. What is your emotional response to this image? What details of the image contribute to your response to it?
2. Characterize the graphic violence represented by the picture. Do you see any paradox in people's accepting this kind of violence while ordinarily condemning violence in films?
3. Comment on the perspective from which the image is viewed. What is the effect of the close-up of Jesus's upper body?

Responding to Visuals

Children watch television in the village of Cabrespine in France, August 1998. Source: Patrick Zachmann/Magnum Photos

1. What do the children's expressions indicate about their television viewing experience?
2. What details of the setting does the photographer include? Do the children seem comfortable in this setting?
3. Can you guess from the children's faces what they are watching? Does it matter that we do not know what program they are watching?
4. What do you think the photographer's purpose is for taking the photograph?

CHAPTER

⑩

THE ARTS

Humans have always used a variety of creative ways in which to express themselves imaginatively through such forms as storytelling, drawing, painting, sculpture, and music. Researchers have discovered paintings in prehistoric caves that provide evidence of the earliest humans' compulsion to tell stories or depict significant aspects of their lives through pictures, while people today argue that videogames, Internet websites, and other digital forms are the latest developments in mankind's quest to express itself aesthetically.

Literature has long been regarded as a significant art form. Indeed, some would claim that imaginative writing, whether it be a short story, a novel, a poem, or some other form of creative expression, is just as crucial to the nurturing of the human soul as are visual arts and music. Certainly Michael Chabon in "Solitude and the Fortresses of Youth" believes this is so. He uses personal experience to explain why he believes young people should not be unduly punished for writing violent material. The force of his own imagination, he writes, was "nourished, stoked and liberated" by everything he read, including stories depicting "human beings in the most extreme situations and states of emotion—horror stories; accounts of madness and despair." Elsewhere in this textbook, in the section on the natural sciences, several people whose chief interests are science and scientific writing explore the nature of human intelligence as measured by an ability to create metaphor and to think in imaginative ways. Whatever its form, imagination and creativity are clearly important components of human identity. As you read Chabon's essay, think about the degree to which you would describe yourself as creative and consider whether you agree with his point about censorship and the arts.

Robert Hughes's discussion of prehistoric cave paintings in "Behold the Stone Age" remarks on the timelessness of the impulse to create. Because the very nature of artistic expression changes over time from culture to culture and from generation to generation within each culture, art provides a rich record of the lives of humans and their relationship with their world from the very earliest period of human existence. As you read Hughes's essay, consider whether you agree with him on the implications of the cave paintings. Can you think of other such discoveries that reveal something of the nature of both prehistoric humans and humans today? Consider, too, how society might be changed without art—or even how your own life might be changed if art were not a part of it. Think, too, of the variety of artistic forms familiar to you. Can any one in particular be said to reflect the essence of your culture? Why or why not?

As you will see, the essays in this chapter raise some intriguing questions, such as, how artists benefit society? Would society lose its soul without artists? Harold M. Williams seems to think the latter, for he asserts in the opening paragraph of his essay "Don't Ignore the Arts" that "the arts define what is meant by civilization." He explains in the rest of his essay why he feels so strongly about the place of the arts in the curriculum. As you read what Williams has to say, think about the place of the arts in your own education, and explore your own attitude toward the arts. Similarly, the assumption behind Daniel E. Gawthrop's "The National Endowment for Football—We're Fighting the Wrong Battle" is that the arts have great social importance. Writing to an audience of like-minded individuals, he suggests that the decrease in arts funding begun by Congress can be offset if arts educators convince the public that arts is as important a social element as, say, football. He argues that no amount of government funding can convince people arts are important and that the most important task is sharing how the arts enrich all lives. His goal is a lofty one, so as you read, consider how possible you think it is for him and his colleagues to reach that goal.

The subject of art and artists is so vast that these few readings serve only to indicate the breadth and depth of possible related topics and issues. Despite the persistence of art throughout time, the role of the artist in society and the relative value of art often are frequently debated topics. Tastes change and differ from generation to generation and individual to individual, as do values and beliefs about what is important to sustain and nurture a society and the standards by which people judge the merits of works of art. Determining what makes an artwork "good" or "bad" is often a subjective response to the art rather than a conscious application of objective standards. Do you have trouble determining whether a new movie, painting, or song is a good or bad one? How do you judge such works? As you consider the points made by the writers in this section, also think about the kinds of creative art that appeal to you, including what imaginative writing you like to read and perhaps write yourself. Think about the role that all of these forms of expression play in humans' lives: How might their absence affect humanity? Do you think your life would be impoverished without art, music, and literature? Why or why not?

SOLITUDE AND THE FORTRESSES OF YOUTH

Michael Chabon

Michael Chabon has written numerous articles, stories, novels, screenplays, and teleplays, including the screenplay for the second Spiderman *movie. His collections of short stories include* A Model World and Other Stories *(1991) and* Werewolves in their Youth: Stories *(1999). His novels include* The Mysteries of Pittsburg *(1988);* Wonder Boys *(1995); and* The Amazing Adventures of Kavalier & Clay *(2000), which won the Pulitzer Prize for fiction in 2001. This essay was published in the April 13, 2004, issue of the* New York Times.

Earlier this month my local paper, the *San Francisco Chronicle*, reported that a college student had been expelled from art school here for submitting a story "rife with gruesome details about sexual torture, dismemberment and bloodlust" to his creative writing class. The instructor, a poet named Jan Richman, subsequently found herself out of a job. The university chose not to explain its failure to renew Ms. Richman's contract, but she intimated that she was being punished for having set the tone for the class by assigning a well-regarded if disturbing short story by the MacArthur-winning novelist David Foster Wallace, "Girl with Curious Hair." Ms. Richman had been troubled enough by the student's work to report it to her superiors in the first place, in spite of the fact that it was not, according to the *Chronicle*, "the first serial-killer story she had read in her six semesters on the faculty at the Academy of Art University."

Homicide inspectors were called in; a criminal profiler went to work on the student. The officers found no evidence of wrongdoing. The unnamed student had made no threat; his behavior was not considered suspicious. In the end, no criminal charges were brought.

In this regard, the San Francisco case differs from other incidents in California, and around the country, in which students, unlucky enough to have as literary precursor the Columbine mass-murderer Dylan Klebold, have found themselves expelled, even prosecuted and convicted on criminal charges, because of the violence depicted in their stories and poems. The threat posed by these prosecutions to civil liberties, to the First Amendment rights of our young people, is grave enough. But as a writer, a parent and a former teenager, I see the workings of something more iniquitous: not merely the denial of teenagers' rights in the name of their own protection, but the denial of their humanity in the name of preserving their innocence.

4   It is in the nature of a teenager to want to destroy. The destructive impulse is universal among children of all ages, rises to a peak of vividness, ingenuity and fascination in adolescence, and thereafter never entirely goes away. Violence and hatred, and the fear of our own inability to control them in ourselves, are a fundamental part of our birthright, along with altruism, creativity, tenderness, pity and love. It therefore requires an immense act of hypocrisy to stigmatize our young adults and teenagers as agents of deviance and disorder. It requires a policy of dishonesty about and blindness to our own histories, as a species, as a nation, and as individuals who were troubled as teenagers, and who will always be troubled, by the same dark impulses. It also requires that favorite tool of the hypocritical, dishonest and fearful: the suppression of constitutional rights.

We justly celebrate the ideals enshrined in the Bill of Rights, but it is also a profoundly disillusioned document, in the best sense of that adjective. It stipulates all the worst impulses of humanity: toward repression, brutality, intolerance and fear. It couples an unbridled faith in the individual human being, redeemed time and again by his or her singular capacity for tenderness, pity and all the rest, with a profound disenchantment about groups of human beings acting as governments, court systems, armies, state religions and bureaucracies, unchecked by the sting of individual conscience and only belatedly if ever capable of anything resembling redemption.

In this light the Bill of Rights can be read as a classic expression of the teenage spirit: a powerful imagination reacting to a history of overwhelming institutional repression, hypocrisy, chicanery and weakness. It is a document written by men who, like teenagers, knew their enemy intimately, and saw in themselves all the potential they possessed to one day become him. We tend to view idealism and cynicism as opposites, when in fact neither possesses any merit or power unless tempered by, fused with, the other. The Bill of Rights is the fruit of that kind of fusion; so is the teenage imagination.

The imagination of teenagers is often—I'm tempted to say always—the only sure capital they possess apart from the love of their parents, which is a force far beyond their capacity to comprehend or control. During my own adolescence, my imagination, the kingdom inside my own skull, was my sole source of refuge, my fortress of solitude, at times my prison. But a fortress requires a constant line of supply; those who take refuge in attics and cellars require the unceasing aid of confederates; prisoners need advocates, escape plans, or simply a window that gives onto the sky.

8   Like all teenagers, I provisioned my garrison with art: books, movies, music, comic books, television, role-playing games. My secret confederates were the works of Monty Python, H. P. Lovecraft, the cartoonist Vaughan Bodé, and the Ramones, among many others; they kept me watered and fed. They baked files into cakes and, on occasion, for a wondrous moment, made the walls of my prison disappear. Given their nature as human creations, as artifacts and devices of human nature, some of the provisions I consumed were bound to be of a dark, violent, even bloody and horrifying nature; otherwise I would not have cared for them. Tales and displays of violence, blood and horror rang true, answered a need, on some deep, angry level that maybe only those with scant power or capital, regardless of their age, can understand.

It was not long before I began to write: stories, poems, snatches of autobiographical jazz. Often I imitated the work of my confederates: stories of human beings in the most extreme situations and states of emotion—horror stories; accounts of madness and despair. In part—let's say in large part, if that's what it takes to entitle the writings of teenagers to unqualified protection under the First Amendment—this was about expression. I was writing what I felt, what I believed, wished for, raged against, hoped and dreaded. But the main reason I wrote stories—and the reason that I keep on writing them today—was not to express myself. I started to write because once it had been nourished, stoked and liberated by those secret confederates, I could not hold back the force of my imagination. I had been freed, and I felt that it was now up to me to do the same for somebody else, somewhere, trapped in his or her own lonely tower.

We don't want teenagers to write violent poems, horrifying stories, explicit lyrics and rhymes; they're ugly, in precisely the way that we are ugly, and out of protectiveness and hypocrisy, even out of pity and love and tenderness, we try to force young people to be innocent of everything but the effects of that ugliness. And so we censor the art they consume and produce, and prosecute and suspend and expel them, and when, once in a great while, a teenager reaches for an easy gun and shoots somebody or himself, we tell ourselves that if we had only censored his journals and curtailed his music and video games, that awful burst of final ugliness could surely have been prevented. As if art caused the ugliness, when of course all it can ever do is reflect and, perhaps, attempt to explain it.

Let teenagers languish, therefore, in their sense of isolation, without outlet or nourishment, bereft of the only thing that makes it all bearable: knowing that somebody else has felt the way that you feel, has faced it, run from it, rued it, lamented it and transformed it into art; has been there, and returned, and lived, for the only good reason we have: to tell the tale. How confident we shall be, once we have done this, of never encountering the ugliness again! How happy our children will be, and how brave, and how safe!

PERSONAL RESPONSE

What do you think of the case that Chabon mentions in his opening paragraphs? In your opinion, should the student have been expelled for writing his gruesome story? If the teacher's termination was, indeed, a punishment for assigning a violent but disturbing story, as she thinks it was, do you think the punishment just?

QUESTIONS FOR CLASS OR SMALL-GROUP DISCUSSION

1. Explain in your own words what it is that bothers Chabon about the expulsion and/or prosecution of students for writing violent stories and poems. Do you agree with his position on this subject?

2. How do you respond to Chabon's assertion in paragraph 4 that "[i]t is in the nature of a teenager to want to destroy"? Is he correct about that, in your opinion?

3. Explain Chabon's analogy of the Bill of Rights "as a classic expression of the teenage spirit" (paragraph 6). How effective do you find that analogy as a strategy for developing his argument?

4. Comment on Chabon's strategy of using his own experience to further his argument. Does it work to strengthen or weaken the argument?

BEHOLD THE STONE AGE

ROBERT HUGHES

Robert Hughes has been art critic for Time *magazine for over thirty years and author of at least sixteen books, including* The Art of Australia *(1966),* Heaven and Hell in Western Art *(1969),* The Shock of the New *(1981),* The Fatal Shore *(1987), and* A Jerk on One End: Reflections of a Mediocre Fisherman *(1999). He has made dozens of TV documentaries, mainly for the BBC and other English production companies, since the mid-1960s. He became widely known in 1981 as the creator and host of the much acclaimed television history series on modern art,* The Shock of the New. *His 1997 television series on American art and architecture,* Americana Visions, *received equal attention and acclaim, earning him the prestigious Richard Dimbley Award from the British Academy of Film and Television Arts for "the most important personal contribution to factual television" of 1996 to 1997. In 2000, Hughes was honored by the* London Sunday Times *as Writer of the Year. Hughes wrote this cover story for the February 13, 1995, issue of* Time.

Not since the Dead Sea Scrolls has anything found in a cave caused so much excitement. The paintings and engravings, more than 300 of them, amount to a sort of Ice Age Noah's ark—images of bison, mammoths, and woolly rhinoceroses, of a panther, an owl, even a hyena. Done on the rock walls with plain earth pigments—red, black, ocher—they are of singular vitality and power, and despite their inscrutability to modern eyes, they will greatly enrich our picture of Cro-Magnon life and culture.

When the French government last month announced that a local official, Jean-Marie Chauvet, had discovered the stunning Paleolithic cave near Avignon, experts swiftly hailed the 20,000-year-old paintings as a trove rivaling—and perhaps surpassing—those of Lascaux and Altamira. "This is a virgin site—it's completely intact. It's great art," exulted Jean Clottes, an adviser to the French Culture Ministry and a leading authority on prehistoric art. It has also reopened some of the oldest and least settled of questions: When, how, and above all why did Homo sapiens start making art?

In the span of human prehistory, the Cro-Magnon people who drew the profusion of animals on the bulging limestone walls of the Chauvet cave were fairly late arrivals. Human technology—the making of tools from stone—had already been in existence for nearly two million years. There are traces of symbolism and ritual in burial sites of Neanderthals, an earlier species, dating back to 100,000 B.P. (before the present). Not only did the placement of the bodies seem meaningful, but so did the surrounding pebbles and bones with fragmentary patterns scratched on them. These, says Clottes, "do indicate that the Neanderthals had some creative capacity."

4   Though the dates are vastly generalized, most prehistorians seem to agree that art—communication by visual images—came into existence somewhere around 40,000 B.P. That was about the time when Cro-Magnons, Homo sapiens, reached Ice Age Europe, having migrated from the Middle East. Some experts think the Cro-Magnons brought a weapon that made Neanderthals an evolutionary has-been: a more advanced brain, equipped with a large frontal lobe "wired" for associative thinking. For art, at its root, is association—the power to make one thing stand for and symbolize another, to create the agreements by which some marks on a surface denote, say, an animal, not just to the markmaker but to others.

Among the oldest types of art is personal decoration—ornaments such as beads, bracelets, pendants, and necklaces. The body was certainly one of the first surfaces for symbolic expression. What did such symbols communicate? Presumably the wearer's difference from others, as a member of a distinct group, tribe, or totemic family: that he was a bison-man, say, and not a reindeer-man.

The Cro-Magnons were not the inarticulate Alley Oops of popular myth. They were nomadic hunter-gatherers with a fairly developed technology. They wore animal-skin clothing and moccasins tailored with bone needles, and made beautiful (and highly efficient) laurel-leaf-shaped flint blades. Living in small groups, they constructed tents from skins, and huts from branches and (in what is now Eastern Europe) mammoth bones.

Most striking was their yearning to make art in permanent places—the walls of caves. This expansion from the body to the inert surface was in itself a startling act of lateral thinking, an outward projection of huge cultural consequence, and Homo sapiens did not produce it quickly. As much time elapsed between the first recognizable art and the cave paintings of Lascaux and Altamira, about fifteen to twenty millenniums, as separates Lascaux (or Chauvet) from the first TV broadcasts. But now it was possible to see an objective image in shared space, one that was not the property of particular bodies and had a life of its own; and from this point the whole history of human visual communication unfolds.

8   We are apt to suppose that Cro-Magnon cave art was rare and exceptional. But wrongly; as New York University anthropologist Randall White points out, more than 200 late–Stone Age caves bearing wall paintings, engravings, bas-relief decorations, and sculptures have been found in southwestern Europe alone. Since the discovery of Lascaux in 1940, French archaeologists have been finding an average of a cave a year—and, says professor Denis Vialou of Paris's Institute of Human Paleontology, "there are certainly many, many more to be discovered, and while many might not prove as spectacular as Lascaux or Chauvet, I'd bet that some will be just as exciting."

No doubt many will never be found. The recently discovered painted cave at Cosquer in the south of France, for instance, can be reached only by scuba divers. Its entrance now lies below the surface of the Mediterranean; in the Upper Paleolithic period, from 70,000 B.P. to 10,000 B.P., so much of Europe's water was locked up in glaciers that the sea level was some 300 feet lower than it is today.

Why the profuseness of Cro-Magnon art? Why did these people, of whom so little is known, need images so intensely? Why the preponderance of animals over human images? Archaeologists are not much closer to answering such questions than they were a half-century ago, when Lascaux was discovered.

Part of the difficulty lies in the very definition of art. As anthropologist Margaret Conkey of the University of California, Berkeley puts it, "Many cultures don't really produce art, or even have any concept of it. They have spirits, kinship, group identity. If people from highland New Guinea looked at some of the Cro-Magnon cave art, they wouldn't see anything recognizable"—and not just because there are no woolly rhinos in New Guinea either. Today we can see almost anything as an aesthetic configuration and pull it into the eclectic orbit of late-Western "art experience"; museums have trained us to do that. The paintings of Chauvet strike us as aesthetically impressive in their power and economy of line, their combination of the sculptural and the graphic—for the artists used the natural bulges and bosses of the rock wall to flesh out the forms of the animals' rumps and bellies. But it may be that aesthetic pleasure, in our sense, was the last thing the Ice Age painters were after.

12   These were functional images; they were meant to produce results. But what results? To represent something, to capture its image on a wall in colored earths and animal fat, is in some sense to capture and master it; to have power over it. Lascaux is full of nonthreatening animals, including wild cattle, bison, and horses, but Chauvet

pullulates with dangerous ones—cave bears, a panther, and no fewer than fifty woolly rhinos. Such creatures, to paraphrase Claude Lévi-Strauss, were good to think with, not good to eat. We can assume they had a symbolic value, maybe even a religious value, to those who drew them, that they supplied a framework of images in which needs, values, and fears—in short, a network of social consciousness—could be expressed. But we have no idea what this framework was, and merely to call it *animistic* does not say much.

Some animals have more than four legs, or grotesquely exaggerated horns; is that just style, or does it argue a state of ritual trance or hallucination in the artists? No answer, though some naturally occurring manganese oxides, the base of some of the blacks used in cave paintings, are known to be toxic and to act on the central nervous system. And the main technique of Cro-Magnon art, according to prehistorian Michel Lorblanchet, director of France's National Center of Scientific Research, involved not brushes but a kind of oral spray-painting—blowing pigment dissolved in saliva on the wall. Lorblanchet, who has re-created cave paintings with uncanny accuracy, suggests that the technique may have had a spiritual dimension: "Spitting is a way of projecting yourself onto the wall, becoming one with the horse you are painting. Thus the action melds with the myth. Perhaps the shamans did this as a way of passing into the world beyond."

Different hands (and mouths) were involved in the production, but whose hands? Did the whole Cro-Magnon group at Chauvet paint, or did it have an élite of artists, to be viewed by nonartists as something like priests or professionals? Or does the joining of many hands in a collaborative work express a kind of treaty between rival groups? Or were the paintings added to over generations, producing the crowded, palimpsest-like effect suggested by some of the photos? And so on.

A mere picture of a bison or a woolly rhino tells us nothing much. Suppose, France's Clottes suggests, that 20,000 years from now, after a global cataclysm in which all books perished and the word vanished from the face of the earth, some excavators dig up the shell of a building. It has pointy ogival arches and a long axial hall at the end of which is a painting of a man nailed to a cross. In the absence of written evidence, what could this effigy mean? No more than the bison or rhino on the rock at Chauvet. Representation and symbolism have parted company.

16   Chauvet cave could be viewed as a religious site—a Paleolithic cathedral. Some have even suggested that a bear's skull found perched on a rock was an "altar." Says Henry de Lumley, director of France's National Museum of Natural History: "The fact that the iconography is relatively consistent, that it seems to obey certain rules about placement and even the way animals are drawn . . . is evidence of something sacred." Yet nobody lived in the cave, and no one in his right mind could imagine doing so; the first analyses of the contents have yielded no signs of human habitation, beyond the traces of animal-fat lamps and torches used by temporary visitors, and some mounds of pigmented earth left behind by the artists.

Modern artists make art to be seen by a public, the larger (usually) the better. The history of public art as we know it, across the past 1,000 years and more, is one of increasing access—beginning with the church open to the worshippers and ending with the pack-'em-in ethos of the modern museum, with its support-system of orientation courses, lectures, films, outreach programs, and souvenir shops. Cro-Magnon cave art was probably meant to be seen by very few people, under conditions of extreme difficulty and dread. The caves may have been places of initiation and trial, in which consciousness was tested to an extent that we can only dimly imagine, so utterly different is our grasp of the world from that of the Cro-Magnons.

Try to imagine an art gallery that could be entered only by crawling on your belly through a hole in the earth; that ramified into dark tunnels, a fearful maze in the earth's bowels in which the gallerygoer could, at any moment, disturb one of the bears whose claw marks can still be seen on the walls; where the only light came from flickering torches, and the bones of animals littered the uneven floor. These are the archaic conditions that, one may surmise, produced the array of cave fears implanted in the human brain—fears that became absorbed into a later, more developed culture in such narratives as that of the mythical Cretan labyrinth in whose core the terrible Minotaur waited. Further metabolized, and more basically misunderstood, these sacred terrors of the deep earth undergird the Christian myth of hell. Which may, in fact, be the strongest Cro-Magnon element left in modern life.

PERSONAL RESPONSE

Describe your own interests in the visual arts by explaining whether you like art in general and who, if any, are your favorite artists and works of art.

QUESTIONS FOR CLASS OR SMALL-GROUP DISCUSSION

1. This essay raises a number of questions about the purpose and nature of Cro-Magnon art. What implications do you think those questions have for art today? Explain your answer.

2. What impact, if any, do you think the discovery of the paintings in a Paleolithic cave in France will have on people today? What do you think modern humans can learn from them?

3. In what ways has art remained essentially the same since the period that Hughes describes in this essay? What significant changes do you see? Be as specific as possible in your answer.

4. Hughes describes the paintings in the French cave and theorizes why they were painted. Can you offer any other plausible reasons for the cave paintings? Explain your answer in detail.

DON'T IGNORE THE ARTS

HAROLD M. WILLIAMS

Harold M. Williams, former chairman of the United States Securities and Exchange Commission, served as president and chief executive officer of the J. Paul Getty Trust, Santa Monica, California, for fifteen years until his retirement in 1998. He is author of The Getty Center:

Design Process, Making Architecture (1997), a two-volume chronicle of the building of the Getty Center from site and architect selection through design and construction. This essay first appeared in USA Today *in 1995.*

It is difficult to imagine a society without the arts. What dark and empty souls would populate an environment without paintings, statues, architecture, drama, music, dances, or poems? The arts define what is meant by *civilization.* They are part of the foundation and the framework of culture. As a universal language through which individuals can express common aspirations, the arts are a channel to understanding and appreciating other cultures. To be conversant with the arts is to be a civilized person.

The arts are a basic and central medium of human communication and understanding. They are how people talk to each other. The arts are the languages of civilization—past and present—through which they express their anxieties, hungers, hopes, and discoveries. They are the means of listening to dreams—of expressing imagination and feelings.

The arts reaffirm humanity. They are the glue that holds society together. While improvement in the three *Rs* may enable Americans to compete more effectively in the world economically and technologically, they do not feed the human spirit. The most vital stages in the history of any society are marked by a flourishing of the arts. When most material goods have turned to dust, it is the arts that remain as testimony to the dreams and passions of the past.

4   Nobel Prize-winning physicist Richard Feynman decided to learn how to draw at the age of forty-four. He eventually got quite good at it, even though he confessed to having been terrible at art in high school. Later, Feynman, who was a brilliant teacher and thinker in mathematics and physics at California Institute of Technology, explained why he had taken up art so late in life. He wanted to express the awe he felt about the glories of the universe, he said. Art, he felt, might be the only way he could reveal this emotion to someone who might share it.

Feynman, of course, wasn't the first or last scientist to seek a perspective on his life through the arts. He discovered late what many others are lucky enough to know intuitively—that the arts are key to building the metaphorical bridges that link individuals to their own creative powers and to each other.

Americans live in a society that is communicating more and more through visual images. Daily, they are bombarded by a constantly changing torrent of messages from billboards, architecture, magazines, four-color newspapers, television, and films. New technology controlled by computers combines words, pictures, and sound to convey information at a breathtaking pace. Computers, with their power to manufacture and animate images, are creating entirely new art forms.

Consider, also, that American civilization is increasingly diverse, mixing cultures from Europe, Africa, the Far East, and Latin America. Each group sends its own messages and images, jostling to preserve and advance its own identity. Meanwhile, many of the surviving messages from past civilizations exist in visual form.

8   In short, to be educated is to be visually literate—to understand the historical and cultural context of the message, make aesthetic judgments about what one sees,

and sort out these images in order to tell the good from the bad, the fake from the genuine, and interpret accurately the signals of other cultural groups in search of common humanity. Armed with an ability to make judgments, an educated person will learn to construct sound value systems for any event or object, whether it is art or not.

It seems fair to ask then, if the arts occupy such a central role in human life, shouldn't they have a central place in education? If children are not taught to look and understand what they see, isn't this a failure to prepare them for life in contemporary society? Aren't they being sent into the modern world without a complete education?

If a purpose of education is to ensure the continuity of the democratic system and its values from one generation to the next, then why aren't schools teaching the things that bring Americans closest to the core of their cultural experience? If the United States is spending its resources on a back-to-basics education, why the tendency to ignore something as basic to human development and culture as the study of the arts?

Access to the wealth of American culture and the cultivation of the sensibilities, human imagination, and judgment are not peripheral educational aims. The arts represent a form of thinking and a way of knowing and, as such, their presence in the schools is as basic as anything can be.

12   Ernest Boyer of the Carnegie Foundation for the Advancement of Teaching put it well in his study, *High School.* "The arts are essential parts of the human experience, they are not a frill. We recommend that *all* students study the arts to discover how human beings communicate not only with words, but through music, dance, and the visual arts. During our visits we found the arts to be shamefully neglected. Courses in the arts were the last to come and first to go."

In 1988, the National Endowment for the Arts released the results of a two-year study, *Toward Civilization: A Report on Arts Education.* Its assessment was that "basic arts education does not exist in the United States today."

With the emphasis on improving the three *Rs,* many schools have cut back on what they consider to be "frills," including the arts. The result is that "the artistic heritage that is ours and the opportunities to contribute significantly to its evolution are being lost to our young people." Not only does the absence or meagerness of the arts in the schools deny children access to the vast treasury of American and world culture, but without it there is no replenishing of the infrastructure to assure the cultural future of the country.

If the arts are so basic to becoming an educated person, why are they ignored in American schools? Elliot W. Eisner of Stanford University examined this question in his book, *The Enlightened Eye.* Among the reasons why the arts are ignored were, first, because there is a tendency to regard them as dealing with emotion, rather than the mind, and useful primarily as a release from the serious work of getting educated. This view fails to recognize that creation of images is a matter of mind that calls for inventive problem-solving capacities, analytic and synthetic forms of reasoning, and the exercise of judgment. Psychologists and educators recognize that intelligence extends beyond verbal and mathematical reasoning.

16   A second cause is that they are not assessed formally and, as a consequence, do not promote students' academic upward mobility. The arts carry little, if any, weight

in college admissions decisions. If arts courses are viewed by college admissions offices as not having much value, it is to be expected that they will be of little importance to schools, upwardly mobile students, or their parents. The attitude on the part of universities carries through into teacher training, which pays little, if any, attention to preparing general education teachers to present the arts competently in the classroom.

A third reason follows from the view held by many art educators that, to the extent that art is taught, it should focus on developing the students' creative abilities. As such, many have resisted including any structure or content for fear it would stifle creativity. The result is programs lacking substance and perceived as not worthy of inclusion in the curriculum.

There are values to be realized in addition to the direct benefits of arts education. Skillfully taught and integrated into the curriculum, the arts can help to achieve many of the aims of educational reform. Studying them can empower children to see and make valid judgments about their environment. The arts also can provide an effective bridge to understanding and appreciating other cultures.

Further, a growing body of evidence from the classroom indicates that strengths gained in the study of art carry over into other subject areas. One of the most convincing testimonials to this comes from New Jersey Assemblywoman Maureen Ogden: "Compare two similar schools; one with strong arts curricula and one without. You'll soon discover that there are nonartistic benefits that make the school with arts curricula a higher performance environment. Most importantly, in such settings the kids are excited about learning. Teachers attribute higher test scores in other traditional subjects to the integration of the arts for learning science, math, reading, and the like. And if that isn't enough, go into a multicultural setting and you will witness a common language that enhances cultural understanding and appreciation. You can see a path to heightened self-esteem that permeates those tough social programs areas we would prefer to ignore."

20   There are reports that students' vocabulary and writing skills improve after having been in a substantive art program. Teachers involved in these initiatives have come to recognize their worth, and faculty in some schools have begun to correlate arts education more closely with other studies such as history or biology.

In 1993, the UCLA Center for the Study of Evaluation conducted an evaluation of the educational impact of the Los Angeles Music Center's Artist in Residence and Teacher (ART) Partnerships. The report found improvement and growth in all areas of the study, including students' cognitive, thinking, and social skills, self-expression, and attitude development.

In cognitive skills, students learned from the factual knowledge and abilities presented by the artists and showed overall improvement in academic knowledge and skills. Their thinking skills also improved, as they made progress in problem-solving. Moreover, they were able to use the information and skills learned in other subjects, as well as outside of school. In the area of self-expression, students improved in both written and oral communication. They learned how to express themselves better in writing, speaking in front of others, and acting out their feelings. Finally, attitude development showed improvement, with gains in motivation and self-confidence, as well as work habit/cooperation report card grades.

What does all this signify for America's schools and children? It means that it is possible to make a difference, that the arts do change lives, and that youngsters will grow through the arts, transforming their own lives and that of their community.

24   During the early 1980s, the J. Paul Getty Trust surveyed the state of art education in America's public schools. The picture generally was bleak. The results were consistent with the later findings reported by Elliot Eisner and the National Endowment for the Arts study. Nevertheless, through discussions with art experts and educators, it was found that there were some exciting trends afoot. New ideas and lines of research were developing that, fortified by subsequent research, were beginning to jell into a comprehensive strategy called discipline-based art education, a humanities-based approach that embraced content from art production, history, criticism, and aesthetics. There even were a few schools struggling in isolation to nurture a version of such an integrated, sequential art program into maturity.

In 1982, the trust, through the Getty Center for Education in the Arts, committed itself to helping make such an approach to art education a reality. We are engaged in a long-term effort to serve as a catalyst in furthering the theory and practice of art education in the United States.

Our experience has confirmed the potential of discipline-based art education programs to develop intellectual skills and create opportunities to explore creative self-expression. It now is known, for instance, that involving students in analyzing works of art, whether their own or others, requires functioning at the highest cognitive levels of mental activity.

Children confronted by a work of art in the context of a comprehensive learning program tend to be fascinated and excited by the challenge and mystery of it. Many classroom teachers who have had to learn art content through in-service training in order to participate in a discipline-based program have reported a renewed enthusiasm for their profession.

28   Students asked to consider art from the standpoints of the artist, historian, critic, and aesthetician soon become more perceptive about visual images and more open to different ways of thinking about the same image. The quality of art produced by students improves measurably as they learn about other artists, are required to solve problems, and assess other works of art.

Opening Children's Imaginations

Art history opens the child's imagination to other eras and cultures. If students of the next century are to work and live productively side by side with others from different cultures, they must respect and appreciate cultural differences and, at the same time, discern what they share in common with other peoples. The arts are one of the best ways of achieving this practical goal.

Learning how to critique and judge art sharpens critical faculties by obliging the student to think independently, creatively, and to make reasoned judgments based on his or her knowledge and trained observations. Finally, consideration of aesthetic issues teaches them to be able to deal with the nature and meaning of art in their own lives.

The ability to think critically and creatively and to make informed judgments is vital for young people preparing for the twenty-first century. The world is changing rapidly and so is the workplace. The likelihood of multiple careers during one's life-time will demand flexibility and imagination. In an increasingly multicultural society, young people need language skills and a tolerance of other peoples and customs based on informed understanding.

32   Computer-based technology requires that workers be able to deal with ever more complex and fast-paced systems of symbols and images—the world of Nintendo and MTV grown up. To cope and compete in these surroundings, young people must become visually literate, versed in the language of the arts. Even today, exciting interactive multimedia programs are beginning to enhance the ways children learn. Before long, they permanently may alter the basic nature of the traditional classroom.

There are reasons to be optimistic about the future. Especially encouraging is the number of people who have joined forces to ensure that arts education is a significant part of national education reform. In the spring of 1994, Congress passed Goals 2000: Educate America Act. This law makes the arts one of the core subjects to be included in the curriculum. It marked the first time in three decades that the arts have been included in federal education legislation.

Also in 1994, the first set of national voluntary curriculum standards for what children should know and be able to do in dance, music, theater, and the visual arts were completed and presented to the Secretary of Education. These are significant for two reasons. First, they expect youngsters not only to be able to create and perform in the arts, but also to understand the entire body of work that makes up human intellectual and cultural heritage. They recognize that, when the arts are studied, students involve themselves in a particular set of processes, influences, and meanings. The standards also recognize that art is expressed in various styles, reflects different historical circumstances, and draws on a multitude of social and cultural resources.

In another significant development for arts education, and one that supports the national arts standards, the National Assessment of Educational Progress is developing a new arts assessment to be administered in 1996 to 4th-, 8th-, and 12th-grade students nationwide. The national arts assessment will enable parents, educators, and the general public to evaluate the condition and progress of student achievement in the arts just as is done for all of the other academic subjects named in the National Education Goals.

36   The national voluntary standards in the arts, the new national arts assessment, and state curriculum frameworks of more than thirty states that recommend a comprehensive approach to arts education instruction reflect a recognition among educational policy makers and the public that the cognitive and affective contributions of the arts are significant enough to be part of every child's schooling from kindergarten through 12th grade.

Americans can have any kind of schools they want, if they make up their minds to do it. They have the freedom to be outspoken advocates for including the arts and humanities in the curriculum. They can form alliances with like-minded individuals and groups. They can seek out successful programs and hold them up as examples. When they finally succeed in raising the arts and humanities to their rightful, and necessary, place in education, they have done a great service not only to countless generations of students to come, but to the cause of democracy.

PERSONAL RESPONSE

Describe the art education you have experienced. Are you satisfied with the quality and quantity of that instruction? In what ways have you benefited—or not—from the art instruction you have received? Do you anticipate taking any more courses in the arts?

QUESTIONS FOR CLASS OR SMALL-GROUP DISCUSSION

1. What do you think Williams means when he says: "The arts define what is meant by *civilization*. [. . .] To be conversant with the arts is to be a civilized person" (paragraph 1)? Do you agree or disagree with him?

2. Explain what this statement means to you: "[T]he arts are key to building the metaphorical bridges that link individuals to their own creative powers and to each other" (paragraph 5). Do you think Williams is overstating the importance of the arts?

3. Find the reasons Williams gives to explain why the arts have been ignored in American schools (paragraph 15). How effective are those reasons as supporting proofs for his thesis?

4. What, according to Williams, "are [the] values to be realized in addition to the direct benefits of art education" (paragraph 18)? Are you persuaded by his evidence?

THE NATIONAL ENDOWMENT FOR FOOTBALL—WE'RE FIGHTING THE WRONG BATTLE

DANIEL E. GAWTHROP

Daniel E. Gawthrop is a composer who has received over a hundred commissions to write original music. He is also an announcer/producer for public radio station WETA, Washington, D.C., and has served as a music critic for the Washington Post. *He has twice served on National Endowment for the Arts (NEA) grants panels. This selection first appeared in* Choral Journal, *the official publication of the American Choral Directors Association, in October 1997.*

Why isn't there a National Endowment for Football? Why does the idea make you giggle? Probably because there is no need for an "NEF," since large numbers of people already believe in the importance of football games in their lives and are perfectly willing to support gridiron activities of all kinds. They buy tickets to games in large numbers, watch games on television in vastly larger numbers, play games themselves with their friends and children, and happily, even insistently, support football in the public schools.

When I was in high school, I thought football was terminally stupid. Years later my wife taught me first to understand and later to enjoy the game, and these days I could even be considered a fan. This experience, while not terribly profound, has nonetheless enriched my life in some measure, and I am grateful for it. The enrichment provided by the arts in my life, in dramatic contrast, has been quite profound and far more formative on my character.

This got me thinking: what if we were able to convince a substantial portion of our fellow citizens that the arts deserve a place in their lives at least as significant as, say, football? Could we then not look forward to their buying tickets to arts events in large numbers, watching concerts and ballets and plays on television in vastly larger numbers, playing instruments and singing (and painting and writing and acting) themselves, with their friends and children, and happily, even insistently, supporting the arts in the public schools? At that point the funding problem would be pretty well solved, and there would be no need to beg for alms from Congress year after year, nor any need to risk "governmental control" of the arts.

4   I believe the arts are a critically important component of our culture and that we will all pay a high price if we fail to insist on their remaining in their rightful role as an ennobling and enriching influence in our society. However, I think fighting for public funding (other than for arts education in our public schools, which is critically important) is the wrong battle. By devoting any substantial amount of time and effort to convincing Congress to offer financial support to the arts, we are allowing ourselves to be distracted from a far more important and urgent need.

The real problem is that we live in a society that simply does not value the arts. Until we address and resolve that flaw in our national character, no amount of money, from whatever source, is going to have the desired effect. Meanwhile, if we fight (and even win) a battle for public funding, we are likely to congratulate ourselves for having reached our goal and then relax, without even realizing that our ladder was leaning against the wrong wall all along. If we really want to help people, or if we really want to help the arts, the answer is the same: we must give individuals a reason to value artistic expression. Fail at that, and all else is lost; succeed at that, and funding problems will disappear.

Most National Endowment for the Arts grant money awarded in support of performing ensembles has focused on making artistic experiences available to as wide an audience as possible. On its surface this seems both reasonable and public-spirited; unfortunately, it rather misses the point. One old saw maintains, "If nobody wants to come, no one will make them."

We need to be asking ourselves two related questions: First, why would we wish to experience this exhibit, play, concert, or other artistic event, and second, how can we evoke the same desires in someone else, someone who has not yet caught the vision? Once we have found a way to convert our society into avid arts enthusiasts, it will take over the funding process, quite voluntarily, without government involvement.

8   The bottom line here is that no amount of government-supported art is going to change the fundamental character of our society. While we're busy fighting for federal money, we're failing to do the things that will make that fundamental change. It should he noted that during the period when federal funding for the NEA was

increasing each year, audiences (especially young audiences) were dwindling and music programs in the public schools were disappearing. If the goal of federal funding was to increase public awareness and involvement with the arts, it failed conclusively, even spectacularly. That's why I think government funding is a red herring.

I say, let's quit worrying about "sending a message to the rest of the world" and get on with the important task we urgently need to complete: converting the heathen. Let's eliminate the self-flagellation over the fact that European arts presentations all rely on government funding and get busy turning out a generation of Americans who understand and appreciate the arts as much as they appreciate the Dallas Cowboys and their cheerleaders. Let's quit trying to get the government to throw money at the arts to spare us the unpleasant necessity of rolling up our sleeves and getting personally involved in the big job of sharing what we understand (and what our fellow citizens don't) about the importance of the arts in everyone's lives.

We need to change the focus of our attention from a distant, unconcerned Congress to local communities, and start changing people, one at a time, by the strength of our examples and our convictions. We need to quit demanding leadership from Washington, from the very folks who got us where we are now, and start exhibiting some leadership of our own. After all, the real arts experts won't be found in think tanks: they're too busy teaching in our public schools, directing our church and community choirs, writing poems and music and books, and sketching and painting and so forth.

The people in our towns and villages who don't (yet) share our vision and understanding are not going to be converted by an NEA grant. We need to invite them, often and fervently, to our concerts and recitals. When they get there, they must be asked to do something: clap in time, sing along, jingle their keys and coins to accompany some rhythmic piece, or any of a thousand other clever ways of getting them involved that you will think of and the government won't.

12   Involvement will bring them back. Once they're coming back, we need to find ways to encourage their own artistic expressions, however simple, because once they've tasted that, you'll never be able to take it away from them again: they'll become your fans, supporters, singers, board members, volunteer committee members, and more. Before you know it, your community will be supporting the arts in hundreds of ways that are not only better suited to your needs than anything the NEA can provide, but which also create side-effects and ripples throughout the community that will amplify and multiply your original investment.

My wife remembers being taken to local symphony concerts as a very young child. Her father took her home at intermission and returned for the second half of the program. A few years of this kind of exposure turned her into an avid listener who was eager to be allowed to stay for the entire concert.

There were no federal grants in those days to bring symphony players into her school, and if there had been, they would not have had the same effect as those repeated exposures, which also carried the psychological impact of her parents' physical presence and obvious sincere interest. It led to instrumental training in elementary school and high school, to playing in a major symphony orchestra, and to a lifelong commitment to support arts institutions of all kinds. That's the progression we need to make our goal.

Bringing a few musicians, or even an entire orchestra, into a school once or twice a year, however worthwhile, simply cannot be expected to create this effect for more than a very few students. Unless they're singing every day, being exposed to musical masterworks regularly, and playing instruments from an early age, the occasional appearance of a few musicians in their midst will be treated as a mystical event with no relevance.

16   I heard a story about a fellow who walked into an art museum and stopped in front of a painting so valuable there was a guard permanently posted beside it. The man glanced casually at the painting and mumbled, "I don't see what's so hot about that." Overhearing this, the guard smiled and replied, "Ah, but don't you wish you did?"

If people in your community don't see what's so hot about the arts, an NEA grant won't fix it. Government money won't fix it. You must fix it.

PERSONAL RESPONSE

Gawthrop says that the arts have had a profound formative influence on his life. What would you identify as the most formative influence on your life?

QUESTIONS FOR CLASS OR SMALL-GROUP DISCUSSION

1. How does Gawthrop's title reflect his content? What relationship does it have with his proposition or claim?

2. To what extent do you agree with Gawthrop that "the arts are a critically important component of our culture" (paragraph 4).

3. Describe your community's level of involvement in promoting the arts.

4. What actions does Gawthrop tell his audience of other arts professionals that they need to take to achieve their goal of "turning out a generation of Americans who understand and appreciate the arts as much as they appreciate the Dallas Cowboys" (paragraph 9)? Do you think his goal is realistic? Is it possible to "change the fundamental character of our society" (paragraph 8)?

○ PERSPECTIVES ON THE ARTS ○
Suggested Writing Topics

1. Argue your position on the subject of violence in any of the creative arts— poetry, drama, short story, novel, dance, the visual arts. Is the expulsion of students or firing of teachers, as described in Michael Chabon's "Solitude and the Fortresses of Youth" justified in uncertain and dangerous times?

2. If you have found that a particular form of creative art is a way to express yourself or use your imagination, as Michael Chabon in "Solitude and the Fortresses of Youth" did with writing, explain what that art is and how it enables you to find self-expression.

3. In "Behold the Stone Age," Robert Hughes points out that the oldest form of art is personal decoration. The body is still being used as a surface for symbolic expression by some young people, who use such techniques as branding, piercing, and tattooing. Defend or attack these practices by considering their relative artistic or creative merits.

4. In an argumentative essay, answer the question posed by Harold M. Williams in "Don't Ignore the Arts": "Shouldn't [the arts] have a central place in education?" (paragraph 9).

5. Expand on either or both of these statements from Harold M. Williams's "Don't Ignore the Arts": "The arts define what is meant by *civilization*" (paragraph 1) and "The arts reaffirm humanity" (paragraph 3).

6. Drawing on at least two of the selections in this chapter, explain your viewpoint on the importance of art. Be sure to defend your position by supplying evidence not only from the essays but also from your own observations.

7. Survey a group of your friends and acquaintances for their opinions of the place of an artist's private beliefs and behavior in judging the artist's work. Then report the results of your survey in an essay that synthesizes the comments and those of the people you interview.

8. Who do you think are today's most creative people? You might highlight a particular group of people (artists, musicians) or a particular person. Give supporting evidence to substantiate your viewpoint.

9. Define *excellence* in relation to a specific art form (for instance, a painting, a novel, a poem, a song, or a film) by stating the criteria you use for judging that abstract quality and by giving examples you believe best illustrate it.

10. Select a work of art in any medium—painting, music, the theatre, dance, literature—and analyze its importance as a work of art, including what it means to you personally.

11. Answer the question: In what ways do the arts—music, art, drama, literature—contribute to the culture of a people?

12. Explore the question of what makes some art live for all time and other art disappear. What makes a "timeless" work of art? Select a particular painting as an example and explain, in as much detail as possible, why you believe as you do.

13. Define *art* (an admittedly abstract term but one that people never tire of wrestling with), and explain what you think is gained by a culture's interest in and support of art and what you think would be lost without it. As an alternative, argue that nothing is gained by a culture's art and that little or nothing would be lost without it. Make sure you explain why you feel as you do on this subject.

Research Topics

1. Select an issue or question related to the broad subject of the role of the artist in society to research and then argue your position on that issue. For instance, what is the connection between artists' moral nature and their work?

Do you think that an artist's private morality should (or does) influence the way his or her work is perceived? What is the connection between an artist's public life and private behavior? Consider whether evidence of immorality affects or alters in any way the quality of a person's work.

2. In recent years, some people have been highly critical of what they see as obscenity or immorality in contemporary art. The works of Robert Mapplethorpe, for instance, were the object of such widespread, heated public debate that the National Endowment for the Arts was threatened with funding cuts because of similar projects it had supported with grants. Research the issue of censorship in the arts, and write an opinion paper on the subject. Consider: Does society have a moral obligation to limit what people can say, do, or use in their art, or do First Amendment rights extend to any subject or medium an artist wants to use?

3. Robert Hughes in "Behold the Stone Age" offers his theory about the nature and purpose of prehistoric art based on an interpretation of cave drawings discovered in France. Such discoveries of prehistoric cave drawings that are fairly sophisticated in technique and meaning have led some art historians to suggest that art did not necessarily develop progressively, as has been commonly believed. Research this topic by reading about some of the prehistoric cave drawings that have been discovered and the theories of art historians about their importance. Then weigh the evidence and arrive at your own opinion about the nature and purpose of prehistoric art or its place in the historical development of art.

4. Harold M. Williams states in "Don't Ignore the Arts" that "a growing body of evidence from the classroom indicates that strengths gained in the study of art carry over into other subject areas" (paragraph 19). Research the role of the arts in strengthening students' abilities in other subject areas. You may want to begin by locating the studies Williams cites in his essay and then continuing your search to find more recent studies.

5. Research the contributions to art of a well-known artist or performer. Although you will want to provide a brief biographical sketch, your paper should focus on assessing the particular way(s) the artist had an effect on not only his or her own specialty but also "the arts" in general.

RESPONDING TO VISUALS

"The new ballet will have quite an effect on you." Source: Henderson Advertising for the South Carolina Ballet

1. What is the purpose of this advertisement?
2. Does the stance of the mechanic strike you as amusing or odd?
3. How do the mechanic and his environment function in relation to what the advertisement is promoting?
4. What is the target audience of the advertisement? How effectively do you think it reaches that audience?

RESPONDING TO VISUALS

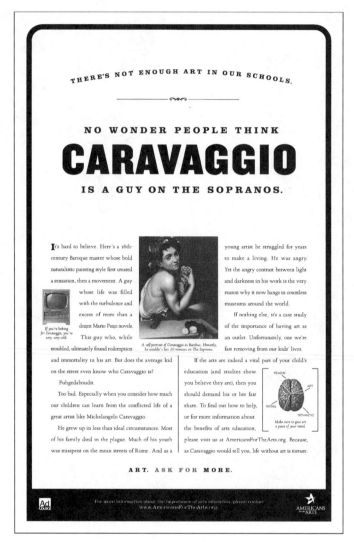

"There's Not Enough Art In Our Schools." Source: Ad Council and Americans for the Arts

1. How does the ad use the reference to *The Sopranos* to make its point about Caravaggio?
2. How effectively does the ad engage viewers?
3. The Ad Council of America created this advertising campaign to aid Americans for the Arts in its efforts to promote the arts in schools. How likely is the ad to achieve that goal?
4. How do the various images in the ad contribute to its overall effect?

E-Readings Online for Part Two
InfoTrac College Edition

http://www.infotrac-college.com

(Search for each article by author or title after entering your Infotrac College Edition password.)

Chapter 7 Music and Video Games

Hip-hop, rap music, and video games are integral parts of America's pop culture, and because of their widespread popularity, they are also the subject of much scrutiny. With lyrics that are quite explicit about sex and violence and that use language that some groups find offensive, such music is often accused of having negative influences on the young people who listen to it. Therefore, it is useful to consider what not only media commentators and social critics but also academic researchers have to say about the music and its effects, negative or positive, on those who listen to it. The first three articles all discuss the results of studies of rap music and its possible effects on young people, including what questions remain unanswered and results that are open to interpretation. The final reading looks specifically at video games in terms of their depiction of a potentially bleak and frightening future as humans battle aliens and intergalactic space monsters. Its author investigates the possible negative effects of these violent video games on young people's views of their own futures.

○

Jason D. Haugen

"Unladylike Divas": Language, Gender, and Female Gangsta Rappers

Examines the way in which female rappers adapt traditionally male gangsta rap narratives for their own music style.

○

The Brown University Child and Adolescent Behavior Letter

New Research Explores Effects of Rap Music on Adolescents

Reports results of a study on the psychological effects of rap music on young African-American women.

○

RONALD ROACH

Decoding Hip-hop's Cultural Impact: Scholars are Poised to Take a Close Look at the Influence of Hip-hop on the Social Identity, Values of Today's Youth

Reviews the current research on the questions raised by critics of hip-hop culture and its influence on young people.

○

THE ECONOMIST

Dip into the Future, Far as Cyborg Eye can See: And Wince

Discusses the possible effects on young people of video games' depiction of an apocalyptic future.

QUESTIONS FOR DISCUSSION OR WRITING

1. Select from any of the articles an opinion or viewpoint that you feel strongly about—either positively or negatively—and explain your reaction to it. Imagine that you are having a dialogue with the person whose opinion you are responding to. What would you say to that person?

2. What is your opinion of the lyrics that critics find offensive? For instance, do you think that gangsta rap is hostile toward women? Are the lyrics morally questionable?

3. Do your own informal analysis of a specific rap piece by taking into consideration the questions that researchers ask about such music. What images are portrayed? What messages are conveyed?

4. Conduct your own informal survey of currently popular video games and analyze their content. Are the games potentially harmful to young people's behavior and outlook on life? Do they have socially redeeming benefits?

Chapter 8 Media Studies

The term "media literacy" comes up frequently in media studies courses and articles on the media. It refers not only to the study of media in its various forms and its effects on audiences but also to the development of skills in the use of all kinds of media. These readings address audiences made up of adults in authority roles and explain the importance of those adults' becoming media literate, particularly in dealing with media violence and young people's exposure to it. The first two are directed toward audiences made up of educators; the third targets pediatric nurses who in turn will advise parents about the potential effects on their children of exposure to media violence. As you read, try to put yourself in the position of a member of the targeted audience. How does that change, if at all, your perception of the topic and the information you are being given?

○

ROYAL VAN HORN

Sex, Potato Chips, and Media Literacy

Urges teachers to become media literate in order to better understand the psychological influence of the mass media on young people.

○

ERICA SCHARRER, LEDA COOKS, AND QIANQING REN

A Media Literacy Project on Violence and Conflict

Describes a short curriculum on media violence and interpersonal conflict, using college students working with sixth-grade students.

○

MARY MUSCARI

Media Violence: Advice for Parents

Offers practical suggestions for advice that pediatric nurses can give to parents to protect their children from the harmful effects of media violence.

QUESTIONS FOR DISCUSSION OR WRITING

1. Are you "media literate"? Are your teachers? Do you agree with Royal Van Horn that there is a sense of urgency for teachers to become media literate?

2. Imagine that you are preparing to give a talk to a group of children about the possible dangers of exposure to media violence. What would you say to them? What details, facts, or references to studies might you include in such a talk?

3. Mary Muscari suggests a variety of steps parents can take to reduce children's exposure to negative media influences. What do you think of her advice? Which of the things she suggests do you believe are useful? Which do you think would be ineffectual?

Chapter 9 Film and Television

Reality television has become a strong fixture in prime-time programming, with creators of television shows creating more new non-scripted reality shows each season. Cultural critics decry such programs, lamenting what they see as the mindless, empty, and meaningless content of such shows. Yet reality television shows are very popular, draw huge viewing audiences, and are so pervasive that they seem to dominate the television listings on many nights of the week. Whether you love them or hate them, they seem to be firmly entrenched in popular culture, at least for the time being. Similarly, in the movie industry, documentary films or films about real-life people have stirred public debate and promoted widespread discussion of such hot topics as politics and religion, as two recently released pictures illustrate. Michael Moore's *Fahrenheit 9/11* documents the Bush administration's decisions and actions in a decidedly controversial manner, while Mel Gibson's *The Passion of the Christ,* also controversial, promoted widespread and often heated discussion of fundamental religious beliefs. These readings discuss either reality television programming or documentary films and are representative of a large number of similar articles on both television and film.

○

GARY HOPPENSTAND

Television as Metaphor

Argues that reality television represents the worst of popular culture.

○

NANCY FRANKLIN

American Idol

Assesses the strengths and weaknesses of the reality television show The Apprentice.

○

CYNTHIA M. FRISBY

Getting Real with Reality TV

Explores reasons why audiences are attracted to reality television programs.

○

GINA MCINTYR

Moore Games: The Controversial Figure Leads a Charge of Nonfiction Filmmakers Responding to Political and Social Turmoil with Feature-length Documentaries

Surveys recent documentary films that tackle political and social issues.

QUESTIONS FOR DISCUSSION OR WRITING

1. Gary Hoppenstand says that "arguably the most pervasive and intolerable product of popular culture's 'lowest common denominator' is reality television." Do you think his position is arguable? Do you agree with him?

2. Psychologists and other experts sometimes suggest that reality television shows can do psychological harm to viewers. In what ways might such television programs do harm to viewers? Do reality shows have any positive benefits?

3. How do you account for the popularity of such controversial films as *Fahrenheit 9/11* and *The Passion of the Christ?* What attracts audiences to them? Why is there such widespread, heated debate about them?

Chapter 10 The Arts

People who work with and appreciate the arts are sometimes called upon to explain why the arts in their various forms are important or what contributions they make to society, especially in difficult times. Those who are unconvinced of the importance of the arts ask, When the nation's economy is in a slump or the country is involved in international conflict, what good are the arts then? The authors of these articles believe very strongly in the benefits of the arts even in—perhaps especially in—times of trouble, and they provide some insights into what the arts can contribute. All of them also write of the role of the arts in individual self-expression in a variety of contexts, and they raise for discussion some of the issues associated with that self-expression.

○

DAVID MCCULLOUGH

The Future of Imagination

Explains the importance of arts education in nurturing the imagination and teaching students about their culture and its aesthetics.

○

ARTHUR C. DANTO

Art & the Towering Sadness

Comments on the responses of art in the wake of the September 11 attacks on New York City and Washington, D.C.

○

DORINNE DORFMAN

Balancing the Bittersweet: Regulating Content in Student Art

An art teacher explains her struggle with "regulating" controversial student work.

QUESTIONS FOR DISCUSSION OR WRITING

1. Which of the readings do you think would be most effective in persuading a skeptical or indifferent audience that the arts are important? Why?
2. What is your opinion of the practice of regulating the content of student work in elementary or secondary school? Do you accept that it is the teacher's responsibility to direct or adjust student content and that such guidance is not censorship?
3. How can art help an individual, a community, or even an entire nation deal with a catastrophe such as the September 11 terrorist attacks? Has art ever helped you through a difficult time?

PART THREE

SOCIAL AND BEHAVIORAL SCIENCES

CHAPTER

11

EDUCATION

Education is a complex and crucially important subject. Without education, people face obstacles to participating fully in society. Because of its importance, education is also the subject of controversy. People are divided on issues such as what material and activities are appropriate for the classroom, what methods of delivering material work best, how much homework ought to be required of students, and what skills and knowledge students must demonstrate to go on to subsequent educational levels. Periodically, philosophies of education change, curricula are restructured, classrooms are transformed, and instructors learn new approaches to teaching their subject matter. As a student who has gone through many years of education, beginning in the primary grades, you are uniquely positioned to comment on this subject. You have been immersed in education and are presumably currently enrolled in at least one class, the course for which you are using this textbook. In the essays in this chapter, writers express their strong opinions on the subject of education. All criticize certain aspects of the educational system in America, so you are likely to find yourself either nodding your head in agreement or shaking your head in disagreement with what they say.

The first essay in this chapter, David Brooks' "One Nation, Enriched by Biblical Wisdom," addresses the controversial issue of religion in public schools. The question of whether students should be allowed to pray in schools or recite the Pledge of Allegiance, specifically the phrase "one nation, under God," has caused much debate for decades. The furor over school prayer has resulted in lawsuits seeking to block schools from allowing public prayer or recitation of God's name. One such case went to the United States Supreme Court, and Brooks' commentary for the *New York Times* appeared the day before the Court began to hear arguments in the *Elk Grove United School District v. Newdow* case. He makes an intriguing point about the issue by looking at it by way of a book about the civil rights movement.

Following Brooks' essay, Marianne M. Jennings's "The Real Generation Gap" is bound to evoke strong responses from many readers. At the time she wrote the essay, Jennings used a term that was popular at the time, "Generation X." Although the term is now outdated, her criticisms of what schools are teaching young people are still relevant. She believes that young people are ignorant, unskilled, and unthinking and that they are being indoctrinated into a condition of passivity that she refers to as "amoral darkness." She calls for outspoken criticism of the curricula in elementary and secondary schools to bring attention to the plight of America's young people.

Next, in a short but pointed essay by a well-known historian, public television host, and biographer, "No Time to Read?" reminds us of the importance of reading books. David McCullough urgently and fervently advises his audience to "read for pleasure. Read what you like and all that you like. Read literally to your heart's content." For him, books are our most important source of education. The same is true for the author of the final essay in this chapter, Andrew Solomon, whose essay "The Closing of the American Book" explains his belief that a number of national crises have been caused by Americans' decreasing interest in reading.

As you read these selections, think about your own education, the courses you have taken, your classroom activities, the teachers who have taught you, and your own reading habits. Where do you find yourself agreeing with the authors, and where do you disagree? Are your experiences similar to or different from what they describe? What is your own philosophy of education? How important do you believe education is to your well-being and sense of self? How important is reading to you?

ONE NATION, ENRICHED BY BIBLICAL WISDOM
DAVID BROOKS

David Brooks is a senior editor at The Weekly Standard, *a contributing editor at* Newsweek *and the* Atlantic Monthly, *and the "Machine Age" columnist for the* New York Times Magazine. *He is also a regular commentator on National Public Radio, CNN's* Late Edition *and* The NewsHour with Jim Lehrer. *He is editor of the anthology* Backward and Upward: The New Conservative Writing *(1996) and author of* Bobos In Paradise: The New Upper Class and How They Got There *(2000). "One Nation, Enriched by Biblical Wisdom" first appeared in the* New York Times *on March 23, 2004.*

Tomorrow the Supreme Court will hear arguments about whether it is constitutional for public school teachers to lead the Pledge of Allegiance, including the phrase "one nation under God," in their classrooms. So tonight's reading assignment is *A Stone of Hope* by David L. Chappell.

A Stone of Hope is actually a history of the civil rights movement, but it's impossible to read the book without doing some fundamental rethinking about the role religion can play in schools and public life.

According to Chappell, there were actually two camps within the civil rights movement. First, there were the mainstream liberals, often white and Northern. These writers and activists tended to have an optimistic view of human nature. Because racism so fundamentally contradicted the American creed, they felt, it would merely take a combination of education, economic development and consciousness-raising to bring out the better angels in people's nature.

4   The second group, which we might today call the religious left, was mostly black and Southern. Its leaders, including Martin Luther King Jr., drew sustenance from a prophetic religious tradition, and took a much darker view of human nature.

King wrote an important essay on Jeremiah, the "rebel prophet" who saw that his nation was in moral decline. King later reminded readers that human beings are capable of "calculated cruelty as no other animal can practice." He and the other leaders in the movement did not believe that education and economic development would fully bring justice, but believed it would take something as strong as a religious upsurge. Because the experiences of the Hebrew prophets had taught them to be pessimistic about humanity, the civil rights leaders knew they had to be spiritually aggressive if they wanted to get anything done.

Chappell argues that the civil rights movement was not a political movement with a religious element. It was a religious movement with a political element.

If you believe that the separation of church and state means that people should not bring their religious values into politics, then, if Chappell is right, you have to say goodbye to the civil rights movement. It would not have succeeded as a secular force.

8   But the more interesting phenomenon limned in Chappell's book is this: King had a more accurate view of political realities than his more secular liberal allies because he could draw on biblical wisdom about human nature. Religion didn't just make civil rights leaders stronger—it made them smarter.

Whether you believe in God or not, the Bible and commentaries on the Bible can be read as instructions about what human beings are like and how they are likely to behave. Moreover, this biblical wisdom is deeper and more accurate than the wisdom offered by the secular social sciences, which often treat human beings as soulless utility-maximizers, or as members of this or that demographic group or class.

Whether the topic is welfare, education, the regulation of biotechnology or even the war on terrorism, biblical wisdom may offer something that secular thinking does not—not pat answers, but a way to think about things.

For example, it's been painful to watch thoroughly secularized Europeans try to grapple with Al Qaeda. The bombers declare, "You want life, and we want death"— a (fanatical) religious statement par excellence. But thoroughly secularized listeners lack the mental equipment to even begin to understand that statement. They struggle desperately to convert Al Qaeda into a political phenomenon: the bombers must be expressing some grievance. This is the path to permanent bewilderment.

12   The lesson I draw from all this is that prayer should not be permitted in public schools, but maybe theology should be mandatory. Students should be introduced to the prophets, to the Old and New Testaments, to the Koran, to a few of the commentators who argue about these texts.

From this perspective, what gets recited in the pledge is the least important issue before us. Understanding what the phrase "one nation under God" might mean— that's the important thing. That's not proselytizing; it's citizenship.

PERSONAL RESPONSE

Do you believe that public-school children should be allowed to repeat the Pledge of Allegiance? Write for a few minutes explaining your answer.

QUESTIONS FOR CLASS OR SMALL-GROUP DISCUSSION

1. Analyze the use that Brooks makes of David L. Chappell's book, *A Stone of Hope*. How does Brooks use his references to that book to forward his argument?

2. Given the constraints of writing a newspaper column (limited space, short paragraphs), how convincingly do you think that Brooks argues his central position on the issue of prayers and reciting the Pledge of Allegiance in public schools?

3. Explain what you think Brooks means in his closing paragraph when he says that "what gets recited in the pledge is the least important issue before us." Why is "understanding what the phrase 'one nation under God' might mean" more important, according to Brooks?

THE REAL GENERATION GAP

MARIANNE M. JENNINGS

Marianne M. Jennings has taught legal and ethical studies and business at Arizona State University since 1977. Author of more than 130 articles and six textbooks, she is also a columnist for the Arizona Republic, *and her articles have appeared in the* Wall Street Journal, *the* Chicago Tribune, *and numerous other U.S. newspapers. A collection of her essays,* Nobody Fixes Real Carrot Sticks Anymore, *was published in 1994. Her most recent book is* A Business Tale: A Story of Ethics, Choices, Success, and a Very Large Rabbit *(2003). "The Real Generation Gap" was delivered at a Shavano Institute for National Leadership seminar sponsored by Hillsdale College, "Heroes for a New Generation and a New Century." The text of this talk was reprinted in the August 1998 edition of* Imprimis, *a monthly publication of Hillsdale College.*

Born in 1980, today's college freshmen are part of "Generation X." They came into the world long after Vietnam, Richard Nixon, and Watergate. They never saw Senator Sam Ervin's eyebrows. Can you imagine? They were also born after *Saturday Night Fever*. They do not know John Travolta has had two movie careers. Nor do they know what it is like to live in a society in which marriage is the predominant social institution. Unfortunately, they do know about broken homes and "single-parent families." And they know what it is like to be the children of child care because 67 percent of them have mothers working outside their homes.

The members of Generation X know a lot about Madonna, Princess Diana, G.I. Jane, Michael Jackson, Michael Jordan, and Mike Tyson. They know nothing at all about Kate Smith, Mother Teresa, Rosie the Riveter, John Wayne, Babe Ruth, and Audie Murphy. Almost without exception, their favorite role models are the type of celebrities seen on MTV, ESPN, and the cover of *People*.

One disturbing poll reveals that nearly 100 percent of today's youth can name the "Three Stooges," but not even 1 percent can name three justices on the U.S. Supreme Court. Seventy-three percent want to start their own businesses, but 53 percent voted for small business foe Bill Clinton. Only 19 percent attend church regularly. Only 1 percent include a member of the clergy on their lists of most admired individuals.

4   What all these statistics tell us is that the gap between generations is wider than ever before. There are five areas in which the gap is most pronounced: skills, knowledge, critical thinking, work, and morality.

The Skills Gap

Iowa test scores have been a standard measurement of academic achievement for many decades. And what they have been measuring lately is frightening. Students who should be scoring at the ninetieth percentile are barely scoring at the seventieth; those who should be at the seventieth are hovering between the thirtieth and fortieth. Between 70 and 90 percent of all students entering the California State University system have to take some form of remedial course work in basic subjects like English and math. Eighty-seven percent of students entering New York community colleges flunk the placement test—they can't even pass the test that would put them into remedial courses! As New York Mayor Rudolph Guiliani observed several years ago, if skills actually determined entrance into the New York system of higher education, three of every four students would probably be denied admission. (The state has recently begun to administer such tests, and it appears that Guiliani was right.) It is also a matter of public record that national ACT and SAT college entrance test scores are steadily declining despite "adjustments" designed to boost them artificially.

Yet one-third of many high schools' students maintain 4.0 (straight A) grade point averages. Why? Because grade inflation, which occurs at every level of education, is rampant. My daughter Sarah has been in the public school system since the third grade, and she is living proof. She has consistently received good grades without the benefit of a good education.

When she enrolled in an algebra class in the eighth grade, I offered to help her with her homework. She took me up on this offer one evening when we were sitting together at the kitchen table. The first problem was: "What is 10 percent of 470?" I was stunned to discover that Sarah couldn't solve it without the aid of a calculator. Another problem involved determining 25 percent of a given figure. She not only didn't know the answer, but she didn't know that this percentage could be expressed as "one-quarter" or "one-fourth."

8

Here was my own flesh and blood—my straight-A student! I couldn't help asking, "Are the other kids this dumb?" Without missing a beat, Sarah replied, "Oh, they're much dumber." She may be right. On the most recent International Math and Science Survey, which tests students from forty-two countries, one-third of all American high school seniors could not compute the price of a $1,250 stereo that was discounted by 20 percent.

The Knowledge Gap

Algebra is not the only area where today's students have trouble. Hillsdale College President George Roche writes, "Tens of thousands of students do not know when Columbus sailed to the New World, who wrote the Declaration of Independence, or why the Civil War was fought." Part of the problem is that most parents don't realize that what is being taught in modern public schools is actually widening the knowledge gap between them and their children.

One of the most popular history textbooks, produced as a result of the campaign for national education standards in the late 1980s, disparages the "Father of Our Country." George Washington was not, the authors of *The United States: In the Course of Human Events* contend, really successful as a soldier, as a politician, or as a human being. Much is made of Thomas Jefferson's subjective observation that Washington was possessed of "a heart that was not warm in its affections."

How is Generation X ever going to find out that Washington the general did more than any individual to win the war that established our nation? Or that Washington the president risked his reputation and his career to ensure that we would have limited government, a sound economy, and a virtuous citizenry? Or that Washington the man constantly performed acts of kindness and charity for others, including Jefferson? It certainly isn't going to learn such important lessons from a textbook that claims Washington was not much of a man because he did not, in modern lingo, "feel our pain."

12   Special sections in each chapter feature biographies of people who have made a difference in history. Almost all are politically correct minorities and/or females. One, for example, is a female astronaut. The authors allege that she was unfairly excluded from Project Mercury because she had no flight experience. This, of course, is characterized as an insufficient reason to deny her the "right" to participate.

The seventeenth-century English philosopher John Locke is not mentioned—there is no room, evidently, to discuss his significant role in bringing about the Enlightenment or the American Revolution. Famous religious leaders are also ignored, although the authors do bow to the ancient gods of primitive peoples. Pre-Columbian cultures like the Toltecs are praised for their lavishly decorated temples, their calendars, their games—so what if they practiced human sacrifice?

This best-selling textbook reveals a glimpse of the version of history—or rather, non-history—Generation X is being taught. I should know. Last summer, I took Sarah, then fourteen years old, on a tour of Boston, Massachusetts. I carefully explained the historic significance of each site to her. After several hours, she said, "Now, Mom, what war was this?" While I was still in a state of shock we arrived at the Old North Church and listened to a tour guide tell the story of Paul Revere. Sarah's question this time was, "What side was he on?" I asked incredulously, "What exactly did you do in the advanced placement U.S. history class you just completed?" Her response was, "I made a great many charts, and I did a lot of little projects with painting."

I do not mean to pick on Sarah. She and her peers are victims of a pernicious system that has turned traditional liberal arts education on its head. The situation is no better in higher education. At some colleges and universities, professors deliver lectures on the "the Apostle Paul as a Homosexual" and "Jesus Acted Up: A Gay and Lesbian Manifesto." Stanford University achieved notoriety a decade ago for its course, "Black Hair as Culture and History." A current survey on American religion at another school fails to mention Catholicism. One new cutting-edge psychology course is titled, "Gender Discrepancies and Pizza Consumption."

16   Before long, the loss of knowledge may even make simple conversation impossible. In my classroom, I cannot say, "Never look a gift horse in the mouth," or my students will give me a blank stare. I cannot say, "Me thinks thou dost protest too much," or at least one will inevitably respond, "Excuse me, Professor Jennings, shouldn't that be, 'I thinks?' " The literary shorthand of our culture is being lost. This is no small loss either, for words are symbols of important ideas.

The Critical Thinking Gap

Indoctrination is partly to blame for the knowledge gap. This is not a new trend in education. When I was in school, I was taught about "global cooling," and my teachers predicted that the earth was going to be frozen over in a new ice age. Today, my children are told that global warming is going to bring on an ecological apocalypse. But the level of indoctrination has risen sharply. Environmentalism has become an obsession with the teachers of Generation X. They constantly bombard students with dire warnings about pollution, scarce resources, and weather-related disasters. A recent cartoon sums up the attitude the students typically develop. It shows a little girl declaring to her mother that her day in school was a bust: "We didn't do anything to save mankind or the environment. We wasted the whole day on reading and math."

Indoctrination makes students passive receivers of information. As such docile participants, most public school students are incapable of independent thought—of drawing logical inferences or exhibiting other critical thinking skills. They are also incapable of looking at a statement and determining its validity. I refer to this as the "frou-frou head" problem, because students are so lacking in skills and knowledge and are so indoctrinated by politically correct thinking that they are not able to think clearly or make sound, well-informed judgments.

High school freshman Nathan Zohmer of Idaho recently conducted an experiment in science class that reveals the serious nature of this problem. He told classmates and teachers that they should sign his petition to ban a dangerous substance, "dihydrogen monoxide," which causes excessive vomiting and sweating. He informed them that dihydrogen monoxide is a component in acid rain. In its gaseous state, it can cause serious burns. Accidental inhalation can kill. To make matters worse, it contributes to soil erosion, decreases the effectiveness of automobile brakes, and its presence has been detected in some terminal cancer tumors.

20   Forty-seven of the fifty students and teachers signed the petition with no questions asked. Not one thought to inquire, "Just what *is* dihydrogen monoxide?" If they had, they would have discovered they had signed a petition calling for a ban on H_2O—water.

The Work Ethic Gap

Then there is the work ethic gap. In a recent survey, 80 percent of Generation X respondents said they want an active social life, while only 37 percent admit success at work is important. More adult males are living at home with their parents than at any time in our country's history. Why this staggering statistic? Moms and dads provide comfortable room and board while salaries can be used for fun. The desire for independence is missing along with the drive for achieving that independence.

There is no longer a stigma attached to joining the welfare rolls or reneging on financial obligations. Personal bankruptcies are at an all-time high. What is unique about these bankruptcies is the fact that the majority are not the result of the loss of a job or health problems; they involve one or two wage earners who have simply overextended themselves. Credit card debt, which has skyrocketed in recent years, is mainly held by those whose annual income exceeds $50,000. Evidently, the willingness to save and to delay gratification, the drive for success, and the concern for reputation are fast disappearing in a culture that condones irresponsible spending.

The average time for completion of a bachelor's degree is 5.5 years, so most students are not on a fast track. And they have developed some bad habits by the time they get into college. One is whining. As long as there have been students there has been whining—about workload, about subjects, about grades. But now there is *pre-emptive whining*. Even before the semester begins, even before papers and tests are handed back, students come into my office at Arizona State University with a laundry list of complaints.

24 Last year, one-third of my students protested their grades. In my first twenty years of teaching, not a single student questioned my judgment, but I expect half of my students to do so in the next ten. They are infected with an entitlement mentality. Good grades are not earned by hard work and subject mastery but by signing up to take the class.

I once counseled a graduate student who was doing poorly by saying: "Look, the problem is that you have a lack of depth when it comes to your studies. You have no knowledge base on which you can draw. You are going to have to start reading." He said with some surprise, "What do you mean? Books?"

A recent study analyzing the habits of elementary school children revealed that the average time spent on homework is ten minutes. Worse yet, the same study found that schools are increasingly adopting a "no homework" policy. Perhaps the saddest aspect of this situation is the reason more assignments are not given: Parents complain about the work their children are given.

Following last spring's final exams, a student came to my office and said, "You made us stretch to the maximum. It wasn't a bad feeling." Unfortunately, most students do not understand the pride that comes with conquering what seems to be impossible. Generation X is filled with self-esteem but bereft of knowledge.

28 In the math survey mentioned earlier, students from around the world were asked how they felt they had done upon completion of the exam. While the scores proved that the United States finished in the bottom third of all countries participating, it did finish first in terms of students' perception of personal performance. Americans exhibited the highest self-esteem while students from Japan and Singapore, who finished in the top two slots, were the least arrogant about their performance.

The Morality Gap

The most grievous problem is the morality gap. Sarah is a basketball player and a devoted fan of *Sports Illustrated*. Recently, she shared with me one of the magazine's top stories, which summarized a poll of 1,000 Olympic athletes. One of the questions posed was, "If we could give you a drug that would guarantee your victory at the Olympic Games but would also guarantee your death in five years, would you take it?" Fifty-four percent said yes.

Another survey conducted by the Lutheran Brotherhood asked, "Are there absolute standards for morals and ethics or does everything depend on the situation?"

Seventy-nine percent of the respondents in the eighteen to thirty-four age group said that standards did not exist and that the situation should always dictate behavior. Three percent said they were not sure.

If this poll is correct, 82 percent of all students believe that right and wrong are relative terms and that morality is a ridiculous concept. This is the den of lions into which I walk every day. It is called the modern American classroom.

32   When I finish teaching a course, I ask my students to fill out a written evalua- tion form. Many of them comment, "This business ethics class was really fascinating. I had never heard these ideas before." Mind you, I am not teaching quantum physics—I am presenting simple, basic ideas and principles that should be followed in the marketplace: Be honest. Treat other people the way that you want to be treated. Work hard. Live up to your obligations.

Comedian Jay Leno revealed during one of his street interviews on the *Tonight Show* that the same young people don't seem to know the Ten Commandments. What they do know about morality is what they have picked up in scattered, discon- nected bits from parents, friends, television, and magazines. And a good deal of this is immoral rather than moral. As a result, Generation X lacks a solid moral founda- tion for its views on school, work, marriage, family, and community.

Closing the Generation Gap

Are there ways to close the yawning generation gap, which is really the sum of all these smaller gaps? Of course there are. We live in a miraculous age. Great changes have revolutionized the way we live. I started law school with an electric typewriter— state-of-the-art back then. Now I have a computer, a fax machine, and electronic mail. The tools of high technology allow for improved education, wider access to knowledge, more work productivity, and greater freedom to make moral decisions. But these same tools also demand greater personal responsibility.

Is Generation X ready? I don't know. Remember the 1986 disaster at the Cher- nobyl nuclear plant in Ukraine? The world's worst nuclear accident did not happen because nuclear power is a flawed technology. It happened because a handful of young, cocky engineers chose to disregard established safety parameters while per- forming a routine test of equipment. Ironically, the test was designed to provide power to operate the reactor core cooling system in the event of an emergency. The engineers' carelessness and arrogance, which caused the release of large quantities of radioactive substances into the atmosphere, has since caused the death, pain, and suf- fering of innocent victims in Belarus, Ukraine, and Russia.

36   Look at what happened to Barings Bank, the venerable institution that financed the Napoleonic wars. It went bankrupt in 1995 because one trader, twenty-eight-year old Nick Leeson, was able to sit in front of his computer and violate the prime ethi- cal rule of banking: You don't take other people's money and recklessly gamble with it. He made a $27 billion bet that the Japanese stock market would rally after the Kobe earthquake. The market dropped instead, and Barings's losses reached a stag- gering $1.3 billion.

At the end of 1997, twenty-nine-year-old Marisa Baridis entered a guilty plea when she was charged with selling inside information. For $2,000 to $10,000 a tip, she and her friends made a dramatic impact on the stock market by using nonpublic information to take advantage of others. Ms. Baridis, who profited handsomely from such cheating, was the compliance officer for the investment bank and brokerage house of Morgan Stanley. She enjoyed a great deal of technological access to confidential information and a great deal of unilateral authority. In a tape-recorded conversation, she referred to insider trading as the "illegalist [sic] thing you can do," but, lacking the basic values of fairness and honesty, she easily dismissed the law she was responsible for enforcing. She also cost shareholders and companies millions of dollars.

High technology demands *more* individual judgment and *more* moral accountability. Generation X boasts thousands of techno-wise youth. But it is missing real wisdom, informed by a strong education and a strong spiritual ethic. When I point this out to some of my students and colleagues, they say, "Hey, don't shove that Judeo-Christian stuff down our throats! We don't want that." Then I remind them that this "stuff" exists everywhere, and that it has been considered vital to civil society for centuries. I challenge them to name one country in the world where bribery and cheating are legal and approved by the populace. I tell them to examine the most basic ethical principles of Moses and Jesus and compare them to those of Aristotle, Confucius, and Mohammed. The major religions of the world are in agreement on certain universals that have stood the test of time.

One such standard of university morality is what is referred to by Christians as the "Golden Rule": Do unto others as you would have them do unto you. The same notion of fairness can be found in the basic tenets of Buddhism, Judaism, Hinduism, and even in philosophy in the form of Kant's "categorical imperative." Throughout time, this simple test of ethics has been recognized in various cultures as a means of preserving civility, decency, and morality. Its beauty lies in its simplicity. Its profundity lies in its universal recognition and adherence.

Parents as Teachers

40   As parents we have to stand up and be counted. When our children come home from school, as my daughter did one day, spinning yarns about Ethan Allen and the "Green Mountain Persons," we have to set the record straight. Truth matters. It was Ethan Allen and the "Green Mountain Boys," and this fact is not a slight to women. When preschoolers are exposed to storybooks on "alternative" lifestyles and early sex education (endorsed by the National Education Association, by the way), we must sound our objections loudly and clearly. We must exert pressure on superintendents, principals, and teachers. We must take the initiative and run for positions on school boards and city councils.

We must also seize moments of morality with our children to teach them the difference between right and wrong and impose punishments when they stray from moral principles. Most important, we must restore the twin notions that being judgmental is not the same as being narrow-minded and that expressing moral outrage is not a form of "hate speech." What a different world we would have if choosing right and rejecting wrong were not considered fanatical!

When I graduated from law school, a speaker offered nine words I have never forgotten: "Truth is violated by falsehood but outraged by silence." The past twenty-five years have been filled with falsehoods about our history and our culture. Generation X has never lived in a time of truth. Condemning immorality has become virtually the only sin, so it has not even witnessed the courage of conviction. We have been silent as an entire generation has seen truth repeatedly violated.

There is a difference between holding beliefs and being valiant in defending beliefs. As parents, struggling to close the generation gap, we must be valiant in defending our beliefs. Indeed, this is a call to action for all who guide our youth and offer them instruction. When immorality and adultery are described as "private" and therefore "irrelevant" in the public square, with no impact on character and leadership, we must shout from the rooftops, "Personal conduct *is* character! Character does matter!" When the lessons of history, literature, science, and religion are distorted, attacked, or lost in the shuffle, we must rescue them. It is time to break our silence and confront those who have perpetrated so many myths, so much fraud, and so little substance for so long.

44   It is still possible to reclaim Generation X from the hopelessly flawed indoctrination it has experienced. But reclaiming our children will require the type of introspection that results in moral courage and is followed by the expression of moral outrage. One of my students commented to me at the end of a semester, "You've dispelled so many myths. Now I know morality in business is not a crime." And I responded, "It's even better, son. Neither is the moral life a sin." Breaking our silence will allow truth to emerge, and its rare and illuminating quality will attract the attention and devotion of a generation trained and raised in amoral darkness.

PERSONAL RESPONSE

Explore your immediate response to Jennings's criticism of the educational backgrounds of today's college freshmen. How do you respond to her opening paragraphs about young people, their role models, and their failure to recognize the names of people who served as role models for her generation?

QUESTIONS FOR CLASS OR SMALL-GROUP DISCUSSION

1. Jennings identifies five areas where she believes "the gap between generations is wider than ever before" (paragraph 4). Summarize her central point about each of those five areas and then discuss them in turn. Do you think her remarks accurately reflect your own educational experience? Do you agree with her generalizations?

2. In paragraphs 1, 2, 3, and 9, Jennings names people and events that she claims today's generation of young people do not know. Is her claim right in your case? How many of them do you recognize or know? Do you agree with her implication that not knowing who those people are, or certain facts about the historical events that she names, is a mark of ignorance?

3. Jennings maintains that "political correctness" is "a pernicious system that has turned traditional liberal arts education on its head" (paragraph 15). What is your opinion of that statement?

NO TIME TO READ?

David McCullough

David McCullough is a biographer, historian, lecturer, and teacher. He holds twenty-one honorary degrees and has received many awards for his writing, including Pulitzer Prizes for his widely acclaimed biographies Truman *(1992) and* John Adams *(2001). His other books include* The Path Between the Seas *(1977), chronicling the building of the Panama Canal;* Mornings on Horseback *(1981), on the life of the young Theodore Roosevelt; and* Brave Companions *(1992), essays on heroic figures of the past and present. McCullough is also well known to viewers of PBS as the host of* The American Experience *and numerous PBS documentaries. "No Time to Read?" appeared in the April 18, 2000, issue of* Family Circle.

Once upon a time in the dead of winter in the Dakota territory, Theodore Roosevelt took off in a makeshift boat down the Little Missouri River in pursuit of a couple of thieves who had stolen his prized rowboat. After several days on the river, he caught up and got the draw on them with his trusty Winchester, at which point they surrendered. Then Roosevelt set off in a borrowed wagon to haul the thieves cross-country to justice. They headed across the snow-covered wastes of the Badlands to the railhead at Dickinson, and Roosevelt walked the whole way, the entire 40 miles. It was an astonishing feat, what might be called a defining moment in Roosevelt's eventful life. But what makes it especially memorable is that during that time, he managed to read all of *Anna Karenina*.

I often think of that when I hear people say that they haven't time to read.

Reportedly, the average American does have time to watch 28 hours of television every week, or approximately four hours a day. The average person, I'm told, reads at a rate of 250 words per minute. So, based on these statistics, were the average American to spend those four hours a day with a book instead of watching television, he or she could, in a week, read: the complete poems of T. S. Eliot; two plays by Thornton Wilder, including *Our Town;* the complete poems of Maya Angelou; Faulkner's *The Sound and the Fury; The Great Gatsby;* and The Book of Psalms.

4   That's all in one week.

But a week is a long time by today's standards, when information is available at the touch of a finger. Information has become an industry, a commodity to be packaged, promoted and marketed incessantly. The tools for "accessing" data grow ever more wondrous and ubiquitous and essential if we're to keep in step, we've come to believe. All hail the web, the Internet, the Information Highway.

We're being sold the idea that information is learning, and we're being sold a bill of goods.

Information isn't learning. It isn't wisdom. It isn't common sense necessarily. It isn't kindness. Or good judgment. Or imagination. Or a sense of humor. Or courage. Information doesn't tell us right from wrong.

8   Knowing the area of the state of Connecticut in square miles, or the date on which the United Nations Charter was signed, or the jumping capacity of a flea may be useful, but it isn't learning of itself.

The greatest of all avenues to learning—to wisdom, adventure, pleasure, insight, to understanding human nature, understanding ourselves and our world and our place in it—is in reading books.

Read for life, all your life. Nothing ever invented provides such sustenance, such infinite reward for time spent, as a good book.

Read for pleasure. Read what you like, and all you like. Read literally to your heart's content. Let one book lead to another. They nearly always do.

12   Take up a great author, new or old, and read everything he or she has written. Read about places you've never been. Read biography, history. Read books that changed history: Tom Paine's *Common Sense;* the autobiography of Frederick Douglass; Rachel Carson's *Silent Spring.*

Read those books you know you're supposed to have read and imagine as dreary. A classic may be defined as a book that stays long in print, and a book stays long in print only because it is exceptional. Why exclude the exceptional from your experience?

Go back and read again the books written supposedly for children, especially if you think they are only for children. My first choice would be *The Wind in the Willows.* There's much, very much, you can learn in the company of Toad, Rat and Mole.

And when you read a book you love—a book you feel has enlarged the experience of being alive, a book that "lights the fire"—then spread the word.

16   To carry a book with you wherever you go is old advice and good advice. John Adams urged his son, John Quincy, to carry a volume of poetry. "You'll never be alone," he said, "with a poet in your pocket."

PERSONAL RESPONSE

Do you read books for pleasure during your leisure time? If so, what do you like to read? If not, why not?

QUESTIONS FOR CLASS OR SMALL-GROUP DISCUSSION

1. How effective do you find McCullough's opening anecdote about Theodore Roosevelt?

2. Do you agree with McCullough that, on the "idea that information is learning, [. . .] we're being sold a bill of goods" (paragraph 6)? Do you agree with him that "[i]nformation isn't learning" (paragraph 7)?

3. Discuss the extent to which you agree with McCullough's implication that people would have time to read books if they just took the time.

4. Have you read any of the books or any works by the authors that McCullough names? What authors have you heard about whose books you would like to read (paragraph 12)? What books do you "know you're supposed to

have read and imagine as dreary" (paragraph 13)? Which of the books for children, besides *The Wind in the Willows,* do you think McCullough may have in mind when he says to read the "books written supposedly for children" (paragraph 14)?

THE CLOSING OF THE AMERICAN BOOK

Andrew Solomon

Andrew Solomon studied at Yale University and Jesus College, Cambridge, England. He is a regular contributor to the New Yorker, Art Forum, *and the* New York Times Magazine. *He is author of two nonfiction books,* The Irony Tower: Soviet Artists in a Time of Glasnost *(1991) and* The Noonday Demon: An Atlas of Depression *(2001), which won the National Book Award and was a finalist for the Pulitzer Prize. His novel,* The Stone Boat *(1994), was a finalist for the* Los Angeles Times *First Fiction Award. "The Closing of the American Book" was published in the* New York Times *on July 10, 2004.*

A survey released on Thursday reports that reading for pleasure is way down in America among every group—old and young, wealthy and poor, educated and uneducated, men and women, Hispanic, black and white. The survey, by the National Endowment for the Arts, also indicates that people who read for pleasure are many times more likely than those who don't to visit museums and attend musical performances, almost three times as likely to perform volunteer and charity work, and almost twice as likely to attend sporting events. Readers, in other words, are active, while nonreaders—more than half the population—have settled into apathy. There is a basic social divide between those for whom life is an accrual of fresh experience and knowledge, and those for whom maturity is a process of mental atrophy. The shift toward the latter category is frightening.

Reading is not an active expression like writing, but it is not a passive experience either. It requires effort, concentration, attention. In exchange, it offers the stimulus to and the fruit of thought and feeling. Kafka said, "A book must be an ice ax to break the seas frozen inside our soul." The metaphoric quality of writing—the fact that so much can be expressed through the rearrangement of 26 shapes on a piece of paper—is as exciting as the idea of a complete genetic code made up of four bases: man's work on a par with nature's. Discerning the patterns of those arrangements is the essence of civilization.

The electronic media, on the other hand, tend to be torpid. Despite the existence of good television, fine writing on the Internet, and video games that test logic, the electronic media by and large invite inert reception. One selects channels, but then the information comes out preprocessed. Most people use television as a means of turning their minds off, not on. Many readers watch television without peril; but for those for whom television replaces reading, the consequences are far-reaching.

4   My last book was about depression, and the question I am most frequently asked is why depression is on the rise. I talk about the loneliness that comes of spending the day with a TV or a computer or video screen. Conversely, literary reading is an entry into dialogue; a book can be a friend, talking not at you, but to you. That the rates of depression should be going up as the rates of reading are going down is no happenstance. Meanwhile, there is some persuasive evidence that escalating levels of Alzheimer's disease reflect a lack of active engagement of adult minds. While the disease appears to be determined in large part by heredity and environmental stimulants, it seems that those who continue learning may be less likely to develop Alzheimer's.

So the crisis in reading is a crisis in national health.

I will never forget seeing, as a high school student on my first trip to East Berlin, the plaza where Hitler and Goebbels had burned books from the university library. Those bonfires were predicated on the idea that texts could undermine armies. Soviet repression of literature followed the same principle.

The Nazis were right in believing that one of the most powerful weapons in a war of ideas is books. And for better or worse, the United States is now in such a war. Without books, we cannot succeed in our current struggle against absolutism and terrorism. The retreat from civic to virtual life is a retreat from engaged democracy, from the principles that we say we want to share with the rest of the world. You are what you read. If you read nothing, then your mind withers, and your ideals lose their vitality and sway.

8   So the crisis in reading is a crisis in national politics.

It is important to acknowledge that the falling-off of reading has to do not only with the incursion of anti-intellectualism, but also with a flawed intellectualism. The ascendancy of poststructuralism in the 1980's coincided with the beginning of the catastrophic downturn in reading; deconstructionism's suggestion that all text is equal in its meanings and the denigration of the canon led to the devaluation of literature. The role of literature is to illuminate, to strengthen, to explain why some aspect of life is moving or beautiful or terrible or sad or important or insignificant for people who might otherwise not understand so much or so well. Reading is experience, but it also enriches other experience.

Even more immediate than the crises in health and politics brought on by the decline of reading is the crisis in national education. We have one of the most literate societies in history. What is the point of having a population that can read, but doesn't? We need to teach people not only how, but also why to read. The struggle is not to make people read more, but to make them want to read more.

While there is much work to be done in the public schools, society at large also has a job. We need to make reading, which is in its essence a solitary endeavor, a social one as well, to encourage that great thrill of finding kinship in shared experiences of books. We must weave reading back into the very fabric of the culture, and make it a mainstay of community.

12   Reading is harder than watching television or playing video games. I think of the Epicurean mandate to exchange easier for more difficult pleasures, predicated on the understanding that those more difficult pleasures are more rewarding. I

think of Walter Pater's declaration: "The service of philosophy, of speculative culture, towards the human spirit is to rouse, to startle it to a life of sharp and eager observation. . . . The poetic passion, the desire of beauty, the love of art for its own sake, has most; for art comes to you professing frankly to give nothing but the highest quality to your moments as they pass." Surely that is something all Americans would want, if we only understood how readily we might achieve it, how well worth the effort it is.

PERSONAL RESPONSE

Write for a few minutes in response to Solomon's opening paragraph. Do you identify yourself as a reader? If you do, are you also "active" in the way that Solomon means it? If you are not a reader, have you "settled into apathy"?

QUESTIONS FOR CLASS OR SMALL-GROUP DISCUSSION

1. What do you think of the conclusions that Solomon draws about the decline in Americans' reading for pleasure? Are the conclusions warranted, or do you think that he makes hasty conclusions based on too little data?

2. In paragraph 7, Solomon writes: "Without books, we cannot succeed in our current struggle against absolutism and terrorism." Explain in your own words what you understand him to mean by that statement. To what extent do you agree with him?

3. In paragraph 10, Solomon says that "[w]e need to teach people not only how, but also why to read." How would you answer the question, "Why do we need to read?"

4. Solomon says that we need to make reading a social activity by weaving it "back into the very fabric of culture, and make it a mainstay of community" (paragraph 11). How do you think such a goal could be accomplished?

○ PERSPECTIVES ON EDUCATION ○
Suggested Writing Topics

1. Explain what you see as the role of parents in children's education.

2. Write a paper defining *education,* using specific examples to illustrate general or abstract statements.

3. Read David L. Chappell's *A Stone of Hope,* as discussed in David Brooks' "One Nation, Enriched by Biblical Wisdom" and analyze it in terms of Brooks' remark: [B]ut it's impossible to read the book without doing some fundamental rethinking about the role religion can play in schools and public life."

4. Select a statement from Marianne M. Jennings's "The Real Generation Gap" with which you strongly agree or disagree. You may want to pick one of the five areas she discusses and respond to her on the general issue, or you may want to select a specific statement and respond to it. Consider, for instance, her allegations that today's young people have been "indoctrinated," that "political correctness" is "a pernicious system," or that today's young people are "a generation trained and raised in amoral darkness."

5. Argue in support of or against this statement from David McCullough's "No Time to Read?": "The greatest of all avenues to learning [. . .] is in reading books" (paragraph 9).

6. Select one of the crises mentioned by Andrew Solomon in "The Closing of the American Book" and write an essay expanding on reasons why not reading has led to the crisis.

7. Write a paper exploring the rewards of reading, using specific examples to illustrate general or abstract statements.

8. Write a paper about a book that had a profound effect on you. Explain briefly what the book is and what it is about, but focus on aspects of it that affected you. Perhaps it moved you emotionally as no other book has or it directed you on a specific path in life.

9. Some people argue that not everyone deserves to go to college and that admitting average or mediocre students into colleges has debased American higher education. Argue in support of or against that position.

10. Describe a teacher who made an impression and had a significant effect on you. What made that teacher so important to you? Try to explain not only physical characteristics but, more importantly, personality features and admirable qualities. If a particular incident was especially significant in your relationship, narrate what happened.

11. Assume the role of a student member of the curriculum task force for a department or unit at your university such as business, foreign languages, education, mathematics, computer science, history, music, physics, or your major area, if you have declared one. Your committee has been asked to consider adding a multicultural component to the required courses for the major without dropping any of the courses already required. What recommendations for or against such an addition would you make? In your recommendations, take into consideration the viewpoint of Marianne M. Jennings in "The Real Generation Gap."

12. Imagine that the number of students admitted to college directly after high school has been limited to the upper 33 percent of all graduating seniors and that you do not meet the requirements for admission to college. Under special circumstances, students who fall below the 33 percent mark may be admitted. In a letter to the admissions officer at the college of your choice, argue that you should be admitted despite your class ranking and give reasons why you would make a good student.

Research Topics

1. Research the tracking systems used in many schools. Find opinions supporting and opposing such systems, consider their advantages and disadvantages, and arrive at your own conclusion based on your reading.

2. Research the Supreme Court case of *Elk Grove United School District v. Newdow*, analyze the arguments on both sides, and come to your own conclusion about the phrase "under God" in the Pledge of Allegiance.

3. Spend some time searching the Internet or going through your library's catalog of books and periodicals on the subject of education. You will find a very large number of subtopics under that broad heading. Select a seemingly controversial subtopic that interests you. Keep searching until you have narrowed your focus to one specific aspect of the subject that is suitable for your research project.

4. Research the conflict of traditional versus revisionist curriculum. Interview educators and read periodical articles from the last several years on *political correctness,* defenses for or against *the canon,* or related topics.

5. Both Brooks, McCullough, and Solomon find fault with the electronic media. Research the subject of the role of television or of the Internet in American popular culture in relationship to the reading habits of Americans.

6. Research the controversy over prayer in public schools and explain your own position on the topic.

RESPONDING TO VISUALS

Boring class, circa 1950s. Source: H. Armstrong Roberts/CORBIS

1. What do you think the photographer wanted to convey with this picture?
2. Although the caption describes the photograph as that of a boring class, what other emotions do the facial expressions of the students suggest? What does their body language reveal about how they view this particular classroom experience?
3. If you had not been told the date that the photograph was taken, what aspects of the classroom and students would give you clues that it is not recent?
4. Why do you think the teacher is not shown in the photograph?

RESPONDING TO VISUALS

During the Supreme Court hearings on the "Under God" clause of the U.S. Pledge of Allegiance, opponents hold vigil in front of the Supreme Court in Washington, D.C. Wednesday, March 24, 2004. Source: Shawn Thew/EPA/Landov

1. Supporters of the Pledge of Allegiance say that the words "under God" are political, historical, or ceremonial, that is, anything but religious. What do the signs indicate about how opponents of the pledge view those words?
2. How does the composition of the photograph convey its message?
3. What is the effect of foregrounding the protestors and placards with the Supreme Court building in the background?

CHAPTER

12

POVERTY AND HOMELESSNESS

Once largely ignored, the issues of poverty, homelessness, and welfare have prompted heated discussion in recent years. At the community level, social workers and staff members at shelters for the homeless and impoverished struggle to meet the needs of desperate people, while at the state and federal levels, legislators argue over whether to cut welfare funding. The numbers of people in poverty, especially women and children, continue to rise. Many families whose incomes provide just enough for basic necessities, such as shelter and food, are only a paycheck or two away from living on the streets. Worse, a growing number of the nation's poor actually work full-time. Compounding the difficulty of these issues are certain attitudes toward or stereotyped beliefs about people on welfare or living on the streets. Charges of laziness and fraud are often leveled at welfare recipients, despite studies that demonstrate that the vast majority of people on welfare want to work and live independent lives.

The essays in this chapter examine some of the issues associated with poverty and homelessness. First, Anna Quindlen in "Our Tired, Our Poor, Our Kids" looks at the plight of homeless mothers and children in America. She points out some of the effects of homelessness on children, emphasizes the importance of affordable housing, and touches on the effects of welfare reform on homelessness. Closely related to Quindlen's opinion piece is an editorial published in *America* magazine. "Still Hungry, Still Homeless" comments on the rise of poverty and homelessness in the United States, notes the increase in requests for emergency housing and food, and, like Quindlen, mentions the effect of welfare reform on this serious social problem.

Following these two readings on homelessness and hunger in America is a classic *satire* (a writing mode whose principle means of persuasion is to ridicule its subject to bring about change) by Jonathan Swift in which he offers a unique solution to the problem of poverty in early 18th-century Ireland. Written when Ireland was a far poorer country than England, its population largely Catholic, and its primary occupation agricultural, "A Modest Proposal" takes a satiric look at ways to solve the very serious problem of poverty and its attendant woes. In its structure and use of logic, the essay is also a model of persuasion.

Next, Melanie Scheller's highly personal essay, "On the Meaning of Plumbing and Poverty," makes concrete and vivid some of the generalizations of Quindlen's essay and the *America* editorial. By presenting graphic, painful details, Scheller conveys a very real sense not only of the experience of a child living in poverty but also of the shame and diminished self-esteem she carried with her as a result of living in homes without indoor plumbing.

Finally, in "The Singer Solution to World Poverty," Peter Singer broadens the focus of the chapter to world poverty while addressing his essay to the American middle class. Using the logic of his training as a utilitarian philosopher, Singer offers a hypothetical ethical scenario to raise readers' awareness of what he sees as their moral responsibility to donate to world aid funds for poor and starving children.

As you read these essays, think about your own attitudes toward welfare, homelessness, and poverty. Do the Quindlen essay and the *America* editorial in any way reinforce or change your attitudes? Does Swift's satire suggest some real solutions to the problems? Are you moved by Scheller's personal essay? Does Singer persuade you to donate to charities?

OUR TIRED, OUR POOR, OUR KIDS

ANNA QUINDLEN

Anna Quindlen began her journalism career at the New York Post *and then became deputy metropolitan editor of the* New York Times. *In 1986, she began her syndicated column "Life in the Thirties" and a few years later "Public and Private," for which she won a Pulitzer Prize in 1992. Currently she contributes* Newsweek's *prestigious back-page column,* The Last Word, *every other week. Her columns are collected in* Living Out Loud *(1988),* Thinking Out Loud *(1992), and* Loud and Clear *(2004). She has written the following novels:* Object Lessons *(1991),* One True Thing *(1994),* Black and Blue *(1998),* Blessings *(2003), and* Being Perfect *(2004). Among her nonfiction books are* How Reading Changed My Life *(1998),* A Short Guide to a Happy Life *(2000), and* Imagining London: A Tour of the World's Greatest Fictional City *(2004). This essay appeared in the March 12, 2001, issue of* Newsweek.

Six people live here, in a room the size of the master bedroom in a modest suburban house. Trundles, bunk beds, dressers side by side stacked with toys, clothes, boxes, in tidy claustrophobic clutter. One woman, five children. The baby was born in a shelter. The older kids can't wait to get out of this one. Everyone gets up at 6 A.M., the little ones to go to day care, the others to school. Their mother goes out to look for an apartment when she's not going to drug-treatment meetings. "For what they pay for me to stay in a shelter I could have lived in the Hamptons," Sharanda says.

Here is the parallel universe that has flourished while the more fortunate were rewarding themselves for the stock split with SUVs and home additions. There is a boom market in homelessness. But these are not the men on the streets of San Francisco holding out cardboard signs to the tourists. They are children, hundreds of thousands of them, twice as likely to repeat a grade or be hospitalized and four times as likely to go hungry as the kids with a roof over their heads. Twenty years ago New York City provided emergency shelter for just under a thousand families a day; last month it had to find spaces for 10,000 children on a given night. Not since the Great Depression have this many babies, toddlers and kids had no place like home.

Three mothers sit in the living room of a temporary residence called Casa Rita in the Bronx and speak of this in the argot of poverty. "The landlord don't call back when they hear you got EARP," says Rosie, EARP being the Emergency Assistance Rehousing Program. "You get priority for Section 8 if you're in a shelter," says Edna, which means federal housing programs will put you higher on the list. Edna has four kids, three in foster care; she arrived at Casa Rita, she says, "with two bags and a baby." Rosie has three; they share a bathroom down the hall with two other families. Sharanda's five range in age from 13 to just over a year. Her eldest was put in the wrong grade when he changed schools. "He's humiliated, living here," his mother says.

4   All three women are anxious to move on, although they appreciate this place, where they can get shelter, get sober and keep their kids at the same time. They

remember the Emergency Assistance Unit, the city office that is the gateway to the system, where hundreds of families sit every day surrounded by their bags, where children sleep on benches until they are shuffled off dull-eyed for one night in a shelter or a motel, only to return as supplicants again the next day.

In another world middle-class Americans have embraced new-home starts, the stock market and the Gap. But in the world of these displaced families, problems ignored or fumbled or unforeseen during this great period of prosperity have dovetailed into an enormous subculture of children who think that only rich people have their own bedrooms. Twenty years ago, when the story of the homeless in America became a staple of news reporting, the solution was presented as a simple one: affordable housing. That's still true, now more than ever. Two years ago the National Low Income Housing Coalition calculated that the hourly income necessary to afford the average two-bedroom apartment was around $12. That's more than twice the minimum wage.

The result is that in many cities police officers and teachers cannot afford to live where they work, that in Las Vegas old motels provide housing for casino employees, that in shelters now there is a contingent of working poor who get up off their cots and go off to their jobs. The result is that if you are evicted for falling behind on your rent, if there is a bureaucratic foul-up in your welfare check or the factory in which you work shuts down, the chances of finding another place to live are very small indeed. You're one understanding relative, one paycheck, one second chance from the street. And so are your kids.

So-called welfare reform, which emphasizes cutbacks and make-work, has played a part in all this. A study done in San Diego in 1998 found that a third of homeless families had recently had benefits terminated or reduced, and that most said that was how they had wound up on the street. Drugs, alcohol and domestic abuse also land mothers with kids in the shelter system or lead them to hand their children over to relatives or foster homes. Today the average homeless woman is younger than ever before, may have been in foster care or in shelters herself and so considers a chaotic childhood the norm. Many never finished high school, and have never held a job.

8   Ralph Nunez, who runs the organization Homes for the Homeless, says that all this calls for new attitudes. "People don't like to hear it, but shelters are going to be the low-income housing of the future," he says. "So how do we enrich the experience and use the system to provide job training and education?" Bonnie Stone of Women in Need, which has eight other residences along with Casa Rita, says, "We're pouring everything we've got into the nine months most of them are here—nutrition, treatment, budgeting. By the time they leave, they have a subsidized apartment, day care and, hopefully, some life skills they didn't have before."

But these organizations are rafts in a rising river of need that has roared through this country without most of us ever even knowing. So now you know. There are hundreds of thousands of little nomads in America, sleeping in the back of cars, on floors in welfare offices or in shelters five to a room. What would it mean, to spend your childhood drifting from one strange bed to another, waking in the morning to try to figure out where you'd landed today, without those things that confer security and happiness: a familiar picture on the wall, a certain slant of light through a curtained window? "Give me your tired, your poor," it says on the base of the Statue of Liberty, to welcome foreigners. Oh, but they are already here, the small refugees from the ruin of the American dream, even if you cannot see them.

PERSONAL RESPONSE

What image of the homeless did you have before reading this essay? Has your understanding of them changed in any way now that you have read it? If so, in what way has it changed? If not, explain why.

QUESTIONS FOR CLASS OR SMALL-GROUP DISCUSSION

1. Were you surprised by this statement: "Not since the Great Depression have this many babies, toddlers and kids had no place like home" (paragraph 2)? What effect do you think Quindlen hopes to achieve by mentioning the Great Depression?

2. Explain why, according to Quindlen, there are so many homeless women and children in America. What is the effect of homelessness on children? Are you persuaded of the seriousness of the problem?

3. What does Quindlen mean by the term *working poor* (paragraph 6)?

4. Quindlen uses the term *so-called* to describe welfare reform (paragraph 7). Why do you think she does that? What fault does she find with welfare reform? Do you agree with her?

STILL HUNGRY, STILL HOMELESS

AMERICA MAGAZINE EDITORIAL

America *magazine describes itself as a journal of opinion on current events, historical events, spiritual events, family, books, film, and television for Catholic people. This editorial appeared in the magazine's February 5, 2001, issue.*

One might think that last year's particularly strong economy would have led to a reduction in the number of requests for emergency food and shelter. In fact, however, the year 2000 actually saw a rise in both areas. This was among the sad findings of the United States Conference of Mayors' annual survey of 25 cities around the country, which was released in late December.

Officials in the survey cities estimated that requests for emergency food assistance jumped by 17 percent—the second highest rate of increase since 1992. Over half of the people seeking help were children and their parents: a particularly disturbing finding, given the need for parents to be able to provide adequate and nutritious food for their children. A third of the adults, moreover, were employed. This reflects the fact that minimum wage jobs at $5.50 an hour cannot cover the cost of living for most Americans. Mirroring the conclusions of the mayors' report, Catholic Charities USA found in its own year-end survey that its agencies had seen what it termed "a startling 22 percent increase in the use of their emergency services."

How could this be, in the face of what many politicians have trumpeted as our unprecedented level of prosperity? Ironically, the mayors' report points out that the very strength of the economy has been partly to blame. Seeing that the earnings of middle-class Americans have risen, landlords have been quick to realize that they can charge much higher rents. But for families at the bottom of the economic ladder, whose earnings did not increase, the consequence has been an ever more desperate search for housing within their income range; it is a search that has sometimes ended in homelessness. Even those lucky enough to have Section 8 vouchers have discovered that apartment owners often refuse to accept them, knowing that they can command higher prices than the government's reimbursement rate for the vouchers. Thus, in nearly half the survey cities, the report cites housing costs as a primary reason for the increase in requests for emergency food and shelter.

4   Welfare reform has played its part in this bleak scenario. People leaving Temporary Assistance for Needy Families (T.A.N.F.) may indeed have full-time jobs that pay above the minimum wage and yet still not be making enough to lift them above the poverty line. And all too frequently, they are unaware that despite being employed, they may still be eligible for the food stamps (and Medicaid) that could tide them over from one month to the next. Government agencies are not as aggressive as they should be in promoting these programs among the working poor. True, the number of food assistance facilities has increased, but the strain on their limited resources is so great that half the cities report that these facilities must either send people away or reduce the amount of what they can provide.

The same situation applies to emergency housing requests. Nearly a quarter of them, says the mayors' report, went unmet. Turned-away families in San Antonio, for instance, found themselves obliged to sleep in cars or parks, under bridges or in already doubled- or tripled-up substandard housing. Even when they can be accommodated, in 52 percent of the cities homeless families may have to break up, with older male youths and fathers sent elsewhere.

The outlook for the future is not bright. Almost three-fourths of the survey cities expect a rise in the demand for emergency food. As the officials in Boston put it, "the number of pantries increases every year, and [yet] the requests for assistance have increased by as much as 40 percent." Nor, they add, do they "see any relief in the near future." Again, there as elsewhere, high housing costs, along with low-paying jobs, lead the list of causes for more hunger and homelessness. The answer is implied in the comments of the respondents from Burlington, Vt.: "Without a significant commitment to building a significant number of new and affordable housing units, homelessness will continue to rise." The new secretary-designate of the Department of Housing and Urban Development, Mel Martinez, said at his Senate confirmation hearing that he would try to make more housing available to low-income Americans. We hope that he will act on his words. For many years, however, Congress has shown little interest in this neglected area of American life.

In releasing its annual report in December, Fred Kammer, S.J., president of Catholic Charities USA, spoke of its findings as "a story about . . . escalating need in a land of skyrocketing wealth." He recalled Bill Clinton's promise to "end welfare as we know it." That has happened, but the rise in requests for emergency food and housing calls into question the effectiveness of welfare reform. The real goal, Father Kammer concluded, should be to "end poverty as we know it." Now is the time for Congress to take the strong measures needed to assist the most vulnerable members of society.

PERSONAL RESPONSE

Are you surprised that the numbers of hungry and homeless people in America are rising? Write for a few minutes on your reaction to that fact or to any other part of the essay that caught your attention as you read it.

QUESTIONS FOR CLASS OR SMALL-GROUP DISCUSSION

1. How does the editorial account for the fact that requests for emergency food and shelter continue to rise despite a strong economy (paragraph 1)? That is, what factors account for the high numbers of children and their parents, including employed adults, seeking emergency aid?

2. The editorial comments that "the rise in requests for emergency food and housing calls into question the effectiveness of welfare reform" (paragraph 7). Why has the welfare reform program not worked, according to the editorial? What do you know about the welfare reform program? Do you think it is a good plan, or do you find fault with it, too?

3. Are you persuaded that "now is the time for Congress to take the strong measures needed to assist the most vulnerable members of society" (paragraph 7)? What measures does the editorial suggest would be appropriate? How effective do you think those measures would be?

4. Can you offer any other solutions to the problem of homelessness and poverty in America besides the ones suggested in this article?

A MODEST PROPOSAL

For Preventing the Children of Poor People in Ireland from Being a Burden to their Parents or Country, and for Making them Beneficial to the Public

JONATHAN SWIFT

Jonathan Swift (1667–1745) was an Irish author and journalist who served as dean of St. Patrick's Cathedral (Dublin) from 1713 to 1742. Widely regarded as the foremost prose satirist in the English language, he is perhaps best known for Gulliver's Travels *(1726), which follows the travels of Lemuel Gulliver to a land of dwarfs ("Lilliputians"), a land inhabited by giants ("Brobdingnagians"), and a land where horses ("Houyhnhnms") are more intelligent than humans. Among his many other works are* The Battle of the Books *(1697), which pits modern versus ancient literature, and a religious satire,* A Tale of a Tub *(1704). "A Modest Proposal" was published as a pamphlet in 1729.*

It is a melancholy object to those who walk through this great town or travel in the country, when they see the streets, the roads, and cabin doors, crowded with beggars of the female sex, followed by three, four, or six children, all in rags and importuning every passenger for an alms. These mothers, instead of being able to work for their honest livelihood, are forced to employ all their time in strolling to beg sustenance for their helpless infants: who as they grow up either turn thieves for want of work, or leave their dear native country to fight for the Pretender in Spain, or sell themselves to the Barbadoes.

I think it is agreed by all parties that this prodigious number of children in the arms, or on the backs, or at the heels of their mothers, and frequently of their fathers, is in the present deplorable state of the kingdom a very great additional grievance; and, therefore, whoever could find out a fair, cheap, and easy method of making these children sound, useful members of the commonwealth, would deserve so well of the public as to have his statue set up for a preserver of the nation.

But my intention is very far from being confined to provide only for the children of professed beggars; it is of a much greater extent, and shall take in the whole number of infants at a certain age who are born of parents in effect as little able to support them as those who demand our charity in the streets.

4   As to my own part, having turned my thoughts for many years upon this important subject, and maturely weighed the several schemes of other projectors, I have always found them grossly mistaken in the computation. It is true, a child just dropped from its dam may be supported by her milk for a solar year, with little other nourishment; at most not above the value of 2 shillings, which the mother may certainly get, or the value in scraps, by her lawful occupation of begging; and it is exactly at one year old that I propose to provide for them in such a manner as instead of being a charge upon their parents or the parish, or wanting food and raiment for the rest of their lives, they shall on the contrary contribute to the feeding, and partly to the clothing, of many thousands.

There is likewise another great advantage in my scheme, that it will prevent those voluntary abortions, and that horrid practice of women murdering their bastard children, alas! too frequent among us! sacrificing the poor innocent babes I doubt more to avoid the expense than the shame, which would move tears and pity in the most savage and inhuman breast.

The number of souls in this kingdom being usually reckoned one million and a half, of these I calculate there may be about two hundred thousand couple whose wives are breeders; from which number I subtract thirty thousand couples who are able to maintain their own children, although I apprehend there cannot be so many, under the present distresses of the kingdom; but this being granted, there will remain an hundred and seventy thousand breeders. I again subtract fifty thousand for those women who miscarry, or whose children die by accident or disease within the year. There only remains one hundred and twenty thousand children of poor parents annually born. The question therefore is, how this number shall be reared and provided for, which, as I have already said, under the present situation of affairs, is utterly impossible by all the methods hitherto proposed. For we can neither employ them in handicraft or agriculture; we neither build houses (I mean in the country) nor cultivate land: they can very seldom pick up a livelihood by stealing, till they arrive at six years old, except where they are of towardly parts, although I confess they learn the rudiments much earlier, during which time, they can however be properly looked upon only as probationers, as I have been informed by a principal gentleman in the county of Cavan, who protested to me that he never knew above one or two instances under the age of six, even in a part of the kingdom so renowned for the quickest proficiency in that art.

I am assured by our merchants, that a boy or a girl before twelve years old is no salable commodity; and even when they come to this age they will not yield above three pounds, or three pounds and half-a-crown at most on the exchange; which cannot turn to account either to the parents or kingdom, the charge of nutriment and rags having been at least four times that value.

8   I shall now therefore humbly propose my own thoughts, which I hope will not be liable to the least objection.

I have been assured by a very knowing American of my acquaintance in London, that a young healthy child well nursed is at a year old a most delicious, nourishing, and wholesome food, whether stewed, roasted, baked, or boiled; and I make no doubt that it will equally serve in a fricassee or a ragout.

I do therefore humbly offer it to public consideration that of the hundred and twenty thousand children already computed, twenty thousand may be reserved for breed, whereof only one-fourth part to be males; which is more than we allow to sheep, black cattle or swine; and my reason is, that these children are seldom the fruits of marriage, a circumstance not much regarded by our savages, therefore one male will be sufficient to serve four females. That the remaining hundred thousand may, at a year old, be offered in the sale to the persons of quality and fortune through the kingdom; always advising the mother to let them suck plentifully in the last month, so as to render them plump and fat for a good table. A child will make two dishes at an entertainment for friends; and when the family dines alone, the fore or hind quarter will make a reasonable dish, and seasoned with a little pepper or salt will be very good boiled on the fourth day, especially in winter.

I have reckoned upon a medium that a child just born will weigh 12 pounds, and in a solar year, if tolerably nursed, increaseth to 28 pounds.

12   I grant this food will be somewhat dear, and therefore very proper for landlords, who, as they have already devoured most of the parents, seem to have the best title to the children.

Infant's flesh will be in season throughout the year, but more plentiful in March, and a little before and after; for we are told by a grave author, an eminent French physician, that fish being a prolific diet, there are more children born in Roman Catholic countries about nine months after Lent than at any other season; therefore, reckoning a year after Lent, the markets will be more glutted than usual, because the number of popish infants is at least three to one in this kingdom: and therefore it will have one other collateral advantage, by lessening the number of papists among us.

I have already computed the charge of nursing a beggar's child (in which list I reckon all cottagers, laborers, and four-fifths of the farmers) to be about two shillings per annum, rags included; and I believe no gentleman would repine to give ten shillings for the carcass of a good fat child, which, as I have said, will make four dishes of excellent nutritive meat, when he hath only some particular friend or his own family to dine with him. Thus the squire will learn to be a good landlord, and grow popular among his tenants; the mother will have eight shillings net profit, and be fit for work till she produces another child.

Those who are more thrifty (as I must confess the times require) may flay the carcass; the skin of which artificially dressed will make admirable gloves for ladies, and summer boots for fine gentlemen.

16   As to our city of Dublin, shambles may be appointed for this purpose in the most convenient parts of it, and butchers we may be assured will not be wanting; although I rather recommend buying the children alive, and dressing them hot from the knife, as we do roasting pigs.

A very worthy person, a true lover of his country, and whose virtues I highly esteem, was lately pleased in discoursing on this matter to offer a refinement upon my scheme. He said that many gentlemen of this kingdom, having of late destroyed their deer, he conceived that the want of venison might be well supplied by the bodies of young lads and maidens, not exceeding fourteen years of age nor under twelve; so great a number of both sexes in every country being now ready to starve for want of work and service; and these to be disposed of by their parents, if alive, or otherwise by their nearest relations. But with due deference to so excellent a friend and so deserving a patriot, I cannot be altogether in his sentiments; for as to the males, my American acquaintance assured me, from frequent experience, that their flesh was generally tough and lean, like that of our schoolboys by continual exercise, and their taste disagreeable; and to fatten them would not answer the charge. Then as to the females, it would, I think, with humble submission be a loss to the public, because they soon would become breeders themselves; and besides, it is not improbable that some scrupulous people might be apt to censure such a practice (although indeed very unjustly), as a little bordering upon cruelty; which, I confess, hath always been with me the strongest objection against any project, however so well intended.

But in order to justify my friend, he confessed that this expedient was put into his head by the famous Psalmanazar, a native of the island Formosa, who came from thence to London above twenty years ago, and in conversation told my friend, that in his country when any young person happened to be put to death, the executioner sold the carcass to persons of quality as a prime dainty; and that in his time the body of a plump girl of fifteen, who was crucified for an attempt to poison the emperor, was sold to his imperial majesty's prime minister of state, and other great mandarins of the court, in joints from the gibbet, at four hundred crowns. Neither indeed can I deny, that if the same use were made of several plump young girls in this town, who without one single groat to their fortunes cannot stir abroad without a chair, and appear at playhouse and assemblies in foreign fineries which they never will pay for, the kingdom would not be the worse.

Some persons of a desponding spirit are in great concern about that vast number of poor people, who are aged, diseased, or maimed, and I have been desired to employ my thoughts what course may be taken to ease the nation of so grievous an encumbrance. But I am not in the least pain upon that matter, because it is very well known that they are every day dying and rotting by cold and famine, and filth and vermin, as fast as can be reasonably expected. And as to the young laborers, they are now in as hopeful a condition; they cannot get work, and consequently pine away for want of nourishment, to a degree that if at any time they are accidentally hired to common labor, they have not strength to perform it; and thus the country and themselves are happily delivered from the evils to come.

20   I have too long digressed, and therefore shall return to my subject. I think the advantages by the proposal which I have made are obvious and many, as well as of the highest importance.

For first, as I have already observed, it would greatly lessen the number of papists, with whom we are yearly overrun, being the principal breeders of the nation as well as our most dangerous enemies; and who stay at home on purpose with a design to deliver the kingdom to the Pretender, hoping to take their advantage by the absence of so many good protestants, who have chosen rather to leave their country than stay at home and pay tithes against their conscience to an episcopal curate.

Secondly, The poorer tenants will have something valuable of their own, which by law may be made liable to distress and help to pay their landlord's rent, their corn and cattle being already seized, and money a thing unknown.

Thirdly, Whereas the maintenance of an hundred thousand children, from two years old and upward, cannot be computed at less than ten shillings a-piece per annum, the nation's stock will be thereby increased fifty thousand pounds per annum, beside the profit of a new dish introduced to the tables of all gentlemen of fortune in the kingdom who have any refinement in taste. And the money will circulate among ourselves, the goods being entirely of our own growth and manufacture.

24   Fourthly, The constant breeders, beside the gain of eight shillings sterling per annum by the sale of their children, will be rid of the charge of maintaining them after the first year.

Fifthly, This food would likewise bring great custom to taverns; where the vintners will certainly be so prudent as to procure the best receipts for dressing it to perfection, and consequently have their houses frequented by all the fine gentlemen, who justly value themselves upon their knowledge in good eating: and a skilful cook, who understands how to oblige his guests, will contrive to make it as expensive as they please.

Sixthly, This would be a great inducement to marriage, which all wise nations have either encouraged by rewards or enforced by laws and penalties. It would increase the care and tenderness of mothers toward their children, when they were sure of a settlement for life to the poor babes, provided in some sort by the public, to their annual profit instead of expense. We should see an honest emulation among the married women, which of them could bring the fattest child to the market. Men would become as fond of their wives during the time of their pregnancy as they are now of their mares in foal, their cows in calf, their sows when they are ready to farrow; nor offer to beat or kick them (as is too frequent a practice) for fear of a miscarriage.

Many other advantages might be enumerated. For instance, the addition of some thousand carcasses in our exportation of barreled beef, the propagation of swine's flesh, and improvement in the art of making good bacon, so much wanted among us by the great destruction of pigs, too frequent at our tables; which are no way comparable in taste or magnificence to a well-grown, fat, yearling child, which roasted whole will make a considerable figure at a lord mayor's feast or any other public entertainment. But this and many others I omit, being studious of brevity.

28 After all, I am not so violently bent upon my own opinion as to reject any offer proposed by wise men, which shall be found equally innocent, cheap, easy, and effectual. But before something of that kind shall be advanced in contradiction to my scheme, and offering a better, I desire the author or authors will be pleased maturely to consider two points. First, as things now stand, how they will be able to find food and raiment for an hundred thousand useless mouths and backs. And secondly, there being a round million of creatures in human figure throughout this kingdom, whose whole subsistence put into a common stock would leave them in debt two millions of pounds sterling, adding those who are beggars by profession to the bulk of farmers, cottagers, and laborers, with their wives and children who are beggars in effect: I desire those politicians who dislike my overture, and may perhaps be so bold as to attempt an answer, that they will first ask the parents of these mortals, whether they would not at this day think it a great happiness to have been sold for food, at a year old in the manner I prescribe, and thereby have avoided such a perpetual scene of misfortunes as they have since gone through by the oppression of landlords, the impossibility of paying rent without money or trade, the want of common sustenance, with neither house nor clothes to cover them from the inclemencies of the weather, and the most inevitable prospect of entailing the like or greater miseries upon their breed for ever.

I profess, in the sincerity of my heart, that I have not the least personal interest in endeavoring to promote this necessary work, having no other motive than the public good of my country, by advancing our trade, providing for infants, relieving the poor, and giving some pleasure to the rich. I have no children by which I can propose to get a single penny; the youngest being nine years old, and my wife past childbearing.

PERSONAL RESPONSE

At what point did you realize that Swift is not serious in his proposal to use toddlers for food? How effective do you find his rather unusual suggestion, even though he is being satirical, in stirring sympathy for the deplorable condition of the people of Ireland?

QUESTIONS FOR CLASS OR SMALL-GROUP DISCUSSION

1. Where does Swift state his thesis? What are the main points of his argument? Where does he offer counter-arguments? How does he address those points?

2. What are Swift's real views on how to solve the problem of poverty in Ireland? For instance, what is Swift's real opinion of the rich, such as landowners and the gentlemen he refers to? How does he really feel about the poor?

3. Why does Swift dismiss some alternative solutions to the problem? Which suggestions does he make throughout that would really contribute to helping Ireland?

4. When Swift wrote "A Modest Proposal," the word "modest" meant simple, easy to achieve, and not likely to be met with opposition. Does that meaning accurately describe what he says? Other words or terms may need explanation, such as "papists" (paragraph 13) (supporters of the Pope and a term that was insulting to Catholics) and "Pretender" (paragraph 21) (a reference to James Stuart, a Catholic who claimed or "pretended to" both the English and Scottish thrones). Locate other words that are unfamiliar or whose historic references you may not know, find out their meanings, and share your findings with the class.

5. Where does Swift use irony (saying one thing but meaning another), understatement (saying less than he means), and overstatement (saying more than he means) in "A Modest Proposal"?

6. What comment does Swift make on the following: religious differences; views of marriage; men's treatment of women, their children, and their livestock; family life of the impoverished; Americans.

ON THE MEANING OF PLUMBING AND POVERTY

MELANIE SCHELLER

Melanie Scheller is a writer whose essay "On the Meaning of Plumbing and Poverty" first appeared in the North Carolina Independent Weekly *in 1990.*

Several years ago I spent some time as a volunteer on the geriatric ward of a psychiatric hospital. I was fascinated by the behavior of one of the patients, an elderly woman who shuffled at regular intervals to the bathroom, where she methodically flushed the toilet. Again and again she carried out her sacred mission as if summoned by some supernatural force, until the flush of the toilet became a rhythmic counterpoint for the ward's activity. If someone blocked her path or if, God forbid, the bathroom was in use when she reached it, she became agitated and confused.

Obviously, that elderly patient was a sick woman. And yet I felt a certain kinship with her, for I too have suffered from an obsession with toilets. I spent much of my childhood living in houses without indoor plumbing and, while I don't feel compelled to flush a toilet at regular intervals, I sometimes feel that toilets, or the lack thereof, have shaped my identity in ways that are painful to admit.

I'm not a child of the Depression, but I grew up in an area of the South that had changed little since the days of the New Deal. My mother was a widow with six children to support, not an easy task under any circumstances, but especially difficult in rural North Carolina during the 1960s. To her credit, we were never seriously in danger of going hungry. Our vegetable garden kept us stocked with tomatoes and string beans. We kept a few chickens and sometimes a cow. Blackberries were free for the picking in the fields nearby. Neighbors did their good Christian duty by bringing us donations of fresh fruit and candy at Christmastime. But a roof over our heads—that wasn't so easily improvised.

4 Like rural Southern gypsies, we moved from one dilapidated Southern farmhouse to another in a constant search for a decent place to live. Sometimes we moved when the rent increased beyond the $30 or $40 my mother could afford. Or the house burned down, not an unusual occurrence in substandard housing. One year, when we were gathered together for Thanksgiving dinner, a stranger walked in without knocking and announced that we were being evicted. The house had been sold without our knowledge and the new owner wanted to start remodeling immediately. We tried to finish our meal with an attitude of thanksgiving while he worked around us with his tape measure.

Usually, we rented from farm families who'd moved from the old home place to one of the brick boxes that are now the standard in rural Southern architecture. The old farmhouse wasn't worth fixing up with a septic tank and flush toilet, but it was good enough to rent for a few dollars a month to families like mine. The idea of tenants' rights hadn't trickled down yet from the far reaches of the liberal North. It never occurred to us to demand improvements in the facilities. The ethic of the land said we should take what we could get and be grateful for it.

Without indoor plumbing, getting clean is a tiring and time-consuming ritual. At one point, I lived in a five-room house with six or more people, all of whom congregated in the one heated room to eat, do homework, watch television, dress and undress, argue, wash dishes. During cold weather we dragged mattresses from the unheated rooms and slept huddled together on the floor by the woodstove. For my bathing routine, I first pinned a sheet to a piece of twine strung across the kitchen. That gave me some degree of privacy from the six other people in the room. At that time, our house had an indoor cold-water faucet, from which I filled a pot of water to heat on the kitchen stove. It took several pots of hot water to fill the metal washtub we used.

Since I was a teenager and prone to sulkiness if I didn't get special treatment, I got to take the first bath while the water was still clean. The others used the water I left behind, freshened up with hot water from the pot on the stove. Then the tub had to be dragged to the door and the bath water dumped outside. I longed to be like the woman in the Calgon bath oil commercials, luxuriating in a marble tub full of scented water with bubbles piled high and stacks of thick, clean towels nearby.

8   People raised in the land of the bath-and-a-half may wonder why I make such a fuss about plumbing. Maybe they spent a year in the Peace Corps, or they backpacked across India, or they worked at a summer camp and, gosh, using a latrine isn't all that bad. And of course it's *not* that bad. Not when you can catch the next plane out of the country, or pick up your duffel bag and head for home, or call mom and dad to come and get you when things get too tedious. A sojourn in a Third World country, where everyone shares the same primitive facilities, may cause some temporary discomfort, but the experience is soon converted into amusing anecdotes for cocktail-party conversation. It doesn't corrode your self-esteem with a sense of shame the way a childhood spent in chronic, unrelenting poverty can.

     In the South of my childhood, not having indoor plumbing was the indelible mark of poor white trash. The phrase "so poor they didn't have a pot to piss in" said it all. Poor white trash were viciously stereotyped, and never more viciously than on the playground. White-trash children had cooties—everybody knew that. They had ringworm and pink-eye—don't get near them or you might catch it. They picked their noses. They messed in their pants. If a white-trash child made the mistake of catching a softball during recess, the other children made an elaborate show of wiping it clean before they would touch it.

     Once a story circulated at school about a family whose infant daughter had fallen into the "slop jar" and drowned. When I saw the smirks and heard the laughter with which the story was told, I felt sick and afraid in the pit of my stomach. A little girl had died, but people were laughing. What had she done to deserve that laughter? I could only assume that using a chamber pot was something so disgusting, so shameful, that it made a person less than human.

     My family was visibly and undeniably poor. My clothes were obviously hand-me-downs. I got free lunches at school. I went to the health department for immunizations. Surely it was equally obvious that we didn't have a flush toilet. But, like an alcoholic who believes no one will know he has a problem as long as he doesn't drink in public, I convinced myself that no one knew my family's little secret. It was a form of denial that would color my relationships with the outside world for years to come.

12   Having a friend from school spend the night at my house was out of the question. Better to be friendless than to have my classmates know my shameful secret. Home visits from teachers or ministers left me in a dither of anticipatory anxiety. As they chattered on and on with Southern small talk about tomato plants and relish recipes, I sat on the edge of my seat, tensed against the dreaded words, "May I use your bathroom, please?" When I began dating in high school, I'd lie in wait behind the front door, ready to dash out as soon as my date pulled in the driveway, never giving him a chance to hear the call of nature while on our property.

     With the help of a scholarship I was able to go away to college, where I could choose from dozens of dormitory toilets and take as many hot showers as I wanted, but I could never openly express my joy in using the facilities. My roommates, each a pampered only child from a well-to-do family, whined and complained about having to share a bathroom. I knew that if I expressed delight in simply having a bathroom,

I would immediately be labeled as a hick. The need to conceal my real self by stifling my emotions created a barrier around me and I spent my college years in a vacuum of isolation.

Almost twenty years have passed since I first tried to leave my family's chamber pot behind. For many of those years, it followed behind me—the ghost of chamber pots past—clanging and banging and threatening to spill its humiliating contents at any moment. I was convinced that everyone could see it, could smell it even. No college degree or job title seemed capable of banishing it.

If finances had permitted, I might have become an Elvis Presley or a Tammy Faye Baker, easing the pain of remembered poverty with gold-plated bathtub fixtures and leopard-skinned toilet seats. I feel blessed that gradually, ever so gradually, the shame of poverty has begun to fade. The pleasures of the present now take priority over where a long-ago bowel movement did or did not take place. But, for many Southerners, chamber pots and outhouses are more than just memories.

16   In North Carolina alone, 200,000 people still live without indoor plumbing. People who haul their drinking water home from a neighbor's house or catch rainwater in barrels. People who can't wash their hands before handling food, the way restaurant employees are required by state law to do. People who sneak into public restrooms every day to wash, shave, and brush their teeth before going to work or to school. People who sacrifice their dignity and self-respect when forced to choose between going homeless and going to an outhouse. People whose children think they deserve the conditions in which they live and hold their heads low to hide the shame. But they're not the ones who should feel ashamed. No, they're not the ones who should feel ashamed.

PERSONAL RESPONSE

What do you think of Scheller's experiences growing up in poverty? Can you sympathize with her? Do you recall a particular period or occasion in your life when you felt a similar sense of shame or acute awareness of yourself in relation to others?

QUESTIONS FOR CLASS OR SMALL-GROUP DISCUSSION

1. Summarize in your own words the effects of poverty on Scheller, and then discuss your own reactions to what she describes.
2. In paragraph 8, Scheller says that people wonder why she "make[s] such a fuss about plumbing." Indeed, she writes about a subject that people seldom discuss in either conversation or writing. How well do you think she has handled her subject? Does she convince you of her reasons for making the fuss?
3. Scheller concludes by repeating "they're not the ones who should feel ashamed" (paragraph 16). Who does she imply should feel ashamed? Do you agree with her on this point?

THE SINGER SOLUTION TO WORLD POVERTY

Peter Singer

Peter Singer, an Australian-born philosopher and bioethicist, is author of the highly influential book Animal Liberation *(1975). He has served as president of the International Association of Bioethics and as editor of its official journal,* Bioethics. *Among his dozen or so other books are* How Are We to Live?: Ethics in an Age of Self Interest *(1993),* Rethinking Life and Death: The Collapse of Our Traditional Ethics *(1995),* Writings on an Ethical Life *(2000), and* The President of Good and Evil *(2004). Singer is on the faculty at the Center for Human Values at Princeton University. This essay appeared in the September 5, 1999, issue of* New York *Times Magazine.*

In the Brazilian film *Central Station,* Dora is a retired schoolteacher who makes ends meet by sitting at the station writing letters for illiterate people. Suddenly she has an opportunity to pocket $1,000. All she has to do is persuade a homeless nine-year-old boy to follow her to an address she has been given. (She is told he will be adopted by wealthy foreigners.) She delivers the boy, gets the money, spends some of it on a television set, and settles down to enjoy her new acquisition. Her neighbor spoils the fun, however, by telling her that the boy was too old to be adopted—he will be killed and his organs sold for transplantation. Perhaps Dora knew this all along, but after her neighbor's plain speaking, she spends a troubled night. In the morning Dora resolves to take the boy back.

Suppose Dora had told her neighbor that it is a tough world, other people have nice new TVs too, and if selling the kid is the only way she can get one, well, he was only a street kid. She would then have become, in the eyes of the audience, a monster. She redeems herself only by being prepared to bear considerable risks to save the boy.

At the end of the movie, in cinemas in the affluent nations of the world, people who would have been quick to condemn Dora if she had not rescued the boy go home to places far more comfortable than her apartment. In fact, the average family in the United States spends almost one-third of its income on things that are no more necessary to them than Dora's new TV was to her. Going out to nice restaurants, buying new clothes because the old ones are no longer stylish, vacationing at beach resorts—so much of our income is spent on things not essential to the preservation of our lives and health. Donated to one of a number of charitable agencies, that money could mean the difference between life and death for children in need.

4   All of which raises a question: In the end, what is the ethical distinction between a Brazilian who sells a homeless child to organ peddlers and an American who already has a TV and upgrades to a better one—knowing that the money could be donated to an organization that would use it to save the lives of kids in need?

Of course, there are several differences between the two situations that could support different moral judgments about them. For one thing, to be able to consign a child to death when he is standing right in front of you takes a chilling kind of heartlessness; it is much easier to ignore an appeal for money to help children you will never meet. Yet for a utilitarian philosopher like myself—that is, one who judges whether acts are right or wrong by their consequences—if the upshot of the American's failure to donate the money is that one more kid dies on the streets of a Brazilian city, then it is, in some sense, just as bad as selling the kid to the organ peddlers. But one doesn't need to embrace my utilitarian ethic to see that, at the very least, there is a troubling incongruity in being so quick to condemn Dora for taking the child to the organ peddlers while, at the same time, not regarding the American consumer's behavior as raising a serious moral issue.

In his 1996 book, *Living High and Letting Die,* the New York University philosopher Peter Unger presented an ingenious series of imaginary examples designed to probe our intuitions about whether it is wrong to live well without giving substantial amounts of money to help people who are hungry, malnourished, or dying from easily treatable illnesses like diarrhea. Here's my paraphrase of one of these examples:

Bob is close to retirement. He has invested most of his savings in a very rare and valuable old car, a Bugatti, which he has not been able to insure. The Bugatti is his pride and joy. In addition to the pleasure he gets from driving and caring for his car, Bob knows that its rising market value means that he will always be able to sell it and live comfortably after retirement. One day when Bob is out for a drive, he parks the Bugatti near the end of a railway siding and goes for a walk up the track. As he does so, he sees that a runaway train, with no one aboard, is running down the railway track. Looking farther down the track, he sees the small figure of a child very likely to be killed by the runaway train. He can't stop the train and the child is too far away to warn of the danger, but he can throw a switch that will divert the train down the siding where his Bugatti is parked. Then nobody will be killed—but the train will destroy his Bugatti. Thinking of his joy in owning the car and the financial security it represents, Bob decides not to throw the switch. The child is killed. For many years to come, Bob enjoys owning his Bugatti and the financial security it represents.

8   Bob's conduct, most of us will immediately respond, was gravely wrong. Unger agrees. But then he reminds us that we, too, have opportunities to save the lives of children. We can give to organizations like Unicef or Oxfam America. How much would we have to give one of these organizations to have a high probability of saving the life of a child threatened by easily preventable diseases? (I do not believe that children are more worth saving than adults, but since no one can argue that children have brought their poverty on themselves, focusing on them simplifies the issues.) Unger called up some experts and used the information they provided to offer some plausible estimates that include the cost of raising money, administrative expenses, and the cost of delivering aid where it is most needed. By his calculation, $200 in donations would help a sickly two-year-old transform into a healthy six-year-old—offering safe passage through childhood's most dangerous years. To show how practical philosophical argument can be, Unger even tells his readers that they can easily donate funds by using their credit card and calling one of these toll-free numbers: (800) 367-5437 for Unicef; (800) 693-2687 for Oxfam America.

Now you, too, have the information you need to save a child's life. How should you judge yourself if you don't do it? Think again about Bob and his Bugatti. Unlike Dora, Bob did not have to look into the eyes of the child he was sacrificing for his own material comfort. The child was a complete stranger to him and too far away to relate to in an intimate, personal way. Unlike Dora, too, he did not mislead the child or initiate the chain of events imperiling him. In all these respects, Bob's situation resembles that of people able but unwilling to donate to overseas aid and differs from Dora's situation.

If you still think that it was very wrong of Bob not to throw the switch that would have diverted the train and saved the child's life, then it is hard to see how you could deny that it is also very wrong not to send money to one of the organizations listed above. Unless, that is, there is some morally important difference between the two situations that I have overlooked.

Is it the practical uncertainties about whether aid will really reach the people who need it? Nobody who knows the world of overseas aid can doubt that such uncertainties exist. But Unger's figure of $200 to save a child's life was reached after he had made conservative assumptions about the proportion of the money donated that will actually reach its target.

12   One genuine difference between Bob and those who can afford to donate to overseas aid organizations but don't is that only Bob can save the child on the tracks, whereas there are hundreds of millions of people who can give $200 to overseas aid organizations. The problem is that most of them aren't doing it. Does this mean that it is all right for you not to do it?

Suppose that there were more owners of priceless vintage cars—Carol, Dave, Emma, Fred and so on, down to Ziggy—all in exactly the same situation as Bob, with their own siding and their own switch, all sacrificing the child in order to preserve their own cherished car. Would that make it all right for Bob to do the same? To answer this question affirmatively is to endorse follow-the-crowd ethics—the kind of ethics that led many Germans to look away when the Nazi atrocities were being committed. We do not excuse them because others were behaving no better.

We seem to lack a sound basis for drawing a clear moral line between Bob's situation and that of any reader of this article with $200 to spare who does not donate it to an overseas aid agency. These readers seem to be acting at least as badly as Bob was acting when he chose to let the runaway train hurtle toward the unsuspecting child. In the light of this conclusion, I trust that many readers will reach for the phone and donate that $200. Perhaps you should do it before reading further.

Now that you have distinguished yourself morally from people who put their vintage cars ahead of a child's life, how about treating yourself and your partner to dinner at your favorite restaurant? But wait. The money you will spend at the restaurant could also help save the lives of children overseas! True, you weren't planning to blow $200 tonight, but if you were to give up dining out just for one month, you would easily save that amount. And what is one month's dining out, compared to a child's life? There's the rub. Since there are a lot of desperately needy children in the world, there will always be another child whose life you could save for another $200. Are you therefore obliged to keep giving until you have nothing left? At what point can you stop?

16   Hypothetical examples can easily become farcical. Consider Bob. How far past losing the Bugatti should he go? Imagine that Bob had got his foot stuck in the track of the siding, and if he diverted the train, then before it rammed the car it would also amputate his big toe. Should he still throw the switch? What if it would amputate his foot? His entire leg?

As absurd as the Bugatti scenario gets when pushed to extremes, the point it raises is a serious one: Only when the sacrifices become very significant indeed would most people be prepared to say that Bob does nothing wrong when he decides not to throw the switch. Of course, most people could be wrong; we can't decide moral issues by taking opinion polls. But consider for yourself the level of sacrifice that you would demand of Bob, and then think about how much money you would have to give away in order to make a sacrifice that is roughly equal to that. It's almost certainly much, much more than $200. For most middle-class Americans, it could easily be more like $200,000.

Isn't it counterproductive to ask people to do so much? Don't we run the risk that many will shrug their shoulders and say that mortality, so conceived, is fine for saints but not for them? I accept that we are unlikely to see, in the near or even medium-term future, a world in which it is normal for wealthy Americans to give the bulk of their wealth to strangers. When it comes to praising or blaming people for what they do, we tend to use a standard that is relative to some conception of normal behavior. Comfortably off Americans who give, say, 10 percent of their income to overseas aid organizations are so far ahead of most of their equally comfortable fellow citizens that I wouldn't go out of my way to chastise them for not doing more. Nevertheless, they should be doing much more, and they are in no position to criticize Bob for failing to make the much greater sacrifice of his Bugatti.

At this point various objections may crop up. Someone may say: "If every citizen living in the affluent nations contributed his or her share I wouldn't have to make such a drastic sacrifice, because long before such levels were reached, the resources would have been there to save the lives of all those children dying from lack of food or medical care. So why should I give more than my fair share?" Another, related objection is that the government ought to increase its overseas aid allocations, since that would spread the burden more equitably across all taxpayers.

20   Yet the question of how much we ought to give is a matter to be decided in the real world—and that, sadly, is a world in which we know that most people do not, and in the immediate future will not, give substantial amounts to overseas aid agencies. We know, too, that at least in the next year, the United States government is not going to meet even the very modest United Nations–recommended target of 0.7 percent of gross national product; at a moment it lags far below that, at 0.09 percent, not even half of Japan's 0.22 percent or a tenth of Denmark's 0.97 percent. Thus, we know that the money we can give beyond that theoretical "fair share" is still going to save lives that would otherwise be lost. While the idea that no one need do more than his or her fair share is a powerful one, should it prevail if we know that others are not doing their fair share and that children will die preventable deaths unless we do more than our fair share? That would be taking fairness too far.

Thus, this ground for limiting how much we ought to give also fails. In the world as it is now, I can see no escape from the conclusion that each one of us with wealth surplus to his or her essential needs should be giving most of it to help people suffering from poverty so dire as to be life-threatening. That's right: I'm saying that you shouldn't buy that new car, take that cruise, redecorate the house, or get that pricey new suit. After all, a $1,000 suit could save five children's lives.

So how does my philosophy break down in dollars and cents? An American household with an income of $50,000 spends around $30,000 annually on necessities, according to the Conference Board, a nonprofit economic research organization. Therefore, for a household bringing in $50,000 a year, donations to help the world's poor should be as close as possible to $20,000. The $30,000 required for necessities holds for higher incomes as well. So a household making $100,000 could cut a yearly check for $70,000. Again, the formula is simple: Whatever money you're spending on luxuries, not necessities, should be given away.

Now, evolutionary psychologists tell us that human nature just isn't sufficiently altruistic to make it plausible that many people will sacrifice so much for strangers. On the facts of human nature, they might be right, but they would be wrong to draw a moral conclusion from those facts. If it is the case that we ought to do things that, predictably, most of us won't do, then let's face that fact head-on. Then, if we value the life of a child more than going to fancy restaurants, the next time we dine out we will know that we could have done something better with our money. If that makes living a morally decent life extremely arduous, well, then that is the way things are. If we don't do it, then we should at least know that we are failing to live a morally decent life—not because it is good to wallow in guilt but because knowing where we should be going is the first step toward heading in that direction.

24   When Bob first grasped the dilemma that faced him as he stood by that railway switch, he must have thought how extraordinarily unlucky he was to be placed in a situation in which he must choose between the life of an innocent child and the sacrifice of most of his savings. But he was not unlucky at all. We are all in that situation.

PERSONAL RESPONSE

Do you contribute to charities? If not, are you moved to start doing so after reading this essay? Why do you think more people do not contribute to charities, especially if they could, as Singer argues, help improve life for the world's impoverished children?

QUESTIONS FOR CLASS OR SMALL-GROUP DISCUSSION

1. How effective do you find the opening example from the film *Central Station?* Does it help clarify for you the thesis of Singer's essay? Do you agree with Singer that the failure to donate money to a charity that would save a Brazilian child from starvation is "just as bad as selling the kid to organ peddlers" (paragraph 5)?

2. Comment on the hypothetical scenario from Peter Unger's book that Singer paraphrases in paragraph 7. Do you agree that "Bob's conduct . . . was gravely wrong" and that failure to donate money to charities that would save children's lives is equally wrong (paragraph 8)? How persuasive do you find Singer's discussion of the ethical implications of failing to donate to charities?

3. Discuss your answer to this question: "While the idea that no one need to do more than his or her fair share is a powerful one, should it prevail if we know that others are not doing their fair share and that children will die preventable deaths unless we do more than our fair share?" (paragraph 20).

4. To what extent do you agree with Singer that "we ought to do things that, predictably, most of us won't do" (paragraph 23)? How persuasive do you find Singer's argument to be?

○ PERSPECTIVES ON POVERTY AND HOMELESSNESS ○

Suggested Writing Topics

1. Taking into consideration Anna Quindlen's "Our Tired, Our Poor, Our Children," the editorial "Still Hungry, Still Homeless," and Melanie Scheller's "On the Meaning of Plumbing and Poverty," explore the effects of poverty on self-esteem or other aspects of the well-being of children.

2. Drawing on the readings in this chapter, consider the problems associated with meeting the needs of welfare recipients, impoverished families, or homeless people. What possible solutions are there to the problems? Can you propose additional suggestions for reducing the large numbers of people in poverty or without homes?

3. With Anna Quindlen's "Our Tired, Our Poor, Our Children" and the editorial "Still Hungry, Still Homeless" in mind, write your own opinion piece on the subject of poverty and homelessness in America.

4. Write a letter to Melanie Scheller in response to her essay "On the Meaning of Plumbing and Poverty."

5. Write an essay showing the relevance of Jonathan Swift's "A Modest Proposal" to the problem of poverty and homelessness today.

6. If you have ever experienced the effects of poverty, too little income, not enough work, or a need to juggle child care with the demands of a job, write an essay describing that experience, how you felt about it, and how you handled it.

7. Create a different hypothetical situation similar to Peter Unger's scenario of Bob and his Bugatti in "The Singer Solution to World Poverty." Detail the moral dilemma of your own scenario and discuss the ethical implications of various responses to the dilemma.

8. Select a social issue and write a satire proposing a solution, in the manner of Jonathan Swift's "A Modest Proposal."

9. Working in small groups and drawing on the essays in this chapter, create a scenario involving one or more of the following people: a welfare recipient or a homeless person, a welfare caseworker or a staff member at a homeless shelter, a police officer, and either or both a wealthy person and a working-class person with a regular income and a home. Provide a situation, create dialogue, and role-play in an effort to understand the varying perspectives of different people on the issue of welfare or homelessness. Then present your scenario to the rest of your classmates. For an individual writing project, do an analysis of the scenario or fully develop the viewpoint of the person whose role you played.

Research Topics

1. Research your state's policy on welfare, including residency requirements, eligibility for payments, monitoring of recipients, and related issues. Then write a paper outlining your opinion of your state's welfare policy, including any recommendations you would make for changing it.

2. From time to time, politicians propose establishing orphanages that would house not only orphaned children but also the children of single parents on welfare or parents deemed unfit to raise their children. Research this subject, and then write a paper in which you argue for or against the establishment of such orphanages. Make sure you consider as many perspectives as possible on this complex issue, including the welfare of the child, the rights of the parent or parents, and society's responsibility to protect children.

3. Research the subject of poverty in America. Focus your research on a particular group, such as children, women, two-parent families, or single-parent families, or target a particular aspect of the subject such as the effects of race, parental education, or employment on poverty.

4. Research an area of public policy on welfare reform, child welfare, homelessness, family welfare, food stamps, job training, or any other issue related to any reading in this chapter.

RESPONDING TO VISUALS

"Some families go out for dinner every night." Source: Henderson Advertising for Project Host Soup Kitchen

1. What is the point of this public service advertisement?
2. In what ways does the ad engage readers?
3. Do you find the text of the advertisement effective?
4. What do you think is the story of the two people in the picture? Why does the photographer place them at the side of the picture instead of the center?

RESPONDING TO VISUALS

A homeless person begging for money. Source: Thomson Corporation/Heinle Image Resource Bank

1. What does the homeless person's body language say about him?
2. What can you tell about the man from the way he is dressed and his facial features? What does the man's sign add to your understanding of him?
3. How does the photographer's perspective affect the way viewers see and respond to the man's situation?
4. Is there any irony in the contrast between the man and the sign behind him?

CHAPTER

13

CRIMINAL BEHAVIOR

America has one of the highest rates of violent crime in the world. Although the national crime rate has fallen slightly in recent years, the number of murders and rapes in some areas of the country continues to be alarmingly high. Muggings, armed robbery, and drug trafficking imperil city living. In many large cities, people live in dread and fear, shutting themselves up in their homes at night or arming themselves in case of attack. But crime is not limited to large cities. Small towns have also been shocked and dismayed by violent crimes such as kidnapping, murder, and rape in their own communities. Children have been abducted from their own bedrooms or neighborhoods and discovered later, murdered, or never found again. Even very young children have murdered other children. Perhaps most dramatic of all have been the school shootings of recent years.

Murders of children inevitably lead to renewed debate over the death penalty, as such crimes are particularly heinous. Thus the first two essays in this chapter address the subject of capital punishment. Joshua Green believes that liberals and conservatives are both wrong about the death penalty. In "Deadly Compromise," he details what he sees as flaws in the current reasoning of both proponents and opponents of the death penalty and suggests what he thinks should be done to correct the system. Then, John O'Sullivan in "Deadly Stakes: The Debate over Capital Punishment" presents his case for the death penalty. Using specific cases of the murders of children in both the United States and Britain as a starting point, he critiques the arguments of those opposed to capital punishment and seeks to persuade his audience that the death penalty is justified. In reading these essays, consider your own position on the death penalty and whether you are persuaded by either or both of their authors.

Next in the chapter is an essay on school shootings, which, during a recent dramatic period of such crimes, drew intense media attention and prompted heartfelt discussions among families, school officials, community members, and national leaders. In his essay "There Are No Lessons to be Learned from Littleton," Gary Kleck looks at possible causes of school violence in the United States, examines potential consequences of such acts, and considers what lessons, if any, can be learned from them. His conclusions may surprise you.

Finally, broadening the focus of the chapter, "What's Wrong with America and Can Anything Be Done about It?" by Wayne M. Barrett and Bernard Rowe traces the antecedents of a host of social problems, including crime and violence, to a decline in decency and discipline. They suggest a number of remedies that may seem controversial to many readers. Although their essay was published over a decade ago, many of the social problems they discuss are still prevalent. As you read what these authors say, consider whether you agree or disagree with them. If you disagree, what do you think are causes and possible solutions for the nation's serious social problems?

DEADLY COMPROMISE

Joshua Green

Joshua Green is a senior editor of The Atlantic *and a contributing editor of the* Washington Monthly. *He has also written for the* New Yorker, *the* New York Times, Playboy, Slate, *and other publications, and he moonlights as a pop music critic for* Westword *in Denver.*

Previously, he was a staff writer at The American Prospect *and an editor at the satirical weekly,* The Onion. *This article appeared in the* Washington Monthly *in November 1999.*

In the long-running battle over America's death penalty, two trends have emerged to stoke passions on opposing sides of the debate. An alarming number of men—82—have been freed from death row, or about one for every seven executed. At the same time, the rate of executions has slowed to a trickle as death row inmates languish on average for more than a decade before their sentence is carried out. Two recent examples bear out the problems in our current capital justice system.

In 1978, Robert Alton Harris, a 26-year-old paroled murderer, kidnapped two California teenagers in the parking lot of a fast-food restaurant. He drove to a remote canyon where he killed the two boys, then finished the hamburgers they'd been eating and drove off. Harris was later caught robbing a bank. He confessed to the murders and was sentenced to death in 1979. Yet he managed to delay his execution for 13 years by repeatedly manipulating the appeals system. Harris and his lawyers challenged the quality of his psychiatric evaluation, claimed California's gas chamber was unconstitutional, and argued that the death penalty discriminated against younger killers, males, and those who killed whites. Each of these claims stalled his execution. In a flurry of last-minute appeals, the Supreme Court overturned four separate stays on the night of Harris' execution before it took the unprecedented step of forbidding lower courts to issue further stays. By the time he was finally put to death in 1992, Harris had managed to get more than 20 appeals.

Like Harris, Aaron Patterson's case centered on a murder confession. He was subsequently sentenced to death for the 1986 stabbing deaths of an elderly Chicago couple. But Patterson is one of Illinois' "Death Row 10," a group facing execution who claim their confessions were beaten out of them by a notorious Chicago police lieutenant since fired for abuse and torture. No physical evidence connects Patterson to the murders. The knife was never found. A fingerprint at the scene—not a match—has inexplicably disappeared. The lone witness against him, a teenager who claims police coerced her testimony, has tearfully recanted.

4   While Harris is a metaphor for the conservative case against the current capital justice system, Patterson's case has been seized upon by abolitionists. Both are justified in their outrage. More than 20 years after its reinstatement, the death penalty is an unwieldy and ineffective compromise between the roughly 70 percent of Americans who favor capital punishment and the minority who fiercely oppose it. The present system is, quite literally, the worst of both worlds. While an ideological battle has been waged in court, a bottleneck has developed in the nation's prisons. Currently, 3,565 inmates sit on death row, and new arrivals average 300 annually. Yet despite rising numbers of death sentences, executions have never topped 100 in a single year. Everyone is being sentenced to death and no one is dying.

Death Born Again

In the landmark 1972 case of *Furman vs. Georgia,* the Supreme Court struck down the death penalty on four grounds: it was imposed arbitrarily; used unfairly against minorities and the poor; its infrequent use made it an ineffective deterrent; and lastly, state-sanctioned killing was no longer acceptable behavior. The decision resulted in tremendous uncertainty. Each justice filed a separate opinion, an unprecedented move in 20th century jurisprudence, yielding the longest written decision in Supreme Court history. The length is indicative of the decision's complicated rationale. While the case for abolition earned the five votes necessary, the motivation for each vote varied. This uncertainty left the door open for states to write new death penalty laws that might pass constitutional muster.

Abolition was never very popular. Polls taken in March 1972, shortly before *Furman* was decided, showed a 50 percent approval rating for capital punishment; that number jumped to 57 percent by November. Within the year, 19 state legislatures passed retooled death penalty statutes they hoped would meet the vague standard of constitutionality hinted at in *Furman*. By the time the Court allowed the modern death penalty by upholding, *Gregg vs. Georgia* in 1976, 35 states had passed new death penalty laws. They have been in dispute ever since, and the result is today's beleaguered system. Shortly after *Gregg*, the court acceded to death penalty opponents by outlawing mandatory death sentences and instituting complex safeguards. This gave rise to a problem that still hampers the courts: Unable to abolish capital punishment in the legislature, defense lawyers have sought to institute a de facto halt to executions by stalling cases in court. The more savvy, like Harris' lawyers, quickly mastered the art of "sandbagging," or using delay tactics to stop an execution. By filing spurious last-minute appeals and repeatedly seeking reversals on obscure technical grounds, activist lawyers (and some judges) could bring the system to its knees. Angered by this end run around the law, conservatives have limited the appeals process at the state and federal levels and expanded the scope of crimes punishable by death. The unfortunate result, as federal prosecutor David Lazarus wrote in this magazine last year ("Mortal Combat," June 1998), is that abolitionists have clogged the courts with endless litigation and slowed the number of actual executions to a trickle. The average delay from sentencing to execution has grown from six years in 1985, to eight years in 1990, to 11 years today.

The Art of Delay

Delays in death penalty cases are caused in part by the tacit acceptance of such maneuvers by liberal judges. The most famous examples are former Supreme Court justices William Brennan, Jr. and Thurgood Marshall, who voted against every death sentence that came before them. Recent limits to federal appeals should eventually block some avenues for delay. But as old methods are thwarted, new ones crop up. Kent Scheidegger, legal director for the conservative Criminal Justice Legal Foundation, cites as an example an increase in the use of "Ford claims"—assertions that a prisoner has gone insane since sentencing and therefore can't be executed under the Eighth Amendment. (This is a particularly savvy ploy, because arguing that insanity occurred after the trial phase means the claim isn't subject to a limit on appeals.)

8   Other recent tools that have been used for manipulation are Marsden and Faretta motions, which a defendant can use to fire his lawyer and represent himself. In a notorious California capital case, the defendant filed numerous such motions, going so

far as to sue two court-appointed defenders for $1 million in an effort to delay his sentence. Common sense needn't be a requirement for a claim—a Montana prisoner, who'd held off his execution through two decades of appeals, finally argued that the length of time he'd had to endure on death row was unconstitutional.

Though liberals are commonly faulted for delays, conservatives also slowed the process by making access to court-appointed attorneys more difficult for the poor. In 1995 more than a quarter of California's capital defendants didn't have a lawyer and their cases couldn't begin until one was assigned. And, with conservative anger buttressing support for prosecutors' win-at-all-costs attitude, unscrupulous prosecutors regularly tie up capital cases by fighting defense requests for information.

Innocence Expired

The unfortunate response to dilatory tactics has been to curtail the judicial process by implementing strict time limits. Thirty-six of the 38 death penalty states impose deadlines for presenting new evidence following a conviction. The strictest such law is Virginia's notorious "21-Day Rule," which limits the introduction of new evidence to 21 days after trial. Other states have similar limits that range from 30 days to a year. These laws were intended to establish finality in all criminal cases and most predate the modern death penalty. But they have recently been championed by conservatives as a way to combat delays in execution, despite the obvious risk they carry of killing or imprisoning innocent people.

In recent years, the law's shortcomings have become apparent. Virginia's 21-Day Rule, for example, forbids new DNA evidence from being introduced more than three weeks after trial. And, amazingly, the law doesn't even make provisions for illegally suppressed evidence—such evidence is considered "new" in Virginia and therefore is inadmissible. (A prisoner would instead have to file a federal appeal.) The problem was ably summed up in a defense attorney's testimony before a Virginia legislative committee: "After 21 days, no court in this state, nor any judicial forum afterwards, can save you from execution based on the proof that you are innocent."

12   The circuit court that oversees this system—referred to locally as "the rocket docket"—has succeeded in speeding the processing time of death penalty defendants. Capital cases in Virginia move much more quickly than they do elsewhere. But the results come at a price. One of the most controversial examples is the case of Earl Washington, Jr., a mildly retarded man sentenced to death for the 1982 rape-murder of a Virginia woman. A concerned prosecutor later ordered DNA tests, unavailable at the time, that provided strong evidence Washington is innocent. But because the evidence appeared after the 21-day deadline, Washington had no avenue for appeal. The only recourse for a prisoner with exculpatory evidence is gubernatorial clemency. But governors aren't part of the judiciary and can't order a new trial. And of course they're heavily subject to political pressure. On the last day of his term, Virginia Governor Douglas Wilder commuted Washington's sentence to life in prison. But with no judicial outlet to order a new case, Washington remains in prison.

Such problems are exacerbated by the fact that many prisoners can't find attorneys for post-conviction hearings—in 1995 Congress eliminated the resource centers that once provided them. Without an attorney, the possibility of correcting a mistake like the one in Washington's case all but disappears. State post-conviction review is the first opportunity to present claims of ineffective counsel and the last chance to investigate claims like actual innocence and prosecutorial misconduct. Ironically, the Supreme Court has affirmed that indigent death row inmates have a right to counsel at federal appeals. But without a lawyer at the state level, their claims will doubtless never make it that far.

Fools on the Hill

While state legislatures have failed to improve the system, reforms at the federal level have also been woefully misguided. In the mid-1980s federal judges couldn't find enough qualified lawyers to handle death penalty cases. Attorneys assigned by the court were expensive and didn't necessarily provide competent counsel. So in 1988, at the behest of federal judges, Congress created legal resource centers to process and defend the poor. By most accounts, these centers served their purpose.

But in the tough-on-crime environment of the early '90s, the centers became a political football. Congressman Bob Ingis (R-South Carolina) branded them "think tanks for legal theories that would frustrate the implementation of all death sentences." In 1996, citing fiscal priorities, Congress eliminated federal funding for resource centers—$20 million for 21 centers nationwide. Budget hawks figured they'd won a double victory. They reasoned that by choking off agencies that represent death row inmates they'd rid themselves of an impediment to executions, while saving taxpayers millions in the process.

That thinking backfired. A critical function of resource centers—one intended by federal judges—was to keep the appellate system functioning smoothly. With organizational support, full-time lawyers kept tabs on death row cases, filed appeals promptly and steered capital defendants through the complicated legal system. Qualified representation meant indigent defendants didn't require the court's help. The infusion of lawyers trained in capital cases helped offset the costly and often inexperienced court-appointed lawyers who otherwise handled capital cases. Resource centers were a government program that worked. So their elimination had the opposite of the intended effect—it slowed the pace of appeals and increased the likelihood of error.

Other measures were similarly misguided. In 1994, by threatening to block the federal crime bill, congressional Republicans forced passage of the Federal Death Penalty Act, making 54 new crimes death-penalty eligible. The law was largely a symbolic measure—there hadn't been a federal execution in 31 years. Yet death-penalty offenses suddenly came to include drug dealing crimes, conspiracy to commit murder even if no murder was committed, and such rarely committed crimes as murder of a federal poultry inspector. The broadened scope only added to the courts' burden. Federal death sentences soared from 28 the year before the law, to 153 in 1997. Even conservatives thought the law frivolous. "It was an easy way to appear tough," said Scheidegger. "Congress enacted a long string of federal death penalty crimes, most of which are entirely unnecessary, so that they could go back and claim to be tough on the death penalty. It was a rather cynical ploy."

Cynical but costly. Last fall, a judicial conference report determined the average cost of prosecuting a federal death penalty case to be $365,000. The same case cost $218,112 to defend. But if a sentence other than death were sought, the defense costs dropped to $55,772. Factored out for the additional convictions, that's a $73 million price tag on a measure that did little more than let congressmen flex their muscles.

Congress responded to the Oklahoma City bombing with its most ambitious reforms to date. The Antiterrorism and Effective Death Penalty Act of 1996 limited to one the number of appeals a prisoner could file in federal court, barring exceptional circumstances, and placed a one-year time limit on their ability to do so. Conservatives believed this would eliminate sandbagging and streamline the appellate process. "No delay in disposition shall be permissible because of general congestion of the court's calendar," the law read.

20   But like earlier efforts, the Act's aim was largely misdirected—a disingenuous marriage of death penalty and terrorism law that represented a large political compromise. Sponsors touted a connection between terrorists like Timothy McVeigh and speedier laws which, they suggested, would bring criminals to justice. The bill was rushed to passage before the first anniversary of the bombings. But the death penalty "reform" on which the law hinged mainly affected state court cases, where the overwhelming majority of death row inmates are sentenced. Terrorists like McVeigh are prosecuted in federal court.

Problems at the Source

If one source of the problem is in congress, another is at the local level where most death penalty cases originate. Here, too, there is need for reform. The rate and effectiveness with which the death penalty is used varies drastically from states like Ohio, which has executed just one person since reinstatement, to Virginia and Texas, which together have executed 247 people (44 percent of all executions). In recent years, the scrutiny surrounding cases like Aaron Patterson's has made Illinois ground zero for the death penalty debate. The state's 12 exonerations are symptomatic of the problems in the way cases are prosecuted and defended.

Patterson's case illustrates many of these problems. To begin with, he was represented by public defenders and was therefore an easier target. Numerous studies have shown that public defenders often lack the skill, resources, and commitment to defend capital cases properly. Not surprisingly, 90 percent of current death row inmates didn't have a private attorney. As prosecutor David Lazarus has noted, "Clients of the world's great defense attorneys (and even the good ones) don't receive death sentences. Almost without exception, a prerequisite for receiving a death sentence is the inability to hire a lawyer sufficiently talented or motivated to mount a credible defense." Public defenders, he continues, will "substantially increase the probability that a defendant will be convicted of capital murder as opposed to some appropriate lesser offense."

Overzealous prosecutors are another problem. Tenet number one for the career-minded prosecutor is "get tough on crime." While ambitious prosecutors often tout their death penalty convictions, they're far less likely to question whether such convictions are cost effective or necessary. The number of death sentences later reversed suggests that in many cases they're grossly unfair: 40 percent of death row cases are vacated at some point in the appeals process. This can occur ten or even 15 years down the line, at enormous cost to taxpayers and tremendous injustice to defendants. But as a rule, prosecutors don't abandon death penalty cases for fear of appearing soft on crime. Federal judge Alex Kozinski has pointed out that while 80 to 90 percent of all criminal cases end in plea bargains, capital cases almost always go to trial. There is little justification for this discrepancy, given that plea-bargaining death penalty cases would limit costs and nullify the issue of protracted appeals.

24   The tough-on-crime mentality also infects state lawmakers who, like congress, can broaden statutes to include more death penalty crimes. Illinois, which in 1977 had seven crimes that qualified for death, today boasts 19. Often, new additions are an ill-considered reaction to high-profile crimes like last year's murder of a neighborhood activist in Chicago, which prompted legislators to make killing an activist a death penalty offense. Such moves are well intentioned but only hamper an overburdened system. Prosecutorial excesses also run up costs. While defense lawyers are commonly faulted for delays, prosecutors share the blame. Because of their never-say-die attitude toward upholding convictions, they often drag their feet when exculpatory evidence raises questions of innocence. Prosecutors fought to prevent DNA testing that ultimately freed Ronald Jones, the last man to walk off Illinois' death row. Jones spent nearly two years on death row after tests proved his innocence because prosecutors were unwilling to abandon their case.

In fairness, Illinois has taken steps to address the most serious shortcomings, and other states would do well to follow its lead. Recognizing the need for adequate representation of the poor, the state legislature stepped in to save Illinois' legal resource center when federal funding ended. The result is the Capital Litigation Division of the Illinois State Appellate Defender's Office, essentially a state-funded resource center.

Illinois also joined New York in passing a provision for post-conviction DNA testing. The law acts as a safeguard against mistaken convictions by allowing inmates to petition for DNA analysis of evidence used to convict them. No other state has used DNA to uncover more wrongly convicted defendants than Illinois. Perhaps most noteworthy in the near term is Illinois' activist community. It has played a part in freeing all of the 12 released death row inmates and forced many of the positive changes in the criminal justice system.

Finally, most of the state's major media outlets have given nuanced coverage to death penalty law and have provided detailed reporting on flaws and abuses. This is in marked contrast to the national media, which eagerly covers high-profile exonerations but shies away from stories that don't rise to the level of a 60 Minutes piece. Consider, for example, the sloppiness of the May 31 *Newsweek* feature on Aaron Patterson and Northwestern University professor David Protess' efforts to free him. "The *Newsweek* article had by my count and my students' count 21 factual errors in three pages," Protess says. "In the entire time that I've been involved in this, I've never seen an article more off-base than that." The author wrote that Patterson "consented to an oral confession," which he did not. She also wrote that the jury "found it hard to believe that Patterson, the son of a Chicago police lieutenant, would be mistreated." In fact, the jury never heard any evidence of physical abuse, thanks to a pretrial ruling. If journalists were to cover the death penalty as thoroughly as they've covered welfare reform, such carelessness would be less common, and the shortcomings of the death penalty system would be a far more prominent public concern.

On the Merits

28   Pragmatism should eclipse the battle between the extremes of liberalism and conservatism that have reigned on the death penalty. Since courts have been unable to speed processing time adequately, the solution is to reduce the number of death sentences handed down. The first step is to provide resources for the system to function properly, then to enact laws that ensure it does so in a timely manner. Improvements should begin with the resurrection of legal resource centers. Qualified resource center attorneys would prevent prosecutors from running up capital convictions against unprepared or unqualified public defenders. In fact, the motivation for ambitious prosecutors would shift from quantity of convictions to quality. They'd need to be certain of an airtight case before seeking the death penalty, since failing to win a conviction is a political embarrassment. This might even have the secondary effect of removing the stigma attached to settling dubious capital cases.

Resource centers would have a trickle-down effect that would alleviate problems later in the justice cycle: only the most deserving killers would be executed; more convictions would be upheld; having competent lawyers at trial would eliminate the claims of incompetent counsel that delay so many cases today. Cases would proceed more quickly because defendants wouldn't have to wait years for the court to assign them an attorney. And fewer convictions and appeals would curtail the staggering cost to taxpayers.

Even the most conservative estimate of savings is substantial. Federal Judge Kozinski estimates each death penalty case (in state court) costs taxpayers $1 million. If each case were thought of as a million-dollar tax increase, prosecutors would have to be much more discriminating. Cutting the number of death sentences in half would save $150 million each year. To put that figure in perspective, resource centers would need to prevent just 20 cases a year to cover the funding Congress cut for them in 1995. States need to institute minimum qualifications for defense lawyers. Studies show that often it's the worst lawyers, not the worst criminals, who draw death sentences—a fact illustrated in the death penalty case of George McFarland in Texas, whose lawyer repeatedly fell asleep in court ("It's boring," he explained to the *Houston Chronicle*). This reform too would cut time and cost. The Justice Department concluded last fall: "Assuring appropriate resources for the defense at the trial stage minimizes the risk of time-consuming and expensive post-conviction litigation." States could also place time limits on appeals (some already do) to force delay-minded defendants to air their claims early on, rather than withhold them for time-consuming appeals. Appeals could also be bundled and made at one time, rather than sequentially. An exception would of course be made for evidence discovered after conviction. Conservatives, no matter how justified their frustration over delays, should not perpetuate a system that refuses to hear exculpatory evidence.

By amending laws like Virginia's 21-Day Rule to allow a judge to rule on credible new evidence, lawmakers would remove a major incentive for delay. The amendment should mirror new programs like one in Illinois that allows post-conviction DNA testing. As a final safeguard, Illinois' attorney general has proposed a board to review capital cases before execution—an idea endorsed by both the state bar association and conservatives like Scheidegger.

None of these improvements will come without political leadership. So politicians sincere about being tough on crime need to be held accountable for the problem. This spring the Texas legislature unanimously passed a bill that would have created an agency to match indigent capital defendants with qualified lawyers. (That Texas, which leads the nation in executions, could pass such a bill unanimously is an indication of how badly it is needed). Nevertheless, Governor Bush vetoed it in June. Undoubtedly, he intended to send a message to voters. But his veto killed a practical, bipartisan agreement that would have hastened justice and likely saved lives. Voters should send their own message right back.

32   The way to repair the "machinery of death" is to shift resources to points earlier in the criminal justice cycle. Only then, with the chance for error greatly diminished, would faster processing be justified. Proponents of capital punishment would have an efficient and equitable system, while opponents could argue abolition purely on its merits. With violent crime at its lowest rate in 25 years, there is no better time for sensible reform.

PERSONAL RESPONSE

Explain whether, after reading this article, you feel that you have a clearer picture of the issues associated with capital punishment.

QUESTIONS FOR CLASS OR SMALL-GROUP DISCUSSION

1. How effective do you find Green's use of examples of death-row cases? How do the opening examples (paragraphs 2 and 3) provide background information for his thesis?

2. What is the "deadly compromise" of the title? What examples does Green use to illustrate the problems inherent in the compromise?

3. Explain what Green means when he says that "reforms at the federal level have . . . been woefully misguided" (paragraph 15).

4. What problems with handling capital crimes does Green find at the state level?

5. What solutions does Green recommend for ending "the battle between the extremes of liberalism and conservativism that have reigned on the death penalty" (paragraph 30)? What do you think of his recommendations? Are you persuaded by his evidence and moved to agree with him?

DEADLY STAKES: THE DEBATE
OVER CAPITAL PUNISHMENT

JOHN O'SULLIVAN

John O'Sullivan is editor-in-chief of The National Interest. *He was editor of* National Review *from 1988 to 1997 and in 1998 was named editor-at-large. His previous posts have included special adviser to Prime Minister Margaret Thatcher, associate editor of the London* Times, *assistant editor of the London* Daily Telegraph, *and editor of* Policy Review. *He was made a Commander of the British Empire in 1991. He lectures on British and American politics. This opinion piece appeared in* National Review Online *on August 30, 2002.*

By a terrible and macabre coincidence both the American and British peoples have found themselves confronted in the last few days with the chilling evil of child murder—and with the grave dilemma of exactly how to punish and deter it.

Last week a California jury found David Westerfield guilty of the kidnapping and murder of his neighbor's daughter, seven-year-old Danielle Van Dam, while in Britain the entire nation was convulsed for weeks over two missing ten-year-old girls. A nationwide hunt ended when their charred remains were found in a ditch. A school janitor has now been charged with their murders and, in a horrible echo of the "Moors Murders" four decades ago, his girlfriend is suspected of complicity in their deaths. In both cases, it seems that the general public would like to see the death penalty imposed for these and similar crimes. If so, their wishes are almost certain to be thwarted by political elites.

In Britain this elite opposition is quite open. Though polls show that 82 percent of the British would like to see the death penalty restored, the politicians refuse to even to discuss the matter. Their reluctance is reinforced by strong pressure from the European Union that has decreed the death penalty to be incompatible with membership in its civilized ranks. Indeed, EU ambassadors troop annually to the State Department to protest the continued use of capital punishment in the U.S.—and the Secretary of State replies apologetically that this is not really a matter for the federal government. In California, the opposition is more subtle—perhaps because it is carried out in the obscurity of a tortuous appeals process. This is likely to ensure that even if Westerfield is sentenced to death, he will probably die of old age as courts endlessly debate his rights.

4   Since this looks embarrassingly like an undemocratic contempt for majority opinion, opponents of capital punishment realize that they need formidable arguments to justify it. The arguments they use are as follows: that justifying the death penalty on the retributive grounds that the punishment should fit the crime is barbaric; that it does not deter potential murderers as its advocates claim; that there are no other arguments that might justify the state taking a life; that it risks killing the wrongly convicted; and, all in all, that it is a cruel punishment incompatible with a civilized society.

Are these arguments formidable? Well, they are repeated so frequently and in tones of such relentless moral self-congratulation that they doubtless come to seem formidable after a while. But they wilt upon examination. Let us take them in turn: Take retribution. This turns out to be a more complex argument that its opponents may have bargained for. To begin with, far from being cruel or barbaric, retribution is an argument that limits punishment as much as it extends it. We do not cut off hands for parking offenses even though that would undoubtedly halt such offenses overnight. Why? Because we recognize that it would violate retributive norms: It would be excessive in comparison to the crime and therefore cruel.

By the same logic, the death penalty is sometimes the only punishment that seems equal to the horror of a particular crime—a cold-blooded poisoning, say, or the rape and murder of a helpless child, or the mass murders of the Nazis and the Communists. Significantly, such civilized nations as the Danes and the Norwegians, which had abolished the death penalty before the First World War, restored it after 1945 in order to deal equitable justice to the Nazis and their collaborators. Was that an excessive response to millions of murders? Was it cruel, unusual, barbaric, uncivilized? Or a measured and just response to vast historic crimes?

Even abolitionists find it hard to reply to these questions because they differ among themselves about whether or not to stress the cruelty of the death penalty. Sometimes they assert that it is uniquely cruel; sometimes, however, they claim to favor lifetime imprisonment on the grounds that it is actually harsher than a quick trip to God or oblivion. Acting on the same grounds, retentionists can reasonably (and, I think, correctly) maintain that death is more merciful than lifetime incarceration (especially when that incarceration is accompanied by sadistic brutality from other inmates.)

8   But this particular dispute is likely to be moot since, as soon as capital punishment is safely outlawed, the ACLU and its camp-followers will immediately file suit to have the courts declare life without parole to be a cruel and unusual punishment outlawed by the U.S. Constitution. In the British debates of the 1970s over whether or not terrorist murderers should face execution, I well remember being assured by politicians who later served as Northern Ireland ministers that convicted murderers would have to serve their full sentence; for there was simply no legal way of releasing them beforehand. Ho Hum. Those same murderers are now walking the streets of Belfast "on license." The Grim Reaper grants no paroles.

So how about the argument from deterrence? Perhaps the loudest and most confident claim made by abolitionists is that there is "no evidence" that the death penalty is a deterrent to potential murders. If that were so, of course, it would hardly be a decisive point in itself. Mere lack of evidence would not establish the reverse proposition—it would not prove that capital punishment was NOT a deterrent. As it happens, however, this claim of "no evidence" is false.

Last year, a trio of economists from Emory University, Hashem Dezhbakhsh, Paul Rubin, and Joanna Melhop Shepherd, released a study—"Does Capital Punishment Have a Deterrent Effect?"—that concluded on the basis of careful statistical analysis of the recent (i.e. since the restoration of capital punishment in the 1970s) evidence that there was a very significant deterrent effect. Summarizing their conclusions, the statistician Iain Murray of the Statistical Assessment Service in Washington reported that "each execution deters other murders to the extent of saving between eight and twenty-eight innocent lives—with a best-estimate average of eighteen lives saved per execution." On this reasoning, if the 3,527 prisoners now on death row in the U.S. were to be executed, then something like 63,000 lives would be saved! Even if we scale down these estimates sharply, we are left with a very strong argument for capital punishment derived from social concern for the lives of potential victims and the distress of their families. (Mr. Murray is himself an opponent of capital punishment on religious grounds; so he deserves particular credit for his intellectual honesty.)

So, if opponents of the death penalty are to continue to disparage the deterrent argument, they will have to overturn this new research. Mere repetition of past assertions will not be enough. That brings us to what is genuinely the strongest argument of the abolitionists—wrongful execution. For it must certainly be admitted that an innocent man might be wrongly convicted and executed, that we can never entirely eliminate that risk, and that such a miscarriage of justice would be shameful. For that very reason we take extreme measures to avoid it. As a result, only a handful of such miscarriages of justice are known to have happened; none of them has happened since the restoration of capital punishment in the U.S. in 1976; and the science of DNA has now added a further barrier to such terrible mistakes. The recent release of man as a result of DNA evidence, cited by Rod Dreher (in *The Corner*) as justifying his opposition to the death penalty, in reality strengthens the case for it since it makes future errors even less likely than they were before.

12   Even though wrongful executions are exceedingly rare, we know a great deal about them. Yet we hear little or no mention of their exact equivalent on the other side of the argument—namely, murders committed by those who have already committed a murder, served their sentence, and been released to murder again (or who have murdered an inmate or guard in prison). That is curious. For a few years ago there were 820 people in U.S. prisons who were serving time for their second murder of this kind. If the death penalty had been applied after their first murders, their 820 subsequent victims would be alive today. That figure is not a statistical inference but an absolute certainty. Of course, it is intellectually possible for abolitionists to argue that it is better to acquiesce reluctantly in the murder of 820 innocent men than to execute mistakenly one innocent man—but somehow I doubt if that argument, stated so plainly, would convince the democratic majority.

What those 820 murders establish is that, contra the abolitionists, there is another strong argument for capital punishment. It is known technically as the argument from incapacitation (i.e., dead men commit no murders.) And that argument alone is more than adequate justification for capital punishment.

That is perhaps why we never hear of it.

Where, then, does that leave the final, broad conclusion that capital punishment is incompatible with a civilized society? Well, to answer that, we must have some idea of what abolitionists mean by "a civilized society." Do they mean a society that has a written language, at least an oral historical tradition, social institutions that claim a monopoly of force and violence, and similar social inventions? It would seem not since such societies have almost invariably imposed the death penalty, sometimes for crimes much less serious than murder. Indeed, the replacement of private vendettas by state executions is as good a definition of the birth of civil society as political scientists can come up with.

16   Do they then mean a society marked by gentle manners, courtesy, low levels of private violence, and declining crime? If so, that argument too backfires on them. Britain in the 1930s and America in the 1950s were societies that had achieved high levels of social tranquility by comparison with their own pasts and the standards of other advanced societies. Yet they employed the death penalty for serious crimes—indeed, murder trials were among the gripping social entertainments of those days. And as the death penalty was gradually abolished (formal abolition generally following on a growing reluctance to impose it except in the most terrible cases), so crime and violence rose, and so society became increasingly brutalist in its popular culture—the violence of films and television making the murder trials of the 1930s seem, well, civilized by comparison.

Britain is still in the midst of this perverse experiment that combines official squeamishness with rising levels of violent crime; America began to restore the death penalty in the 1970s—and 20 years later violent crime began to fall.

What the "civilized" argument boils down to in the end, as the late Ernest Van Den Haag used to point out in his intellectual demolitions of the abolitionist case, is the circular logic that capital punishment is incompatible with a civilized society because a civilized society is one that rejects capital punishment. Or, to put the abolitionist case as simply as possible: "People like us don't like capital punishment."

A genuinely civilized society would take a very different view of the evidence cited above. It would pay more attention to the cries of the victims than to its own squeamishness. And it would transfer its compassion from the David Westerfields of this world to the Danielle Van Dams. For if the death penalty would certainly have saved 820 innocent lives, and might arguably save tens of thousands of innocent lives in the future, almost certainly at the cost of no innocent lives at all, then surely a society that shrinks from using it deserves to be called sentimentalist and cruel rather than civilized. And if in addition it ignores majority opinion in order to indulge its refined sensibilities, then it deserves to be called undemocratic too.

20   When next the EU ambassadors come calling at the State Department to complain of executions in Texas, Colin Powell might tell them exactly that.

PERSONAL RESPONSE

Write for a few minutes explaining your views on the death penalty. Has this essay changed your opinion in any way?

QUESTIONS FOR CLASS OR SMALL-GROUP DISCUSSION

1. How does O'Sullivan use the murders of children in both America and Britain to argue his position on capital punishment?

2. State the arguments that opponents of capital punishment typically use to argue their position. What does O'Sullivan have to say about each of those points? How valid or sound do your find his reasoning on each point?

3. Assess the strengths and weaknesses of O'Sullivan's argument. Which is his weakest point? Which is his most persuasive point? Are you convinced to agree with him?

THERE ARE NO LESSONS TO BE LEARNED FROM LITTLETON

GARY KLECK

Gary Kleck, author of Point Blank: Guns and Violence in America *(1991) and* Targeting Guns: Firearms and Their Control *(1997), is a professor in the School of Criminology and Criminal Justice at Florida State University. He is co-author, with Don B. Kates Jr., of* The Great American Gun Debate: Essays on Firearms and Violence *(1997) and* Armed: New Perspectives on Gun Control *(2001). This essay was first published in the winter/spring 1999 issue of* Criminal Justice Ethics.

On April 21, 1999, two young men armed with guns and explosives murdered 13 people, wounded 31 others, and then committed suicide in a high school in Littleton, Colorado. This mass shooting had been preceded by three other highly publicized mass shootings in schools involving adolescent boys in the preceding year-and-a-half in Pearl, Mississippi; West Paducah, Kentucky; and Jonesboro, Arkansas (and there had been at least seven other multi-victim school shootings in the six years before that), and was followed by two more occurring within a month in Springfield, Oregon, and Conyers, Georgia.

In the aftermath of this spate of murders, a wave of commentary followed, in which journalists and other writers of every ideological stripe explained to their readers what lessons were to be learned from Littleton or, more broadly, from this cluster of massacres. In a typical commentary, a writer would diagnose one or more key problems that supposedly contributed to the killings, and then prescribe one or more solutions. The diagnoses and solutions generally fitted remarkably well with preexisting news media themes, reflecting either an impressive ability of news providers to identify causes and solutions in advance or a tendency to exclude the solutions that do not easily fit the themes.

A partial list of the problems that have been blamed for the recent mass killings in schools would include: guns, "assault weapons," large-capacity ammunition magazines, lax regulation of gun shows; the failure of parents to secure guns, school cliques, and the exclusion of "outsiders"; bullying and taunting in schools, especially by high school athletes; inadequate school security, especially a lack of metal detectors, armed guards, locker searches, and so forth; excessively large high schools; inadequate monitoring of potentially violent students by schools; lazy, uninvolved Baby Boomer parents and correspondingly inadequate supervision of their children; young killers not being eligible for the death penalty; a lack of religion, especially in schools; violent movies and television; violent video games; violent material and communications on the World Wide Web/Internet (including bomb-making instructions); anti-Semitism, neo-Nazi sentiments, and Hitler worship; "Industrial" music, Marilyn Manson's music, and other "dark" variants of rock music; Satanism; "Goth" culture among adolescents; and Southern culture.

4   The purpose of this essay is not to sort out which diagnoses are correct. Many of them are plausible, and some are probably even accurate. Likewise, some of the proposed preventive measures may well be effective. Rather, my main point is that it is generally a mistake to diagnose the causes of violence and crime, or to identify effective ways to reduce violence and crime, via a focus on unusual, heavily publicized violent events, because diagnoses and prescriptions developed or promoted in the immediate aftermath of such events are especially likely to be irrelevant or even counterproductive.

A casual consumer of the flood of news coverage of these shootings could easily draw the conclusion that violence in schools is a growing problem or that youth violence, gun violence, or violence in general has been increasing. In fact, these are the recent trends in violence:

- the homicide rate dropped by a third from 1991 to 1998,
- the juvenile share of arrests for violent crime has been declining since 1992,
- gun violence, and the gun share of violent crimes, has been declining since 1993,
- the lethality of gun crime (the share ending in death) has been declining since the mid-1970s,
- mass murder has been declining for decades (the share of homicide victims killed in incidents with four or more victims dropped in half between 1976 and 1994), and
- school gun violence has generally declined since national statistics were first gathered for the 1992–1993 school year.

In sum, the cluster of mass shootings in schools that occurred in the late 1990s may well be one of the few forms of violence that have been increasing in recent years. Even gun homicides in schools have generally been declining in recent years, despite the massacres. Indeed, excluding the Littleton killings, U.S. schools experienced just two gun homicides during the 1998–1999 school year, which would have been the lowest total since national statistics were first compiled. While some of these facts were mentioned occasionally in news stories about these events, many writers nevertheless offered explanations for the nonexistent "trend" in youth/school/gun violence.

Misdescription of the phenomenon to be explained leads to misdiagnosis of its causes. If there is no increase in youth/school/gun violence, it is fruitless to search for contributing factors that have been increasing in recent years. The only kind of violence that did increase was mass shootings in schools, (so far) only for a very short period of time. Thus, long-term or significant social trends may be irrelevant to these murders, however relevant some of them may be to more commonplace forms of violence. Rather, this short-term clustering may largely reflect an endogenous process by which each new act is triggered by news media accounts of the previous ones. Adolescent boys, faced with powerlessness and anonymity, and otherwise unhappy for a multitude of diverse reasons, recognize that fame, importance, and a sort of immortality have been the rewards for previous mass killers and realistically anticipate the same rewards for themselves if they copy their actions. This process can perpetuate itself until the news media loses interest or competing stories push schoolyard massacres off the front pages.

8   A tragedy that has already occurred obviously cannot be prevented by any actions taken now. Therefore, actions will prevent harm only to the extent that the events they can effectively head off are likely to be repeated in the future. Yet, the more bizarre an event, the less likely it is to be repeated. Thus, because bizarre events are unlikely to be repeated in quite the same way in the future, the more narrowly a preventive measure is tailored to the specifics of such events, the less likely it is to save lives.

One might argue that while commentary on these media-heavy tragedies might not successfully identify measures that could prevent such events in the future, analysis of the extraordinary events might identify measures that could prevent more commonplace kinds of violence. This might make sense if the heavily publicized events closely resembled more ordinary acts of violence, but in many important ways they do not.

Particular violent events are heavily covered by the news media precisely because they are unusual and thus unrepresentative of broader categories of crime and violence. For example, violent incidents with many victims are the ones most likely to be covered heavily. Yet less than one percent of Americans who are murdered are killed in incidents with four or more dead victims (often regarded by experts as the admittedly arbitrary cutoff between mass killings and "ordinary" homicides). Only two percent are killed in incidents with more than two victims, and these are most commonly killings within families. Their high body count itself makes mass killings unusual and unrepresentative of murder or violence in general.

This would not be problematic if the causes of, and likely solutions to, mass killings matched closely with likely causes and solutions to "ordinary" violence, but mass killings differ from ordinary violence in crucial ways. For example, mass killings are almost invariably planned, while other homicides and assaults are rarely planned. Likewise, firearms are virtually a necessity to killing large numbers of people in a single incident, but far less essential for killing a single person. Further, mass killers often come from middle-class backgrounds and have little prior record of criminal behavior, while these things are rarely true of "ordinary" killers.

12   A particularly worrisome implication is that a focus on mass murders tends to distract attention from the role of underclass poverty in generating the "ordinary" violence that accounts for almost all of its casualties. There really was a recent increase in juvenile violence, especially with guns, but it was confined to the period from 1985 to 1991, and it had little to do with middle class–linked causes, and everything to do

with the collapse of the legitimate economy in America's inner city ghettoes and the resultant rise of the crack economy to fill the vacuum.

Just as few homicides involve large numbers of victims, very few occur in schools. Schools continue to be the safe havens that they were traditionally perceived to be, however much media coverage of these killings has eroded that perception. While there is serious violence in a few schools, and considerable gun violence outside of schools, gun violence in schools is extremely rare. In the 1996–97 school year, 90 percent of public schools did not experience a single serious violent crime (murder, rape, sexual battery, robbery, or attack with a weapon) regardless of gun involvement, and over 99.99 percent have never had a homicide. The violence that does occur in schools is mostly unarmed fighting (including a good deal of bullying), while gun violence, even among adolescents, is almost entirely confined to places other than schools. Less than one in 400 adolescent gun homicides in 1994 occurred in a school or on school grounds.

The school shootings triggered a barrage of transparently irrelevant proposed solutions, tossed out without regard to their relevance to the events that supposedly occasioned the proposals. Mississippi responded to the Pearl shootings by making murder on school property a capital offense, even though premeditated murder, regardless of location, was already a capital offense in Mississippi. The killers in this incident, moreover, were ineligible for the death penalty because of their ages, eleven and thirteen; the minimum age for the death penalty was left unchanged.

Following the first four of these shootings, members of Congress were pushing a bill that would "crack down" on dealers who sell firearms to children even though none of these cases involved a dealer selling a gun to a child. After the shooting in West Paducah, in which the killer was armed with five firearms and shot eight different people in the school lobby, newspapers reported that the school system was considering installing metal detectors. The stories did not explain how metal detectors could prevent attacks by those willing to shoot their way into a school.

16   After it was found that such transfers were involved in the Littleton case, some analysts proposed restricting sales at gun shows. Gun show sales, however, had nothing at all to do with any of the other high-profile school shootings. The most common modes of acquisition of guns by shooters were theft (the West Paducah, Jonesboro, and Conyers shootings, as well as a somewhat less prominent case in Edinboro, Pennsylvania), while the Springfield shooter was given his guns by his father. Further, even in the Littleton case the three longguns that accounted for all of the deaths were purchased on the killers' behalf by the eighteen-year-old girlfriend of one of the shooters. Under both Colorado and federal law, she would have been eligible to purchase the same guns from any gun store. Further, one of the two killers turned eighteen before the shootings and was likewise eligible to buy longguns from any gun store.

Consequently, regulation of gun shows was totally irrelevant to preventing any of these massacres. One irony of addressing such proposals in the context of mass killings, however, is that some of them make sense, but not in connection with mass killings. As a result, some people will reject the value of a measure with regard to ordinary violence because it is irrelevant to the unusual events at hand. A prime example is extending background checks to private gun transfers at gun shows. The Littleton and other mass shootings are the worst possible examples of cases in which the background checks could succeed since determined killers who plan their murders over a long period of time are the people least likely to be blocked from getting a gun by background checks. As a long-time advocate of extending background checks to all private transfers of guns, not just the few that take place at gun shows, I worry that the real merits of such a step will be obscured by the inane debate over the nonexistent link between gun shows and the Littleton massacre. More broadly, mass killings and other premeditated murders are the very worst examples for buttressing a case in favor of gun control because they involve the perpetrators most strongly motivated and able to evade the controls.

Even under the best of circumstances, the lessons one could derive from the examination of individual violent events are inherently ambiguous. The fact that violence did occur necessarily means that all existing preventive measures failed. This can lead to any of a number of very different conclusions: (1) we need different preventive measures, (2) we need more of the existing measures, or (3) nothing can be done. The ongoing issue most frequently linked to the school shootings was gun control, and reactions by those on both sides of that issue were predictable. Pro-gun people concluded that despite the existence of laws completely prohibiting the purchase and carrying of guns by minors, youthful killers got guns anyway; therefore gun control is ineffective. Meanwhile, pro-control people concluded that if existing gun controls failed, it showed that stronger measures were called for—anything from tougher controls over gun shows and laws requiring guns to be kept locked to lawsuits against gun companies supposedly marketing guns to juveniles.

Assessments of preventive measures based on a narrow focus on violent events that did occur, however, are inherently misleading because they necessarily focus only on the failures of preventive efforts. One cannot infer how much success a policy has had by counting its failures. Successes of preventive measures, unlike failures, usually cannot be observed directly. Instead, they can be detected only indirectly through careful comparison of persons, places, and times subject to the preventive measures with those not subject to them.

20   Diagnosis of the causes of violence is similarly distorted by a narrow focus on the attributes of a few violent actors, distracting attention from violent actors who lacked the attributes, and from the even larger number of people who had the attributes but were not violent.

Those who propose preventive measures in the context of these mass shootings can plausibly assert that the irrelevance of their proposals to these incidents does not matter because the proposals are meritorious with respect to more common sorts of violence. If that is the case, however, honest advocates should show why their proposals are relevant to more ordinary violence and not coast dishonestly on the emotional momentum created by extraordinary violent events that their policies could not prevent. It would, however, be naive to expect those playing hard-ball politics to follow the intellectually honest path since they will be loathe to forego exploiting the emotional power that comes from tying their recommendations to the most horrific and frightening crimes.

One might justify drawing lessons from high-profile tragedies by arguing that one should make use of the temporarily elevated level of concern about violence to advance worthy solutions that might not prevent unusual events like those that just occurred, but would be effective in the long run with more mundane crimes.

This argument, however, would seem to depend on the dubious premise that people make wise choices in times of fear and hysteria (sometimes euphemistically referred to as "intense public concern"). Unfortunately, frightened people often favor actions that make them feel better over those that would actually make them safer, if the actions can be implemented quickly and easily and are touted as producing results immediately.

24   People are less likely to be in a logical or critical frame of mind in the aftermath of the most ghastly crimes, a situation that smart advocates exploit. In such a context, people are more willing to believe that "something must be done," and not look too closely at the details and full set of consequences of proposed solutions. Decisions about serious matters should not be made in the sort of overheated aftermath in which demagoguery flourishes. Such an atmosphere is more conducive to lynch mob justice and empty, politically easy gestures than to wise public policy.

Littleton and the other school shootings do raise serious issues, some largely ignored by the news media, and others only briefly mentioned and obscured by the noisy debates over the irrelevancies. These issues might include school bullying and taunting, male-on-female teen dating violence, and violence-saturated entertainment disseminated by profit-hungry corporations. But we will be best able to separate the issues that matter from the ones that do not if we learn our lessons from careful analysis of "ordinary" crime and violence rather than from the freakish events chosen for our attention by the news media.

PERSONAL RESPONSE

Are you convinced that "there are no lessons to be learned from Littleton"? If not, what lessons do you think we can learn from the Littleton, Colorado, shooting in particular or from school shootings in general?

QUESTIONS FOR CLASS OR SMALL-GROUP DISCUSSION

1. Locate Kleck's thesis and consider how effectively he supports that thesis as you discuss the essay. To what extent did/do you believe that "violence in schools is a growing problem or that youth violence, gun violence, or violence in general has been increasing"? Were you surprised by the statistics that Kleck cites in paragraphs 5, 6, 10, and 13? Are you persuaded that there is no " 'trend' in youth/school/gun violence"?

2. How convinced are you by Kleck's argument against the position that "commentary on these media-heavy tragedies [. . .] could prevent such events in the future" (paragraph 9)? What differences does Kleck see between "mass killings" and " 'ordinary' violence"?

3. According to Kleck, what are the "transparently irrelevant proposed solutions" to the problem of school shootings (paragraph 14)? Discuss your views on his evidence. To what extent do you agree with him that the proposed solutions are irrelevant to the problem?

4. In paragraphs 18–24, Kleck states some of the lessons people say we could learn from the school shootings and then rejects each in turn. Summarize what those lessons are and why he rejects them. To what extent do you agree with his arguments on these points?

WHAT'S WRONG WITH AMERICA AND CAN ANYTHING BE DONE ABOUT IT?

Wayne M. Barrett and Bernard Rowe

Wayne M. Barrett is Managing Editor of USA Today *magazine and writes often of sports, especially hockey and baseball. Bernard Rowe, a British citizen, is a retired chartered accountant (the British term for what Americans call a CPA or Certified Public Accountant) and a textile industry consultant who lives in Valley Stream, New York. They wrote this essay for* USA Today *in 1994.*

It is a clichéd tale as old as the hills. The elder generation looks at society's youngsters and shakes its head in disappointed wonder and disgust. "When I was a kid . . . ," the admonition inevitably begins. Today, however, the Establishment is in no position to criticize anyone or anything. If American youth is poisoned with skewed values and a lack of respect, one doesn't have to look very far to see where such behavior originates. Consider the following incidents:

- Unmarried pregnant teenage girls, no longer outcasts among their high school peers, instead are made cheerleaders and crowned homecoming queens by court order.

- The Chief Council for the President of the United States commits suicide and, before the body is even cold, Clinton administration officials rifle through his office to remove all "incriminating" paperwork that related to the chief executive and first lady.

- In 1993, New York Mets outfielder Vince Coleman threw an M-80 firecracker into a crowd of fans outside Dodger Stadium in Los Angeles. A handful of people, including a little girl, were injured in the explosion. In response to the heat the Mets took following this ugly and unforgivable occurrence, the club's vice president of baseball operations, Gary Hunsicker, stated: "This incident didn't happen during working hours. It didn't happen in the clubhouse. It only involves the Mets because he is an employee of the Mets. This is Vince Coleman's incident. This is Vince Coleman's problem."

- *The Program,* a Disney movie about a college football team, contained a scene in which a drunken player lies on a busy highway's dividing line, with traffic zooming past. A New Jersey man and Pennsylvania teenager, imitating the dangerous stunt, were killed, while a New York teenager was paralyzed. The film's producers and distributors were blamed. (The scene subsequently was removed from the film and videotape version.)
- A New York City mugger was awarded $4,300,000 by the state's Court of Appeals, which ruled that the arresting officer used too much force by shooting him. The U.S. Supreme Court refused to overturn the decision.
- A 1993 survey released by Who's Who among American High School Students found that the nation's top secondary school pupils get their good grades the old-fashioned way—they cheat. Eighty percent said cheating was common at their schools, and 78 percent admitted to doing so themselves.
- The handshake, long the symbol of sportsmanship and good will, has been banned at the closing of school sporting events in California's Ventura County. It seems that some players were spitting in their hands before shaking or slapping opponents in the face during the post-game ritual.
- Madison Square Garden Network announcer John Andariese has covered the National Basketball Association since 1972. Recently, he compared the "old days" to contemporary times, where players "diss" each other with trash talk. Bench-clearing brawls often are the result. "It wasn't that long ago when respect came from winning the game; a series; a championship. Self-respect was about being part of the game; now it's a reason to be thrown out of the game. "Today, self-respect is so misplaced," he told the *New York Post.* "It's about putting your own feelings above all else. The individual's interests, including commercial interests, come before the team. . . . We've made heroes out of guys who do bad things; selfish things. The attention they receive is often equated with their ability to be entertaining, and that's when commercial opportunities present themselves."
- Fox Television, in a live update on the New York Rangers' fifty-four-year quest for the Stanley Cup, cut to a reporter outside Madison Square Garden just before the opening faceoff of Game 5 of the finals. No sooner did the camera go on than a bunch of Big Apple rooters standing behind the reporter started chanting: "Let's Go Rangers! F— Vancouver!" Loudly, over and over again. Did Fox switch back to the studio? Of course not. Instead, the obscene chant came cascading right into the viewer's living room, over and over.
- Fallen football hero O. J. Simpson, wanted by the Los Angeles Police on a double-murder charge, took cops on a cross-county highway chase, captured live by news helicopter cameras. As O. J.'s car passed under an overpass, a group of revelers cheered him on, apparently delighted to be part of the action.

It all comes down to a breakdown in discipline and the advent of liberalism. The general idea is of total *laissez-faire*—the concept that everyone has a personal right to do whatever he or she wants. America has institutionalized selfishness.

People need not look out for anyone but themselves. My interest then becomes myself. I no longer have to worry about anyone else. When there is the understanding that people just live for themselves, when that attitude permeates a society, individuals attempt to protect themselves without regard for others. If they can't protect their rights in a civilized way, they're prepared to carry it through using a violent route, oftentimes with little or no regard for right and wrong, or how that action will impact upon themselves or those around them. After all, that person reasons, I'm free and have my own rights.

4   One can track this growth in liberalism with the breakdown of the great religions. The church taught a certain level of morals. "Thou shalt not steal" didn't come from the schools. Parents taught that. They took their kids to church, synagogue, or the mosque, and the youngsters were taught there that you mustn't kill; you mustn't do certain things. Along came liberalism, and no one bothered to teach those things anymore. This effectively has led to a bankrupt society. True, there are numerous social welfare programs, but, because Americans have let go of all other moral values, much of the good that these programs could have generated or produced has been lost.

There used to be corporal punishment in the schools. If teachers tried that today, they would be sued. If parents do it, they risk having the state take away their offspring. Accordingly, such discipline wasn't only given up in school, but in the home as well.

Everywhere, there is unbridled freedom bordering on license. Children are allowed to watch any television program, no matter what it is. By allowing kids unrestricted access to TV, the movies, and new computer information systems, they not only are being exposed to greater knowledge, they are being exposed to all of the world's ills without countervailing criticism. No one comes on at the end to say, "This is wrong; this should not have happened." No one tries to utilize the media to show youngsters a piece of news that might be startling and use it as a lesson, asking them: "What happens if . . . ?"

Not surprisingly, then, the nation's work ethic has suffered as well. Today, employees have rights against their employer, oftentimes out of balance with what rights should be. True, there was a time when employers exploited individuals, and the unions had to right major wrongs. People were made to work in a certain way that was beyond what was reasonable. The unions have come full circle and introduced a system whereby the employees almost control what they will do, what rights they have, and how much they will work.

8   Within the workplace, certain individuals may be motivated, but they often are held back by the others, who complain, "What are you doing? Why are you being so productive? If management sees this, it will want more from us." They then will use whatever means are at their disposal—violence not excepted—to stop the more productive workers. While the advent of unions brought back a certain sense of balance, it took away the decency of the individual, which no longer counts.

When individuals are institutionalized, it effectively removes a lot of their creativity and motivation. There is a tremendous loss, especially in the aspect of discipline. Doing what management wants is only one facet of discipline. The other is fulfilling your moral obligation when you take on a job or assignment.

That the work ethic has been weakened by Western society becomes particularly noticeable in considering newcomers to our shores. Immigrant labor has not been subject to generations of this kind of influence, so they come to this country willing to work, willing to give it their best. They feel they owe it. They have a job. They're determined to achieve for themselves, their families, and the relatives back home. They are willing to work hard, sacrificing and doing without for years.

These people never remove the yoke from their shoulders. They were born into societies where children, parents, and grandparents lived in one community. Children knew that, as they grew up, they had an obligation to take care of their parents. Today, as youngsters grow up and go to college, their main concern is for themselves and their own well-being.

12   Marriage is another dying institution. Today, many people decide to live together to see if they're compatible. Does that produce the best results? Obviously not. "If we live together," the attitude goes, "why should I commit myself? Why should I assume responsibility? Indeed, why should I give of myself more than I need to so that I can still have the physical contact my desires require without having to give a financial or moral commitment to just one person or to the children who may come from this relationship? I can come and go as I please. If someone better arrives on the scene, I can go with him or her."

Such an attitude inevitably leads to a lack of discipline and responsibility for another. If children see their parents act this way, why should they be any different? When they go to school, why should they care about their friends? Why do they have to worry that other kids may be hurt? To take it a step further, why would it worry them if they hurt other youngsters?

Meanwhile, lawsuit mania has gripped America. The phenomenon goes back to the same issue: I have a right! I'm entitled to sue for anything and everything that may impinge upon that right, no matter what society's needs.

Take the Rodney King case. This is a man who everyone agrees required force to be subdued after a high-speed auto chase, but excessive force was used by the Los Angeles police. There was a wrong committed here, but remember, King was in the wrong, too. Conceding that he had inflicted upon him a certain amount of pain, he did deserve something for his suffering. He should have been given a small amount of financial compensation, but not a seven-digit settlement.

16   This is a man who in his lifetime never dreamed of earning that kind of money or had been deprived of anything resembling that sort of income. He probably is way better off having been subjected to physical abuse at the hands of the police. That doesn't justify the wrong, but neither does it justify a multimillion-dollar lawsuit. It's not an issue of civil rights. The system has been made to look stupid. The courts and lawyers should be viewed with a certain amount of integrity. Once respect has disappeared, so has the sense of honesty.

Now, consider the impact of the legal system on physicians. Much of what the medical profession does today simply is to avoid lawsuits, because it's a "cover yourself just in case" kind of world. This is the price society pays for allowing malpractice lawyers to reach for the moon. The measure of compensation should be related to what is right and what is wrong. Instead, the dollar amounts are astronomical. In the end, society pays. When individuals who have observed the system at work find themselves with the potential for a claim, however spurious, they say, "Well, it's my turn to exploit it now." There are bumper stickers that sum it up quite succinctly: "Hit me; I need the cash." That's not what society should be all about.

The Drug Scourge

The drug problem in America also can be traced back to a lack of discipline, lack of education, and lack of knowledge between right and wrong. Again there is the attitude: I have rights. I want to take drugs. Meanwhile, the government says they must be outlawed. A tremendous amount of resources have been sunk into the war on drugs, with no victory in sight. As a result of interdictment efforts, however, drugs are becoming more and more expensive, and more and more people are turning to crime to finance their drug habits. One way of looking at it is the government has made criminals out of noncriminals.

When addicts kill for drug money, people act perplexed and ask, "How on Earth did this happen?" Actually, the surprise is that it doesn't happen more often. As the situation worsens, society does what it absolutely shouldn't—legislate against its own people.

20   In a society pervasive with so many freedoms, government simply can't say, with regard to drugs, "No, you can't do what you want." It hasn't worked and won't work. The easy solution is to legalize drugs. There's a strong case for that. Fundamentally, the price of drugs would drop to next to nothing. Sell it like alcohol and cigarettes, with a label: "Warning—this stuff may kill you." The criminals peddling it will be out of business overnight. The people addicted to it no longer will have to commit crimes to obtain it. If they want to rot their bodies and minds, or even kill themselves, let them.

Making drugs illegal recalls an old Hebrew saying: "Stolen waters are sweet." If you tell people they can't have drugs, especially in a *laissez-faire* society such as ours, the response will be, "I'll show you what I can have." Yet, if you were to say, "Take this poison," people would respond, "Are you crazy?"

Here is where education can be so valuable. Morality can be introduced into many subjects. So can the concepts of quality, decency, right, and wrong. Programs can be designed so that almost every teacher and every subject can introduce moral values.

In the old days, a child was told, "Sit here and pay attention." If a student dozed off or talked during lessons, there was instant retribution. To some extent, such a system was shown to have been very successful, though many children failed to achieve their full potential. Nevertheless, it certainly gave kids a better education than they're getting today.

24   Contemporary students, as they grow older and become more mature, discover that much of school has been a waste of time. They didn't learn very much, and thus have very little respect for teachers. Think what's going to happen when they have children to send to school. Can they convincingly tell their kids, "You must respect your teacher"? Absolutely not. Yet, the system doesn't change, except to give children more rights and greater freedom, and only in the negative form.

What is the price society pays?—criminals in the classroom. Never before did children come to school armed in order to protect themselves. Walk the streets of New York and you will see thousands of kids there on a normal school day. These youngsters have grown up with zero discipline. What happens when they get older?

In the past, the military system, while far from perfect, accomplished two things: It made people live a disciplined life and took them off the streets. American society has abandoned another of the fortresses of discipline. For whatever bad or good influence it had, the military at least showed people they couldn't do whatever they wanted. It also often gave them a vocation.

Discipline and decency are disappearing from the family as well. So much used to take place within the network of the family, including the education of the children. Parents sat down with them and went through their homework, helped them with assignments, and saw to it that they were progressing. Today, too many parents are jealous of their time. Watching a favorite TV show becomes more important than helping with their offspring's homework.

28   Children today seem to be kept only out of a grudging obligation. Parents will send their kids off to a private high school if they can afford it, or, in the summer, to camp. Look at it from the youngsters' viewpoint. They no longer see the constant cohesive unit of the family. On the contrary, they remember that their father sent them money and took care of their economic needs. The child comes to regard the economic thread as what is important. "My father was busy chasing the dollar. He gave me food. He sent me to camp. But other than that, I didn't really need him. I didn't need my mother, either." When there's a substitute for everything and children don't see the need for the family unit, it is an unreasonable expectation that they, in turn, will grow up and create a proper family unit.

Children very quickly perceive the way adults are. Parents who have no time for their kids and show no interest in them, who don't give up their time to help others, can't expect their children to grow up and do that. As a result, society winds up with a next generation whose main interests are themselves. They are liberated, free, have rights they are entitled to, and only have to make sure they will have means to provide for themselves. In their old age, they will not be able to depend on their children, anymore than their parents can depend on them.

A Revolution Is Needed

There has to be a total revolution in this country in attitudes and outlook. If we don't come up with a quick, solid remedy, some very serious unwanted changes will take place, almost as great as what happened in the Soviet Union. When the American dream bursts, there's no predicting exactly where the pieces will fall.

Most of the standard remedies already have been tried. We have raised and lowered taxes, adjusted interest rates, added police officers in an effort to promote law and order, poured more money into the educational system, and interdicted the traffic of narcotics, even attempting to impede their flow at the source by shipping drug enforcement agents overseas. The net effect has been minor.

32   Some success stories can be demonstrated, but, overall, it's hard to dispute that the United States is a nation in decline. Fundamentally, there's a perception by most

Americans that we are worse off than we were, and our hopes for the future are dim. Gone are the days when we looked to the future and saw the Great American Promise.

The basic ingredient for a happy society is that anyone who wishes to work should be able to find a job. In the United States today, unemployment is rampant, layoffs are all too common, and jobs flow overseas. One problem is lack of productivity by American workers.

Industry, struggling to survive in the face of cheap foreign competition, has changed its methods. Massive layoffs have resulted, and a healthier type of American company is emerging. "Leaner and meaner" is the cliché. Industry can look forward to reduced costs, and therefore be more competitive.

Government, meanwhile, remains extremely wasteful, maintaining multiple employees for each one required in industry. The numbers range all the way from twenty-five to fifty, depending on which survey one chooses to read or believe. Even in the face of all the cuts in the private sector, there's been virtually no drastic actions by the federal, state, or city government. They all remain overbloated. Elected officials are afraid to antagonize the army of civil servants and refuse to reduce their own staffs.

36   The public does not have confidence in the government or in the economy. People don't have the confidence that the future will be brighter. The key to reversing this malaise is that good jobs must be provided. How this can be accomplished is no secret. Too much of the employment in this country has been lost to foreigners. The United States exported many of its jobs through various government policies, often in the name of helping developing countries. At the same time, it allowed tremendous amounts of imports, often undercutting American companies.

America has a great history of charity, and many countries of the world are grateful, but the United States is in a time of crisis. The way to ensure that America will be here tomorrow to continue its tradition of decency and kindness is to make sure that many of those jobs exported overseas are returned home.

How can that be accomplished? The simplest way, one guaranteed to produce an almost immediate effect, is by imposing strict import controls. The United States should turn to its major trading partners—Taiwan, Korea, Japan, and China, which account for a very large part of the trade deficit—and say to them, "You may export into the United States, dollar for dollar, what you purchase from America." It is ludicrous to think that the United States should allow a two- or three-to-one ratio of imports to exports. Under the dollar-for-dollar proposal, there would be an immediate shortage of many products and some short-term price increases. However, people can survive without a new camera this month or maintain their cars for another six months—or purchase an American car—until things stabilize.

The United States would have to maintain this policy for a minimum of three years, then ease off in increments of no greater than 10 percent. Then, the manufacturers and entrepreneurs will feel secure in the knowledge that, if they produce goods in this country, they will have a local market and potential for export. They will be willing to invest in the necessary plant and machinery—almost immediately—to manufacture goods. Meanwhile, foreign companies should be encouraged with incentives to introduce more and more production in the United States. A new flow of jobs will be created within an extremely short period of time.

40   One important side effect may be a reduction in crime. American youths—especially minorities—face high rates of unemployment, poor prospects, and a lack of interest in life. Providing them with reasonably paying productive jobs can help make them feel they are valued members of society.

Next is the issue of taxation. Practically speaking, Americans don't like paying taxes and, above all, feel that much of what they pay is wasted. So long as there's mismanagement in government, there is resentment on the part of taxpayers. People recognize the need to finance national and local services, so they are prepared to pay, but there's the general sense out there—and not without justification—that the U.S. taxpayer isn't getting value for the buck.

Another major irritant is that the burden of taxation does not seem to be shared by all. There is massive avoidance of taxation in many industries, and the government doesn't even want to admit the scale of avoidance because it's embarrassingly large. People accept the idea of being taxed if everyone shares the burden. One way is to generate a taxation system that virtually encompasses the entire country. Take certain industries and tax them at source. This is not a value-added tax, which runs through all the multiple stages of production and becomes very expensive to collect. The United States has to look for something that is simple, efficient, and easy to collect.

For example, the utility companies could be taxed very highly. Abolish income tax altogether and corporation taxes because they require massive administration, massive collection systems, massive policing and effectively turn the nation into a country of crooks. Under the new plan, every electric bill would be taxed heavily. Oil, if it's imported, would be taxed at the ports; domestic oil wells, at the source. There's no reason Americans can't pay up to $4 a gallon for gas as they do in many European countries. Everyone would be caught up in the net because nobody can avoid electricity or phone bills. Among the benefits would be a very simple method of collection. A far smaller IRS would emerge.

44   Right now, America is a nation in crisis, so all the old rules are off. An enormous number of government employees no longer would be necessary. Within industry, a tremendous amount of money is spent to assist in the collection of taxes. There would be substantial savings there. As government expenses go down, revenues could be rebudgeted.

As for the poor, government now pays out a substantial amount in welfare and other social programs. Instead of money, services should be provided. It would be a cleaner system, with much less fraud. A lot of the people on such programs have been shown to take the money and use it in ways that don't necessarily benefit their welfare.

Undoubtedly, a system that sucks in the needy, while failing to show them a way out, is inherently flawed. Temporary and short-term help must be axiomatic to the system. All who enter must be encouraged to leave as soon as possible. Life within the system can not be made more comfortable than outside it. There must be an end to the credo: "We are better off on welfare than at work." To achieve this, all citizens—on welfare and off—should be issued identity cards with photos. Such a card would be required in all dealings with officialdom as well as the maintenance of bank accounts, financial securities, homes, and other assets and liabilities. In order to secure welfare benefits, a potential recipient would have to submit to a means test to be verified by the identity card. If, and while, assets remain below established criteria, appropriate benefits would be granted, and only for that period.

These benefits would be distributed on community campuses, as it is vitally important to establish appropriate homes to house welfare recipients. All beneficiaries would be required to live on campus and to participate in maintaining it based on their abilities. The campus would be sparsely, yet adequately, furnished and would provide food prepared in a communal kitchen. The cash allowance would be extremely limited, sufficient for only the barest of necessities (which, for the most part, already would be supplied on campus). There would be counselors available to assist with interviews and appropriately sponsored job training. Travel to and from such locations would be arranged by the counselor social workers using vouchers instead of cash.

48   This system would be managed by appropriate community boards. Its members—all volunteers—would be drawn from the community, industry, local government, clergy, and the judiciary. The government would pay 50 percent of the cost, the balance to be covered by regional utilities and local donations.

It's Time to Bring Back the Draft

What should be done about the military? The first thing to do is forget about the idea of a volunteer army. The United States must reintroduce the draft. The purpose of conscription is two-fold. There is an immediate problem with a generation that has grown up without discipline. The best thing America can do about it is to draft youths aged seventeen to twenty-one for a period of eighteen months to two years. Run them through military training and teach them what they didn't learn in school. The military could be used to handle works projects. After a certain number of months in initial basic training, a schedule could be set up allocating perhaps two days a week for military training, four days for production, and one day off.

The military also could be used for policing. If an area is out of control, like Los Angeles during the Rodney King riots, call in the Army. In New York, for example, the police don't have the numbers to cope with street crime. Hire the military. Have a soldier on every corner twenty-four hours a day. See how anxious street thugs are to mug someone when they see an armed soldier standing on the corner.

Congress has passed numerous law enforcement bills, many calling for more prisons, which already are draining too much revenue. Obviously, there is a great need to put away people who are dangerous to society. The numbers being seen now, though, in terms of percentage of the general population in prison, is very high, and they are costing society a fortune.

52   America's criminal justice system has several significant flaws. It fails to convey the impression that justice is done, that it is swift, and that it acts as a deterrent to potential perpetrators. Speed is essential to an effective system of justice. "Delay defeats equity" is a long-held maxim of law. It also is vital to remember the victim. At present, virtually no effort is made to compensate the victim. Adoption of the following will improve the situation:

- Abolish the jury system. It is time-consuming, expensive, allows for clever manipulation of jurors by attorneys, and suggests that, having heard and understood the evidence, judges are incapable of rendering a fair verdict.
- Establish a court of petty/small crimes that can deal swiftly with many of the lesser cases in a manner similar to small claims court.
- Require mandatory sentencing for violent crimes without parole.
- Institute capital punishment for all deliberate murders. A death sentence should be subject to immediate priority appeals and then followed right away by execution. Keeping inmates on death row for years is immoral, cruel, and wasteful.
- Enact caning or birching for thieves. Besides being a just punishment, it will avoid clogging up the prison system.
- Make prison labor tougher. Prisoners should be made to work long and hard as part of their sentence. The soft and easy jobs presently offered do not make jail a place to avoid at any cost. The proceeds from this labor should pay for prisoner upkeep, and the balance should be turned over to crime victims as partial compensation.
- Community service sentences need to be stricter. Whenever criminals today are sentenced to community service, it usually means some cushy job with the Red Cross or similar agency. Let community service provide meaningful work for a city or state agency, such as sanitation, road repair, graffiti scrubbing, etc. Any wages earned would help compensate victims.
- Lower the age for adult crime. Anyone fourteen years old and up should be treated as an adult. Children below that age should be limited to a flogging (under appropriate medical supervision).

America needs a better way to educate the nation's youth; a revamped military system; vastly altered social services; a slimmed down, more efficient bureaucracy; a stronger, more caring family unit; and a revitalized economy with no income taxes that nevertheless generates enough revenue to erase the deficit almost overnight. Will any of it happen, and, if it did, would society's ills be cured? If America is to be saved, we must try.

PERSONAL RESPONSE

What is your response to Barrett and Rowe's assertion in their first paragraph that "American youth is poisoned with skewed values and a lack of respect"?

QUESTIONS FOR CLASS OR SMALL-GROUP DISCUSSION

1. Discuss the authors' contention that America's abandonment of decency and discipline and its adoption of liberalism have led to an "institutionalized selfishness" (paragraph 2). Do you think their examples in the opening section are ample evidence of "skewed values and a lack of respect"? Do you agree that Americans are, in general, a selfish people? How do Barrett and Rowe connect this allegation with the gun-control issue?

2. Summarize the complaints Barrett and Rowe lodge against American society. Which ones do you support? Which ones do you question? Explain your answers.

3. What do you think of the solution Barrett and Rowe propose for the drug problem in America? Do you favor legalization of drugs? If so, would you legalize all or just some drugs? Explore the pros and cons of this issue.

4. Do you agree with Barrett and Rowe that "there has to be a total revolution in this country in attitudes and outlook" (paragraph 30)? Explain why or why not. Do you agree with the changes they call for, or would you suggest others?

5. How do you feel about Barrett and Rowe's proposal that America bring back the draft and the uses to which they propose putting the military?

6. What do you think of the solutions Barrett and Rowe propose for the high crime rate in this country? Which would you favor? Do any seem extreme to you?

○ PERSPECTIVES ON CRIMINAL BEHAVIOR ○

Suggested Writing Topics

1. Argue for or against capital punishment, drawing on Joshua Green's "Deadly Compromise" and/or John O'Sullivan's "Deadly Stakes: The Debate over Capital Punishment" where appropriate.

2. Write an essay on a topic suggested by Gary Kleck's "There Are No Lessons to be Learned from Littleton," such as the effects of the way news media report school violence or what he says about adolescent boys and violence.

3. Select one specific aspect of the problem of crime and violence in America. Write a paper assessing the seriousness of the problem you choose and offering possible solutions, to the degree that you can identify possible solutions.

4. Select any of the readings in the chapter and write a critique of or response to it.

5. Argue for or against the legalization of certain drugs, such as marijuana.

6. Argue for or against reinstating the draft in America.

7. Argue for or against stricter gun control laws, taking into consideration what Gary Kleck says about that subject.

8. Respond to the allegation by Wayne M. Barrett and Bernard Rowe in "What's Wrong with America?" that American young people are disrespectful and lack values.

9. Select any of the complaints about America that Wayne M. Barrett and Bernard Rowe make in "What's Wrong with America?" and respond by explaining the extent to which you agree with them. For instance, consider any of these statements: "America has institutionalized selfishness" (paragraph 3);

"Everywhere there is unbridled freedom bordering on license" (paragraph 6); "[America's] work ethic has suffered" (paragraph 7); "[L]awsuit mania has gripped America" (paragraph 14); America's drug problem "can be traced back to a lack of discipline, lack of education, lack of knowledge between right and wrong" (paragraph 18).

10. Conduct a classroom forum on the problem of inner-city violence. In preparation, decide what aspects of the problem you want to address in the forum and from which perspectives you will examine the problem. Consider including the perspectives of law-enforcement officers, sociologists, behavioral scientists, educators, and social workers. For a writing assignment, examine one aspect of the problem of inner-city violence and offer solutions for it, taking into consideration two or more of the essays in this chapter.

Research Topics

1. In paragraph 3 of "There Are No Lessons to Be Learned from Littleton," Gary Kleck catalogues a list of problems that are often mentioned when looking for something to blame for school shootings. These include the availability and ease of accessing guns, school cliques, lax parental supervision, bullying in schools, lax school security, lack of religion in schools, the Internet, neo-Naziism, and Satanism, among others. Select one of those subjects as a beginning point for research, framing your questions and narrowing your focus as you read and discover more about your subject.

2. Research recent statistics on serious crimes such as armed robbery, rape, murder, and assault with a deadly weapon and argue ways to reduce the rates of these violent crimes in America.

3. Research the controversy over gun control and arrive at your own position on the subject.

4. Argue for or against the legalization of marijuana, using source materials to support your argument.

5. Research the social conditions at the root of crime in America.

6. Research the efficacy of capital punishment or life in prison as deterrents.

7. Research the subject of reform in the penal system and arrive at your own conclusion about the best way to proceed.

RESPONDING TO VISUALS

Ruth Snyder, the second woman electrocuted at Sing Sing prison in New York, January 12, 1928. The picture was taken by a Daily News *reporter who secretly took the snapshot at the moment Snyder was dying. For years afterward, witnesses were searched as they entered and asked to raise their hands during the execution to prevent pictures being taken. Source: 2002 Daily News LP*

1. This picture ran on the front page of the *Daily News* the day after it was taken and was so popular that the newspaper had to run an additional 750,000 copies. Why do you think the public was so interested in this picture?

2. What is your opinion of the reporter who sneaked the camera in and took the picture?

3. How might this picture be used to argue the position of those opposed to the death penalty?

4. How might this picture be used to argue the position of those who support the death penalty?

RESPONDING TO VISUALS

"In a community with guns, everyone's a target." Source: MRA for the Syracuse Partnership to Reduce Juvenile Gun Violence and the Rosamond Gifford Foundation. Photo by Chip East.

1. What is the message of this advertisement?
2. What details of the advertisement help convey its message?
3. What is the function of the bullet-ridden stop sign?
4. What audience is the advertisement aimed at? How effectively do you think the ad reaches that audience?

CHAPTER

(14)

GENDER AND SEX ROLES

Many people use the word *gender* interchangeably with the word sex, but the two have different meanings. Sex is a biological category; a person's sex—whether male or female—is genetically determined. On the other hand, gender refers to the socially constructed set of expectations for behavior based on one's sex. Masculinity and femininity are gender constructs whose definitions vary and change over time and with different cultures or groups within cultures. What is considered appropriate and even desirable behavior for men and women in one culture may be strongly inappropriate in another. Like other cultures, American culture's definitions of masculinity and femininity change with time, shaped by a number of influences, such as parental expectations, peer pressure, and media images. We are born either male or female, and most of us learn to behave in ways consistent with our society's expectations for that sex.

The first two essays look at sexual stereotyping and its effects on both males and females, although in vastly different ways. First, Megan Rosenfeld's "Reexamining the Plight of Young Males" argues that researchers should pay more attention to how boys are being raised. Noting that studies of the effects of sexual stereotyping on boys have long been neglected in deference to studies of girls, she quotes a number of authors and researchers who are starting to investigate the conflicting messages that boys get from parents, peers, and popular culture. Next, looking at just one small aspect of popular culture in "You Can Never Have Too Many," best-selling author Jane Smiley muses on the presence of Barbie dolls in her household as her daughters were growing up. Far from criticizing them for setting up an impossible model of femininity for impressionable young girls, Smiley sees Barbie dolls as aids to helping girls figure out who they are and what they want to be. "Barbies are all right with me," she says. Try to recall your early childhood, the toys you played with, the games you played, and your playmates. How accurately do Rosenfeld's and Smiley's observations match your own experiences or observations?

The focus of the chapter shifts to the subject of marriage with Howard Moody's "Sacred Rite or Civil Right?" Moody asserts that gay marriages show why we need to separate church and state. He gives a historical overview of the roles that both church and state have played in establishing the nature of heterosexual marriage, stressing the differences between the religious definition of marriage and the state's definition. At the heart of his essay is the question of what marriage is, so you may want to think about your own definition of marriage as you read the essay.

The chapter concludes with Whitney Mitchell's "Deconstructing Gender, Sex, and Sexuality as Applied to Identity." Mitchell objects to the way those terms are applied to individuals and believes that they "rob individuals of their dignity as human beings." As you read the essay, consider your feelings about being male or female, recalling especially situations when you were identified on the basis of that characteristic alone.

REEXAMINING THE PLIGHT OF YOUNG MALES

Megan Rosenfeld

Megan Rosenfeld, now a freelance writer, was for many years a Washington Post *staff writer. "Reexamining the Plight of Young Males" first appeared in the* Washington Post *on March 26, 1998.*

Two decades of study about the sexual stereotyping of girls is now inspiring a new subject for gender research: boys. Our boys are in trouble, say a vanguard of researchers, and it's time to pay attention to how we are raising them.

The case begins with numbers. Boy babies die in greater numbers in infancy, and are more fragile as babies than girls. Boys are far more likely than girls to be told they have learning disabilities, to be sent to the principal's office, to be given medication for hyperactivity or attention deficit disorder, to be suspended from high school, to commit crimes, to be diagnosed as schizophrenic or autistic. In adolescence, they kill themselves five times more often than girls do. In adulthood, they are being incarcerated at ever-increasing rates, abandoning families, and becoming more likely to be both the perpetrators and victims of violence.

Some psychologists and educators studying boys argue that because of the way we parent and educate boys, combined with biology and an overlay of popular culture, male children do not fully develop their capacity for emotional depth and complexity. As a result, they are less able than they need to be to navigate the turmoil of adolescence, to develop healthy adult relationships, in some cases to survive at all. While the simple hierarchy of male authority and dominance in our society is becoming obsolete, the men of tomorrow are not being trained for a world in which their traditional survival mechanisms—like physical strength, bluster and bullying—no longer prevail. Meanwhile, traditionally male virtues like courage and determination are too often neglected.

4   "An enormous crisis of men and boys is happening before our eyes without our seeing it. There's been an extraordinary shift in the plate tectonics of gender; everything we ever thought is open for examination," said Barney Brawer, a longtime educator. Brawer is managing the boys component of the Harvard Project on Women's Psychology, Boys' Development, and the Culture of Manhood, which is headed by Carol Gilligan, whose research helped shape the new understanding of girls. For two years the project has held a series of discussions and lectures, sponsored mothers-of-sons support groups, and designed research projects. The public interest in their work has taken the academics by surprise. "It's almost more than we can handle," Brawer said.

A few miles away in Newton, Mass., psychologist William S. Pollack is also worrying about boys and writing a book about them. So are Michael Thompson and Dan Kindlon, also psychologists, and consultants to all-boys schools in the Boston area. Publishers have forked over six-figure advances for these books, due out later this year, hoping to replicate the financial bonanza of Mary Pipher's bestseller on girls, *Reviving Ophelia*.

"We've become very clear about what we want for girls," Brawer said. "We are less clear about what we want for boys."

"Politically Incorrect"

"It's politically incorrect to be a boy," says the mother of an 18-month-old male. Boys are the universal scapegoats, the clumsy clods with smelly feet who care only about sports and mischief. They are seen as "toxic," says Pollack, creatures "who will infect girls with some kind of social cooties." But could it be they are just as much victims of gender stereotyping as girls have been? As their sisters grow up with more options and opportunities than they used to have, boys may be feeling the tightening noose of limited expectations, societal scorn and inadequate role models.

8   "Why is there always a bad boy in every one of my classes, every year, but no bad girls?" a second-grade girl asked Kindlon, who with Thompson is writing a book called *Raising Cain: Protecting the Emotional Life of Boys*. Thompson jokes that the subtitle of the book should really be "how to raise your son so he won't turn out like your husband."

"Our beliefs about maleness, the mythology that surrounds being male, has led many boys to ruin," writes Geoffrey Canada in the newly published *Reaching Up for Manhood: Transforming the Lives of Boys in America*. "The image of male as strong is mixed with the image of male as violent. Male as virile gets confused with male as promiscuous. Male as adventurous equals male as reckless. Male as intelligent often gets mixed with male as arrogant, racist, and sexist."

Said Pollack: "If girls were killing themselves in these numbers we'd recognize this as a public health issue in our society."

A survey on gender by the *Washington Post*, Henry J. Kaiser Family Foundation and Harvard University showed that most parents feel they treat their sons and daughters equally. Still, most parents know that Jack will heedlessly jump off just about anything or pick up a block and make it a gun, while 4-year-old Jill insists on wearing her party dress and wrapping her toy animals in blankets. But while Jill can keep or abandon party dresses as she wishes Jack is often forbidden a toy gun, or he's told repeatedly to sit down and stop running around.

12   A 16-year-old boy in Washington remembers his elementary school as a place without male teachers, where by sixth grade (age 11 or 12) boys were assumed to be the troublemakers. One day a girl sitting next to him made him laugh by sticking a pencil up her nose. When the teacher reprimanded him, the boy blamed his friend and her pencil antics. But the girl denied doing anything—and the teacher believed her and not him. She sent him to sit in the hall for lying. "That kind of thing happened all the time," he said. "It made me not respect teachers very much."

Barb Wilder-Smith is a Boston-area teacher who became interested in researching boys after she gave birth to two of them—and realized she didn't know much about them. Three years ago she took her then 5-year-old to buy a new bike. At the time, his favorite color was pink and he wanted a pink bike. She and her husband were content to let him make his own color choice.

"But the salesman said he couldn't have a pink bike, pink was a girl color, and he had to have a red or blue bike," Wilder-Smith said. "My son looked at him and said, 'That's ridiculous, colors aren't boys or girls, and pink is my favorite color.'"

The boy got his pink bike. But he was teased so much by other children, who called this 5-year-old gay, that he put a sign on his bicycle basket. It read:

I like pink.

I am still a boy.

I have a penis.

Now he is 8, and doesn't let anyone know he likes pink. It was the girls who hassled him about it most mercilessly. Girls who wear blue all the time.

Talking About Differences

16   Considerable trepidation surrounds this new interest in boys. Some parents are afraid that it's about having their boys grow up "to be sweet and nice and good," as Wilder-Smith put it, and will endanger their sons. Feminists of both genders worry that the hard-won changes that benefit girls will be pitted against newly defined needs of boys, and that the old canards about biology being destiny will come back from the near-dead. Some are resentful that attention is being directed toward boys when girls have had only "a nanosecond in the history of educational reform," as Gabrielle Lange wrote in the American Association of University Women magazine "Outlook." Researchers into boys' behavior fear they will be tagged as anti-female, and they tread cautiously into the politically and emotionally loaded field of gender study.

"For 30 years it has been politically unacceptable to talk about [neurological or biological] differences," said Thompson, who has worked as a clinical psychologist with both coed and all-boys schools. But now, he and others note, the scientific community seems more willing to acknowledge that there are differences between males and females. The question is what the significance of these differences is.

Diane F. Halpern, a psychology professor at California State University in San Bernardino, recently surveyed current studies of differences between male and female intelligence. She found that women do better in tasks that test language abilities, fine motor tasks, perceptual speed, decoding nonverbal communication, and speech articulation. Men are superior in "visual working memory," tasks that require moving objects, aiming, fluid reasoning, knowledge of math, science and geography, and general knowledge. At the same time males have more mental retardation, attention deficit disorders, delayed speech, dyslexia, stuttering, learning disabilities and emotional disturbances.

Girls' brains are stronger in the left hemisphere, which is where language is processed, while boys' are more oriented to the right hemisphere, the spatial and physical center. Recent advances in brain study have shown that the two hemispheres are better connected in females, which may eventually explain why the genders show different patterns in cognitive tests.

20   "Boys' early experience of school is being beaten by girls at most things," Thompson said. "The first thing we do in school is make them read and sit still, two things they are generally not as good at."

Boys score better on achievement tests, but girls get better grades—another pattern that inspires all sorts of interpretations. Since boys are bigger risk-takers, perhaps they guess more on tests and by the law of averages get enough right answers. Halpern suggested that since most standardized tests are multiple choice, and female strength tends to be in writing, perhaps they lose out that way. Conversely, since sitting still, neatness and studiousness are rewarded in classroom grades, maybe boys are inadvertently penalized in that arena. It also has been demonstrated repeatedly that scores can change with the right training.

Boys and Learning

Why are so many more boys—six times more—diagnosed with learning disabilities? No one knows for sure, but there are some theories. One is that the standards for diagnosing LD are so loose that disruptive boys are classified to get them to special help and out of the classroom. "The system has shaped the definition rather than the other way around," said Ken Kavale, an expert in learning disabilities who teaches graduate school at the University of Iowa.

Douglas Fuchs, a professor at the Kennedy Center Institute on Education and Learning at Peabody College of Vanderbilt, thinks learning disabilities are over-diagnosed and may be related to early language differences. Millions of boys are now taking Ritalin to treat attention deficit and hyperactivity.

24   No one questions that many boys are legitimately learning disabled—neurolog-ically mis-wired in ways that make traditional learning difficult. But there may be other factors that affect a boy's ability to be successful in school.

Pollack's theory, based on his years of research and clinical practice, is that many boys' problems are rooted in a too-early separation from their mother's nurturing. While boy babies start out with a wider emotional range—more sounds, expressions and wails—parents tend to give them less adoring interaction after about the age of 6 months, he says. Even though boy babies are more physically fragile, he believes that adults tend to think of them as being bigger and tougher, and also to soothe them into quietness rather than try to understand their noise. Boys are so traumatized by this "disruption of their early holding environment" that they harden up and with-draw, which has repercussions for the rest of their lives, Pollack suggests.

Another question is whether we have failed to appreciate the language of boys because so much of it is either violent in imagery or oblique in approach. Wilder-Smith recalled getting a note from one of the 5-year-old boys whose fantasy play-acting she recorded for a year in a Boston school.

"Have a Hindenburg Exploding Life!" the boy Tyler wrote. Wilder-Smith wasn't sure at first if this note was meant affectionately; after she thought about it she realized it was. It just wasn't her kind of language. But she has come to believe that what appears to be violent play or imagery to a woman may be a valuable tool to a boy, his way of conquering fear and his smallness in the universe. Removing that out-let may end up making boys more violent rather than less, she thinks.

28   Barney Brawer likes to use the example of a Vermont farmer working on a bro-ken tractor. His son may spend the day at his side, and yet they may exchange no more than a dozen words. But the son has seen a great deal—perseverance, problem solv-ing (or trying to), engine repair. "We've lost a lot of that kind of communicating," he says.

Boys exhibit different signs of depression, says Pollack, whose book *Real Boys: Rescuing Our Sons from the Myths of Boyhood* will be published later this year. Thus we often fail to recognize them because they are not as evident as the symptoms com-mon to girls—who in adolescence and adulthood are diagnosed with depression at far higher rates than males. "Our view of depression has been feminized," he said. "Boys may have a moody withdrawal rather than tears."

After spending a year observing in a Boston public school, Wilder-Smith is among those who think we may need to reevaluate our attitudes about boy aggression and action. Too often, she suspects, the mothers and female teachers who statistically spend the most time with young boys believe that the key to producing a nonviolent adult is to remove all conflict—toy weapons, wrestling and shoving, imaginary explosions and crashes—from a boy's life.

"I've watched teachers who have the rule with creative writing that there's 'no killing in stories,'" she said. "One boy said, 'But the bad guy! He has to die somehow!' Finally the teacher said the bad guy could die, and allowed him to be run over by a truck. . . . They can't draw it [violence], they can't write about it, they can't act it out."

32   "We do take away a lot of the opportunity to do things boys like to do," said Carol Kennedy, a school principal in Missouri with 34 years' experience in education. "That is be rowdy, run and jump and roll around. We don't allow that." Educator Vivian Gussin Paley once put a running track in her kindergarten classroom. The girls ran around it in laps. The boys chased each other. They all seemed to like it.

Mass media ill-serve both genders, researchers say. Many believe that violence on television encourages aggressive behavior in boys and girls, but they have no conclusive proof of a connection. There is more evidence backed up by teachers that television has encouraged shorter attention spans and a need for artificial excitement. While girls are surrounded by television shows and books in which boys are almost always the protagonist, the hero and the main ingredient, boys rarely get a positive cultural message that it's okay to be afraid or sad, to not be athletic, to have a girl for a friend, or to enjoy writing poetry.

New Pressures

It is no secret that modern life has produced a new style of childhood. But some aspects of contemporary life may exact particular hardships for boys that are rarely acknowledged by those in authority.

For example, divorce in many cases not only removes a boy's primary role model from his daily life, it often brings additional burdens from his mother. He becomes the "man of the family," a role he is generally not prepared to handle. School principals dealing with boys who are sent to their office with behavior problems are finding that many of them are in this situation.

36   "The responsibilities most of our young boys are having placed on them is different than ever before," said principal Kennedy. "Mother is sharing things with that boy that almost makes him a partner rather than a son. . . . We find that even in elementary school, when a boy is taking on the role of being the major babysitter, he is often paying more attention to what happens at home than at school. It's more of a boy problem because a mother can see the boy as head of household, or man of the family, and doesn't tend to do that with a girl."

Unsupervised play is another issue—the lack of it, that is. Researchers like Brawer suspect that while too many hours are being idled away alone, indoors, in front of a television set, too few are being spent outdoors in time-honored games of exploration, mock warfare, fort building, sneaking around, inventing ball games and so forth. Because many parents today are legitimately afraid of criminals and bad drivers careening down neighborhood streets, boys—and girls—are rarely allowed the freedom to investigate and master their home turf in a way that once provided a rehearsal for the real world.

So the questions mount. Brawer, who is writing a dissertation on Attention Deficit and Hyperactivity Disorder, notes that in the 1,700 studies on the subject that he has found, the word "father" is mentioned only three times. "The neurobiological crowd doesn't believe in Freudian language," he said. "But if you look at the conditions under which kids are more or less likely to have problems, the indicators go way down when the father is in the home. This is an area we need to study."

What messages do mothers inadvertently send when they recoil from their son's wish to have a toy gun or his desire to be a ballerina for Halloween? How do fathers restrict a boy's emotional vocabulary when they say "big boys don't cry"? Should some boys, as Thompson and Kindlon suggest, start school at 8 rather than 5 or 6 years of age?

40   "It may still be a man's world, but it's not a boy's," Pollack said. "He's been sat on so long he'll push to keep the dominance. Recognizing boys' pain is the way to change society."

PERSONAL RESPONSE

Select a statement, example, or reference in this essay that particularly impressed you, either favorably or unfavorably, and respond to or explore it.

QUESTIONS FOR CLASS OR SMALL-GROUP DISCUSSION

1. Where does Rosenfeld state her thesis? Are you persuaded that her argument is valid?

2. How effective do you find the anecdote about the little boy wanting a pink bicycle in supporting Rosenfeld's position? What do you think of her other evidence?

3. Do your own experiences and observations bear out Rosenfeld's comment, "As their sisters grow up with more options and opportunities than they used to have, boys may be feeling the tightening noose of limited expectations, society scorn, and inadequate role models" (paragraph 7). What examples or anecdotes can you provide that support or refute that statement?

4. How effective do you find Rosenfeld's concluding paragraphs, especially her implications about the role of fathers? Can you suggest any answers to the questions she asks in the next-to-last paragraph?

YOU CAN NEVER HAVE TOO MANY

JANE SMILEY

Jane Smiley is the author of many novels, including The Greenlanders *(1988),* A Thousand Acres *(1991),* Moo *(1995),* The All-True Travels and Adventures of Lidie Newton *(1998),* Horse Heaven

(2000), and Good Faith *(2003). She published a memoir,* A Year at the Race: Reflections on Horses, Humans, Love, Money, and Luck, *in 2004. This essay was first published in a collection of essays entitled* The Barbie Chronicles, *edited by Yona Zeldis McDonough (1999).*

For my daughter's sixteenth birthday, my six-year-old son wanted to give her a Barbie. I greatly guided him toward the Rapunzel Barbie, whose hair was so long that her head was cocked backward on her neck, or the Birthday Wishes Barbie, in a massive organdy skirt. The one he finally chose was Baywatch Barbie. Okay, she had a dolphin with her. I am willing to admit that that might have been the draw. But you know, Barbies are all right with me. I may have had more Barbies pass through my house than anyone. I like to think so.

I was slightly too old for Barbie myself when they first came out in 1959—I was more of a stuffed-animal girl, anyway—so my first real Barbie experience came when my now–twenty-year-old daughter was three. My First Barbie came home, and was disrobed. The clothes were lost. I spent the required amount of time deploring Barbie's proportions and coloring and the fact that her feet can wear only high heels. Barbie could not have been shaped more differently from me, or have a more different *weltanschauung* from mine, but, hey, here she came with all her stuff.

The one I still remember most fondly was Twirly Curls Barbie. Like Rapunzel Barbie, Twirly Curls Barbie had a serious neck problem because of the weight of her hair. But she came with an intriguing pink-and-cream machine that attached to the ends of a couple of hanks of hair and twisted them together in a chignon. The catch was that the hair had to be neatly combed for the machine to work, an impossible task for a four-year-old, so I spent a lot of time combing the doll until I gave up. My daughters were not in the habit of shaving their Barbies' heads, but they could have. It's a good idea.

4   Both my girls went through periods where they would wear only pink and purple. I chalk this up to the Barbie influence. Both of them learned how to put on makeup before kindergarten. Lucy could apply lipstick with her eyes closed by the time she was five.

I don't wear makeup. Nor do I have any gowns, bikinis, pink high heels, floral accessories or feminine furniture (like a dressing table or a pink chaise longue). There are no blonds in my family. I could never wear short shorts or feather boas or halter tops. In other words, if my daughters were to learn certain Hollywood-inspired essentials of American womanhood, it wasn't going to be from me, but from Barbie.

And so the Barbies came through the house in a flood. And I am here to tell you that Doctor Barbie was not one of them. Frilly, sexy, pink, purple, bedizened and bejeweled were the preferred Barbies at my house, the more rhinestones the better. We had dozens, because, frankly, Barbies are cheap in more ways than one. My daughters had three mothers: me; their stepmother, who was not unlike me stylistically; and Barbie.

A friend of mine (male) maintains that Barbies have such staying power because they are the only anatomically adult dolls available, and children can manipulate and control them as they cannot the other adults in their lives. But I think girls like Barbie because through her they can try on a no-holds-barred, all-stops-out model of femininity, and that is something they need to do, especially if their own mothers are more androgynous-looking and sober-dressing than Barbie can be. The more a girl is drawn to Barbie, the less she should be deprived of her, no matter what the child's mother's own values are. Longing is more likely to breed attachment than satisfaction is.

8   Finally, after seventeen years, the Barbies in my house went the way of all flesh. In their last year with us, they were subject to any number of tragic narratives, at least partly inspired by that disguised Barbie literature, *Sweet Valley High*. I discovered the older girls showing the younger girls how to bandage the Barbies with toilet paper (gruesomely decorated with red nail polish) when they happened to get into alcohol-related car crashes with Ken.

My older daughter wandered in the land of Barbie for many years—after all, Nancy Drew is a Barbie; Elizabeth and Jessica, the *Sweet Valley High* twins, are Barbies; Cinderella, Sleeping Beauty, and Beauty of *Beauty and the Beast* all are Barbies. The prettiest girl in school, always a blond, or so it seems, is a Barbie, too. All the blonds on TV and in the movies are Barbies. A girl has to have a Barbie doll in order to decide whether she herself wants to be a Barbie.

On one hand, she has the ever-present mom, who is wearing jeans, cutting her hair ever shorter, getting glasses at forty if not sooner, driving a dark-colored sedan, going to work or cleaning the house, or, worse, espousing all kinds of selfless values of hard work, charity, civic virtue, environmental responsibility.

On the other hand, she has the ever-present Barbie, a tireless consumer whose favorite color is pink, whose jeans are much harder to get on her than her ballet tutu, whose hair requires constant care, and who has more high heels than any First Lady of the Philippines who ever lived. Barbie represents, in every way, getting what you want when you want it, no matter who objects.

12   Just after she stopped reading *Sweet Valley High* and passed her Barbies down to her younger sister, my older daughter changed her views on her future. No longer did she plan to be a fashion consultant or a Hollywood movie star. No longer did beauty school attract her. She began to read authors like Sandra Cisneros and books like *Our Bodies, Ourselves*. She began her collection of all the works of U2, a band Barbie would never understand. She became socially conscious. She got to be the editor of her high-school newspaper, not because it was a status position, but because she had views she wanted to air on homophobia, the environment and women's rights.

Now she is planning to go to graduate school and law school and become an expert on women's health issues, perhaps adolescent health issues like anorexia and bulimia. She can go on for hours about women's problems with appearance and self image. Barbie should be proud. My daughter wouldn't have gotten here without her.

Have we ever known a Barbie who, in the end, was cherished? I don't think so. More than all the other dolls in the toy box, perhaps because she isn't cuddly or sweet, Barbie is meant to be fiddled with, thought about, manipulated, done to. All of this aids in a girl's making up her mind about who she is and what she wants. That Barbie is a genius.

PERSONAL RESPONSE

What is your opinion of Barbie dolls?

QUESTIONS FOR CLASS OR SMALL-GROUP DISCUSSION

1. Explain what you think Smiley means when she writes: "I spent the required amount of time deploring Barbie's proportions and coloring and the fact that her feet can wear only high heels" (paragraph 2).

2. What do you think Smiley means when she writes: "The more a girl is drawn to Barbie the less she should be deprived of her, no matter what the child's mother's own values are" (paragraph 7). Do you agree with her?

3. To what extent do you agree with Smiley when she writes: "A girl has to have a Barbie doll in order to decide whether she herself wants to be a Barbie" (paragraph 9)?

SACRED RITE OR CIVIL RIGHT?

HOWARD MOODY

Howard Moody is minister emeritus of Judson Memorial Church in New York City. Author of several books, including two with Arlene Carmen on abortion rights and prostitution and a collection of his essays, The God-Man of Galilee: Studies in Christian Living *(1983), he lectures, preaches, and writes often on issues of ethics and social policy. "Sacred Rite or Civil Right?" was first published in the July 5, 2004, issue of* The Nation.

If members of the church that I served for more than three decades were told I would be writing an article in defense of marriage, they wouldn't believe it. My reputation was that when people came to me for counsel about getting married, I tried to talk them out of it. More about that later.

We are now in the midst of a national debate on the nature of marriage, and it promises to be as emotional and polemical as the issues of abortion and homosexuality have been over the past century. What all these debates have in common is that they involved both the laws of the state and the theology of the church. The purpose of this writing is to suggest that the gay-marriage debate is less about the legitimacy of the loving relationship of a same-sex couple than about the relationship of church and state and how they define marriage.

In Western civilization, the faith and beliefs of Christendom played a major role in shaping the laws regarding social relations and moral behavior. Having been nurtured in the Christian faith from childhood and having served a lifetime as an ordained Baptist minister, I feel obligated first to address the religious controversy concerning the nature of marriage. If we look at the history of religious institutions regarding marriage we will find not much unanimity but amazing diversity—it is really a mixed bag. Those who base their position on "tradition" or "what the Bible says" will find anything but clarity. It depends on which "tradition" in what age reading from whose holy scriptures.

4   In the early tradition of the Jewish people, there were multiple wives and not all of them equal. Remember the story of Abraham's wives, Sara and Hagar. Sara couldn't get pregnant, so Hagar presented Abraham with a son. When Sara got angry with Hagar, she forced Abraham to send Hagar and her son Ishmael into the wilderness. In case Christians feel superior about their "tradition" of marriage, I would remind them that their scriptural basis is not as clear about marriage as we might hope. We have Saint Paul's conflicting and condescending words about the institution: "It's better not to marry." Karl Barth called this passage the Magna Carta of the single person. (Maybe we should have taken Saint Paul's advice more seriously. It might have prevented an earlier generation of parents from harassing, cajoling and prodding our young until they were married.) In certain religious branches, the church doesn't recognize the licensed legality of marriage but requires that persons meet certain religious qualifications before the marriage is recognized by the church. For members of the Roman Catholic Church, a "legal divorce" and the right to remarry may not be recognized unless the first marriage has been declared null and void by a decree of the church. It is clear that there is no single religious view of marriage and that history has witnessed some monumental changes in the way "husband and wife" are seen in the relationship of marriage.

In my faith-based understanding, if freedom of choice means anything to individuals (male or female), it means they have several options. They can be single and celibate without being thought of as strange or psychologically unbalanced. They can be single and sexually active without being labeled loose or immoral. Women can be single with child without being thought of as unfit or inadequate. If these choices had been real options, the divorce rate may never have reached nearly 50 percent.

The other, equally significant choice for people to make is that of lifetime commitment to each other and to seal that desire in the vows of a wedding ceremony. That understanding of marriage came out of my community of faith. In my years of ministry I ran a tight ship in regard to the performance of weddings. It wasn't because I didn't believe in marriage (I've been married for sixty years and have two wonderful offspring) but rather my unease about the way marriage was used to force people to marry so they wouldn't be "living in sin."

The failure of the institution can be seen in divorce statistics. I wanted people to know how challenging the promise of those vows was and not to feel this was something they had to do. My first question in premarital counseling was, "Why do you want to get married and spoil a beautiful friendship?" That question often elicited a thoughtful and emotional answer. Though I was miserly in the number of weddings I performed, I always made exceptions when there were couples who had difficulty finding clergy who would officiate. Their difficulty was because they weren't of the same religion, or they had made marital mistakes, or what they couldn't believe. Most of them were "ecclesiastical outlaws," barred from certain sacraments in the church of their choice.

8   The church I served had a number of gay and lesbian couples who had been to-gether for many years, but none of them had asked for public weddings or blessings on their relationship. (There was one commitment ceremony for a gay couple at the end of my tenure.) It was as though they didn't need a piece of paper or a ritual to symbolize their lifelong commitment. They knew if they wanted a religious cere-mony, their ministers would officiate and our religious community would joyfully witness.

It was my hope that since the institution of marriage had been used to exclude and demean members of the homosexual community, our church, which was open and affirming, would create with gays and lesbians a new kind of ceremony. It would be an occasion that symbolized, between two people of the same gender, a covenant of intimacy of two people to journey together, breaking new ground in human rela-tionships—an alternative to marriage as we have known it.

However, I can understand why homosexuals want "to be married" in the old-fashioned "heterosexual way." After all, most gays and lesbians were born of married parents, raised in a family of siblings; many were nourished in churches and syna-gogues, taught about a living God before Whom all Her creatures were equally loved. Why wouldn't they conceive their loving relationships in terms of marriage and fam-ily and desire that they be confirmed and understood as such? It follows that if these gays and lesbians see their relationship as faith-based, they would want a religious ceremony that seals their intentions to become lifelong partners, lovers and friends, that they would want to be "married."

Even though most religious denominations deny this ceremony to homosexual couples, more and more clergy are, silently and publicly, officiating at religious ritu-als in which gays and lesbians declare their vows before God and a faith community. One Catholic priest who defied his church's ban said: "We can bless a dog, we can bless a boat, but we can't say a prayer over two people who love each other. You don't have to call it marriage, you can call it a deep and abiding friendship, but you can bless it."

12   We have the right to engage in "religious disobedience" to the regulations of the judicatory that granted us the privilege to officiate at wedding ceremonies, and suffer the consequences. However, when it comes to civil law, it is my contention that the church and its clergy are on much shakier ground in defying the law.

In order to fully understand the conflict that has arisen in this debate over the nature of marriage, it is important to understand the difference between the religious definition of marriage and the state's secular and civil definition. The government's interest is in a legal definition of marriage—a social and voluntary contract between a man and woman in order to protect money, property and children. Marriage is a civil union without benefit of clergy or religious definition. The state is not interested in why two people are "tying the knot," whether it's to gain money, secure a dynasty or raise children. It may be hard for those of us who have a religious or romantic view of marriage to realize that loveless marriages are not that rare. Before the Pill, preg-nancy was a frequent motive for getting married. The state doesn't care what the com-mitment of two people is, whether it's for life or as long as both of you love, whether it's sexually monogamous or an open marriage. There is nothing spiritual, mystical or romantic about the state's license to marry—it's a legal contract.

Thus, George W. Bush is right when he says that "marriage is a sacred institution" when speaking as a Christian, as a member of his Methodist church. But as President of the United States and leader of all Americans, believers and unbelievers, he is wrong. What will surface in this debate as litigation and court decisions multiply is the history of the conflict between the church and the state in defining the nature of marriage. That history will become significant as we move toward a decision on who may be married.

After Christianity became the state religion of the Roman Empire in AD 325, the church maintained absolute control over the regulation of marriage for some 1,000 years. Beginning in the sixteenth century, English kings (especially Henry VIII, who found the inability to get rid of a wife extremely oppressive) and other monarchs in Europe began to wrest control from the church over marital regulations. Ever since, kings, presidents and rulers of all kinds have seen how important the control of marriage is to the regulation of social order. In this nation, the government has always been in charge of marriage.

16   That is why it was not a San Francisco mayor licensing same-sex couples that really threatened the President's religious understanding of marriage but rather the Supreme Judicial Court of Massachusetts, declaring marriage between same-sex couples a constitutional right, that demanded a call for constitutional amendment. I didn't understand how important that was until I read an op-ed piece in the *Boston Globe* by Peter Gomes, professor of Christian morals and the minister of Memorial Church at Harvard University, that reminds us of a seminal piece of our history:

> The Dutch made civil marriage the law of the land in 1590, and the first marriage in New England, that of Edward Winslow to the widow Susannah White, was performed on May 12, 1621, in Plymouth by Governor William Bradford, in exercise of his office as magistrate.
>   There would be no clergyman in Plymouth until the arrival of the Rev. Ralph Smith in 1629, but even then marriage would continue to be a civil affair, as these first Puritans opposed the English custom of clerical marriage as unscriptural. Not until 1692, when Plymouth Colony was merged into that of Massachusetts Bay, were the Clergy authorized by the new province to solemnize marriages. To this day in the Commonwealth the clergy, including those of the archdiocese, solemnize marriage legally as agents of the Commonwealth and by its civil authority. Chapter 207 of the General Laws of Massachusetts tells us who may perform such ceremonies.

Now even though it is the civil authority of the state that defines the rights and responsibilities of marriage and therefore who can be married, the state is no more infallible than the church in its judgments. It wasn't until the mid-twentieth century that the Supreme Court declared antimiscegenation laws unconstitutional. Even after that decision, many mainline churches, where I started my ministry, unofficially discouraged interracial marriages, and many of my colleagues were forbidden to perform such weddings.

The civil law view of marriage has as much historical diversity as the church's own experience because, in part, the church continued to influence the civil law. Although it was the Bible that made "the husband the head of his wife," it was common law that "turned the married pair legally into one person—the husband," as Nancy Cott documents in her book *Public Vows: A History of Marriage and the Nation* (an indispensable resource for anyone seeking to understand the changing nature of marriage in the nation's history). She suggests that "the legal doctrine of marital unity was called coverture . . . [which] meant that the wife could not use legal avenues such as suits or contracts, own assets, or execute legal documents without her husband's collaboration." This view of the wife would not hold water in any court in the land today.

As a matter of fact, even in the religious understanding of President Bush and his followers, allowing same-sex couples the right to marry seems a logical conclusion. If marriage is "the most fundamental institution of civilization" and a major contributor to the social order in our society, why would anyone want to shut out homosexuals from the "glorious attributes" of this "sacred institution"? Obviously, the only reason one can discern is that the opponents believe that gay and lesbian people are not worthy of the benefits and spiritual blessings of "marriage."

At the heart of the controversy raging over same-sex marriage is the religious and constitutional principle of the separation of church and state. All of us can probably agree that there was never a solid wall of separation, riddled as it is with breaches. The evidence of that is seen in the ambiguity of tax-free religious institutions, "in God we trust" printed on our money and "under God" in the Pledge of Allegiance to our country. All of us clergy, who are granted permission by the state to officiate at legal marriage ceremonies, have already compromised the "solid wall" by signing the license issued by the state. I would like to believe that my authority to perform religious ceremonies does not come from the state but derives from the vows of ordination and my commitment to God. I refuse to repeat the words, "by the authority invested in me by the State of New York, I pronounce you husband and wife," but by signing the license, I've become the state's "handmaiden."

20   It seems fitting therefore that we religious folk should now seek to sharpen the difference between ecclesiastical law and civil law as we beseech the state to clarify who can be married by civil law. Further evidence that the issue of church and state is part of the gay-marriage controversy is that two Unitarian ministers have been arrested for solemnizing unions between same-sex couples when no state licenses were involved. Ecclesiastical law may punish those clergy who disobey marital regulations, but the state has no right to invade church practices and criminalize clergy under civil law. There should have been a noisy outcry from all churches, synagogues and mosques at the government's outrageous contravention of the sacred principle of the "free exercise of religion."

I come from a long line of Protestants who believe in "a free church in a free state." In the issue before this nation, the civil law is the determinant of the regulation of marriage, regardless of our religious views, and the Supreme Court will finally decide what the principle of equality means in our Constitution in the third century of our life together as a people. It is likely that the Commonwealth of Massachusetts will probably lead the nation on this matter, as the State of New York led to the Supreme Court decision to allow women reproductive freedom.

So what is marriage? It depends on whom you ask, in what era, in what culture. Like all words or institutions, human definitions, whether religious or secular, change with time and history. When our beloved Constitution was written, blacks, Native Americans and, to some extent, women were quasi-human beings with no rights or privileges, but today they are recognized as persons with full citizenship rights. The definition of marriage has been changing over the centuries in this nation, and it will change yet again as homosexuals are seen as ordinary human beings.

In time, and I believe that time is now, we Americans will see that all the fears foisted on us by religious zealots were not real. Heterosexual marriage will still flourish with its statistical failures. The only difference will be that some homosexual couples will join them and probably account for about the same number of failed relationships. And we will discover that it did not matter whether the couples were joined in a religious ceremony or a secular and civil occasion for the statement of their intentions.

PERSONAL RESPONSE

Explain whether you believe that the issue of how marriage is defined by church and state is relevant to the issue of same-sex marriage.

QUESTIONS FOR CLASS OR SMALL-GROUP DISCUSSION

1. Locate Moody's central purpose and discuss whether you are persuaded that his position is valid.
2. What distinctions does Moody draw between the state's definition of marriage and that of the church?
3. To what extent are you convinced that "the state has no right to invade church practices and criminalize clergy under civil law" (paragraph 20)?
4. How would you answer the question, "So what is marriage?" (paragraph 22)?

DECONSTRUCTING GENDER, SEX, AND SEXUALITY AS APPLIED TO IDENTITY

WHITNEY MITCHELL

Whitney Mitchell of Nashville, Tennessee, received honorable mention in the thirteen-to-seventeen-year-old age category of the 2001 Humanist Essay Contest for Young Women and Men of North America for this essay. It was published in the July–August 2002 issue of The Humanist. The Humanist *is a social-issues–oriented bimonthly that applies the philosophy of Humanism to current matters of concern.*

By nature, we as humans have a need to identify ourselves and others in broad and exclusionary/inclusionary terms. But then, "human nature" is actually nothing more than human habit. Every set of standards that we as a society currently use to identify ourselves is coupled with an opposing set: good versus bad, female versus male, hetero versus homo. This system of duality in the everyday assessment of ourselves and those around us holds the power to rob individuals of their dignity as human beings.

What we must understand is that, just because an individual doesn't fit one set of standards, the individual doesn't then automatically fit the opposite standards. Specifically, the female/male binary is constructed as a natural occurrence and presumed to be unchangeable. However, intersexuality, by definition, offers clear evidence to the contrary. It serves as an opportunity to disprove the concepts of what is "natural" and to disrupt the hetero-normative systems of sex, gender, and sexuality. It presents the possibility of proving gender to be nothing more than something abstract and conceptual. Analyzing intersexuality therefore provides greater opportunities for individual liberty and social understanding.

Gender, as it stands, is currently defined by society in the simplest terms of female and male. However, gender only exists because our society, consciously or unconsciously, wills it to. What makes a woman is her specific social relation to a man, and what makes a man is his specific social relation to a woman. To refuse to be a woman, however, doesn't mean that one becomes a man. It only means that one refuses one's designated ideological, political, and economic characteristics as identity and thus refuses gender.

4   Therefore, if the class of "man" were to disappear, if it were no longer used, then the same would occur with the class of "woman." Gender would no longer be able to leave anyone behind, condemning them as sick or mentally ill for not fitting our standards. (Transgender identity and expression are the psychiatric classification under the Diagnostic Codes 302.3, transvestic fetishism; and 302.85, gender identity disorder.) Identity could exist independently of gender. However, because we continue to use gender classifications, people who don't identify with such labels are left in a state of confusion, with no language to use in claiming their own identities.

Our society commonly uses the equation gender = sex. This is a naive and oversimplified statement. It further categorizes individuals by way of black-and-white, unrealistic standards. It is difficult for most people to understand that individuals exist who identify as men with vaginas and women with penises. Therefore gender and sex aren't interchangeable terms. The difference is as simple as that between the mind and the body. Where gender is a device used for identification of the mind and emotions, sex is about biology and comfort within one's own body.

Here the concept of gender as changeable and subjective raises questions about sex reassignment surgery (SRS). However, just as the assumption that gender is the same as sex is naive, so is the assumption that a change in gender requires a change in sex as well. An individual born biologically female who, gender-wise, only feels comfortable identifying as male, doesn't necessarily desire SRS in order to become physically male. The individual's body could feel completely comfortable and right despite a discomfort with gender. Therefore the gender that an individual identifies with doesn't always indicate any information regarding the sex of the individual's body. This realization provides an alternative way of seeing individuals independent of society's standards.

By the same token, gender doesn't always indicate any information about an individual's sexuality. The existence of transgendered individuals and transsexual individuals promotes confusion regarding sexuality. Any speculation about the sexual orientation of a trans-individual is as ignorant as the speculation of the sexual orientation of any individual. Just as any individual identifying as male might be attracted to males or females, an individual having had male-to-female SRS may be attracted to males or females. Identification of sexual orientation occurs independently of gender or sex identification, despite whether such identifications change from those assigned at birth. Thus, gender identity is about comfort or discomfort within the established gender roles of society. Sex identity is about comfort within the body. And identification of sexual orientation is more about experiences outside of the self and the body; it isn't about comfort so much as it is about individual desire and attraction.

8   Now that we've clarified the differences between gender, sex, and sexuality, it is obvious why these terms are inefficient for identifying people. They tell us nothing about a person because they are all noninclusive concepts created by humans out of convenience and discomfort. Personally, I've found that the less I use these terms to identify myself, the more comfortable with myself I become and the less I feel the need to identify at all. Thus, not really identifying with any current social role allows for a new liberation uninhibited by the standards of others. As the poet Eileen Myles said: "If we don't define who we are, we are everything. Once we define ourselves, we are nothing."

PERSONAL RESPONSE

Did your parents or care givers treat you differently on the basis of your sex? Were you assigned a "gender identity" that you were comfortable with?

QUESTIONS FOR CLASS OR SMALL-GROUP DISCUSSION

1. What assumptions about the traditional definitions of sex, gender, and sexuality does Mitchell object to?

2. In the conclusion, Mitchell writes that "it is obvious why these terms [gender, sex, and sexuality] are inefficient for identifying people." Is it clear to you? Has Mitchell fully clarified that the differences among those three terms clearly demonstrated their inefficiency for identifying people? Does Mitchell's use of the abstract concept "comfort" to distinguish among those terms help clarify those definitions for you?

3. Do you think it possible for any society, but especially American society, to do away with assigning sex roles? How possible do you think it would be to raise a child not to be conscious of gender? What advantages and disadvantages do you see in having a "genderless" society?

○ PERSPECTIVES ON GENDER AND SEX ROLES

Suggested Writing Topics

1. Read any of the books that Megan Rosenfeld mentions in "Reexamining the Plight of Young Males" and write a critique of it.

2. Explain why you agree or disagree with the opinions in Jane Smiley's "You Can Never Have Too Many."

3. Define "marriage," taking into account Howard Moody's article "Sacred Rite or Civil Right?"

4. Write an essay defining and distinguishing among the terms "sex," "gender," and "sexuality," as Whitney Mitchell does in "Deconstructing Sex, Gender, and Sexuality as Applied to Identity."

5. Drawing on two or more of the essays in this chapter, write a reflective essay in which you explore your own concepts of masculinity and femininity (and perhaps androgyny) and the way in which that concept has shaped the way you are today.

6. Consider to what degree you think that sex determines destiny.

7. Conduct an investigative analysis of any of the following for their depiction of female and male sex roles: fairy tales, children's stories, advertising images, music videos, television programs, or film. Do you find stereotyped assumptions about masculinity and femininity? In what ways do you think the subject of your analysis reinforces or shapes cultural definitions of masculinity and femininity?

8. Examine media images for the ways in which gays and lesbians are portrayed. Focus on a particular medium, such as print advertisements, television situation comedies, or film.

9. Explore ways in which you would like to see definitions of masculinity and femininity changed. How do you think relationships between the sexes would be affected if those changes were made?

10. Write a personal narrative recounting an experience in which you felt you were being treated unfairly or differently from persons of the other sex. What was the situation, how did you feel, and what did you do about it?

11. Explain the degree to which you consider gender issues to be important. Do you think too much is made of gender? Does it matter whether definitions of masculinity and femininity are rigid?

12. Argue the case for or against same-sex marriage to an audience of judges sitting on a state's Supreme Court, trying to decide whether to legalize it.

Research Topics

1. Research the history of the contemporary women's movement, the men's movement, or the gay rights movement in America and report on its origins, goals, and influence. You will very likely have to narrow your scope,

depending on the time you have for the project and the nature of your purpose.

2. Research the subject of bisexuality, making sure to include differing viewpoints, and then explain your own viewpoint on the topic, supporting your position with relevant source materials.

3. Through research and interviews, write a paper on some aspect of the gay and lesbian experience in America.

4. Research the subject of sex-role stereotyping in books, movies, or other media.

5. Research the shifting views of both the church and the state on marriage. You may want to begin with Nancy Cott's *Public Vows: A History of Marriage and the Nation* that Howard Moody recommends in "Sacred Rite or Civil Right?"

6. Update the statistics used by Megan Rosenfeld in "Reexamining the Plight of Young Males" and conduct research that seeks to support or refute her contention that male children "are less able than they need to be to navigate the turmoil of adolescence, to develop healthy adult relationships, in some cases survive at all" (paragraph 3).

RESPONDING TO VISUALS

Two vegetarian Playboy centerfolds promote meat-free hot dogs for People for the Ethical Treatment of Animals (PETA). Source: Robert Sebree/Getty Images

1. PETA's goal is to prevent the abuse of animals. How well do you think this poster promotes that goal?
2. How does the poster use sex to convey its message?
3. Why is one of the women posed so closely to the grill?

RESPONDING TO VISUALS

These two women, who have been together for 51 years, embrace after their marriage at City Hall. They were the first legally married same-sex couple in San Francisco. Gay marriages were later voided by the California State Supreme Court. Source: Liz Mangelsdorf/San Francisco Chronicle/CORBIS

1. What comment does the photographer make by selecting for his subject an older couple who have been together for 51 years?
2. In what way does this photograph get at the heart of the issue of gay marriage?
3. How do the facial expressions and body language of both the married couple and their witnesses reveal the emotional nature of the event?

CHAPTER

(15)

RACE AND ETHNICITY IN AMERICA

Racial or ethnic heritage is as important to shaping identity as are sex and social class. One's race or ethnicity can also influence quality of life, educational opportunity, and advancement in employment. American society has a long history of struggling to confront and overcome racism and discrimination on the basis of ethnic heritage. Beginning well before the Civil War, American antislavery groups protested the enslavement of African Americans and worked to abolish slavery in all parts of the country. Other groups besides African Americans have experienced harsh treatment and discrimination solely because of their color or ethnic heritage.

These groups include Chinese men brought to America to help construct a cross-country railroad in the nineteenth century, European immigrants who came to America in large numbers near the end of the nineteenth century in search of better lives than

they could expect in their homelands, Japanese men who came in the twentieth century to work at hard labor for money to send home, and Latinos/Latinas and Hispanics
migrating north to America. As a result of the heightened awareness of the interplay of
race, class, and gender, schools at all levels, from elementary through postgraduate,
have incorporated course materials on race, class, and/or gender or created whole
courses devoted to those important components of individual identities and histories.

The chapter begins with George Henderson's "Race in America," which provides a
succinct historical overview of immigration to America. Henderson maintains that
America has never truly been a melting pot and that its history has always been composed of migrants, immigrants, and slaves. Observing that America is "at a crossroads
in its race relations," Henderson reviews several options for where we can go from here.
Following Henderson's piece is the first article in a series by the *Washington Post* on the
effects of recent increases in the numbers of immigrants on American life today and in
the future. William Booth in "One Nation, Indivisible: Is It History?" contrasts the effects
of the first great wave of immigration to America in the period between 1890 and 1920
with the recent second great wave of immigration, as he explores the question of
whether America is truly a "melting pot." As you read his article, keep in mind the question posed by its title and consider whether you think, as the writer implies, that the
concept of America as a single, indivisible nation is soon to be a matter of history, not
fact.

The next two essays take as their subjects specific American groups, Hispanics and
blacks, and the difficulties they encounter living in a predominantly white society. In
"Hispanics and the American Dream," Linda Chavez writes fervently of the particular
strengths of Hispanics in America. She argues that "policy prescriptions offered by many
Hispanic advocacy organizations and most politicians seem oddly out of sync," charging
that current policies perpetuate demeaning stereotypes. Alex Kotlowitz, in "Colorblind,"
focuses on two towns across the river from one another, "whose only connections are
two bridges and a powerful undertow of contrasts." As he researched the circumstances
surrounding the death of a black teenager, Kotlowitz discovered a history of racial hostility between the two towns. His interviews with both blacks and whites led him to conclude that only when the members of both groups question their own perspectives can
they learn to understand each other. "It's all about perspective," he insists.

The final reading in this chapter addresses the subject of affirmative action. In "How
Much Diversity Do You Want from Me?" Perry Bacon, Jr., comments on a Supreme

Court opinion by Justice Sandra Day O'Connor, in which she remarks on the " 'unique experience of being a racial minority'." Bacon, Jr., explains that her "diversity rationale" puts tremendous pressure on minorities to "deliver diversity." He raises some interesting questions about what it means to belong to a racial minority as he explains some of the situations he has personally experienced.

RACE IN AMERICA
George Henderson

George Henderson is Director of Advanced Studies and reformer Dean of the College of Liberal Arts at the University of Oklahoma, where he is also a professor of human relations, education, and sociology. Henderson has served as a race-relations consultant to many national and international organizations. He is the author of more than 70 articles and 29 books, including Cultural Diversity in the Workplace *(1994);* Social Work Interventions: Helping People of Color *(1994);* Migrants, Immigrants and Slaves *(1995);* Human Relations Issues in Management *(1996);* Our Souls to Keep: Black/White Relations in America *(1999); and* Ethnicity and Substance Abuse *(2002). He also co-edited, with Grace Xuequin Ma,* Rethinking Ethnicity and Health Care: A Sociocultural Perspective *(1999). This essay appeared in a special issue on race in America in the Spring 2000 issue of* National Forum.

Because of intermarriage, most Americans have multiple ethnic and racial identities. Some persons of mixed lineage prefer to assume culturally nondescript identities. For example, they have become "white people," "black people," "Indians," "Latinos," "Asians," or just plain "Americans" in order to somehow deflect from themselves any connection with their ancestors. The task of tracing their families has become too taxing or too insignificant. Even so, the effects of ethnicity and race are pervasive: disparate patterns of community relationships and economic opportunities haunt us. At some time in their history, all ethnic groups in the United States have been the underclass. Also, at different times, all ethnic groups have been both the oppressed and the oppressors.

Ethnicity is the most distinguishing characteristic of Americans, where we are sorted primarily on the basis of our cultural identities or nationalities. An ethnic group is a culturally distinct population whose members share a collective identity and a common heritage. Historically, the overwhelming majority of ethnic groups emerged in the United States as a result of one of several responses to the following processes: (1) migration, (2) consolidation of group forces in the face of an impending threat from an aggressor, (3) annexation or changes in political boundary lines, or

(4) schisms within a church. Hence, "ethnic minority" presupposes people different from the mainstream or dominant cultured persons.

But it is the erroneous belief that people who come to America can be placed in categories based on their unique gene pools that has resulted in the most blatant instances of discrimination. Races, however defined, do not correspond to genetic reality because inbreeding world populations share a common gene pool. A much more practical dictum, and one that has often been ignored throughout American history, is that all people belong to the same species. Unfortunately, too few individuals believe that the only race of any significance is the human race.

A Brief History

4   At the time of the American Revolution, the American population was largely composed of English Protestants who had absorbed a substantial number of German and Scotch-Irish settlers and a smaller number of French, Dutch, Swedes, Poles, Swiss, Irish, and other immigrants. The colonies had a modest number of Catholics, and a smaller number of Jews. Excluding Quakers and Swedes, the colonists treated Native Americans with contempt and hostility, and engaged in wars against them that bordered on genocide. They drove natives from the coastal plains in order to make way for a massive white movement to the West. Although Africans, most of whom were slaves, comprised one-fifth of the American population during the Revolution, they, similar to Indians, were not perceived by most white colonists as being worthy of assimilation.

The white peoples of the new nation had long since crossed Caucasian lines to create a conglomerate but culturally homogeneous society. People of different ethnic groups—English, Irish, German, Huguenot, Dutch, Swedish—mingled and intermarried. English settlers and peoples from western and northern Europe had begun a process of ethnic assimilation that caused some writers to incorrectly describe the nation as melted into one ethnic group: American. In reality, nonCaucasian Americans were not included in the Eurocentric cultural pot.

During the 150 years immediately following the Revolution, large numbers of immigrants came to the United States from eastern European countries. They were the so-called "new immigrants." During the latter part of that period, slaves were emancipated, numerous Indian tribes were conquered and forced to relocate to reservations, portions of Mexico's land were taken, and Asians began emigrating to the United States. The English language and English-oriented cultural patterns grew even more dominant. Despite a proliferation of cultural diversity within the growing ethnic enclaves, Anglo-conformity ideology spawned racist notions about Nordic and Aryan racial superiority. This ideology gave rise to nativist political agendas and exclusionist immigration policies favoring western and northern European immigrants.

Non-English-speaking western Europeans and northern Europeans were also discriminated against. The slowness of some of those immigrants, particularly Germans, to learn English, their tendency to live in enclaves, and their establishment of ethnic-language newspapers were friction points. Such ethnic-oriented lifestyles prompted many Americanized people to chide: "If they don't like it here, they can go back to where they came from." But that solution was too simplistic. Immigrants from all countries and cultures, even those who were deemed socially and religiously undesirable, were needed to help build a nation—to work the farms, dig the ore, build the railroads and canals, settle the prairies, and otherwise provide human resources.

8   Beginning in the 1890s, immigrants from eastern and southern Europe were numerically dominant. That set the stage for racist statements about inferior, darker people threatening the purity of blond, blue-eyed Nordics or Aryans through miscegenation. Intermixture was perceived as a deadly plague. Although the immigrants from eastern and southern Europe were not suitable marriage partners, their critics stated, they could be properly assimilated and amalgamated. This kind of ethnocentrism prevented large numbers of other immigrants and indigenous peoples of color from becoming fully functioning citizens. And the legacy for the children of people denied equal opportunities was second-class citizenship. We can easily document the negative effects of second-class citizenship: abhorrent inequalities, unwarranted exclusions, and atmospheres of rejection.

Immigrants who lived in remote, isolated areas were able to maintain some semblance of being ethnic nations within America. But the growth of cities brought about the decline of farming populations and ethnic colonies. A short time was required for the white immigrants who settled in cities to discard their native languages and cultures. But it is erroneous to think of any ethnic group as melting away without leaving a trace of its cultural heritage. All ethnic groups have infused portions of their cultures into the tapestry of American history.

Early twentieth-century eastern European immigrants were a very disparate mixture of peoples. They came from nations that were trying to become states—Poland, Czechoslovakia, Lithuania, and Yugoslavia; from states trying to become nations—Italy, Turkey, and Greece; and from areas outside the Western concept of either state or nation. All of them included people such as Jews who did not easily fit into any of those categories. Through social and educational movements, laws, and superordinate goals such as winning wars and establishing economic world superiority, eastern Europeans and other white ethnic groups were able to enter mainstream America.

The cultures and colors of Third World ethnic groups were in stark contrast to European immigrants. Those differences became obstacles to assimilation and, more importantly, to people of color achieving equal opportunities. Nonwhite groups in the United States occupied specific low-status niches in the workplace, which in turn resulted in similarities among their members in such things as occupations, standard of living, level of education, place of residence, access to political power, and quality of health care. Likenesses within those groups facilitated the formation of stereotypes and prejudices that inhibited the full citizenship of nonwhite minorities.

12   Immigrants who held highly esteemed occupations—lawyers, artists, engineers, scientists, and physicians—became Americanized much faster than those who held less esteemed positions—unskilled laborers, farm workers, coal miners, and stock clerks. But even in those instances there were pro-European biases and stereotypes. For example, French chefs, Italian opera singers, Polish teachers, German conductors, and Russian scientists were more highly recruited than Africans, Hispanics, and Asians who had the same skills. Racial and quasi-racial groups—including American Indians, Mexican Americans, Asian Americans, African Americans, and Puerto

Ricans—were not nearly so readily absorbed as various Caucasian ethnic groups. And that is generally the situation today. Despite numerous and impressive gains during the past century, a disproportionate number of peoples of color are still treated like pariahs.

What Does the Future Hold?

If U.S. Census Bureau population projections are correct, our nation is undergoing mind-boggling demographic changes: Hispanics will triple in numbers, from 31.4 million in 1999 to 98.2 million in 2050; blacks will increase 70 percent, from 34.9 million to 59.2 million; Asians and Pacific Islanders will triple, from 10.9 million to 37.6 million; Native Americans and Alaska Natives will increase from approximately 2.2 million to 2.6 million. During the same period, the non-Hispanic white population will increase from 196.1 million to 213 million. Also, the foreign-born population, most of them coming from Asia and Latin America, will increase from 26 million to 53.8 million. The non-Hispanic white population will decrease from 72 percent of the total population in 1999 to 52 percent in 2050, and the nation's workforce will be composed of over 50 percent racial and ethnic minorities and immigrants. Who then will be the pariahs?

Without equal opportunities, the melting pot will continue to be an unreachable mirage, a dream of equality deferred, for too many people of color. This does not in any way detract from the significance of the things minorities have achieved. Ethnic-group histories and lists of cultural contributions support the contention that each group is an integral part of a whole nation. Although all American ethnic minority groups have experienced continuous socioeconomic gains, the so-called "playing field" that includes white participants is not yet level. Simply stated, the rising tide of economic prosperity has not yet lifted the masses of people of color. Whatever our life circumstances, the citizens of the United States are bound together not as separate ethnic groups but as members of different ethnic groups united in spirit and behavior and locked into a common destiny.

There is little doubt that our nation is at a crossroads in its race relations. Where we go from here is up to all of us. We can try segregation again, continuance of the status quo, silence in the face of prejudice and discriminatory practices, or activism. The choice is ours.

16   Segregation of ethnic minorities is not a redeeming choice for the United States. It did not work during earlier times, and it will not work now. There have never been separate but equal majority-group and minority-group communities in the United States. And the pretense of such a condition would once again be a particularly pernicious injustice to all citizens. Racial segregation diminishes both the perpetrators and their victims. Preserving the status quo in education, employment, health care, and housing, which so often is little more than codified racial discrimination, is not justice for minorities either.

Inaction by people who witness oppressive acts is equally unacceptable. Even though they may be shocked and frustrated by the problems, standing in wide-eyed horror is not an adequate posture to assume. While they may be legally absolved of any wrongdoing, these silent people must come to terms with what others believe to be their moral culpability. Of course, silence may be prudent. Usually, there is a high price to be paid by those who would challenge racism in community institutions. Friends, jobs, promotions, and prestige may be lost. Furthermore, few victories come easily, and most of the victors are unsung heroes.

Individuals who choose to challenge purveyors of bigotry and unequal opportunities must also take care that in their actions to redress racial injustices, they do not emulate the oppressors whom they deplore. That might makes right, that blood washes out injustices—these too are false strategies for achieving justice. "It does not matter much to a slave what the color of his master is," a wise black janitor once said. We, the descendants of migrants, immigrants, and slaves, can build a better nation— a place where all people have safe housing, get a top-quality education, do meaning-ful work for adequate wages, are treated fairly in criminal-justice systems, have their medical needs met, and in the end die a timely death unhurried by bigots. This is the kind of history that should be made.

PERSONAL RESPONSE

Noting that America is "at a crossroads in its race relations," Henderson identifies four options for "where we can go from here" (paragraph 15). Explain which option you think you will choose and why.

QUESTIONS FOR CLASS OR SMALL-GROUP DISCUSSION

1. State in your own words what you understand Henderson to mean when he says that "all ethnic groups [in America] have been both the oppressed and the oppressors" (paragraph 1). What examples does he give? Can you provide other examples that either support or refute that statement?

2. Do you agree with Henderson on the following point: "But it is the erro-neous belief that people who come to America can be placed in categories based on their unique gene pools that has resulted in the most blatant in-stances of discrimination" (paragraph 3)? How does being "placed in cate-gories" result in discrimination?

3. State in your own words why America is not, according to Henderson, a true melting pot. To what extent do you agree with him? In preparation for your answer to this question, make sure you understand what these words and terms mean: *ethnic enclave, nativist,* and *exclusionist* (paragraph 6); *misce-genation, ethnocentrism,* and *second-class citizenship* (paragraph 8).

4. In his discussion of options for where we can go from here, Henderson says of those who choose activisim: "Individuals who choose to challenge pur-veyors of bigotry and unequal opportunities must also take care that in their actions to redress racial injustices, they do not emulate the oppressors whom they deplore" (paragraph 18). What do you understand him to mean by that statement? Why might people working against oppression become oppres-sors themselves?

ONE NATION INDIVISIBLE: IS IT HISTORY?

WILLIAM BOOTH

William Booth is a Washington Post *staff writer. This article was the first in a series examining the effects of changing demographics on American life. It appeared in the Sunday, February 22, 1998, issue of the* Washington Post.

At the beginning of this century, as steamers poured into American ports, their steerages filled with European immigrants, a Jew from England named Israel Zangwill penned a play whose story line has long been forgotten, but whose central theme has not. His production was entitled "The Melting Pot" and its message still holds a tremendous power on the national imagination—the promise that all immigrants can be transformed into Americans, a new alloy forged in a crucible of democracy, freedom, and civic responsibility. In 1908, when the play opened in Washington, the United States was in the middle of absorbing the largest influx of immigrants in its history—Irish and Germans, followed by Italians and East Europeans, Catholics and Jews—some eighteen million new citizens between 1890 and 1920.

Today, the United States is experiencing its second great wave of immigration, a movement of people that has profound implications for a society that by tradition pays homage to its immigrant roots at the same time it confronts complex and deeply ingrained ethnic and racial divisions. The immigrants of today come not from Europe but overwhelmingly from the still developing world of Asia and Latin America. They are driving a demographic shift so rapid that within the lifetimes of today's teenagers, no one ethnic group—including whites of European descent—will comprise a majority of the nation's population.

This shift, according to social historians, demographers, and others studying the trends, will severely test the premise of the fabled melting pot, the idea, so central to national identity, that this country can transform people of every color and background into "one America." Just as possible, they say, is that the nation will continue to fracture into many separate, disconnected communities with no shared sense of commonality or purpose. Or perhaps it will evolve into something in between, a pluralistic society that will hold onto some core ideas about citizenship and capitalism, but with little meaningful interaction among groups.

4   The demographic changes raise other questions about political and economic power. Will that power, now held disproportionately by whites, be shared in the new America? What will happen when Hispanics overtake blacks as the nation's single largest minority? "I do not think that most Americans really understand the historic changes happening before their very eyes," said Peter Salins, an immigration scholar who is provost of the State Universities of New York. "What are we going to become? Who are we? How do the newcomers fit in—and how do the natives handle it—this is the great unknown."

Fear of strangers, of course, is nothing new in American history. The last great immigration wave produced a bitter backlash, epitomized by the Chinese Exclusion

Act of 1882 and the return, in the 1920s, of the Ku Klux Klan, which not only targeted blacks, but Catholics, Jews, and immigrants, as well. But despite this strife, many historians argue that there was a greater consensus in the past on what it meant to be an American, a yearning for a common language and culture, and a desire—encouraged, if not coerced by members of the dominant white Protestant culture—to assimilate. Today, they say, there is more emphasis on preserving one's ethnic identity, of finding ways to highlight and defend one's cultural roots.

Difficult to Measure

More often than not, the neighborhoods where Americans live, the politicians and propositions they vote for, the cultures they immerse themselves in, the friends and spouses they have, the churches and schools they attend, and the way they view themselves are defined by ethnicity. The question is whether, in the midst of such change, there is also enough glue to hold Americans together. Black community activist Nathaniel J. Wilcox in Miami says, "Hispanics don't want some of the power, they want all the power." "As we become more and more diverse, there is all this potential to make that reality work for us," said Angela Oh, a Korean American activist who emerged as a powerful voice for Asian immigrants after the Los Angeles riots in 1992. "But yet, you witness this persistence of segregation, the fragmentation, all these fights over resources, this finger-pointing. You would have to be blind not to see it."

It is a phenomenon sometimes difficult to measure, but not observe. Houses of worship remain, as the Rev. Martin Luther King Jr. described it three decades ago, among the most segregated institutions in America, not just by race but also ethnicity. At high school cafeterias, the second and third generation children of immigrants clump together in cliques defined by where their parents or grandparents were born. There are television sit-coms, talk shows, and movies that are considered black or white, Latino or Asian. At a place like the law school of the University of California at Los Angeles, which has about one thousand students, there are separate student associations for blacks, Latinos, and Asians with their own law review journals.

8   It almost goes without saying that today's new arrivals are a source of vitality and energy, especially in the big cities to which many are attracted. Diversity, almost everyone agrees, is good; choice is good; exposure to different cultures and ideas is good. But many scholars worry about the loss of community and shared sense of reality among Americans, what Todd Gitlin, a professor of culture and communications at New York University, calls "the twilight of common dreams." The concern is echoed by many on both the left and the right, and of all ethnicities, but no one seems to know exactly what to do about it.

Academics who examine the census data and probe for meaning in the numbers already speak of a new "demographic balkanization," not only of residential segregation, forced or chosen, but also of a powerful preference to see ourselves through a racial prism, wary of others, and, in many instances, hostile. At a recent school board meeting in East Palo Alto, California, police had to break up a fight between Latinos and blacks, who were arguing over the merits and expense of bilingual education in a school district that has shifted over the past few years from majority African American to majority Hispanic. One parent told reporters that if the Hispanics wanted to learn Spanish they should stay in Mexico.

The demographic shifts are smudging the old lines demarcating two historical, often distinct societies, one black and one white. Reshaped by three decades of rapidly rising immigration, the national story is now far more complicated. Whites currently account for 74 percent of the population, blacks 12 percent, Hispanics 10 percent, and Asians 3 percent. Yet according to data and predictions generated by the U.S. Census Bureau and social scientists poring over the numbers, Hispanics will likely surpass blacks early in the next century. And by the year 2050, demographers predict, Hispanics will account for 25 percent of the population, blacks 14 percent, Asians 8 percent, with whites hovering somewhere around 53 percent. As early as next year, whites will no longer be the majority in California; in Hawaii and New Mexico this is already the case. Soon after, Nevada, Texas, Maryland, and New Jersey are also predicted to become "majority minority" states, entities where no one ethnic group remains the majority.

Effects of 1965 Law

The overwhelming majority of immigrants come from Asia and Latin America—Mexico, the Central American countries, the Philippines, Korea, and Southeast Asia. What triggered this great transformation was a change to immigration law in 1965, when Congress made family reunification the primary criterion for admittance. That new policy, a response to charges that the law favored white Europeans, allowed immigrants already in the United States to bring over their relatives, who in turn could bring over more relatives. As a result, America has been absorbing as many as one million newcomers a year, to the point that now almost one in every ten residents is foreign born. These numbers, relative to the overall population, were slightly higher at the beginning of this century, but the current immigration wave is in many ways very different, and its context inexorably altered, from the last great wave.

12   This time around tensions are sharpened by the changing profile of those who are entering America's borders. Not only are their racial and ethnic backgrounds more varied than in decades past, their place in a modern postindustrial economy has been recast. The newly arrived today can be roughly divided into two camps: those with college degrees and highly specialized skills, and those with almost no education or job training. Some 12 percent of immigrants have graduate degrees, compared to 8 percent of native Americans. But more than one-third of the immigrants have no high school diploma, double the rate for those born in the United States. Before 1970, immigrants were actually doing better than natives overall, as measured by education, rate of home ownership, and average income. But those arriving after 1970 are younger, more likely to be underemployed, and live below the poverty level. As a group, they are doing worse than natives. About 6 percent of new arrivals receive some form of welfare, double the rate for U.S.-born citizens. Among some newcomers—Cambodians and Salvadorans, for example—the numbers are even higher.

With large numbers of immigrants arriving from Latin America, and segregating in barrios, there is also evidence of lingering language problems. Consider that in Miami, three-quarters of residents speak a language other than English at home, and 67 percent of those say that they are not fluent in English. In New York City, four of every ten residents speak a language other than English at home, and of these, half said they do not speak English well.

It is clear that not all of America is experiencing the impact of immigration equally. Although even small midwestern cities have seen sharp changes in their racial and ethnic mix in the past two decades, most immigrants continue to cluster into a handful of large, mostly coastal metropolitan areas: Los Angeles, New York, San Francisco, Chicago, Miami, Washington, D.C., and Houston. They are home to more than a quarter of the total U.S. population and more than 60 percent of all foreign-born residents. But as the immigrants arrive, many American-born citizens pour out of these cities in search of new homes in more homogeneous locales. New York and Los Angeles each lost more than one million native-born residents between 1990 and 1995, even as their populations increased by roughly the same numbers with immigrants. To oversimplify, said University of Michigan demographer William Frey, "For every Mexican who comes to Los Angeles, a white native-born leaves."

Most of the people leaving the big cities are white, and they tend to be working class. This is an entirely new kind of "white flight," whereby whites are not just fleeing the city centers for the suburbs but also are leaving the region and often the state. "The Ozzies and Harriets of the 1990s are skipping the suburbs of the big cities and moving to more homogeneous, mostly white smaller towns and smaller cities and rural areas," Frey said. They're headed to Atlanta, Las Vegas, Phoenix, Portland, Denver, Austin, and Orlando, as well as smaller cities in Nevada, Idaho, Colorado, and Washington. Frey and other demographers believe the domestic migrants—black and white—are being "pushed" out, at least in part, by competition with immigrants for jobs and neighborhoods, political clout and lifestyle. Frey sees in this pattern "the emergence of separate Americas, one white and middle-aged, less urban and another intensely urban, young, multicultural, and multiethnic. One America will care deeply about English as the official language and about preserving social security. The other will care about things like retaining affirmative action and bilingual education."

Ethnic Segregation

16   Even within gateway cities that give the outward appearance of being multicultural, there are sharp lines of ethnic segregation. When describing the ethnic diversity of a bellwether megacity such as Los Angeles, many residents speak roaringly of the great mosaic of many peoples. But the social scientists who look at the hard census data see something more complex. James P. Allen, a cultural geographer at California State University–Northridge, suggests that while Los Angeles, as seen from an airplane, is a tremendously mixed society, on the ground, racial homogeneity and segregation are common. This is not a new phenomenon; there have always been immigrant neighborhoods. Ben Franklin, an early proponent of making English the official language, worried about close-knit German communities. Sen. Daniel Patrick Moynihan

(D–N.Y.) described the lingering clannishness of Irish and other immigrant populations in New York in *Beyond the Melting Pot*, a benchmark work from the 1960s that he wrote with Nathan Glazer.

But the persistence of ethnic enclaves and identification does not appear to be going away and may not in a country that is now home to not a few distinct ethnic groups, but to dozens. Hispanics in Los Angeles, to take the dominant group in the nation's second largest city, are more segregated residentially in 1990 than they were ten or twenty years ago, the census tracts show. Moreover, it is possible that what mixing of groups that does occur is only a temporary phenomenon as one ethnic group supplants another in the neighborhood.

If there is deep-seated ethnic segregation, it clearly extends to the American workplace. In many cities, researchers find sustained "ethnic niches" in the labor market. Because jobs are often a matter of whom one knows, the niches were enduring and remarkably resistant to outsiders. In California, for example, Mexican immigrants are employed overwhelmingly as gardeners and domestics, in apparel and furniture manufacturing, and as cooks and food preparers. Koreans open small businesses. Filipinos become nurses and medical technicians. African Americans work in government jobs, an important niche that is increasingly being challenged by Hispanics who want in.

UCLA's Roger Waldinger and others have pointed to the creation, in cities of high immigration, of "dual economies." For the affluent, which includes a disproportionate number of whites, the large labor pool provides them with a ready supply of gardeners, maids, and nannies. For businesses in need of cheap manpower, the same is true. Yet there are fewer "transitional" jobs—the blue-collar work that helped Italian and Irish immigrants move up the economic ladder—to help newcomers or their children on their way to the jobs requiring advanced technical or professional skills that now dominate the upper tier of the economy.

A Rung at a Time

20   Traditionally, immigration scholars have seen the phenomenon of assimilation as a relentless economic progression. The hard-working new arrivals struggle along with a new language and at low-paying jobs in order for their sons and daughters to climb the economic ladder, each generation advancing a rung. There are many cases where this is true. More recently, there is evidence to suggest that economic movement is erratic and that some groups—particularly in high immigration cities—can get "stuck." Among African Americans, for instance, there emerge two distinct patterns. The black middle class is doing demonstrably better—in income, home ownership rates, education—than it was when the demographic transformation (and the civil rights movement) began three decades ago. But for African Americans at the bottom, research indicates that immigration, particularly of Latinos with limited education, has increased joblessness and frustration.

In Miami, where Cuban immigrants dominate the political landscape, tensions are high between Hispanics and blacks, said Nathaniel J. Wilcox, a community activist there. "The perception in the black community, the reality, is that Hispanics don't want some of the power, they want all the power," Wilcox said. "At least when we were going through this with the whites during the Jim Crow era, at least they'd hire us. But Hispanics won't allow African Americans to even compete. They have this feeling that their community is the only community that counts."

Yet many Hispanics too find themselves in an economic "mobility trap." While the new immigrants are willing to work in low-end jobs, their sons and daughters, growing up in the barrios but exposed to the relentless consumerism of popular culture, have greater expectations, but are disadvantaged because of their impoverished settings, particularly the overwhelmed inner-city schools most immigrant children attend. "One doubts that a truck-driving future will satisfy today's servants and assemblers. And this scenario gets a good deal more pessimistic if the region's economy fails to deliver or simply throws up more bad jobs," writes Waldinger, a professor of sociology and director of center for regional policy studies at the University of California–Los Angeles.

Though there are calls to revive efforts to encourage "Americanization" of the newcomers, many researchers now express doubt that the old assimilation model works. For one thing, there is less of a dominant mainstream to enter. Instead, there are a dozen streams, despite the best efforts by the dominant white society to lump groups together by ethnicity. It is a particularly American phenomenon, many say, to label citizens by their ethnicity. When they lived in El Salvador, for example, they saw themselves as a nationality. When they arrive in the United States, they become Hispanic or Latino. So too with Asians. Koreans and Cambodians find little in common, but when they arrive here they become "Asian," and are counted and courted, encouraged or discriminated against as such. "My family has had trouble understanding that we are now Asians, and not Koreans, or people from Korea or Korean Americans, or just plain Americans," said Arthur Lee, who owns a dry cleaning store in Los Angeles. "Sometimes, we laugh about it. Oh, the Asian students are so smart! The Asians have no interest in politics! Whatever. But we don't know what people are talking about. Who are the Asians?"

24   Many immigrant parents say that while they want their children to advance economically in their new country, they do not want them to become "too American." A common concern among Haitians in South Florida is that their children will adopt the attitudes of the inner city's underclass. Vietnamese parents in New Orleans often try to keep their children immersed in their ethnic enclave and try not to let them assimilate too fast.

Hyphenated Americans

One study of the children of immigrants, conducted six years ago among young Haitians, Cubans, West Indians, Mexicans, and Vietnamese in South Florida and southern California, suggests the parents are not alone in their concerns. Asked by researchers Alejandro Portes and Ruben Rumbauthow how they identified themselves, most chose categories of hyphenated Americans. Few choose "American" as their identity. Then there was this—asked if they believe the United States is the best country in the world, most of the youngsters answered: no.

PERSONAL RESPONSE

Does the fact that many immigrant parents say "they do not want [their children] to become 'too American' " (paragraph 24) surprise you? How important do you consider your race or ethnicity to your identity? Is the neighborhood where you grew up largely composed of a particular racial or ethnic group, or does it have a mixed population?

QUESTIONS FOR CLASS OR SMALL-GROUP DISCUSSION

1. State in your own words what is meant by the terms *melting pot* (paragraphs 1 and 3) and *pluralistic society* (paragraph 3). What does *demographic balkanization* (paragraph 9) mean?

2. How, according to Booth, does the second great wave of immigration differ from the first great wave? What possible effect do social historians and demographers see in this second wave?

3. How has the 1965 immigration law affected American demographics?

4. In what ways, according to Booth, is America still a highly segregated country? Explain whether your own observations and/or experiences support his assertions.

5. Summarize Booth's discussion of terminology for various racial or ethnic groups (paragraphs 23–25). What effect do you think labels or identity markers have on members of those groups?

HISPANICS AND THE AMERICAN DREAM

LINDA CHAVEZ

Linda Chavez is president of the Center for Equal Opportunity in Washington, D.C., and writes a weekly column for USA Today. *She regularly appears on* The McLaughlin Group, CNN & Co., *and* The NewsHour with Jim Lehrer. *Her books include* Out of the Barrio: Toward a New Politics of Hispanic Assimilation *(1992) and* From Sugar Daddies to Uncle Sam *(1999). This essay was first published in* Imprimis *in 1996.*

The more than twenty-one million Hispanics now living in the United States are fast becoming the nation's largest minority group. Some demographers can already see the day when one of three Americans will be of Hispanic descent. Will this mean a divided nation with millions of unassimilated, Spanish-speaking, poor, uneducated Hispanics living in the barrios? Well, here is one reply:

> Each decade offered us hope, but our hopes evaporated into smoke. We became the poorest of the poor, the most segregated minority in schools, the lowest paid group in America, and the least educated minority in this nation.

This pessimistic view of Hispanics' progress—offered in 1990 by the president of the National Council of La Raza, one of the country's leading Hispanic civil rights groups—is the prevalent one among Hispanic leaders and is shared by many outside the Hispanic community as well. Hispanics are widely perceived as the dregs of society with little hope of participating in the American Dream.

The trouble with this perception is that it is wrong. The success of Hispanics in the United States has been tremendous. They represent an emerging middle class that is a valuable addition to our culture and our economy. However, their story has been effectively suppressed by Hispanic advocates whose only apparent interest is in spreading the notion that Latinos cannot make it in this society. This has been an easy task since the Hispanic poor, who, although they only constitute about one-fourth of the Hispanic population, are visible to all. These are the Hispanics most likely to be studied, analyzed, and reported on, and certainly they are the ones most likely to be read about. A recent computer search of stories about Hispanics in major newspapers and magazines over a twelve-month period turned up more than eighteen hundred stories in which the words *Hispanic* or *Latino* occurred in close connection with the word *poverty*. In most people's minds, the expression "poor Hispanic" is almost redundant.

Has Hispanics' Progress Stalled?

4   Most Hispanics, rather than being poor, lead solidly lower middle- or middle-class lives, but finding evidence to support this thesis is sometimes difficult. Of course, Hispanic groups vary one from another, as do individuals within any group. Most analysts acknowledge, for example, that Cubans are highly successful. Within one generation, they have virtually closed the earnings and education gap with other Americans. Although some analysts claim their success is due exclusively to their higher socioeconomic status when they arrived, many Cuban refugees—especially those who came after the first wave in the 1960s—were in fact skilled or semiskilled workers with relatively little education. Their accomplishments in the United States mainly are attributable to diligence and hard work.

Cubans have tended to establish enclave economies, in the traditional immigrant mode, opening restaurants, stores, and other émigré-oriented services. Some Cubans have even formed banks, specializing in international transactions attuned to Latin American as well as local customers, and others have made major investments in real estate development in South Florida. These ventures have provided not only big profits for a few Cubans but jobs for many more. By 1980, there were eighteen thousand Cuban-owned businesses in Miami, and about 70 percent of all Cubans there owned their own homes.

But Cubans are, as a rule, dismissed as the exception among Hispanics. What about other Hispanic groups? Why has there been no "progress" among them? The largest and most important group is the Mexican American population. Its leaders have driven much of the policy agenda affecting all Hispanics, but the importance of Mexican Americans also stems from the fact that they have had a longer history in the United States than any other Hispanic group. If Mexican Americans whose families have lived in the United States for generations are not yet making it in this society, they may have a legitimate claim to consider themselves a more or less permanently disadvantaged group.

That is precisely what Mexican American leaders suggest is happening. Their "proof" is that statistical measures of Mexican American achievement in education, earnings, poverty rates, and other social and economic indicators have remained largely unchanged for decades. If Mexican Americans had made progress, it would show up in these areas, so the argument goes. Since it doesn't, progress must be stalled. In the post–civil rights era, it is also assumed that the failure of a minority to close the social and economic gap with whites is the result of persistent discrimination. Progress is perceived not in absolute but in relative terms. The poor may become less poor over time, but so long as those on the upper rungs of the economic ladder are climbing even faster, the poor are believed to have suffered some harm, even if they have made absolute gains and their lives are much improved. But in order for Hispanics (or any group on the lower rungs) to close the gap, they would have to progress at an even greater rate than non-Hispanic whites.

8   Is this a fair way to judge Hispanics' progress? No. It makes almost no sense to apply this test today (if it ever did) because the Hispanic population itself is changing so rapidly. In 1959, 85 percent of all persons of Mexican origin living in the United States were native-born. Today, only about two-thirds of the people of Mexican origin were born in the United States, and among adults barely one in two was born here. Increasingly, the Hispanic population, including that of Mexican origin, is made up of new immigrants, who, like immigrants of every era, start off at the bottom of the economic ladder. This infusion of new immigrants is bound to distort our image of progress in the Hispanic population if, each time we measure the group, we include people who have just arrived and have yet to make their way in this society.

In 1980, there were about 14.6 million Hispanics living in the United States; in 1990, there were nearly twenty-one million, representing an increase of 44 percent in one decade. At least one-half of this increase was the result of immigration, legal and illegal. Not surprisingly, when these Hispanics—often poorly educated with minimal or no ability to speak English—are added to the pool being measured, the achievement level of the whole group falls. Yet no major Hispanic organization will acknowledge the validity of this reasonable assumption. Instead, Hispanic leaders complain, "Hispanics are the population that has benefited least from the American economy."

In fact, a careful examination of the voluminous data on the Hispanic population gathered by the Census Bureau and other federal agencies shows that, as a group, Hispanics have made significant progress and that most of them have moved into the social and economic mainstream. In most respects, Hispanics—particularly those born here—are very much like other Americans: They work hard, support their own families without outside assistance, have more education and higher earnings than their parents, and own their own homes. In short, they are pursuing the American Dream with increasing success.

The Hispanic Family

No institution is more important to the success of Hispanics (or any group) than the family. Studies published in the early 1990s reported that 73 percent of all

Mexican-origin families and 77 percent of all Cuban-origin families consist of married couples. Only 20 percent of the Mexican-origin and 19 percent of the Cuban-origin families are headed by women with no husband present. While out-of-wedlock births to Mexican-origin women are higher than those to white women generally, they fall considerably short of the number of such births to black women, and Hispanic children born out of wedlock are still likely to grow up in families with two parents.

12   The babies of Mexican-origin women, even those who have received little or no prenatal care, are generally quite healthy. There is also a lower infant mortality rate and smaller incidence of low birth weight, a common predictor of health problems, than among blacks and whites. While researchers are not sure what accounts for the apparent health of even poor Mexican babies, one reason may be that their mothers are less likely to drink, smoke, or use drugs, and they place special emphasis on good nutrition while pregnant.

In general, Hispanic families are somewhat more traditional than non-Hispanic families: Men are expected to work to support their families and women to care for children. Hispanic families tend to be child-centered, which increases the importance of women's role as child bearers. Hispanics are also more likely than other Americans to believe that the demands and needs of the family should take precedence over those of the individual. In an earlier age this attitude was common among other ethnic groups—Italians, for example. Today, however, it runs counter to the dominant culture of individualism characteristic of American life and may even impede individual success. This perhaps explains why so many young Hispanics are starting to drop out of school to take jobs, a decision that has some immediate financial benefits for the family but is detrimental to the individual in the long run. Nonetheless, Hispanics' attachment to family is one of their most positive cultural attributes. Family members are expected to help each other in times of financial or other need, which some analysts believe explains why so many Mexican-origin families shun welfare even when their poverty makes them eligible for assistance.

Hispanics and Public Policy

For most Hispanics, especially those born in the United States, the last few decades have brought greater economic opportunity and social mobility. They are building solid lower middle- and middle-class lives that include two-parent households, with a male head who works full-time and earns a wage commensurate with his education and training. Their educational level has been steadily rising, their earnings no longer reflect wide disparities with those of non-Hispanics, and their occupational distribution is coming to resemble more closely that of the general population. They are buying homes—42 percent of all Hispanics owned or were purchasing their homes in 1989, including 47 percent of all Mexican Americans—and moving away from inner cities. Even in areas with very high concentrations of Hispanics, like Los Angeles, the sociologist Douglas Massey reports, "segregation [is] low or moderate on all dimensions." And, in what is perhaps the ultimate test of assimilation, about one-third of all U.S.-born Hispanics under the age of thirty-five are marrying non-Hispanics.

In light of these facts, the policy prescriptions offered by many Hispanic advocacy organizations and by most politicians seem oddly out of sync. They rely too much on government programs of doubtful efficacy like affirmative action, welfare, and bilingual public education. And they perpetuate demeaning stereotypes of the very people they claim they are championing. What they should be doing instead is promoting tax reform, deregulation, enterprise zones, English instruction, and private education—all of which will help Hispanics help themselves.

16   Groups do not all advance at precisely the same rate in this society—sometimes because of discrimination, sometimes because of other factors. As Thomas Sowell and others have pointed out, no multiethnic society in the world exhibits utopian equality of income, education, and occupational status for every one of its ethnic groups. What is important is that opportunities be made available to all persons, regardless of race or ethnicity. Ultimately, however, it will be up to individuals to take advantage of those opportunities. Increasing numbers of Hispanics are doing just that. And no government action can replace the motivation and will to succeed that propels genuine individual achievement.

PERSONAL RESPONSE

Are you convinced by Chavez's argument? Has your understanding of Hispanics changed or been reinforced as a result of reading this essay? Explain your answer. If you are Hispanic, describe your feelings as you read the essay.

QUESTIONS FOR CLASS OR SMALL-GROUP DISCUSSION

1. How does Chavez answer the question she poses in paragraph 1: "Will this [the possibility that one day one of three Americans will be of Hispanic descent] mean a divided nation with millions of unassimilated, Spanish-speaking, poor, uneducated Hispanics living in the barrios?"

2. Chavez notes in paragraph 3 that a recent search of stories in periodicals over a one-year period "turned up more than eighteen hundred stories in which the words *Hispanic* or *Latino* occurred in close connection with the word *poverty*." Discuss the implications of this statement.

3. What Hispanic group does Chavez use as an outstanding example of an exception to the popular perception of Hispanics? In what other ways are stereotypes of any racial or ethnic group reinforced, consciously or unconsciously, by the media?

4. In her next-to-last paragraph, Chavez says that such programs as affirmative action, welfare, and bilingual public education are "of doubtful efficacy." Do you agree with her that those programs are not very effective or useful?

COLORBLIND

ALEX KOTLOWITZ

Alex Kotlowitz's investigative articles appear regularly in such national magazines as the New Yorker *and the* New York Times Sunday Magazine. *Formerly a staff writer for the* Wall Street Journal, *he is the author of* There are No Children Here: The Story of Two Boys Growing up in the Other America *(1992):* The Other Side of the River: A Story of Two Towns, a Death and America's Dilemma *(1998); and* Never a City So Real: A Walk in Chicago *(2004). This essay appeared in the January 11, 1998, issue of the* New York Times Magazine.

One Christmas day seven years ago, I'd gone over to the Henry Horner Homes in Chicago to visit with Lafeyette and Pharoah, the subjects of my book *There Are No Children Here*. I had brought presents for the boys, as well as a gift for their friend Rickey, who lived on the other side of the housing complex, an area controlled by a rival gang. Lafeyette and Pharoah insisted on walking over with me. It was eerily quiet, since most everyone was inside, and so, bundled from the cold, we strolled toward the other end in silence. As we neared Damen Avenue, a kind of demilitarized zone, a uniformed police officer, a white woman, approached us. She looked first at the two boys, neither of whom reached my shoulder, and then directly at me. "Are you O.K.?" she asked.

About a year later, I was with Pharoah on the city's North Side, shopping for hightops. We were walking down the busy street, my hand on Pharoah's shoulder, when a middle-aged black man approached. He looked at me, and then at Pharoah. "Son," he asked, "are you O.K.?"

Both this white police officer and middle-aged black man seemed certain of what they witnessed. The white woman saw a white man possibly in trouble; the black man saw a black boy possibly in trouble. It's all about perspective—which has everything to do with our personal and collective experiences, which are consistently informed by race. From those experiences, from our histories, we build myths, legends that both guide us and constrain us, legends that include both fact and fiction. This is not to say the truth doesn't matter. It does, in a big way. It's just that getting there may not be easy, in part because everyone is so quick to choose sides, to refute the other's myths and to pass on their own.

4   We'd do well to keep this in mind as we enter the yearlong dialogue on race convened by President Clinton. Yes, conversation is critical, but not without self-reflection, both individually and communally. While myths help us make sense of the incomprehensible, they can also confine us, confuse us, and leave us prey to historical laziness. Moreover, truth is not always easily discernible—and even when it is, the prism, depending on which side of the river you reside on, may create a wholly different illusion. Many whites were quick to believe Susan Smith, the South Carolina mother who claimed that a black man had killed her children. And with the

reawakening of the Tawana Brawley case, we learn that, although a grand jury has determined otherwise, many blacks still believe she was brutally raped by a group of white men. We—blacks and whites—need to examine and question our own perspectives. Only then can we grasp each other's myths and grapple with the truths.

In 1992, I came across the story of a sixteen-year-old black boy, Eric McGinnis, whose body had been found a year earlier floating in the St. Joseph River in southwestern Michigan. The river flows between Benton Harbor and St. Joseph, two small towns whose only connections are two bridges and a powerful undertow of contrasts.

St. Joseph is a town of nine thousand and, with its quaint downtown and brick-paved streets, resembles a New England tourist haunt. But for those in Benton Harbor, St. Joseph's most defining characteristic is its racial makeup: It is 95 percent white. Benton Harbor, a town of twelve thousand on the other side of the river, is 92 percent black and dirt poor. For years, the municipality so hurt for money that it could not afford to raze abandoned buildings.

Eric, a high-school sophomore whose passion was dancing, was last seen at the Club, a teenage nightspot in St. Joseph, where weeks earlier he had met and started dating a white girl. The night Eric disappeared, a white man said he caught the boy trying to break into his car and chased him—away from the river, past an off-duty white deputy sheriff. That was the last known moment he was seen alive, and it was then that the myths began.

8   I became obsessed with Eric's death, and so for five years moved in and out of these two communities, searching for answers to both Eric's disappearance and to matters of race. People would often ask which side of the river I was staying on, wanting to gauge my allegiance. And they would often ask about the secrets of those across the way or, looking for affirmation, repeat myths passed on from one generation to the next.

Once, during an unusually bitter effort by white school-board members to fire Benton Harbor's black superintendent, one black woman asked me: "How do you know how to do this? Do you take lessons? How do you all stick together the way you do?" Of course, we don't. Neither community is as unified or monolithic as the other believes. Indeed, contrary to the impression of those in St. Joseph, the black community itself was deeply divided in its support for the superintendent, who was eventually fired.

On occasion, whites in St. Joseph would regale me with tales of families migrating to Benton Harbor from nearby states for the high welfare benefits. It is, they would tell me, the reason for the town's economic decline. While some single mothers indeed moved to Benton Harbor and other Michigan cities in the early eighties to receive public assistance, the truth is that in the thirties and forties factories recruited blacks from the South, and when those factories shut down, unemployment, particularly among blacks, skyrocketed.

But the question most often asked was: "Why us? Why write about St. Joseph and Benton Harbor?" I would tell them that while the contrasts between the towns seem unusually stark, they are, I believe, typical of how most of us live: physically and spiritually isolated from one another.

12   It's not that I didn't find individuals who crossed the river to spend time with their neighbors. One St. Joseph woman, Amy Johnson, devotes her waking hours to a Benton Harbor community center. And Eric McGinnis himself was among a handful of black teenagers who spent weekend nights at the Club in St. Joseph. Nor is it that I didn't find racial animosity. One St. Joseph resident informed me that Eric got what he deserved: "That nigger came on the wrong side of the bridge," he said. And Benton Harbor's former school superintendent, Sherwin Allen, made no effort to hide his contempt for the white power structure.

What I found in the main, though, were people who would like to do right but don't know where to begin. As was said of the South's politicians during Jim Crow, race diminishes us. It incites us to act as we wouldn't in other arenas: clumsily, cowardly, and sometimes cruelly. We circle the wagons, watching out for our own.

That's what happened in the response to Eric's death. Most everyone in St. Joseph came to believe that Eric, knowing the police were looking for him, tried to swim the river to get home and drowned. Most everyone in Benton Harbor, with equal certitude, believes that Eric was killed—most likely by whites, most likely because he dated a white girl. I was struck by the disparity in perspective, the competing realities, but I was equally taken aback by the distance between the two towns—which, of course, accounts for the myths. Jim Reeves, the police lieutenant, who headed the investigation into Eric's death, once confided that this teenager he'd never met had more impact on him than any other black person.

I'm often asked by whites, with some wonderment, how it is that I'm able to spend so much time in black communities without feeling misunderstood or unwelcomed or threatened. I find it much easier to talk with blacks about race than with fellow whites. While blacks often brave slights silently for fear that if they complain they won't be believed, when asked, they welcome the chance to relate their experiences. Among whites, there's a reluctance—or a lack of opportunity—to engage. Race for them poses no urgency; it does not impose on their daily routines. I once asked Ben Butzbaugh, a St. Joseph commissioner, how he felt the two towns got along. "I think we're pretty fair in this community," he said. "I don't know that I can say I know of any out-and-out racial-type things that occur. I just think people like their own better than others. I think that's pretty universal. Don't you? . . . We're not a bunch of racists. We're not anything America isn't." Butzbaugh proudly pointed to his friendship with Renée Williams, Benton Harbor's new school superintendent. "Renée was in our home three, four, five days a week," he noted. "Nice gal. Put herself through school. We'd talk all the time." Williams used to clean for Butzbaugh's family.

16   As I learned during the years in and out of these towns, the room for day-to-day dialogue doesn't present itself. We become buried in our myths, certain of our truths—and refuse to acknowledge what the historian Allan Nevins calls "the grains of stony reality" embedded in most legends. A quarter-century ago, race was part of everyday public discourse; today it haunts us quietly, though on occasion—the Rodney King beating or the Simpson trial or Eric McGinnis's death—it erupts with jarring urgency. At these moments of crisis, during these squalls, we flail about, trying to find moral ballast. By then it is usually too late. The lines are drawn. Accusations are hurled across the river like cannon fire. And the cease-fires, when they occur, are

just that, cease-fires, temporary and fragile. Even the best of people have already chosen sides.

PERSONAL RESPONSE

If you are black or white, describe your feelings as you read this essay and your perspective of the tension between the two groups. If you are neither black nor white, explain your perspective of the tension between whites and blacks.

QUESTIONS FOR CLASS OR SMALL-GROUP DISCUSSION

1. Locate Kotlowitz's central idea or thesis, and then summarize his viewpoint on that issue. What is your opinion of his viewpoint? Do you agree or disagree with him? To what extent do your own observations or experiences support his conclusions?

2. Discuss your understanding of this statement: "It's all about perspective—which has everything to do with our personal and collective experiences, which are consistently informed by race. From those experiences, from our histories, we build myths, legends that both guide us and constrain us, legends that include both fact and fiction" (paragraph 3). Then explain the extent to which you agree with Kotlowitz.

3. Explain the reference to Jim Crow in paragraph 13, and then respond to Kotlowitz's statement that "race diminishes us. It incites us to act as we wouldn't in other arenas: clumsily, cowardly, and sometimes cruelly."

4. Are you surprised by Kotlowitz's comment in paragraph 15 that he finds it "much easier to talk with blacks about race than with fellow whites"? Does his explanation seem plausible to you? To what extent is your own experience or observation similar to his?

HOW MUCH DIVERSITY DO YOU WANT FROM ME?

Perry Bacon, Jr.

Perry Bacon, Jr. has been a correspondent in Time *Magazine's Washington bureau since 2002, covering education policy, diplomatic issues, and politics. He graduated from Yale University with distinction in political science, interning at the* Louisville Courier Journal, National Journal, *and the* Washington Post *before joining* Time. *"How Much Diversity do you want from Me?" was published in the July 7, 2003, issue of* Time.

I'm from Louisville, Ky., attended Yale University and work as a *Time* journalist. Since I haven't met any other person who shares these three characteristics, I suppose

I add some diversity to most discussions I'm a part of. But at most colleges and workplaces in America, something else about me would make me add much more diversity. I'm black. And as Justice Sandra Day O'Connor wrote in a landmark Supreme Court opinion last week, borrowing language from a lower court, once a few people like me are sitting in a classroom, "discussion is livelier, more spirited and simply more enlightening and interesting." In her defense of affirmative action, O'Connor argued that our presence "helps to break down racial stereotypes and 'enables [students] to better understand persons of different races.'" And since nearly every major employer in America has a diversity policy, I will be expected to share what O'Connor calls the "unique experience of being a racial minority" with my coworkers as well.

O'Connor says other traits bring diversity too. But let's be honest here. Growing up on a farm in Arizona might help broaden a resume, but checking "black" has the effect of leapfrogging me over many comparable applicants gunning for a prestigious school or job. Although I'm sure my race improved my odds of being admitted to Yale and hired at *Time*, I don't carry around the "stigma" that Justice Clarence Thomas claims all blacks do because of affirmative action, wondering if they received a benefit based on merit or race. For me, the question has never been "Do I belong?" but rather "Since I'm here in part to contribute diversity, how do I do that?" O'Connor's diversity rationale doesn't just pressure colleges to admit more minority students. It gives me and other underrepresented minority students an added burden: delivering diversity. It creates expectations that I have a uniquely black viewpoint to contribute and that part of my responsibility as a student or worker is to do that.

At Yale, I often felt obligated to present these diverse views. On the campus paper there, I edited feature stories and had little desire to influence other sections of the paper. But when some minority students complained about the lack of diversity in our coverage and on our staff, I felt dutybound to press other editors to cover minorities more and explore ways to recruit more black students. When students debated whether Yale should have a day off for Martin Luther King Jr. Day, I saw this as a largely symbolic issue that I wasn't passionately interested in. But eventually I found myself questioning how anyone could not agree that we should have this day off, in part because I felt that as one of the few blacks around I should be speaking up.

4   As a full-time journalist, I feel these same pressures. Since I'm more interested in politics than in racial issues, am I fulfilling my sociojournalistic mission? I suppose I could bring a black perspective by talking to more minority sources or by closely examining how Bush Administration policies affect minorities. But isn't this something a white reporter could do too? Similarly, if you're white and discussing racial profiling in a class, isn't it part of your role as a student to think about how you would feel about this issue if you were black? This is a core problem with O'Connor's diversity rationale. It suggests that only a black person can articulate what it means to be black and that others shouldn't bother to try. Further, O'Connor suggests that simply by attending a law school with a "critical mass" of blacks, Hispanics and Native Americans, you come away understanding the perspectives of minorities. But the fact is, a Michigan Law School student would learn a lot more about the "unique experience" of blacks in America if he spent a day at an inner-city school in Detroit than he would

in a torts class with me. In fact, a white person who grew up poor has an equally or perhaps more diverse perspective, and yet my blackness counts so much more in affirmative action.

Maybe O'Connor really believes in this diversity notion. But here's what I suspect she and other affirmative-action proponents really think: nearly 27% of the population is black or Hispanic, but few of these minorities are in the upper ranks of most fields, in part because of past discrimination or current inequalities. And they think that the leadership class of our society should look like the rest of it. It's a laudable goal, and it's why I remain at least a tepid supporter of affirmative action. But let's stop using this notion of diversity to sidestep the real issue. Colleges don't want more minority students so we can all hold hands and sing "It's a Small World." Why can't we just say what the real goal is: the creation of a multiethnic elite. I think young minorities can help form that elite. But I want to join that elite and be expected to deliver the "unique experience" of my whole life rather than an assumed experience based solely on the color of my skin.

PERSONAL RESPONSE

What is your opinion of affirmative action?

QUESTIONS FOR CLASS AND SMALL-GROUP DISCUSSION

1. To what extent do you agree with Justice O'Connor's estimation of affirmative action, as reported by Bacon, Jr., in paragraph 1? Do you agree with Bacon, Jr., that her rationale puts undue pressure on minorities to deliver diversity (paragraph 2)?

2. Where do you position yourself on Justice Clarence Thomas's claim (as reported by Bacon, Jr.) that blacks are stigmatized, "wondering if they received a benefit based on merit or race" (paragraph 2)?

3. To what extent do you agree with Bacon, Jr., that the "real goal" of affirmative action is "the creation of a multiethnic elite" (paragraph 5)?

○ PERSPECTIVES ON RACE AND ETHNICITY IN AMERICA ○

Suggested Writing Topics

1. Compare what Linda Chavez, in "Hispanics and the American Dream," says about Hispanics and assimilation into American society with the developments that William Booth discusses in "One Nation, Indivisible: Is It History?"

2. Refer to the comments of at least two writers in this chapter as you discuss the subject of stereotypes and prejudice. As you plan your essay, consider the following questions: Where do people get prejudices? What aspects of

American culture reinforce and/or perpetuate stereotypes? How can you personally work against stereotyping and prejudice?

3. Explore your position on the issue of a "melting pot" (a society in which minorities are assimilated into the dominant culture) versus pluralism (a society in which ethnic and racial groups maintain separate identities, with no dominant culture). Take into consideration the views of two or more authors in this chapter.

4. Several of the authors in this chapter touch on the issue of labels. Synthesize their discussions into your own analysis of the role labels play in one's identity, self-esteem, and/or self-concept.

5. Interview at least one other person whose racial or ethnic heritage is different from yours about some of the points raised in at least two of the essays in this chapter. Then write an essay explaining what you learned and how the interview has in any way changed your own views on the issue of racism.

6. Write a reflective essay on your own cultural heritage, explaining your family's background and how you feel about that heritage.

7. Explain the importance of race or ethnicity to your own self-identity. Is it as important as your sex, your job, your socioeconomic level, or your educational level?

8. Alex Kotlowitz writes in "Colorblind": "We—blacks and whites—need to examine and question our own perspectives. Only then can we grasp each other's myths and grapple with the truths" (paragraph 4). Write an essay responding to that statement in which you try to sort out the two perspectives and offer some possible ways for the two groups to begin understanding one another.

9. Write a letter to the editor of the *New York Times Magazine* in which you explain your response to Alex Kotlowitz's viewpoint in "Colorblind," or, referring to his article where relevant, explain your own theory on the conditions that prevent blacks and whites in America from understanding one another's perspectives.

10. Write an essay exploring the role of racial and ethnic diversity in your educational experiences in high school and college. Consider these questions: How diverse are the student populations of schools you have attended? How large a component did multiculturalism play in the curricula of courses you have taken? Have you been satisfied with that aspect of your education?

11. Respond to Linda Chavez's claim, in "Hispanics and the American Dream," that public policies like affirmative action, welfare, and bilingual public education are ineffective and, worse, "perpetuate demeaning stereotypes of the very people they claim they are championing" (paragraph 15).

12. Narrate your first experience with prejudice, discrimination, or bigotry, as either a witness or a victim. Describe in detail the incident and how it made you feel.

13. Explain the effects of racial prejudice on a person or a group of people familiar to you.

14. Write an essay in which you suggest ways for countering prejudice or ethnic and racial hatred in the United States.

Research Topics

1. As a starting point for a research project, read Linda Chavez's *Out of the Barrio: Toward a New Politics of Hispanic Assimilation* or Alex Kotlowitz's *There Are No Children Here: The Story of Two Boys Growing Up in the Other America* or *The Other Side of the River: A Story of Two Towns, a Death, and America's Dilemma.* You may decide to find out more about a major point the author makes, or something the author mentions may lead you to a suitable topic. If the book has a bibliography, you have an excellent list of potential resources for your project.

2. Research one aspect of the subject of immigration raised by William Booth in "One Nation, Indivisible: Is It History?" or Linda Chavez in "Hispanics and the American Dream."

3. Research and write a paper on one of the following topics related to some of the essays in this chapter: Jim Crow; the influx of Chinese immigrants to America in the nineteenth century; the Chinese Exclusion Act of 1882 and its implications for Japanese immigrants; the Japanese religion Shinto; the internment of people of Japanese ancestry in America during World War II; or the economic, political, or historical relationship of the United States with Puerto Rico, Cuba, Central America, or Mexico.

4. Research the subject of multiculturalism in American education by reading expressions of differing opinions on the subject.

5. Select a topic from any of the Suggested Writing Topics and expand it to include library research, Internet research, and/or interviews.

6. Select one of the following groups to whom the U.S. federal government has made reparations and research reasons why those reparations were made: Japanese Americans interned in American prisons camp during World War II or the Sioux Indians whose lands were confiscated in 1877.

RESPONDING TO VISUALS

A friend comforts the Iraqi-born owner, right, of a restaurant burned by apparently racially motivated arson, Plymouth, Massachusetts, September 19, 2001. Source: William B. Plowman/Getty Images

1. What emotions does the photograph evoke in you?
2. The restaurant owner had received threatening telephone calls for days before the fire. How does that knowledge affect your understanding of this photograph?
3. Why did the photographer choose this particular moment to take his picture? What does it convey that a picture of the restaurant ruins alone would not?

RESPONDING TO VISUALS

Advertising postcard for Elliott's White Veneer, circa 1935. Source: Lake County Museum/ CORBIS

1. What is the message of this advertisement?
2. What is your opinion of the way the African Americans are portrayed in this ad?
3. What stereotypes does the advertisement play on?

CHAPTER

(16)

TERRORISM AND WAR

Terrorism is a sinister and reprehensible expression of hatred or vengeance. Terrorists, whether individuals or groups, target specific enemies and contrive to cause destruction, create havoc, and in general make a spectacular and grisly statement. Acts of terrorism are not new to this century nor the last, but they do seem to have grown more deadly, more widespread, and increasingly more difficult to combat. Nations, religions, and groups of assorted allegiances and identities have all been victims of numerous violent acts over time.

America is one nation that has experienced terrorism both abroad and at home. For instance, in 1979, militant students in Tehran stormed the U.S. Embassy there and held 52 hostages for 444 days. In 1983, a suicide-bomb attack destroyed the U. S. Embassy in Beirut, killing 63. That same year, also in Beirut, Hezbollah suicide bombers claimed responsibility for blowing up U. S. and French military headquarters, killing 241

U. S. and 58 French servicemen. In 1988, Pan Am flight 103, on its way to the United States, exploded over Lockerbie, Scotland, killing 270 people. On American soil, in 1993 a bomb in the underground garage of the World Trade Center killed six and injured more than 1,000 people; in 1995, a truck bomb destroyed a federal building in Oklahoma City, killing 168 and injuring more than 600.

By far the largest acts of terrorism in terms of lives lost and effects on the economy, the way people live, and American society in countless ways have been the September 11, 2001, attacks on the World Trade Center in New York City and the Pentagon in Washington, D.C. Those attacks have had profound effects on America and both its allies and foes. Many countries around the world expressed not only their shock and outrage at the terrorism on American soil but also their deep sympathy for the families, friends, and loved ones of those who lost their lives or were injured in the attacks.

The first two essays in this chapter represent different perspectives on the tragic events of September 11. Written less than two weeks later, Barbara Kingsolver's "A Pure, High Note of Anguish" seeks to offer words of consolation by answering questions that her five-year-old asked about the terrorist attacks. As you read her essay, think about how you might answer the questions posed by that child and whether your answers would differ from Kingsolver's. Then, writing less than three weeks after the event, Arundhati Roy in "The Algebra of Infinite Justice" offers an alternate view of the aftermath of the events of September 11 in her comments on Operation Enduring Freedom, the United States' military operation in Afghanistan in retaliation for the terrorist attacks of September 11. She makes a number of predictions about the effects of the United States' war on terrorism; as you read, ask yourself which, if any, have come true.

The other readings comment on the controversy over war photographs, particularly the photographs of prisoner abuse at the Abu Ghraib prison in Iraq and those of flag-draped coffins of Americans killed in the war with Iraq. First, Jeff Jacoby expresses his rage at the widespread distribution of the Abu Ghraib images. In "The Images We See and Those We Don't," he explains why he believes it was wrong to publish them. Then Charles Paul Freund in "Flag-Draped Memories" writes of the history of wartime photography, looking especially at the struggle to control war imagery during the Second World War. In doing so, he sheds light on the controversy over the publication of photographs of flag-draped coffins. The articles in this group will give you much to think about as you formulate or confirm your own viewpoint of the implications of war imagery.

A PURE, HIGH NOTE OF ANGUISH

BARBARA KINGSOLVER

Barbara Kingsolver's articles, book reviews, and short stories have appeared in numerous magazines and journals. Her novels include Animal Dreams *(1987),* The Bean Trees *(1988),* Pigs in Heaven *(1993),* The Poisonwood Bible *(1998), and* Prodigal Summer *(2000). Collections of her stories are in* Homeland and Other Stories *(1989), while a collection of her poems appears in* Another America *(1992). Among her nonfiction titles are* High Tide in Tucson: Essays from Now or Never *(1996),* Holding the Line Women in the Great Arizona Mine Strike of 1983 *(1996),* Last Stand: America's Virgin Lands *(2002), and* Small Wonder: Essays *(2002). "A Pure, High Note of Anguish" was published on September 23, 2001, in the* Los Angeles Times.

I want to do something to help right now. But I can't give blood (my hematocrit always runs too low), and I'm too far away to give anybody shelter or a drink of water. I can only give words. My verbal hemoglobin never seems to wane, so words are what I'll offer up in this time that asks of us the best citizenship we've ever mustered. I don't mean to say I have a cure. Answers to the main questions of the day—Where was that fourth plane headed? How did they get knives through security?—I don't know any of that. I have some answers, but only to the questions nobody is asking right now but my 5-year old. Why did all those people die when they didn't do anything wrong? Will it happen to me? Is this the worst thing that's ever happened? Who were those children cheering that they showed for just a minute, and why were they glad? Please, will this ever, ever happen to me?

There are so many answers, and none: It is desperately painful to see people die without having done anything to deserve it, and yet this is how lives end nearly always. We get old or we don't, we get cancer, we starve, we are battered, we get on a plane thinking we're going home but never make it. There are blessings and wonders and horrific bad luck and no guarantees. We like to pretend life is different from that, more like a game we can actually win with the right strategy, but it isn't. And, yes, it's the worst thing that's happened, but only this week. Two years ago, an earthquake in Turkey killed 17,000 people in a day, babies and mothers and businessmen, and not one of them did a thing to cause it. The November before that, a hurricane hit Honduras and Nicaragua and killed even more, buried whole villages and erased family lines and even now, people wake up there empty-handed. Which end of the world shall we talk about? Sixty years ago, Japanese airplanes bombed Navy boys who were sleeping on ships in gentle Pacific waters. Three and a half years later, American planes bombed a plaza in Japan where men and women were going to work, where schoolchildren were playing, and more humans died at once than anyone thought possible. Seventy thousand in a minute. Imagine. Then twice that many more, slowly, from the inside.

There are no worst days, it seems. Ten years ago, early on a January morning, bombs rained down from the sky and caused great buildings in the city of Baghdad to fall down—hotels, hospitals, palaces, buildings with mothers and soldiers inside—and here in the place I want to love best, I had to watch people cheering about it. In Baghdad, survivors shook their fists at the sky and said the word "evil." When many lives are lost all at once, people gather together and say words like "heinous" and "honor" and "revenge," presuming to make this awful moment stand apart somehow from the ways people die a little each day from sickness or hunger. They raise up their compatriots' lives to a sacred place—we do this, all of us who are human—thinking our own citizens to be more worthy of grief and less willingly risked than lives on other soil. But broken hearts are not mended in this ceremony, because, really, every life that ends is utterly its own event—and also in some way it's the same as all others, a light going out that ached to burn longer. Even if you never had the chance to love the light that's gone, you miss it. You should. You bear this world and everything that's wrong with it by holding life still precious, each time, and starting over.

4   And those children dancing in the street? That is the hardest question. We would rather discuss trails of evidence and whom to stamp out, even the size and shape of the cage we might put ourselves in to stay safe, than to mention the fact that our nation is not universally beloved; we are also despised. And not just by "The Terrorist," that lone, deranged non-man in a bad photograph whose opinion we can clearly dismiss, but by ordinary people in many lands. Even by little boys—whole towns full of them it looked like—jumping for joy in school shoes and pilled woolen sweaters.

There are a hundred ways to be a good citizen, and one of them is to look finally at the things we don't want to see. In a week of terrifying events, here is one awful, true thing that hasn't much been mentioned: Some people believe our country needed to learn how to hurt in this new way. This is such a large lesson, so hatefully, wrongfully taught, but many people before us have learned honest truths from wrongful deaths. It still may be within our capacity of mercy to say this much is true: We didn't really understand how it felt when citizens were buried alive in Turkey or Nicaragua or Hiroshima. Or that night in Baghdad. And we haven't cared enough for the particular brothers and mothers taken down a limb or a life at a time, for such a span of years that those little, briefly jubilant boys have grown up with twisted hearts. How could we keep raining down bombs and selling weapons, if we had? How can our president still use that word "attack" so casually, like a move in a checker game, now that we have awakened to see that word in our own newspapers, used like this: Attack on America.

Surely, the whole world grieves for us right now. And surely it also hopes we might have learned, from the taste of our own blood, that every war is both won and lost, and that loss is a pure, high note of anguish like a mother singing to any empty bed. The mortal citizens of a planet are praying right now that we will bear in mind, better than ever before, that no kind of bomb ever built will extinguish hatred.

"Will this happen to me?" is the wrong question, I'm sad to say. It always was.

PERSONAL RESPONSE

Write for a few minutes about your emotions when you heard the news of the September 11, 2001, terrorist attacks against the United States.

QUESTIONS FOR CLASS OR SMALL-GROUP DISCUSSION

1. Kingsolver says that she wants "to do something to help" and "can only give words" (paragraph 1). How helpful do you find her words? If you find her words helpful, locate a passage that you find particularly effective. If you do not believe they help, explain why not.

2. Explain the title of the essay. How is it related to Kingsolver's central purpose?

3. What do you think Kingsolver means by her concluding sentence? Why is " 'Will this happen to me?' " the "wrong question"?

4. How would you answer the questions that Kingsolver's five-year-old asks (paragraph 1)?

THE ALGEBRA OF INFINITE JUSTICE

ARUNDHATI ROY

Arundhati Roy was trained as an architect but became known for her filmscripts. She was the first Indian woman to win England's prestigious Booker Prize for her novel The God of Small Things *(1999), which sold six million copies and has been translated into forty languages. She is also author of* The Cost of Living *(1999),* Power Politics *(2001),* War Talk, *(2003), and* An Ordinary Person's Guide to Empire *(2004), among other works. This article was first published in* The Guardian *of London on September 29, 2001.*

In the aftermath of the unconscionable September 11 suicide attacks on the Pentagon and the World Trade Center, an American newscaster said: "Good and evil rarely manifest themselves as clearly as they did last Tuesday. People who we don't know massacred people who we do. And they did so with contemptuous glee." Then he broke down and wept.

Here's the rub: America is at war against people it doesn't know, because they don't appear much on TV. Before it has properly identified or even begun to comprehend the nature of its enemy, the US government has, in a rush of publicity and embarrassing rhetoric, cobbled together an "international coalition against terror," mobilized its army, its air force, its navy and its media, and committed them to battle.

The trouble is that once America goes off to war, it can't very well return without having fought one. If it doesn't find its enemy, for the sake of the enraged folks back home, it will have to manufacture one. Once war begins, it will develop a momentum, a logic and a justification of its own, and we'll lose sight of why it's being fought in the first place.

4   What we're witnessing here is the spectacle of the world's most powerful country reaching reflexively, angrily, for an old instinct to fight a new kind of war. Suddenly, when it comes to defending itself, America's streamlined warships, cruise missiles and F-16 jets look like obsolete, lumbering things. As deterrence, its arsenal of nuclear bombs is no longer worth its weight in scrap. Box-cutters, penknives, and cold anger are the weapons with which the wars of the new century will be waged. Anger is the lock pick. It slips through customs unnoticed. Doesn't show up in baggage checks.

Who is America fighting? On September 20, the FBI said that it had doubts about the identities of some of the hijackers. On the same day President George Bush said, "We know exactly who these people are and which governments are supporting them." It sounds as though the president knows something that the FBI and the American public don't.

In his September 20 address to the US Congress, President Bush called the enemies of America "enemies of freedom". "Americans are asking, 'Why do they hate us?' " he said. "They hate our freedoms—our freedom of religion, our freedom of speech, our freedom to vote and assemble and disagree with each other." People are being asked to make two leaps of faith here. First, to assume that The Enemy is who the US government says it is, even though it has no substantial evidence to support that claim. And second, to assume that The Enemy's motives are what the US government says they are, and there's nothing to support that either.

For strategic, military and economic reasons, it is vital for the US government to persuade its public that their commitment to freedom and democracy and the American Way of Life is under attack. In the current atmosphere of grief, outrage and anger, it's an easy notion to peddle. However, if that were true, it's reasonable to wonder why the symbols of America's economic and military dominance—the World Trade Center and the Pentagon—were chosen as the targets of the attacks. Why not the Statue of Liberty? Could it be that the stygian anger that led to the attacks has its taproot not in American freedom and democracy, but in the US government's record of commitment and support to exactly the opposite things—to military and economic terrorism, insurgency, military dictatorship, religious bigotry and unimaginable genocide (outside America)? It must be hard for ordinary Americans, so recently bereaved, to look up at the world with their eyes full of tears and encounter what might appear to them to be indifference. It isn't indifference. It's just augury. An absence of surprise. The tired wisdom of knowing that what goes around eventually comes around. American people ought to know that it is not them but their government's policies that are so hated. They can't possibly doubt that they themselves, their extraordinary musicians, their writers, their actors, their spectacular sportsmen and their cinema, are universally welcomed. All of us have been moved by the courage and grace shown by firefighters, rescue workers and ordinary office staff in the days since the attacks.

8   America's grief at what happened has been immense and immensely public. It would be grotesque to expect it to calibrate or modulate its anguish. However, it will

be a pity if, instead of using this as an opportunity to try to understand why September 11 happened, Americans use it as an opportunity to usurp the whole world's sorrow to mourn and avenge only their own. Because then it falls to the rest of us to ask the hard questions and say the harsh things. And for our pains, for our bad timing, we will be disliked, ignored and perhaps eventually silenced.

The world will probably never know what motivated those particular hijackers who flew planes into those particular American buildings. They were not glory boys. They left no suicide notes, no political messages; no organization has claimed credit for the attacks. All we know is that their belief in what they were doing outstripped the natural human instinct for survival, or any desire to be remembered. It's almost as though they could not scale down the enormity of their rage to anything smaller than their deeds. And what they did has blown a hole in the world as we knew it. In the absence of information, politicians, political commentators and writers (like myself) will invest the act with their own politics, with their own interpretations. This speculation, this analysis of the political climate in which the attacks took place, can only be a good thing.

But war is looming large. Whatever remains to be said must be said quickly. Before America places itself at the helm of the "international coalition against terror," before it invites (and coerces) countries to actively participate in its almost godlike mission—called Operation Infinite Justice until it was pointed out that this could be seen as an insult to Muslims, who believe that only Allah can mete out infinite justice, and was renamed Operation Enduring Freedom—it would help if some small clarifications are made. For example, Infinite Justice/Enduring Freedom for whom? Is this America's war against terror in America or against terror in general? What exactly is being avenged here? Is it the tragic loss of almost 7,000 lives, the gutting of five million square feet of office space in Manhattan, the destruction of a section of the Pentagon, the loss of several hundreds of thousands of jobs, the bankruptcy of some airline companies and the dip in the New York Stock Exchange? Or is it more than that? In 1996, Madeleine Albright, then the US secretary of state, was asked on national television what she felt about the fact that 500,000 Iraqi children had died as a result of US economic sanctions. She replied that it was "a very hard choice," but that, all things considered, "we think the price is worth it." Albright never lost her job for saying this. She continued to travel the world representing the views and aspirations of the US government. More pertinently, the sanctions against Iraq remain in place. Children continue to die.

So here we have it. The equivocating distinction between civilization and savagery, between the "massacre of innocent people" or, if you like, "a clash of civilizations" and "collateral damage." The sophistry and fastidious algebra of infinite justice. How many dead Iraqis will it take to make the world a better place? How many dead Afghans for every dead American? How many dead women and children for every dead man? How many dead mojahedin for each dead investment banker? As we watch mesmerized, Operation Enduring Freedom unfolds on TV monitors across the world. A coalition of the world's superpowers is closing in on Afghanistan, one of the poorest, most ravaged, war-torn countries in the world, whose ruling Taliban government is sheltering Osama bin Laden, the man being held responsible for the September 11 attacks.

12   The only thing in Afghanistan that could possibly count as collateral value is its citizenry. (Among them, half a million maimed orphans. There are accounts of hobbling stampedes that occur when artificial limbs are airdropped into remote, inaccessible villages.) Afghanistan's economy is in a shambles. In fact, the problem for an invading army is that Afghanistan has no conventional coordinates or signposts to plot on a military map—no big cities, no highways, no industrial complexes, no water treatment plants. Farms have been turned into mass graves. The countryside is littered with land mines—10 million is the most recent estimate. The American army would first have to clear the mines and build roads in order to take its soldiers in.

Fearing an attack from America, one million citizens have fled from their homes and arrived at the border between Pakistan and Afghanistan. The UN estimates that there are eight million Afghan citizens who need emergency aid. As supplies run out—food and aid agencies have been asked to leave—the BBC reports that one of the worst humanitarian disasters of recent times has begun to unfold. Witness the infinite justice of the new century. Civilians starving to death while they're waiting to be killed.

In America there has been rough talk of "bombing Afghanistan back to the stone age." Someone please break the news that Afghanistan is already there. And if it's any consolation, America played no small part in helping it on its way. The American people may be a little fuzzy about where exactly Afghanistan is (we hear reports that there's a run on maps of the country), but the US government and Afghanistan are old friends.

In 1979, after the Soviet invasion of Afghanistan, the CIA and Pakistan's ISI (Inter Services Intelligence) launched the largest covert operation in the history of the CIA. Their purpose was to harness the energy of Afghan resistance to the Soviets and expand it into a holy war, an Islamic jihad, which would turn Muslim countries within the Soviet Union against the communist regime and eventually destabilize it. When it began, it was meant to be the Soviet Union's Vietnam. It turned out to be much more than that. Over the years, through the ISI, the CIA funded and recruited almost 100,000 radical mojahedin from 40 Islamic countries as soldiers for America's proxy war. The rank and file of the mojahedin were unaware that their jihad was actually being fought on behalf of Uncle Sam. (The irony is that America was equally unaware that it was financing a future war against itself.)

16   In 1989, after being bloodied by 10 years of relentless conflict, the Russians withdrew, leaving behind a civilization reduced to rubble.

Civil war in Afghanistan raged on. The jihad spread to Chechnya, Kosovo and eventually to Kashmir. The CIA continued to pour in money and military equipment, but the overheads had become immense, and more money was needed. The mojahedin ordered farmers to plant opium as a "revolutionary tax." The ISI set up hundreds of heroin laboratories across Afghanistan. Within two years of the CIA's arrival, the Pakistan-Afghanistan borderland had become the biggest producer of heroin in the world, and the single biggest source of the heroin on American streets. The annual profits, said to be between $100bn and $200bn, were ploughed back into training and arming militants.

In 1995, the Taliban—then a marginal sect of dangerous, hardline fundamentalists—fought its way to power in Afghanistan. It was funded by the ISI, that old cohort of the CIA, and supported by many political parties in Pakistan. The Taliban unleashed a regime of terror. Its first victims were its own people, particularly women. It closed down girls' schools, dismissed women from government jobs, and enforced sharia laws under which women deemed to be "immoral" are stoned to death, and widows guilty of being adulterous are buried alive. Given the Taliban government's human rights track record, it seems unlikely that it will in any way be intimidated or swerved from its purpose by the prospect of war, or the threat to the lives of its civilians.

After all that has happened, can there be anything more ironic than Russia and America joining hands to re-destroy Afghanistan? The question is, can you destroy destruction? Dropping more bombs on Afghanistan will only shuffle the rubble, scramble some old graves and disturb the dead.

20   The desolate landscape of Afghanistan was the burial ground of Soviet communism and the springboard of a unipolar world dominated by America. It made the space for neocapitalism and corporate globalization, again dominated by America. And now Afghanistan is poised to become the graveyard for the unlikely soldiers who fought and won this war for America.

And what of America's trusted ally? Pakistan too has suffered enormously. The US government has not been shy of supporting military dictators who have blocked the idea of democracy from taking root in the country. Before the CIA arrived, there was a small rural market for opium in Pakistan. Between 1979 and 1985, the number of heroin addicts grew from zero to one-and-a-half million. Even before September 11, there were three million Afghan refugees living in tented camps along the border. Pakistan's economy is crumbling. Sectarian violence, globalization's structural adjustment programs and drug lords are tearing the country to pieces. Set up to fight the Soviets, the terrorist training centers and madrasahs, sown like dragon's teeth across the country, produced fundamentalists with tremendous popular appeal within Pakistan itself. The Taliban, which the Pakistan government has supported, funded and propped up for years, has material and strategic alliances with Pakistan's own political parties.

Now the US government is asking (asking?) Pakistan to garotte the pet it has hand-reared in its backyard for so many years. President Musharraf, having pledged his support to the US, could well find he has something resembling civil war on his hands.

India, thanks in part to its geography, and in part to the vision of its former leaders, has so far been fortunate enough to be left out of this Great Game. Had it been drawn in, it's more than likely that our democracy, such as it is, would not have survived. Today, as some of us watch in horror, the Indian government is furiously gyrating its hips, begging the US to set up its base in India rather than Pakistan. Having had this ringside view of Pakistan's sordid fate, it isn't just odd, it's unthinkable, that India should want to do this. Any third world country with a fragile economy and a complex social base should know by now that to invite a superpower such as America in (whether it says it's staying or just passing through) would be like inviting a brick to drop through your windscreen.

24   Operation Enduring Freedom is ostensibly being fought to uphold the American Way of Life. It'll probably end up undermining it completely. It will spawn more anger and more terror across the world. For ordinary people in America, it will mean

lives lived in a climate of sickening uncertainty: will my child be safe in school? Will there be nerve gas in the subway? A bomb in the cinema hall? Will my love come home tonight? There have been warnings about the possibility of biological warfare—smallpox, bubonic plague, anthrax—the deadly payload of innocuous crop-duster aircraft. Being picked off a few at a time may end up being worse than being annihilated all at once by a nuclear bomb.

The US government, and no doubt governments all over the world, will use the climate of war as an excuse to curtail civil liberties, deny free speech, lay off workers, harass ethnic and religious minorities, cut back on public spending and divert huge amounts of money to the defense industry. To what purpose? President Bush can no more "rid the world of evil-doers" than he can stock it with saints. It's absurd for the US government to even toy with the notion that it can stamp out terrorism with more violence and oppression. Terrorism is the symptom, not the disease. Terrorism has no country. It's transnational, as global an enterprise as Coke or Pepsi or Nike. At the first sign of trouble, terrorists can pull up stakes and move their "factories" from country to country in search of a better deal. Just like the multi-nationals.

Terrorism as a phenomenon may never go away. But if it is to be contained, the first step is for America to at least acknowledge that it shares the planet with other nations, with other human beings who, even if they are not on TV, have loves and griefs and stories and songs and sorrows and, for heaven's sake, rights. Instead, when Donald Rumsfeld, the US defense secretary, was asked what he would call a victory in America's new war, he said that if he could convince the world that Americans must be allowed to continue with their way of life, he would consider it a victory.

The September 11 attacks were a monstrous calling card from a world gone horribly wrong. The message may have been written by Bin Laden (who knows?) and delivered by his couriers, but it could well have been signed by the ghosts of the victims of America's old wars. The millions killed in Korea, Vietnam and Cambodia, the 17,500 killed when Israel—backed by the US—invaded Lebanon in 1982, the 200,000 Iraqis killed in Operation Desert Storm, the thousands of Palestinians who have died fighting Israel's occupation of the West Bank. And the millions who died, in Yugoslavia, Somalia, Haiti, Chile, Nicaragua, El Salvador, the Dominican Republic, Panama, at the hands of all the terrorists, dictators and genocidists whom the American government supported, trained, bankrolled and supplied with arms. And this is far from being a comprehensive list.

28   For a country involved in so much warfare and conflict, the American people have been extremely fortunate. The strikes on September 11 were only the second on American soil in over a century. The first was Pearl Harbor. The reprisal for this took a long route, but ended with Hiroshima and Nagasaki. This time the world waits with bated breath for the horrors to come.

Someone recently said that if Osama bin Laden didn't exist, America would have had to invent him. But, in a way, America did invent him. He was among the jihadis who moved to Afghanistan in 1979 when the CIA commenced its operations there. Bin Laden has the distinction of being created by the CIA and wanted by the FBI. In the course of a fortnight he has been promoted from suspect to prime suspect and then, despite the lack of any real evidence, straight up the charts to being "wanted dead or alive."

From all accounts, it will be impossible to produce evidence (of the sort that would stand scrutiny in a court of law) to link Bin Laden to the September 11 attacks. So far, it appears that the most incriminating piece of evidence against him is the fact that he has not condemned them.

From what is known about the location of Bin Laden and the living conditions in which he operates, it's entirely possible that he did not personally plan and carry out the attacks—that he is the inspirational figure, "the CEO of the holding company." The Taliban's response to US demands for the extradition of Bin Laden has been uncharacteristically reasonable: produce the evidence, then we'll hand him over. President Bush's response is that the demand is "non-negotiable."

32   (While talks are on for the extradition of CEOs—can India put in a side request for the extradition of Warren Anderson of the US? He was the chairman of Union Carbide, responsible for the Bhopal gas leak that killed 16,000 people in 1984. We have collated the necessary evidence. It's all in the files. Could we have him, please?)

But who is Osama bin Laden really? Let me rephrase that. What is Osama bin Laden? He's America's family secret. He is the American president's dark doppelgänger. The savage twin of all that purports to be beautiful and civilized. He has been sculpted from the spare rib of a world laid to waste by America's foreign policy: its gunboat diplomacy, its nuclear arsenal, its vulgarly stated policy of "full-spectrum dominance," its chilling disregard for non-American lives, its barbarous military interventions, its support for despotic and dictatorial regimes, its merciless economic agenda that has munched through the economies of poor countries like a cloud of locusts. Its marauding multinationals who are taking over the air we breathe, the ground we stand on, the water we drink, the thoughts we think. Now that the family secret has been spilled, the twins are blurring into one another and gradually becoming interchangeable. Their guns, bombs, money and drugs have been going around in the loop for a while. (The Stinger missiles that will greet US helicopters were supplied by the CIA. The heroin used by America's drug addicts comes from Afghanistan. The Bush administration recently gave Afghanistan a $43m subsidy for a "war on drugs" . . .).

Now Bush and Bin Laden have even begun to borrow each other's rhetoric. Each refers to the other as "the head of the snake." Both invoke God and use the loose millenarian currency of good and evil as their terms of reference. Both are engaged in unequivocal political crimes. Both are dangerously armed—one with the nuclear arsenal of the obscenely powerful, the other with the incandescent, destructive power of the utterly hopeless. The fireball and the ice pick. The bludgeon and the axe. The important thing to keep in mind is that neither is an acceptable alternative to the other.

President Bush's ultimatum to the people of the world—"If you're not with us, you're against us"—is a piece of presumptuous arrogance. It's not a choice that people want to, need to, or should have to make.

PERSONAL RESPONSE

Select a statement or passage that you feel strongly about, either positively or negatively, and explain your response to it.

QUESTIONS FOR CLASS AND SMALL-GROUP DISCUSSION

1. Explain the title.

2. What is Roy's perception of the United States? For instance, why do you think she says that America did not know its enemy because they have not been on television (paragraphs 2 and 26)? What does she say about America's aggressive foreign policy?

3. Roy asks a number of questions, as in paragraphs 5 and 10. Select one of these or any of her other questions and formulate a possible answer.

4. What do you think Roy means when she says that the belief motivating the hijackers on September 11 "has blown a hole in the world as we knew it" (paragraph 9)?

5. Writing just weeks after the events of September 11, 2001, Roy makes a number of assumptions or predictions about what would happen. Which of her assumptions have been realized? For instance, look at what she says about the probable effects of Operation Enduring Freedom and the government's using "the climate of war as an excuse to curtail civil liberties." Find other places where she predicts what will happen and discuss whether they have, in fact, happened.

THE IMAGES WE SEE AND THOSE WE DON'T

JEFF JACOBY

Jeff Jacoby was chief editorial writer for the Boston Herald *from 1987 until becoming an op-ed columnist for* The Boston Globe *in 1994. Trained as a lawyer, he has been a political commentator for Boston's National Public Radio affiliate and was host of "Talk of New England," a weekly television program, for several years. In 1999, Jacoby became the first recipient of the Breindel Award for Excellence in Opinion Journalism. "The Images We See and Those We Don't" first appeared in the May 13, 2004, issue of* The Boston Globe.

The death of Nicholas Berg is a horror. It is a bitter reminder of why we are at war— something that much of America's political and media elite, in their binge of outrage and apology over the Abu Ghraib abuses, have lately seemed all too willing to forget.

I don't for a moment minimize the awfulness of what some American soldiers did to their Iraqi captives in that prison. Their offenses may have fallen far short of the savagery that Abu Ghraib was notorious for under Saddam Hussein, but in their cruelty and urge to humiliate and in the sadistic glee with which they posed for those photographs, they reek of the depravity we went to Iraq to uproot. As one who believes that this war was necessary above all on moral grounds, I'm sickened by what they did.

But I'm sickened as well by the relish with which this scandal is being exploited by those who think that the defeat of the Bush administration is an end that justifies just about any means. I'm sickened by the recklessness of the media, which relentlessly flogged the graphic images from Abu Ghraib, giving them an in-your-face prominence that couldn't help but exaggerate their impact. And I'm sickened by the thought of how much damage this feeding frenzy may have done to the war effort. We do remember the war effort, don't we? Surely we haven't forgotten the jetliners smashing into the twin towers and Pentagon, and 3,000 innocents dying in a single morning. Or the monstrous Saddam, who filled mass graves to bursting, invaded two neighboring countries, and avidly sought weapons of mass destruction. Or the reason why 130,000 US soldiers are on the line in Iraq: because establishing a democratic beachhead in the Middle East is critical to cutting off the terrorists' oxygen—the backing they get from dictatorial regimes.

4   My sense is that the public hasn't lost sight of any of this. But for weeks now, a goodly swath of the chattering class has been treating the war as little more than a rhetorical backdrop against which to score political points or increase market share.

Newsweek's Eleanor Clift, for instance, reacted to the Abu Ghraib revelations with a column urging the Democratic presidential candidate to milk the moment for all it was worth. "If ever there was a moment for John Kerry to come out swinging, this is it," she wrote. "It is the biggest story of the war, and he is essentially silent." There are many thoughtful things one might say about Abu Ghraib, but only someone eager for the US campaign in Iraq to fail and George W. Bush to be defeated could possibly describe it as "the biggest story of the war."

Besides, the Kerry campaign has hardly been silent on the prison scandal. It is using it as a fund-raising hook, sending out mass e-mails urging supporters to petition for Donald Rumsfeld's resignation—and to donate money to the Kerry campaign.

Poor Nick Berg. The anybody-but-Bush crowd isn't going to rush to publicize his terrible fate with anything like the zeal it brought to the abused prisoners story. CBS and *The New Yorker* couldn't resist the temptation to shove the Abu Ghraib photos into the public domain—and the rest of the media then made sure the world saw them over and over and over. But when it comes to video and stills of Al Qaeda murderers severing Berg's head with a knife and brandishing it in triumph for the camera, the Fourth Estate is suddenly squeamish.

8   As I write on Wednesday afternoon, the CBS News website continues to offer a complete "photo essay" of naked Iraqi men being humiliated by Americans in a variety of poses. But the video of Berg's beheading, CBS says, "is too gruesome to show." No other network and no newspaper that I have seen shows the gory pictures, either.

What exactly is the governing rule here? That incendiary images sure to enrage our enemies and get more Americans killed should be published while images that show the world just how evil those enemies really are should be suppressed? Offensive and shocking pictures that undermine the war effort should be played up but offensive and shocking pictures that remind us why we're at war in the first place shouldn't get played at all?

Yes, Virginia, there really is a gaping media double standard. News organizations will shield your tender eyes from the sight of a Berg or a Daniel Pearl being decapitated, or of Sept. 11 victims jumping to their deaths, or of the mangled bodies on the USS Cole, or of Fallujans joyfully mutilating the remains of four lynched US civilians. But they will make sure you don't miss the odious behavior of Americans or American allies, no matter how atypical that misbehavior may be or how determined the US military is to uproot and punish it.

We are at war with a vicious enemy, and propaganda in wartime is a weapon whose consequences can be deadly. Nick Berg lost his life because the Abu Ghraib pictures were turned into a worldwide media event. Yes, those who did so were sheltered by the First Amendment. That makes what they did not better but worse.

PERSONAL RESPONSE

What is your opinion on the issue of whether the photos from the Abu Ghraib prison scandal should be published? Is publishing the photos the same as siding with the enemy, as Jacoby suggests?

QUESTIONS FOR CLASS OR SMALL-GROUP DISCUSSION

1. Explain in your own words why Jacoby objects to the publication of the images of prisoner abuse at Abu Ghraib.
2. What strategies does Jacoby use argue his position? Do you find him convincing and his position valid?
3. Jacoby says in paragraph 9 that there is "a gaping media double standard." Do you agree with Jacoby on this point? What examples can you give from personal observation?

FLAG-DRAPED MEMORIES

CHARLES PAUL FREUND

Charles Paul Freund, a Reason *senior editor, has also written for many periodicals, including the* Washington Post, *the* New Republic, *the* New York Times, Village Voice, Esquire, Columbia Journalism Review, American Film, *and newspapers throughout the United States. A long-time documentary filmmaker, Freund has written many film scripts for Universal Studios' Documentary Division, United Press International Television News, and the United States Information Agency. "Flag-Draped Memories" was published in the April 28, 2004, issue of* Reason.

Three months after the war began, a New York newspaper bitterly attacked the administration's handling of unpleasant military news. "Their 'information' is treacle for children," thundered the angry editorialist, who compared the military's growing edifice of information control to the work of Nazi propagandist Joseph Goebbels. Other publications agreed that war news was being "dry-cleaned" by the government, which had yet to release a single image of an American military death. Indeed, there were rumors that a paranoid White House was planting informants in newsrooms and even tapping reporters' phones. It was 1942.

You'll find that portrait of an earlier generation of wartime Americans, their press, and their government in George Roeder's invaluable study *The Censored War: American Visual Experience During World War Two* (1993). One lesson to be taken is that Americans don't entirely trust their state, even when it is engaged in an effort that most of them support. That is especially true when the state's effort is military, as the recent controversy concerning images of Iraq's flag-draped coffins—and thus the struggle over the control of war imagery—illustrates once again.

The struggle for war image control began when a camera was first aimed at soldiers in Crimea, but that struggle is hardly founded on the absolutes implied by arguments like the one over the war coffins. The simple version of this and similar debates—that the state must hide its dead or risk growing opposition to its war—is a misleading simplification of a complex phenomenon. Yet both the state, which wants to limit these images' exposure, and war critics, who want them disseminated, are acting as if the reaction to such images is Pavlovian.

4   The historic role of war imagery is actually filled with contradictions. The state doesn't always try to hide its war dead; sometimes it is anxious to display them. Viewers of such images are not always repelled or demoralized by them; they have had many other reactions, including an increased support for war. The press is not always anxious to reproduce such images for either sensational or political purposes; it may well prefer to ignore them entirely. The war images we see are not always documentary evidence of war's carnage; some famous images may well have been misidentified, and some photographers have even arranged and rearranged the dead like so many props. For that matter, images, however harrowing, are not necessarily more revealing of war's atrocities than words.

World War II, a singularly misperceived experience, offers telling illustrations of many of the complexities involving both the control of war images and the reaction to them. As Roeder recounts, for the first two years of that war there was not a single documentary image of American death released to the public. This was a continuation of the policy adopted during World War I, when the American government censored all such images throughout the conflict.

The reason Franklin Roosevelt followed Woodrow Wilson's censorship example, it appears, is that FDR was uncertain of continued public support, especially for the war in Europe. Until mid-1942, the war news was nearly all bad, and a significant number of Americans thought an overextended U.S. should have concentrated on Japan, which had attacked the country. Nearly a third of the populace favored making some accommodation with Nazi Germany and extricating the U.S. military from Europe. The administration feared that images of the war's dead would demoralize the country and further erode support for the war's broad strategy. War photographers (who, like war reporters, wore uniforms) often had to send their unexposed rolls of film to the Pentagon for processing.

By late 1943, however, FDR's administration and the military had completely changed their minds. Americans, they decided, had by then become too complacent about the war. Much of the war news had been positive, and the government was worried about increasing work absenteeism. What Americans needed, thought the state, was a display of military sacrifice. So the Pentagon quickly released hundreds of images of dead soldiers to remind civilians that the war remained a deadly business still to be decided. As it happens, many publications refused to publish the images; their editors feared such pictures would "disturb" readers. But some of the country's largest-circulation periodicals, such as *Life*, did run them, and they were widely seen.

8   There is, of course, an apparent contradiction between these two approaches. If FDR's original view—that death images would demoralize the public—was valid, displaying them in the latter part of the war (when the vast majority of U.S. war deaths occurred) risked undermining the American military's demands for uncondi- tional surrender, at least in Europe. If his later, revised view—that death images would increase public fervor—was correct, then displaying them in the first, dark months of the war might well have helped counteract the effect of so much negative military news. (After all, "noble sacrifice" against great odds was the underlying theme of many early Hollywood war movies.)

There is an obvious third proposition: Neither of these generalizations about the effect of death imagery was necessarily correct. While there is often a plain and un- changing personal meaning in such images of death, there is no inevitable political meaning in them; rather, their political meaning and impact can change according to their context. The most important factor in that context is probably not whether a given conflict appears to be going well but whether the viewer of such images believes the war's cause to be just and its pursuit purposeful. If you believe that about the Iraq war, then you probably interpret the coffin images a certain way; if you don't, you probably see a different picture.

Hiding such imagery, as many administrations have done, is in the end an act of self-defeating censorship, one that invites legitimate questions about what else the state might be hiding about the war and about the state's attitude toward the citizens it is sending into battle. At the same time, disseminating such images as an act of war criticism is reductionist and prone to backfire, because such an act seeks to impose a single political meaning—often involving victimhood or exploitation—on images whose meaning is fluid.

Whether such images portray honorable sacrifice or something very different de- pends on how the viewers perceive the war itself, and not, as some involved in this de- bate seem to believe, the other way around.

PERSONAL RESPONSE

Should war imagery be controlled? Should the press have full freedom to publish any images it wants to, or should the government monitor what gets released to the public?

QUESTIONS FOR CLASS OR SMALL-GROUP DISCUSSION

1. Freund says that the debate over war-image control is often viewed simplis- tically but that it is really "a complex phenomenon" (paragraph 3). Explain what makes it a complex issue, according to Freund.

2. What is the "apparent contradiction between" two approaches to publishing war death images that Freund mentions in paragraph 8?

3. Freund maintains that "[t]here is an obvious third proposition" in the controversy over publishing war-death imagery (paragraph 9). Explain what it is and whether you agree with him.

4. To what extent do you agree with Freund's conclusion about the effects of hiding war images?

○ PERSPECTIVES ON TERRORISM AND WAR ○

Suggested Writing Topics

1. Write an opinion essay in response to Arundhati Roy's "The Algebra of Infinite Justice" or Jeff Jacoby's "The Images We See and Those We Don't."

2. Referring to the readings in this chapter, compare and contrast views on the publication of photographs of the Abu Ghraib prison abuse or the flag-draped coffins of American soldiers killed in the war and explain your own position on their publication.

3. Explore the effects of the September 11, 2001, terrorist attacks on America. In what ways did they change America?

4. Analyze the responses of people in other nations to the September 11 terrorist attacks.

5. Write a reflective essay on the nature of heroism and extraordinary sacrifice as demonstrated during the September 11 terrorist attacks or after them.

6. Write an essay explaining your viewpoint on the issue of how far the state should be allowed to restrict civil liberties for the sake of national security.

7. Write a personal essay explaining your feelings about the September 11 terrorist attacks and/or how you see them affecting you or your generation in the years to come.

8. Select a statement from any of the readings in this chapter and write an essay in response to it.

9. Write a critique of George Roeder's *The Censored War: American Visual Experience During World War Two,* as mentioned by Charles Paul Freund in Flag-Draped Memories (paragraph 2).

Research Topics

1. Research the effects of the September 11 terrorist attacks in New York and Washington on the American economy, the American image abroad, or America's role in international politics. All of these topics are broad, so after selecting one, narrow it down further. For instance, you might begin by asking what the economic effects of the attacks were on the airline industry, investment firms, or the Stock Exchange, and then further narrow your focus as you begin reading on the subject.

2. Research the subject of what led to the events of September 11. What motivated the terrorist attacks? How can one explain why they happened?

3. Research the question of whether there is a double standard in war reporting, as charged by Jeff Jacoby in "The Images We See and Those We Don't."

4. Conduct research to support or refute Charles Paul Freund's comment in "Flag-Draped Memories" that "the struggle for war image control . . . [is] a complex phenomenon" (paragraph 3).

5. Research the costs of the war on terrorism and do an analysis of the economics of such a war.

6. Research the role of other nations in coalition-building following the terrorist attacks in New York and Washington.

7. Research the subject of how extremist Muslims contrast with moderate and secularist Muslims. Look at the beliefs and actions of both and identify major areas of difference.

8. Following the terrorist attacks against New York and Washington, the North Atlantic Treaty Organization (NATO) invoked article 5 of its mutual defense treaty. Research the purpose of NATO and assess its role in the aftermath of the September 11 attacks.

RESPONDING TO VISUALS

Sculpture in a park near the World Trade Center, September 11, 2001. Source: Susan Meiselas/Magnum Photos

1. How does the photographer use the sculpture to comment on the terrorist attacks against the twin towers of the World Trade Center? What details combine to make that comment?
2. Would the effect of the picture be different if a human or humans were in it instead of a sculpture?
3. How does the photographer use lines and shapes in the composition of the photograph?

RESPONDING TO VISUALS

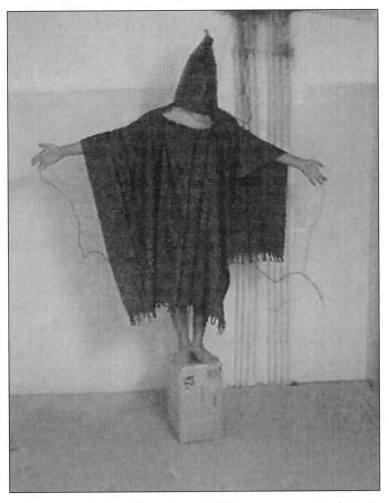

A prisoner being tortured in Iraq, November 4, 2003. The prisoner was made to stand on the box for about an hour and was told he would be electrocuted if he fell. Source: EPA/Landov

1. What details of the photograph contribute to its overall effect?
2. How does the image reveal the power relationship between the person who took the photograph and the prisoner?
3. What are the implications of this photograph in terms of the war in Iraq, the behavior of U.S. soldiers, and the treatment of prisoners of war?
4. Why do you think that, for many people, this photograph has become the iconic image of the war in Iraq

CHAPTER

17

AMERICA ABROAD IN
POLITICAL SCIENCE

In recent years, international relations have become an extremely important branch of political science, the study of politics, and the workings of the government. America's role as a superpower puts it in the position of being closely scrutinized by leaders, journalists, and ordinary citizens around the world. What America does politically is extremely important to other countries because America's actions are likely to affect them either directly or indirectly in many ways, especially economically and politically. The term *global village,* coined a few decades ago to describe the myriad links among the world's nations, is particularly apt when considering international relations and the perception that other countries have of America. Its political events are reported almost instantaneously around the globe by satellite, and magazines and newspapers also play crucial roles in conveying certain images of America and Americans to other nations.

Other nations pay close attention to American politics and America's foreign policy, as the first two essays in this chapter indicate. Although Timothy Garton Ash's "Fortress America" was written before the 2004 presidential election, he makes some interesting observations about U. S. foreign policy and how America is perceived abroad. His immediate subject is the 2004 presidential race, but his broader subject is American foreign policy. Next, Joseph S. Nye, Jr., in "The Decline of America's Soft Power," writes of the unpopularity of American policies abroad. Nye believes that in order to succeed in the war on terrorism, the United States must be able to persuade other nations to support them. In Nye's view, the government's ability to do that is in sharp decline, and his essay makes recommendations for what America must do to turn that decline around. Ask yourself as you read these essays just what the implications of the American image abroad are for American politics.

"Voices from Abroad," which follows Nye's essay, is a compilation of comments from Americans living abroad. New Englanders living in other countries were asked to describe how people in the countries they are living in perceive America. Their remarks, as compiler Chris Berdik notes, indicate just how pervasive is America's influence on people in other nations of the world. The final essay, Pico Iyer's "Selling Our Innocence Abroad," examines the image of America abroad as represented by American popular culture. Iyer points out that the products of America's popular culture—its movies, songs, magazines, T-shirts, and the like—make up "the largest single source of America's export earnings." These products of American pop culture convey an image that helps perpetuate certain notions about America as a land of glamour, wealth, excitement, and even a kind of innocence. Hollywood, Broadway, and Nashville have particular influence in conveying this image, according to Iyer. Before you read his essay, think about what Hollywood suggests to you. Do you think of glamour, of classic films and famous stars, or do you think of cheap sensationalism, escapism, and money-hungry exploiters out to become rich in any way they can? What picture of America do you think today's Hollywood stars, pop recording artists, and famous Broadway actors project?

FORTRESS AMERICA

Timothy Garton Ash

Timothy Garton Ash is a senior fellow at the Hoover Institution, direc-
tor of the European Studies Centre, and Gerd Bucerius Senior Research
Fellow in Contemporary History of St. Antony's College, Oxford Uni-
versity. He is the author of eight books: Und Willst Du Nicht Mein
Brüder Sein . . . Die DDR Heute *(1981);* The Polish Revolution:
Solidarity, 1980–82 *(1983);* The Uses of Adversity: Essays on the
Fate of Central Europe *(1989);* The Magic Lantern: The Revolution of 1989 as Witnessed in Warsaw, Budapest, Berlin, and Prague
(1990); In Europe's Name: Germany and the Divided Continent
(1993); The File: A Personal History *(1998);* History of the
Present: Essays, Sketches, and Dispatches from Europe in the
1990s *(1999); and* Free World: America, Europe and the Surprising Future of the West *(2004). He frequently writes for leading news-*
papers and magazines and is a regular contributor to the New York
Review of Books. *This essay was first published in the July 22, 2004,*
issue of The Guardian.

I have just entered the United States. Since I was on a so-called J-1 visa, this was quite
an achievement. First I had to fill in a form asking my host university to send me another form. Armed with that form, I filled in three further forms, including such obviously relevant information as my brother's telephone number, and the names of two
people who could verify this information. Then I had to go to Barclays bank to get a
special receipt for paying the fee. Then I had to supply a passport photograph 2 inches
square in which "the head (measured from the top of the hair to the bottom of the
chin) should measure between 1 inch to 1½ inches (25mm to 35mm) with the eye
level between 1¹¹⁄₁₈ inch to 1½ inches (28mm and 35mm) from the bottom of the
photo." Only a few photoshops do these and, once found, Snappy Snaps charged me
£24.99 for a double set. Snappy, indeed. The first time you apply, you also have to go
for an interview at the embassy.

Finally armed with this precious patent of nobility, I arrived at San Francisco airport, where I was fingerprinted and photographed. Last year, I was taken aside for further investigation, while at the next desk an official of the department of homeland
security reduced a girl to a nervous wreck by intrusive questioning about what she
would be up to with her American boyfriend. And she, like me, was from Britain, the
United States' closest ally. Imagine what it's like if you come from Libya or Iran.

Yes, I know that the United States was attacked by terrorists on September 11
2001, and some of those terrorists had entered the US on J-1 visas. I understand, obviously, that the country has had to tighten up its security controls. But this is more
than just a personal grouse. Heads of leading American universities have publicly
complained that such bureaucratic and intrusive procedures are reducing the number
of foreign students willing and able to come to study in the US. (I have heard it
argued in London that this creates a significant opportunity for British universities.)

This raises the larger question of whether the United States' "soft power," its power to attract others and to get them to do what it wants because they find it attractive, has been diminished by the way the Bush administration has reacted to the 9/11 attacks. That, in turn, raises the even larger question of who is winning this "war": al-Qaida or the US?

4   "God bless America," wrote the poet Philip Larkin, "so large, so friendly and so rich." And American hyperpower, by contrast with the one-dimensional superpower of the Soviet Union, has always depended on having all three dimensions: military, economic and "soft." The soft power of a country is more difficult to measure than its military or economic power, but one yardstick is what I call the "Statue of Liberty test." In this test, countries are rated by the number of people outside who want to get into them, divided by the number of people inside who want to get out. Thus, during the cold war, many people wanted to emigrate from the Soviet Union, while very few wanted to go and live there, whereas hundreds of millions wanted to enter America and very few to leave it. By this rough measure, America still has bags of soft power.

Yet its overall attractiveness surely has been diminished, not just by such bureaucratic procedures, but by Guantánamo, by Iraq, by a certain harsh, militarist, nationalist approach to world affairs, and by a mistaken belief that the "war on terror" can be won mainly, if not solely, by military, intelligence and police means.

If you look at the results of the worldwide survey conducted by the Pew Research Centre, you can see that resentment of America around the world has reached unprecedented levels in the last two years. The Bush administration has imperilled the economic dimension of American power, by running up $500bn trade and budget deficits while increasing military spending to $400bn, and it has largely neglected the third, soft dimension. Meanwhile, even the one in five Americans who possess a passport have become more reluctant to travel outside North America. To give just one small example: American customers of Avis car rentals in Europe are down 40% on 2000 levels. There's a real sense of a "Fortress America."

Could the liberal, multilateralist, French-speaking John Kerry, who launches his campaign in earnest at the Democrats' convention in Boston next week, change all this, and restore a Kennedyesque glow to America's image in the world? I find many people in Europe already answer that question with a firm no. Something deeper has changed, they say. Even if America reverts to its previous form, attitudes towards America will not.

8   But I wouldn't be so sure. Perhaps it's just the effect of sitting here in the Californian sunshine, watching this extraordinary multi-ethnic society working all around me, but I think America's underlying attractions are still all there—damaged by 9/11, diminished by economic competition from booming Asia, but still formidable. If Kerry can summon a spark of charisma, aided by his appealing running mate John Edwards, and if the monstrous ego of Ralph Nader will kindly fall under an appropriately eco-friendly bus, the Democrat has a chance of reminding us that the other America still exists. And much of the world, even the Arab and Muslim world, will respond.

Which is why, if Osama bin Laden is still in a fit state to make political calculations, he must be backing an election victory for George Bush. The object of the terrorist is often to reveal the "true" repressive character of the state against which the terror is directed, and thus win further support for the terrorists' cause. If the United States had just acted in Afghanistan, and then concentrated on hoovering-up the remains of al-Qaida, the United States might clearly be winning the war on terror today. But, as bin Laden must have hoped, the Bush administration overreacted, and thus provided, in Iraq and Guantánamo, recruiting sergeants for al-Qaida of which Osama could only dream.

So in this looking-glass world of backhanded ironies, Republicans are covertly supporting their most extreme opponent, Ralph Nader, because he will take votes from John Kerry, and al-Qaida terrorists will be backing Bush, because he's their best recruiter. But can they do anything to affect the outcome of an American presidential election? Of course they can. A major terrorist attack on the American homeland a few days before November 2 would almost certainly not have the effect that the Madrid pre-election bombing had, sending swing voters to the anti-war opposition.

In a recent opinion poll for the *Economist,* handling the war on terror was one of the few areas in which American voters favoured Bush over Kerry. It seems likely there would be a wave of patriotic solidarity with the incumbent. In short, Bush's election chances may depend on the ruthless ingenuity of al-Qaida, while Kerry's election chances may depend on the ability of Bush's department of homeland security to combat it.

PERSONAL RESPONSE

Do you agree that "the Bush administration overreacted" to the September 11 terrorist attacks (paragraph 7)? Explain your answer.

QUESTIONS FOR CLASS OR SMALL-GROUP DISCUSSION

1. What is the purpose of the opening anecdote? How does it relate to Garton Ash's thesis or central point?

2. In what ways does Garton Ash suggest that America is a "fortress" (title)?

3. Explain the references to Guantánamo and Iraq in paragraph 4. What do you think Garton Ash means when he says that America has "a certain harsh, militarist, nationalist approach to world affairs" (paragraph 4)? Do you agree with him?

4. What does Garton Ash mean when he says that al-Qaida terrorists are George W. Bush's "best recruiter" (paragraph 8)? Are you convinced that his point is valid?

THE DECLINE OF AMERICA'S SOFT POWER

JOSEPH S. NYE, JR.

Joseph S. Nye, Jr., was Assistant Secretary of Defense in the Clinton Administration and currently is Dean of Harvard University's John F.

Kennedy School of Government. He is author of The Paradox of American Power: Why the World's Only Superpower Cannot Go It Alone *(2002) and* Soft Power: The Means to Success in World Politics *(2004). This essay appeared in the May–June 2004 issue of* Foreign Affairs.

Anti-Americanism has increased in recent years, and the United States' soft power—its ability to attract others by the legitimacy of U.S. policies and the values that underlie them—is in decline as a result. According to Gallup International polls, pluralities in 29 countries say that Washington's policies have had a negative effect on their view of the United States. A Eurobarometer poll found that a majority of Europeans believes that Washington has hindered efforts to fight global poverty, protect the environment, and maintain peace. Such attitudes undercut soft power, reducing the ability of the United States to achieve its goals without resorting to coercion or payment.

Skeptics of soft power (Secretary of Defense Donald Rumsfeld professes not even to understand the term) claim that popularity is ephemeral and should not guide foreign policy. The United States, they assert, is strong enough to do as it wishes with or without the world's approval and should simply accept that others will envy and resent it. The world's only superpower does not need permanent allies; the issues should determine the coalitions, not vice-versa, according to Rumsfeld.

But the recent decline in U.S. attractiveness should not be so lightly dismissed. It is true that the United States has recovered from unpopular policies in the past (such as those regarding the Vietnam War), but that was often during the Cold War, when other countries still feared the Soviet Union as the greater evil. It is also true that the United States' sheer size and association with disruptive modernity make some resentment unavoidable today. But wise policies can reduce the antagonisms that these realities engender. Indeed, that is what Washington achieved after World War II: it used soft-power resources to draw others into a system of alliances and institutions that has lasted for 60 years. The Cold War was won with a strategy of containment that used soft power along with hard power.

4   The United States cannot confront the new threat of terrorism without the cooperation of other countries. Of course, other governments will often cooperate out of self-interest. But the extent of their cooperation often depends on the attractiveness of the United States.

Soft power, therefore, is not just a matter of ephemeral popularity; it is a means of obtaining outcomes the United States wants. When Washington discounts the importance of its attractiveness abroad, it pays a steep price. When the United States becomes so unpopular that being pro-American is a kiss of death in other countries' domestic politics, foreign political leaders are unlikely to make helpful concessions (witness the defiance of Chile, Mexico, and Turkey in March 2003). And when U.S. policies lose their legitimacy in the eyes of others, distrust grows, reducing U.S. leverage in international affairs.

Some hard-line skeptics might counter that, whatever its merits, soft power has little importance in the current war against terrorism; after all, Osama bin Laden and his followers are repelled, not attracted, by American culture and values. But this claim ignores the real metric of success in the current war, articulated in Rumsfeld's now-famous memo that was leaked in February 2003: "Are we capturing, killing or deterring and dissuading more terrorists every day than the madrassas and the radical clerics are recruiting, training and deploying against us?"

The current struggle against Islamist terrorism is not a clash of civilizations; it is a contest closely tied to the civil war raging within Islamic civilization between moderates and extremists. The United States and its allies will win only if they adopt policies that appeal to those moderates and use public diplomacy effectively to communicate that appeal. Yet the world's only superpower, and the leader in the information revolution, spends as little on public diplomacy as does France or the United Kingdom—and is all too often outgunned in the propaganda war by fundamentalists hiding in caves.

Lost Savings

8   With the end of the Cold War, soft power seemed expendable, and Americans became more interested in saving money than in investing in soft power. Between 1989 and 1999, the budget of the United States Information Agency (USIA) increased ten percent; resources for its mission in Indonesia, the world's largest Muslim nation, were cut in half. By the time it was taken over by the State Department at the end of the decade, USIA had only 6,715 employees (compared to 12,000 at its peak in the mid-1960s). During the Cold War, radio broadcasts funded by Washington reached half the Soviet population and 70 to 80 percent of the population in Eastern Europe every week; on the eve of the September 11 attacks, a mere two percent of Arabs listened to the Voice of America (VOA). The annual number of academic and cultural exchanges, meanwhile, dropped from 45,000 in 1995 to 29,000 in 2001. Soft power had become so identified with fighting the Cold War that few Americans noticed that, with the advent of the information revolution, soft power was becoming more important, not less.

It took the September 11 attacks to remind the United States of this fact. But although Washington has rediscovered the need for public diplomacy, it has failed to master the complexities of wielding soft power in an information age. Some people in government now concede that the abolition of USIA was a mistake, but there is no consensus on whether to recreate it or to reorganize its functions, which were dispersed within the State Department after the Clinton administration gave in to the demands of Senator Jesse Helms (R-N.C.). The board that oversees the VOA, along with a number of specialized radio stations, has taken some useful steps—such as the establishment of Radio Sawa to broadcast in Arabic, Radio Farda to broadcast in Farsi, and the Arabic-language TV station Al Hurra. The White House has created its own Office of Global Communications. But much more is needed, especially in the Middle East.

Autocratic regimes in the Middle East have eradicated their liberal opposition, and radical Islamists are in most cases the only dissenters left. They feed on anger toward corrupt regimes, opposition to U.S. policies, and popular fears of modernization. Liberal democracy, as they portray it, is full of corruption, sex, and violence—an impression reinforced by American movies and television and often exacerbated by the extreme statements of some especially virulent Christian preachers in the United States.

Nonetheless, the situation is not hopeless. Although modernization and American values can be disruptive, they also bring education, jobs, better health care, and a range of new opportunities. Indeed, polls show that much of the Middle East craves the benefits of trade, globalization, and improved communications. American technology is widely admired, and American culture is often more attractive than U.S. policies. Given such widespread (albeit ambivalent) moderate views, there is still a chance of isolating the extremists.

12   Democracy, however, cannot be imposed by force. The outcome in Iraq will be of crucial importance, but success will also depend on policies that open regional economies, reduce bureaucratic controls, speed economic growth, improve educational systems, and encourage the types of gradual political changes currently taking place in small countries such as Bahrain, Oman, Kuwait, and Morocco. The development of intellectuals, social groups, and, eventually, countries that show that liberal democracy is not inconsistent with Muslim culture will have a beneficial effect like that of Japan and South Korea, which showed that democracy could coexist with indigenous Asian values. But this demonstration effect will take time—and the skillful deployment of soft-power resources by the United States in concert with other democracies, nongovernmental organizations, and the United Nations.

First Responders

In the wake of September 11, Americans were transfixed by the question "Why do they hate us?" But many in the Middle East do not hate the United States. As polls consistently show, many fear, misunderstand, and oppose U.S. policies, but they nonetheless admire certain American values and aspects of American culture. The world's leader in communications, however, has been inept at recognizing and exploiting such opportunities.

In 2003, a bipartisan advisory group on public diplomacy for the Arab and Muslim world found that the United States was spending only $150 million on public diplomacy in majority-Muslim countries, including $25 million on outreach programs. In the advisory group's words, "to say that financial resources are inadequate to the task is a gross understatement." They recommended appointing a new White House director of public diplomacy, building libraries and information centers, translating more Western books into Arabic, increasing the number of scholarships and visiting fellowships, and training more Arabic speakers and public relations specialists.

The development of effective public diplomacy must include strategies for the short, medium, and long terms. In the short term, the United States will have to become more agile in responding to and explaining current events. New broadcasting units such as Radio Sawa, which intersperses news with popular music, is a step in the right direction, but Americans must also learn to work more effectively with Arab media outlets such as Al Jazeera.

16   In the medium term, U.S. policymakers will have to develop a few key strategic themes in order to better explain U.S. policies and "brand" the United States as a democratic nation. The charge that U.S. policies are indifferent to the destruction of

Muslim lives, for example, can be countered by pointing to U.S. interventions in Bosnia and Kosovo that saved Muslim lives, and to assistance to Muslim countries for fostering development and combating AIDS. As Assistant Secretary of State for Near Eastern Affairs William Burns has pointed out, democratic change must be embedded in "a wider positive agenda for the region, alongside rebuilding Iraq, achieving the president's two-state vision for Israelis and Palestinians, and modernizing Arab economies."

Most important will be a long-term strategy, built around cultural and educational exchanges, to develop a richer, more open civil society in Middle Eastern countries. To this end, the most effective spokespeople are not Americans but indigenous surrogates who understand American virtues and faults. Corporations, foundations, universities, and other nongovernmental organizations—as well as governments—can all help promote the development of open civil society. Corporations can offer technology to modernize educational systems. Universities can establish more exchange programs for students and faculty. Foundations can support institutions of American studies and programs to enhance the professionalism of journalists. Governments can support the teaching of English and finance student exchanges.

In short, there are many strands to an effective long-term strategy for creating soft-power resources and the conditions for democracy. Of course, even the best advertising cannot sell an unpopular product: a communications strategy will not work if it cuts against the grain of policy. Public diplomacy will not be effective unless the style and substance of U.S. policies are consistent with a broader democratic message.

Ante Up

The United States' most striking failure is the low priority and paucity of resources it has devoted to producing soft power. The combined cost of the State Department's public diplomacy programs and U.S. international broadcasting is just over a billion dollars, about four percent of the nation's international affairs budget. That total is about three percent of what the United States spends on intelligence and a quarter of one percent of its military budget. If Washington devoted just one percent of its military spending to public diplomacy—in the words of Newton Minnow, former head of the Federal Communications Commission, "one dollar to launch ideas for every 100 dollars we invest to launch bombs"—it would mean almost quadrupling the current budget.

20   It is also important to establish more policy coherence among the various dimensions of public diplomacy, and to relate them to other issues. The Association of International Educators reports that, despite a declining share of the market for international students, "the U.S. government seems to lack overall strategic sense of why exchange is important. . . . In this strategic vacuum, it is difficult to counter the day-to-day obstacles that students encounter in trying to come here." There is, for example, little coordination of exchange policies and visa policies. As the educator Victor Johnson noted, "While greater vigilance is certainly needed, this broad net is catching all kinds of people who are no danger whatsoever." By needlessly discouraging people from coming to the United States, such policies undercut American soft power.

Public diplomacy needs greater support from the White House. A recent Council on Foreign Relations task force recommended the creation of a "White House Public Diplomacy Coordinating Structure," led by a presidential designee, and a nonprofit "Corporation for Public Diplomacy" to help mobilize the private sector. And ultimately, a successful strategy must focus not only on broadcasting American messages, but also on two-way communication that engages all sectors of society, not just the government.

It Goes Both Ways

Above all, Americans will have to become more aware of cultural differences; an effective approach requires less parochialism and more sensitivity to perceptions abroad.

The first step, then, is changing attitudes at home. Americans need a better understanding of how U.S. policies appear to others. Coverage of the rest of the world by the U.S. media has declined dramatically since the end of the Cold War. Training in foreign languages has lagged. Fewer scholars are taking up Fulbright visiting lectureships. Historian Richard Pells notes "how distant we are from a time when American historians—driven by a curiosity about the world beyond both the academy and the United States—were able to communicate with the public about the issues, national and international, that continue to affect us all."

24   Wielding soft power is far less unilateral than employing hard power—a fact that the United States has yet to recognize. To communicate effectively, Americans must first learn to listen.

PERSONAL RESPONSE

Nye concludes by saying that Americans "will have to become more aware of cultural differences" (paragraph 22). Assess your own awareness of other cultures.

QUESTIONS FOR CLASS OR SMALL-GROUP DISCUSSION

1. What do you understand Nye to mean by the term "soft power"? In contrast, what is "hard power"?
2. To what extent do you agree that "soft power" is vitally important to the interests of the United States? Do you side with skeptics of or with believers in the efficacy of soft power in guiding foreign policy?
3. Summarize each of the recommendations that Nye makes for short, medium, and long-term strategies for developing effective public diplomacy (paragraphs 15–18) and then state your views on each of those recommendations.
4. Analyze Nyes' argumentative strategies. Where does he acknowledge the positions of those opposed to his? Does he address those positions to your satisfaction? Overall, are you convinced that America needs to strengthen its soft power?

VOICES FROM ABROAD

CHRIS BERDIK

Chris Berdik is a freelance writer living in Massachusetts. He has written for a number of periodicals, including Boston Magazine, Mother Jones, *and* The Boston Globe. *He compiled these selections, which have been edited for space and clarity. "Voices from Abroad" ran in the June 27, 2004, issue of* The Boston Globe.

At few other times in history has the view of the United States around the globe been so polarized. We are envied; we are loathed; we are wanted and needed; we are cast aside as bullies. But we Americans here, on the inside, get only the views on our own streets and our computer screens, in our newspapers, on our televisions and radios, and from the mouths of our leaders. But how are we viewed by people outside our borders?

New Englanders who live overseas share today's perceptions of America. These voices include a Marblehead woman managing a medical clinic in Israel, a Boston consultant helping artisans in Panama, and newlyweds from New Hampshire teaching English in Brazil. What this diverse group of people is hearing, seeing, and reporting challenges the often insular assumptions that we have about our nation.

FRANCE: Cara Fraley, 30

"I have not had one person insult me"

Cara Fraley is a biochemist who met her husband, Andrew, while the two were in graduate school at Boston College. They both work at the Universite Louis Pasteur in Strasbourg, France (not far from the German border), where they have lived for two years. They plan to return to Boston in the fall.

4   "The impression I've gotten from the French who are from Alsace is that they are grateful to the US for liberating them during World War II. Being on the border of Germany, they certainly had more than their fair share of suffering.

"The general impression people have given me about the current events in Iraq reflects those of their government—against the war. To their credit, I have not had one person insult me or try to dredge up politics with me. I've felt the French to be very polite about the whole situation.

"Convenience is not a concern for the average person here. I do miss the conveniences that are available in the States. On Sundays, there is no grocery shopping, most pharmacies are closed, and other stores are closed. However, I do appreciate the importance that is put on family life and will miss it on our return to the US.

"I've begun to comprehend just how isolated the US is from the rest of the world. With our isolation and with our being the most powerful and most developed country in the world, I think Americans tend to assume everyone is like we are, want to be more like us, or to just not think about the differences in general.

8   "I've also realized that while the US is isolated, we truly are a melting pot of ethnicities. This is our tradition, and I think it is fantastic."

BRAZIL: Kerry and Abel McClennen, both 26

Civics lesson

Newlyweds Kerry and Abel McClennen have been teaching English in Brazil for the last several months. Abel, a Holliston native, lived in New England his entire life, while Kerry is from the Chicago area. They were both teachers at a public high school in New Hampshire.

Abel: "The common joke among Brazilians when they first meet Americans is 'Oh, gringo, how are things going in the land of Mr. Bush? Any new wars?'

"The American dollar and pop culture, however, seem to make any and all Brazilians dizzy with excitement. Many popular radio stations down here broadcast only American music, and the main television station will publicize most tales of American tragedy in a Fox News sort of way. American news, presidential elections, and sports take center stage many times on the evening national news. In short, the US economy and capitalism are a bait that most any Brazilian would snatch if given the opportunity.

12   "When they look past the stable economy, the education, the lack of poverty, and less-corrupt government, they see war and big cars and consumerism that they don't want to be a part of but at the same time are jealous of. Although most Americans could not care less about what Brazil thinks about them, Brazilians are very curious about how Americans see them: 'Do they think Brazil is just a big jungle?' 'What Brazilian singers are popular in the States?' 'Do you guys study Brazilian history in school?' 'Do Americans really think that the capital of Brazil is Buenos Aires?' "

GERMANY: Christine Louise Hohlbaum, 35

"Greeted with open arms"

Before moving to a rural town in Germany in 2003, Christine Louise Hohlbaum lived in Somerville for six years. She worked at Putnam Investments and then directed a host-family program for international students in Massachusetts. Married with two children, Hohlbaum has authored two books about parenting, including *Diary of a Mother.*

"I live in a rural Bavarian cow town (1,500 inhabitants), and I have been greeted with open arms. In fact, people love the English language. A fellow American who lives down the street from me offers English classes for preschoolers and grade-school children. Her classes are booked every year. People's desire for their young children to learn English is so strong that a group of young mothers asked me to run an English-language play group in Freising. I now get paid to play with six little German 4-year-olds and to sing in my slippers.

"However, when it comes to Bush and his foreign policy, forget it! People are extremely negative about his claims. What changed for me was that I looked at the world with open eyes. While I love my country with all my heart, I am always left in shock for the first week when I go back to the States to visit. Everything appears so large; the people move fast, the cars drive slowly."

FRANCE: Sara Sagoff Mitter, 66

Model and menace

16   Moving to Paris 30 years ago was a fluke, says writer Sara Sagoff Mitter, who was born in Cambridge and raised in Brookline. Her husband had a one-year, renewable visiting lectureship in theoretical physics at the Universite Paris. The couple stayed on in France, although every year Mitter brought her two children back to the Boston area to visit family and friends.

"Where I live now, in the south of France, an American is seen as someone quite ignorant of the world outside continental USA; well-intentioned perhaps, but brash and a bit naive, characteristics that are reflected back in our clichéd images of Frenchies. America the political, military, economic, and cultural heft of the USA looms large in France, looms large as a model and as a menace. New York and San Francisco fascinate; Hollywood films predominate; fashion, music, and lifestyles made in USA find instant favor.

"Thus it was no surprise that September 11 had such reverberations in France. On September 12, in my mailbox was a card with a message of sympathy from a neighbor I hardly knew. Most of my compatriots had similar experiences—in some cases, a first sign of their being identified as US nationals. It hadn't much mattered before. But it has continued to matter since, and particularly since the start of the Bush administration's build up to invade—'liberate'—Iraq and bulldoze the world into the new American century."

ISRAEL: Bret Stephens, 30

An emotional disconnect

Bret Stephens attended the Middlesex School in Concord and then received degrees from the University of Chicago and the London School of Economics. He is a former editor at the *The Wall Street Journal* and is editor in chief of *The Jerusalem Post*, an English-language daily in Israel, where he lives with his wife and baby daughter.

20   "On the evening of September 11, 2001, I walked the streets of Jerusalem to get local reaction to the attacks. On the Arab side, the general feeling was that America got what it deserved. On the Israeli side, there was a sense of vindication bordering on conceit. 'Now they'll know what it's like,' they said. Israel is probably the world's most pro-American country. But emotionally, there's a gap. Israelis think they live in the real world, whereas Americans only tune in to it.

"Living abroad puts American political debate in a certain perspective. Americans sometimes talk about the country as if it were hopelessly split between red states and blue, blacks and whites, Rush Limbaugh and Al Franken. From the distance of the Middle East, you all look, sound, and think pretty much alike: smart-alecky, optimistic, a bit brash. Which is good news, actually."

PANAMA: Giselle Leung, 28

"Panamanians think that all Americans are white"

Born in Hong Kong and having spent her teenage years in New York City, Giselle Leung graduated from Harvard in 1998. She worked as a business consultant in Boston before joining the Peace Corps in 2002. She was assigned to Panama, where she lives and works in a community of subsistence farmers and helps female artisans find markets for traditional clothing and crafts.

"A convincing combination of first hand encounters and American sitcoms and movies gives them the predominant notion that the United States is a land of the rich. Most Panamanians I know recall fondly the good old times when Americans, representing both the business and military sectors, would compensate them for manual labor in relatively exorbitant sums that are hardly imaginable today. This, along with the luxury cars, nice clothes, and big suburban houses they see on TV, has led more than a handful of Panamanians to ask me, *'Hay pobreza en los Estados Unidos?'* Is there poverty in the US? Housing projects, urban poverty, welfare mothers, and ghettos are not images that are readily accessible to my local friends.

24   "In this small Panamanian rural community where I am writing, most people reacted with slight confusion, befuddlement, or plain incredulousness when I told them that I'm from the United States at my initial arrival. Why? I certainly don't look the part of an American: I do not have fair skin, blond hair, and blue eyes. And this points to the widespread misconception among Panamanians regarding the social makeup of the United States. Panamanians think that all Americans are white. To those who do not know me, they assume that I am from China or Japan and think, 'How strange that she speaks fluent English and hangs out with gringos.'

"First of all, I am much more keenly aware and appreciative of the ethnic diversity found among American people; their affable coexistence and the general acceptance on the part of the society is something that I had previously taken for granted. Sure, the United States has its share of racial problems, but there is something admirable in knowing that when a multitude of people, of all different colors and ethnicities, are riding the T or walking through downtown Boston, no one would consciously question who the 'real Americans' are. When I traveled to Boston last December after having been away for 15 months, I found myself happily indulged in my uninterrupted existence as an Asian American. No one called out *'Chinita.'* I remember being on the Green Line, observing the faces of fellow riders, and thinking, 'It's beautiful to have all these different people around me.'

"Whereas Panamanians view the US as a land of the rich, I have, in turn, come to see it as a land of abundance and excess. I asked myself when I was home: Where else in the world can one find shiitake mushrooms, French foie gras, organic soy milk, and Australian shiraz all under one roof? We Americans are truly fortunate to have such easy access to the bountiful variety of products.

"On the other hand, because I have seen how people can lead happy and fulfilled lives while living simply, I have also become more cognizant of the excess in American life. Is a large Frappuccino really worth $4? Is it absolutely necessary to have bigger, more monstrous, and environmentally unsound SUVs?"

FRANCE: Carlos Joly, 57

"The impression the French have had of America was awe, respect, and admiration"

28   Carlos Joly was born in Buenos Aires but grew up in New York City. He was a graduate student in philosophy at Harvard in the late 1960s and early 1970s and has since gone on to be an institutional investment manager, university lecturer, and author. He's lived abroad since 1986, first in Norway and now in Paris.

"The dominant impression the French have had of America was awe, respect, and admiration. Awe at the economic power of the US, respect for its scientific achievements, and admiration for its can-do attitude in all walks of life, including the arts. Since Bush became president, this has changed. Many people fear the US's reckless bumbling getting into the war in Iraq and now the disaster from going it alone. In France, I have never come across anti-American sentiment like the negativism people in the US have shown toward the French as such."

CHINA: Lorraine Shang-Huei Chao, 32

Impressions of the "easy life"

Lorraine Shang-Huei Chao was born in Boston and raised in Newton. After earning bachelor's and master's degrees, she worked as a teacher in Connecticut and California. Two years ago, she headed overseas. She teaches at the Shanghai American School.

"The impression that everyone in America enjoys the easy life is common. They find it hard to understand why I would give up what they imagine to be a comfortable, perhaps even pampered life. Another common impression of America, or Americans, is that they are gregarious, loud, and outgoing. Several months ago, I introduced two friends to each other, one local and one American, Sarah. After Sarah left, my friend commented, covering her mouth and giggling, 'She really laughs with her mouth wide open. So loud, just like in the movies.'

32   "The grandmas and grandpas in my apartment complex walk or bicycle to the vegetable market daily. What would they think of going online and ordering a week's worth of food from an e-grocer? While I do miss some of the conveniences, I also feel that this ever-increasing level of convenience and comfort can engender an increasingly demanding society, one whose citizens are so used to advancement that they take the basics for granted. That was me.

"I read the newspaper, but never with the respect for the First Amendment that I've developed living in China. My deepest new appreciation is that, in America, there is opportunity for people to create and walk their own path and an understanding that this is natural. I miss this especially when I am the one, the only one in the group, who is laughing (out loud) with a big, wide-open mouth."

ISRAEL: Judith Prager-Berkowitz, 45

"Americans' attitudes are very provincial"

Judith Prager-Berkowitz was born in Salem and grew up in Marblehead. A resident of Israel since 1981, she is married with three children and manages a medical clinic in Jerusalem.

"Here in Israel, I think that most people have a very positive attitude toward the United States. Politically, as one of our only allies, people realize how lucky we are to have America as our friend. Culturally, people are very attracted to many aspects of American culture. Over the years, there has been a proliferation of many American chains like McDonald's and Kentucky Fried Chicken. My impressions of America have changed tremendously over the years. As large-scale as America is, or maybe because of its large scale, Americans' attitudes are very provincial. I think the majority of Americans understand very little of what goes on in the world."

CAMBODIA: Scott Worden, 29

Leveling the field

36   Scott Worden grew up in Stow and is a graduate of Harvard Law School. Last year, while working as an associate at an international law firm in New York, he received a fellowship to work with the Cambodian Defenders Project, a nongovernmental organization representing victims of human rights abuses in Cambodian courts.

"America and Americans are perhaps the most respected foreign nationality in Cambodia. In a culture that sees virtue in power and wealth, America is the paragon of both. Americans are admired for their education and mobility. A Khmer colleague who is generally quite liberal in his views told me that he likes George Bush, 'because he is strong.'

"America is one of Cambodia's largest financial donors, both through USAID and through its participation in the World Bank. Numerous government agencies and US-based NGOs promote and protect Cambodians' civil and human rights, including strong support for justice of the victims of the Khmer Rouge. And America is home to many of the refugees who fled the Khmer Rouge regime (in fact, Lowell has one of the largest overseas Cambodian communities).

"The strongest new impression I've formed of America since moving to Cambodia is that Americans have no idea what a tremendous impact the United States has on the personal lives of people living in less-developed countries until they live there. What many Americans might view as an arcane policy debate over foreign aid can mean the difference between whether organizations like the Cambodian Defenders Project succeeds or fails. Without US diplomatic and financial support, there may be no trials for victims of the Khmer Rouge."

RUSSIA: John Rose, 44

"Struck by the intensity of American patriotism"

40   The iron curtain had not yet fallen when John Rose expanded his Boston-based advertising agency to Moscow. At the time, says Rose, who was born in Chelsea and attended Boston College, Russians didn't understand the concept of marketing and promotion. They learned quickly, and today, says Rose, advertising in Russia is an almost $3 billion industry. Rose and his wife have one son.

"Western movies and television had not yet invaded the Soviet Union when I first arrived. So I observed with fascination as 'advertising' became Russia's window to the West—and particularly America. It was not uncommon to find magazine ads framed on walls in Russian apartments. In those early days, I was often the first American encountered by the Russians I met. And I found them very welcoming and fascinated with all things American. I still do.

"Until I lived abroad, I hadn't realized how much people are struck by the intensity of American patriotism. Long before the 9/11 attacks, several Russians who had visited the US (particularly American suburbs) mentioned the number of flags they saw on houses, buildings, cars. Stars and stripes everywhere.

"I have come to realize how lucky we are. It's just so much easier to live in America than anywhere else. We have everything we need so close at hand. Russia has come a long way from the days when I used to bring my own toilet paper and peanut butter. If every American could live abroad for a time, I'm certain there would be a lot less complaining.

44   "During my time away, I have also come to understand why the world views Americans as arrogant. And why that makes us easy targets for ridicule when we falter. As a nation, we have so much for which to be proud. But swaggering seldom wins friends."

POLAND: Sandra F. Nicholson, 37

America is still viewed as a "land of opportunity"

Stoneham native Sandra F. Nicholson has lived in Poland since 2002. She moved there with her husband, a State Department employee who works at the US Embassy in Warsaw. Nicholson, who has three children, is the director of the International Preschool of Warsaw. She still refers to the Boston area as her home and hopes one day to return.

"[The Poles] still view us as a land of opportunity. When I drop my husband off at the embassy, the never-ending line of people trying to get visas so they can go to America never ceases to amaze me. They have to pay the visa application fee, which equates to what many Poles earn in a week, in hopes of getting the visa and knowing this does not guarantee a visa, just a chance to apply.

"I have a housekeeper over here in Poland, a luxury I could never afford in the States. I talk with her and hear she lives with no heat through a Polish winter, as her furnace broke, and she cannot afford to fix it. I know others who have a residence which has never had heat. These are normal day-to-day conditions for people here, not viewed as particular hardships, just part of life, which I think many Americans would find extremely difficult to live with. I love America and think we are still the best country in the world, but I do not think many Americans truly know how good we really have it."

BANGLADESH: Michelle LaBonte, 45

A belief in democracy

48   Michelle LaBonte was born and raised in Oxford, Massachusetts, received an MBA from Boston College, and worked for Texas Instruments in Attleboro until she joined the Foreign Service in 1989. Her assignments have included Jamaica,

Romania, Madagascar, Niger, and, most recently, Bangladesh. Along with her husband and two sons, she is moving back to the United States this summer.

"The people of Bangladesh have a warm place in their hearts for Americans. We have been solid development partners in the country since its turbulent birth in 1971. Bangladeshis believe in democracy, free speech, and are tolerant and respectful of diverse religions and ethnic groups. They admire Americans for our values and our leadership in those areas. On the other hand, many Bangladeshis view the global war on terror, Middle East policy, and now activities in Iraq as biased and anti-Muslim.

"Most Bangladeshis—like most Americans—are not focused on distant foreign-policy issues; they are concerned about their families, education, increasing crime, and jobs. Their impressions of the US are based on their personal experiences with those of us working and living here, particularly the many wonderful people involved in things like rural electrification, community health, gender issues, eliminating child labor, and the Peace Corps."

TURKEY: Linda Boulden, 21

"Many disagree with Bush and his actions"

Linda Boulden grew up in Norfolk and is a management and journalism student at Boston University. She spent her spring term in Turkey as an exchange student and took classes in liberal arts, Middle Eastern studies, and Turkish.

52 "I didn't know what to expect coming to the Middle East, given America's role in the region's current instability. With blond hair, fair skin, and green eyes, I am clearly not a native, and many inquire where I'm from. When I answer 'America,' they immediately ask my opinion of [President George W.] Bush. Many disagree with Bush and his actions but do not blame the situation on America or its people. In fact, most people I've encountered do not hate America; rather, they see it as a land of opportunity and hope to travel and work there when they leave the university.

"While Turkey is an amazing country, my experiences here have made me only appreciate America and my freedoms more. Seventy percent of the economy is informal, giving the government little revenue to provide public services."

EGYPT: Kathleen Moynihan, 40

Missing an opportunity to show our principles

On the wall of Kathleen Moynihan's Cairo office is a photograph of a cellist sitting in the destroyed National Library in Sarajevo. His hand is over his eyes, but his bow is poised to play. To Moynihan, born and raised in Boston and now a deputy regional director for Catholic Relief Services for Europe, the Middle East, and North Africa, the photo represents the "amazing range of human potential for destruction and divinity."

"I have started to tell lies to Cairo taxi drivers or Iraqi nationals, because I don't want the situation to become heated about US policy in this part of the world. I don't lie because I am a coward but because I am exhausted at the disconnect between the values that most American citizens hold in their hearts and our international policies. I believe we missed an opportunity to send a clear message about our country's resolve, as well as the principles we hold dear, in the aftermath of 9/11.

56   "Many people in this part of the world were not surprised; they knew we would choose instead to take revenge. These same detractors think of America as a wealthy, spoiled family. But we are also a family that has the ability to solve problems in creative and groundbreaking ways. I will forever believe that we are a fundamentally good nation."

JAPAN: Holly Salmon, 29

"I am constantly amazed by how everyone follows the rules"

Holly Salmon graduated from Wellesley College in 1997 and has worked as a conservation technician at the Isabella Stewart Gardner Museum and other Boston-area museums. Through a scholarship, Salmon is studying Japanese lacquer production and restoration in Kyoto.

"They find my need for a 'mattress' (a 2-inch piece of foam) underneath my futon to be a bit wimpy. But more than anything, they are very interested in my eating habits. There is a general assumption that Americans are squeamish about Japanese food. My sensei [her teacher] still takes great pleasure in giving me some new delicacy to try.

"Everyone wants to know if I like Bush. Most people I have encountered here don't like him and do not want to be involved in the Iraqi conflict. Once, a taxi driver asked if I own a gun. Despite my insistence that I have never owned or even shot a gun, he went to a lot of trouble to explain that you cannot own a gun in Japan, nor can you even carry a concealed large knife. And he kept insisting that if I had any weapons on me, that this was unacceptable in Japan.

60   "There is also a universal sense of propriety that I know I will miss when I return to America. I am constantly amazed by how everyone follows the rules here. Rarely will you see anyone jaywalking in Japan. Even if there are no cars to be seen, most Japanese people will wait for the light to turn green."

HAITI: Todd Holmes, 38

Hunger and want

During the February rebellion in Haiti, Todd Holmes, a senior program manager for Catholic Relief Services, was evacuated to the Dominican Republic. From there, he continued to manage the logistics of US food donations to Haiti for nearly 170,000 people. Holmes grew up in North Attleborough and worked in Boston as a Peace Corps recruiter in the 1990s. He is now back in Haiti.

"Haiti is a country where almost everyone has family living in the US, primarily in the Boston, New York, or Miami area. Most Haitians I know travel to the US, and many others want to get visas to be able to better their education or just chances of having a better life free from hunger, want, or fear. Chances for advancement in Haiti are limited. The attraction of jobs, no matter how menial, with regular pay is a motivating factor, especially since it offers the possibility of sending remittances to help family back in Haiti make ends meet. Haiti is fraught with infrastructure problems, lack of electricity, clean water, basic medical and dental care, as well as trained professionals: All feed the desire to emigrate.

"Living away for nearly nine years in lesser-developed countries has definitely colored the way I look at my country and culture. Having grown up in New England and been raised on a farm in a hardworking family, I realize how much of the do-it-yourselfness runs in my veins. Americans are a can-do people, on the forefront of innovation, questioning why we do things, looking to do them better, trying to make our country and, by extension, the world a better place."

BRITAIN: Gary Siegei, 47

Conflicted emotions

64   Gary Siegel grew up in upstate New York but moved to Boston in 1980 to attend graduate school in engineering at Northeastern University. In 2002, he moved with his family to Britain on an overseas assignment from his employer, the environmental and energy consulting firm ENSR International (based in Westford).

"Everyone seems to know so much more about us than we do about them. Our news and culture are everywhere. They see all our television shows, have opinions on all our sports, know all about our politicians. Every one of my daughter's friends has been talking about the last episode of *Friends,* and they like going on dates to Pizza Hut and Starbucks.

The British "like America for what we are, and at the same time they strongly dislike what they see as our heavy-handedness and one-track mind in international affairs and, to them, selfishness. All my friends think that Americans are afraid to leave the US, and that if we did we might have a better idea of how the rest of the world sees us.

"People here tend to make fun of our limited vacation time and holidays compared to their six weeks' vacation and numerous holidays. But whenever I try to give an explanation as to why America is where it is today, I end up talking about our collective work ethic and the freedom we have to exercise our entrepreneurial abilities that have been the prime reason for this.

68   "When I was living in the US, I found [our] decisiveness and independence a strength; now that I have been away, I can understand how this appears to come across as arrogance, and it is what leads to the negative feelings that are toward our government."

PERSONAL RESPONSE

Which of the comments about how other people view America surprised you the most? Which pleased you the most?

QUESTIONS FOR CLASS AND SMALL-GROUP DISCUSSION

1. What do these anecdotes suggest about how other countries view America? Do you see any common threads running throughout them? How do others view American foreign policy? How do they view America's popular culture?

2. Judith Prager-Berkowitz, living in Israel, says, "I think the majority of Americans understand very little of what goes on in the world." To what extent do you agree with her?

3. Select one country represented in this collection, find out more about how its people view America, and report your findings to the class.

4. Is there a country whose viewpoint you are interested in that is not represented here? If so, find out about its views of American foreign policy and report your findings to your class.

SELLING OUR INNOCENCE ABROAD

Pico Iyer

Pico Iyer was born in England to Indian parents and studied at Oxford and Harvard Universities. He is author of a novel, Abandon: A Romance *(2003), and the following nonfiction books:* Video Night in Kathmandu: And Other Reports from the Not-So-Far-East *(1988),* The Lady and the Monk: Four Seasons in Kyoto *(1991),* Falling Off the Map: Some Lovely Places of the World *(1994),* Tropical Classical: Essays from Several Directions *(1997),* The Global Soul: Jet Lag, Shopping Malls, and the Search for Home *(2000),* Sun after Dark: Flights into the Foreign *(2004), and* The Contagion of Innocence *(1991), from which the following piece is excerpted. Iyer lives in the United States and writes for* Time *magazine.*

There is a genuine sense in many parts of the world that America is being left behind by the rise of a unified Europe and the new East Asian powers. The largest debtor nation in the world, where ten million blacks live in poverty and whose capital, run by a cocaine addict, had a murder rate during the Eighties higher than that of Sri Lanka or Beirut, seems an unlikely model for emulation. And yet America maintains a powerful hold on the world's imagination.

A visitor today in Vietnam, one of the last of America's official enemies, will find crowds in Hue, in waterside cafes, desperate to get a glimpse of Meryl Streep on video; at night, in Dalat, he will hear every last word of "Hotel California" floating across Sighing Lake. In Bhutan, where all the citizens must wear traditional medieval dress and all the buildings must be constructed in thirteenth-century style—in Bhutan, perhaps the most tightly closed country in the world, which has never seen more than three thousand tourists in a single year—the pirated version of Eddie Murphy's *Coming to America* went on sale well before the video had ever come to America.

All this, of course, is hardly surprising and hardly new. Pop culture makes the world go round, and America makes the best pop culture. By now, indeed, such products represent the largest single source of America's export earnings, even as America remains the single most popular destination for immigrants. The more straitened or shut off a culture, the more urgent its hunger for the qualities it associates with America: freedom, wealth, and modernity. The Japanese may be the leaders in technology, the Europeans may have a stronger and more self-conscious sense of their aesthetic heritage, yet in the world of movies and songs and images America is still, and long will continue to be, the Great Communicator. The capital of the world, as Gore Vidal has said, is not Washington but Hollywood. And however much America suffers an internal loss of faith, it will continue to enjoy, abroad, some of the immunity that attaches to all things in the realm of myth. As much as we—and everyone else—assume that the French make the best perfumes and the Swiss the finest watches, the suspicion will continue that Americans make the best dreams.

4   As borders crumble and cultures mingle, more and more of us are becoming hyphenated. I, perhaps, am an increasingly typical example: entirely Indian by blood, yet unable to speak a word of any Indian language; a British citizen, born and educated in England, yet never having really worked or lived in the country of my birth; an American permanent resident who has made his home for two-thirds of his life in America, in part because it feels so little like home; and a would-be resident of Japan. As people like me proliferate, and Filipinos in San Francisco marry Salvadorans, and Germans in Japan take home women from Kyoto, the global village becomes internalized, until more and more of us are products of everywhere and citizens of nowhere.

And though Paris, Tokyo, and Sydney are all in their way natural meeting points for this multipolar culture, America, as the traditional land of immigrants, is still the spiritual home of the very notion of integration. Everyone feels at home in only two places, Milos Forman has said: at home and in America. That is one reason why America's domination of pop culture is unlikely to subside, even if the reality of American power increasingly seems a thing of the past. The notion of America itself attracts more and more people to come and revive or refresh the notion of America. And the more international a culture is, the more, very often, it draws from the center of internationalism—the United States. The French may rail against cultural imperialism and try to enforce a kind of aesthetic protectionism by striving to keep out *le burger* and *le video*. But as soon as Madonna shows up in Cannes—so efficient is her command of all the media and so self-perpetuating her allure—she sets off the biggest stir in thirty years.

Madonna's global appeal is not unlike that of the Kentucky Fried Chicken parlor in Tiananmen Square: Both provide a way for people to align themselves, however fleetingly, with a world that is—in imagination at least—quick and flashy and rich. The lure of the foreign is quickened by the lure of the forbidden.

I got my own best sense of this in a friend's apartment in Havana some years ago. My friend was an intellectual dissident, fluent in several languages, eager to talk about Spinoza and Saroyan, and able to make a living by reading people's futures from their photographs and translating the latest Top 40 hits—recorded from radio stations in Miami—into Spanish. One night, trying to convey his desperation to escape, he pulled out what was clearly his most precious possession: a copy of Michael Jackson's album *Bad,* on which he had scrawled some heartfelt appeals to Jackson to rescue him. He did not, I suspect, know that Jackson was reclusive, eccentric, and about as likely to respond to political appeals as Donald Duck. What he did know was that

Jackson was black, rich, and sexually ambiguous—all things that it is not good to be in Castro's Cuba. What he also knew was that Jackson had succeeded on his own terms, an individual who had proved himself stronger than the system. The less my friend knew about Jackson the man, the closer he could feel to Jackson the symbol. And so it is with America: Since the America that he coveted does not quite exist, it is immutable, a talisman that will fail him only if he comes here.

8   People everywhere, whatever their circumstances, will always have a hunger for innocence, and America seems to have a limitless supply of that resource. Somehow the moguls of Hollywood and Broadway and Nashville—perhaps because they were immigrants themselves, with half a heart on the streets they left—have never lost their common touch: *E.T.* and *Back to the Future* strike universal chords as surely as *Gone with the Wind* and *Casablanca* did half a century ago. These stories continue to affect us because they speak to our most innocent dreams. To renounce them would be to renounce our own innocence.

PERSONAL RESPONSE

What does the term *global village* (paragraph 4) mean to you?

QUESTIONS FOR CLASS OR SMALL-GROUP DISCUSSION

1. What do you think of Milos Forman's comment that everyone feels "at home" in America (paragraph 5)? Do you agree with the statement? If so, why do you think America makes people feel at home? If not, what do you think prevents people from feeling at home in America?

2. In what way is America "the center of internationalism" (paragraph 5) and Hollywood "the capital of the world" (paragraph 3)?

3. What dreams and myths do you think America represents to people around the world (paragraph 3)?

4. In what way or ways do you think the films Iyer mentions in the last paragraph "speak to our most innocent dreams"? Can you name any more recent films as examples of the kind of innocence Iyer is referring to?

5. How does the innocent image of America that some movies portray fit with the "quick and flashy and rich" image of Madonna and Kentucky Fried Chicken (paragraph 6)? That is, how can America seem both "innocent" and "forbidden" to foreigners?

○ PERSPECTIVES ON AMERICA ABROAD IN POLITICAL SCIENCE ○

Suggestions for Writing

1. Explain the effect that America's wealth, power, commercialism, or any other aspect of its culture has on the way America is perceived by people in other nations.

2. Interview people who have immigrated to America to learn their reasons for coming to this country. Find out what images they had of America before they came and whether their impressions have changed now that they are living here.

3. If you are familiar with the difficulties a foreigner has had adjusting to life in your own country, tell about that person's experiences. Or, if you have personally experienced life as a foreigner in a country not your own, describe that experience.

4. Write an essay explaining why you think America's popular culture appeals to people in other countries.

5. Select a recent popular film and analyze the image of America that it projects, or, do a close analysis of a person or object from popular culture that you think represents an aspect of American culture.

6. Define *global village,* citing specific examples from your own experiences or observations.

7. Analyze an American book or story for the image it projects of America. Try to view the book or story objectively, as if you were a foreigner looking for information about America. What impression do you think a foreigner reading the same book or story would get of America?

8. Explore the subject of cultural stereotypes by looking at the way in which Americans stereotype people in a particular foreign country. What accounts for the stereotype? How does it prevent full understanding of the culture? What can you do to help dispel the stereotype?

9. Write a paper explaining your position on the question of whether America is responsible for defending weaker countries from oppression.

10. Interview foreign students on your campus to gather their impressions of American people and culture, and write an essay in which you summarize your findings and analyze reasons to account for those impressions. Incorporate into your paper the views of one or more of the writers in this chapter.

11. Describe your own friendship with a person from a foreign country, including what you see as the benefits of such a relationship.

12. If you have traveled abroad, write an essay about that experience, focusing on what you learned about another country and what you see as the benefits of foreign travel.

Research Topics

1. Research the subject of America's "soft power" in the period following the September 11, 2001, terrorist attacks on American soil.

2. Research the subject of anti-Americanism in countries other than America, whether it exists and, if so, why it exists and how strong it is.

3. Pico Iyer, in "Selling Our Innocence Abroad," describes America as "the center of internationalism" (paragraph 5). Conduct library research on this subject with a view to either supporting or refuting Iyer's assertion.

4. Conduct library research to expand on the views expressed by writers in this chapter of the American image abroad. From your research, draw some conclusions about that image. Do you find one particular image or many images? What aspects of America are responsible for the image or images? Does the image of America differ from country to country or even from continent to continent? You should be able to narrow your focus and determine a central idea for your paper after your preliminary search for sources and early review of the materials.

5. Research the subject of U. S. relations with Japan, China, the Soviet Union, the Middle East, or another foreign country that may figure importantly in the future of the United States. On the basis of your research, assess the importance to the United States of strengthening such relations and the potential effects of allowing relations with that country to deteriorate.

6. Research the conditions surrounding America's involvement in Bosnia, Kuwait, or Kosovo. Limit your focus to one aspect of the subject, such as what led to America's involvement, what America's involvement meant to American citizens, or effects on the country of America's intervention. Then argue the extent to which you support that involvement.

RESPONDING TO VISUALS

Protesters burn an American flag during demonstrations in the western Pakistani city of Peshawar, October 12, 2001. Source: Reuters/CORBIS

1. What is going on in this picture? Select details that convey the overall meaning of the picture.
2. What are the implications of the many cameras and video recorders at this event? Does the rhetorical effectiveness of flag burning depend on its being photographed? Does a gesture such as burning a flag need to be recorded visually in order to be effective? How does capturing the event on film or tape aid its effectiveness as a public expression of protest?
3. How would the meaning of the image change if the photographer had done a close-up of the burning flag, excluding the crowd?

RESPONDING TO VISUALS

Two Afghan women study in a classroom at the Afghan Police Academy in Kabul, December 8, 2003. They are part of a group of 70 women being trained at the policy academy. Source: Shah Marai/AFP/Getty Images

1. What do the women's faces reveal about how they view their classroom experience?
2. After the fall of the Taliban regime in Afghanistan, women began returning to school and work in large numbers. What do the looks on the men's faces suggest about how they view the women in their classroom?
3. How does the perspective of the photographer convey the mixed emotions of classroom members?

E-Readings Online for Part Three
InfoTrac College Edition

http://www.infotrac-college.com
(Search for each article by author or title after entering your Infotrac College Edition password.)

Chapter 11 Education

Selecting appropriate classroom materials is one of the most important responsibilities of an instructor, as course materials are a key factor in the successful classroom experience for students and teachers alike. Censorship or limitations on what teachers are allowed to teach can therefore be a real issue in education, and it occurs at all levels—elementary school, middle school, high school, and even college. Parents or concerned adults have challenged such books as J. K. Rowling's popular Harry Potter series for possibly enticing young children to dabble in witchcraft and Mark Twain's *Huckleberry Finn* for racism and insensitive language. The matter of censorship is likely to arise in relation to the school newspaper as well. Editors and reporters for such papers are sometimes warned not to write on certain taboo subjects. Libraries, bookstores, and other organizations work to focus attention on the restrictions to freedom of information and violations of rights that result from censorship. On the other hand, those calling for censorship or banning of books feel just as strongly about their reasons, which often include the well-being of students and the preservation of values. These articles comment on the issues associated with censorship in the classroom and on school newspapers and with the banning of the works of a popular author of books for young people.

○

SKIP LOWERY

Censorship: Tactics for Defense

Offers reasons for censorship in schools and practical suggestions for ways teachers can deal with it.

○

LISA WATTS

The Case They've Waited For?

Four high-school students sue their school district for violating their First Amendment rights.

○

JUDY BLUME

Places I Never Meant to Be: A Personal View

One of most banned American authors shares her frustration over book banning in the United States.

QUESTIONS FOR DISCUSSION OR WRITING

1. What reasons are most commonly cited for banning books in schools? What is your opinion of those reasons?
2. Under what conditions, if any, would you support the banning of books?
3. To what extent do you believe that school newspaper editors and reporters should have complete freedom of choice in the subjects reported in their newspapers?

Chapter 12 Poverty and Homelessness

Over half a million American families, including almost a million children, live on the streets or in shelters. Often, though not always, these are single-parent families with several children. The parents are unable to find employment, struggle to feed and clothe their children, and cannot afford health care for themselves or their families. Their children may not be going to school and often suffer emotional trauma from living in impoverished conditions. The plight of families who have no homes counters a prevailing stereotype of the drug- or alcohol-addicted person who will not work and begs for money to feed his or her habit. While such persons do exist, the picture of homeless people is much broader and much more complex. Families become homeless for a variety of reasons, and not always for reasons that one might think of. For instance, a significant number of homeless people were actually employed full- or part-time when they lost their home and a large percentage of them have at least a high-school education. These articles look at the issues facing homeless families, including possible causes and solutions to their circumstances.

○

LESLIE KAUFMAN

Surge in Homeless Families Sets Off Debate on Cause

Looks at the debate over what causes families to become homeless and features the experiences of two such families.

○

RALPH DA COSTA NUNEZ AND LAURA M. CARUSO

Are Shelters the Answer to Family Homelessness?

Surveys the plight of American families who become homeless and suggests a way to provide affordable housing for them.

○

YVONNE VISSING

The Yellow School Bus Project: Helping Homeless Students Get Ready for School

Describes a model collaborative project that helps homeless students succeed in school and feel good about themselves.

QUESTIONS FOR DISCUSSION OR WRITING

1. What do these articles tell you about who becomes homeless and why? Do they help dispel any stereotypical images of "typical" homeless persons that you may have had?

2. What solutions to meeting the needs of homeless families, particularly children, do these articles suggest? Do you have any other suggestions for meeting those needs?

3. Do you know anyone who is homeless, or are there homeless people in your community? Does anything in these articles apply to the people you know or know of?

Chapter 13 Criminal Behavior

Violent crimes have been a part of society from the beginning of mankind, and American society is no exception. Indeed, America often ranks at the top in terms of numbers of violent crimes per capita. Researchers and analysts in criminal justice, psychology, sociology, and other disciplines interested in the study of human behavior try to understand why people commit violent crimes. They look at a number of factors, depending upon their professional training and interests. Childhood, family life, marital status, interpersonal relationships, and a host of other aspects of human experience may be the key to understanding the criminal mind. Such understanding might lead to insights that help determine which predictive indicators may potentially identify who is likely to commit crimes, which in turn might lead to effective preventive measures. The problem is a complex one, because all kinds of people commit violent crimes, and in many cases there are no predictive factors or logical explanations. The first article in this group is actually a three-part look at how America compares with other countries in terms of numbers and kinds of crimes committed. The next looks at the effects of family life on men as it examines the social and cultural conditions that historically bred violence, and the third explores the ethical and moral implications should human behavioral genetics research develop an ability to successfully predict violent behavior even before conception.

○

UNITED PRESS INTERNATIONAL

America the Crime-free, in 3 parts

Dispels the prevailing stereotype of America as a lawless country by comparing America's crime rates to those of both developed and developing countries.

○

DAVID T. COURTWRIGT

Violence in America: What Human Nature and the California Gold Rush Tell Us about Crime in the Inner City

Looks at the importance of stable family life and marriage in reducing violence in society, using the California gold rush era as a historical example.

○

DAVID WASSER

Is there Value in Identifying Individual Genetic Predispositions to Violence?

Asks what we should do, either individually or collectively, if human behavioral genetics makes it possible to predict who will act violently.

QUESTIONS FOR DISCUSSION OR WRITING

1. What insights do these articles give you into crime in America? What do you think would have to change in American society before the rate of violent crimes can be significantly reduced?
2. Which of the cultural causes cited as factors to explain why people commit violent crimes do you find particularly compelling, and why?
3. What do you think of the answer David Wasser gives to the question posed in his title, "Is there Value in Identifying Individual Genetic Predispositions to Violence?" How would you answer the question?

Chapter 14 Gender and Sex Roles

The issue of same-sex marriage has gained national attention in recent years, with some cities and states moving quickly to pass laws that either legalize or make illegal the union between people of the same sex. Arguments on both sides wrangle with such considerations as the definition of marriage, the nature of the family, and responsibilities to children. Those opposed to same-sex marriage believe the basic foundation of society would be threatened, while those in favor argue just the opposite. These selections provide a wide spectrum of opinions. The first details reasons why arguments of those in favor of same-sex marriage are flawed and argues against legalizing it. The next is a personal essay by a lesbian who has been in a committed relationship for over three decades. She wonders more about the homophobia and gay bashing that a national debate about legalizing same-sex marriage might generate. Finally, the forum on marriage presents the views of fifteen writers and scholars about the broader purposes of marriage and whether legalizing gay marriage would threaten or strengthen those purposes.

○

STANLEY N. KURTZ

What Is Wrong with Gay Marriage

Provides a detailed explanation of why he is opposed to same-sex marriage.

○

CATHARINE R. STIMPSON

To Wed is to Lose One's Precious Distance from Conformity

Explains her conflicting feelings about legalizing same-sex marriage.

○

ELLEN WILLIS ET AL.

Can Marriage be Saved? A Forum

Writers and scholars offer their thoughts on the institution of marriage.

QUESTIONS FOR DISCUSSION OR WRITING

1. What issues seem to you most important in the debate over same-sex marriage?

2. What, if any, new points for consideration have these readings raised for you? If you are familiar with all of the arguments in these readings, who do you believe expresses the key ones most clearly and forcefully?

3. Whose opinion in the forum "Can Marriage be Saved" do you most agree with? Explain your answer.

Chapter 15 Race and Ethnicity in America

The question of reparations to minority groups who have been mistreated or discriminated against has come up many times in recent history. The U. S. government has made reparations and apologized to the Sioux Indians whose lands were illegally seized by the government in 1877, and it has done the same to Japanese Americans who were interned in American prison camps during World War II. President Clinton was apologetic about African slavery. For some time, people have suggested that the U. S. government make reparations to black Americans for slavery and its aftermath. Other approaches to the problem of how to deal with the fact that blacks were horribly wronged by slavery have been suggested as well. The writers of these articles look at various aspects of the question by giving an overview of the issues involved and representing voices both in favor of and against reparations.

○

CAROL M. SWAIN

Do Blacks Deserve a National Apology?

Asks the question, Should today's citizenry be held morally and financially accountable for the misdeeds of America's forefathers?

○

ROBINSON RANDALL

Reparations—More than Just a Check

Argues that "even the making of a well-reasoned case for restitution will do wonders for the spirit of African Americans."

○

CHARLES J. OGLETREE JR. AND E.R. SHIPP

Does America Owe Us?

A Harvard law professor and a Pulitzer Prize–winning journalist discuss the pros and cons of reparations.

QUESTIONS FOR DISCUSSION OR WRITING

1. Should the federal government make a monetary payment to African Americans to make up for their historical mistreatment?

2. To what extent do you agree that problems facing African Americans today are the result of slavery?

3. Assume the role of a member of a panel to consider a national apology to blacks. What questions would you ask? What would you take into consideration to make your decision? Do you think the federal government should apologize?

Chapter 16 Terrorism and War

Following the terrorist attacks on September 11, 2001, in New York City and Washington, D.C., the United States went on high alert. Terrorism was on everyone's mind as people struggled to come to terms with the deadliest attacks ever on American soil. The President declared a war on terrorism, Congress passed the Patriot Act and established the Department of Homeland Security, and America went to war against first Afghanistan and then Iraq. These readings look at different aspects of those events. The first explains the distinctions between the words "terror" and "terrorism" and what they suggest about the battle that the United States has undertaken, while the next advises against being too fearful in a struggle that is likely to last a long time. The third reviews five books on the war on terrorism and draws attention to the multifaceted issues associated with that war. The final piece argues that the Patriot Act, passed 45 days after the September 11, 2001, attacks, is "a grab bag of enhanced police and prosecution powers."

○

GEOFFREY NUNBERG

How Much Wallop Can a Simple Word Pack?

Examines the implications of the words "war on terror" versus "war on terrorism."

○

WILLIAM GREIDER

Under the Banner of the "War" on Terror

Warns Americans that a " 'war on terror' is useful for the President, but irrational for the nation."

○

P. W. Singer

The War on Terrorism: The Big Picture

Reviews five recent books that address the issues associated with the war on terrorism.

○

Timothy Egan

Sensing the Eyes of Big Brother, and Pushing Back

Criticizes the United States' Patriot Act.

QUESTIONS FOR DISCUSSION OR WRITING

1. What, if any, civil liberties would you be willing to give up in order to prevent or fight terrorism?
2. Review the consequences that William Greider says have resulted from the President's declaring a war on terrorism. How accurate to you think he is in assessing those consequences?
3. Of the issues raised by these writers, which do you think are the most pressing?

Chapter 17 America Abroad in Political Science

Because America is such a vast and rich nation and a powerful political force throughout the world, other countries inevitably have strong opinions about how they perceive it. This perception is influenced by many factors, including how close a country's ties are to America and whether a country is ideologically or politically in line with America. At times, other nations have viewed America with envy, sympathy, awe, displeasure, or even hatred, as the terrorist events of September 11, 2001, revealed so shockingly. This last emotion is difficult for many Americans to accept, and many writers have explored reasons to account for it. Furthermore, America's military response to the terrorist attacks has led to growing anti-American sentiments in countries throughout the world. These readings address that topic, beginning with an article that attempts to explain both the cultural and political divide between America and other nations. The next suggests that it is the cultural differences between America and other nations that explains their political differences. The last insists that it is fruitless to try to explain anti-Americanism: it is inevitable, and Americans would do well to ignore it.

○

THE ECONOMIST MAGAZINE

On the Rise; Anti-Americanism

Warns not to let criticism of America get out of hand.

○

RUSSELL A. BERMAN

Differences in American and European Worldviews

Examines deep-seated cultural differences between Europe and America.

○

CHARLES KRAUTHAMMER

To Hell with Sympathy

Expresses the opinion that whatever goodwill America earned on 9/11 is gone and that it is time to move on.

QUESTIONS FOR DISCUSSION OR WRITING

1. How might America persuade other nations that its goals and the methods for attaining them are sound? Do you agree with the *Economist* article that America must "make a greater effort" and "bend over backwards to nurture friendships"?

2. What, according to Russell A. Berman, are the differences between American and European worldviews? Does his article help explain to your satisfaction why anti-Americanism is growing in Europe?

3. What is your opinion of Charles Krauthammer's position that hatred of America is inevitable and that "its roots are envy and self-loathing"?

PART FOUR

SCIENCE AND TECHNOLOGY

CHAPTER

18

DIGITAL TECHNOLOGY AND THE INTERNET

Digital technology is constantly changing, with new, ever-faster programs emerging frequently. Although early researchers recognized the potential of computers, no doubt few of them envisioned the staggering capabilities of what they can do or the extent to which they would be so closely and inextricably linked with people's everyday lives. Increasingly sophisticated computers make child's play of activities that just a few years ago were challenging or impossible tasks. Young children today learn skills—sometimes before they enter school—that many of their grandparents will never even try to learn. Indeed, computer technology has advanced at such a rapid rate that its powers seem unlimited, a prospect that fills some with eager anticipation and leaves others feeling intimidated and frightened.

"Cyberspace," a word coined by author William Gibson in his sci-fi novel *Neuro-mancer,* commonly refers to the non-physical space and sense of community created by Internet users around the world, the virtual "world" that users inhabit when they are online. People can communicate on the Internet through e-mail and at websites; they can conduct research, shop, play games, and do any number of activities that people have been accustomed to do in physical space. The difference, of course, is that all those activities take place by pressing keys on a keyboard or moving a mouse around. Such convenience has changed the way many people conduct their lives, most would say in a positive way. However, the high-tech capabilities of the Internet have also led to problems.

One large problem for creators of intellectual property—books, movies, music, television programs, and computer programs, among others—is the pirating of copy-righted material. Music downloading was perhaps the first area in which the problem became apparent, and measures were put in place to protect that material. Now, certain technologies make it possible to illegally upload or download films in a matter of seconds; whole books can be scanned without their authors' or publishers' permission and made available to anyone with Internet access. A strong advocate for restraints on movie piracy has been Jack Valenti, past president of the Motion Picture Association of America. His "Thoughts on the Digital Future of Movies, the Threat of Piracy, the Hope of Redemption" represents his testimony before a Senate Committee hearing on the effects of Internet piracy on the entertainment industry. In it, Valenti spells out the dangers of movie piracy and steps that need to be taken to protect the rights of copyright holders.

In the next article in this chapter, Steven Levy uses personal experience to explain why he opposes piracy of intellectual property. In "The Day I Got Napsterized: First They Came for Metallica. Then They Came for Tom Clancy. And Then They Came for Me," he recounts his quick shift from being complacent about Internet intellectual-property de-bates to being a strong fighter in defense of artists' rights. He writes, "For authors like me—as musicians have already learned—the intellectual-property wars cannot be a spectator sport."

The focus of the chapter shifts from Internet theft to Internet websites, with articles on blogging and the act of creating a website. Geoffrey Nunberg's "Blogging in the Global Lunchroom" comments on the widespread presence of blogs on the Internet and explains how the language of public discourse used in blogging is different from other public discourse. Then, Meghan Daum, in "My Website, My Self," recounts her experience in creating her own website. It should, she felt, represent the "true" Meghan Daum, but just who the "true" Meghan Daum is turned out to be the most challenging question of all.

THOUGHTS ON THE DIGITAL FUTURE OF MOVIES, THE THREAT OF PIRACY, THE HOPE OF REDEMPTION

JACK VALENTI

Jack Valenti is past president and chief executive officer of the Motion Picture Association of America. A former wartime bomber pilot, political consultant, and White House Special Assistant, he is author of four books: The Bitter Taste of Glory *(1971),* A Very Human President *(1975),* Speak Up with Confidence *(2002), and the political novel* Protect and Defend *(1992). This statement was presented to the Permanent Subcommittee on Investigations, a subcommittee of the Senate Committee on Governmental Affairs during a hearing entitled "Privacy & Piracy: The Paradox of Illegal File Sharing on Peer-to-Peer Networks and the Impact of Technology on the Entertainment Industry." Valenti presented his statement at the hearing on September 30, 2003.*

The peril of piracy and the value of movies and intellectual property to this nation

It was said that during World War I, French General Foch, later to be Supreme Allied Commander, was engaged in a furious battle with the Germans. He wired military headquarters, "My right is falling back, my left is collapsing, my center cannot hold, I shall attack!"

Some say this version is apocryphal. I choose to believe it is true, because that is precisely the way I feel about the assault on the movie industry by 'file-stealers,' a rapidly growing group whose mantra is "I have the technological power to use as I see fit and I will use it to upload and download movies, no matter who owns them for I don't care about ownership."

To paraphrase Mr. Churchill, I did not become the head of the Motion Picture Association to preside over a decaying industry. I am determined to join with my colleagues in making it plain that we will not allow the movie industry to suffer the pillaging that has been inflicted on the music industry. This Committee understands, I do believe, that the movie industry is under attack. And this Committee would agree, I do believe, that we must counter these attacks NOW with all the resolve and imagination we can summon. To remain mute, inert, to casually attend the theft of our movies would be a blunder too dumb to comprehend.

4   This is not a peculiarly Hollywood problem. It is a national issue that should concern the citizens of this free and loving land. Why? Because the Intellectual Property community is America's greatest trade export and an awesome engine of growth, nourishing the American economy. Intellectual Property (movies, TV programs, home video, books, music, computer software) brings in more international revenues than agriculture, aircraft, automobiles and auto parts—it is also responsible for over five percent of the GDP—it is creating NEW jobs at THREE times the rate of the rest of the economy, at a time when we are suffering some 2 million job losses. The movie industry alone has a surplus balance of trade with every single country in the world. I don't believe any other American enterprise can make that statement—and at a time when this country is bleeding from a $400 billion-plus deficit balance of trade.

The very future of this awesome engine of economic growth is at stake. Happily, our movies draw large crowds to the theaters. But record box-office revenues should not blind anyone to the fact that the movie industry sits on a fragile fiscal bottom. The average film costs over $90 million to make and market. Only one in ten films ever gets this investment returned through theatrical exhibition. Films have to journey through many market venues—premium and basic cable, satellite delivery, home video, network and individual TV stations, international—in order to try to recoup the private risk capital that brings a movie to life.

If a film is kidnapped early in that journey, it's obvious the worth of that film can be fatally depleted long before it can retrieve its investment. Piracy means fewer people buying DVDs, less revenue, and fewer movies being made. Especially hurt will be creative ventures outside the mainstream that involve greater financial risk.

Add to that the fact that in this country almost one million men and women work in some aspect of the movie industry. These are not high-salaried jobs. They are held by ordinary Americans with families to feed, kids to send to college and mortgages to pay. Their jobs, their livelihoods, are put to extreme peril if we bear witness to the slow undoing of one of America's most valuable job-producing industries.

The onslaught grows in force and speed

8   An outside research group has estimated that 400,000 to 600,000 films are being illegally abducted every day. We know this will increase exponentially in the future. The speed of broadband is nothing compared to the supersonic download speeds being developed right now.

Scientists at CalTech have announced "FAST," an experimental program that can download a DVD quality movie in five seconds! Another experiment at Internet II has dispatched 6.7 gigabytes—more than a typical movie—halfway around the world in one minute! Internet II has conducted new experiments that will make that earlier triumph seem like a slow freight train. These technologies are not decades away. What is experiment today will be in the marketplace a few years from now. Can anyone deny that these huge download speeds brood over our future? Can anyone deny that when one can upload and download movies in seconds or minutes the rush to illegally obtain films will reach the pandemic stage? Can anyone deny the degrading impact this will have on the movie industry? And can anyone deny that limitless stealing of creative works will have a soiling impact on the national economy?

Not only is this piracy endemic in the United States, it flourishes abroad, though most of the pilfering is in the analog format: videocassettes and optical discs, as well as counterfeiting of DVDs. A good part of that thievery springs from organized criminal organizations. We have organized anti-piracy operations throughout the world. We are partnered with local groups in Japan, Great Britain, Germany, France, Italy, in Latin America and other countries where we are every day vigilant, for like virtue we are every day besieged. We estimate that we lose some $3.5 billion annually in analog and optical disc piracy.

We also know that much of the hard-goods pirated products, especially of films in theatrical release, are the result of people illegally camcording movies in theaters, and then distributing them over the Internet. Then they are stamped onto optical disks and sold for pennies on the streets of Asia and Eastern Europe, even before the movie has a chance to open in those countries. It is not pleasant for legitimate dealers and distributors to watch this breakdown in law and ethics.

12   What incentive will companies have to create, nourish and market digital movies online when they are kidnapped and flung around the world? Can high-value legitimate creative works live in an environment of abundant theft unchecked and growing? Will legitimate sites (which I will describe below) stand a chance of success competing against blinding-fast speeds of downloads and all for "free"? How does anyone answer that?

President Kennedy once told a story about a French general in Algeria who ordered his gardener to plant a certain species of tree to line the pebbled drive to his chateau. The gardener, astonished, said, "But mon General, that tree takes fifty years to bloom." To which the General responded, "Ah, we haven't a moment to lose. Plant them today." Precisely the way the movie industry addresses its future—we must plant today the barriers and rebuttals to movie stealing that will go on unchecked tomorrow unless we move with swiftness, resolve and efficiency.

The dark world of Peer-to-Peer (P2P) so-called file-swapping sites

We know that the infestation of P2P not only threatens the well-being of the copyright industries but consumers and their families as well. As hearings in the House and Senate have conclusively established, downloading KaZaa, Gnutella, Morpheus, Grockster, etc., can lay bare your most private financial and personal information to identity thieves. It can bring into your home and expose your children to pornography of the most vile and depraved character imaginable. Most insidious of all, the pornography finds its way to your children disguised as wholesome material: your son or daughter may "search" for "Harry Potter" or "Britney Spears," and be confronted with files that contain bestiality or child pornography. The pornography distributed through P2P networks is so horrific that the District Attorney from Suffolk County, New York, recently called it the worst his office had ever seen on the Internet. And the most disturbing fact of all is that any 10-year old can easily and swiftly bring down this unwelcome perversion.

Therefore, the business model that current P2P networks celebrate as "the digital democracy" is built on the fetid foundation of pornography and pilfered copyrighted works.

16   I invite members of this Committee to go online to KaZaa and see for yourself the mammoth menu of copyrighted works available FREE, as well as an endless listing of the most throat-choking child porn. It's all there, joyously defiant, enticing all to enter and take whatever you want, risk-free. What a wonderful world we live in!

What would be amusing if it were not so unhelpful are the outcries from critics whose hidden objective is to brutalize and shrink the value of copyright if not totally banish it from the Constitution. They always piously insist they are "opposed to violation of copyright" and then move quickly to defend the right of anyone to use P2P file-swapping sites without regard to who owns the material. Anyone who reads their testimony and dissertations will find, in the words of Horace Walpole, "that they swarm with loose and foolish observations."

The amazing Internet and how the movie industry wants to use it

The Internet, without doubt, is the greatest delivery system yet known to this planet. It has the potential to reshape how we communicate, how we buy and how to enlarge the dispatch of knowledge on a scale never before exhibited.

The movie industry is eager to use the Internet to deploy our movies, thousands of titles of every genre, to homes in this country and around the world. We want to give American families additional options for watching movies. They can make their choices easily, as well, when they want to see a movie. All at fair and reasonable prices, a phrase to be defined by the consumer and no one else.

20   Already, the industry is working on VideoOnDemand (VOD), so that everything is instantaneous. The consumer clicks a button and the movie is on the screen.

Now available are sites for legitimate movie viewing such as MovieLink, CinemaNow and others. You can call them up immediately and browse through their catalogue titles available. And it's legitimate, not illegal.

There is only one barrier to expand this immense bounty of movies and other entertainment for consumers. It is a forest thickly crowded with outlaws whose mission in life is to hijack movies and upload them to the Internet; then the feeding begins with illegal downloads. Once we defeat this illegitimacy, the consumers of America will be the cheerful beneficiaries of a never-ending source of high-value entertainment in a lawful environment.

What the movie industry is doing to baffle piracy

What is the movie industry doing to find rebuttals to piracy? We are working to address the corrosive effects of piracy by actively and expensively pursuing a comprehensive plan on multiple fronts with every tool we have at our disposal. We have launched an attack on a broad front to go on the offensive against thievery:

> (1) We are trying to educate the public about copyright and explain why it is important to the nation. We have created TV public service announcements (I hope you have seen them), and have joined with colleagues in exhibition who are showing

trailers in their theaters. We are in an alliance with Junior Achievement and one million students in grades five through nine, to explain and educate why copyright is central to intellectual property growth, and why filching movies in digital form by uploading and downloading on the Net is not only just plain wrong, but has a malignant effect on the future of American consumers.

(2) We have been meeting with a committee representing the nation's universities. These educational institutions are confronted with huge increased costs for large amounts of storage space and bandwidth in their state-of-the-art broadband systems, which are devoured by P2P networks. Most universities are now offering to students a catalogue which outlines that taking movies and music off the Net is an infringement of copyright and carries penalties. These codes of conduct inform students so they are aware that what they might consider to be okay and easy, is a violation of copyright and has to be taken seriously.

(3) We are investing all our anti-piracy resources to lift the level of law enforcement not only here but in other countries on every continent. In every region of the globe the MPAA has anti-piracy personnel working closely with law enforcement and local governments to keep pirate activity at bay. It's our intention to invest these efforts with more energy and resolve.

(4) We are embarking on a new project—technological research. We aim to enlist the finest brains of the best in the high-technology field to develop technological measures and means to baffle piracy. At the same time we are continuing to work with the most inventive men and women in the IT and CE sectors. By embracing these innovative scientists, I believe we can extract from this research more than a few counter-measures to put together a technological framework where all our industries can thrive, to the benefit of consumers. We are hopeful, very hopeful.

The role of the Congress

24   The Congress plays a vital role in establishing legitimacy to the marketplace. Through hearings like this, a forum is provided to explore and probe key issues, and allow debate to take place so that all viewpoints are heard and weighed.

Hearings to date in both chambers have exposed the economic dangers of piracy and its links to organized crime and terrorism. Also the hearings have brought to the ken of the public threats to consumers and the economy by piracy on a swollen scale and pornography easily available to youngsters.

I am sure this Committee understands that in 1998 many meetings took place between all the parties involved in the DMCA [Digital Millennium Copyright Act] legislation. I know very well because I was personally present and active in those meetings. In our conclusions, the ISPs [Internet Service Providers] got what they very much wanted, a safe harbor from liability. The copyright holder was given the tools necessary to identify infringers operating in cyberspace. The ISPs were in agreement with the details of the DMCA because they loved that which benefited them. It is wrong for ISPs to revisit an agreement they approved without hesitation.

Copyright holders have a firm belief that the Congress will never approve any legislation to strip copyright holders of their rights, and will never allow America's greatest trade export to become the victim of theft. This we believe.

PERSONAL RESPONSE

What are your views on movie piracy? Do you agree with Valenti that it is a serious problem that needs to be stopped?

QUESTIONS FOR CLASS OR SMALL-GROUP DISCUSSION

1. How effective is Valenti's opening anecdote about General Foch? Is it relevant to his subject and appropriate for his audience?

2. What strategies does Valenti use to convince his audience of the seriousness of the problem of movie piracy? That is, how persuasively does he demonstrate "the perils of piracy" and "the value of movies and intellectual property to this nation"?

3. What do you think of the movie industry's plans to "go on the offensive against thievery" (paragraph 23)? How effective do you think those measures will be in baffling piracy?

4. Where do you position yourself in the debate over movie piracy?

THE DAY I GOT NAPSTERIZED: FIRST THEY CAME FOR METALLICA. THEN THEY CAME FOR TOM CLANCY. AND THEN THEY CAME FOR ME.

STEVEN LEVY

Steven Levy, a senior editor and chief technology writer for Newsweek, *was a long-time writer of the "Iconoclast" column for* Macworld *magazine. His books include* Hackers: Heroes of the Computer Revolution *(1984);* Artificial Life: A Report from the Frontier Where Computers Meet Biology *(1992);* Insanely Great: The Life and Times of MacIntosh, the Computer That Changed Everything *(1993); and* Crypto: How the Code Rebels Beat the Government—Saving Privacy in the Digital Age *(2001). This article appeared in the May 28, 2001, issue of* Newsweek.

As a spectator, I found it easy to be sanguine about the raging Internet intellectual-property debates. I'd tempered my ecstasy during the heady exultations of the "information wants to be free"-bies, and kept my emotional powder dry as apocalyptic content owners warned that wanton file-sharing would mean the death of creativity. Basically, my take was that the Net had simply opened up a powerful mode of distribution, most fully realized in the Napsterlike peer-to-peer (P2P) model, where everybody could help spread the word (and the music). Artists and merchants alike would eventually figure out how to reap bucks from that bounty, and until then I'd sit back and enjoy the fun as Metallica and Courtney Love duked it out.

That was before I got P2P'd. And like facing a hangman's noose, being pirated on the Net has a way of focusing one's attention.

I first got wind of my own Napsterish problem a few months back when I stumbled on a message posted in an Internet discussion group that mentioned my 1984 book "Hackers." Some helpful soul informed the group that one could get the whole tome free, simply by going to a certain website. Huh?

4   Indeed, the entire text of "Hackers" was posted for all the world to download. And the web address revealed a most unexpected host for the giveaway: Stanford University. How did my copyrighted work find its way there? A few minutes of clicking revealed that this particular server had some connection to the chair of the university's program in history and philosophy of science, Tim Lenoir. So I called him to ask if he'd any idea who'd done this.

"I scanned your book," he said. Then came the apologies. The professor professed to be a big fan of my work, and (erroneously) assuming that it was out of print, spent a few hours to suck the words from each page of my book, submit it to a program that converted it to text and posted it for the benefit of his students only. The fact that anyone in the world could get to it, he said, was a mistake: he had not intended Stanford University to become an unofficial global distributor of "Hackers," charging nothing and, of course, paying no royalties. Lenoir promised to remove the book from the site, and we had a pretty good conversation about what might be fair use of electronic texts in an educational setting. By the time I hung up the phone, I felt somewhat less violated. Still, I wondered whether his "mistake" had cost me book sales.

My benign outlook dissolved about a week later when I received an e-mail from an English reader informing me that "in some kind of ironic but illegal turn, your book 'Crypto' has been . . . posted onto the newsgroup alt.binaries.e-book." This was the work I had published just weeks before, still selling briskly at $25.95 a pop! I knew all too well where the aforementioned irony came from. One topic I'd discussed in "Crypto" was the use of cyberanonymity, a means of cloaking the origin of an electronic missive. The purloiner of my own book called himself Stormysky, and carefully hid his tracks. Using those techniques, a number of Internet repositories had emerged as thriving underground book dumps where free-riders could download the texts of hundreds of recent tomes. Author Harlan Ellison calls the alt-scanners "rodents without ethic or understanding." A talk with my publisher's lawyer was even more dispiriting. "We're seeing this problem all the time," he moaned; he'd had little success in stemming the tide of purloined works by the likes of Tom Clancy. (So what were my chances?)

Though the technologies of anonymity wouldn't let me trace this particular rodent, it was possible to send him e-mail. Stormysky replied promptly, assuring me that he'd posted my book not to hurt me but to express his notion that the Internet was about sharing—and also as a protest against the intention of publishers to lock up intellectual property on the Net. If publishers have their way, Stormysky warned, they would limit the uses of books so that traditional consumer rights—lending a book to a friend, or even getting access to the book after a specified period—might be lost.

8   I actually agree with those sentiments, but also think I'm entitled to some payment for my work—and wonder what will happen when electronic reading devices

become more convivial, and downloaders of these files won't pay a penalty in eye-strain. Unfortunately, my new friend's protest contradicted his belief that "authors should receive monetary compensation for their creations." Grappling with this concept, he graciously agreed not to post any more of my work to newsgroups.

Forgive me, Stormy, if I'm feeling less than grateful. But I do appreciate the wake-up call. For authors like me—as musicians have already learned—the intellectual-property wars cannot be a spectator sport. I need to speak up more forcefully on the issues, and petition vociferously for creative business models—even if they require drastically altering the ones that have evolved over decades. Publishers mainly want control, and the consumers mainly want convenience and value, if not freebies. But it's the artists who are on the firing line, eager to win audiences but concerned about maintaining our credit ratings. We have to muscle our way into the center of the quest for a solution that somehow exploits the distribution power of the Net while assuring that our audiences pay us something for the experience. Otherwise, we'll just be P'd on.

PERSONAL RESPONSE

Write for a few minutes on your view of the Napster controversy that Levy refers to in his title and opening paragraph, whether you used its services before it was made illegal or not.

QUESTIONS FOR CLASS OR SMALL-GROUP DISCUSSION

1. Does Levy fully explain the controversy over P2P technology, including the viewpoints of both artists and consumers? State in your own words what the various viewpoints are.

2. Comment on the tone and point of view of this essay. What effect is achieved by using first-person point of view and personal experience?

3. Levy quotes author Harlan Ellison as referring to alt-scanners as " 'rodents without ethic or understanding' " (paragraph 6). Do you think Ellison's description of alt-scanners is fair?

4. Do you agree with Levy's position in defense of his copyrighted material? Are there any circumstances in which you think it would be acceptable to copy creative works without paying for them?

BLOGGING IN THE GLOBAL LUNCHROOM

Geoffrey Nunberg

Geoffrey Nunberg is a senior researcher at the Center for the Study of Language and Information at Stanford University, and a Consulting Full Professor of Linguistics at Stanford University. Until 2001, he was a principal scientist at the Xerox Palo Alto Research Center, working on the development of linguistic technologies. Nunberg serves as usage editor and chair of the usage panel of the American Heritage Dictionary and has written on language and other topics for a variety of periodicals, including a regular feature on language for the "Week in Review" section of the Sunday New York Times. *He is author of* The Future of the Book *(1996),* The Way We Talk Now *(2001), and* Going Nucular *[sic]:* Language, Politics, and Culture in Controversial Times *(2004). Nunberg does a regular language feature on the NPR program* Fresh Air, *where this commentary was broadcast on April 20, 2004.*

Over the last couple of months, I've been posting on a group blog called languagelog.org, which was launched by a couple of linguists as a place where we could vent our comments on the passing linguistic scene.

Still, I don't quite have the hang of the form. The style that sounds perfectly normal in a public radio feature or an op-ed piece comes off as distant and pontifical when I use it in a blog entry. Reading over my own postings, I recall what Queen Victoria once said about Gladstone: "He speaks to me as if I were a public meeting."

I'm not the only one with this problem. A lot of newspapers have been encouraging or even requiring their writers to start blogs. But with some notable exceptions, most journalists have the same problems that I do. They do all the things you should do in a newspaper feature. They fashion engaging leads, they develop their arguments methodically, they give context and background, and tack helpful ID's onto the names they introduce—"New York Senator Charles E. Schumer (D)."

4 That makes for solid journalism, but it's not really blogging. Granted, that word can cover a lot of territory. A recent Pew Foundation study found that around three million Americans have tried their hands at blogging, and sometimes there seem to be almost that many variants of the form. Blogs can be news summaries, opinion columns, or collections of press releases, like the official blogs of the presidential candidates. But the vast majority are journals posted by college students, office workers, or stay-at-home moms, whose average readership is smaller than a family Christmas letter. (The blog hosting site livejournal.com reports that two-thirds of bloggers are women—I'm not sure what to make of that proportion.)

But when people puzzle over the significance of blogs nowadays, they usually have in mind a small number of A-List sites that traffic in commentary about politics, culture, or technology—blogs like Altercation, Instapundit, Matthew Yglesias, Talking Points or Doc Searls. It's true that bloggers like these have occasionally come up with news scoops, but in the end they're less about breaking stories than bending them. And their language is a kind of anti-journalese. It's informal, impertinent, and digressive, casting links in all directions. In fact one archetypal blog entry consists entirely of a cryptic comment that's linked to another blog or a news item—"Oh, please," or "He's married to her?"

That interconnectedness is what leads enthusiasts to talk about the blogosphere, as if this were all a single vast conversation—at some point in these discussions, somebody's likely to trot out the phrase "collective mind." But if there's a new public sphere assembling itself out there, you couldn't tell from the way bloggers address their readers—not as anonymous citizens, the way print columnists do, but as co-conspirators who are in on the joke.

Taken as a whole, in fact, the blogging world sounds a lot less like a public meeting than the lunchtime chatter in a high-school cafeteria, complete with snarky comments about the kids at the tables across the room. (Bloggers didn't invent the word snarky, but they've had a lot to do with turning it into the metrosexual equivalent of bitchy. On the Web, blogs account for more than three times as large a share of the total occurrences of snarky as of the occurrences of irony.)[1]

8   Some people say this all started with Mickey Kaus's column in *Slate*, though Kaus himself cites the old *San Francisco Chronicle* columns of Herb Caen. And Camille Paglia not surprisingly claims that her column in *Salon.com* was the first true blog, and adds that the genre has been going downhill ever since.

But blogs were around on the web well before Kaus or Paglia first logged in.[2] And if you're of a mind to, you can trace their print antecedents a lot further back than Caen or Hunter S. Thompson. That informal style recalls the colloquial voice that Addison and Steele devised when they invented the periodical essay in the early 18th century, even if few blogs come close to that in artfulness. Then too, those essays were written in the guise of fictive personae like Isaac Bickerstaff and Sir Roger de Coverly, who could be the predecessors of pseudonymous bloggers like Wonkette, Atrios, or Skippy the Bush Kangaroo, not to mention the mysterious conservative blogger who goes by the name of Edward Boyd.[3]

For that matter, my languagelog co-contributor Mark Liberman recalls that Plato always had Socrates open his philosophical disquisitions with a little diary entry, the way bloggers like to do: "I went down yesterday to see the festival at the Peiraeus with Glaucon, the son of Ariston, and I ran into my old buddy Cephalus and we got to talking about old age . . ."

Of course whenever a successful new genre emerges, it seems to have been implicit in everything that preceded it. But in the end, this is a mug's game, like asking whether the first SUV was a minivan, a station wagon, or an off-road vehicle.

12   The fact is that this is a genuinely new language of public discourse—and a paradoxical one. On the one hand, blogs are clearly a more democratic form of expression than anything the world of print has produced. But in some ways they're also more exclusionary, and not just because they only reach about a tenth of the people who use the web.[4] The high, formal style of the newspaper op-ed page may be nobody's native language, but at least it's a neutral voice that doesn't privilege the speech of any particular group or class. Whereas blogspeak is basically an adaptation of the table talk of the urban middle class—it isn't a language that everybody in the cafeteria is equally adept at speaking. Not that there's anything wrong with chewing over the events of the day with the other folks at the lunch table, but you hope that everybody in the room is at least reading the same newspapers at breakfast.[5]

Notes

[1]This is a rough estimate, arrived at by taking the proportion of total Google hits for a word that occurs in a document that also contains the word blog:

snarky: 87,700

snarky + blog: 32,600 (37%)

irony: 1,600,000

irony + blog: 168,000 (10.5%)

Of course the fact that the word blog appears in a page doesn't necessarily mean that it is a blog, but it turns out that more than 90 percent of the pages containing the word are blog pages, and in any case, the effect would be the same for both terms. And while some part of this variation no doubt reflects the status of snarky as a colloquial word that is less likely to show up in serious literary discussions and the like, the effect is nowhere near so marked when we look at the word bitchy:

bitchy: 250,000

bitchy + blog: 43,700 (17.5%)

That is, the specialization to blogs is more than twice as high for snarky as for bitchy, even though both are colloquial items.

[2]Many have given credit for inventing the genre to Dave Winer, whose *Scripting News* was one of the earliest weblogs, though Winer himself says that the first weblog was Tim Berners-Lee's page at CERN. But you could argue that blog has moved out from under the derivational shadow of its etymon—the word isn't just a truncation of weblog anymore. In which case, the identity of the first "real blog" is anybody's guess—and it almost certainly will be.

[3]James Wolcott makes a similar comparison in the current *Vanity Fair*, and goes so far as to suggest that "If Addison and Steele, the editors of *The Spectator* and *The Tatler*, were alive and holding court at Starbucks, they'd be WiFi-ing into a joint blog." That's cute, but I think it gets Addison and Steele wrong—the studied effusions of Isaac Bickertaff and Sir Roger de Coverly may have sounded like blogs, but they were fashioned with an eye towards a more enduring literary fame. Which is not to say that blogs couldn't become the basis for a genuine literary form. As I noted in a "Fresh Air" piece a few years ago that dealt more with blogs as personal journals:

> There's something very familiar about that accretion of diurnal detail. It's what the novel was trying to achieve when eighteenth-century writers cobbled it together out of subliterary genres like personal letters, journals, and newspapers, with the idea of reproducing the inner and outer experience that makes up daily life. You wonder whether anything as interesting could grow up in the intimate anonymity of cyberspace. (See "I Have Seen the Future, and It Blogs," in Going Nucular, *PublicAffairs*, May, 2004.)

So it's not surprising that a number of fictional blogs ("flogs"? "blictions"?) have begun to emerge, adapting the tradition of the fictional diary that runs from Robinson Crusoe to Bridget Jones' Diary. As to whether that will ultimately amount to "anything as interesting" as the novel, the jury is likely to be out for a while.

[4]The Pew study found that 11% of Internet users have read the blogs or diaries of other Internet users.

[5]For a diverting picture of the blogosphere-as-lunchroom, see Whitney Pastorek's recent piece in the *Village Voice,* "Blogging Off."

PERSONAL RESPONSE

Do you read (or have you read) blogs? Have you ever posted a comment at a blog?

QUESTIONS FOR CLASS OR SMALL-GROUP DISCUSSION

1. How effective is Nunberg's title? In what ways does it reflect the content and focus of his talk?

2. What seems to account for the popularity of blogs and the variety of people who post them? In paragraph 4, Nunberg notes that "two-thirds of bloggers are women—I'm not sure what to make of that proportion." What do you make of it?

3. Is Nunberg's language appropriate to his subject? Define these words and terms: "blogosphere" (paragraph 6), "snarky" and "metrosexual" (paragraph 7). Who are Addison and Steele (paragraph 9)? What is the point of Nunberg's reference to them?

4. Does Nunberg convincingly explain the paradox he sees in this "new language of public discourse" (paragraph 12)? How would you explain it in your own words?

MY WEBSITE, MY SELF

Meghan Daum

Meghan Daum is the author of an essay collection, My Misspent Youth *(2001) and a novel* The Quality of Life Report *(2004). A former columnist for* Self Magazine, *she has contributed to National Public Radio's* Morning Edition *and* This American Life *and has written for* The New Yorker, Harper's, GQ, *and* Vogue, *among other periodicals. She can be reached at her website:* <www.meghandaum.com>.

I thought I knew myself. Then I put three letters before my name and I disappeared entirely. Who knew "www" could provoke such an identity crisis? It was as if I'd been given the opportunity to choose a new name and couldn't decide between Mary or Moonbeam, as if I was on a makeover show and weighing the advantages of a Kate Winslet-ish nose or a Kate Hudson-esque chin. But this was much more metaphysical than that. A website was a chance to receive a Total Reputation Makeover. Gone would be the horrifying debris washed up by the ruthless surf of Google. The nasty customer reviews would be conveniently omitted and replaced by carefully selected encomiums. The out-of-context quotes from newspaper interviews would be traded for witty, eloquent statements custom written for the homepage. Unfortunate mug shots would be eclipsed by a strategically lit and suitably hot photo of myself. In other words, the website would set the record straight. Thought you knew who I was? Visit meghandaum.com and think again!

Of course, that assumes a lot of people know who I am to begin with, which they don't, and barring some future involvement in a government sex scandal (meghangate.com), probably never will. After all, I'm a writer. As Gore Vidal said, "Saying you're a very famous novelist is like saying you're a famous ceramicist." The goal here isn't fame. The goal is professional and creative sustainability. Or more than two people showing up at book signings. Or being able to afford car insurance. Or the car wash. And while having a website may not hold the key to that goal, it seems increasingly clear that not having one is a form of self-sabotage tantamount to not having a cell phone.

I won't ask why websites for authors—or for anyone—are necessary these days because they're really not. The whole idea of "necessary" is quaint. The web has turned us into a nation of hobbyists. It's as if we're all attending a high school in which only electives are offered.

4   Still, some electives are more elective than others, and herein lies the conundrum of the artist's website. Though most writers, musicians, and artists spare the public our high school poetry or 1970s-era family photos, we don't exactly offer much that's particularly useful. My website features no mortgage calculator or Atkins recipes, nor is there any online-dating component or opportunity to buy a kitchen appliance and then rate it by number of stars. It's merely a website about me, the explaining of me, the showing of me, the providing of links to a sampling of my works—two books, a couple of magazine essays that don't embarrass me, a rather cringe-inducing "what the critics said" link that includes the kind of disembodied, ellipses-laden quotes that could just as easily be talking about a really ripe tomato. Incidentally, tomatoes have their own website, **www.tomato.org,** which is sponsored by the California Tomato Commission. It has some interesting stuff on it and I wish I'd looked at it before I designed my site.

I wish I'd looked at a lot of sites before I embarked on my own. Maybe I could have avoided reverting back to pre-adolescent levels of inquiry along the lines of "if I were a wallpaper pattern, what kind would I be?" Maybe I could have spared my patient and very capable designers hours of time wasted at the hands of my indecision and my habit of describing navigation bars as "those scrolly things" and links as "those things that go to other things."

But my ignorance of the web paled in comparison to my ignorance of (cue the synthesizer) . . . myself. What was my look? My tone? My ratio of crowd-pleasing genericness to take-it-or-leave-it edginess? Was it best to stick with the tried-and-true hybrid of biography and promotion ("Meghan Daum was born in 1970 and excelled in English and now writes books, *buy them now*"), or did I dare attempt to be hip as well as promotional ("A little bit ribald, a little bit renegade, Meghan Daum is an acid-tongued princess of noir, *buy her books now, super saver shipping!*")?

The alternating satisfaction and discomfort I feel toward my website runs, predictably, in direct proportion to the alternating satisfaction and discomfort I feel about my work, my career, my entire being. Depending on my mood, I am convinced the site needs to be funnier, cooler, more minimalist, less minimalist, more informative, less revealing, and/or displaying different fonts or colors. Surfing the Internet, I find the site of a Pulitzer-winning author. It's a funky yet cerebral presentation with whimsical cartoons and a refreshing absence of author photos and within seconds I decide mine should be exactly like that. Five minutes later I stumble upon the site for a '70s punk music icon and am certain I would be better off with an entirely white screen with tiny lowercase letters displaying only my initials and perhaps an arcane quotation from Quentin Crisp.

8   As things turned out, I ended up with a site that resembles an amalgam of the Sundance catalog, *Real Simple,* and an Anthropologie store. This is because my designers followed my instructions to the letter, responding to my blurted-out declaration of "I like shabby chic!" with a design scheme that I suspect has led a number of people to attempt to order ottomans from **www.meghandaum.com.** Imagine their disappointment when they end up with a measly book.

Imagine my disappointment when the launch of my website transforms me into neither a Pulitzer Prize winner nor a punk icon. The design scheme of my living room also remains a pale shadow of my homepage. All working artists grapple with the fallout of presenting work to the public. The degree to which people "get it" is occasionally exhilarating (the glowing newspaper review, the audience that appears to be on laughing gas) and mostly horrifying (the vitriolic online customer review, the ubiquitous question "Do you write mysteries or romance?"). This lack of control over audience response can be uncomfortable, even debilitating. The website, thus, is not just a promotional tool but an opportunity for creative people to attempt to explain ourselves, to set the record straight, to re-create our images by suggesting that we are in fact something entirely different from what our publicist, agent, or mother assumes us to be.

Like all technological "advances," the artist's website makes us wonder how anyone ever got along, or at least forged a career, without one. After all, visual artists can now display high-resolution JPEGs of their work, musicians can offer downloadable (and crappy-sounding) samples of their songs, and, for my part, I no longer spend hours making photocopies of my magazine clippings since editors can ostensibly go to my site. But convenience aside, these websites suggest a lack of faith in the audience's ability to interpret the work on its own. It is no longer enough for us to present our work; we must now tell people how to read, see, or hear it. As if prefacing every offering with a press release, we must emphasize that we're "a satirist," "an abstract impressionist," "an award-winning Claymation animator," "a klezmer drummer." (Don't know what klezmer is? No worries, we'll explain that, too.)

The opportunity to educate the public is both tempting and troubling. As much as I relish the chance to use my website as a partisan clearinghouse of my work, I must admit that it's also a vain act of self-defense. The degree to which I feel compelled to be my own publicist is proportional to the degree to which I don't entirely trust my readers and would-be readers to grasp or even like my work without the benefit of my helpful reader's guide. This reveals both a pitiful insecurity on my part and, I daresay, a growing need for artists to not only create their art but to advertise, market, and hand-sell it. The pragmatist in me says this is a necessary evil. It is, after all, presumptuous to think we can hole up in our garrets, writing our books and throwing our pots with no thought to how our work might reach the public. But in our effort to brand ourselves, are we relying on links and bios and design elements to express ideas that, back in the old days, resided solely in the work itself?

12   Unless someone on the MacArthur committee stumbles upon my website and is jazzed enough by my color scheme to give me a genius award, the value of artists' websites will probably remain, like the work itself, in the eye of the beholder. And unless I start selling ottomans, it's unlikely that I'll generate enough traffic to effect any increase in sales or exposure. But, like decorating a house, the process of designing the site taught me a thing or two about myself. Lesson one: If I were a wallpaper pattern it would probably not be the pattern you see on my site. Lesson two: Sometimes you just have to live with the wallpaper you have.

PERSONAL RESPONSE

Visit Daum's website at <www.meghandaum.com> and analyze its rhetorical effectiveness.

QUESTIONS FOR CLASS OR SMALL-GROUP DISCUSSION

1. In what sense can a website be "a chance to receive a Total Reputation Makeover" (paragraph 1)? How does Daum's title relate to her central point?

2. In what way does Daum mean that, for writers, not having a website "is a form of self-sabotage"? Do you agree with her on that point?

3. To what degree do you agree with Daum when she says that artists' "websites suggest a lack faith in the audience's ability to interpret the work on its own" (paragraph 10).

4. Explain the two lessons that Daum learned while designing her website (paragraph 12).

○ PERSPECTIVES ON DIGITAL TECHNOLOGY AND THE INTERNET ○
Suggested Writing Topics

1. Argue your position on the issue of peer-to-peer technology and file-swapping.

2. Argue your position on the quandary that Steven Levy describes in "The Day I Got Napsterized . . ." between wanting to support the free sharing intellectual property and wanting to prevent wholesale giving away of his work (paragraphs 7 and 8).

3. Explain the characteristics of a blog that you particularly like to visit, or follow the postings at one blog for a week and do an analysis of the site.

4. Write an analysis of a website that you think is especially well done.

5. Write a process paper explaining how to create an effective website.

6. Drawing on at least one of the readings in this chapter, explore the impact of digital technology on an aspect of contemporary culture.

7. Drawing on at least one of the readings in this chapter, explain how digital technology raises issues for copyright holders.

8. Explain the importance of high-tech digital systems in your life.

9. Write an essay explaining what you see as the benefits and/or dangers of the Internet.

10. Explain the direction you see digital technology going in over the next decade or two.

Research Topics

1. Research the economic impact of movie piracy on the entertainment industry.

2. Jack Valenti in "Thoughts on the Digital Future of Movies . . ." refers to the "dark world of Peer-to-Peer (P2P) so-called file-swapping sites." Research to either substantiate or refute Valenti's view on the danger that P2P technology and P2P file-swapping sites pose to individuals.

3. Research efforts by the film industry to protect itself from piracy. Which efforts promise to be most effective? Which have proven useless?

4. Research the efforts of rock groups such as Metallica and Pearl Jam to use the Internet to distribute their music while protecting themselves from piracy.

5. Research the role of blogs as "a new language of public discourse" (Geoffrey Nunberg's "Blogging in the Global Lunchroom").

6. Research an area of computer technology that is still in the experimental stages or still being refined.

7. Research the impact of technology in one of the following areas: marketing, shopping, entertainment, scholarship/research, American culture, education, or government and politics.

8. Research a problem associated with the Internet such as the availability of pornography for children, the potential dangers of e-mail, or privacy issues.

RESPONDING TO VISUALS

A vendor sells illegal bootleg DVDs on Canal Street, Manhattan, New York. Source: Ei Katsumata/Alamy

1. What aspects of the picture indicate that the vendor is selling illegally?
2. Why did the photographer choose this perspective rather than focus, say, on the vendor or on the DVDs exclusively?
3. How does the picture comment on the practice of selling bootlegged DVDs?

RESPONDING TO VISUALS

Tribal boys with a laptop in Australia. Source: Robert Essel NYC/CORBIS

1. What is your reaction to this picture?
2. What is the purpose of the picture?
3. What contrasts in the picture does the photographer emphasize?
4. What do you think the boys are doing with the laptop? Does it matter that we do not know?

CHAPTER
19

NATURAL SCIENCES

The natural sciences include such disciplines as biology, physics, astronomy, and chemistry. Their inquiry focuses on the workings and phenomena of the natural world, from the ocean floor to the farthest galaxies of the universe. Two essays in this chapter cover that range and hint at the enormous possibility for increasing human knowledge of the world we inhabit; the other two comment on the subject of people's readiness to accept anything offered as "science" and the ways to counter that gullibility. The authors reprinted here share a belief in the wonders and joy of science and in the close relationship of science and creative imagination.

For instance, Jacob Bronowski, in "The Reach of the Imagination," emphasizes the imaginative component of scientific thinking as he explains the workings of the imagination and why he believes it marks the chief difference between humans and other animals. Consider whether you agree with him on this point. Do other differences of equal importance distinguish humans' superiority over other animals? To what extent do you agree with him about the imaginative and creative components of science and its link with the humanities?

"The Chemist" is written by a scientist who works to popularize science and enhance its accessibility to the public. In this brief chapter from his book celebrating the truly interdisciplinary nature of life today, chemist Roald Hoffmann explores the metaphor of discovery used by scientists from historical, psychological, philosophical, and sociological perspectives. As you read the essay, think about the broader issue raised by Hoffmann, that is, the interconnectedness of the disciplines. Do you see such a connection in the courses you are now taking? Another writer who is excited about science is Matt Ridley. In his article, "The Year of the Genome," he celebrates the results of both the public and the private research into the human genome, gives a brief history of the history of discoveries in genetics, and suggests that we are now at "the beginning of a whole new way of understanding human biology."

The final two writers represented in this chapter, one a scientist herself and the other a science journalist, address the issue of the general public's being too willing to accept what they call "junk science" or "pseudoscience." Lee Ann Fisher Baron in "The Influence of 'Junk Science' and the Role of Science Education" discusses some of the unfounded scientific claims that too many people believe. Her examples of how "junk science" claims persuade people to buy certain products include some very popular items such as fat-free foods and herbal supplements. The examples cited by the other writer, Boyce Rensberger in "The Nature of Evidence," also have widespread followers: parapsychology and UFOs. Baron and Rensberger both suggest reasons to account for the general public's "gullibility" and offer steps that educators, scientists, and journalists can take to better inform people about the nature of evidence.

THE REACH OF THE IMAGINATION

Jacob Bronowski

Jacob Bronowski (1908–1974) was a Polish-born American scientist whose television series Ascent of Man *(1974) combined art, philosophy, and science to explain the connections between science and the humanities. His books include* The Common Sense of Science *(1951),* Science and Human Values *(1959), and* William Blake, a Man with a Mask *(1965). This essay was originally delivered as the Blashfield Address at a meeting of the American Academy of Arts and Letters and the National Institute of Arts and Letters in May 1966. It was reprinted in the spring 1990 issue of* American Scholar.

For three thousand years, poets have been enchanted and moved and perplexed by the power of their own imagination. In a short and summary essay I can hope at most to lift one small corner of that mystery; and yet it is a critical corner. I shall ask, What goes on in the mind when we imagine? You will hear from me that one answer to this question is fairly specific: which is to say, that we can describe the working of the imagination. And when we describe it as I shall do, it becomes plain that imagination is a specifically *human* gift. To imagine is the characteristic act, not of the poet's mind, or the painter's, or the scientist's, but of the mind of man.

My stress here on the word *human* implies that there is a clear difference in this between the actions of men and those of other animals. Let me then start with a classical experiment with animals and children which Walter Hunter thought out in Chicago about 1910. That was the time when scientists were agog with the success of Ivan Pavlov in forming and changing the reflex actions of dogs, which Pavlov had first announced in 1903. Pavlov had been given a Nobel Prize the next year, in 1904; although in fairness I should say that the award did not cite his work on the conditioned reflex, but on the digestive gland.

Hunter duly trained some dogs and other animals on Pavlov's lines. They were taught that when a light came on over one of three tunnels out of their cage, that tunnel would be open; they could escape down it, and were rewarded with food if they did. But once he had fixed that conditioned reflex, Hunter added to it a deeper idea: He gave the mechanical experiment a new dimension, literally—the dimension of time. Now he no longer let the dog go to the lighted tunnel at once; instead, he put out the light, and then kept the dog waiting a little while before he let him go. In this way Hunter timed how long an animal can remember where he has last seen the signal light to his escape route.

4   The results were and are staggering. A dog or a rat forgets which one of three tunnels has been lit up within a matter of seconds—in Hunter's experiment, ten seconds at most. If you want such an animal to do much better than this, you must make the task much simpler: You must face him with only two tunnels to choose from. Even so, the best that Hunter could do was to have a dog remember for five minutes which one of two tunnels had been lit up.

I am not quoting these times as if they were exact and universal: They surely are not. Hunter's experiment, more than fifty years old now, had many faults of detail. For example, there were too few animals, they were oddly picked, and they did not all behave consistently. It may be unfair to test a dog for what he saw, when he commonly follows his nose rather than his eyes. It may be unfair to test any animal in the unnatural setting of a laboratory cage. And there are higher animals, such as chimpanzees and other primates, which certainly have longer memories than the animals that Hunter tried.

Yet when all these provisos have been made (and met, by more modern experiments) the facts are still startling and characteristic. An animal cannot recall a signal from the past for even a short fraction of the time that a man can—for even a short fraction of the time that a child can. Hunter made comparable tests with six-year-old children, and found, of course, that they were incomparably better than the best of his animals. There is a striking and basic difference between a man's ability to imagine something that he saw or experienced, and an animal's failure.

Animals make up for this by other and extraordinary gifts. The salmon and the carrier pigeon can find their way home as we cannot: They have, as it were, a practical memory that man cannot match. But their actions always depend on some form of habit: on instinct or on learning, which reproduce by rote a train of known responses. They do not depend, as human memory does, on calling to mind the recollection of absent things.

8   Where is it that the animal falls short? We get a clue to the answer, I think, when Hunter tells us how the animals in his experiment tried to fix their recollection. They most often pointed themselves at the light before it went out, as some gun dogs point rigidly at the game they scent—and get the name *pointer* from the posture. The animal makes ready to act by building the signal into its action. There is a primitive imagery in its stance, it seems to me; it is as if the animal were trying to fix the light on its mind by fixing it in its body. And indeed, how else can a dog mark and (as it were) name one of the three tunnels, when he has no such words as *left* and *right*, and no such numbers as *one, two, three?* The directed gesture of attention and readiness is perhaps the only symbolic device that the dog commands to hold on to the past, and thereby to guide himself into the future.

I used the verb *to imagine* a moment ago, and now I have some ground for giving it a meaning. *To imagine* means to make images and to move them about inside one's head in new arrangements. When you and I recall the past, we imagine it in this direct and homely sense. The tool that puts the human mind ahead of the animal is imagery. For us, memory does not demand the preoccupation that it demands in animals, and it lasts immensely longer, because we fix it in images or other substitute symbols. With the same symbolic vocabulary we spell out the future—not one but many futures, which we weigh one against another.

I am using the word *image* in a wide meaning, which does not restrict it to the mind's eye as a visual organ. An image in my usage is what Charles Peirce called a *sign*, without regard for its sensory quality. Peirce distinguished between different forms of signs, but there is no reason to make his distinction here, for the imagination works equally with them all, and that is why I call them all *images*.

Indeed, the most important images for human beings are simply words, which are abstract symbols. Animals do not have words, in our sense: There is no specific center for language in the brain of any animal, as there is in the human being. In this respect at least we know that the human imagination depends on a configuration in the brain that has only evolved in the last one or two million years. In the same period, evolution has greatly enlarged the front lobes in the human brain, which govern the sense of the past and the future; and it is a fair guess that they are probably the seat of our other images. (Part of the evidence for this guess is that damage to the front lobes in primates reduces them to the state of Hunter's animals.) If the guess turns out to be right, we shall know why man has come to look like a highbrow or an egghead: because otherwise there would not be room in his head for his imagination.

12   The images play out for us events which are not present to our senses, and thereby guard the past and create the future—a future that does not yet exist, and may never come to exist in that form. By contrast, the lack of symbolic ideas, or their rudimentary poverty, cuts off an animal from the past and the future alike, and imprisons him in the present. Of all the distinctions between man and animal, the characteristic gift which makes us human is the power to work with symbolic images: the gift of imagination.

This is really a remarkable finding. When Philip Sidney in 1580 defended poets (and all unconventional thinkers) from the Puritan charge that they were liars, he said that a maker must imagine things that are not. Halfway between Sidney and us, William Blake said, "What is now proved was once only imagined." About the same time, in 1796, Samuel Taylor Coleridge for the first time distinguished between the passive fancy and the active imagination, "the living Power and prime Agent of all human Perception." Now we see that they were right, and precisely right: The human gift is the gift of imagination—and that is not just a literary phrase.

Nor is it just a literary gift; it is, I repeat, characteristically human. Almost everything that we do that is worth doing is done in the first place in the mind's eye. The richness of human life is that we have many lives; we live the events that do not happen (and some that cannot) as vividly as those that do; and if thereby we die a thousand deaths, that is the price we pay for living a thousand lives. (A cat, of course, has only nine.) Literature is alive to us because we live its images, but so is any play of the mind—so is chess: The lines of play that we foresee and try in our heads and dismiss are as much a part of the game as the moves that we make. John Keats said that the unheard melodies are sweeter, and all chess players sadly recall that the combinations that they planned and which never came to be played were the best.

I make this point to remind you, insistently, that imagination is the manipulation of images in one's head; and that the rational manipulation belongs to that, as well as the literary and artistic manipulation. When a child begins to play games with things that stand for other things, with chairs or chessmen, he enters the gateway to reason and imagination together. For the human reason discovers new relations between things not by deduction, but by that unpredictable blend of speculation and insight that scientists call *induction,* which—like other forms of imagination—cannot be formalized. We see it at work when Walter Hunter inquires into a child's memory, as much as when Blake and Coleridge do. Only a restless and original mind would have asked Hunter's questions and could have conceived his experiments, in a science that was dominated by Pavlov's reflex arcs and was heading toward the behaviorism of John Watson.

16   Let me find a spectacular example for you from history. What is the most famous experiment that you had described to you as a child? I will hazard that it is the experiment that Galileo is said to have made in Sidney's age, in Pisa about 1590, by dropping two unequal balls from the Leaning Tower. There, we say, is a man in the modern mold, a man after our own hearts: He insisted on questioning the authority

of Aristotle and St. Thomas Aquinas, and seeing with his own eyes whether (as they did) the heavy ball would reach the ground before the light one. Seeing is believing.

Yet seeing is also imagining. Galileo did challenge the authority of Aristotle, and he did look at his mechanics. But the eye that Galileo used was the mind's eye. He did not drop balls from the Leaning Tower of Pisa—and if he had, he would have got a very doubtful answer. Instead, Galileo made an imaginary experiment in his head, which I will describe as he did years later in the book he wrote after the Holy Office silenced him: *Discorsi . . . intorno a due nuove scienze,* which was smuggled out to be printed in the Netherlands in 1638.

Suppose, said Galileo, that you drop two unequal balls from the tower at the same time. And suppose that Aristotle is right—suppose that the heavy ball falls faster, so that it steadily gains on the light ball, and hits the ground first. Very well. Now imagine the same experiment done again, with only one difference: This time the two unequal balls are joined by a string between them. The heavy ball will again move ahead, but now the light ball holds it back and acts as a drag or brake. So the light ball will be speeded up and the heavy ball will be slowed down; they must reach the ground together because they are tied together, but they cannot reach the ground as quickly as the heavy ball alone. Yet the string between them has turned the two balls into a single mass which is heavier than either ball—and surely (according to Aristotle) this mass should therefore move faster than either ball? Galileo's imaginary experiment has uncovered a contradiction; he says trenchantly, "You see how, from your assumption that a heavier body falls more rapidly than a lighter one, I infer that a (still) heavier body falls more slowly." There is only one way out of the contradiction: The heavy ball and the light ball must fall at the same rate, so that they go on falling at the same rate when they are tied together.

This argument is not conclusive, for nature might be more subtle (when the two balls are joined) than Galileo has allowed. And yet it is something more important: It is suggestive, it is stimulating, it opens a new view—in a word, it is imaginative. It cannot be settled without an actual experiment, because nothing that we imagine can become knowledge until we have translated it into, and backed it by, real experience. The test of imagination is experience. But then, that is as true of literature and the arts as it is of science. In science, the imaginary experiment is tested by confronting it with physical experience; and in literature, the imaginative conception is tested by confronting it with human experience. The superficial speculation in science is dismissed because it is found to falsify nature; and the shallow work of art is discarded because it is found to be untrue to our own nature. So when Ella Wheeler Wilcox died in 1919, more people were reading her verses than Shakespeare's; yet in a few years her work was dead. It had been buried by its poverty of emotion and its trivialness of thought: which is to say that it had been proved to be as false to the nature of man as, say, Jean Baptiste Lamarck and Trofim Lysenko were false to the nature of inheritance. The strength of the imagination, its enriching power and excitement, lies in its interplay with reality—physical and emotional.

20   I doubt if there is much to choose here between science and the arts: The imagination is not much more free, and not much less free, in one than in the other. All great scientists have used their imagination freely, and let it ride them to outrageous

conclusions without crying "Halt!" Albert Einstein fiddled with imaginary experiments from boyhood, and was wonderfully ignorant of the facts that they were supposed to bear on. When he wrote the first of his beautiful papers on the random
movement of atoms, he did not know that the Brownian motion which it predicted
could be seen in any laboratory. He was sixteen when he invented the paradox that he
resolved ten years later, in 1905, in the theory of relativity, and it bulked much larger
in his mind than the experiment of Albert Michelson and Edward Morley which had
upset every other physicist since 1881. All his life Einstein loved to make up teasing
puzzles like Galileo's, about falling lifts and the detection of gravity; and they carry
the nub of the problems of general relativity on which he was working.

Indeed, it could not be otherwise. The power that man has over nature and himself, and that a dog lacks, lies in his command of imaginary experience. He alone has
the symbols which fix the past and play with the future, possible and impossible. In
the Renaissance, the symbolism of memory was thought to be mystical, and devices
that were invented as mnemonics (by Giordano Bruno, for example, and by Robert
Fludd) were interpreted as magic signs. The symbol is the tool which gives man his
power, and it is the same tool whether the symbols are images or words, mathematical signs or mesons. And the symbols have a reach and a roundness that goes beyond
their literal and practical meaning. They are the rich concepts under which the mind
gathers many particulars into one name, and many instances into one general induction. When a man says *left* and *right,* he is outdistancing the dog not only in looking
for a light; he is setting in train all the shifts of meaning, the overtones and the am-
biguities, between *gauche* and *adroit* and *dexterous,* between *sinister* and the sense of
right. When a man counts *one, two, three,* he is not only doing mathematics; he is on
the path to the mysticism of numbers in Pythagoras and Vitruvius and Kepler, to the
Trinity and the signs of the Zodiac.

I have described imagination as the ability to make images and to move them
about inside one's head in new arrangements. This is the faculty that is specifically
human, and it is the common root from which science and literature both spring and
grow and flourish together. For they do flourish (and languish) together; the great
ages of science are the great ages of all the arts, because in them powerful minds have
taken fire from one another breathless and higgledy-piggledy, without asking too
nicely whether they ought to tie their imagination to falling balls or a haunted island.
Galileo and Shakespeare, who were born in the same year, grew into greatness in the
same age; when Galileo was looking through his telescope at the moon, Shakespeare
was writing *The Tempest* and all Europe was in ferment, from Johannes Kepler to Peter Paul Rubens, and from the first table of logarithms by John Napier to the Autho-
rized Version of the Bible.

Let me end with a last and spirited example of the common inspiration of literature and science, because it is as much alive today as it was three hundred years ago.
What I have in mind is man's ageless fantasy, to fly to the moon. I do not display this
to you as a high scientific enterprise; on the contrary, I think we have more important
discoveries to make here on earth than wait for us, beckoning, at the horned surface
of the moon. Yet I cannot belittle the fascination which that ice-blue journey has had
for the imagination of men, long before it drew us to our television screens to watch

the tumbling astronauts. Plutarch and Lucian, Ariosto and Ben Jonson wrote about it, before the days of Jules Verne and H. G. Wells and science fiction. The seventeenth century was heady with new dreams and fables about voyages to the moon. Kepler wrote one full of deep scientific ideas, which (alas) simply got his mother accused of witchcraft. In England, Francis Godwin wrote a wild and splendid work, *The Man in the Moone,* and the astronomer John Wilkins wrote a wild and learned one, *The Discovery of a New World.* They did not draw a line between science and fancy; for example, they all tried to guess just where in the journey the earth's gravity would stop. Only Kepler understood that gravity has no boundary, and put a law to it—which happened to be the wrong law.

24   All this was a few years before Isaac Newton was born, and it was all in his head that day in 1666 when he sat in his mother's garden, a young man of twenty-three, and thought about the reach of gravity. This was how he came to conceive his brilliant image, that the moon is like a ball which has been thrown so hard that it falls exactly as fast as the horizon, all the way round the earth. The image will do for any satellite, and Newton modestly calculated how long therefore an astronaut would take to fall round the earth once. He made it ninety minutes, and we have all seen now that he was right; but Newton had no way to check that. Instead he went on to calculate how long in that case the distant moon would take to round the earth, if indeed it behaves like a thrown ball that falls in the earth's gravity, and if gravity obeyed a law of inverse squares. He found that the answer would be twenty-eight days.

In that telling figure, the imagination that day chimed with nature, and made a harmony. We shall hear an echo of that harmony on the day when we land on the moon, because it will be not a technical but an imaginative triumph, that reaches back to the beginning of modern science and literature both. All great acts of imagination are like this, in the arts and in science, and convince us because they fill out reality with a deeper sense of rightness. We start with the simplest vocabulary of images, with *left* and *right* and *one, two, three,* and before we know how it happened the words and the numbers have conspired to make a match with nature: We catch in them the pattern of mind and matter as one.

PERSONAL RESPONSE

Do you consider yourself imaginative? Write for a few minutes on how you use your own imagination.

QUESTIONS FOR CLASS OR SMALL-GROUP DISCUSSION

1. What is Bronowski's thesis or central idea? How do his examples function to illustrate or support that thesis? For instance, what is the point of telling his audience about Walter Hunter's experiments beginning in paragraph 2? Where else do you find examples used effectively?

2. What strategies does Bronowski use to define the words "to imagine," "image," and "imagination"?

3. Bronowski's essay was written before the first moon landing (see paragraphs 23 to 25). If Bronowski were writing today, what example do you think he would use in his closing paragraphs to demonstrate that scientific achievement is the result of both technology and imagination? What examples would you use? Why?

4. Discuss the ways in which scientists you know about are (or were) imaginative, making sure you explain why you think so.

5. Working with members of a small group, interview a scientist about the importance of the imagination in his or her work. Before the interview, work in your group to draw up a list of appropriate questions. Select one member to set up the appointment, one to ask the questions, one to record the answers, and one to report to the rest of the class the results of your interview.

THE CHEMIST

ROALD HOFFMANN

Roald Hoffmann is the Frank H. T. Rhodes Professor of Humane Letters and Professor of Chemistry at Cornell University, and the only person ever to have received the American Chemical Society's awards in three different specific subfields of chemistry. In 1981, he shared the Nobel Prize in Chemistry with Kenichi Fukui. He was responsible for a twenty-six part PBS television series designed to explain chemistry to high-school and junior-college students and has worked actively to popularize chemistry. He is author, with Vivian Torrence as artistic collaborator, of Chemistry Imagined: Reflections on Science *(1993), from which this essay is taken.*

In describing what they do, scientists have by and large bought the metaphor of discovery and artists that of creation. The cliché "uncovering the secrets of nature" has set, like good cement, in our minds. But I think that the metaphor of discovery is effective in describing only part of the activity of scientists, and a smaller piece still of the work of chemists. The historical, psychological, philosophical, and sociological reasons for the ready acceptance of the metaphor deserve a closer look.

History and Psychology

The rise of modern science in Europe coincided with the age of geographical exploration. Men set foot on distant shores, explored *terra incognita*. Even in our century, a man I was named after first sailed the Northwest passage and reached the South Pole. Voyages of discovery, maps filled in—those are powerful images indeed. So is penetration into a royal tomb full of glistening gold vessels. It's no surprise that these metaphors were and are accepted by (predominantly male) scientists as appropriate descriptors of their generally laboratory-bound activity. Is there some vicarious sharing of imagined adventures at work here?

Philosophy

The French rationalist tradition, and the systematization of astronomy and physics before the other sciences, have left science with a reductionist philosophy at its core. There is supposed to exist a logical hierarchy of the sciences, and understanding is to be defined solely in vertical terms as reduction to the more basic science. The more mathematical, the better. So biological phenomena are to be explained by chemistry, chemistry by physics, and so on. The logic of a reductionist philosophy fits the discovery metaphor—one digs deeper and discovers the truth.

4   But reductionism is only one face of understanding. We have been made not only to disassemble, disconnect, and analyze but also to build. There is no more stringent test of passive understanding than active creation. Perhaps *test* is not the word here, for building or creation differs inherently from reductionist analysis. I want to claim a greater role in science for the forward, constructive mode.

Sociology

Those philosophers of science who started out as practicing scientists have generally, I believe, come from physics and mathematics. The education of professional philosophers is likely to favor the same fields; quite understandably, there is a special role for logic in philosophy. No wonder that the prevailing ideology of reasoning in the underlying scientific areas of expertise of philosophers of science has been extended by them, unrealistically I believe, to all science.

What is strange is that chemists should accept the metaphor of discovery. Chemistry is the science of molecules (up to a hundred years ago one would have said *substances* or *compounds*) and their transformations. Some of the molecules are indeed *there*, just waiting to be "known" by us, their static properties—what atoms are in them, how the atoms are connected, the shapes of molecules, their splendid colors—and in their dynamic characteristics—the molecules' internal motions, their reactivity. The molecules are those of the earth—for instance, simple water and complex malachite. Or of life—relatively simple cholesterol and more complicated hemoglobin. The discovery paradigm certainly applies to the study of these molecules.

But so many more molecules of chemistry are made by us, in the laboratory. We're awfully prolific. A registry of known, well-characterized compounds now numbers nearly ten million. These were not on earth before. It is true that their constitution follows underlying rules, and if Chemist A had not made such-and-such a molecule on a certain day, then it is likely to have been synthesized a few days or decades later by Chemist B. But it is a human being, a chemist, who chooses the molecule to be made and a distinct way to make it. This work is not so different from that of the artist who, constrained by the physics of pigment and canvas, shaped by his or her training, nevertheless creates the new.

8   Even when one is clearly operating in the discovery mode in chemistry, elucidating the structure or dynamics of a known, naturally occurring molecule, one usually has to intervene with created molecules. I recently heard a beautiful lecture by Alan Battersby, an outstanding British organic chemist, on the biosynthesis of uroporphyrinogen-III. (Even in the trade, the name of this molecule is abbreviated as uro'gen-III.) It's not a glamorous molecule, but it should be: for from this precursor

plants make chlorophyll, the basis of all photosynthetic activity. All cells use another uro'gen-III derivative in cytochromes for electron transport. And the crucial iron-containing, oxygen-carrier piece of hemoglobin derives from this small disk-shaped molecule.

Uro'gen-III, pictured [here], is made from four rings, called *pyrroles*, themselves tied into a larger ring. Note the markers A and P in each ring. They're in the same order as one goes around the ring (from about 10 o'clock), except for the last set, which are "reverse." So the markers read A, P, A, P, A, P, P, A.

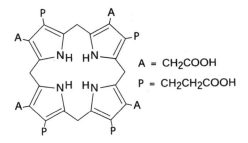

A = CH₂COOH

P = CH₂CH₂COOH

How this natural molecule is assembled, within us, is clearly a discovery question. In fact, the four pyrrole rings are connected up, with the aid of an enzyme, into a chain, then cyclized. But the last ring is first put in "incorrectly," that is, with the same order of the A, P labels as in the other rings: A, P, A, P, A, P, A, P. Then, in a fantastic separate reaction sequence, just that last ring, with its attached labels, is flipped into position.

This incredible but true story was deduced by Battersby and his coworkers using a sequence of synthetic molecules, not natural ones, which were made slightly different from the natural ones. Each was designed to test some critical part of the natural process in the living system. Each was then treated under the physiological conditions to allow the sequence of the natural events to be traced out. Using molecules we've made, we've learned how nature builds a molecule that makes life possible.

12   The synthesis of molecules puts chemistry very close to the arts. We create the objects that we or others then study or appreciate. That's exactly what writers, composers, visual artists, all working within their areas, working perhaps closer to the soul, do. I believe that, in fact, this creative capacity is exceptionally strong in chemistry. Mathematicians also study the objects of their own creation, but those objects, not to take anything away from their uniqueness, are mental concepts rather than real structures. Some branches of engineering are actually close to chemistry in this matter of synthesis. Perhaps this is a factor in the kinship the chemist–narrator feels for the builder Faussone, who is the main character in Primo Levi's novel *The Monkey's Wrench*.

In the building of theories and hypotheses, even more than in synthesis, the act is a creative one. One has to imagine, to conjure up a model that fits often irregular observations. There are rules; the model should be consistent with previously received reliable knowledge. There are hints of what to do; one sees what was done in related problems. But what one seeks is an explanation that was not there before, a connection between two worlds. Often, actually, it's a metaphor that serves as the clue: "Two interacting systems, hmm . . . , let's model them with a resonating pair of harmonic oscillators, or . . . a barrier penetration problem." The world out there is moderately chaotic, frighteningly so, in the parts we do not understand. We want to see a pattern in it. We're clever, we "connoisseurs of chaos," so we find/create one. Had more philosophers of science been trained in chemistry, I'm sure we would have a very different paradigm of science before us.

Is art all creation? I don't think so. In substantial measure it is discovery, of the deep truths of what is also around us, often overlapping, but more often reaching outside the set of problems that science has set for itself to try to understand. Art aspires to discover, explore, unravel—whatever metaphor you please—the non-unique, chanced, irreducible world within us.

PERSONAL RESPONSE

Despite the widespread influence of chemistry in almost every aspect of our lives, most people know very little about it. Discuss what difference it makes that few people have any serious understanding of chemistry. Do you think it ought to be a required subject in high school? Why or why not?

QUESTIONS FOR CLASS OR SMALL-GROUP DISCUSSION

1. What do you think Hoffman means when he writes, "There is no more stringent test of passive understanding than active creation" (paragraph 4)? Can you think of examples from your own experience that illustrate the statement?

2. How does Hoffman show the connections between what chemists do and what artists do? Do you think the metaphors of discovery and of creation are appropriate for both, as Hoffmann suggests? Why or why not?

3. Hoffmann says of uro'gen-III, "It's not a glamorous molecule, but it should be" (paragraph 8). How does he attempt to prove that point? Are you convinced?

4. List all the things you can think of that are in some way touched by chemistry. Volunteer to read your list aloud and see how long a list of items you and your classmates can come up with.

THE YEAR OF THE GENOME

MATT RIDLEY

Matt Ridley holds a Ph.D. in zoology and is a former science editor, Washington correspondent, and U.S. editor for the Economist. *He is author of* The Red Queen: Sex and the Evolution of Human Nature *(1994),* The Origins of Virtue: Human Instincts and the Evolution of Cooperation *(1997), and* Genome: The Autobiography of a Species in 23 Chapters *(2000). This article was published in the January 2001 issue of* Discover.

Imagine that one day there lands upon earth an alien spacecraft stuffed with a million crumpled pieces of paper, each covered in text written in an unknown script. The best brains in the world are put to the task of deciphering the code, which takes 10 years. But it takes another 40 years to smooth out all of the pages, translate them in English, sort them, and publish them as a vast book. Then, at long last, the task is done, and we sit down to read the book from beginning to end. It contains thousands of stories about the past, the present, and the future of humankind, from the origin of life to the recipe for curing cancer.

What an extraordinary and unlikely tale. And yet that is essentially what happened this year. After 50 years of preparation, we have suddenly been placed in the position of being able to read the entire genetic story of human beings—the genome.

On June 26 Francis Collins, head of the Human Genome Project, and Craig Venter, head of Celera Genomics, jointly announced that they had completed the reading of a "rough draft" of the human genome—the complete set of human DNA. The announcement came at least two years earlier than expected and marked a dead heat in a fiercely contested scientific marathon.

4   The researchers on the Human Genome Project had been working toward a complete human sequence since the late 1980s. In early 1998, with less than 10 percent of the job done, scientists were predicting that it would take seven more years. Then Venter announced that he would undertake to do the job by 2001, using private funds.

Twice before he had delivered on equally dramatic promises. In 1991 he invented a quick way to find human genes, using expressed sequence tags, after the senior scientists at the Human Genome Project had said it wouldn't work. In 1995, he invented a new "shotgun" technique for sequencing DNA and read the full genome of a bacterium while the establishment was still dismissing the technique as unworkable.

So Venter's threat was serious. The Human Genome Project reorganized its efforts, and the race was on. In the end, both projects announced together that they had finished a rough draft last June. A rough draft is a sequence with 91 percent of the letters in the right place, each letter having been read and reread between five and seven times. Plenty of gaps remain, but they amount to less than 10 percent of the text.

This announcement was the beginning of a whole new way of understanding human biology. Everything we have laboriously discovered hitherto about how our bodies work will be dwarfed by the knowledge tumbling from the genome.

8   It was also the end to a great detective story. In 1860, Gregor Mendel made the bizarre discovery that inheritance comes in tiny particles called genes that do not decay with age, or blend with one another. In 1953, James Watson and Francis Crick made the even more unexpected discovery that those particles are actually digital

messages written along strands of DNA in code, using a four-letter chemical alpha-bet. In 1961, Marshall Nirenberg and Johann Matthaei cracked the first "word" in that code, revealing exactly how DNA instructs the cell to build proteins. It was then inevitable—if mind-boggling—that one day we would read all the genetic messages that a human body inherits. Now we have.

But, of course, the genome announcement is just a beginning. For the document that has been produced—a 3.3-billion-letter book, as long as 900 Bibles—is almost entirely mysterious. We do not know even the basic facts about it, such as how many genes it contains—although the guesses are converging on a figure of 38,000—let alone what each gene is and how genes interact with one another. We do not know why the genes are hidden in great stretches of apparently meaningless text, or so-called junk DNA. We stand on the brink of a continent of new knowledge.

Most people do not see the genome in such romantic terms. They want to know how it will help cure cancer; they speculate about customized medicine, with drugs designed for the individual, not the population. They worry that it will lead to de-signer babies for the rich or to a lessening of respect for the disabled; they fear the patenting of genes by private corporations; they predict that medical insurance may cease to be offered by insurance companies to those whose risks are known and high.

All these are real issues. The medical possibilities and ethical fears that dominate the debate are by no means trivial. But there is a larger philosophical truth missed. The genome represents an unprecedented draft of self-knowledge for humankind with implications that stretch far beyond medicine. It promises to tell us new things about our past as a species, and it promises new insights into philosophical conun-drums, not least of which is the puzzle of free will.

12   We have been misled into thinking that genetics is all about disorders. Geneti-cists have so far concentrated on genes that are linked to disease: first the simple but rare inherited diseases like cystic fibrosis (the gene for which is on chromosome 7) or Huntington's (chromosome 4), then the environmental diseases for which different people inherit different susceptibilities, such as Alzheimer's (chromosome 19) or breast cancer (chromosomes 13 and 17). More recently, they have begun to seek genes that affect our behavior, prompting us to be dyslexic (chromosome 6), homosexual (perhaps on the X chromosome), adventurous (chromosome 11), or even highly reli-gious (no map location yet).

A well-studied example of a human gene is the ACE gene on chromosome 17, which seems to predict physical performance. According to a group of scientists at University College, London, possessing one version of this gene rather than another dramatically improves the ability to increase muscle strength with training and in-creases the mechanical efficiency of trained muscle. Mountain climbers, rowers, and other athletes tend to have this high-performance version of the gene. Likewise, one version of the APOE gene on chromosome 19 predicts the likelihood of a boxer suf-fering from premature Alzheimer's disease. A person with the "wrong" versions of both these genes would be well advised not to become an athlete in a contact sport.

But that word "wrong" is all wrong, is it not? There is still too much tendency to think in terms of genetic divergence from the presumed norm. Back in the Stone Age, the low-performance version of the ACE gene might have resisted starvation better, and the risky version of the APOE gene might have had some other advantage. Besides, to define a gene as an "Alzheimer's gene" or a "dyslexia gene" is a bit like defining the heart as a "heart-attack organ." This is misleading. Neither blue nor brown eyes (a gene somewhere on chromosome 15) are normal. With the genome in hand, we can see genes in better context. We can study how and why all human beings inherit a musical sense, rather than why some people are more musical than others.

Genes are windows on the past. Some reflect the history of infectious disease in different tribes. The A and B blood groups (chromosome 9) protect against cholera; the cystic fibrosis and Tay-Sachs (15) mutations may protect against tuberculosis; the sickle-cell (11) and thalassemia (16) mutations protect against malaria. Hence the prevalence of these particular mutations in certain peoples.

16   Other genes tell a story of responses to culture. The fact that adult Europeans are twice as likely as Asians to tolerate lactose in milk (no location yet) reflects a much longer history of dairy farming in the West; the ability to dehydrogenate alcohol (chromosome 4) is more common in people with a history of drinking fermented fluids; the prevalence of the blond-hair gene in young northern Europeans (perhaps on chromosome 15?) may reflect a sexual preference for youthful mates.

Still others tell of events long before recorded history. The unusual genes of the Basque people mirror the unique nature of their language and suggest that they are descendants of pre-agricultural Europeans. The astonishing similarity between embryonic-development genes called Hox genes in fruit flies and people (chromosomes 2, 7, 9, 12, and 17) tells us that the common ancestor of people and insects was a segmented animal; yet this animal lived more than 600 million years ago and left no fossils. The genome is going to be a treasure trove of such stories.

Science has a habit of addressing problems raised by philosophy. It may not be too much to claim that the mystery of free will has been recast by recent discoveries in genetics, which have exposed the myth that genes are puppet masters and we are their puppets. Take, as an example, the various learning mutations that have been discovered in fruit flies and subsequently in mice and people (chromosomes 2 and 16). These are found in genes that are central to memory and learning, many of them part of the CREB (cyclic-AMP response elements binding protein) system in the brain. The mutations reveal that every time a person learns something, he has to switch on some of these genes in order to lay down new connections between brain cells.

That sounds like dull molecular plumbing. But actually it is revolutionary philosophy. In attempting to answer the question of whether we possess free will, the Scottish philosopher David Hume impaled himself on the following dilemma: Either our actions are determined, in which case we are not responsible for them, or they are the result of random events, in which case we are also not responsible for them. But the CREB genes show how to escape this fix. If genes are at the mercy of behavior, but behavior is also at the mercy of genes, then our actions can be determined by forces that originate within us as well as by outside influences. The will is therefore a mixture of instincts and outside influences. This makes it deterministic and responsible, but not predictable.

20   Curiously, the free will story brings us to cancer, which is where the whole genome project started. Cancer researchers first suggested sequencing the human

genome in the mid-1980s. They were just beginning to realize that cancer was a wholly genetic process. Genetic, but not hereditary. Most cancer is not inherited—though there are well-known mutations that increase susceptibility to cancer, such as BRCA1 and BRCA2, both of which are associated with breast cancer.

Yet cancer is a disease of the genes. Like free will, it is a process mediated by the genes but not caused by them. Like the CREB genes of memory, changes in cancer genes are the consequence, not the cause, of environmental effects. Cigarette smoke, for example, causes cancer by mutating genes inside human cells called oncogenes, which encourage cells to multiply, and tumor-suppressor genes, which prevent them from multiplying. To turn malignant, a tumor must evolve with at least one oncogene jammed in the "on" position and at least one tumor-suppressor gene jammed in the "off" position.

Little wonder that President Clinton, announcing the genome last June, mused that one day people may know cancer only as a star sign, not a disease. That was going much too far, because cancer is also a disease of aging: Its incidence increases steadily with age. Rendering it easily curable will only increase its incidence. Nonetheless, by identifying all oncogenes and tumor-suppressor genes and understanding how they work, the Human Genome Project will transform cancer therapy. Already, drugs based on the most famous of the tumor-suppressors, p53 (chromosome 17), are in early clinical trials.

The human genome opens a world of medical opportunity, of commercial promise, of ethical danger, and of social challenge. It is also a cornucopia of scientific possibilities that ranks alongside the revolutions wrought by Euclid, Copernicus, Newton, Darwin, and Einstein. It is a fitting bang with which to start a new millennium.

PERSONAL RESPONSE

How do you feel about genetics research? Do you think the potential good of such research outweighs the potential for devastating misuse?

QUESTIONS FOR CLASS OR SMALL-GROUP DISCUSSION

1. How effective is the opening analogy? Does it make clear for you what the " 'rough draft' of the human genome" is (paragraph 3)?

2. Discuss what Ridley has to say about the larger implications of the genome, beyond medical possibilities. To what extent do you agree with him that those things are larger in implication than either "the medical possibilities or ethical issues fears" (paragraph 11)?

3. What do you understand Ridley to mean by the following statement: "We have been misled into thinking that genetics is all about disorders" (paragraph 12)?

4. How effective is Ridley's final paragraph? What does it suggest about the potential and challenges opened by the completion of the human genome?

THE INFLUENCE OF "JUNK SCIENCE" AND THE ROLE OF SCIENCE EDUCATION

LEE ANN FISHER BARON

Lee Ann Fisher Baron is Professor of Natural Science at Hillsdale College, where she has taught since 1989. Recipient of many awards for her teaching and work in science education, Baron has developed programs to interest middle-school girls in scientific careers and written laboratory study guides for high-school summer science camps, among other things. This essay is based on a presentation Baron did for a seminar on "junk science" held at Hillsdale College, and it was published in Imprimis *in February 2001.*

Science is exciting partly because single discoveries can change the course of history. Think of the effects on human health and longevity of the discovery of antibiotics, the multi-faceted impact on our lives of the discovery of polymers, or the far-reaching importance of the Human Genome Project. Unfortunately, however, most of the "revolutionary discoveries" made throughout history have turned out to be wrong.

Error is a regular part of science. That is why reports of new findings or discoveries, no matter where or how widely they are reported, should be regarded with healthy skepticism. The proper scientific approach to such claims involves a set of procedures called the scientific method. This method requires the design of tests or experiments that can be repeated with the same results by anyone. These tests must also contain controls to ensure that the results are statistically significant.

Let me illustrate the importance of controls by describing briefly an experiment in which my daughter participated as a subject some years ago at the University of Michigan Medical School. Its purpose was to determine whether the vaccine for tuberculosis could lengthen the interval during which newly-diagnosed type 1 diabetics do not experience severe high or low blood sugar. The subjects were divided into a group of those who received the vaccine and a control group of those who received a placebo. The subjects did not know who got the vaccine and, just as importantly, neither did the researchers—a type of control referred to as a "double-blind." By using two groups, the researchers were able to measure the "placebo effect"—a phenomenon in which patients improve because they falsely believe that they are receiving medicine. And by keeping themselves ignorant of the breakdown of the groups, the researchers were prevented from reading their hypotheses into the results.

"Junk Science"

4   Most erroneous conclusions by scientists are discovered during the process of publishing their research. Other scientists review submitted articles, often repeating any relevant tests or experiments and always evaluating the conclusions that have been drawn from them. So-called "junk science" bypasses this system of peer review. Presented directly to the public by people variously described as "experts" or "activists,"

often with little or no supporting evidence, this "junk science" undermines the ability of elected representatives, jurists, and others—including everyday consumers—to make rational decisions.

An example of "junk science" I like to use with my students is the myth of "fat-free foods" invented by the food industry with the help of federal regulators. By regulatory definition, these foods may contain monoglycerides and diglycerides, but not triglycerides. From the point of view of solid science this definition makes no practical sense, given that the body metabolizes mono-, di- and triglycerides in essentially the same way. Meanwhile unwary consumers take the "fat-free" label as a license to eat these foods to excess, and Americans are more obese now than ever before.

A more amusing example is "Vitamin O," a wonder supplement advertised to "maximize your nutrients, purify your blood stream, and eliminate toxins and poisons—in other words, [to supply] all the processes necessary to prevent disease and promote health." It was described on its label as "stabilized oxygen molecules in a solution of distilled water and sodium chloride." In other words, the 60,000 consumers purchasing "Vitamin O"—to the tune of $20 a month—were taking salt water! Although this product was legally exempted from certain FDA requirements by virtue of its status as a "natural" diet supplement, the FTC was able to file a complaint against it in 1999, based on false claims by its promoters that it was being used by NASA astronauts. Otherwise "Vitamin O" would still be one of the world's best-selling placebos.

The potential lasting power of "junk science" is demonstrated by the story of German physician Samuel Hahnemann, who took quinine back in 1776 to investigate its use against malaria. After taking the quinine he experienced chills and fever, which are the symptoms of malaria. For this he concluded, wrongly, that "likes cure likes," i.e., that diseases should be treated with medicines that produce similar symptoms to the diseases. In the course of testing this theory with other herbal remedies, Hahnemann discovered that many "natural" herbs are toxic and made his patients worse. To reduce the toxic effects, he diluted the remedies until they seemed to be working. On that basis he formulated a "law of infinitesimals" stating that higher dilutions of herbal cures increase their medicinal benefits. To be fair, Hahnemann conducted these experiments more than 70 years before scientists understood that a dilution weaker than one part in 6.02×10^{23} may not contain even a single molecule of the dissolved substance. Thus he did not realize that upon administering to his patients 30x preparations—dilutions of one part herb to 10^{30} parts water—the placebo effect was all that was really left to measure.

8   Incredibly, homeopathic medicine today still relies on Hahnemann's theories. Not only does it often come in 30× preparations, it comes in 200c dilutions—solutions of one part herb to 100 parts of water 200 times, resulting in one molecule of the herb per 10^{400} molecules of water! Modern homeopathists obviously can't deny that such preparations are beyond the dilution limit, but they insist that the dilutions still work because their water or alcohol/water mixtures somehow "remember" the herbs. Despite this preposterous claim, the market for these remedies is enormous.

Just as many homeopathic preparations are diluted to the point that they are nothing but water, many "natural" herbs on the market contain drugs and chemicals which interact with the human body like prescription drugs. For example, Echinacea stimulates the immune system, which could prove harmful to people with type 1 diabetes, rheumatoid arthritis, or other autoimmune diseases. It is therefore unwise—to put it gently—to take herbal remedies or supplements of any kind without consulting a doctor and/or the *Physician's Desk Reference for Herbal Medicines*. But many Americans do so, equating "natural" with "harmless" and "good."

Cause and Solution

I have addressed here the corrupting influence of "junk science" in the area of consumer foods, vitamins and diet supplements. The same dynamic increasingly affects other aspects of our individual and collective lives as well. But I believe the root cause is the same: Americans are losing the common-sense skepticism toward scientific claims that animates the scientific method itself. And one of the reasons for this is a slow but steady degradation of our educational system. In short, as Charles J. Sykes explains in *Dumbing Down Our Kids*, theories such as "outcome-based education," "cooperative learning," and "maximization of self-esteem" are fast replacing reading, writing, and arithmetic as the goals of education.

Anecdotal evidence of this trend is vast and compelling. For instance, when average SAT math scores fell from 500 to 424, the College Board responded by allowing the use of calculators. When that didn't work, they "recentered" the test by adding approximately 20 points to the math scores (while also adding 80 points on the verbal side, for a total of 100), regardless of achievement. At the state level, many high school competency exams are written at an eighth-grade level. And coloring for credit in elementary-level math classes is now fairly common. Is it any wonder that so many of the kids we now graduate from high school enter the workforce unable to add in their heads or make correct change, or arrive at college incapable of solving the simplest equations?

12   The situation is no better in the sciences. Students at a Seattle middle school spend two weeks studying the eating habits of birds by trying to pick up Cheerios with tongue depressors, toothpicks, spoons, and clothespins between their teeth. "Educationalists" call this creative and engaging. But it doesn't create useful or important knowledge. And surely it is not true that such activity is more engaging than learning about Newton's Laws or DNA.

A popular high school chemistry book moves from "Supplying Our Water Needs," which includes a discussion of acid raid, to "Chemistry and the Atmosphere," which addresses the ozone layer. This approach would not be all bad if the chemistry behind these issues was rigorously taught and if important topics unrelated to social controversies were also included. Unfortunately they are not. When I called the American Chemical Society—which, sadly, produced this textbook—one of those responsible justified its approach by pointing out that most high school graduates don't pursue science in college. Furthermore, he said, students introduced to chemistry in this way enjoy it more and find it easier to handle, resulting in higher self-esteem. I asked if it had occurred to him that perhaps students don't pursue college science because they don't obtain the requisite skills or knowledge in high school. Regardless, when the American Chemical Society endorses a high school science text that doesn't even list the scientific method in its index, we shouldn't be surprised that so many Americans gorge themselves on "fat-free foods," throw their money at "Vitamin O," or risk their health by taking "natural" herbs without investigating their effects.

The solution to the problem I have outlined is easy to see, and is by no means impossible to accomplish. Individually, we must be careful to take our bearings from the scientific method when confronted with scientific claims, employing healthy skepticism and asking questions before believing what we hear or read. Together, we must work diligently to revive real standards in primary and secondary science education.

PERSONAL RESPONSE

Baron begins with the statement, "Science is exciting" and then goes on to add that science is exciting in part because of discoveries that change humans' lives. Do you find science exciting? What discovery or breakthrough would you like to see scientists make that would change our lives significantly?

QUESTIONS FOR CLASS OR SMALL-GROUP DISCUSSION

1. How does Baron illustrate the difference between "junk science" and proper science? Are you satisfied with her explanation of "the scientific method" (paragraph 2)?

2. Comment on the examples of junk science that Baron gives. Why do you think people so readily accept what they hear and read about such things? Were you surprised by her examples of homeopathic medicine and herbal remedies and supplements? Many people are firm believers in their benefits. What is your viewpoint on them?

3. Baron blames Americans' lack of commonsense skepticism in part on the content of high-school science classes and textbooks. Discuss your own high-school science classes and the textbooks you used. Were your experiences similar to or different from the ones she describes?

THE NATURE OF EVIDENCE

BOYCE RENSBERGER

Boyce Rensberger wrote for the Washington Post *and the* New York Times *before becoming director of the Knight Science Journalism Fellowships program at the Massachusetts Institute of Technology. His books, which explain science to the lay reader, include* Instant Biology: From Single Cells to Human Beings, and Beyond *(1995) and* Life Itself: Exploring the Realm of the Living Cell *(1997). Rensberger*

*also was head writer of a PBS science series for children, 3-2-1-Con-
tact! This article appeared in the July 7, 2000, issue of Science.*

"You just want to sell newspapers," a scientist hissed at me at a meeting not long ago. "That's your bottom line." The event was one of many efforts around the United States to bridge the gap that supposedly exists between scientists and science journalists.

"Well, yes," I replied. We do like to sell newspapers or attract viewers, just as much as the average scientist likes to have a big turnout for his talk at the annual meeting. But that is not the main motivation for me and my science-writing colleagues as we sift among the many scientific developments of the moment and single out a select few for our scarce column inches or minutes of airtime.

We write about science because we love science and want to communicate our fascination with the natural world. And we write about science and technology because we believe that the more people know and understand, the better informed public opinion will be. Of course, we must also cover the harms or the risks that some technologies pose. We do this not because we question the overall value of science or technology but because the watchdog role is an integral part of journalism.

4   There are those in science who believe that journalists have become careless and irresponsible, that we devote our words and pictures to half-baked research, even antiscientific claims. Critics point to the popularity of parapsychology, UFOs, and other forms of pseudoscience and insist that if interest in them rises, it does so at the expense of interest in real science. Some see the rise of public opposition to genetic engineering—prominently covered in the new media—as another worrisome symptom. Often mixed into this criticism is the allegation that Americans are woefully uneducated about science, especially compared with people in other countries.

My experience as a science journalist has led me to some rather different views. I find that the situation is more hopeful, and that the weakness in the public's understanding of science lies in an area not often addressed in interactions between scientists and journalists—the nature of evidence.

But first, take the claim that Americans are more ignorant of science than are people in other countries. According to a National Science Foundation (NSF) report,* American adults understand basic scientific facts at least as well as those in most other developed countries. A set of nine science-based questions was asked of adults in 11 European countries, Canada, Japan, and the United States. Denmark scored at the top, followed a point or two behind by the Netherlands, the United States, and, ever so slightly lower, Great Britain.

The same NSF study found that 70% of American adults say they are "interested" in science but that only 48% consider themselves "informed" about scientific matters. When I speak to editors, encouraging them to improve their science coverage, I use these figures to suggest that the public is not being well served. People say

*Science and Engineering Indicators 1998 (National 5 Science Foundation, Washington, DC. 1998).

they are interested in science but realize they don't know much. Therefore, I surmise, they want to know more.

8   When NSF surveyors asked specific questions—such as what the term "molecule" means, or whether light or sound travels faster—they found a composite score of only 57% correct answers. The score was even worse when people were asked about the nature of scientific inquiry—for example, to define an experiment or a hypothesis. Only 27% of the sample gave passable answers. In sum, Americans are overwhelmingly interested in science but don't understand it and know even less about how it is done.

In these data, I believe, lies the reason for the popularity of pseudoscience. Without a grasp of scientific ways of thinking, the average person cannot tell the difference between science based on real data and something that resembles science—at least in their eyes—but is based on uncontrolled experiments, anecdotal evidence, and passionate assertions. They like it all.

The claim, for example, that brains can transmit information telepathically, strikes them as no less believable than the claim that whole stars can collapse into infinitesimal points. Many among the public have not yet learned that what makes science special is that evidence has to meet certain standards.

My own encounters with believers in pseudoscience—based on anecdotal evidence, to be sure—are consistent with the view that many adults are fascinated by claims that the world is filled with wonders and that some of them remain inexplicable. No problem there. But instead of dismissing such people as hopelessly beyond the pale, both scientists and journalists need to find ways of teaching them how to think more rigorously.

12   First, I suggest, journalists need to learn more about scientific methods and thinking. Most full-time science writers are already up on this, but nonspecialist journalists seldom are, and it is increasingly common that they cover stories with science content. It is important that we educate these nonspecialist journalists.

Second, when scientists talk to journalists, they ought to move beyond the highlights of their findings and wade into the methods, taking the initiative to ensure that the reporter understands why the results may be believed. Journalists, then, must make it a point to explain in their stories, somehow, that the new finding is founded on a plausible base of evidence.

PERSONAL RESPONSE

Rensberger writes: "Americans are overwhelmingly interested in science but don't understand it and know even less about how it is done" (paragraph 8). To what extent does this statement describe you?

QUESTIONS FOR CLASS OR SMALL-GROUP DISCUSSION

1. Rensberger says that "the weakness in the public's understanding of science lies in an area not often addressed between scientists and journalists—the nature of evidence" (paragraph 5). How does he define that term?

2. Do you find Rensberger's use of his own experiences and observations an effective rhetorical strategy? Is it appropriate for his subject?

3. How does Rensberger use exemplification to define "pseudoscience"? What other examples of pseudoscientific subjects or beliefs can you name?

4. Rensberger offers two ways that he thinks scientists and journalists can teach the general public "how to think more rigorously" (paragraph 11). Discuss his suggestions and the likelihood of his plan succeeding.

○ PERSPECTIVES ON NATURAL SCIENCES ○

Suggested Writing Topics

1. The writers in this chapter share a firm belief in the importance of science. Argue either in support of or against the position that one of them takes on the value of science by first summarizing his or her position and then explaining why you do or do not support that viewpoint.

2. Write an essay that draws a comparison between science and the arts.

3. In Jacob Bronowski's "The Reach of the Imagination," he asks what was the most famous scientific experiment that you had described to you as a child (paragraph 16). Write about your own experience by stating what the experiment was, how you heard about it, how it impressed you, and what it means to you now, looking back on that experience.

4. Drawing from your own experience or observations, write an essay that illustrates this statement from Roald Hoffman's "The Chemist": "There is no more stringent test of passive understanding than active creation" (paragraph 4).

5. Write an essay on the subject of "junk science" and/or "pseudoscience," drawing on both Lee Ann Fisher Baron's "The Influence of 'Junk Science' and the Role of Science Education" and Boyce Rensberger's "The Nature of Evidence."

6. Define the abstract term *imagination,* using examples from both science and the humanities to illustrate what you mean.

7. Support or argue against Roald Hoffmann's assertion that art is not all creation but "in substantial measure it is discovery" ("The Chemist," paragraph 14).

8. Explore the connections between two essays in this chapter by comparing and contrasting them. Consider what ideas their authors have in common, how they differ, and what their observations have taught you about the natural sciences.

9. Write a personal essay in which you explore your own interest in and involvement with science.

10. Write an essay explaining how just one scientific discipline has an effect on your everyday life.

Research Topics

1. Select one of the many scientific discoveries that have "change[d] the course of human history" (Lee Ann Fisher Baron, "The Influence of 'Junk Science' and the Role of Science Education," paragraph 1) and research its discovery and how it changed humans' lives.

2. Research the history of important discoveries that led to the genome project, especially those of people mentioned in paragraph 8 of Matt Ridley's "The Year of the Genome": Gregor Mendel, James Watson and Francis Crick, and/or Marshall Nirenberg and Johann Matthaei.

3. Read about research into how the brain works or the results of neurological damage, and write a paper that not only reports your findings but that also takes a position on some aspect of the subject. For example, Oliver Sacks's *The Man Who Mistook His Wife for a Hat* is a fascinating account of Sacks's work with people who have suffered damage to parts of their brains. To make this subject suitable for a research paper, you might begin by finding out what controversies surround treatment for neurological damage and then reading opposing opinions on the controversy. Once you have read enough opposing viewpoints to form your own opinion, take a side and explain why you have chosen that position.

4. Scientists know much more about how the brain works now than they did when Jacob Bronowski wrote "The Reach of the Imagination." Research the latest thinking about the way the brain works, for example in relation to Bronowski's conjecture about the importance of the frontal lobe in imaginative thinking. Explore differing theories, take a position, and explain why you believe as you do.

5. Jacob Bronowski, Roald Hoffmann, and Boyce Rensberger were all involved in television series intended to popularize science for laypeople. Research the life and efforts of one of these men, or do a comparative analysis of two or all three of them. In addition to reading about their television work, locate contemporary reviews of the programs. Then draw your own conclusions about their success or failure.

6. Read about the efforts of schools to encourage students to take math and science classes. Find out the rationale for such programs and what steps they have taken to increase interest in the subjects. Then draw your own conclusions about the relative importance of increasing enrollment in math and science courses and in improving test scores in those subjects.

RESPONDING TO VISUALS

An illustration of the human genome. Source: Carol & Mike Werner/Index Stock Imagery

1. What does this illustration suggest about the relationship between humans and the human genome?
2. What are the implications of the letters on the human figure?
3. How does the illustrator arrange images on the page for the best effect?
4. Why does the illustrator use this particular rendering of the human figure?

RESPONDING TO VISUALS

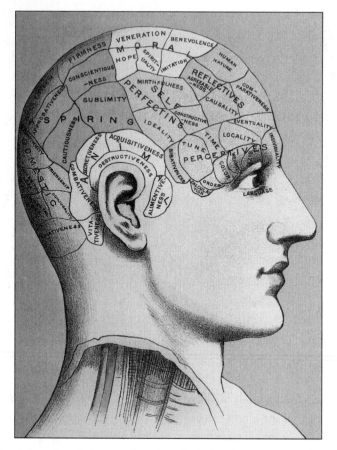

Diagram of the human head, showing the phrenological regions corresponding to various human capacities. Source: Bettmann/CORBIS

1. When it was first introduced in the late 18th century, phrenology (the study of the shape and protuberances of the head) was believed to be the latest advancement in neurology. However, by the end of the 19th century, phrenology had been discredited. How is the drawing a classic example of pseudoscience?

2. On the basis of the drawing, what specific things did scientists and laypeople apparently believe that the shape of the head revealed about a person?

3. Despite the fact that phrenology was discredited over a century ago, belief in it persists yet today. Why do you think that some people still believe that the bumps on a person's head reveal personality?

4. What connections might there be between phrenology and, say, palm reading, astrology, or even herbal remedies or crystal therapy?

CHAPTER

BIOETHICS

Research into the complex structure of the human body since James D. Watson and Francis Crick discovered in 1953 that deoxyribonucleic acid (DNA) molecules arrange themselves in a double helix has made enormous advances. The discovery of this pattern in DNA, a substance that transmits the genetic characteristics from one generation to the next, earned Watson and Crick a Nobel Prize in 1962. Their discovery led other scientists to work on such things as recombinant DNA and gene splicing in the 1970s and eventually to the Human Genome Project, whose goal was to map the entire sequence of human DNA. A genome is the complete set of instructions for making a human being. Each nucleus of the one hundred trillion cells that make up the human body contains this set of instructions, which are written in the language of DNA. This major undertaking by scientists around the world promises to provide medical doctors with the tools to predict the development of human diseases. When the project began in

1988, scientists thought that it would take fifteen years to complete, but the project progressed faster than first predicted and was finished well ahead of schedule.

Now that the human code has been mapped, scientists can begin to better understand how humans grow, what causes human diseases, and what new drugs would combat those diseases by either preventing or curing them. Scientists already are able to identify variations or defects in the genetic makeup of certain cells in human bodies that may result in diseases with genetic origins. Eventually, they will be able to develop tests of an individual's likelihood of developing one of thousands of inherited diseases such as sickle-cell anemia, cystic fibrosis, or muscular dystrophy, and even heart disease or cancer. Because more than 30,000 genes make up the "instruction manual" for the human body, it will take some time before all of them are codified and their functions known. The Human Genome Project raised a number of difficult ethical questions, however, as the essays in this chapter indicate. One of the most controversial steps forward in the potential of scientists to manipulate genes is the capacity to clone living creatures, though gene therapy has other potential uses.

The first essay, James Pethokoukis's "Our Biotech Bodies, Ourselves," gives an overview of the debate over how far science should be allowed to go to cure human disease and enhance human life. Although human cloning is obviously a red-flag issue, other developments, either a reality or a possibility, cause people to think seriously about placing limits on scientists who are working on genetic engineering, stem-cell therapy, and neuropharmacology, among other areas of research.

The next two essays, by James D. Watson and Ian Wilmut, respectively, were written for a special *Time* magazine issue on the future of medicine. Wilmut is the Scottish embryologist who cloned the first mammal, the famous sheep Dolly. Watson and Wilmut hold different opinions on just what should and what should not be done with research into human cloning. Then, Jeff Lyon's "Playing God: Has Science Gone Too Far?" looks at the ethical and moral issues of human cloning, gene therapy, and stem-cell research. His article reports the opinions of many people, including representatives of several major religions, in answer to this question: "Is it right for scientists to assume powers that many people believe should belong only to God?" As you read the essays in this chapter, ask yourself the questions that their authors raise: Just how far should science be allowed to go?

OUR BIOTECH BODIES, OURSELVES

JAMES PETHOKOUKIS

James Pethokoukis is a senior writer at U. S. News & World Report; *he also writes the* Next News *science and technology column for the* U. S. News *website. "Our Biotech Bodies, Ourselves" was first published in* U. S. News & World Report *on May 31, 2004.*

What if, by taking a drug, you could possess an IQ of 250? Or by tinkering with your genes, have the athletic prowess of a decathlete? Or by injecting yourself with stem cells, live to be 160? Would you do it? Would these enhancements make you less human? If everyone did this, would the world become a paradise full of self-actualized superpeople? Or a dystopian Stepford society devoid of essential human values such as compassion for the less blessed?

What seems like fodder for a science fiction potboiler has become a matter of deadly serious debate among scientists and ethicists. In a speech last year before a gathering of enhancement advocates, William Sims Bainbridge, a deputy director at the National Science Foundation who studies the societal impact of technology, warned that "scientists may be forced into rebellion in order to carry out research prohibited unnecessarily by powerful institutions."

A few months later, Leon Kass, chair of the President's Council on Bioethics, was expressing the advisory panel's profound "disquiet" with a biotech-enabled, post-human future that "cheapens rather than enriches America's most cherished ideals." The council's 325-page report, "Beyond Therapy: Biotechnology and the Pursuit of Happiness," takes a decidedly dim view of the impact of such issues as radical life extension, mood- and intelligence-enhancing drugs, and genetic therapies.

4   At the core of the conflict lies a fundamental question: How far should homo sapiens be allowed to go? Nascent technologies like genetic engineering, stem-cell therapy, and neuropharmacology promise not only to cure our diseases but to enhance our bodies, even to turn us all into the Six Million Dollar Man—better, stronger, and faster.

Clash. But not everyone thinks humans should be bioengineered. "Our increasing ability to alter our biology and open up the processes of life is now fueling a new cultural war," says Gregory Stock, director of the University of California–Los Angeles's Program on Medicine, Technology, and Society and author of the proenhancement book *Redesigning Humans.*

Yet isn't arguing about whether mankind should transform itself into a race of superhumans a little like arguing about whether the first Mars colony should have a bicameral or unicameral legislature? Kass doesn't think so. "These topics are not futuristic," he says. "Some of these issues are already here. Choosing the sex of your children is here. The use of stimulants on children to improve performance is here. Steroid use is here. Drugs that affect mood and temperament are here. . . . There is something profound going on here that will affect our identities and the society we live in."

Indeed, there are hints that genetic engineering might be able to alter mankind in some astounding ways. Researchers at the University of Pennsylvania have boosted levels of a protein in mice that makes them more muscular throughout life. Southern Illinois University scientists extended one mouse's life span to nearly twice the normal length.

8   But governments around the world are already putting brakes on this type of research, especially as it applies to humans. President Bush famously banned the federal funding of research on new embryonic stem-cell lines in 2001. A year later, the South Korean government raided BioFusion Tech, a company backed by the Raelian religious sect, after the group announced that a Korean woman would give birth to a clone—even though cloning isn't illegal there. And at least 17 countries have banned germ-line modification, which alters reproductive cells so that genetic tweaks will be passed down to future generations.

"How we respond to these threats to enhancement today will lay the groundwork for dealing with the ones that emerge in the future," says enhancement activist James Hughes, a lecturer in health policy at Trinity College in Hartford, Conn. Political scientist Francis Fukuyama agrees that policies need to be shaped before these technologies fully ripen—although Fukuyama, member of the bioethics council and author of *Our Posthuman Future,* counts himself a bioconservative. "If you don't shake people up now, then you will get these gradual changes that are going to end up leading us to a place that we're not going to be comfortable with," he says.

Side effects. Why worry about human enhancement? After all, what's not to like about, say, doubling the average human life span? But the bioethics council wonders in its report whether we would achieve a "stretched rubber band" version of longevity in which our active, healthy years would be extended, but so would our years of decline and decay. "Having many long, productive years, with the knowledge of many more to come, would surely bring joy to many of us," says panel member William Hurlbut, a bioethicist at Stanford University. "But in the end, these techniques could also leave the individual somewhat unhinged from the life cycle. Do I want to live to be 100? Sure. But to 250 or some other dramatic extension? No."

Bioconservatives acknowledge, however, that human enhancement may be inevitable. Even Kass admits that the council's report focused on the problems of enhancement rather than its benefits because the advantages of longer lives and better brains are so obvious "they don't need articulating." It's easy to argue the "con" position, says UCLA's Stock, about issues like the use of embryonic stem cells as long as the benefits are merely theoretical. Once those benefits become tangible, though, "the debate will be over," says Stock. Indeed, the potential therapeutic value of stem-cell research has already prompted more than 200 House members and Nancy Reagan to urge Bush to alter his ban.

12   With the proliferation of plastic surgery, for example, or the use of Ritalin by achievement-crazed students hoping to score better on the SAT, enhancement seems to be the wave of the future. Even Bush's Department of Commerce appears to be buying into it. In a 2002 joint report with the National Science Foundation (coauthored by Bainbridge among others), the agency recommended a national research-and-development effort to enhance humanity in order to create a world where human

brains communicate directly with machines, and scientists "control the genetics of humans" to make bodies "more durable, healthier . . . and more resistant to many kinds of stress, biological threats, and aging processes." If successful, the effort will "create a golden age that would be a turning point for human productivity and quality of life."

Or not. Science could render all this high-flying rhetoric just that. Stem-cell and protein therapies, after all, have yet to spawn any successful treatments for disease, much less provide the catalyst for launching a new stage of human evolution. In 2000, researchers used gene therapy to cure two French boys of an inherited immune-system disorder but in the process gave them leukemia. Who knows what other dangerous side effects these new therapies will bring? It is, as they say, too early to tell—but judging by the intensity of the debate, not any too early to fight.

PERSONAL RESPONSE

How would you answer the questions Pethokoukis asks in his opening paragraph: If it were possible, would you take a drug to enhance your IQ, tinker with your genes to have athletic prowess, or have an injection that would let you live to be 160?

QUESTIONS FOR CLASS OR SMALL-GROUP DISCUSSION

1. Why do you think Pethokoukis begins his essay with a series of rhetorical questions? How effective is paragraph 1 as an introduction to the essay?

2. What strategies does Pethokoukis use to explain the controversy among scientists and ethicists over biotech possibilities? Can you restate in your own words the major issues in the conflict over biotech possibilities?

3. In paragraph 11, Pethokoukis notes that there is no argument over the benefits of enhancement because they are so obvious. What are some of the benefits? With so many benefits, why are people opposed to human enhancement?

4. Select one of the arguments against human enhancement that Pethokoukis mentions and explain where you position yourself on the issue.

ALL FOR THE GOOD

JAMES D. WATSON

James D. Watson, with Francis Crick, discovered in 1953 that DNA molecules arrange themselves in a double helix. In 1962, Watson, Crick, and a British biophysicist, Maurice Wilkins, shared the Nobel Prize in medicine for their work on DNA. In 1968 Watson became director of the Cold Springs Harbor Laboratory of Quantitative Biology, in New York State. He published The Double Helix, *his best-selling story of the discovery of the structure of DNA, in 1968. His other books include* Genes, Girls and Gamow: After the Double Helix *(2002) and, with Andrew Berry,* DNA: The Secret of Life *(2003). A recipient of the Presidential Medal of Freedom and author of many scientific papers, Watson directed the Human Genome Project from 1988 to 1992. He wrote this piece for* Time *magazine's January 11, 1999, issue on the future of medicine.*

There is lots of zip in DNA-based biology today. With each passing year it incorporates an ever increasing fraction of the life sciences, ranging from single-cell organisms, like bacteria and yeast, to the complexities of the human brain. All this wonderful biological frenzy was unimaginable when I first entered the world of genetics. In 1948, biology was an all too descriptive discipline near the bottom of science's totem pole, with physics at its top. By then Einstein's turn-of-the-century ideas about the interconversion of matter and energy had been transformed into the powers of the atom. If not held in check, the weapons they made possible might well destroy the very fabric of civilized human life. So physicists of the late 1940s were simultaneously revered for making atoms relevant to society and feared for what their toys could do if they were to fall into the hands of evil.

Such ambivalent feelings are now widely held toward biology. The double-helical structure of DNA, initially admired for its intellectual simplicity, today represents to many a double-edged sword that can be used for evil as well as good. No sooner had scientists at Stanford University in 1973 begun rearranging DNA molecules in test tubes (and, equally important, reinserting the novel DNA segments back into living cells) than critics began likening these "recombinant" DNA procedures to the physicist's power to break apart atoms. Might not some of the test-tube-rearranged DNA molecules impart to their host cells disease-causing capacities that, like nuclear weapons, are capable of seriously disrupting human civilization? Soon there were cries from both scientists and nonscientists that such research might best be ruled by stringent regulations—if not laws.

As a result, several years were to pass before the full power of recombinant-DNA technology got into the hands of working scientists, who by then were itching to explore previously unattainable secrets of life. Happily, the proposals to control recombinant-DNA research through legislation never got close to enactment. And when anti-DNA doomsday scenarios failed to materialize, even the modestly restrictive governmental regulations began to wither away. In retrospect, recombinant-DNA may rank as the safest revolutionary technology ever developed. To my knowledge, not one fatality, much less illness, has been caused by a genetically manipulated organism.

4   The moral I draw from this painful episode is this: Never postpone experiments that have clearly defined future benefits for fear of dangers that can't be quantified. Though it may sound at first uncaring, we can react rationally only to real (as opposed to hypothetical) risks. Yet for several years we postponed important experiments on the genetic basis of cancer, for example, because we took much too seriously spurious arguments that the genes at the root of human cancer might themselves be dangerous to work with.

Though most forms of DNA manipulation are now effectively unregulated, one important potential goal remains blocked. Experiments aimed at learning how to insert functional genetic material into human germ cells—sperm and eggs—remain off limits to most of the world's scientists. No governmental body wants to take responsibility for initiating steps that might help redirect the course of future human evolution. These decisions reflect widespread concerns that we, as humans, may not have the wisdom to modify the most precious of all human treasures—our chromosomal "instruction books." Dare we be entrusted with improving upon the results of the several million years of Darwinian natural selection? Are human germ cells Rubicons that geneticists may never cross?

Unlike many of my peers, I'm reluctant to accept such reasoning, again using the argument that you should never put off doing something useful for fear of evil that may never arrive. The first germ-line gene manipulations are unlikely to be attempted for frivolous reasons. Nor does the state of today's science provide the knowledge that would be needed to generate "superpersons" whose far-ranging talents would make those who are genetically unmodified feel redundant and unwanted. Such creations will remain denizens of science fiction, not the real world, far into the future. When they are finally attempted, germ-line genetic manipulations will probably be done to change a death sentence into a life verdict—by creating children who are resistant to a deadly virus, for example, much the way we can already protect plants from viruses by inserting antiviral DNA segments into their genomes.

If appropriate go-ahead signals come, the first resulting gene-bettered children will in no sense threaten human civilization. They will be seen as special only by those in their immediate circles, and are likely to pass as unnoticed in later life as the now grownup "test-tube baby" Louise Brown does today. If they grow up healthily gene-bettered, more such children will follow, and they and those whose lives are enriched by their existence will rejoice that science has again improved human life. If, however, the added genetic material fails to work, better procedures must be developed before more couples commit their psyches toward such inherently unsettling pathways to producing healthy children.

8   Moving forward will not be for the faint of heart. But if the next century witnesses failure, let it be because our science is not yet up to the job, not because we don't have the courage to make less random the sometimes most unfair courses of human evolution.

PERSONAL RESPONSE

Are you as comfortable with the possibility that something might go wrong in "gene-bettered children" as Watson seems to be (paragraph 7)? What is your opinion on that point?

QUESTIONS FOR CLASS OR SMALL-GROUP DISCUSSION

1. How successfully do you believe Watson has defended his position on genetic engineering? What strategies does he use for persuading his audience to agree with him?

2. How effective is the comparison that Watson makes between the public response to physicists' learning how to make the atomic bomb in the 1940s and biologists' ability to do recombinant-DNA procedures in the 1970s? Are you persuaded that the issues are the same? If so, what are their similarities? If not, how do they differ?

3. To what extent do you agree with Watson when he writes: "Never postpone experiments that have clearly defined future benefits for fear of dangers that can't be quantified" (paragraph 4)?

4. Comment on Watson's response to those who believe that humans "may not have the wisdom to modify the most precious of all human treasures—our chromosomal 'instruction book' " (paragraph 5). Do you share his view on this point?

DOLLY'S FALSE LEGACY

IAN WILMUT

Ian Wilmut is the Scottish embryologist whose team of researchers, in 1996, was the first to clone a mammal from fully differentiated adult mammary cells. Wilmut holds a Ph.D. in animal genetic engineering from Darwin College, University of Cambridge, and has been a researcher at the Animal Research Breeding Station (now known as the Roslin Institute) in Edinburgh, Scotland, since 1974. He is co-author of The Second Creation: Dolly and the Age of Biological Control *(2000) and has been editor of the* Journal of Reproduction Fertility *since 1993. This essay appeared in the January 11, 1999, issue of* Time *magazine.*

Overlooked in the arguments about the morality of artificially reproducing life is the fact that, at present, cloning is a very inefficient procedure. The incidence of death among fetuses and offspring produced by cloning is much higher than it is through natural reproduction—roughly 10 times as high as normal before birth and three times as high after birth in our studies at Roslin. Distressing enough for those working with animals, these failure rates surely render unthinkable the notion of applying such treatment to humans.

Even if the technique were perfected, however, we must ask ourselves what practical value whole-being cloning might have. What exactly would be the difference between a "cloned" baby and a child born naturally—and why would we want one?

The cloned child would be a genetically identical twin of the original, and thus physically very similar—far more similar than a natural parent and child. Human personality, however, emerges from both the effects of the genes we inherit (nature) and environmental factors (nurture). The two clones would develop distinct personalities, just as twins develop unique identities. And because the copy would often be born in a different family, cloned twins would be less alike in personality than natural identical twins.

4 Why "copy" people in the first place? Couples unable to have children might choose to have a copy of one of them rather than accept the intrusion of genes from a donor. My wife and I have two children of our own and an adopted child, but I find it helpful to consider what might have happened in my own marriage if a copy of me had been made to overcome infertility. My wife and I met in high school. How would she react to a physical copy of the young man she fell in love with? How would any of us find living with ourselves? Surely the older clone—I, in this case—would believe that he understood how the copy should behave and so be even more likely than the average father to impose expectations upon his child. Above all, how would a teenager cope with looking at me, a balding, aging man, and seeing the physical future ahead of him?

Each of us can imagine hypothetical families created by the introduction of a cloned child—a copy of one partner in a homosexual relationship or of a single parent, for example. What is missing in all this is consideration of what's in the interests of the cloned child. Because there is no form of infertility that could be overcome only by cloning, I do not find these proposals acceptable. My concerns are not on religious grounds or on the basis of a perceived intrinsic ethical principle. Rather, my judgment is that it would be difficult for families created in this way to provide an appropriate environment for the child.

Cloning is also suggested as a means of bringing back a relative, usually a child, killed tragically. Any parent can understand that wish, but it must first be recognized that the copy would be a new baby and not the lost child. Herein lies the difficulty, for the grieving parents are seeking not a new baby but a return of the dead one. Since the original would be fondly remembered as having particular talents and interests, would not the parent expect the copy to be the same? It is possible, however, that the copy would develop quite differently. Is it fair to the new child to place it in a family with such unnatural expectations?

What if the lost child was very young? The shorter the life, the fewer the expectations parents might place on the substitute, right? If a baby dies within a few days of birth and there is no reason to think that death was caused by an inherited defect, would it then be acceptable to make a copy? Is it practical to frame legislation that would prevent copying of adults or older children, but allow copying of infants? At what age would a child be too old to be copied in the event of death?

8 Copying is also suggested as a means by which parents can have the child of their dreams. Couples might choose to have a copy of a film star, baseball player or scientist, depending on their interests. But because personality is only partly the result of genetic inheritance, conflict would be sure to arise if the cloned child failed to develop the same interests as the original. What if the copy of Einstein shows no interest in science? Or the football player turns to acting? Success also depends upon fortune. What of the child who does not live up to the hopes and dreams of the parent simply because of bad luck?

Every child should be wanted for itself, as an individual. In making a copy of oneself or some famous person, a parent is deliberately specifying the way he or she wishes that child to develop. In recent years, particularly in the U.S., much importance has been placed on the right of individuals to reproduce in ways that they wish. I suggest that there is a greater need to consider the interests of the child and to reject these proposed uses of cloning.

By contrast, human cloning could, in theory, be used to obtain tissues needed to treat disorders such as Parkinson's disease and diabetes. These diseases are associated with cell types that do not repair or replace themselves, but suitable cells will one day be grown in culture. These uses cannot be justified now; nor are they likely to be in the near future.

Moreover, there is a lot we do not know about the effects of cloning, especially in terms of aging. As we grow older, changes occur in our cells that reduce the number of times they can reproduce. This clock of age is reset by normal reproduction during the production of sperm and eggs; that is why children of each new generation have a full life span. It is not yet known whether aging is reversed during cloning or if the clone's natural life is shortened by the years its parent has already lived. Then there is the problem of the genetic errors that accumulate in our cells. There are systems to seek out and correct such errors during normal reproduction; it is not known if that can occur during cloning. Research with animals is urgently required to measure the life span and determine the cause of death of animals produced by cloning.

12   Important questions also remain on the most appropriate means of controlling the development and use of these techniques. It is taken for granted that the production and sale of drugs will be regulated by governments, but this was not always the case. A hundred years ago, the production and sale of drugs in the U.S. was unregulated. Unscrupulous companies took the opportunity to include in their products substances, like cocaine, that were likely to make the patients feel better even if they offered no treatment for the original condition. After public protest, championed by publications such as the *Ladies' Home Journal,* a federal act was passed in 1906. An enforcement agency, known now as the FDA, was established in 1927. An independent body similar to the FDA is now required to assess all the research on cloning.

There is much still to be learned about the biology associated with cloning. The time required for this research, however, will also provide an opportunity for each society to decide how it wishes the technique to be used. At some point in the future, cloning will have much to contribute to human medicine, but we must use it cautiously.

PERSONAL RESPONSE

Does it surprise you that the man who cloned the first mammal is so cautious about the possibility of cloning humans? What do you think of his caution?

QUESTIONS FOR CLASS OR SMALL-GROUP DISCUSSION

1. Assess the effectiveness of Wilmut's title and his opening paragraph. How do they serve to introduce his subject and the position he takes on it?

2. How persuasive do you find Wilmut's reasons for why people might want to clone themselves or their children? Do any of the possible reasons seem more valid to you than others?

3. Wilmut suggests certain ways that human cloning might be used besides cloning entire humans. What do you think of those uses of the technology?

4. Wilmut states that there are important questions that need to be considered before proceeding with the technology to clone humans. What are those questions? To what extent do you agree with him that these questions are weighty enough to postpone research until they are answered?

PLAYING GOD: HAS SCIENCE GONE TOO FAR?

JEFF LYON

Jeff Lyon, with Peter Gorner, wrote Altered Fates: Gene Therapy and the Retooling of Human Life *(1995). He and Gorner won a Pulitzer Prize for journalism in 1987 for the stories on which this book was based. Lyon is a science writer for the* Chicago Tribune *and writes extensively on genetic engineering. This article was published in* Woman's Day *in July, 2001.*

Until recently, human cloning wasn't something most adults expected to see in their lifetimes. Even five years ago, many scientists believed it would still be another 20 years or more before they figured out how to clone any species of mammal—that is, how to get a single cell from an adult animal to generate a whole new animal. But that assumption was demolished in February 1997, when British embryologist Ian Wilmut, Ph.D., announced that he and colleagues at the Roslin Institute in Edinburgh, Scotland, had successfully cloned a sheep: the now world-famous Dolly.

Since then the floodgates have opened, and cattle, goats, mice and pigs have all been cloned. Dogs haven't been cloned yet, but researchers at Texas A & M University are working on it. And now it seems it may not be long before the ultimate line is crossed.

Last January Panos Zavos, Ph.D., then professor of reproductive physiology at the University of Kentucky, announced that he was leaving his position to team up with Severino Antinori, M.D., an Italian fertility specialist, to try to clone a human by 2003. Their purpose, he said, is to help infertile couples who want a genetically related child.

4   And last fall a sect called the Raelians, based in Montreal, announced that an American couple had paid the sect $500,000 to clone their deceased baby girl and that Brigitte Boisselier, Ph.D., the sect's scientific director, had agreed to attempt it. The Raelians believe all life on earth was created by aliens through genetic engineering. They endorse cloning and claim to have the scientific know-how and enough potential surrogate mothers to achieve their goal.

Welcome to the future, where science fiction becomes science fact and researchers and ordinary citizens alike must wrestle with a question that has profound meaning for humankind: Should scientists be allowed to pursue research that may one day enable them to shape and even create life? Or to put it another way: Is it right for scientists to assume powers that many people believe should belong only to God?

Less than a decade ago, this question would have prompted an automatic answer from most people: No, it shouldn't be allowed—not that it is likely to happen any time soon. But in a swift and startling turnabout, the answer to that question has become less clear, even as scientists are taking baby steps toward making such things happen.

Last March, Dr. Boisselier and Dr. Zavos both appeared before a congressional panel investigating whether to draft a law banning human-cloning experiments in the United States—a measure President Bush has said he would sign. The U.S. Food and Drug Administration prohibits these experiments, but a federal law would carry more weight and be a stronger deterrent against conducting this work. Of course, scientists would still be free to work in countries that look upon this research more favorably.

8   "Those that say ban it, those would not be the Neil Armstrongs that would fly us to the moon," Dr. Zavos said, adding that it would be difficult, if not impossible, to stop the science of cloning now. "The genie's out of the bottle," he said. And as if to prove his point, last January Britain became the first nation to legalize cloning human embryos for limited research purposes.

Yet, even as the likelihood of human cloning becomes more real, the science is still rudimentary. Most cloned animals die in the womb, and even those that initially seem healthy often develop fatal defects of the heart, lungs, kidney, brain and immune system down the road. Something about cloning seems to disrupt normal gene activation in the developing fetus. This could prove catastrophic if an attempt is made to clone a human. Dr. Wilmut has said that trying it now would be "criminally irresponsible."

Nor is cloning the only sign that humans are assuming powers once relegated to the Almighty. Last September six-year-old Molly Nash of Englewood, Colorado, was given a blood transfusion that doctors hoped would help cure her of Fanconi's anemia. This rare, often fatal, hereditary disease causes the bone marrow to fail to produce blood cells and platelets. The transfused blood came from her baby brother, Adam. It had been collected from his umbilical cord at the time of his birth. Adam had been conceived in a laboratory dish with other embryos produced by his parents' eggs and sperm. He had been implanted in his mother's womb because he was disease free and because his tissue and blood type matched his sister's—in other words, so he could be her donor. The other embryos were discarded. Cord blood is rich in stem cells, the mother cells found in various organs that generate the functional cells of those organs. It was hoped that Adam's stem cells would generate functioning bone marrow and a healthy new blood supply for Molly.

The procedure seems to have worked. Tests done in January found that almost all of Molly's bone marrow came from Adam. "While we will continue to monitor Molly, especially over this first critical year, her prognosis looks great," said John Wagner, M.D., a transplant specialist at the University of Minnesota Medical School, who performed the transfusion. The Nashes did not doubt they had done the right thing. "You could say it was an added benefit to have Adam be the right bone-marrow type, which would not hurt him in the least and would save Molly's life," Lisa, their mother, said in September. "We didn't have to think twice about it." But some ethicists were concerned. Would children now be bred for their biological usefulness?

12   Stem cells, meanwhile, are the focus of another scientific endeavor that rivals cloning in its potential to bestow Godlike powers on human beings. Researchers hope someday to be able to direct a person's stem cells to grow new organs and tissue for that person in a lab. The cells could be told to grow a liver for someone who needs a transplant, for example, or brain cells for someone with Alzheimer's disease. And because the cells would contain the person's own DNA, there would be no problem with tissue rejection.

Advances in genetic engineering and gene therapy are also transforming the nature of life and the way we live. Researchers have already created genetically altered seeds and grains designed to produce hardier plants and bigger harvests—and American consumers are already eating some of this altered produce without knowing it. And despite a tragic setback in September 1999, when 18-year-old Jesse Gelsinger of Tucson, Arizona, died during a gene-therapy experiment at the University of Pennsylvania, research is also moving forward in developing safer, more effective ways to deliver healthy new genes into a patient's cells.

Thanks to the Human Genome Project, the ongoing effort to codify and learn the function of the more than 30,000 genes that make up the instruction manual for the human body, researchers are also zeroing in on which genes cause and can cure various diseases. In a few years it may be possible for people to go to a doctor's office and, in the time it takes to read this article, get a full lab report detailing their genetic predisposition to various diseases. If the report noted a susceptibility to lung cancer, for example, they would then be counseled not to smoke. In the not-too-distant future, scientists could also have the power to design smarter, more attractive and athletic offspring by tinkering with a child's genetic makeup before or after birth. Such powers would enable them to change the course of human evolution, and to do it in a matter of generations.

And then there is the ultimate quest: to create life itself. In 1953 researchers at the University of Chicago mixed methane, ammonia, hydrogen and water—the ingredients of the so-called "primordial soup" that existed on the young earth—and passed an electric current through it to simulate lightning. To their amazement, they found traces of amino acids—the chemical building blocks of life—in the residue. Now, a team of scientists headed by a brilliant maverick named J. Craig Venter, Ph.D., director of the Institute for Genomic Research in Rockville, Maryland, is conducting another experiment.

16   Working with a harmless species of bacteria called *Mycoplasma genitalium* that has only 517 genes—the fewest of any known organism—Dr. Venter and his colleagues disrupted the microbe's genes one by one to see which it needed to survive. In a paper published in the December 1999 issue of *Science* they estimated that *M. genitalium* needs 265 to 350 of its genes to stay alive. The next task, they wrote, is

to narrow down that number as a "first step" toward "engineering" a cell with "a minimum genome" in the lab: in other words, manufacturing a living microbe.

That's as far as Dr. Venter has taken the research. The question is whether anyone should take it any further. In the issue of *Science* containing his paper, a panel of bioethicists—thinkers who specialize in weighing the thorny issues raised by modern medicine and biology—addressed this point at his request. They did not give a thumbs-down to the experiment. Instead, they gave it a conditional thumbs-up. The prospect of humans creating a life form "does not violate any fundamental moral precepts," the authors wrote. But they did raise questions they felt needed to be considered, such as whether the new technology would "be used for the benefit of all" and the possibility that it could be misused to create new biological weapons.

It must be said that even if scientists do pursue this goal, achieving it is probably years off. The genes essential to sustain *M. genitalium,* for example, include at least 100 whose function is unknown. If science cannot yet understand the workings of a cell with a paltry 500 genes—even a fruit fly has more than 10,000—it can hardly claim mastery of biology. The task would also require an expertise in the workings of cells and gene activation that is still beyond us. But most people thought cloning a mammal was decades away when Dolly was cloned. And even if the breakthrough is far off, the seeming lack of opposition to it is striking.

"A couple of years ago I'd have opposed this experiment," says Arthur Caplan, Ph.D., director of the University of Pennsylvania Center for Bioethics, who co-headed the panel that evaluated Dr. Venter's experiment. "I think society's becoming used to genetic tinkering. Despite all our religious grounding, we are becoming increasingly secular in thinking that life is not a mystery beyond our understanding. I have been told that creating life violates God's will and that it's unnatural. But I've heard no persuasive arguments for banning these experiments. There are certainly issues that demand attention if the research is to proceed. But they are safety questions. For example, you could make things that get out of the containment facility or that pose a threat because they have properties we don't understand. There is also the possibility of misapplication in the weapons and terrorism area. It needs comment and oversight to make sure no one does anything nasty or dangerous. But those risks aren't so great that you can't proceed."

20   Different people simply have different beliefs about how life came to exist and where humans fit in the grand design. "I see life as a process of chemistry," says Norman Pace, Ph.D., a professor of molecular, cellular and developmental biology at the University of Colorado who is involved in his own quest to isolate the minimal components of life in the lab. "I see life as chemicals talking to one another in sophisticated ways developed through natural selection. Much of it we don't yet understand, but that doesn't mean it's a spiritual matter. These spiritual issues are human inventions."

Even if God exists, say others, we can't call these pursuits "playing God" because they don't reflect how God operates. "In nature, chance determines things," says R. Alta Charo, J.D., professor of law and medical ethics at the University of Wisconsin Law School. "I believe that the essence of God is to let the odds play out." In contrast, she says, "It is the essential attribute of being human to make choices, to exercise control, to have dominion over the natural world." She sees these quests as "completely consistent with what it means to be humans on this planet. I believe knowledge is an intrinsic good and that until it is shown to cause harm, it should be encouraged. I believe we should have eaten the apple."

Not everyone shares these views. Lori Andrews, Ph.D., a professor of law at the Chicago–Kent College of Law in Chicago and a legal specialist in new reproductive technologies, thinks ethicists have become too accepting of a whole laundry list of unsettling scientific quests. "It's like we've become deadened to the ethical dimensions of this," she says. "We're viewing biology as playing with Tinker Toys. There seems to be less resistance to the whole idea of tampering with life."

Dr. Andrews cites the news last January that researchers at Oregon Health Sciences University in Portland had produced a genetically altered rhesus monkey—one of humankind's closest relatives—by inserting a jellyfish gene into a monkey egg before it was fertilized. ANDi, as the monkey was named, is the first "transgenic" primate: the first to have genes of another species in every cell of his body. Lead researcher Gerald Schatten, Ph.D., said the long-term goal is to create monkeys that have been modified to develop disease traits for use in studying new treatments. Is that a good goal? Does it justify creating ANDi? An ethicist at the university acknowledged that some people think "maybe we shouldn't do this on nonhuman primates." Dr. Andrews is more outspoken. "The day you start doing genetic engineering on monkeys," she says, "humans can't be far behind."

24   Richard Hayes, former assistant political director of the Sierra Club, finds the lack of loud public debate about these technologies "chilling" and holds bioethicists partly to blame. "Many of these academics have become almost apologists for genetic engineering and cloning," says Hayes, now executive director of the Exploratory Initiative on the New Human Genetic Technologies, a network of professionals and activists interested in stimulating that debate. "You rarely find a bioethicist who thinks there's anything fundamentally wrong with these technologies. In Europe it's very different, because they had the Nazi Holocaust. But here we have consumer-driven markets."

Not all bioethicists fit this mold, of course. Leon Kass, M.D., Ph.D., the Addie Clark Harding professor in the Committee on Social Thought at the University of Chicago, is one who doesn't. It worries him, he says, "that the scientists' view of what they're doing could rapidly become the public's view, and that kind of shrunken understanding of what life is—that it's nothing but chemicals—could spread even further in the culture than it already has. It seems to support the materialist view of life—which, even though I'm a trained scientist, I regard as false and inadequate."

Dr. Kass argues further that making a microbe in a lab is not really creating life. "It's a gross exaggeration. It's like reproducing a Mozart symphony. You haven't written the score; you are merely recopying it. I'm bothered that we are coming under the illusion that because we know how to reproduce a few things, we are absolutely in charge. It's a form of hubris and folly." Besides, he says, even if a scientist could create a human from scratch, "would he really be the author or just the instrument of God's handiwork?"

Lisa Sowle Cahill, Ph.D., J. Donald Monan chair of theology at Boston College and former president of the Catholic Theological Society of America, wonders about this, too. "The Bible says we are created in the image of God and God is the Creator," she says. "Does that mean only God creates? Or does it mean that because we are made in God's image we share that ability?" If so, who is to say which of our efforts do and don't cross the line? "Are we playing God when we wipe out smallpox or cure cancer? Why is it wrong to put a jellyfish gene in a monkey?" It makes us uncomfortable for many reasons, she says, "but defining why it is wrong is more difficult—for me, anyway."

28   Like many religions, the Catholic Church "doesn't have a final position on a lot of these questions," says Dr. Cahill. "It cautiously welcomes new genetic therapies, but it is concerned about protecting human life and has ruled out research using human embryos. Other things are not settled."

But religion can guide and prod people to think in ways they otherwise might not. "It is the nature of religion to be conservative," says Harold S. Kushner, Rabbi Laureate of Temple Israel in Natick, Massachusetts, and author of the forthcoming *Living a Life That Matters: Resolving the Conflict between Conscience and Success.* "Religion says, 'Wait a minute, there are time-tested values here which we should be very slow to disregard.' I'd hope our experience with polluted air and toxic and nuclear waste would have taught us not to go where we can just because we can. I'd hope for a self-imposed moratorium on doing what's possible until we figure out whether we really want to do it."

"In vitro fertilization is wonderful," says Rabbi Kushner. "DNA repair is good. My wife and I had a son who died of a genetic disease, and the idea of fixing what's missing and giving an innocent child life is exciting. But it is one thing to repair, and another to let parents make sure they have perfect children. My concern is we will lose the knack of loving children who are less than perfect. And my concern with cloning is less ambivalent. I mind very much if we clone people. The whole idea of God's plan for humanity, which calls for people to have children and die, means that one generation, scarred and wearied by its experience, gives way to another that's born fresh and innocent and full of promise. Once you start fooling with that, I think you undermine what God had in mind for the human race. As for creating life artificially, there is something special about humans being created out of an act of love, not chemistry."

Dr. Kass agrees. There is a difference between using new technologies to cure disease and "using them to engineer so-called improvements," he says. "As a species we don't have the wisdom to know what an improvement would be. The better path is caution and humility before these awesome powers we may never fully understand." Indeed, says Rabbi Kushner, "A scientist ought to stand in awe of the things modern science can do and realize that he has seen the face of God, he hasn't become God."

32   One thing is clear. These technologies are here to stay, and it's up to all of us to decide what to do with them. "We want to support the most creative and compassionate science possible," says Laurie Zoloth, Ph.D., head of the Jewish Studies department at San Francisco State University. "The bold scientific approach allowed Pasteur and Salk to take leaps that advanced the cause of humankind. But the human

capacity for error is enormous. And the human capacity for terrible moral choices is also great. We live in a society in which some 44 million people have too little access to health care. And now we're developing technologies that may give enormous life-shaping power to people who have the money to control it. So there is a lot to be cautious about."

Hayes is more blunt. "What's at stake is our common human future. Genetic modification could lead to the creation of separate genetic castes and social division beyond anything in history. There's no reason to go down this road. We need to summon the maturity to use our technology in ways that affirm rather than degrade humanity. We have to decide which uses we approve of and which we oppose."

The only way we can do that, says Dr. Zoloth, is through an "enormous national conversation. All we have is the ability to keep talking and raising fears and hopes and encouraging scientists to stop and reflect." History shows we can achieve great things if we keep talking. "When we wanted to think about race, we had a transformative national conversation. The civil-rights movement was America at its best. The Vietnam war sparked such a conversation. Now we need to have one about genetics. This is exactly the moment when we must decide who controls this technology and on behalf of whom. The need cannot be overestimated. This is far too important to leave in the hands of market forces alone."

PERSONAL RESPONSE

Write for a few minutes in answer to the question posed by the title of this article.

QUESTIONS FOR CLASS OR SMALL-GROUP DISCUSSION

1. How successfully does Lyon present the views of representatives from various religious bodies in answer to his overarching question about whether humans should be trying to do those things that many people believe only God should do? Is quoting specific people directly a more effective writing strategy than merely summarizing the issues?

2. Lyon reports that a panel of bioethicists did not give "thumbs down" to Dr. J. Craig Venter's question about whether he should continue his experiments on creating life in the laboratory. What is your response to the panel's opinion? Do you agree that "the prospect of humans creating a life form 'does not violate any fundamental moral precepts'" (paragraph 17)?

3. What do you think about continuing research similar to that done with ANDi, the first "'transgenic'" monkey (paragraph 23)? Why do you think there is "a lack of loud public debate about" this and other technologies mentioned in the article (paragraph 24)?

4. Discuss your position on the subject of stem-cell research, which Lyon mentions in paragraph 9, after first explaining just where the controversy lies, what benefits the research would have, and what problems might result from it.

○ PERSPECTIVES ON BIOETHICS ○

Suggested Writing Topics

1. Compare and contrast the views of James D. Watson in "All for the Good" and Ian Wilmut in "Dolly's False Legacy" on the subject of human cloning. Whom do you find more persuasive?

2. Drawing on at least two of the essays in this chapter, explain where you stand on one of the questions raised in the readings in this chapter about the implications and dangers of genetics research.

3. Write a response to James D. Watson ("All for the Good"), Ian Wilmut ("Dolly's False Legacy"), or any of the people quoted in Jeff Lyon's "Playing God: Has Science Gone Too Far?" Explain where you agree, where you disagree, and where you have real concerns about what the person says. Be sure to state why you believe as you do.

4. Write an essay in which you explain what other issues, besides the ones identified by the authors of the articles in this chapter, need to be looked at closely. For instance, do you think care must be taken to make the results of genetic research available to everyone while protecting the rights of both researchers who make the discoveries and companies that want to profit from them?

5. Argue your position on one of these issues or any other raised by the essays in this chapter: stem-cell research, physician-assisted suicide, universal health care, access to expensive treatments for self-induced health problems, embryo research, mandatory testing for HIV diseases, or compulsory genetic screening for certain risk groups, as part of premarital examinations, or of donees for in vitro embryo fertilization.

6. Conduct a class forum on the ethical, social, and/or legal problems that are associated with the Human Genome Project, human cloning, stem-cell research, and/or other genetics research. For a writing project, summarize the views of your classmates, and state your own position on the subject.

7. Invite professionals to speak to your class on the ethical, social, and legal problems associated with the Human Genome Project or stem-cell research. For instance, you might invite a molecular biologist, an ethics professor, or someone else familiar with genetics research or the Human Genome Project to speak. An alternative is to interview such a person. For a writing project, draw on the views of the professionals who visit your class or whom you interview as you explain your own position on the subject.

Research Topics

1. Research one of the issues suggested by the readings in this chapter: stem-cell research, physician-assisted suicide, universal health care, access to expensive treatments for self-induced health problems, embryo research, mandatory testing for HIV diseases, and compulsory genetic screening for

certain risk groups or during premarital examinations; the status of genetic disease and genetic therapy; or the process of social negotiation of scientific knowledge.

2. Research the Human Genome Project, and write a paper in which you elaborate on its main objectives, provide representative views on the controversy surrounding it, and explain your own position and why you believe as you do.

3. Jeff Lyon in "Playing God: Has Science Gone Too Far?" refers to a special issue of *Science* in which a panel of bioethicists considered whether Dr. J. Craig Venter should continue his research on engineering a living microbe. Read the opinions of that panel as a starting point for your thinking and then conduct further research on the debate over whether humans should attempt to create life.

4. Research some aspect of the history and/or practice of eugenics, such as the program of Nazi Germany under Hitler or in the U. S. programs for forced sterilization for mentally ill patients.

RESPONDING TO VISUALS

A human in a Petri dish. Source: Image Source/CORBIS

1. What is the message of this image?
2. What is the symbolic significance of the naked human inside a Petri dish?
3. Why do you suppose an adult was used inside the Petri dish instead of a baby?

RESPONDING TO VISUALS

Medical finger-pointing. Source: Created by Joyce Hesselberth ©Images.com/CORBIS

1. What is the function of the eyes and the broken lines linked to various body parts?
2. How do the pointing fingers function?
3. What is the effect of the syringes and scalpel in combination with the staring eyes and pointing fingers?
4. What comment does this drawing make on medicine?

CHAPTER

21

PUBLIC HEALTH

Epidemics, pandemics, and plagues have been much dreaded realities from the very beginning of human existence. Consider such major outbreaks of disease as the bubonic plague in thirteenth- and fourteenth-century Europe; cholera epidemics in various parts of the world from time to time, up to the present; the smallpox epidemic that swept Sweden in 1764; the typhus epidemic that killed more than three million Russians during World War I; or the influenza plague of 1918 to 1919 that killed more than 20 million people around the world. More recently, untreatable, deadly viruses have infected populations in certain areas of the world, worrying health officials that they may spread elsewhere. The Ebola virus in Africa, for instance, produces acute suffering in its victims, most of whom die within days of being infected. Viruses are particularly difficult to contain, because they live inside body cells, where antibiotics cannot reach them. Worse, once a person is infected with a virus, it can continue to live in the body's cells, waiting to strike again many years later.

Even such previously treatable diseases as herpes, hepatitis, and chicken pox are becoming resistant to treatment and causing deaths in increasingly higher numbers. Cases of deaths caused by herpes simplex 1 (HSV1) and related members of the herpes family, such as cytomegalovirus (CVM), chicken pox, and genital herpes (HSV2), have been reported. Although certain groups such as pregnant women are particularly vulnerable to these diseases, these and other viruses pose a considerable threat to the general population. More than three million Americans are believed to harbor the mysterious and deadly hepatitis C virus, for instance, with even more people harboring the less-mysterious but potentially life-threatening hepatitis A and hepatitis B viruses.

This chapter features articles on issues related to several aspects of public health, both national and global, beginning with Charles Krauthammer's "Smallpox Shots: Make Them Mandatory." Smallpox was supposedly eradicated for good almost three decades ago, but the possibility that hostile nations might be developing strains to attack the U. S. leads Krauthammer to argue that preventive vaccinations should be reintroduced and made mandatory, not voluntary.

Another serious public-health issue is the rising cost of U. S. health care. Arnold S. Relman gives an overview of the current health-care system in "Restructuring the U.S. Health Care System." Relman outlines the problems inherent in rising health-care costs and discusses the perspectives of insurance companies, physicians, and patients. He concludes by recommending a restructuring of the system that he believes would benefit all parties.

The focus then shifts to global health concerns with Richard D. Smith's "Global Public Goods and Health." Smith explains what "global public goods" are and suggests applying that model to global health issues. Next, Wayne Ellwood in "We All Have AIDS" argues that AIDS is everyone's problem. Noting that "AIDS spreads along the fault line of poverty, gender and class inequality," he explains how those social inequalities nurture the disease in sub-Saharan Africa and certain Asian countries and makes a plea for the world community to help curb this enormous global health problem.

The last article in the chapter, Johanna McGeary's "Death Stalks a Continent," elaborates on Ellwood's piece by giving another look at the AIDS epidemic in Africa. McGeary explains how the region's social dynamics "colluded to spread the disease and help block effective intervention." Her article tells the personal stories of disease victims and reports the viewpoints of both care takers and those who may be responsible for spreading the disease. Both Ellwood's and McGeary's articles site ignorance of how sexually transmitted diseases are spread as one of the major causes of the epidemic.

SMALLPOX SHOTS: MAKE THEM MANDATORY

CHARLES KRAUTHAMMER

Charles Krauthammer is a contributing editor to the New Republic *and writes a weekly syndicated column for the* Washington Post. *A political scientist, psychiatrist, journalist, and speech writer, Krauthammer won a Pulitzer Prize in 1981 for his commentary on politics and society. He has published a book,* Cutting Edges: Making Sense of the Eighties *(1985). While serving as Chief Resident in Psychiatry at Massachusetts General Hospital, he published scientific papers, including his co-discovery of a form of bipolar disease, that continue to be cited in psychiatric literature. In 2001, he was appointed to the President's Council on Bioethics. Krauthammer also contributes to* Time *magazine, where the following essay appeared in December 2002.*

The eradication of smallpox was one of humanity's great success stories. After thousands of years of suffering at the hands of the virus, the human race gathered all its wit and cunning and conquered the scourge, eradicating it forever. Well, forever lasted less than 25 years. It does not bode well for the future of our species that it took but a blink of the eye for one of history's worst killers to make a comeback—not on its own, mind you, but brought back by humans to kill again.

During the age of innocence—the '90s, during which it seemed history had ended—the big debate was whether the two remaining known stocks of smallpox in the world, one in Russia and the other in the U.S., should be destroyed. It seemed like a wonderful idea, except that no one could be absolutely sure that some smallpox stores had not fallen into other hands. In fact, we now think Iraq is working on weaponizing smallpox, and perhaps North Korea and others too.

The danger is greater now than ever—first, and ironically, because of our very success in eradicating it in the past. People today have almost no experience with, and therefore no immunity to, the virus. We are nearly as virgin a population as the Native Americans who were wiped out by the various deadly pathogens brought over by Europeans. Not content with that potential for mass murder, however, today's bad guys are reportedly trying to genetically manipulate the virus to make it even deadlier and more resistant to treatment. Who knows what monstrosities the monsters are brewing in their secret laboratories.

4   What to do? We have enough vaccine on hand, some diluted but still effective, to vaccinate everyone in the U.S., with more full-strength versions to come. President

Bush has just announced that his Administration will take the concentric-circle approach: mandatory inoculations for certain soldiers, voluntary inoculations for medical and emergency workers, and then inoculations available to, but discouraged for, everybody else.

It sounds good, but it is not quite right. If smallpox were a threat just to individuals, then it could be left up to individuals to decide whether or not they want to protect themselves. When it comes to epidemic diseases, however, we don't leave it up to individuals to decide. The state decides.

Forget about smallpox. This happens every day with childhood diseases. No child can go to school unless he's been immunized. Parents have no choice. Think of it: we force parents to inject healthy children with organisms—some living, some dead—that in a small number of cases will cripple or kill the child. It is an extraordinary violation of the privacy and bodily integrity of the little citizen. Yet it is routine. Why? Because what is at stake is the vulnerability of the entire society to catastrophic epidemic. In that case, individuals must submit.

Which is why smallpox vaccines were mandatory when we were kids. It wasn't left up to you to decide if you wanted it. You might be ready to risk your life by forgoing the vaccine, but society would not let you—not because it was saving you from yourself but because it had to save others from you. The problem wasn't you getting smallpox; the problem was you giving smallpox to others if you got it. Society cannot tolerate that. We forced vaccination even though we knew it would maim and kill a small but certain number of those subjected to it.

8   Today the case for mandatory vaccination is even stronger. This is war. We need to respond as in war. The threat is not just against individuals, but against the nation. Smallpox kills a third of its victims. If this epidemic were to take hold, it could devastate America as a functioning society. And the government's highest calling is to protect society—a calling even higher than protecting individuals.

That is why conscription in wartime is justified. We violate the freedom of individuals by drafting them into combat, risking their lives—suspending, in effect, their right to life and liberty, to say nothing of the pursuit of happiness—in the name of the nation.

Vaccination is the conscription of civilians in the war against bioterrorism. I personally would choose not to receive the smallpox vaccine. I would not have my family injected. I prefer the odds of getting the disease vs. the odds of inflicting injury or death by vaccination on my perfectly healthy child.

Nonetheless, it should not be my decision. When what is at stake is the survival of the country, personal and family calculation must yield to national interest. And a population fully protected from smallpox is a supreme national interest.

12   If it is determined that the enemy really has smallpox and might use it, we should vaccinate everyone. We haven't been called upon to do very much for the country since Sept. 11. We can and should do this.

PERSONAL RESPONSE

Would you choose to have a smallpox vaccination if it were available and voluntary? Explain your answer.

QUESTIONS FOR CLASS OR SMALL-GROUP DISCUSSION

1. Analyze Krauthammer's argumentative strategy. Where does he state his position? What supporting proofs does he provide? What is his chief evidence in support of his position? How convincing is it?

2. How effective is Krauthammer's comparison of mandatory smallpox vaccination to conscription in wartime (paragraph 9)?

3. Are you persuaded by Krauthammer's argument?

RESTRUCTURING THE U.S. HEALTH CARE SYSTEM
Arnold S. Relman

Arnold S. Relman, Professor Emeritus of Medicine and Social Medicine at Harvard Medical School, is the former editor of The New England Journal of Medicine. *This article appeared in the Summer 2003 issue of* Issues in Science and Technology.

The past two decades have seen major economic changes in the health care system in the United States, but no solution has been found for the basic problem of cost control. Per-capita medical expenditures increased at an inflation-corrected rate of about 5 to 7 percent per year during most of this period, with health care costs consuming an ever-growing fraction of the gross national product. The rate of increase slowed a little for several years during the 1990s, with the spread of managed care programs. But the rate is now increasing more rapidly than ever, and control of medical costs has reemerged as a major national imperative. Failure to solve this problem has resulted in most of the other critical defects in the health care system. Half of all medical expenditures occur in the private sector, where employment-based health insurance provides at least partial coverage for most (but by no means all) people under age 65. Until the mid-1980s, most private insurance was of the indemnity type, in which the insurer simply paid the customary bills of hospitals and physicians. This coverage was offered by employers as a tax-free fringe benefit to employees (who might be required to contribute 10 to 20 percent of the cost as a copayment), and was tax-deductible for employers as a business cost. But the economic burden and unpredictability of ever-increasing premiums caused employers ultimately to abandon indemnity insurance for most of their workers. Companies increasingly turned to managed care plans, which contracted with employers to provide a given package of health care benefits at a negotiated and prearranged premium in a price-competitive market.

When the Clinton administration took office in 1993, one of its first initiatives was an ambitious proposal to introduce federally regulated competition among managed care plans. The objective was to control premium prices while ensuring that the public had universal care, received quality care, and could choose freely among care providers. It was hoped that all kinds of managed care plans, including the older not-for-profit plans as well as the more recent plans offered by investor-owned companies, would be attracted to the market and would want to compete for patients on a playing field kept level by government regulations.

But this initiative was sidetracked before even coming to a congressional vote. There was strong opposition from the private insurance industry, which saw huge profit-making opportunities in an unregulated managed care market but not under the Clinton plan. Moreover, the proposed plan's complexity and heavy dependence on government regulation frightened many people—including the leaders of the American Medical Association—into believing it was "socialized medicine."

4   The failure of this initiative delivered private health insurance into the hands of a new and aggressive industry that made enormous profits by keeping the lid on premiums while greatly reducing its expenditures on medical services—and keeping the difference as net income. This industry referred to its expenditures on care as "medical losses," a term that speaks volumes about the basic conflict between the health interests of patients and the financial interests of the investor-owned companies. But, in fact, there was an enormous amount of fat in the services that had been provided through traditional insurance, so these new managed care insurance businesses could easily spin gold for their investors, executives, and owners by eliminating many costs. They did this in many different ways, including denial of payment for hospitalizations and physicians' services deemed not medically essential by the insurer. The plans also forced price discounts from hospitals and physicians and made contracts that discouraged primary care physicians from spending much time with patients, ordering expensive tests, or referring patients to specialists. These tactics were temporarily successful in controlling expenditures in the private sector. Fueled by the great profits they made, managed care companies expanded rapidly. It then consolidated into a relatively few giant corporations that enjoyed great favor on Wall Street, and quickly came to exercise substantial influence over the political economy of U.S. health care.

The other half of medical expenditures is publicly funded, and this sector was not even temporarily successful in restraining costs. The government's initial step was to adopt a method of reimbursing hospitals based on diagnostic related groupings (DRGs). Rather than paying fees for each hospital day and for individual procedures, the government would pay a set amount for treating a patient with a given diagnosis. Hospitals were thus given powerful incentives to shorten stays and to cut corners in the use of resources for inpatient care. At the same time, they encouraged physicians to conduct many diagnostic and therapeutic procedures in ambulatory facilities that were exempt from DRG-based restrictions on reimbursement.

Meanwhile, the temporary success of private managed care insurance in holding down premiums—along with its much-touted (but never proven) claims of higher quality of care—suggested to many politicians that government could solve its health care cost problems by turning over much of the public system to private enterprise. Therefore, states began to contract out to private managed care plans a major part of the services provided under Medicaid to low-income people. The federal government, for political reasons, could not so cavalierly outsource care provided to the elderly under Medicare, but did begin to encourage those over 65 to join government-subsidized private plans in lieu of receiving Medicare benefits. For a time, up to 15 percent of Medicare beneficiaries chose to do so, mainly because the plans promised coverage for outpatient prescription drugs, which Medicare did not provide.

What about attempts to contain the rapidly rising physicians' bills for the great majority of Medicare beneficiaries who chose to remain in the traditional fee-for-service system? The government first considered paying doctors through a DRG-style system similar to that used for hospitals, but this idea was never implemented; and in 1990, a standardized fee schedule replaced the old "usual and customary" fees. Physicians found a way to maintain their incomes, however, by disaggregating (and thereby multiplying) billable services and by increasing the number of visits; and Medicare's payments for medical services continued to rise.

8   Cost-control efforts by for-profit managed care plans and by government have diminished the professional role of physicians as defenders of their patients' interests. Physicians have become more entrepreneurial and have entered into many different kinds of business arrangements with hospitals and outpatient facilities, in an effort not only to sustain their income but also to preserve their autonomy as professionals. Doctor-owned imaging centers, kidney dialysis units, and ambulatory surgery centers have proliferated. Physicians have acquired financial interests in the medical goods and services they use and prescribe. They have installed expensive new equipment in their offices that generates more billing and more income. And, in a recent trend, groups of physicians have been investing in hospitals that specialize in cardiac, orthopedic, or other kinds of specialty care, thus serving as competition for community-based general hospitals for the most profitable patients. Of course, all of these self-serving reactions to the cost-controlling efforts of insurers are justified by physicians as a way to protect the quality of medical care. Nevertheless, they increase the costs of health care, and they raise serious questions about financial influences on professional decisions.

In the private sector, managed care has failed in its promise to prevent sustained escalation in costs. Once all the excess was squeezed out, further cuts could only be achieved by cutting essentials. Meanwhile, new and more expensive technology continues to come online, inexorably pushing up medical expenditures. Employers are once again facing a disastrous inflation in costs that they clearly cannot and will not accept, and they are cutting back on covered benefits and shifting more costs to employees. Moreover, there has been a major public backlash against the restrictions imposed by managed care, forcing many state governments to pass laws that prevent private insurers from limiting the health care choices of patients and the medical decisions of physicians. The courts also have begun to side with complaints that managed care plans are usurping the prerogatives of physicians and harming patients.

In the public sector, a large fraction of those Medicare beneficiaries who chose to shift to managed care are now back with their standard coverage, either because they were dissatisfied and chose to leave their plans or because plans have terminated their government contracts for lack of profit. The unchecked rise in expenditures on the Medicaid and Medicare programs is causing government to cut back on benefits to patients and on payments to physicians and hospitals. Increased unemployment has reduced the numbers of those covered by job-related insurance and thus has expanded the ranks of the uninsured, which now total more than 41 million people. Reduced payments have caused many physicians to refuse to accept Medicaid patients. Some doctors are even considering whether they want to continue taking new elderly patients into their practices who do not have private Medigap insurance to supplement their Medicare coverage.

Major Changes Needed

What will the future bring? The present state of affairs cannot continue much longer. The health care system is imploding, and proposals for its rescue will be an important part of the national political debate in the upcoming election year. Most voters want a system that is affordable and yet provides good-quality care for everyone. Some people believe that modest, piecemeal improvements in the existing health care structure can do the job, but that seems unlikely. Major widespread changes will be needed.

12   Those people who think of health care as primarily an economic commodity, and of the health care system as simply another industry, are inclined to believe in market-based solutions. They suggest that more business competition in the insuring and delivering of medical care, and more consumer involvement in sharing costs and making health care choices, will rein in expenditures and improve the quality of care. However, they also believe that additional government expenditures will be required to cover the poor.

Those people who do not think that market forces can or should control the health care system usually advocate a different kind of reform. They favor a consolidated and universal not-for-profit insurance system. Some believe in funding this system entirely through taxes and others through a combination of taxes and employer and individual contributions. But the essential feature of this idea is that almost all payments should go directly to health care providers rather than to the middlemen and satellite businesses that now live off the health care dollar.

A consolidated insurance system of this kind—sometimes called a single-payer system—could eliminate many of the problems in today's hodgepodge of a system. However, sustained cost control and the realignment of incentives for physicians with the best interests of their patients will require still further reform in the organization of medical care. Fee-for-service private practice, as well as regulation of physician practices by managed care businesses, will need to be largely replaced by a system in which multispecialty not-for-profit groups of salaried physicians accept risk-free prepayment from the central insurer for the delivery of a defined benefit package of comprehensive care.

Such reform, seemingly utopian now, may eventually gain wide support as the failure of market-based health care services to meet the public's need becomes increasingly evident, and as the ethical values of the medical profession continue to erode in the rising tide of commercialism.

PERSONAL RESPONSE

What health plan, if any, do you have? Are you satisfied with your health plan?

QUESTIONS FOR CLASS OR SMALL-GROUP DISCUSSION

1. How effectively does Relman explain the problem of rising health-care costs for all parties concerned? State in your own words what you understand to be the views of physicians, insurers, employers, and the elderly on the current state of health care in the U. S.

2. How well does Relman explain the differences between those who view health care as an economic commodity and those who believe health care should not be market-driven?

3. What is Relman's argumentative strategy? Does he make a persuasive case for health care reform in the U. S.?

4. In his concluding paragraphs, Relman suggests a reform plan that he describes as "seemingly utopian." In what ways is it utopian? What is the likelihood of his plan's succeeding?

GLOBAL PUBLIC GOODS AND HEALTH

RICHARD D. SMITH

Richard D. Smith is Senior Lecturer in Health Economics at the School of Health Policy and Practice, University of East Anglia, England. "Global Public Goods and Health" is an editorial that appeared in the July, 2003, issue of Bulletin of the World Health Organization.

Health improvement requires collective as well as individual action, and the health of poor populations in particular requires collective action between countries as well as within them. Initiatives such as the Global Fund to Fight AIDS, Tuberculosis and Malaria reflect a growing awareness of this fact. However, initiating, organizing and financing collective actions for health at the global level presents a challenge to existing international organizations (1).

The concept of "global public goods" (GPGs) suggests one possible framework for considering these issues (2). In this expression, "goods" encompass a range of physical commodities (such as bread, books and shoes) but include services (such as security, information and travel), distinguishing between private and public goods. Most goods are "private" in the sense that their consumption can be withheld until a payment is made in exchange for them, and once consumed they cannot be consumed again. In contrast, once "public" goods are provided no one can be excluded from consuming them (they are non-excludable), and one person's consumption of them does not prevent anyone else's (they are non-rival in consumption) (3). For example, no one in a population can be excluded from benefiting from a reduction in risk of infectious disease when its incidence is reduced, and one person benefiting from this reduction in risk does not prevent anyone else from benefiting from it as well.

Global public goods are goods of this kind whose benefits cross borders and are global in scope. For example, reductions in carbon dioxide emissions will slow global warming. It will be impossible to exclude any country from benefiting from this, and each country will benefit without preventing another from doing so. Similarly, the eradication of infectious diseases of global scope, such as smallpox or polio, provides a benefit from which no country is excluded, and from which all countries will benefit without detriment to others.

4   However, these attributes of public goods give rise to a paradox: although there is significant benefit to be gained from them by many people, there is no commercial incentive for producing them, since enjoyment cannot be made conditional on payment. With national public goods, the government therefore intervenes either financially, through such mechanisms as taxation or licensing, or with direct provision. But for global public goods this is harder to do, because no global government exists to ensure that they are produced and paid for. The central issue for health-related GPGs is how best to ensure that the collective action necessary, for health is taken at the international level.

Globalization of travel, changes in technology, and the liberalization of trade all affect health. Communicable diseases spread more rapidly, often in drug-resistant form (4), environmental degradation reduces access to clean air and water, and knowledge of traditional and modern health technologies is increasingly patented and thus made artificially excludable (5). However, discussion of GPGs to date has typically been broad-based and multisectoral (for instance on the environment, international security and trade agreements), and most of the discussion within the health sector has been focused on medical technologies (3, 6, 7).

This has left many questions unanswered (8). For example, is health itself a GPG? To what extent does my (national) health depend on your (national) health? How many of the actions necessary to global health—communicable disease control, generation and dissemination of medical knowledge, public health infrastructure—constitute GPGs? What contribution can the GPG concept make to fulfilling these needs? Is international financing for these GPGs best coordinated through voluntary contributions, global taxation systems, or market-based mechanisms? Does the concept of GPGs undermine or support concepts of equity and human rights?

The first large-scale study of the application of the GPG concept to the health sector examines questions such as these, and has just been published (8). The study finds that, while the concept has important limitations, for some areas of health work it can offer guidance in the financing and provision of global health programmes. In these areas it provides a framework for collective action at the global level, demonstrates the advantages for the rich in helping the poor, and provides a rationale for industrialized countries to use national health budgets to complement traditional aid (as seen in the Polio Eradication Initiative (9)). Overall, the GPG concept will be increasingly important as a rationale and a guide for public health work in an era of globalization.

Endnotes[1]

(1.) Drager N. & Beaglehole, R. Globalization: Changing the public health landscape. *Bulletin of the World Health Organization* 2001; 79: 803.

[1]Endnotes are reproduced as originally published and do not conform to either MLA or APA style. [Ed.]

(2.) Kaul I & Faust, M. Global public goods and health: Taking the agenda forward. *Bulletin of the World Health Organization* 2001; 79: 869-74.

(3.) Kaul I, Grunberg I, Stern MA, editors. *Global public goods: International cooperation in the 21st century.* New York: Oxford University Press; 1999.

(4.) Smith RD, Coast J. Antimicrobial resistance: a global response. *Bulletin of the World Health Organization* 2002; 80:126-33.

(5.) Thorsteinsdottir H, Daar A, Smith RD, Singer P. Genomics—a global public good? *Lancet* 2003; 361:891-2.

(6.) Kaul I, Conceicao P, Le Goulven K, Mendoza RU, editors. *Providing global public goods: managing globalization.* New York: Oxford University Press; 2003.

(7.) *Macroeconomics and health: investing in health for economic development. Report of the Commission on Macroeconomics and Health.* Geneva: World Health Organization; 2001.

(8.) Smith RD, Beaglehole R, Woodward D, Drager N, editors. *Global public goods for health: a health economic and public health perspective.* Oxford: Oxford University Press; 2003.

(9.) Aylward B, Acharya A, England S, et al. Achieving global health goals: the politics and economics of polio eradication, *Lancet* (forthcoming).

PERSONAL RESPONSE

Do you agree that the issue of health care requires collective rather than individual action (paragraph 1)? How would you answer Smith's question in paragraph 6: "Is health itself a GPG"?

QUESTIONS FOR CLASS OR SMALL-GROUP DISCUSSION

1. Does Smith clearly define the concept of "global public goods"? How well do his examples in paragraphs 2 and 3 serve to illustrate that concept?
2. How well does Smith explain the paradox that he mentions in paragraph 4?
3. Do you agree with Smith that the GPG model would work in the health sector?
4. What is the rhetorical effect of the series of questions in paragraph 6?

WE ALL HAVE AIDS

Wayne Ellwood

Wayne Ellwood joined the UK-based global issues magazine, New Internationalist, *in 1977 as an editor. In the early 1980s he worked as an assistant producer for the BBC Television series,* Global Report, *traveling to Liberia and Zimbabwe. In 1984 he spent a year in Malaysia, Thailand and Indonesia. In addition, he has traveled for*

New Internationalist in Asia, Africa, the United States, and Australia. He is the editor of The A-Z of World Development *(1995) and author of* The No Nonsense Guide to Globalization *(2001). This article appeared in the June, 2002, issue of* New Internationalist.

They are the dead who walk again: the Lazarus men. Invisible to most of us, these are the gay males, now in their 30s and 40s, who first contracted the HIV virus 10, 15 and even 20 years ago. Through a combination of raw courage, determination and powerful new drug therapies, they have managed to keep the disease at bay.

Steve Mueller is one of those survivors. He is a warm, articulate 42-year-old with sharp, sculpted features, a halo of black curls and a hacking cough—the legacy of a battle with HIV which is not yet over. We're sitting in a crowded lunch spot in the heart of Toronto's Little Italy, straining to hear each other amidst the jangle of crashing cutlery and the hum of animated conversations ricocheting around the room. "I could fill these tables with guys who are gone," he nods, glancing quickly across the crowded restaurant.

Steve has been through a lot since he discovered he was HIV positive back in the early 1990s. Then he was teaching psychology at a small community college in the city, enjoying life, financially secure, with a partner who was an affluent executive in the advertising business. Life was good, he was living "by the rules."

4   Then he got sick and his world shattered. He lost his job; his partner, also HIV positive, died within a year. And then Steve contracted meningitis, one of the often deadly "opportunistic diseases" that strike the battered immune systems of people with HIV.

"The doctors told me in June 1995 that I was unlikely to see Christmas. I'd gone from 180 to 120 lbs and I was still losing weight. Then I started on the AIDS cocktail; it literally pulled me back from the edge. They called guys like me, who were dying and then bounced back, the Lazarus men."

Steve's life, and the lives of many other people with HIV/AIDS (PHAs), was turned around by the discovery of effective "antiretroviral" medications (ARVs) a decade ago. These drugs are not a cure for HIV but they can be a way of controlling the virus, enabling many people to work and lead otherwise normal lives again.

But as important as they've been in the West, they have made scarcely a dent in those parts of the world where HIV rages unchecked. Soon after HIV was identified in North America it leapt from the homosexual to the heterosexual community, and then from the gay "ghettos" of Seattle and New York to the slums of Port-au-Prince, Bangkok and Mumbai.

8   Today, the disease once branded as a "gay plague" has become, overwhelmingly, a heterosexual disease: 75 percent of worldwide HIV transmission is now due to heterosexual sex. And while the spread of HIV across the North has slowed due to vigorous treatment and prevention campaigns, the virus continues to cut a widening swath across the South.

The numbers are brutally stark. Twenty-two million people dead from AIDS-related illnesses since the disease was first discovered just 20 years ago—more people than died in Europe during the Black Death of the Middle Ages. Three million people dead last year alone. Thirty-six million people are now infected—25 million in sub-Saharan Africa where the disease threatens to hobble human development for decades. In Botswana, 36 per cent of adults have the HIV virus, in South Africa more than 5 million people are infected—20 per cent of the adult population. (1)

AIDS is eroding economic progress and fracturing social stability across sub-Saharan Africa and will do so in other parts of the world unless urgent action is taken. Average life expectancy in more than a dozen African countries has dropped by 17 years due to AIDS—from 64 to 47 years. Zimbabweans have to cope both with the septuagenarian autocrat, Robert Mugabe, and with an AIDS epidemic which has shaved 26 years off their average life span. Families without breadwinners are thrown into a downward spiral of poverty and hunger. A quarter of all families in Botswana can expect to lose a wage earner in the next 10 years, slashing household income and forcing those who remain to do whatever they can to make ends meet. According to the UN Food and Agricultural Organization (FAO) more than 16 million farm workers will die from AIDS in the next 20 years with incalculable impact on food production and hunger. The Zambian Government says it has lost one-in-three teachers to AIDS. (1)

"Let us not equivocate," warns Nelson Mandela, "AIDS today in Africa is claiming more lives than the sum total of all wars, famines and floods, and the ravages of such deadly diseases as malaria. It is devastating families and communities."

12   Millions of people are being cut down in their prime leaving a continent of old people and orphans. There are more than 13 million AIDS orphans in Africa—Zambia alone has a million kids who have lost their parents to the virus. With the adult workforce so depleted, more kids are forced to leave school to support brothers and sisters. The Tanzanian sociologist, Gabriel Rugalema, reports that in the province of Kagera in Northwest Tanzania orphans make up nearly 20 per cent of the population. Rugalema worries that AIDS is upending the tribal clan structure and tearing apart the social fabric. It's a catastrophe in the making, a breeding ground for crime and social chaos.

But describing the terrible consequences of this disease doesn't confront the most fundamental question: what's driving the epidemic? Why is it that HIV infection rates vary so dramatically from one part of the globe to another? Just as there is no reason to believe that people are more sexually active in Lusaka than they are in London, so there is no reason to believe that human behaviour is the sole determinant of the rate of infection.

The great French pioneer in epidemiology, Louis Pasteur, wrote: "The microbe is nothing; the terrain, everything." That was Pasteur's way of saying that epidemics are never merely biological. They are shaped and amplified by social forces which are in turn set in motion by economic change. Just as the bubonic plague thrived in the crowded, pestilential European cities which provided the breeding grounds for the rats which spread the disease, so too AIDS spreads along the fault lines of poverty, gender and class inequality.

In recounting the case histories of three of his patients in rural Haiti, the medical anthropologist and doctor Paul Farmer notes that in all three cases "the declining fortunes of the rural poor pushed young adults to try their chances in the city. Once there, all three became entangled in unions that the women, at least, characterized as attempts to emerge from poverty. Each worked as a domestic, but none managed to fulfill the expectation of saving and sending home desperately needed cash. What they brought home, instead, was AIDS." (2)

16   Commercial sex work, urbanization and poverty-driven job migration are exacerbated by imposed economic adjustment policies and debt. Colonialism set the template for African labour migration, tearing men away from their villages and families to work in mines and plantations. The collapse of rural economies across the South in the wake of mechanized farming and the spread of cash-crop exports continued the forced exodus of peasants to the cities in search of work. The South African photographer Gideon Mendel, who has chronicled the AIDS epidemic for more than a decade, has this to say about his country's migrant-labour scheme:

"You go to some of the mines and there are between 20,000 and 30,000 men working there. They go home for two weeks a year. The mines are surrounded by squatter camps full of sex workers, many of whom are infected with HIV. If an evil genius were asked to design an ideal scenario for the spread of AIDS, he couldn't come up with anything better." (3)

More recently, structural-adjustment policies intended to "modernize" Southern economies have accelerated labour migration and urbanization. Spending on health and education has been slashed, fueling illiteracy and ignorance which foils AIDS prevention. In the midst of a skyrocketing AIDS epidemic in the early 1990s the World Bank instructed Kenya that public clinics should charge a user fee of $2.15 for an examination which revealed the presence of sexually-transmitted diseases (STDs). Attendance fell in some cases by as much as 60 per cent. When health clinics are too expensive or too far away, untreated STDs multiply the chances of contracting and spreading the HIV virus. (4) Chronic malnutrition due to poverty weakens natural defenses, making people more vulnerable to infection.

Up to now the ABC of AIDS prevention has focused on changing individual behaviour to arrest the spread of the disease: (A)bstain, (B)e faithful to one partner and use a (C)ondom. This tactic has put a brake on the virus in parts of Africa, notably Uganda and in Asian countries like Thailand and Cambodia. The prevalence of HIV in pregnant women in Cambodia fell from 3.2 to 2.3 per cent from 1997 to 2000 due to a concerted education campaign. (1) And there's no doubt the safe-sex message has helped curb HIV transmission rates across the West, where AIDS deaths and new infection rates have edged steadily downwards over the past decade.

20   But handing out condoms will never be enough. As Pasteur might have said, they may stop the microbe but they don't change the terrain. HIV spreads by exploiting cultural and economic conditions. How do you deal with the claim that in Zimbabwe: "It is very difficult for a man who is married to use a condom with his wife, since condoms are for prostitutes." (5) Or the fact that more knowledge may not result in more use. The Indian journalist, Radhakrishna Rao, writes that "health workers in India speak of how males have worn condoms on their thumbs or middle fingers during coitus, just like in the demonstrations. And one young female AIDS educator who

distributed condoms among women in one of the slums in Hyderabad was aghast to find that many women were not so happy with the 'strange-looking device' as they had difficulty swallowing it." (6)

And then there is the shadow of stigma. As UNAIDS notes: "It is always easier to blame others for the spread of HIV, but progress against the epidemic is only possible when communities own the problem of AIDS themselves." Being honest and open is the first and most important step in dealing with the virus. Yet everywhere HIV-positive people are reluctant to be tested, for fear of censure and discrimination. This sets in motion a cycle of guilt, shame and denial which impedes both treatment and prevention. More than half of a group of HIV-positive women in Kenya hid the news from their partners because they feared they'd be beaten or abandoned. (1) And in Swaziland last year prominent politicians proposed that PHAs should be forced to wear identification badges and be herded into special segregated areas where they would not be able to contaminate "normal people." (7) But prejudice is not confined to the South. A March 2002 survey published by the *American Journal of Public Health* found that half of all Americans still believe they can get HIV through everyday contact with a person infected with the virus and half also support mandatory testing of groups most at risk of HIV infection.

It's no accident that the marginalized and the poor are the ones most deeply affected by the disease. A graph of the rates of incidence in the US is telling—with infection amongst Black and Hispanic populations marching ever upwards while that of White Americans continues to decline. The same is true in Canada for native people, where infection rates jumped 90 per cent from 1996 to 1999. Aboriginal people are 2.8 per cent of the Canadian population but made up nearly 9 per cent of all new HIV infections in 1999. (8)

Poverty doesn't cause AIDS. But it is the ideal incubator. And gender and poverty are inextricably combined: 70 percent of the world's poor are women and poor women are most susceptible to HIV. Violence against women and sexual assault are cornerstones of the AIDS epidemic. Says UN special AIDS envoy Stephen Lewis: "Until there is a much greater degree of gender equality, women will always constitute the greatest number of new infections. You cannot have millions of women effectively sexually subjugated, forced into sex which is risky without condoms, without the capacity to say no, without the right to negotiate sexual relationships."

24   Unequal power relations mean poor women can be more easily abused or coerced into dangerous sexual encounters. Researchers from Soul City, a health-education agency in Cape Town, found "a pervasive sense of male entitlement to sex and the right to discipline disobedient partners." Said one young girl: "When a woman refuses to have sex for no reason, then a man is obliged to beat that woman." (9) Without property or skills, women are forced to sell their bodies to feed themselves and their children—a dismal choice but one which is more lucrative than the alternative. Poverty means sex workers are more concerned with day-to-day survival than the threat of an infection whose deadly consequences lie many years in the future.

Treatment for HIV depends not on medical need but on where you live and how much you can afford to pay. It is unconscionable that millions of AIDS patients across the South suffer and die while drugs which could ease their pain and prolong their lives are denied to them. The death-rate from AIDS in the US dropped by 40 per cent over the last decade as a result of antiretroviral drugs. But the current price for a year of triple combination therapy in the West can be as high as $10,000. Compulsory licensing and the opening of Southern markets to manufacturers of generic drugs could dramatically increase their availability. But even for generics to be affordable in the poorest countries the cost will need to plummet.

There has been a high-profile fight against the giant pharmaceutical companies that control the manufacture of ARVs. Countries like Brazil and India are on the front line of this battle. But the multinationals have mostly held their ground, despite insistent demands from 'treatment action' campaigns in South Africa and elsewhere. The drugs are not a panacea but they do improve quality of life and boost life expectancy. They provide hope in the midst of despair and, critically, offer an incentive to be tested for those who may carry the virus. And visible, effective treatment also helps overcome the social stigma, which is still so pervasive. Treatment benefits communities and individuals, with fewer hospitalizations, fewer deaths, fewer infected infants and fewer orphans. Those treated can support their families and are likely to be less infectious.

UN Secretary-General Kofi Annan has established a global AIDS Fund with an initial target of $10 billion. So far the Fund has garnered about $2.0 billion in pledges. The Bush administration, which came up with $50 billion to fight global terrorism after the 11 September 2001 attack on the US, has committed a mere $200 million. More resources are urgently needed for care and prevention, as well as treatment.

28   The hardest-hit countries can't do it on their own—especially not when global economic conditions are conspiring against them. With healthcare systems limping, debt payments draining national budgets and nations, North and South, diverting millions into antiterrorism measures and military spending, the prospect of more resources to fight AIDS seems slim.

There are no short-term solutions. But there are solutions. Some of the most inspiring efforts are being carried out by PHAs themselves working in small-scale NGOs [non-governmental organizations]. As a group of African women declared at a recent gathering on HIV in Kampala: "Without HIV-positive people, researchers can not do their work. We are the real experts in our communities about how HIV infection affects individuals and their families." (10)

Steve Mueller is one of those experts. Until his latest bout of oesophageal cancer he worked with the Toronto People with AIDS Foundation (PWA)—a lean, street-smart agency offering practical advice on everything from housing to alternative therapies.

"Mentally, AIDS is a huge, stigmatized death sentence," he says. "Suicide is a big concern. So whenever I dealt with clients the first thing I'd say was: 'Like you, I also had to live with the disease.' You have to be a role model; you're sick and you're back in the work force. You might die next week and you might last another 50 years, nobody knows for sure. All kinds of awful things could happen to you and all kinds of wonderful things. But if you jump off a balcony you'll never know."

32   There are also countless successful projects, like Toronto's PWA Foundation, peppered across the South. But they are swamped by the virulence and intensity of

the virus itself. The time for a fully resourced, international, multi-dimensional programme is now. Already the virus is racing through India, China, Russia and Eastern Europe. The AIDS historian, Allan Brandt, wrote these words in 1988:

"In the years ahead we will, no doubt, learn a great deal more about AIDS and how to control it. We will also learn a great deal about the nature of our society from the manner in which we address the disease. AIDS will be the standard by which we measure not only our medical and scientific skill but also our capacity for justice and compassion." (2)

The simple truth of that analysis would not be lost on Steve Mueller.

Endnotes[2]

(1.) *AIDS Epidemic Update,* UNAIDS/WHO, December 2001.

(2.) Paul Farmer, *Infections and Inequalities: The Modern Plagues,* University of California Press, 1999.

(3.) Gideon Mendel, *A Broken Landscape: HIV and Africa,* Network/ActionAid, London, 2001.

(4.) J Collins and B Rau, *AIDS in the Context of Development,* UN Research Institute for Social Development, Paper no 4, December 2000.

(5.) Vincent Mwanma, *Africa Recovery,* December 2001.

(6.) Radhakrishna Rao, "Taming HIV/AIDS in India," unpublished article available on the NI web site: www.newint.org

(7.) Lunga Masuku, Swaziland's AIDS Ambassador, Africa Eye News Service, August 2001.

(8.) HIV/AIDS among aboriginal persons in Canada remains a pressing issue, Health Canada. www.hcsc.gc.ca/hpb/lcdc/bah/epi/aborig_e.html

(9.) Shereen Usdin, "Violence against women is fueling the AIDS epidemic," Soul City Institute for Health and Development Communication, 2001.

(10.) *The Focus on Women Kampala Declaration,* text drafted by 130 Ugandan women at Third International Conference on Global Strategies for the Prevention of HIV Transmission, September, 2001.

PERSONAL RESPONSE

What, if anything, do you think the U. S. should do to help the AIDS victims that Ellwood writes about?

QUESTIONS FOR CLASS OR SMALL-GROUP DISCUSSION

1. How is the impact of the opening paragraphs, especially Ellwood's use of a specific person to illustrate "the Lazarus men"? How does the example of Steve Mueller function in the essay overall?

---

[2]Endnotes are reproduced as originally published and do not conform to either MLA or APA style. [Ed.]

2. What use does Ellwood make of the quotation from Louis Pasteur: "The microbe is nothing; the terrain, everything" (paragraph 14)? How does Ellwood apply that statement to his point about AIDS?

3. Analyze the case that Ellwood makes for the AIDS epidemic's being more than just biological but social and economic as well. What role do gender and poverty play in the AIDS epidemic?

4. Ellwood suggests that the AIDS epidemic in third-world countries is everyone's problem, especially those countries like the U. S. who can afford drugs that would make life easier for AIDS victims. Are you sympathetic with Ellwood's position?

DEATH STALKS A CONTINENT

Johanna McGeary

Johanna McGeary, a Time *magazine reporter, spent a month traveling through South Africa, Botswana, and Zimbabwe doing research for this February 12, 2001, cover story.*

Imagine your life this way. You get up in the morning and breakfast with your three kids. One is already doomed to die in infancy. Your husband works 200 miles away, comes home twice a year and sleeps around in between. You risk your life in every act of sexual intercourse. You go to work past a house where a teenager lives alone tending young siblings without any source of income. At another house, the wife was branded a whore when she asked her husband to use a condom, beaten silly and thrown into the streets. Over there lies a man desperately sick without access to a doctor or clinic or medicine or food or blankets or even a kind word. At work you eat with colleagues, and every third one is already fatally ill. You whisper about a friend who admitted she had the plague and whose neighbors stoned her to death. Your leisure is occupied by the funerals you attend every Saturday. You go to bed fearing adults your age will not live into their 40s. You and your neighbors and your political and popular leaders act as if nothing is happening.

Across the southern quadrant of Africa, this nightmare is real. The word not spoken is AIDS, and here at ground zero of humanity's deadliest cataclysm, the ultimate tragedy is that so many people don't know—or don't want to know—what is happening.

As the HIV virus sweeps mercilessly through these lands—the fiercest trial Africa has yet endured—a few try to address the terrible depredation. The rest of society looks away. Flesh and muscle melt from the bones of the sick in packed hospital wards and lonely bush kraals. Corpses stack up in morgues until those on top crush the identity from the faces underneath. Raw earth mounds scar the landscape, grave after grave without name or number. Bereft children grieve for parents lost in their prime, for siblings scattered to the winds.

4   The victims don't cry out. Doctors and obituaries do not give the killer its name. Families recoil in shame. Leaders shirk responsibility. The stubborn silence heralds victory for the disease: denial cannot keep the virus at bay.

The developed world is largely silent too. AIDS in Africa has never commanded the full-bore response the West has brought to other, sometimes lesser, travails. We pay sporadic attention, turning on the spotlight when an international conference occurs, then turning it off. Good-hearted donors donate; governments acknowledge that more needs to be done. But think how different the effort would be if what is happening here were happening in the West.

By now you've seen pictures of the sick, the dead, the orphans. You've heard appalling numbers: the number of new infections, the number of the dead, the number who are sick without care, the number walking around already fated to die.

But to comprehend the full horror AIDS has visited on Africa, listen to the woman we have dubbed Laetitia Hambahlane in Durban or the boy Tsepho Phale in Francistown or the woman who calls herself Thandiwe in Bulawayo or Louis Chikoka, a longdistance trucker. You begin to understand how AIDS has struck Africa—with a biblical virulence that will claim tens of millions of lives—when you hear about shame and stigma and ignorance and poverty and sexual violence and migrant labor and promiscuity and political paralysis and the terrible silence that surrounds all this dying. It is a measure of the silence that some asked us not to print their real names to protect their privacy.

8   Theirs is a story about what happens when a disease leaps the confines of medicine to invade the body politic, infecting not just individuals but an entire society. As AIDS migrated to man in Africa, it mutated into a complex plague with confounding social, economic and political mechanics that locked together to accelerate the virus's progress. The region's social dynamics colluded to spread the disease and help block effective intervention.

We have come to three countries abutting one another at the bottom of Africa— Botswana, South Africa, Zimbabwe—the heart of the heart of the epidemic. For nearly a decade, these nations suffered a hidden invasion of infection that concealed the dimension of the coming calamity. Now the omni-present dying reveals the shocking scale of the devastation.

AIDS in Africa bears little resemblance to the American epidemic, limited to specific high-risk groups and brought under control through intensive education, vigorous political action and expensive drug therapy. Here the disease has bred a Darwinian perversion. Society's fittest, not its frailest, are the ones who die—adults spirited away, leaving the old and the children behind. You cannot define risk groups: everyone who is sexually active is at risk. Babies too, unwittingly infected by mothers. Barely a single family remains untouched. Most do not know how or when they caught the virus, many never know they have it, many who do know don't tell anyone as they lie dying. Africa can provide no treatment for those with AIDS.

They will all die, of tuberculosis, pneumonia, meningitis, diarrhea, whatever overcomes their ruined immune systems first. And the statistics, grim as they are, may be too low. There is no broad-scale AIDS testing: infection rates are calculated mainly from the presence of HIV in pregnant women. Death certificates in these countries do not record AIDS as the cause. "Whatever stats we have are not reliable," warns Mary Crewe of the University of Pretoria's Center for the Study of AIDS. "Everybody's guessing."

The TB Patient

12   Case No. 309 in the Tugela Ferry Home-Care Program shivers violently on the wooden planks someone has knocked into a bed, a frayed blanklet pulled right up to his nose. He has the flushed skin, overbright eyes and careful breathing of the tubercular. He is alone, and it is chilly within the crumbling mud walls of his hut at Msinga Top, a windswept outcrop high above the Tugela River in South Africa's KwaZulu-Natal province. The spectacular view of hills and veld would gladden a well man, but the 22-year-old we will call Fundisi Khumalo, though he does not know it, has AIDS, and his eyes seem to focus inward on his simple fear.

Before he can speak, his throat clutches in gasping spasms. Sharp pains rack his chest; his breath comes in shallow gasps. The vomiting is better today. But constipation has doubled up his knees, and he is too weak to go outside to relieve himself. He can't remember when he last ate. He can't remember how long he's been sick—"a long time, maybe since six months ago." Khumalo knows he has TB, and he believes it is just TB. "I am only thinking of that," he answers when we ask why he is so ill.

But the fear never leaves his eyes. He worked in a hair salon in Johannesburg, lived in a men's hostel in one of the cheap townships, had "a few" girlfriends. He knew other young men in the hostel who were on-and-off sick. When they fell too ill to work anymore, like him, they straggled home to rural villages like Msinga Top. But where Khumalo would not go is the hospital. "Why?" he says. "You are sick there, you die there."

"He's right, you know," says Dr. Tony Moll, who has driven us up the dirt track from the 350-bed hospital he heads in Tugela Ferry. "We have no medicines for AIDS. So many hospitals tell them, 'You've got AIDS. We can't help you. Go home and die.' " No one wants to be tested either, he adds, unless treatment is available. "If the choice is to know and get nothing," he says, "they don't want to know."

16   Here and in scattered homesteads all over rural Africa, the dying people say the sickness afflicting their families and neighbors is just the familiar consequence of their eternal poverty. Or it is the work of witchcraft. You have done something bad and have been bewitched. Your neighbor's jealously has invaded you. You have not appeased the spirits of your ancestors, and they have cursed you. Some in South Africa believe the disease was introduced by the white population as a way to control black Africans after the end of apartheid.

Ignorance about AIDS remains profound. But because of the funerals, southern Africans can't help seeing that something more systematic and sinister lurks out there. Every Saturday and often Sundays too, neighbors trudge to the cemeteries for costly burial rites for the young and the middle-aged who are suddenly dying so much faster than the old. Families say it was pneumonia, TB, malaria that killed their son, their wife, their baby. "But you starting to hear the truth," says Durban home-care volunteer Busi Magwazi. "In the church, in the graveyard, they saying, 'Yes, she died of AIDS.' Oh, people talking about it even if the families don't admit it."

Ignorance is the crucial reason the epidemic has run out of control. Surveys say many Africans here are becoming aware there is a sexually transmitted disease called AIDS that is incurable. But they don't think the risk applies to them. And their vague knowledge does not translate into changes in their sexual behavior. It's easy to see why so many don't yet sense the danger when few talk openly about the disease. And Africans are beset by so plentiful a roster of perils—famine, war, the violence of desperation or ethnic hatred, the regular illnesses of poverty, the dangers inside mines or on the roads—that the delayed risk of AIDS ranks low.

The Outcast

To acknowledge AIDS in yourself is to be branded as monstrous. Laetitia Hambahlane (not her real name) is 51 and sick with AIDS. So is her brother. She admits it; he doesn't. In her mother's broken-down house in the mean streets of Umlazi township, though, Laetitia's mother hovers over her son, nursing him, protecting him, resolutely denying he has anything but TB, though his sister claims the sure symptoms of AIDS mark him. Laetitia is the outcast, first from her family, then from her society.

20   For years Laetitia worked as a domestic servant in Durban and dutifully sent all her wages home to her mother. She fell in love a number of times and bore four children. "I loved that last man," she recalls. "After he left, I had no one, no sex." That was 1992, but Laetitia already had HIV.

She fell sick in 1996, and her employers sent her to a private doctor who couldn't diagnose an illness. He tested her blood and found she was HIV positive. "I wish I'd died right then," she says, as tears spill down her sunken cheeks. "I asked the doctor, 'Have you got medicine?' He said no. I said, 'Can't you keep me alive?' " The doctor could do nothing and sent her away. "I couldn't face the world," she says. "I couldn't sleep at night. I sat on my bed, thinking, praying. I did not see anyone day or night. I ask God, Why?"

Laetitia's employers fired her without asking her exact diagnosis. For weeks she could not muster the courage to tell anyone. Then she told her children, and they were ashamed and frightened. Then, harder still, she told her mother. Her mother raged about the loss of money if Laetitia could not work again. She was so angry she ordered Laetitia out of the house. When her daughter wouldn't leave, the mother threatened to sell the house to get rid of her daughter. Then she walled off her daughter's room with plywood partitions, leaving the daughter a pariah, alone in a cramped, dark space without windows and only a flimsy door opening into the alley. Laetitia must earn the pennies to feed herself and her children by peddling beer, cigarettes and candy from a shopping cart in her room, when people are brave enough to stop by her door. "Sometimes they buy, sometimes not," she says. "That is how I'm surviving."

Her mother will not talk to her. "If you are not even accepted by your own family," says Magwazi, the volunteer home-care giver from Durban's Sinoziso project who visits Laetitia, "then others will not accept you." When Laetitia ventures outdoors, neighbors snub her, tough boys snatch her purse, children taunt her. Her own kids are tired of the sickness and don't like to help her anymore. "When I can't get up, they don't bring me food," she laments. One day local youths barged into her room, cursed her as a witch and a whore and beat her. When she told the police, the youths returned, threatening to burn down the house.

24   But it is her mother's rejection that wounds Laetitia most. "She is hiding it about my brother," she cries. "Why will she do nothing for me?" Her hands pick restlessly at the quilt covering her paper-thin frame. "I know my mother will not bury me properly. I know she will not take care of my kids when I am gone."

Jabulani Syabusi would use his real name, but he needs to protect his brother. He teaches school in a red, dusty district of KwaZulu-Natal. People here know the disease is all around them, but no one speaks of it. He eyes the scattered huts that make up his little settlement on an arid bluff. "We can count 20 who died just here as far as we can see. I personally don't remember any family that told it was AIDS," he says. "They hide it if they do know."

Syabusi's own family is no different. His younger brother is also a teacher who has just come home from Durban too sick to work anymore. He says he has tuberculosis, but after six months the tablets he is taking have done nothing to cure him. Syabusi's wife Nomsange, a nurse, is concerned that her 36-year-old brother-in-law may have something worse. Syabusi finally asked the doctor tending his brother what is wrong. The doctor said the information is confidential and will not tell him. Neither will his brother. "My brother is not brave enough to tell me," says Syabusi, as he stares sadly toward the house next door, where his only sibling lies ill. "And I am not brave enough to ask him."

Kennedy Fugewane, a cheerful, elderly volunteer counselor, sits in an empty U.S.-funded clinic that offers fast, pinprick blood tests in Francistown, Botswana, pondering how to break through the silence. This city suffers one of the world's highest infection rates, but people deny the disease because HIV is linked with sex. "We don't reveal anything," he says. "But people are so stigmatized even if they walk in the door." Africans feel they must keep private anything to do with sex. "If a man comes here, people will say he is running around," says Fugewane, though he acknowledges that men never do come. "If a woman comes, people will say she is loose. If anyone says they got HIV, they will be despised."

28   Pretoria University's Mary Crewe says, "It is presumed if you get AIDS, you have done something wrong." HIV labels you as living an immoral life. Embarrassment about sexuality looms more important than future health risks. "We have no language to talk candidly about sex," she says, "so we have no civil language to talk about AIDS." Volunteers like Fugewane try to reach out with flyers, workshops, youth meetings and free condoms, but they are frustrated by a culture that values its dignity over saving lives. "People here don't have the courage to come forward and say, 'Let me know my HIV status,' " he sighs, much less the courage to do something about it. "Maybe one day . . ."

Doctors bow to social pressure and legal strictures not to record AIDS on death certificates. "I write TB or meningitis or diarrhea but never AIDS," says South Africa's Dr. Moll. "It's a public document, and families would hate it if anyone knew." Several years ago, doctors were barred even from recording compromised immunity or HIV status on a medical file; now they can record the results of blood tests for AIDS on patient charts to protect other health workers. Doctors like Moll have long agitated to apply the same openness to death certificates.

The Truck Driver

Here, men have to migrate to work, inside their countries or across borders. All that mobility sows HIV far and wide, as Louis Chikoka is the first to recognize. He regularly drives the highway that is Botswana's economic lifeline and its curse. The road runs for 350 miles through desolate bush that is the Texas-size country's sole strip of habitable land, home to a large majority of its 1.5 million people. It once brought prospectors to Botswana's rich diamond reefs. Now it's the link for transcontinental truckers like Chikoka who haul goods from South Africa to markets in the continent's center. And now the road brings AIDS.

Chikoka brakes his dusty, diesel-belching Kabwe Transport 18-wheeler to a stop at the dark roadside rest on the edge of Francistown, where the international trade routes converge and at least 43% of adults are HIV-positive. He is a cheerful man even after 12 hard hours behind the wheel freighting rice from Durban. He's been on the road for two weeks and will reach his destination in Congo next Thursday. At 39, he is married, the father of three and a long-haul trucker for 12 years. He's used to it.

32   Lighting up a cigarette, the jaunty driver is unusually loquacious about sex as he eyes the dim figures circling the rest stop. Chikoka has parked here for a quickie. See that one over there, he points with his cigarette. "Those local ones we call bitches. They always waiting here for short service." Short service? "It's according to how long it takes you to ejaculate," he explains. "We go to the 'bush bedroom' over there [waving at a clump of trees 100 yds. away] or sometimes in the truck. Short service, that costs you 20 rands [$2.84]. They know we drivers always got money."

Chikoka nods his head toward another woman sitting beside a stack of cardboard cartons. "We like better to go to them," he says. They are the "businesswomen," smugglers with gray-market cases of fruit and toilet paper and toys that they need to transport somewhere up the road. "They come to us, and we negotiate privately about carrying their goods." It's a no-cash deal, he says. "They pay their bodies to us." Chikoka shrugs at a suggestion that the practice may be unhealthy. "I been away two weeks, madam. I'm human. I'm a man. I have to have sex." What he likes best is dry sex. In parts of sub-Saharan Africa, to please men, women sit in basins of bleach or saltwater or stuff astringent herbs, tobacco or fertilizer inside their vagina. The tissue of the lining swells up and natural lubricants dry out. The resulting dry sex is painful and dangerous for women. The drying agents suppress natural bacteria, and friction easily lacerates the tender walls of the vagina. Dry sex increases the risk of HIV infection for women, already two times as likely as men to contract the virus from a single encounter. The women, adds Chikoka, can charge more for dry sex, 50 to 60 rands ($6.46 to $7.75), enough to pay a child's school fees or to eat for a week.

Chikoka knows his predilection for commercial sex spreads AIDS; he knows his promiscuity could carry the disease home to his wife; he knows people die if they get it. "Yes, HIV is terrible, madam," he says as he crooks a finger toward the businesswoman whose favors he will enjoy that night. "But, madam, sex is natural. Sex is not like beer or smoking. You can stop them. But unless you castrate the men, you can't stop sex—and then we all die anyway."

Millions of men share Chikoka's sexually active lifestyle, fostered by the region's dependence on migrant labor. Men desperate to earn a few dollars leave their women at hardscrabble rural homesteads to go where the work is: the mines, the cities, the road. They're housed together in isolated males-only hostels but have easy access to prostitutes or a "town wife" with whom they soon pick up a second family and an ordinary STD and HIV. Then they go home to wives and girlfriends a few times a year, carrying the virus they do not know they have. The pattern is so dominant that rates of infection in many rural areas across the southern cone match urban numbers.

36   If HIV zeros in disproportionally on poor migrants, it does not skip over the educated or the well paid. Soldiers, doctors, policemen, teachers, district administrators are also routinely separated from families by a civil-service system that sends them alone to remote rural posts, where they have money and women have no men. A regular paycheck procures more access to extramarital sex. Result: the vital professions are being devastated.

Schoolmaster Syabusi is afraid there will soon be no more teachers in his rural zone. He has just come home from a memorial for six colleagues who died over the past few months, though no one spoke the word AIDS at the service. "The rate here—they're so many," he says, shaking his head. "They keep on passing it at school." Teachers in southern Africa have one of the highest group infection rates, but they hide their status until the telltale symptoms find them out.

Before then, the men—teachers are mostly men here—can take their pick of sexual partners. Plenty of women in bush villages need extra cash, often to pay school fees, and female students know they can profit from a teacher's favor. So the schoolmasters buy a bit of sex with lonely wives and trade a bit of sex with willing pupils for A's. Some students consider it an honor to sleep with the teacher, a badge of superiority. The girls brag about it to their peers, preening in their ability to snag an older man. "The teachers are the worst," says Jabulani Siwela, an AIDS worker in Zimbabwe who saw frequent teacher-student sex in his Bulawayo high school. They see a girl they like; they ask her to stay after class; they have a nice time. "It's dead easy," he says. "These are men who know better, but they still do it all the time."

The Prostitute

The working woman we meet directs our car to a reedy field fringing the gritty eastern townships of Bulawayo, Zimbabwe. She doesn't want neighbors to see her being interviewed. She is afraid her family will find out she is a prostitute, so we will call her Thandiwe. She looked quite prim and proper in her green calf-length dress as she waited for johns outside 109 Tongogaro Street in the center of downtown. So, for that matter, do the dozens of other women cruising the city's dim street corners: not a mini or bustier or bared navel in sight. Zimbabwe is in many ways a prim and proper society that frowns on commercial sex work and the public display of too much skin.

40   That doesn't stop Thandiwe from earning a better living turning tricks than she ever could doing honest work. Desperate for a job, she slipped illegally into South Africa in 1992. She cleaned floors in a Johannesburg restaurant, where she met a cook

from back home who was also illegal. They had two daughters, and they got married; he was gunned down one night at work.

She brought his body home for burial and was sent to her in-laws to be "cleansed." This common practice gives a dead husband's brother the right, even the duty, to sleep with the widow. Thandiwe tested negative for HIV in 1998, but if she were positive, the ritual cleansing would have served only to pass on the disease. Then her in-laws wanted to keep her two daughters because their own children had died, and marry her off to an old uncle who lived far out in the bush. She fled.

Alone, Thandiwe grew desperate. "I couldn't let my babies starve." One day she met a friend from school. "She told me she was a sex worker. She said, 'Why you suffer? Let's go to a place where we can get quick bucks.' " Thandiwe hangs her head. "I went. I was afraid. But now I go every night."

She goes to Tongogaro Street, where the rich clients are, tucking a few condoms in her handbag every evening as the sun sets and returning home strictly by 10 so that she won't have to service a taxi-van driver to get a ride back. Thandiwe tells her family she works an evening shift, just not at what. "I get 200 zim [$5] for sex," she says, more for special services. She uses two condoms per client, sometimes three. "If they say no, I say no." But then sometimes resentful johns hit her. It's pay-and-go until she has pocketed 1,000 or 1,500 Zimbabwe dollars and can go home—with more cash than her impoverished neighbors ever see in their roughneck shantytown, flush enough to buy a TV and fleece jammies for her girls and meat for their supper.

44   "I am ashamed," she murmurs. She has stopped going to church. "Every day I ask myself, 'When will I stop this business?' The answer is, 'If I could get a job' . . . ." Her voice trails off hopelessly. "At the present moment, I have no option, no other option." As trucker Chikoka bluntly puts it, "They give sex to eat. They got no man; they got no work; but they got kids, and they got to eat." Two of Thandiwe's friends in the sex trade are dying of AIDS, but what can she do? "I just hope I won't get it."

In fact, casual sex of every kind is commonplace here. Prostitutes are just the ones who admit they do it for cash. Everywhere there's premarital sex, sex as recreation. Obligatory sex and its abusive counterpart, coercive sex. Transactional sex: sex as a gift, sugar-daddy sex. Extramarital sex, second families, multiple partners. The nature of AIDS is to feast on promiscuity.

Rare is the man who even knows his HIV status: males widely refuse testing even when they fall ill. And many men who suspect they are HIV positive embrace a flawed logic: if I'm already infected, I can sleep around because I can't get it again. But women are the ones who progress to full-blown AIDS first and die fastest, and the underlying cause is not just sex but power. Wives and girlfriends and even prostitutes in this part of the world can't easily say no to sex on a man's terms. It matters little what comes into play, whether it is culture or tradition or the pathology of violence or issues of male identity or the subservient status of women.

Beneath a translucent scalp, the plates of Gertrude Dhlamini's cranium etch a geography of pain. Her illness is obvious in the thin, stretched skin under which veins throb with the shingles that have blinded her left eye and scarred that side of her face. At 39, she looks 70. The agonizing thrush, a kind of fungus, that paralyzed her throat has ebbed enough to enable her to swallow a spoon or two of warm gruel, but most of the nourishment flows away in constant diarrhea. She struggles to keep her hand from scratching restlessly at the scaly rash flushing her other cheek. She is not ashamed to proclaim her illness to the world. "It must be told," she says.

48   Gertrude is thrice rejected. At 19 she bore a son to a boyfriend who soon left her, taking away the child. A second boyfriend got her pregnant in 1994 but disappeared in anger when their daughter was born sickly with HIV. A doctor told Gertrude it was her fault, so she blamed herself that little Noluthando was never well in the two years she survived. Gertrude never told the doctor the baby's father had slept with other women. "I was afraid to," she says, "though I sincerely believe he gave the sickness to me." Now, she says, "I have rent him from my heart. And I will never have another man in my life."

Gertrude begged her relatives to take her in, but when she revealed the name of her illness, they berated her. They made her the household drudge, telling her never to touch their food or their cooking pots. They gave her a bowl and a spoon strictly for her own use. After a few months, they threw her out.

Gertrude sits upright on a donated bed in a cardboard shack in a rough Durban township that is now the compass of her world. Perhaps 10 ft. square, the little windowless room contains a bed, one sheet and blanket, a change of clothes and a tiny cooking ring, but she has no money for paraffin to heat the food that a home-care worker brings. She must fetch water and use a toilet down the hill. "Everything I have," she says, "is a gift." Now the school that owns the land under her hut wants to turn it into a playground and she worries about where she will go. Gertrude rubs and rubs at her raw cheek. "I pray and pray to God," she says, "not to take my soul while I am alone in this room."

Women like Gertrude were brought up to be subservient to men. Especially in matters of sex, the man is always in charge. Women feel powerless to change sexual behavior. Even when a woman wants to protect herself, she usually can't: it is not uncommon for men to beat partners who refuse intercourse or request a condom. "Real men" don't use them, so women who want their partners to must fight deeply ingrained taboos. Talk to him about donning a rubber sheath and be prepared for accusations, abuse or abandonment.

52   A nurse in Durban, coming home from an AIDS training class, suggested that her mate should put on a condom, as a kind of homework exercise. He grabbed a pot and banged loudly on it with a knife, calling all the neighbors into his house. He pointed the knife at his wife and demanded: "Where was she between 4 p.m. and now? Why is she suddenly suggesting this? What has changed after 20 years that she wants a condom?"

Schoolteacher Syabusi is an educated man, fully cognizant of the AIDS threat. Yet even he bristles when asked if he uses a condom. "Humph," he says with a fine snort. "That question is nonnegotiable." So despite extensive distribution of free condoms, they often go unused. Astonishing myths have sprung up. If you don one, your erection can't grow. Free condoms must be too cheap to be safe: they have been stored too long, kept too hot, kept too cold. Condoms fill up with germs, so they spread

AIDS. Condoms from overseas bring the disease with them. Foreign governments that donate condoms put holes in them so that Africans will die. Education programs find it hard to compete with the power of the grapevine.

The Child in No. 17

In crib No. 17 of the spartan but crowded children's ward at the Church of Scotland Hospital in KwaZulu-Natal, a tiny, staring child lies dying. She is three and has hardly known a day of good health. Now her skin wrinkles around her body like an oversize suit, and her twigsize bones can barely hold her vertical as nurses search for a vein to take blood. In the frail arms hooked up to transfusion tubes, her veins have collapsed. The nurses palpate a threadlike vessel on the child's forehead. She mews like a wounded animal as one tightens a rubber band around her head to raise the vein. Tears pour unnoticed from her mother's eyes as she watches the needle tap-tap at her daughter's temple. Each time the whimpering child lifts a wan hand to brush away the pain, her mother gently lowers it. Drop by drop, the nurses manage to collect 1 cc of blood in five minutes.

The child in crib No. 17 has had TB, oral thrush, chronic diarrhea, malnutrition, severe vomiting. The vial of blood reveals her real ailment, AIDS, but the disease is not listed on her chart, and her mother says she has no idea why her child is so ill. She breastfed her for two years, but once the little girl was weaned, she could not keep solid food down. For a long time, her mother thought something was wrong with the food. Now the child is afflicted with so many symptoms that her mother had to bring her to the hospital, from which sick babies rarely return.

She hopes, she prays her child will get better, and like all the mothers who stay with their children at the hospital, she tends her lovingly, constantly changing filthy diapers, smoothing sheets, pressing a little nourishment between listless lips, trying to tease a smile from the vacant, staring face. Her husband works in Johannesburg, where he lives in a men's squatter camp. He comes home twice a year. She is 25. She has heard of AIDS but does not know it is transmitted by sex, does not know if she or her husband has it. She is afraid this child will die soon, and she is afraid to have more babies. But she is afraid too to raise the subject with her husband. "He would not agree to that," she says shyly. "He would never agree to have no more babies."

Dr. Annick DeBaets, 32, is a volunteer from Belgium. In the two years she has spent here in Tugela Ferry, she has learned all about how hard it is to break the cycle of HIV transmission from mother to infant. The door to this 48-cot ward is literally a revolving one: sick babies come in, receive doses of rudimentary antibiotics, vitamins, food; go home for a week or a month; then come back as ill as ever. Most, she says, die in the first or second year. If she could just follow up with really intensive care, believes Dr. DeBaets, many of the wizened infants crowding three to a crib could live longer, healthier lives. "But it's very discouraging. We simply don't have the time, money or facilities for anything but minimal care."

Much has been written about what South African Judge Edwin Cameron, himself HIV positive, calls his country's "grievous ineptitude" in the face of the burgeoning epidemic. Nowhere has that been more evident than in the government's failure

56

to provide drugs that could prevent pregnant women from passing HIV to their babies. The government has said it can't afford the 300-rand-per-dose, 28-dose regimen of AZT that neighboring nations like Botswana dole out, using funds and drugs from foreign donors. The late South African presidential spokesman Parks Mankahlana even suggested publicly that it was not cost effective to save these children when their mothers were already doomed to die: "We don't want a generation of orphans."

Yet these children—70,000 are born HIV positive in South Africa alone every year—could be protected from the disease for about $4 each with another simple, cheap drug called nevirapine. Until last month, the South African government steadfastly refused to license or finance the use of nevirapine despite the manufacturer's promise to donate the drug for five years, claiming that its "toxic" side effects are not yet known. This spring, however, the drug will finally be distributed to leading public hospitals in the country, though only on a limited basis at first.

60   The mother at crib No. 17 is not concerned with potential side effects. She sits on the floor cradling her daughter, crooning over and over, "Get well, my child, get well." The baby stares back without blinking. "It's sad, so sad, so sad," the mother says. The child died three days later.

The children who are left when parents die only add another complex dimension to Africa's epidemic. At 17, Tsepho Phale has been head of an indigent household of three young boys in the dusty township of Monarch, outside Francistown, for two years. He never met his father, his mother died of AIDS, and the grieving children possess only a raw concrete shell of a house. The doorways have no doors; the window frames no glass. There is not a stick of furniture. The boys sleep on piled-up blankets, their few clothes dangling from nails. In the room that passes for a kitchen, two paraffin burners sit on the dirt floor alongside the month's food: four cabbages, a bag of oranges and one of potatoes, three sacks of flour, some yeast, two jars of oil and two cartons of milk. Next to a dirty stack of plastic pans lies the mealy meal and rice that will provide their main sustenance for the month. A couple of bars of soap and two rolls of toilet paper also have to last the month. Tsepho has just brought these rations home from the social-service center where the "orphan grants" are doled out.

Tsepho has been robbed of a childhood that was grim even before his mother fell sick. She supported the family by "buying and selling things," he says, but she never earned more than a pittance. When his middle brother was knocked down by a car and left physically and mentally disabled, Tsepho's mother used the insurance money to build this house, so she would have one thing of value to leave her children. As the walls went up, she fell sick. Tsepho had to nurse her, bathe her, attend to her bodily functions, try to feed her. Her one fear as she lay dying was that her rural relatives would try to steal the house. She wrote a letter bequeathing it to her sons and bade Tsepho hide it.

As her body lay on the concrete floor awaiting burial, the relatives argued openly about how they would divide up the profits when they sold her dwelling. Tsepho gave the district commissioner's office the letter, preventing his mother's family from grabbing the house. Fine, said his relations; if you think you're a man, you look after your brothers. They have contributed nothing to the boys' welfare since. "It's as if we don't exist anymore either," says Tsepho. Now he struggles to keep house for the others, doing the cooking, cleaning, laundry and shopping.

64   The boys look at the future with despair. "It is very bleak," says Tsepho, kicking aimlessly at a bare wall. He had to quit school, has no job, will probably never get one. "I've given up my dreams. I have no hope."

Orphans have traditionally been cared for the African way: relatives absorb the children of the dead into their extended families. Some still try, but communities like Tsepho's are becoming saturated with orphans, and families can't afford to take on another kid, leaving thousands alone.

Now many must fend for themselves, struggling to survive. The trauma of losing parents is compounded by the burden of becoming a breadwinner. Most orphans sink into penury, drop out of school, suffer malnutrition, ostracism, psychic distress. Their makeshift households scramble to live on pitiful handouts—from overstretched relatives, a kind neighbor, a state grant—or they beg and steal in the streets. The orphans' present desperation forecloses a brighter future. "They hardly ever succeed in having a life," says Siphelile Kaseke, 22, a counselor at an AIDS orphans' camp near Bulawayo. Without education, girls falls into prostitution, and older boys migrate illegally to South Africa, leaving the younger ones to go on the streets.

Every day spent in this part of Africa is acutely depressing: there is so little countervailing hope to all the stories of the dead and the doomed. "More than anywhere else in the world, AIDS in Africa was met with apathy," says Suzanne LeClerc-Madlala, a lecturer at the University of Natal. The consequences of the silence march on: infection soars, stigma hardens, denial hastens death, and the chasm between knowledge and behavior widens. The present disaster could be dwarfed by the woes that loom if Africa's epidemic rages on. The human losses could wreck the region's frail economies, break down civil societies and incite political instability.

68   In the face of that, every day good people are doing good things. Like Dr. Moll, who uses his after-job time and his own fund raising to run an extensive volunteer home-care program in KwaZulu-Natal. And Busi Magwazi, who, along with dozens of others, tends the sick for nothing in the Durban-based Sinoziso project. And Patricia Bakwinya, who started her Shining Stars orphan-care program in Francistown with her own zeal and no money, to help youngsters like Tsepho Phale. And countless individuals who give their time and devotion to ease southern Africa's plight.

But these efforts can help only thousands; they cannot turn the tide. The region is caught in a double bind. Without treatment, those with HIV will sicken and die; without prevention, the spread of infection cannot be checked. Southern Africa has no other means available to break the vicious cycle, except to change everyone's sexual behavior—and that isn't happening.

The essential missing ingredient is leadership. Neither the countries of the region nor those of the wealthy world have been able or willing to provide it.

South Africa, comparatively well off, comparatively well educated, has blundered tragically for years. AIDS invaded just when apartheid ended, and a government absorbed in massive transition relegated the disease to a back page. An attempt at a national education campaign wasted millions on a farcical musical. The premature release of a local wonder drug ended in scandal when the drug turned out to be made of industrial solvent. Those fiascoes left the government skittish about embracing expensive programs, inspiring a 1998 decision not to provide AZT to HIV-positive pregnant women. Zimbabwe too suffers savagely from feckless leadership. Even in Botswana, where the will to act is gathering strength, the resources to follow through have to come from foreign hands.

72   AIDS' grip here is so pervasive and so complex that all societies—theirs and ours—must rally round to break it. These countries are too poor to doctor themselves. The drugs that could begin to break the cycle will not be available here until global pharmaceutical companies find ways to provide them inexpensively. The health-care systems required to prescribe and monitor complicated triple-cocktail regimens won't exist unless rich countries help foot the bill. If there is ever to be a vaccine, the West will have to finance its discovery and provide it to the poor. The cure for this epidemic is not national but international.

The deep silence that makes African leaders and societies want to deny the problem, the corruption and incompetence that render them helpless is something the West cannot fix. But the fact that they are poor is not. The wealthy world must help with its zeal and its cash if southern Africa is ever to be freed of the AIDS plague.

PERSONAL RESPONSE

McGeary says that "every day spent in this part of Africa is acutely depressing" (paragraph 68), and most would agree that just reading about what she has witnessed could be depressing as well. What is the effect of this article on you personally?

QUESTIONS FOR CLASS OR SMALL-GROUP DISCUSSION

1. What is the effect of McGeary's using specific people to illustrate the devastation of AIDS? What would be lost if she had not used individual examples but had written in general terms of the large numbers of victims?

2. McGeary writes that AIDS in Africa is "a complex plague with confounding social, economic and political mechanics that locked together to accelerate the virus's progress" (paragraph 8). How well does she explain those "mechanics"? State in your own words what they are.

3. In paragraph 5, McGeary makes this comment: "Think how different the effort would be if what is happening [in the southern quadrant of South Africa] were happening in the West." How different do you think the effort would be?

4. McGeary ends her article by asserting that "the West will have to finance [a vaccine] and provide it to the poor" (paragraph 73). Are you persuaded that developed countries must help Africa fight its epidemic?

○ PERSPECTIVES ON PUBLIC HEALTH ○

Suggested Writing Topics

1. Argue for or against making smallpox vaccinations mandatory.
2. Argue for or against the view that expanding women's rights is an important component in the fight to control the spread AIDS.
3. Argue for or against the right of pharmaceutical companies to hold patents and continue to make large profits on drugs that could help fight AIDS in sub-Saharan countries.
4. Explore the role of drug companies in fighting the global AIDS epidemic.
5. Discuss your views on providing universal access to health care in light of the high cost of health care.
6. Explain your views on how best to educate the public about preventing sexually transmitted diseases.
7. Explain the role you believe that schools and other public institutions should play in disseminating information about sexually transmitted diseases.
8. Argue either for or against programs to distribute free condoms to high-school students.
9. If you know someone with AIDS or another grave illness, describe that person's condition, the problems it poses for the person's family, and your concerns about the person and the illness.

Research Topics

1. Research the viewpoints of drug companies, economists, and health workers, among others, on this question: Should drug companies bear the financial burden of sending lifesaving drugs to developing countries?
2. In combination with library and Internet research, interview public-health officials or representatives from the health center at your campus about a public-health issue. Narrow your focus to one aspect of public health and explain your own view on the topic.
3. Research the controversy over government funding for AIDS research.
4. Research and assess the importance or success of the work of either a national health agency, such as the U. S. Centers for Disease Control (CDC), or an international health agency, such as the World Health Organization (WHO).
5. Research some aspect of the AIDS epidemic in the United States (or another country) and responses by public-health officials to the disease. You will discover many controversies on this subject, so identify one major controversy, explore the issues involved, and arrive at your own position on the subject. You may want to take a historical approach, for instance, by exploring various theories on the origin of AIDS, or you may want to focus on controversial treatments for the disease.

6. Research one of the many contributing factors in the spread of AIDS in Africa that are mentioned by either Wayne Ellwood in "We All Have AIDS" or Johanna McGeary in "Death Stalks a Continent": poverty, gender, class inequality, ignorance, urbanization, colonialism, or the collapse of rural economies.

7. Research a major plague of the past, such as the bubonic plague in thirteenth- and fourteenth-century Europe, cholera epidemics, the smallpox epidemic that swept Sweden in 1764, the typhus epidemic that killed more than three million Russians during World War I, or the influenza plague of 1918 to 1919 that killed more than 20 million people around the world. Determine the consequences for the country (or countries) affected by the plague as well as its possible origins and how it was finally conquered.

RESPONDING TO VISUALS

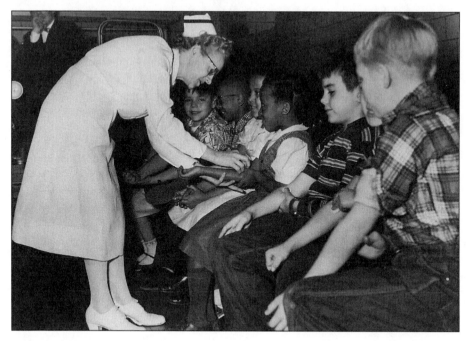

A nurse prepares children for a polio vaccine shot as part of a city-wide testing of the vaccine on elementary school students, February 23, 1954, Pittsburgh, Pennsylvania. Source: Bettmann/CORBIS

1. What is going on in this photograph? State the details that explain what is happening.
2. What aspects of the scene does the photographer emphasize?
3. What do the facial expressions and body language indicate about how both the nurse and the children view this experience?
4. What details give clues that this picture is not current? Could you tell that the photograph was taken in the 1950s if you were not told that in the caption?

RESPONDING TO VISUALS

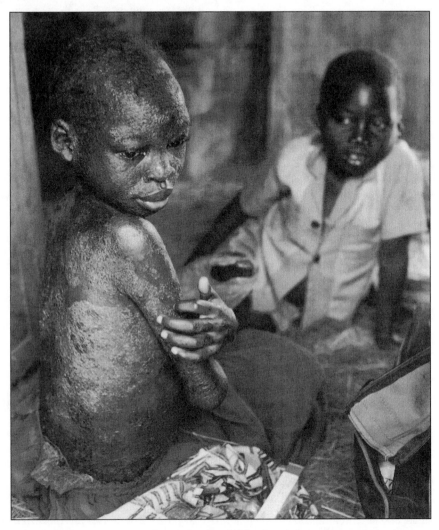

A 13-year-old Tanzanian girl suffering from an AIDS-related skin infection, at her home near Bukoba, Tanzania. She was transmitted AIDS from a blood transfusion from her father to treat malarial anaemia. Her father died from AIDS-related syndrome, and her mother is severely ill from the disease. Source: Gideon Mendel/CORBIS

1. What is your emotional response to the picture?
2. What is the effect of the perspective from which the photograph was taken? What details about the children are revealed from that perspective?
3. Why does the photographer include the child who apparently is not ill? What is the effect of the juxtaposition of the two children?

ENVIRONMENTAL STUDIES

Environmental issues such as depletion of the ozone layer, global warming, deforestation, and air and water pollution are just a few of the many causes for concern over
the health of animal and vegetable life on Earth. Closely connected to these environmental problems is the rapid rate of increase in the world population. As the number of
people grows, pressure increases on natural resources. Will Earth provide enough food
for everyone? How can water supplies be kept safe for drinking? How does pollution
produced by so many humans affect the quality of the air they breathe? How can
people stop the ever-widening hole in the ozone layer that protects us from the harmful rays of the sun? How will future generations sustain the rapidly increasing worldwide

population? These are just some of the questions confronting scientists, civic leaders, and ordinary people everywhere.

Although most people recognize that humans must keep their environments safe, not everyone agrees on either the nature of the problems or the severity of their consequences. For instance, resource depletion and global warming are the subjects of many debates. Researchers and scientists differ in their beliefs on questions such as Earth's ability to sustain life indefinitely and whether Earth is experiencing global warming and, if so, whether the phenomenon is cause for alarm.

In the first piece in this chapter, Aaron Sachs profiles the nineteenth-century scientist Baron Alexander von Humboldt, who, he says, is "the man most responsible for bringing the practice of science into mainstream Western culture." In "Humboldt's Legacy and the Restoration of Science," Sachs maintains that modern science would do well to adopt Humboldt's integrated vision of nature. He laments the relatively low federal allocation for furthering the understanding of the environment, and he believes that ecologists and environmentalists should adopt a broader, interdisciplinary approach to environmental problems.

Next is an essay offering practical guides to conservation in a number of areas. Paul Hawken, in "A Declaration of Sustainability," suggests actions for both individuals and groups to help the environment. According to his "strategies for sustainability," Hawken offers "twelve steps society can take to save the whole enchilada." As you read both Sachs's and Hawken's essays, think about what you already do to conserve resources and help curb environmental problems and whether these writers persuade you to do even more.

The *American Spectator* editorial, "The Galileo of Global Warming," presents a critical view of environmentalists, at least those who maintain that humans are responsible for global warming. The article reviews some of the issues concerning global warming and reports on the findings of scientist Lloyd Keigwin, whose research about Earth's climate discredit the theory that it is humans who cause global warming.

D. Grant DeMan, on the other hand, maintains that he has done all he could to be friendly to the environment but is still being bombarded with messages to do more. He asserts that he is fed up with all those who warn about the dire consequences of careless use of resources. In "Out, Damn Naturalists," he describes his efforts to be environmentally responsible and adds his opinion of environmental activists.

HUMBOLDT'S LEGACY AND THE RESTORATION OF SCIENCE

Aaron Sachs

Aaron Sachs is a research associate at Worldwatch Institute. He is author of Eco-Justice: Linking Human Rights and the Environment *(1994) and co-author of* The Next Efficiency Revolution: Creating a Sustainable Materials Economy *(1990) and* State of the World 1995. *This essay is from the March/April, 1995, issue of* World Watch *magazine.*

On September 15, 1869, the *New York Times* ran a one-word headline: "HUMBOLDT." Every literate American knew the name. "The One Hundredth Birthday of the Philosopher," explained the subtitle. "Celebration Generally Throughout the Country." The story took up the entire front page.

It is unthinkable today that Americans would celebrate the birthday of any dead philosopher, let alone a foreign one. Yet from San Francisco to Peoria to New York, on that Tuesday afternoon, people read speeches, unrolled banners, and unveiled statues in honor of the late Baron Alexander von Humboldt. Of course, Humboldt was much more than a philosopher: He was also an explorer, a geographer, a writer, a naturalist—and the man most responsible for bringing the practice of science into mainstream Western culture.

The word *scientist* first entered the English language in the 1830s, specifically in reference to Humboldt and his disciples—Charles Darwin among them. Originally, then, the term meant "natural scientist." The new profession Humboldt had carved out and popularized took as its goal the transformation of natural history studies, to cover not just the detailed cataloging of the phenomena of the physical world, but also the formulation of a grand, unifying theory that would link all those phenomena together. Humboldt wanted to know what tied the rivers to the trees, how climate influenced vegetation, why particular animals thrived only in particular habitats; he also wanted to reveal humanity's place within these interdependent relationships. And in an early nineteenth-century culture of amateur naturalists obsessed with the romance of the wilderness, his quest struck many chords.

4   Initially, Humboldt earned his fame by exploring the New World between 1799 and 1804, when he surveyed the headwaters of the Orinoco in the jungles of Venezuela and scaled the Andes to heights never before attained in any of the world's mountain ranges. On that trip, between the ages of thirty and thirty-five, the "Rediscoverer of America" witnessed the immense diversity of humanity and nature. He saw just how different life was among the natives of the Venezuelan rainforest and the politicians of the newly formed U.S. Congress—among the insects swarming in marshlands along the Colombian coast and the birds floating above Ecuadorean volcanoes and the wildflowers lining fertile Cuban valleys. Yet he never wavered in his belief that there existed a "chain of connection," that all elements of earthly life, including humans, were "mutually dependent"—and that a knowledge of that

interdependence was the "noblest and most important result" of all scientific inquiry. For the last fifty-five years of his life—he lived to age ninety—he struggled to "recognize unity in the vast diversity of physical phenomena." While acknowledging the world's chaos, he saw within it what the ancient Greeks called a *kosmos,* a beautifully ordered and harmonious system, and he coined the modern word *cosmos* to use as the title of his final, multivolume work—a book Walt Whitman kept on his desk as he was writing *Leaves of Grass.*

Today, most environmentalists would be shocked to learn that nature's interrelationships were once in the mainstream of scientific thought. The dominant theme in science over the past century has been *fission,* the breaking down of life and matter and ideas into their smaller components: Life science and its organic theories have given way to specialization, to microbiology and nuclear physics. In our rush to gain in-depth knowledge about particular elements of a complicated, seemingly chaotic world, we have tacitly decided that it would be futile to try to tie those elements together. Science has lost its delicate balance between chaos and cosmos, between diversity and unity.

It now seems clear that this century-old imbalance is inextricably linked to our global ecological crisis. If we assume that the world on which we depend is utterly chaotic, there is no reason to do anything but try to control and conquer it—which has become science's new goal. And though specialization has proved itself invaluable in the pursuit of knowledge, its narrow, short-range focus, in the absence of a complementary organic approach, is extremely dangerous. We have directed society's accumulated scientific knowledge toward constantly improving our exploitation of each individual natural resource, without recognizing the threat we are posing to the basic ecosystems that create those resources. As Rachel Carson observed in her classic *Silent Spring,* we failed to predict the environmental impacts of extensive pesticide use because chemical companies paid researchers simply to kill pests—and not to worry about the pesticides' effects on other plants and animals, or groundwater supplies, or farmworkers' lungs. Perhaps the highest goal of the environmental movement, then, is to reclaim science, to ensure that we use it not for the domination of nature but for the appreciation of our connectedness to it—to restore, in other words, the legacy that Humboldt tried to leave us.

In the nineteenth century, Humboldt's appeal was wide-ranging. Many people saw him as the world's historian, the man who would explain where we came from and how we fit into the universe. He provided an enthralled public with glimpses of exotic natural worlds they would never see for themselves. Scholars flocked to his study in Germany to soak up his wisdom, to examine his field notes and sprawling maps and native artifacts. And laypeople gathered at the newly opened natural history museums to which Humboldt had donated his famous collections of intricate jungle plants and multicolored birds. By organizing lectures and workshops all over the world, he made huge numbers of people feel involved in the progress of science. Moreover, his theories themselves were attractive for their inclusiveness, their ambitious attempts at painting a unified picture of all the world's complexities.

8   Just as every lowly plant and minute insect had a crucial role in Humboldt's vision of the world, so too did every type of human being, no matter how powerless or

marginalized. Humboldt was a hero to Simon Bolivar, who used the scientist's writings in his campaigns for Latin American independence, to help prove that colonialism was wreaking havoc on both the people and the environment of the New World. And Humboldt was especially popular among Americans, by the time of the 1869 centennial, because he had been one of the world's most outspoken opponents of slavery. "In maintaining the unity of the human race," he had written, "we also reject the disagreeable assumption of superior and inferior peoples." Four years after the end of the Civil War, Americans found in Humboldt's scientific work a parallel to the political heroism of President Lincoln. Both men had staked everything on the concept of Union.

In 1869, Humboldt was as well-known and respected, globally, as Lincoln and Bolivar; he had been as influential in nineteenth-century science as Beethoven had been in music, as Napoleon had been in politics. Darwin once wrote that "my whole career is due to having read and reread" Humboldt's *Personal Narrative to the Equinoctial Regions of America,* and he often sent his manuscripts to the older scientist for comment. When the great theoretician of evolution set off on his voyage aboard *The Beagle,* he brought with him only three books: the Bible, a copy of Milton, and Humboldt's *Narrative.* Humboldt's magnum opus, *Cosmos,* bore the daunting subtitle, "A Sketch of a Physical Description of the Universe," and it had an index that ran to more than one thousand pages. But it was translated into all the major languages and sold hundreds of thousands of copies. "The demand is epoch-making," Humboldt's publisher claimed. "Book parcels destined for London and St. Petersburg were torn out of our hands by agents who wanted their orders filled for the bookstores in Vienna and Hamburg." Science, it seems, could easily have gone in the direction Humboldt was taking it.

Today, Humboldt's name is woven tightly into our geographical fabric: The index of a good atlas might list it some twenty-five times, referring not only to towns like Humboldt, Iowa, and Humboldt, South Dakota, but also to the Humboldt Mountains in China, Venezuela, and Nevada; the Humboldt Current off the coast of Peru; and even a Humboldt Glacier in Greenland. But almost no one today has any idea who Humboldt was.

Science, and Western society in general, underwent a huge transformation toward the end of the nineteenth century. In 1859, Humboldt died, Darwin published *On the Origin of Species,* and the modern age was born—though the full implications of evolution did not become clear until 1871, when Darwin delivered the ultimate comeuppance of his own species in *The Descent of Man.* The theory of evolution was revolutionary both because it directly undermined the centuries-old assumption that there was a divine plan separating human beings from the lowly animals, and because it posed a significant threat to the dearly held Humboldtian notion that nature was fundamentally a harmonious, unified entity. To most educated Westerners, the Darwinian concept of "the struggle for existence" meant that humanity's origins were steeped in animal violence and conflict—that the different facets of nature were not working together to form an organic whole but were competing with each other, fighting over ecological niches, fighting just to survive.

12   The one redeeming element of Darwinism, for many shocked Victorians, was that their civilization had at least seemed to come out of the competition victorious.

In the hands of so-called Social Darwinists, "the struggle for existence" became "the survival of the fittest," and theorizers were quick to assert that Darwin's explanation of biological fitness proved the superiority of white, Christian Europeans. After all, they argued, a careful reading of *On the Origin of Species* revealed that the successful animals were those that had bodies perfectly designed to perform a particular function or adapt to a particular environment. The key to a species' success, in other words, was *specialization*—a word Darwin probably coined in the 1840s. And Europeans were without question becoming the world's experts in specialization.

By the second half of the nineteenth century, specialization was beginning to seep into almost every aspect of Western culture and thought. Graduate schools were offering highly specialized training in narrow professions. Huge new businesses were dividing their production processes into the smallest possible components, with the aim of improving efficiency and becoming more fit competitors in the capitalist economy. Laborers no longer saw products through from start to finish, but rather performed their one limited function, over and over again. By the turn of the century, someone had to coin the term *Renaissance man* to refer to that rare person who hearkened back to the era before intense specialization was the norm, back when most people cultivated a variety of linked interests and skills.

Gradually, Humboldt's bigger picture came to seem neither appealing nor important, since specialization was paying off so well by making labor and the exploitation of nature so much more efficient. Now, Darwinists reasoned, man might be on his way to breaking his connections with animal savagery and freeing himself from all the other harsh forces of nature. Evolutionary progress came to mean the conquest of the natural world by science and technology, and distancing oneself from nature became a cultural imperative. Survival depended on winning an all-out competition with other living things—including other members of our own species. And knowledge depended on the ability to observe nature purely as object, as something unrelated to us and best understood when broken down mechanistically into its smallest components.

The embrace of Darwinism and the transformation of science, then, went hand in hand with rapid industrialization, the rise of free-market capitalism, and the expansion of colonialism. Social Darwinists defended empire-building on the grounds that vigorous self-aggrandizement was only natural. And they used similar arguments to validate their racism: The affluence and technological prowess of the Western world, they argued, proved that the races and nations of the "Third World" really were "less developed." As C. S. Lewis, the British writer and critic, once pointed out, the ironies of this new world order ran deep: "At the moment, then, of man's victory over nature, we find the whole human race subjected to some individual men, and individuals subjected to that in themselves which is purely 'natural'—to their irrational impulses." The leaders of a culture that worshipped civilization and science were calmly calling for the massacre or repression of several indigenous nations in the Americas, the methodical deforestation of the United States, and the military invasion of most of Africa.

16   Of course, given Humboldt's direct influence on Darwin, there had to be elements of the theory of evolution that hearkened back to the elder scientist's approach. Indeed, the most significant implication of the *Origin* may have been its assertion

that man, on the most fundamental level, was but a part of nature—as Humboldt had argued for decades. Some nineteenth-century thinkers, accordingly, managed to find in evolutionary theory a spirit of cooperation and union. To the author and naturalist W. H. Hudson, for instance, Darwin's work meant that "we are no longer isolated, standing like starry visitors on a mountain-top, surveying life from the outside; but are on a level with and part and parcel of it."

Darwin was fascinated with the idea of nature as a "web"—"we may all be netted together," he mused in the late 1830s—and strong ecological currents run through many of his early writings. The word *oecologie* was in fact coined in 1866 by Germany's foremost Darwinian scientist, Ernst Haeckel. And when Haeckel defined his new scientific discipline, he invoked his mentor by name: ecology, he explained, was "the body of knowledge concerning the economy of nature . . . , the study of all those complex interrelations referred to by Darwin."

In the end, however, Darwin chose to focus on the violent, competitive aspects of his theory. He was explicitly lending his support to the colonialist ethic when he asserted the evolutionary doctrine that an "endless number of lower races" had to be "beaten and supplanted" by "the higher civilized races." Such competitive replacement was inevitable, Darwin argued, because niches in the economy of nature were only so big—as he had learned from the work of the Reverend Thomas Malthus. To Darwin, Malthus's 1798 *Essay on Population* proved that no species could rely on the myth of nature's abundance. Since our population seems to grow at a much faster rate than our food supply, Malthus argued, human society is destined to face starvation on a massive scale. Darwin made this doomsday theme the engine of his theory of evolution: Crises caused by environmental constraints brutally forced out the species that could not compete. He considered it part of his mission to convince naive Romantics that, in the words of the evolutionary biologist Stephen Jay Gould, "we should never have sought solace or moral instruction in Nature."

Humboldt, conversely, held up the natural world as a model, as something worthy of our ultimate respect. In his writings, he sought "to depict the contemplation of natural objects as a means of exciting a pure love of nature." Yet he was no naive Romantic. Just as Darwin recognized the organicist ecological perspective, so too did Humboldt recognize the elements of violence, competition, and disunity in nature. After all, he had cut his way through the swarming, dripping jungles of South America, had witnessed such bizarre events as the mass electrocution of several horses by a colony of eels—and he had seen men enslaving other men. While Darwin focused on the disunity, though, and the specialized adaptations of species to local environments, Humboldt focused on the unity, and the global forces that link different environments and their inhabitants together. Both perspectives reveal important truths. Humboldt's ideas were marginalized simply because Darwin's were more fit in the late nineteenth century—because Darwinism in effect captured the essence of the modernizing Western world.

20   In general, Humboldt's work is still marginalized, but where it is known, experts accept it as good, hard science. One representative contribution he made to the development of ecology was his theory relating the geographical distribution of plants to the effects of climate—a radical idea that remains a cornerstone of our understanding of plant ecosystems. At the base of peaks like Mount Chimborazo in the

Ecuadorean Andes, he found the vines and bright orchids and tall hardwoods of the rainforest, while on the snow-clad summit he found only the hardiest mosses and lichens. On mountain after mountain, vegetation got sparser at higher altitudes, as if during his ascent he were walking from the equator to one of the poles: vertical geography mirrored horizontal geography. Humboldt was the first to classify forests as tropical, temperate, or boreal. Climate, he realized, seemed to govern the development of life everywhere; all plants and animals were "subject to the same laws" of temperature.

Humboldt had traveled to a continent less touched by human influence in order to look into the past and discover the forces that had shaped nature into its present form. "In the New World," he wrote, "man and his productions almost disappear amidst the stupendous display of wild, and gigantic nature. . . . On no other part of the globe is [the naturalist] called upon more powerfully to raise himself to general ideas on the cause of phenomena and their mutual connection." This historical technique and his "habit of viewing the Globe as a great whole" allowed Humboldt to identify climate as a unifying global force, proving, in a sense, that we all live under the same roof. Changes in one locale, he pointed out, might cause, or at least signal, changes somewhere else. And by drawing lines on the map connecting points with the same mean temperature—he coined the word *isotherm*—he established permanent scientific structures that would enable future generations to think globally. Humboldt's innovations in the field of comparative climatology underlie current attempts to understand the threat of global warming.

Long before any suspicion of change in the atmosphere, Humboldt was worrying about the effect of humanity's actions on terra firma; his knowledge of ecology translated into a nascent environmentalism. Again, the New World taught him an important lesson. European systems of commerce insulated the wealthy from the ecological consequences of their consumption, but the less developed economies of the Americas could not hide their dependence on surrounding natural systems. A year in Mexico, for instance, showed Humboldt that "the produce of the earth is in fact the sole basis of permanent opulence"—and that we could not afford to use that produce wastefully.

Studying a lake in Venezuela, Humboldt used his ecological perspective to relate the lake's decline to the deforestation of the surrounding watershed. Once deprived of the trees' root systems, he explained, the surrounding soils had a greatly diminished capacity for water retention, so they could no longer recharge the springs that fed the lake. And, meanwhile, because the area was deforested, "the waters falling in rain are no longer impeded in their course; and instead of slowly augmenting the level of the rivers by progressive filtrations, they furrow [the hillsides with] sudden inundations," causing widespread soil erosion. "Hence it results that the destruction of the forests, the want of permanent springs, and the existence of torrents are three phenomena closely connected together." Humboldt saw the social consequences as well: "by felling trees . . . , men in every climate prepare at once two calamities for future generations: the want of fuel and a scarcity of water."

24   Humboldt's fear of resource scarcity reflects his own reading of Malthus's essay, which he called "one of the most profound works of political economy ever written." Yet Humboldt's analysis of environmental limits was far more sophisticated than

Malthus's: To Humboldt, increases in resource consumption reflected not inevitable demographic pressures but simple, conscious decisions. If our population increased to several billion, then perhaps our basic needs might become too much for the earth to handle, but Humboldt realized that the resource scarcities of his own day were caused by overconsumption and mismanagement. Those trees in Venezuela didn't have to be chopped down.

Even more radical was Humboldt's interest in linking such problems to the injustices of colonialism. In his analysis of the resource base of Mexico, which he published as *A Political Essay on the Kingdom of New Spain*—and which ventured into the fields of demography, medicine, anthropology, sociology, political science, economics, agriculture, biology, geology, and geography—Humboldt took great pains to show that it was not necessary for so many Mexicans to go without land and food. His multifaceted approach helped him to see that such outrages were being driven not by population pressures but by basic socioeconomic structures. Many peasants were landless, he explained, because "the property in New Spain . . . is in a great measure in the hands of a few powerful families who have gradually absorbed the smaller estates." And impoverished Mexicans were starving because wealthy landlords grew cash crops for export instead of food crops for domestic consumption. "Whenever the soil can produce both indigo and maize," Humboldt noted indignantly, "the former prevails over the latter, although the general interest requires that a preference be given to those vegetables which supply nourishment to man over those which are merely objects of exchange with strangers."

Humboldt was still a man of his time: In general, he approved of the development of the New World, and he never openly demanded that the Spanish American colonies receive full independence. But his interdisciplinary research did lead him to a scathing critique of colonialism. With the conviction of one who knows his subject thoroughly, Humboldt asserted that "the restless and suspicious colonial policies of the nations of Europe . . . have thrown insurmountable obstacles in the way of the . . . prosperity of their distant possessions. . . . A colony has for ages been considered useful to the parent state only in so far as it supplied a great number of raw materials." Because Humboldt was so aware of the interdependent relationships that governed the world, his science could never have been used to validate dominance over other people or the environment; he knew the Europeans' abuse of other lands would come back to haunt them. Later in the nineteenth century, politicians would repeatedly refer to Darwinism in claiming that certain human and natural resources were expendable for the sake of the evolutionary progress of "the higher civilized races." But according to Humboldt, nothing was expendable.

Today, the destruction of the developing world's environment—the burning of the rainforest, the strip-mining of mountain ranges, the appropriation of valuable croplands for the raising of tradable commodities—is still largely driven by the demands of the world's wealthiest countries. The structure of the global economy dictates that developing nations put all their efforts into raising cash—usually by exporting whatever virgin resources the industrial world might desire. They need the cash to pay off their "debt."

28   Even Humboldt accepted Darwinian conflict and chaos as basic facts of life. The whole time he was working on *Cosmos*—during the last thirty years of his life—he

knew that the grand, unifying theory he sought was unattainable, because the world was too complicated and chaotic and contingent. "Experimental sciences," he wrote, "based on the observation of the external world, cannot aspire to completeness; the nature of things, and the imperfection of our organs, are alike opposed to it. . . . The attempt perfectly to represent unity in diversity must therefore necessarily prove unsuccessful."

The existence of chaos, however, does not invalidate the search for a cosmos. "Even a partial solution," Humboldt wrote, "—the tendency toward a comprehension of the phenomena of the universe—will not the less remain the eternal and sublime aim of every investigation of nature." And modern chaos theory has in fact demonstrated that beneath almost every manifestation of disorder lurks some sort of pattern or equilibrium. As Daniel Botkin, author of *Discordant Harmonies: A New Ecology for the Twenty-First Century*, has noted, it is important for us to realize, with Darwin, that nature is not calm and balanced but rather constantly changing; but we must also understand that "certain rates of change are natural, desirable, and acceptable, while others are not." It is possible to differentiate between natural and unnatural rates of change and to seek to uphold nature's dynamic equilibrium.

Up to now, unfortunately, scientists and policy makers have put far too much emphasis on bracing for disorder—on exploiting and stockpiling natural resources in ever greater quantities, and on stockpiling weapons to defend those resources. The United States, for instance, spends $50 billion annually on the development of defense and space technologies, but less than $2 billion in furthering our understanding of the environment. There is a perfectly straightforward reason why we have more sophisticated techniques for planting land mines in the desert than for planting corn on an erodible hillside.

Restoring the balance of modern science, then, would entail devoting more time and money to the search for order in nature, to the mapping of the world's interconnections. A more prominent, better-funded environmental science could help stop over-exploitation by forcing people to realize that each part of the living world is equally valuable. And a major redistribution of research dollars could produce creative, long-term solutions to the problems inherent in resource extraction. New studies could help us, for instance, to pinpoint sustainable yields from fisheries and water supplies; to harvest crops, including trees, without losing so much soil to erosion; and to harness renewable, efficient forms of energy instead of going to war to ensure a steady supply of oil.

32   In lobbying for the research dollars they deserve, ecologists and environmentalists should begin by spreading an ethic of interdisciplinary cooperation. Their unique perspective, which emphasizes holistic, synthetic thinking, is crucial to scientists and developers alike, who need to understand the full impacts of their work over the long term. Even more important, though, ecologists and environmentalists should extend their interdisciplinary approach to include the public at large. People everywhere need to realize that they have a stake in the direction science is taking. All over the world, people concerned about their environments are already clamoring for more information, so that they can hold developers, corporations, and governments accountable for their actions. But they need more help from the scientists themselves, who too often come across as aloof experts with little interest in the public sphere. Only

by bridging the gap between "laypeople" and "specialists," only by building connections among ourselves, will we be able to alter the scientific research agenda and rebuild our connections with the natural world.

So far, what limited success environmentalists have had in broadening their coalitions and garnering more research grants has been due to their eloquent public warnings about the dangers of ignoring the ecological perspective. Over the last few years, for instance, by pointing out that most rainforests are probably nurturing valuable medicines, food crops, fibers, soil-restoring vegetation, or petroleum substitutes, environmentalists have convinced major drug companies and agribusiness firms to join with indigenous peoples in conserving tropical ecosystems. As the wilderness philosopher Aldo Leopold once noted, "To keep every cog and wheel is the first precaution of intelligent tinkering."

Unfortunately, though, ecological warnings sometimes deteriorate into scare tactics, and a public that already has too much to worry about is quickly becoming disdainful of doomsday scenarios. Well-meaning environmentalists too often claim that if we don't do the right thing immediately, we'll end up fighting each other for whatever resources remain—in other words, we'll be stuck in a world of Malthusian scarcity and Darwinian conflict. Yet the goal of ecological thinking should be to offer an alternative to conflict. If environmentalists truly want to restore science's balance, they will have to go beyond warnings and give us a positive reason to take an interest in scientific research priorities. They will have to popularize science the way Humboldt did—by conveying to people the exhilaration of understanding one's place in the world, the "intellectual delight and sense of freedom" that comes of "insight into universal nature."

Humboldt considered himself above all an educator, and his ultimate goal was to teach people a basic love of nature, something today's environmental movement rarely seems to do. All his life, he encouraged people simply to leave their houses and escape their specialized lifestyles, to experience the wide-open land. Once we were surrounded by nature, Humboldt felt sure, an awareness of our dependence on it would arise in us "intuitively . . . , from the contrast we draw between the narrow limits of our own existence and the image of infinity revealed on every side—whether we look upward to the starry vault of heaven, scan the far-stretching plain before us, or seek to trace the dim horizon across the vast expanse of ocean." That intuition of our indebtedness to the natural world, that recognition of our own smallness, should be the force driving scientific research.

PERSONAL RESPONSE

What did you know about Humboldt before you read this essay? What is your impression of him now that you have read about his work and his importance?

QUESTIONS FOR CLASS OR SMALL-GROUP DISCUSSION

1. What is the impact of Sachs' opening paragraph? What details does Sachs provide throughout the essay to explain why Humboldt was so highly

regarded? Locate a passage that you consider especially significant in describing Humboldt and his influence.

2. Sachs writes in paragraph 19 that the perspectives of both Darwin and Humboldt "reveal important truths." Summarize the different perspectives of those two, and then discuss what truths their differing perspectives reveal.

3. Sachs reports that the United States "spends $50 billion annually on the development of defense and space technologies, but less than $2 billion on furthering our understanding of the environment" (paragraph 30). Are you comfortable with that ordering of priorities? Explain whether you would make any changes in allocations if you had the authority to do so.

4. Sachs maintains that ecologists and environmentalists should spread "an ethic of interdisciplinary cooperation" (paragraph 32). How do you think that might be done?

A DECLARATION OF SUSTAINABILITY

PAUL HAWKEN

Paul Hawken writes frequently of the need for businesses to take social and environmental responsibility. The ideas in this essay, which first appeared in the September/October, 1993, issue of Utne Reader, *are from his book* The Ecology of Commerce: A Declaration of Sustainability *(1993) and from* Our Future and the Making of Things *(1994), which he wrote with William McDonough. His latest book is* Natural Capitalism: Creating the Next Industrial Revolution *(1999).*

I recently performed a social audit for Ben & Jerry's Homemade Inc., America's premier socially responsible company. After poking and prodding around, asking tough questions, trying to provoke debate, and generally making a nuisance of myself, I can attest that their status as the leading social pioneer in commerce is safe for at least another year. They are an outstanding company. Are there flaws? Of course. Welcome to planet Earth. But the people at Ben & Jerry's are relaxed and unflinching in their willingness to look at, discuss, and deal with problems.

In the meantime, the company continues to put ice cream shops in Harlem, pay outstanding benefits, keep a compensation ratio of seven to one from the top of the organization to the bottom, seek out vendors from disadvantaged groups, and donate generous scoops of their profit to others. And they are about to overtake their historic rival Häagen-Dazs, the ersatz Scandinavian originator of super-premium ice cream, as the market leader in their category. At present rates of growth, Ben & Jerry's will be a $1 billion company by the end of the century. They are publicly held, nationally recognized, and rapidly growing, in part because Ben wanted to show that a socially responsible company could make it in the normal world of business.

Ben & Jerry's is just one of a growing vanguard of companies attempting to re-define their social and ethical responsibilities. These companies no longer accept the maxim that the business of business is business. Their premise is simple: Corpora-tions, because they are the dominant institution on the planet, must squarely face the social and environmental problems that afflict humankind. Organizations such as Business for Social Responsibility and the Social Venture Network, corporate "ethics" consultants, magazines such as *In Business* and *Business Ethics,* nonprofits including the Council on Economic Priorities, investment funds such as Calvert and Covenant, newsletters like *Greenmoney,* and thousands of unaffiliated companies are drawing up new codes of conduct for corporate life that integrate social, ethical, and environ-mental principles.

4   Ben & Jerry's and the roughly two thousand other committed companies in the social responsibility movement here and abroad have combined annual sales of ap-proximately $2 billion, or one-hundredth of 1 percent of the $20 trillion sales gar-nered by the estimated eighty million to one-hundred million enterprises worldwide. The problems they are trying to address are vast and unremittingly complex: 5.5 bil-lion people are breeding exponentially, and fulfilling their wants and needs is strip-ping the earth of its biotic capacity to produce life; a climactic burst of consumption by a single species is overwhelming the skies, earth, waters, and fauna.

As the Worldwatch Institute's Lester Brown patiently explains in his annual sur-vey, *State of the World,* every living system on earth is in decline. Making matters worse, we are having a once-in-a-billion-year blowout sale of hydrocarbons, which are being combusted into the atmosphere, effectively double glazing the planet within the next fifty years with unknown climatic results. The cornucopia of resources that are being extracted, mined, and harvested is so poorly distributed that 20 percent of the earth's people are chronically hungry or starving, while the top 20 percent of the population, largely in the north, control and consume 80 percent of the world's wealth. Since business in its myriad forms is primarily responsible for this "taking," it is appropriate that a growing number of companies ask the question, How does one honorably conduct business in the latter days of industrialism and the beginning of an ecological age? The ethical dilemma that confronts business begins with the ac-knowledgment that a commercial system that functions well by its own definitions unavoidably defies the greater and more profound ethic of biology. Specifically, how does business face the prospect that creating a profitable, growing company requires an intolerable abuse of the natural world?

Despite their dedicated good work, if we examine all or any of the businesses that deservedly earn high marks for social and environmental responsibility, we are faced with a sobering irony: If every company on the planet were to adopt the environ-mental and social practices of the best companies—of, say, the Body Shop, Patago-nia, and Ben & Jerry's—the world would still be moving toward environmental degradation and collapse. In other words, if we analyze environmental effects and cre-ate an input–output model of resources and energy, the results do not even approxi-mate a tolerable or sustainable future. If a tiny fraction of the world's most intelligent companies cannot model a sustainable world, then that tells us that being socially responsible is only one part of an overall solution, and that what we have is not a management problem but a design problem.

At present, there is a contradiction inherent in the premise of a socially responsible corporation: to wit, that a company can make the world better, can grow, and can increase profits by meeting social and environmental needs. It is a have-your-cake-and-eat-it fantasy that cannot come true if the primary cause of environmental degradation is overconsumption. Although proponents of socially responsible business are making an outstanding effort at reforming the tired old ethics of commerce, they are unintentionally creating a new rationale for companies to produce, advertise, expand, grow, capitalize, and use up resources: the rationale that they are doing good. A jet flying across the country, a car rented at an airport, an air-conditioned hotel room, a truck full of goods, a worker commuting to his or her job—all cause the same amount of environmental degradation whether they're associated with the Body Shop, the Environmental Defense Fund, or R. J. Reynolds.

8   In order to approximate a sustainable society, we need to describe a system of commerce and production in which each and every act is inherently sustainable and restorative. Because of the way our system of commerce is designed, businesses will not be able to fulfill their social contract with the environment or society until the system in which they operate undergoes a fundamental change, a change that brings commerce and government into alignment with the natural world from which we receive our life. There must be an integration of economic, biologic, and human systems in order to create a sustainable and interdependent method of commerce that supports and furthers our existence. As hard as we may strive to create sustainability on a company level, we cannot fully succeed until the institutions surrounding commerce are redesigned. Just as every act of production and consumption in an industrial society leads to further environmental degradation, regardless of intention or ethos, we need to imagine—and then design—a system of commerce where the opposite is true, where doing good is like falling off a log, where the natural, everyday acts of work and life accumulate into a better world as a matter of course, not a matter of altruism. A system of sustainable commerce would involve these objectives:

1. It would reduce absolute consumption of energy and natural resources among developed nations by 80 percent within forty to sixty years.

2. It would provide secure, stable, and meaningful employment for people everywhere.

3. It would be self-actuating as opposed to regulated, controlled, mandated, or moralistic.

4. It would honor human nature and market principles.

5. It would be perceived as more desirable than our present way of life.

6. It would exceed sustainability by restoring degraded habitats and ecosystems to their fullest biological capacity.

7. It would rely on current solar income.

8. It should be fun and engaging, and strive for an aesthetic outcome.

Strategies for Sustainability

At present, the environmental and social responsibility movements consist of many different initiatives, connected primarily by values and beliefs rather than by design. What is needed is a conscious plan to create a sustainable future, including a set of design strategies for people to follow. For the record, I will suggest twelve.

1. Take Back the Charter. Although corporate charters may seem to have little to do with sustainability, they are critical to any long-term movement toward restoration of the planet. Read *Taking Care of Business: Citizenship and the Charter of Incorporation,* a 1992 pamphlet by Richard Grossman and Frank T. Adams (Charter Ink, Box 806, Cambridge, MA 02140). In it you find a lost history of corporate power and citizen involvement that addresses a basic and crucial point: Corporations are chartered by, and exist at the behest of, citizens. Incorporation is not a right but a privilege granted by the state that includes certain considerations such as limited liability. Corporations are supposed to be under our ultimate authority, not the other way around. The charter of incorporation is a revocable dispensation that was supposed to ensure accountability of the corporation to society as a whole. When Rockwell criminally despoils a weapons facility at Rocky Flats, Colorado, with plutonium waste, or when any corporation continually harms, abuses, or violates the public trust, citizens should have the right to revoke its charter, causing the company to disband, sell off its enterprises to other companies, and effectively go out of business. The workers would have jobs with the new owners, but the executives, directors, and management would be out of jobs, with a permanent notice on their résumés that they mismanaged a corporation into a charter revocation. This is not merely a deterrent to corporate abuse but a critical element of an ecological society because it creates feedback loops that prompt accountability, citizen involvement, and learning. We should remember that the citizens of this country originally envisioned corporations to be part of a public–private partnership, which is why the relationship between the chartering authority of state legislatures and the corporation was kept alive and active. They had it right.

2. Adjust Price to Reflect Cost. The economy is environmentally and commercially dysfunctional because the market does not provide consumers with proper information. The "free market" economies that we love so much are excellent at setting prices but lousy when it comes to recognizing costs. In order for a sustainable society to exist, every purchase must reflect or at least approximate its actual costs, not only the direct cost of production but also the costs to the air, water, and soil; the cost to future generations; the cost to worker health; the cost of waste, pollution, and toxicity. Simply stated, the marketplace gives us the wrong information. It tells us that flying across the country on a discount airline ticket is cheap when it is not. It tells us that our food is inexpensive when its method of production destroys aquifers and soil, the viability of ecosystems, and workers' lives. Whenever an organism gets wrong information, it is a form of toxicity. In fact, that is how pesticides work. A herbicide kills because it is a hormone that tells the plant to grow faster than its capacity to absorb nutrients allows. It literally grows itself to death. Sound familiar? Our daily doses of toxicity are the prices in the marketplace. They are telling us to do the wrong thing for our own survival. They are lulling us into cutting down old-growth forests on the Olympic Peninsula for apple crates, into patterns of production and consumption that are not just unsustainable but profoundly shortsighted and destructive. It is surprising that "conservative" economists do not support or understand this idea, because it is they who insist that we pay as we go, have no debts, and take care of business. Let's do it.

12   **3. Throw Out and Replace the Entire Tax System.** The present tax system sends the wrong messages to virtually everyone, encourages waste, discourages conservation, and rewards consumption. It taxes what we want to encourage—jobs, creativity, payrolls, and real income—and ignores the things we want to discourage—degradation, pollution, and depletion. The present U.S. tax system costs citizens $500 billion a year in record-keeping, filing, administrative, legal, and governmental costs—more than the actual amount we pay in personal income taxes.

The only incentive in the present system is to cheat or hire a lawyer to cheat for us. The entire tax system must be incrementally replaced over a twenty-year period by "Green fees," taxes that are added onto existing products, energy, services, and materials so that prices in the marketplace more closely approximate true costs. These taxes are not a means to raise revenue or bring down deficits, but must be absolutely revenue neutral so that people in the lower and middle classes experience no real change of income, only a shift in expenditures. Eventually, the cost of nonrenewable resources, extractive energy, and industrial modes of production will be more expensive than renewable resources, such as solar energy, sustainable forestry, and biological methods of agriculture. Why should the upper middle class be able to afford to conserve while the lower income classes cannot? So far the environmental movement has only made the world better for upper middle class white people. The only kind of environmental movement that can succeed has to start from the bottom up. Under a Green fee system the incentives to save on taxes will create positive, constructive acts that are affordable for everyone. As energy prices go up to three to four times their existing levels (with commensurate tax reductions to offset the increase), the natural inclination to save money will result in carpooling, bicycling, telecommuting, public transport, and more efficient houses. As taxes on artificial fertilizers, pesticides, and fuel go up, again with offsetting reductions in income and payroll taxes, organic farmers will find that their produce and methods are the cheapest means of production (because they truly are), and customers will find that organically grown food is less expensive than its commercial cousin. Eventually, with the probable exception of taxes on the rich, we will find ourselves in a position where we pay no taxes, but spend our money with a practiced and constructive discernment. Under an enlightened and redesigned tax system, the cheapest product in the marketplace would be best for the customer, the worker, the environment, and the company. That is rarely the case today.

4. Allow Resource Companies to Be Utilities. An energy utility is an interesting hybrid of public–private interests. A utility gains a market monopoly in exchange for public control of rates, open books, and a guaranteed rate of return. Because of this relationship and the pioneering work of Amory Lovins, we now have markets for "negawatts." It is the first time in the history of industrialism that a corporation has figured out how to make money by selling the absence of something. Negawatts are the opposite of energy: They represent the collaborative ability of a utility to harness efficiency instead of hydrocarbons. This conservation-based alternative saves ratepayers, shareholders, and the company money—savings that are passed along to everyone. All resources systems, including oil, gas, forests, and water, should be run by some form of utility. There should be markets in negabarrels, negatrees, and negacoal. Oil companies, for example, have no alternative at present other than to lobby for the absurd, like drilling in the Arctic National Wildlife Refuge. That project, a $40 billion to $60 billion investment for a hoped-for supply of oil that would meet U.S. consumption needs for only six months, is the only way an oil company can make money under our current system of commerce. But what if the oil companies formed an oil utility and cut a deal with citizens and taxpayers that allowed them to "invest" in insulation, super-glazed windows, conservation rebates on new automobiles, and the scrapping of old cars? Through Green fees, we would pay them back a return on their conservation investment equal to what utilities receive, a rate of return that would be in accord with how many barrels of oil they save, rather than how many barrels they produce. Why should they care? Why should we? A $60 billion investment in conservation will yield, conservatively, four to ten times as much energy as drilling for oil. Given Lovins' principle of efficiency extraction, try to imagine a forest utility, a salmon utility, a copper utility, a Mississippi River utility, a grasslands utility. Imagine a system where the resource utility benefits from conservation, makes money from efficiency, thrives through restoration, and profits from sustainability. It is possible today.

5. Change Linear Systems to Cyclical Ones. Our economy has many design flaws, but the most glaring one is that nature is cyclical and industrialism is linear. In nature, no linear systems exist, or they don't exist for long because they exhaust themselves into extinction. Linear industrial systems take resources, transform them into products or services, discard waste, and sell to consumers, who discard more waste when they have consumed the product. But of course we don't consume TVs, cars, or most of the other stuff we buy. Instead, Americans produce six times their body weight every week in hazardous and toxic waste water, incinerator fly ash, agricultural wastes, heavy metals, and waste chemicals, paper, wood, etc. This does not include CO_2 which if it were included would double the amount of waste. Cyclical means of production are designed to imitate natural systems in which waste equals food for other forms of life, nothing is thrown away, and symbiosis replaces competition. Bill McDonough, a New York architect who has pioneered environmental design principles, has designed a system to retrofit every window in a major American city. Although it still awaits final approval, the project is planned to go like this: The city and a major window manufacturer form a joint venture to produce energy-saving super-glazed windows in the town. This partnership company will come to your house or business, measure all windows and glass doors, and then replace them with windows with an R-8 to R-12 energy-efficiency rating within seventy-two hours. The windows will have the same casements, molding, and general appearance as the old ones. You will receive a $500 check on installation, and you will pay for the new windows over a ten- to fifteen-year period in your utility or tax bill. The total bill is less than the cost of the energy the windows will save. In other words, the windows will cost the home or business owner nothing. The city will pay for them initially with industrial development bonds. The factory will train and employ three hundred disadvantaged people. The old windows will be completely recycled and reused, the glass melted into glass, the wooden frames ground up and mixed with recycled resins that are extruded to make the casements. When the city is reglazed, the residents and businesses will pocket an extra $20 million to $30 million every year in money saved on utility bills. After the windows are paid for, the figure will go even higher. The factory, designed to be transportable, will move to another city; the first city will retain an equity interest in the venture. McDonough has designed a win-win-win-win-win system that optimizes a number of agendas. The ratepayers, the homeowners, the renters, the city, the environment, and the employed all thrive because they are "making" money from efficiency rather than exploitation. It's a little like running the industrial economy backwards.

16   **6. Transform the Making of Things.** We have to institute the Intelligent Product System created by Michael Braungart of the EPEA (Environmental Protection Encouragement Agency) in Hamburg, Germany. The system recognizes three types of products. The first are consumables, products that are either eaten, or, when they're placed on the ground, turn into dirt without any bio-accumulative effects. In other words, they are products whose waste equals food for other living systems. At present, many of the products that should be "consumable," like clothing and shoes, are not. Cotton cloth contains hundreds of different chemicals, plasticizers, defoliants, pesticides, and dyes; shoes are tanned with chromium and their soles contain lead; neckties and silk blouses contain zinc, tin, and toxic dye. Much of what we recycle today turns into toxic by-products, consuming more energy in the recycling process than is saved by recycling. We should be designing more things so that they can be thrown away—into the compost heap. Toothpaste tubes and other nondegradable packaging can be made out of natural polymers so that they break down and become fertilizer for plants. A package that turns into dirt is infinitely more useful, biologically speaking, than a package that turns into a plastic park bench. Heretical as it sounds, designing for decomposition, not recycling, is the way of the world around us.

The second category is *durables,* but in this case, they would not be sold, only licensed. Cars, TVs, VCRs, and refrigerators would always belong to the original manufacturer, so they would be made, used, and returned within a closed-loop system. This is already being instituted in Germany and to a lesser extent in Japan, where companies are beginning to design for disassembly. If a company knows that its products will come back someday, and that it cannot throw anything away when they do, it creates a very different approach to design and materials.

Last, there are *unsalables*—toxins, radiation, heavy metals, and chemicals. There is no living system for which these are food and thus they can never be thrown away. In Braungart's Intelligent Product System, unsalables must always belong to the original maker, safeguarded by public utilities called *parking lots* that store the toxins in glass-lined barrels indefinitely, charging the original manufacturers rent for the service. The rent ceases when an independent scientific panel can confirm that there is a safe method to detoxify the substances in question. All toxic chemicals would have molecular markers identifying them as belonging to their originator, so that if they are found in wells, rivers, soil, or fish, it is the responsibility of the company to retrieve them and clean up. This places the problem of toxicity with the makers, where it belongs, making them responsible for full-life-cycle effects.

7. Vote, Don't Buy. Democracy has been effectively eliminated in America by the influence of money, lawyers, and a political system that is the outgrowth of the first two. While we can dream of restoring our democratic system, the fact remains that we live in a plutocracy—government by the wealthy. One way out is to vote with your dollars, to withhold purchases from companies that act or respond inappropriately. Don't just avoid buying a Mitsubishi automobile because of the company's participation in the destruction of primary forests in Malaysia, Indonesia, Ecuador, Brazil, Bolivia, Chile, Siberia, and Papua New Guinea. Write and tell them why you won't. Engage in dialogue, send one postcard a week, talk, organize, meet, publish newsletters, boycott, patronize, and communicate with companies like General Electric. Educate nonprofits, organizations, municipalities, and pension funds to act affirmatively, to support the ecological CERES (formerly *Valdez*) Principles for business, to invest intelligently, and to *think* with their money, not merely spend it. Demand the best from the companies you work for and buy from. You deserve it and your actions will help them change.

20 **8. Restore the "Guardian."** There can be no healthy business sector unless there is a healthy governing sector. In her book *Systems of Survival*, author Jane Jacobs describes two overarching moral syndromes that permeate our society: the commercial syndrome, which arose from trading cultures, and the governing, or guardian, syndrome that arose from territorial cultures. The guardian system is hierarchical, adheres to tradition, values loyalty, and shuns trading and inventiveness. The commercial system, on the other hand, is based on trading, so it values trust of outsiders, innovation, and future thinking. Each has qualities the other lacks. Whenever the guardian tries to be in business, as in Eastern Europe, business doesn't work. What is also true, but not so obvious to us, is that when business plays government, governance fails as well. Our guardian system has almost completely broken down because of the money, power, influence, and control exercised by business and, to a lesser degree, other institutions. Business and unions have to get out of government. We need more than campaign reform. We need a vision that allows us all to see that when Speaker of the House Tom Foley exempts the aluminum industry in his district from the proposed Btu tax, or when Philip Morris donates $200,000 to the Jesse Helms Citizenship Center, citizenship is mocked and democracy is left gagging and twitching on the Capitol steps. The irony is that business thinks that its involvement in governance is good corporate citizenship or at least is advancing its own interests. The reality is that

business is preventing the economy from evolving. Business loses, workers lose, the environment loses.

9. Shift from Electronic Literacy to Biologic Literacy. That an average adult can recognize one thousand brand names and logos but fewer than ten local plants is not a good sign. We are moving not to an information age but to a biologic age, and unfortunately our technological education is equipping us for corporate markets, not the future. Sitting at home with virtual reality gloves, 3D video games, and interactive cable TV shopping is a barren and impoverished vision of the future. The computer revolution is not the totem of our future, only a tool. Don't get me wrong. Computers are great. But they are not an uplifting or compelling vision for culture or society. They do not move us toward a sustainable future any more than our obsession with cars and televisions provided us with newer definitions or richer meaning. We are moving into the age of living machines, not, as Corbusier noted, "machines for living in." The Thomas Edison of the future is not Bill Gates of Microsoft, but John and Nancy Todd, founders of the New Alchemy Institute, a Massachusetts design lab and think tank for sustainability. If the Todds' work seems less commercial, less successful, and less glamorous, it is because they are working on the real problem—how to live—and it is infinitely more complex than a microprocessor. Understanding biological processes is how we are going to create a new symbiosis with living systems (or perish). What we can learn online is how to model complex systems. It is computers that have allowed us to realize how the synapses in the common sea slug are more powerful than all of our parallel processors put together.

10. Take Inventory. We do not know how many species live on the planet within a factor of ten. We do not know how many are being extirpated. We do not know what is contained in the biological library inherited from the Cenozoic age. (Sociobiologist E. O. Wilson estimates that it would take 25,000 person-years to catalog most of the species, putting aside the fact that there are only 1,500 people with the taxonomic ability to undertake the task.) We do not know how complex systems interact—how the transpiration of the giant lily, *Victoria amazonica*, of Brazil's rainforests affects European rainfall and agriculture, for example. We do not know what happens to 20 percent of the CO_2 that is off-gassed every year (it disappears without a trace). We do not know how to calculate sustainable yields in fisheries and forest systems. We do not know why certain species, such as frogs, are dying out even in pristine habitats. We do not know the long-term effects of chlorinated hydrocarbons on human health, behavior, sexuality, and fertility. We do not know what a sustainable life is for existing inhabitants of the planet, and certainly not for future populations. (A Dutch study calculated that your fair share of air travel is one trip across the Atlantic in a lifetime.) We do not know how many people we can feed on a sustainable basis, or what our diet would look like. In short, we need to find out what's here, who has it, and what we can or can't do with it.

11. Take Care of Human Health. The environmental and socially responsible movements would gain additional credibility if they recognized that the greatest amount of human suffering and mortality is caused by environmental problems that are not being addressed by environmental organizations or companies. Contaminated water is killing a hundred times more people than all other forms of pollution combined. Millions of children are dying from preventable diseases and malnutrition. The movement toward sustainability must address the clear and present dangers that people face worldwide, dangers that ironically increase population levels because of their perceived threat. People produce more children when they're afraid they'll lose them. Not until the majority of people in the world, all of whom suffer in myriad preventable yet intolerable ways, understand that environmentalism means improving their lives directly will the ecology movement walk its talk. Americans will spend more money in the next twelve months on the movie and tchotchkes of *Jurassic Park* than on foreign aid to prevent malnutrition or provide safe water.

34   **12. Respect the Human Spirit.** If hope is to pass the sobriety test, then it has to walk a pretty straight line to reality. Nothing written, suggested, or proposed here is possible unless business is willing to integrate itself into the natural world. It is time for business to take the initiative in a genuinely, open process of dialogue, collaboration, reflection, and redesign. "It is not enough," writes Jeremy Seabrook of the British Green party, "to declare, as many do, that we are living in an unsustainable way, using up resources, squandering the substance of the next generation however true this may be. People must feel subjectively the injustice and unsustainability before they will make a more sober assessment as to whether it is worth maintaining what is, or whether there might not be more equitable and satisfying ways that will not be won at the expense either of the necessities of the poor or of the wasting fabric of the planet."

Poet and naturalist W. S. Merwin (citing Robert Graves) reminds us that we have one story, and one story only, to tell in our lives. We are made to believe by our parents and businesses, by our culture and televisions, by our politicians and movie stars that it is the story of money, of finance, of wealth, of the stock portfolio, the partnership, the country house. These are small, impoverished tales and whispers that have made us restless and craven; they are not stories at all. As author and garlic grower Stanley Crawford puts it, "The financial statement must finally give way to the narrative, with all its exceptions, special cases, imponderables. It must finally give way to the story, which is perhaps the way we arm ourselves against the next and always unpredictable turn of the cycle in the quixotic dare that is life; across the rock and cold of lifelines, it is our seed, our clove, our filament cast toward the future." It is something deeper than anything commercial culture can plumb, and it is waiting for each of us.

Business must yield to the longings of the human spirit. The most important contribution of the socially responsible business movement has little to do with recycling nuts from the rainforest, or employing the homeless. Their gift to us is that they are leading by trying to do something, to risk, take a chance, make a change—change. They are not waiting for "the solution," but are acting without guarantees of success or proof of purchase. That is what all of us must do. Being visionary has always been given a bad rap by commerce. But without a positive vision for humankind we can have no meaning, no work, and no purpose.

PERSONAL RESPONSE

In what way or ways has this essay changed or influenced your views about your personal consumption habits and about the steps society must take to require socially responsible actions by businesses? If you are not persuaded by the essay that changes must be made, explain why.

QUESTIONS FOR CLASS OR SMALL-GROUP DISCUSSION

1. How effectively does Hawken define "socially responsible" (paragraph 2)? Can you give examples, other than those Hawken names, of businesses that do not meet this "socially responsible" criterion?

2. In paragraph 8, Hawken lists the objectives involved in his proposed "system of sustainable commerce." Discuss those objectives and the likelihood that the majority of commercial enterprises worldwide would adopt them and work toward such a system.

3. Discuss the twelve steps Hawken lists. Include in your discussion an assessment of how effective you believe the steps to be as reasonable conservation measures, what their adoption would entail, and how likely you think it is that Hawken's recommendations will be adopted.

4. How well does Hawken support the following statements: "Democracy has been effectively eliminated in America by the influence of money, lawyers, and a political system that is the outgrowth of the first two" (paragraph 18) and "Computers are great. But they are not an uplifting or compelling vision for culture or society" (paragraph 20)?

THE GALILEO OF GLOBAL WARMING

AMERICAN SPECTATOR EDITORIAL

American Spectator is a national opinion magazine whose target audience is leaders in business, government, and media. It covers matters of business, politics, economics, foreign policy, and culture. This editorial appeared in the May, 2001, issue of American Spectator.

Now the global warming debate reveals that what Bob Tyrrell calls the plutomores (from the Greek plutos, "riches," and moros, "fools") have reached high positions in the Bush administration. Fooled entirely by the copious press and television coverage of the Democratic victory in Florida, for example, Treasury Secretary Paul O'Neill seems to believe he was summoned to Washington to serve as a token Republican in the administration of Al Gore. The Alcoa corpocrat devoted his first presentation to the Cabinet to an earnest plutomoronic tract on global warming, urging his baffled companions to save the planet from Republican religionists (apparently awaiting the Second Coming in rubber boots on Long Island beaches and golf courses). He all but said the Earth is in the Balance.

O'Neill and his Cabinet colleague Christie Whitman had provided the high point of this comic opera until this month's assault on Exxon Mobil by a group of angry shareholders, including a medley of nuns and Capuchin friars from New Jersey, inspired by Lloyd Keigwin, a good scientist panicked by pressures of political correctness. Collaborating in the panic is a writer from the *Wall Street Journal* named Thaddeus Herrick, who reports lugubriously that Exxon Mobil is "increasingly isolated on the issue, not only from the international scientific community, but also from European competitors . . . which largely accept the premise that the Earth is warming because of heat-trapping greenhouse gases."

Hardly heroic is Exxon Mobil, backpedaling from its denial of global warming risks. Its own plutomores seem increasingly ready to capitulate to the idea that their energy products imperil the planet.

4   Keigwin, though, is the more intriguing case. A 54-year-old oceanographer at Woods Hole Observatory near the Massachusetts Cape, he found a way to concoct a 3,000-year record of the temperatures of the Sargasso Sea near Bermuda through analyzing thermally dependent oxygen isotopes in fossils on the ocean floor. He discovered that temperatures a thousand years ago, during the so-called medieval climate optimum, were two degrees Celsius warmer than today's and that the average temperature over the last three millennia was slightly warmer than today's. Roughly confirming this result are historical records—the verdancy of Greenland at the time of the Vikings, the little ice age of the mid-1700s, a long series of temperature readings collected in Britain over the last 300 years documenting a slow recovery from the ice age, reports of medieval temperatures from a variety of sources, and records of tree rings and ice cores.

These previous findings, echoed by Keigwin's, are devastating to the theory of human-caused global warming. If the Earth was significantly warmer a thousand years ago, if we have been on a rewarming trend for three centuries, if, as other even more voluminous evidence suggests, the Earth has repeatedly seen mini-cycles of warming and cooling of about 1,500 years duration, then any upward drift in temperatures we may be seeing now—included scattered anecdotes of thinning arctic ice—is likely to be the result of such cycles.

Thus the case for human-caused global warming can no longer rest on the mere fact of contemporary warming. To justify drastic action like the Kyoto treaty requiring a reduction in U.S. energy consumption of some 30 percent, unfeasible without destroying the U.S. economy, the human-caused global warming advocates would have to demonstrate a persuasive mechanism of human causation. This they show no sign of being able to do. Grasping the point, scientists at Exxon Mobil recently used the Keigwin data in a *Wall Street Journal* ad and the PC bees hit the fan.

By all reasonable standards, Keigwin is a hero. Not only did he invent an ingenious way to compile an early temperature record, but he made a giant contribution to discrediting a movement that would impose a deadly energy clamp on the world economy. But soon enough his government-financed colleagues began to exert pressure. Was he a tool of the oil companies? Lordy no, he wrote, in an indignant letter to Exxon Mobil, denying that his findings had anything much to do with the global warming issue.

8   As the *Wall Street Journal* reported, "Dr. Keigwin warns that the results are not representative of the Earth as a whole. He says that the importance of his research isn't in the data per se, but rather that marine geologists can undertake such a study at all. . . . He wants to put the issue behind him." Hey, he's got a new government grant to find out "what's causing a substantial warming in the Atlantic Ocean off Nova Scotia." He has not reached any conclusion—but according to the *Journal,* "he gives a nod to global warming concerns, saying 'I'd take a guess.' "

Scores of scientists have been pressured to embrace the cult pressures that befall any critic of the cult of human-caused global warming. In a scientific establishment 50 percent financed by government, few can resist. An eminent scientist who was once the leading critic of global warming had to stop writing on the subject in order to continue his research. The source of the pressure that ended his publications was then-Senator Al Gore. Later this scientist coauthored a key paper with Arthur Robinson—organizer of a petition against Kyoto signed by 17,000 scientists—but had to remove his name under pressure from Washington.

Keigwin's denials of his own significance are all pathetically misleading. The temperature pattern he found in the Sargasso Sea is indeed a global phenomenon. Sallie Baliunas and Willi Soon of Harvard have uncovered a new oxygen isotope study that extends this temperature record another 3,000 years based on six millennia of evidence from peat bogs in northeastern China. The peat bog records both confirm Keigwin and demonstrate an even warmer period that lasted for 2,000 years. During this era, beginning some 4,000 years ago and running until the birth of Christ, temperatures averaged between 1.5 and 3 degrees Celsius higher than they do today.

Summing up the case is an article published earlier this year by Wallace Broecker in the prestigious pages of *Science* entitled "Was the Medieval Warm Period Global?" His answer is a resounding yes. As Craig and Keith Idso report in a March 7 editorial on their Webpage www.co2science.org, Broecker recounts substantial evidence for a series of climatic warmings spaced at roughly 1,500-year intervals. Broecker explains the science of reconstructing the histories of surface air temperatures by examining temperature data from "boreholes." From some 6,000 boreholes on all continents, this evidence confirms that the Earth was significantly warmer a thousand years ago and two degrees Celsius warmer in Greenland. This data, Robinson warns, is less detailed and authoritative than the evidence from the Sargasso Sea and from the Chinese peat bogs. But together with the independent historical record, the collective evidence is irrefutable. Thousands of years of data demonstrate that in the face of a few hundred parts per million increase in CO_2, temperatures today, if anything, are colder than usual. Temperatures in Antarctica, for example, have been falling for the last 20 years. The global satellite record of atmospheric temperature, confirmed by weather balloons, shows little change one way or another for the last three decades. Terrestrial temperature stations, on average, show more warming over the past century, but many are located in areas that were rural when the stations were established and are densely urban today, a change which causes local warming. The dominance of natural cycles globally is not surprising since, as Baliunas and Soon report, the impact of changes in sun energy output are some 70,000 times more significant than all human activity put together.

12   In the end, the global warming panic will take its place in the history books next to other environmental chimeras, such as the threat of DDT (but not of pandemic malaria), the peril of nuclear power (but not of coal mining), the brain-curdling effect of cellphones (but not of far more potent sun rays), the menace of powerlines (but not of poverty), the poison of alar (though not of rotten apple juice), the danger of asbestos in walls (but not of fire), the carcinogenic impact of PCBs (but not of carrots, peanut butter, coffee and other items that test more toxic in the same way) and the horror of radon and other sources of low-level radiation (despite is beneficial effect on health through a process called hormesis).

Overall, the situation is simple. Politicized scientists with government grants and dubious computer temperature models persuaded the world's politicians to make pompous fools of themselves in Kyoto. Socialist politicians were happy to join an absurd movement to impose government regulations over the world energy supply and thus over the world economy. The scientific claims and computer models have now blown up in their faces. But rather than admit error they persist in their fearmongering. When this happened with DDT, hundreds of millions of people died of malaria. They continue to die. How many people would die as a result of an energy clamp on global capitalism?

PERSONAL RESPONSE

Explore your reactions to the position this article takes on the subject of global warming.

QUESTIONS FOR CLASS OR SMALL-GROUP DISCUSSION

1. What evidence does this article present to support its major argument? Are you persuaded by that evidence?

2. Discuss your understanding of the Kyoto Treaty referred to in this article. Did you know that 17,000 scientists had signed a petition against the treaty (paragraph 9)? Does that information in any way change your thinking about the treaty?

3. Comment on the editorial's use of the term *cult* to describe the views of those who believe that there is global warming occurring and that humans are responsible for it (paragraph 9).

4. Look carefully at paragraph 12 and discuss your understanding of the im-
    plications of all of the parenthetical asides. For instance, the editorial ex-
    pands on the second one—"the threat of DDT (but not of pandemic
    malaria)"—in paragraph 13 when it suggests that when DDT was banned,
    it resulted in a resurgence of malaria, which has killed hundreds of millions
    of people. What is your response to that claim and to the implications in
    paragraph 12?

OUT, DAMN NATURALISTS

D. Grant DeMan

*Donald Grant DeMan (1936–2001) had many occupations through-
out his life, including policeman, private investigator, management
consultant, high-school teacher of art, artist, and author. His articles
were published in the* Toronto Globe and Mail, *the* Vancouver Sun,
and the Victoria Times-Colonist. *He was working on a book of 1950s
youth adventures in conjunction with the Sociology Department of the
University of Toronto when he died unexpectedly in 2001. This article
was published in the May 28, 2001, issue of* McLean's *magazine.*

I've had it up to here with politicos, editorialists, naturalists, protesting leftists, right-
ists and plain generic loudmouths bellowing about the damage we do to our earth,
water and air. Do I look like some harebrained game freak? Don't they think by now
I've got the message?

It seems every time I search for news, the latest wailing of some Chicken Little
group is taking up all the space. I'd like to give them space—out there alongside Pluto.
By now, I think we're aware bikes are less damaging than SUV's. It's obvious that if
you cut rainforest above a river the soil will wash downhill. I no longer need to hear
about those things. Smoking is bad. Drinking worse, except it does a little good for
the heart. Drugs devastate so we should either make them legal; hang the dealers; re-
habilitate everybody; or set up more studies.

We are told the world needs fewer people. Then on the next page, we find some
nincompoop praising the latest plan to extend life. "We can all live to be two hundred" raves the headline. Seems to me if the body crush were that severe the press
would be chiding us to live shorter, rather than longer, lives. I've given up fish and
whale products; saved birds until I'm knee-deep in feathers; and now that I've
chucked the rifle, bears are stopping by for beans and rice.

4   But that's not enough.

I now drive weekly less than 10 km. Never take trips on energy-consuming
airplanes, trains, buses or boats. Cut my hair with scissors. Flush every third time.
Seldom shave or shower. Keep the thermostat at zero. Renew the septic system.
Batten all my cracks and generally exist close to a state of donating—rather than

consuming—energy. And don't even ask how often I change my underwear. But is that sufficient? Apparently not. They just keep at it.

The pain inflicted by the tree-hugging onslaught seems even more unbearable than the original issue. For they are lambasting our ecosphere with an around-the-clock verbal First World War cannon barrage, shattering my nerves with posttraumatic stress disorder.

My newspaper is like a harping spouse. I pay for the privilege of being scolded to clean up my act. During sleepless nights, I'm haunted by their clarion call: "Let's make the whole world a natural heritage park." Pipe down, guys, I've planted so much foliage that my place—known hereabouts as "that damn jungle"—grew twice as high as it is long. Thus we live under a permanent risk of being smothered and crushed by a giant fir. So call off the heralding doomsayers, I say. We know about it and are doing it, so please stop.

8   I recycle, walk softly upon the earth, breathe as little as possible and eschew harsh detergents. I refuse all packaged and imported slave-labour food. I make only green investments. I read things online in order to preserve forests, and my only newspaper not available online, I turn into mulch for a hedgerow. I return flyers. I don't own a dishwasher. I mend and fix everything. And I even spit to enrich the soil. I'll bet the farm I pollute less than 99 per cent of those thumping the door and invading my mailbox with their "Protect Momma Earth!" flyers.

For some time, I've absolutely refused to buy anything new for fear it will harm the environment. But what must transpire so the media relents and gets on to something of which we're unaware, like what the government is really up to these days? Just once I'd love to open the op-ed page to a void of environmental rage. Or turn on the television without being harangued.

Hey guys, quit picking on me.

Once more with feeling: it's not my fault!

PERSONAL RESPONSE

What do you do to be environmentally responsible?

QUESTIONS FOR CLASS OR SMALL-GROUP DISCUSSION

1. What, exactly, is DeMan complaining about? Do you agree with him? Is he serious?

2. Explain what you think DeMan means in paragraph 6. What is "the pain inflicted by the tree-hugging onslaught"? What is "the original issue"? Where else does DeMan criticize environmentalists?

3. To what extent do you agree with DeMan about the hypocrisy of complaining about overpopulation while at the same time "praising the latest plan to extend life" (paragraph 3)?

4. What is the effect of DeMan's concluding statement: "Once more with feeling: it's not my fault!"? Is it a fitting conclusion?

○ PERSPECTIVES ON ENVIRONMENTAL STUDIES ○

Suggested Writing Topics

1. Explain your own position on global warming or any of the environmental issues mentioned in the readings.

2. Write an essay that offers possible solutions to one of the major environmental issues confronting people today.

3. Write an essay in response to the *American Spectator* editorial "The Galileo of Global Warming," D. Grant DeMan's "Out, Damn Naturalists," or Paul Hawken's "A Declaration of Sustainability."

4. Taking into account the opinion of Paul Hawken in "A Declaration of Sustainability," argue the extent to which you think pressure from lobbyists should influence the thinking of legislators considering measures that would tighten regulations on environmental issues.

5. Write a letter to the editor of your campus or community newspaper in which you urge students on your campus and citizens in the community to take actions to reverse the current abuse of natural resources. Or, propose practical conservation steps that students on your campus can take.

6. Write a letter to the president of a corporation that you know abuses the environment urging him or her to make changes in the way the company produces its product. If you refuse to buy the product because of its production methods, say so.

7. Although the writers in this chapter address a wide range of environmental issues, these selections do not provide exhaustive coverage. Select an environmental issue that is not addressed in these essays, then explain the problem in detail, and if possible, offer solutions.

Research Topics

1. Research the work of Baron Alexander von Humboldt, Charles Darwin, or Thomas Malthus and write a paper arguing the relevance of their ideas to today's environmental issues.

2. Conduct library research on the impact of socioeconomic inequities on environmental issues and argue your position on the subject. Consider including interviews of environmentalists, sociologists, and/or economists from your campus in your research.

3. Research the Kyoto Treaty referred to in the *American Spectator* editorial "The Galileo of Global Warming," explain the controversy that surrounds the treaty, and explain your own viewpoint on it.

4. Select any of the environmental issues mentioned in this chapter as a research subject. Make sure that you fairly present both sides of the issue as you explain your own position.

RESPONDING TO VISUALS

Mexican Greenpeace activists on deforested land in Ocuyoapan, Lagunas de Zempoala, Mexico, February 3, 2004. Source: Daniel Aguilar/Reuters/Landov

1. Describe the details in the picture.
2. What is the photographer's subject? Is it the SOS sign, or is it something else?
3. How effectively does the activists' banner convey their protest?
4. What does the photograph say about deforestation?

RESPONDING TO VISUALS

The island state of Nauru, the world's smallest republic, has been devastated by phosphate strip mining and was on the verge of financial collapse when this photo was taken, Sept. 11, 2001. Source: Torsten Blackwood/AFP/Getty Images

1. How do the ocean and sky surrounding the island emphasize the devastation on the island itself?
2. What story does this photograph tell about the island?
3. The island, heavily in debt, was threatened with financial ruin but received a reprieve when an Indian business group offered to pay its debts. How does that information in combination with the visual image of the island affect your response to the picture?
4. What questions about the island does the photograph raise?

E-Readings Online for Part Four
InfoTrac College Edition

http://www.infotrac-college.com

(Search for each article by author or title after entering your Infotrac College Edition password.)

Chapter 18 Digital Technology and the Internet

A major concern for parents and other adults is the easy access children have to pornography and other objectionable material on the Internet. This concern led to legislation of the Child Online Privacy Protection Act (COPPA) in 1998 and, in 2003, to the Children's Internet Protection Act (CIPA). This latter federal law forces public libraries to install Internet filters on their publicly accessed computers by withholding federal funding for Internet access to those libraries that do not comply with the law. After a lower court ruled CIPA unconstitutional, the decision made its way to the Supreme Court, who upheld the law. Meanwhile, COPPA, which has been challenged repeatedly, has never been enacted. It, too, has gone to the Supreme Court, who sent it back to lower courts for further trials. As might be expected, there has been a great deal of discussion about these laws, which seem to have honorable intentions but which many say violate First Amendment rights and constitute censorship. These readings address the subjects of both CIPA and COPPA.

○

WILL MANLEY

Intellectual Freedom Begins at Home

Criticizes library professionals for defending an "anything goes" attitude to avoid being branded censors.

○

KAREN G. SCHNEIDER

Let's Begin the Discussion: What Now? Now that CIPA's the Law, Librarians Must Tell ALA Where to Draw the Next Line

Criticizes the legal strategies of the American Library Association in arguing against the Children's Internet Protection Act.

○
Linda Greenhouse

Court, 5–4, Blocks a Law Regulating Internet Access

Provides an overview of the Supreme Court's upholding the block on enforcement of Child Online Protection Act.

QUESTIONS FOR DISCUSSION OR WRITING

1. Summarize the arguments for and against the Children's Internet Protection Act. Which position do you most align yourself with, and why?
2. Summarize the arguments for and against the Child Online Privacy Protection Act and state your own position on the issue.
3. Do you think that filters alone will solve the problem of children's exposure to sexually explicit material on the Internet? Laws such as CIPA and COPPA aside, what actions might help solve the problem?

Chapter 19 Natural Sciences

The term "junk science" applies to claims that purport to be scientific fact but that are, instead, unsubstantiated or erroneous. They may be based on a single study or on studies without peer review, or they may simply be based on no scientific fact at all. The label may be applied to claims that are based on hasty conclusions, broad generalizations, or simplification of complex problems. Such faulty data is often used to advance a particular point of view or special agenda. For instance, many health products claim to do amazing things but turn out to have little or no health benefits at all. Claims for products that perform miracles or promise things too good to be true usually are just that, too good to be true. Such products usually have not been studied or confirmed by legitimate scientific studies and are therefore based on junk science. Questions about the legitimacy or misuse of scientific data often arise in legal and political contexts as well. These articles suggest the range of areas where junk science causes problems.

○
Steven J. Milloy

Statistics Alone Don't Show Causes: How to Spot Junk Science, and Why You Need To

Provides many examples of the effects of junk science.

○

DAVID J. HANSON AND MATT WALCOFF

Age of Propaganda: The Government Attacks Teenage Drinking with Junk Science

Accuses the government of using "slick marketing" to support its position on the drinking age.

○

JOHN E. DODES

Junk Science and the Law

Argues that some courts have "demeaned science and promoted junk science" and that the system must be changed.

QUESTIONS FOR DISCUSSION OR WRITING

1. What do these articles suggest are the dangers of accepting unsubstantiated, pseudoscientific, or "junk science" claims?
2. What do you think are ways to protect yourself from junk science?
3. Do any of the examples of junk science in these articles surprise you? What examples of junk science have you come across in your everyday life?

Chapter 20 Bioethics

Many of the issues engendered by genetic research are controversial, but one of the most controversial is embryonic stem-cell research. People are torn on this issue because, on the one hand it seems to promise enormous progress in medicine, such as making it possible for people with severe spinal-cord injuries to walk again and curing or reversing such deadly diseases as Alzheimer's and Parkinson's. On the other hand, many people find the use of embryonic stem cells to be ethically and morally unacceptable. Recently, researchers have begun to consider the use of adult stem cells, which have no controversy associated with them. However, research on the effectiveness of adult stem cells has so far shown them to be inferior to embryonic stem cells for achieving dramatic medical breakthroughs. Others have tried mixing human cells with other animals' cells to produce a suitable research subject. Much research in this area remains to be done, as these articles suggest. They also suggest the nature and complexity of problems associated with stem-cell research.

○

CLAUDIA KALB

The Life in a Cell

Reports that, along with finding new hope for curing deadly disease, researchers are also finding new controversies.

○

NELL BOYCE

Mixing Species—and Crossing a Line?

Discusses the ethics of implanting stem cells from one animal into another.

○

AMY LAURA HALL

Price to Pay: The Misuse of Embryos

Argues against embryonic stem-cell research.

○

STEVE GLASSNER

Fighting Diseases with Cells: Stem-cell Research: Peril—or Potential?

Argues in favor of embryonic stem-cell research.

QUESTIONS FOR DISCUSSION OR WRITING

1. What do these articles tell you about the controversy over adult versus embryonic stem-cell research?
2. What is your opinion of mixing human and animal cells in the name of scientific research, as reported by Nell Boyce?
3. What persuasive strategies do Amy Laura Hall and Steve Glassner use in their arguments? Which do you find more persuasive? Why?

Chapter 21 Public Health

Although AIDS has been in the forefront of discussions about global health in recent years, other communicable and sometimes deadly diseases plague mankind as well. For a few years, scientists have been predicting an influenza pandemic where up to a third of the world's population would become ill. There have been outbreaks of measles in countries as far apart as Ireland and the Marshall Islands, while tuberculosis is reaching epidemic proportions in some countries. The World Health Organization (WHO) predicts that in the next decade up to 90 million people will contract tuberculosis, with a third of those people dying from it. Another widespread and deadly disease is malaria. WHO predicts that Ethiopia alone will see up to 15 million of its people infected with malaria in the next few years. Diseases like tuberculosis and malaria can be treated; unfortunately, drug-resistant "super bug" strains of both have developed. These readings touch on just a few aspects of the vexing problem of the spread and control of infectious diseases worldwide.

○

ERIC ECKERT

Diseased Societies

Surveys the many contributing factors to the high incidence of infectious diseases in developing nations.

○

LARA E. LASHER, TRACY L. AYERS, PAULI N. AMORNKUL,
MICHELE N. NAKATA, AND PAUL V. EFFLER

Contacting Passengers after Exposure to Measles on an International Flight: Implications for Responding to New Disease Threats and Bioterrorism

Details the attempts to locate passengers who had been exposed to a communicable disease on an international flight and outlines the implications of that event.

○

MICHAEL KREMER

On How to Improve World Health

Explores reasons why there is a lack of research and development on vaccines for diseases that primarily affect poor countries.

○

CHRISTINE GORMAN

Death by Mosquito

Explores reasons why malaria, which can be cured, is killing millions.

QUESTIONS FOR DISCUSSION OR WRITING

1. In what ways have these articles broadened your understanding of the global problem of infectious diseases? How are diseases spread? How do they become drug resistant? Who are their victims?

2. What advice about protecting yourself from deadly diseases do these articles give? What, if anything, can you individually do to help solve this problem? What can your community and your country do?

3. What, if any, good news is there in these articles about combating deadly diseases?

Chapter 22 Environmental Studies

In recent decades, citizens have been made aware of global environmental issues and the importance of taking individual action to help keep the world a safe and healthy place. School children learn about the potential effects of wasting natural resources, waning renewable energy sources, and pollution. Many communities make recycling mandatory and have enacted laws on the handling and disposing of hazardous waste. In addition to individuals and communities, industries and corporations have joined the fight to protect the environment. If owners and upper-level managers have not initiated such measures themselves, pressure from stakeholders, consumers, and employees have been instrumental in persuading them to set corporate social responsibility (CSR) as one of their main goals. Though that goal covers a wide spectrum of issues, including workers' rights, it almost always includes matters of interest to the greater community such as ecosystem conservation, waste management, and environmental planning and monitoring. These articles look at the efforts of corporations to play their part—or avoid it—in protecting the environment and being socially responsible.

○

BJORN STIGSON

Pillars of Change

Reports that business is finally learning that taking care of the environment and meeting social responsibilities makes good business sense.

○

JEREMY KAHN

Stop Me Before I Pollute Again

Profiles the CEO of an electric and gas supplier who wants to compromise with environmentalists.

○

STEPH LAMBERT

Unless: Two Views on Social Responsibility and the Environment

Explains how both Dr. Seuss's Lorax *and Al Gore's* Earth in the Balance *"acknowledge that Western ideals of capitalism and consumerism have been both the cause of and the financial justification for environmental devastation."*

QUESTIONS FOR DISCUSSION OR WRITING

1. How would you define "corporate social responsibility"?

2. What do these articles tell you about why industries must be socially responsible? What do they tell you about steps that industries are taking to help the environment? Is there anything else the companies should be doing?

3. Why do not all companies do the right thing by their communities, especially when it comes to environmental concerns? What are the complicating factors for them?

PART FIVE

BUSINESS AND ECONOMICS

CHAPTER

23

MARKETING AND THE AMERICAN CONSUMER

In their characteristic consumption and materialism, Americans are both the envy of people in other nations and the objects of their criticism. America has long been re-garded as the "land of plenty," with a plethora of products to buy and a standard of liv-ing that allows most citizens to buy them. Yet such plenitude can lead to over-consumption, creating a need to buy for the sake of buying that can become a kind of obsession. Some people seek psychological counseling for this compulsion, whereas others seek financial counseling to manage the debts they have built up as a result of their need to buy things.

Indeed, shopping is so central to the lives of Americans that malls have become more than places to find virtually any product people want and need; they have become social centers, where people gather to meet friends, eat, hang out, exercise, and be entertained. Some regard this penchant for spending money and acquiring goods as a symptom of some inner emptiness, with malls, shopping strips, and discount stores replacing the spiritual centers that once held primary importance in people's lives. Others, especially manufacturers of products and the people who sell them, regard consumerism as a hearty indicator of the nation's economic health.

The selections in this chapter begin with "In Praise of Consumerism," an essay by James B. Twitchell, who writes often on American consumerism and materialism. Twitchell discusses the social aspect of the consumerism concept in America, suggesting that it is the consumer who directs the marketplace, not the manufacturers and marketers of products. "We like having stuff," he asserts. As you read his essay, think about your own spending habits. Do you buy just to have things, or do you buy just those things necessary for living?

In an essay that also acknowledges the influence of advertising but that sees its influence in a different light, Richard Wolkomir and Joyce Wolkomir, in "You Are What You Buy," profile James B. Twitchell, author of "In Praise of Consumerism," based on his book *Lead Us Into Temptation: The Triumph of American Materialism.* Their article provides a historical overview of mass marketing, using many examples of successful advertising campaigns as they follow Twitchell through a Wal-Mart.

In the next article, Kevin O'Rourke, writing for beverage marketers, explains the influence of the hip-hop culture on the urban beverage market. In "The Birth of Hip-Hop," O'Rourke gives many examples of beverages that are being endorsed by hip-hop artists and stresses the overwhelming influence that such endorsements can have on sales. Finally, Phyllis Rose takes an amused look at consumerism in America in "Shopping and Other Spiritual Adventures in America Today."

As you read each of the selections in this chapter, think of your own consumer habits. Are you "addicted" to shopping? Do you like to buy for the sake of buying, whether you need a product or not? Do you buy products that are endorsed by celebrities for that reason alone? Did you (or do you) go to malls in order to socialize, or do you visit them frequently now?

IN PRAISE OF CONSUMERISM

JAMES B. TWITCHELL

James B. Twitchell teaches English and Advertising at the University of Florida. He is author of Carnival Culture: The Trashing of Taste in

America (1992), Adcult USA: The Triumph of Advertising in American Culture *(1995),* Twenty Ads that Shook the World: The Century's Most Groundbreaking Advertising and How It Changed Us All *(2000),* Living it Up: America's Love Affair with Luxury *(2003), and* Branded Nation: The Marketing of Megachurch, College Inc., and Museumworld *(2004). This article, which is based on his book* Lead Us Into Temptation: The Triumph of American Materialism *(1999), appeared in the August/September, 2000, issue of* Reason.

Sell them their dreams, sell them what they longed for and hoped for and almost despaired of having, sell them hats by splashing sunlight across them. Sell them dreams—dreams of country clubs and proms and visions of what might happen if only. After all, people don't buy things to have things. They buy things to work for them. They buy hope—hope of what your merchandise will do for them. Sell them this hope and you won't have to worry about selling them goods.

—Helen Landon Cass

Those words were spoken some years ago by a female radio announcer to a convention of salesmen in Philadelphia. *The Philadelphia Retail Ledger* for June 6, 1923, recorded Ms. Cass' invocations with no surrounding explanation. They were simply noted as a matter of record, not as a startling insight.

There are two ways to read her spiel. You can read it like a melancholy Marxist and see the barely veiled indictment of the selling process. What does she think consumers are—dopes to be duped? What is she selling? Snake oil?

Or you can read it like an unrepentant capitalist and see the connection between consuming goods and gathering meaning. The reason producers splash magical promise over their goods is because consumers demand it. Consumers are not sold a bill of goods; they insist on it. Snake oil to the cynic is often holy water to the eager. What looks like exploiting desire may be fulfilling desire.

4   How you come down in this matter depends on your estimation of the audience. Does the audience manipulate things to make meaning, or do other people use things to manipulate the audience? Clearly, this is a variation of "I persuade, you educate, they manipulate," for both points of view are supportable. Let's split the difference and be done with it.

More interesting to me, however, is to wonder why such a statement, so challenging, so revolutionary, so provocative in many respects was, in the early 1920s, so understandable, so acceptable, even so passe that it appears with no gloss. Why is it that when you read the early descriptions of capitalism, all the current bugaboos—advertising, packaging, branding, fashion, and retailing techniques—seem so much better understood?

And why has the consumer—playing an active, albeit usually secondary, part in the consumptive dyad of earlier interpretations—become almost totally listless in our current descriptions? From Thomas Hobbes in the mid-17th century ("As in other things, so in men, not the seller but the buyer determines the price") to Edwin S. Gingham in the mid-20th century ("Consumers with dollars in their pockets are not, by any stretch of the imagination, weak. To the contrary, they are the most merciless, meanest, toughest market disciplinarians I know"), the consumer was seen as participating in the meaning-making of the material world. How and why did the consumer get dumbed down and phased out so quickly? Why has the hypodermic metaphor (false needs injected into a docile populace) become the unchallenged explanation of consumerism?

I think that much of our current refusal to consider the liberating role of consumption is the result of who has been doing the describing. Since the 1960s, the primary "readers" of the commercial "text" have been the well-tended and -tenured of members of the academy. For any number of reasons—the most obvious being their low levels of disposable income, average age, and gender, and the fact that these critics are selling a competing product, high-cult (which is also coated with its own dream values)—the academy has casually passed off as "hegemonic brainwashing" what seems to me, at least, a self-evident truth about human nature: We like having stuff.

8   In place of the obvious, they have substituted an interpretation that they themselves often call vulgar Marxisms. It is supposedly vulgar in the sense that it is not as sophisticated as the real stuff, but it has enough spin on it to be more appropriately called Marxism lite. Go into almost any cultural studies course in this country and you will hear the condemnation of consumerism expounded: What we see in the marketplace is the result of the manipulation of the many for the profit of the few. Consumers are led around by the nose. We live in a squirrel cage. Left alone we would read Wordsworth, eat lots of salad, and have meetings to discuss Really Important Subjects.

In cultural studies today, everything is oppression and we are all victims. In macrocosmic form, the oppression is economic—the "free" market. In microcosmic form, oppression is media—your "free" TV. Here, in the jargon of this downmarket Marxism, is how the system works: The manipulators, a.k.a. "the culture industry," attempt to enlarge their hegemony by establishing their ideological base in the hearts and pocketbooks of a weak and demoralized populace. Left alone, we would never desire things (ugh!). They have made us materialistic. But for them, we would be spiritual.

To these critics, the masters of industry and their henchmen, the media lords, are predators, and what they do in no way reflects or resolves genuine audience concerns. Just the opposite. The masters of the media collude, striving to infantilize us so that we are docile, anxious, and filled with "reified desire." While we may think advertising is just "talking about the product," that packaging just "wraps the object," that retailing is just "trading the product," or that fashion is just "the style of the product," this is not so. That you may think so only proves their power over you. The marginalized among us—the African American, the child, the immigrant, and especially the female are trapped into this commodifying system, this false consciousness, and this fetishism that only the enlightened can correct. Legendary ad man David Ogilvy's observation that, "The consumer is no fool, she is your wife" is just an example of the repressive tolerance of such a sexist, materialist culture.

Needless to say, in such a system the only safe place to be is tenured, underpaid, self-defined as marginalized, teaching two days a week for nine months a year, and writing really perceptive social criticism that your colleagues can pretend to read. Or rather, you would be writing such articles if only you could find the time.

The Triumph of Stuff

12   The idea that consumerism creates artificial desires rests on a wistful ignorance of history and human nature, on the hazy, romantic feeling that there existed some halcyon era of noble savages with purely natural needs. Once fed and sheltered, our needs have always been cultural, not natural. Until there is some other system to codify and satisfy those needs and yearnings, capitalism—and the culture it carries with it—will continue not just to thrive but to triumph.

In the way we live now, it is simply impossible to consume objects without consuming meaning. Meaning is pumped and drawn everywhere throughout the modern commercial world, into the farthest reaches of space and into the smallest divisions of time. Commercialism is the water we all swim in, the air we breathe, our sunlight and shade. Currents of desire flow around objects like smoke in a wind tunnel.

This isn't to say that I'm simply sanguine about such a material culture. It has many problems that I have glossed over. Consumerism is wasteful, it is devoid of otherworldly concerns, it lives for today and celebrates the body. It overindulges and spoils the young with impossible promises. It encourages recklessness, living beyond one's means, gambling. Consumer culture is always new, always without a past. Like religion, which it has displaced, it afflicts the comfortable and comforts the afflicted. It is heedless of the truly poor who cannot gain access to the loop of meaningful information that is carried through its ceaseless exchanges. It is a one-dimensional world, a wafer-thin world, a world low on significance and high on glitz, a world without yesterdays.

On a personal level, I struggle daily to keep it at bay. For instance, I am offended by billboards (how do they externalize costs?); I fight to keep Chris Whittle's Channel One TV and all placed-based advertising from entering the classroom; political advertising makes me sick, especially the last-minute negative ads; I contribute to PBS in hopes they will stop slipping down the slope of commercialism (although I know better); I am annoyed that Coke has bought all the "pouring rights" at my school and is now trying to do the same to the world; I think it's bad enough that the state now sponsors gambling, do they also have to support deceptive advertising about it?; I despise the way that amateur athletics has become a venue for shoe companies (why not just replace the football with the Nike swoosh and be done with it?); and I just go nuts at Christmas.

16   But I also realize that while you don't have to like it, it doesn't hurt to understand it and our part in it. We have not been led astray. Henry Luce was not far off when he claimed in a February 1941 editorial in *Life* magazine that the next era was to be the American Century: "The Greeks, the Romans, the English and the French had their eras, and now it was ours." Not only that, but we are likely to commandeer much of the 21st century as well.

Almost a decade ago, Francis Fukuyama, a State Department official, contended in his controversial essay (and later book) "The End of History?" that "the ineluctable spread of consumerist Western culture" presages "not just the end of the Cold War, or the passing of a particular period of postwar history, but the end of history as such: that is, the end point of mankind's ideological evolution." OK, such predictions are not new. "The End of History" (as we know it) and "the end point of mankind's ideological evolution" have been predicted before by philosophers. Hegel claimed it had already happened in 1806 when Napoleon embodied the ideas of the French Revolution, and Marx said the end was coming soon with world communism. What legitimizes this modern claim is that it is demonstrably true. For better or for worse, American commercial culture is well on its way to becoming world culture. The Soviets have fallen. Only quixotic French intellectuals and anxious Islamic fundamentalists are trying to stand up to it.

To some degree, the triumph of consumerism is the triumph of the popular will. You may not like what is manufactured, advertised, packaged, branded, and broadcast, but it is far closer to what most people want most of the time than at any other period of modern history.

Trollope and *The Jerk*

Two fictional characters personify to me the great divide: Augustus Melmotte, the protagonist of Anthony Trollope's 19th-century novel, *The Way We Live Now*, and Navin R. Johnson, the eponymous hero of Steve Martin's 1979 movie, *The Jerk*.

20   Melmotte, a Jew, comes from Paris to London with his daughter and his Bohemian wife. When the action of the novel is over and Augustus has committed suicide because he cannot fit in to proper Victorian society, wife and daughter head off to America—to San Francisco, to be exact. Trollope is always exact in letting you know that geography determines character. So too we know that Ruby Ruggles and her bumpkin brother belong at Sheep's Acres Farm and that Roger Carbury should preside over Carbury Hall. Sir Felix Carbury, fallen from grace, must go to Germany—there is no room for his kind, no club that will accept him. Mrs. Hurtle comes from San Francisco and in the end must return there.

Any Trollope lover worth his salt can tell you much about the protagonists simply by such comings and goings. These paths are the code by which our grandparents recognized, in Dominick Dunne's felicitous title, those who are "people like us": our kind/not our kind. The Victorian reading public needed such shorthand because things had no brand personalities—manners, places, sinecures—and bloodlines did. Salaries meant little, accomplishments even less. The central acts of *The Way We Live Now* are the attempts by Augustus Melmotte to buy a titled husband for his daughter and get a named estate for himself. He can't do it, of course—how silly to try, even if he is the "City's most powerful financier." In his world, meaning was generated through such social conventions as the abstract concept of bloodline, the value of patina, your club, owning land, acceptable in-laws, your accent, the seating chart for dinner, the proper church pew—all things Melmotte could never master. It was a stultifying system—a real old-boy network, but one that to Trollope still worked. It was a system presided over by chummy squires, comfortable gentlemen, and twinkling clerics.

Compare that to the world of *The Jerk*. Here, the story is held together by the running joke that when Navin R. Johnson is being the most idiotic, he is really being the most savant. After a series of misadventures, Navin amasses a fortune by inventing a way to keep eyeglasses from slipping down the nose (the "Opti-grab"). He wins the hand of his sweetheart, buys incredibly gauche gold chains, swag lamps, outrageous golf carts, and ersatz Grecian mansions. Surrounded by things, he is finally happy. But then—curses!—he loses his possessions as a google-eyed litigant wins a class action lawsuit because the Opti-grab has made many wearers cross-eyed. Navin's wife is distraught. She bursts into tears. "I don't care about losing the money, it's losing all this stuff."

Navin, as innocent as he is honest, says he doesn't really care about these things, he knows who he is without possessions. His sense of self is certainly not tied to the material world. "I don't want stuff . . . I don't need anything," he says to her as he starts to leave the room in his pajamas. He sees an old ashtray. "Except this ashtray, and that's the only thing I need is this," he says, as he leans over to pick it up. Navin walks to the door. "Well, and this paddle game and the ashtray is all I need. And this, this remote control; that's all I need, just the ashtray, paddle game, and this remote control."

24   Navin is growing progressively more frantic in vintage Steve Martin fashion. He is in the hall now, pajamas down around his knees and his arms full of stuff. "And these matches. Just the ashtray, paddle ball, remote control, and these matches . . . and this lamp, and that's all I need. I don't need one other thing . . . except this magazine." We hear him gathering more things as he disappears down the hall. Navin, jerk enough to think he needs nothing, is sage enough not to leave home without a few of his favorite things.

Augustus Melmotte, certified world-class financier, is forever kept at bay. He never achieves his goal and finally commits suicide. Navin R. Johnson, certified consumer jerk, achieves (if only for a while) the objects of his heart's desire. He finally becomes a bum on Skid Row, true, but a bum who at least can try it all over again. In a consumerist culture, the value-making ligatures that hold our world together come from such conventions as advertising, packaging, branding, fashion, and even shopping itself. It is a system presided over by marketers who deliver the goods and all that is carried in their wake. It is a more democratic world, a more egalitarian world, and, I think, a more interesting world.

That said, commercialism can be a stultifying system too, and wasteful. It would be nice to think that this eternally encouraging market will result in the cosmopolitanism envisioned by the Enlightenment philosophers, that a "universalism of goods" will end in a crescendo of hosannas. It would be nice to think that more and more of the poor and disenfranchised will find their ways into the cycle of increased affluence without contracting "affluenza," the "disease" of buying too much. It would be nice to think that materialism could be heroic, self-abnegating, and redemptive. It would be nice to think that greater material comforts will release us from racism, sexism, and ethnocentricism, and that the apocalypse will come as it did at the end of Shelley's *Prometheus Unbound,* leaving us "Sceptreless, free, uncircumscribed . . . Equal, unclassed, tribeless; and nationless . . . Pinnacled dim in the intense inane."

But it is more likely that the globalization of capitalism will result in the banalities of an ever-increasing, worldwide consumerist culture. Recall that Athens ceased to be a world power around 400 B.C., yet for the next three hundred years Greek culture was the culture of the world. The Age of European Exposition ended in the mid-20th century; the Age of American Markets—Yankee imperialism—is just starting to gather force. The French don't stand a chance. The Middle East is collapsing under the weight of dish antennas and Golden Arches. The untranscendent, repetitive, sensational, democratic, immediate, tribalizing, and unifying force of what Irving Kristol calls the American Imperium need not result in a Bronze Age of culture, however. In fact, who knows what this Pax Americana will result in? But it certainly will not produce what Shelley had in mind.

28   We have been in the global marketplace a short time, and it is an often scary and melancholy place. A butterfly flapping its wings in China may not cause storm clouds over Miami, but a few lines of computer code written by some kid in Palo Alto may indeed change the lives of all the inhabitants of Shanghai.

More important, perhaps, we have not been led into this world of material closeness against our better judgment. For many of us, especially when young, consumerism is not against our better judgment. It is our better judgment. And this is true regardless of class or culture. We have not just asked to go this way, we have demanded. Now most of the world is lining up, pushing and shoving, eager to elbow into the mall. Woe to the government or religion that says no.

Getting and spending have been the most passionate, and often the most imaginative, endeavors of modern life. We have done more than acknowledge that the good life starts with the material life, as the ancients did. We have made stuff the dominant prerequisite of organized society. Things "R" Us. Consumption has become production. While this is dreary and depressing to some, as doubtless it should be, it is liberating and democratic to many more.

PERSONAL RESPONSE

Do you think that consumerism creates artificial values? Do you consider yourself "an unrepentant capitalist" (paragraph 4)? Explain your answer.

QUESTIONS FOR CLASS OR SMALL-GROUP DISCUSSION

1. How does the Helen Landon Cass quotation that precedes the text work to introduce Twitchell's subject? How effective do you find Twitchell's references to Trollope and *The Jerk* (paragraph 20)? What is their function?

2. Look at what Twitchell says in paragraph 4 about consumers demanding that "producers splash magical promise over their goods." What do you think he means when he says that consumers "insist on" a bill of goods and that "what looks like exploiting desire may be fulfilling desire"? To what extent do you agree with him?

3. Comment on Twitchell's use of the phrase "liberating role of consumption" in paragraph 8. Do you agree with him that "we like having stuff"? Do you think it is a fair representation of Americans?

4. What do you think of Twitchell's critique of academics who view consumerism as oppression (paragraphs 8–12)?
5. Twitchell seems to see consumerism as both good and bad. State in your own words what he sees as good about it and what he sees as bad. To what extent do you share his viewpoint?

YOU ARE WHAT YOU BUY

RICHARD WOLKOMIR AND JOYCE WOLKOMIR

Richard Wolkomir and Joyce Wolkomir are writers whose work appears often in Smithsonian *magazine. He is a former editor at the McGraw-Hill Publishing Company, and she is a former* Scholastic Magazines *editor. They are authors of* Junkyard Bandicoots and Other Tales of the World's Endangered Species *(1992). This article was published in the October, 2000, issue of* Smithsonian.

Along with two friends who need a new plastic dish drainer, James Twitchell, a professor of 19th-century poetry at the University of Florida in Gainesville, is visiting a Wal-Mart. Twitchell gazes raptly upon the aisles stacked with TV sets in boxes, and picnic baskets and T-shirts and beach balls. So much mass-produced stuff! Twitchell is energized—as any dedicated scholar would be upon entering an archive packed with new material.

"Look at this wire shopping cart—it's the equivalent of the Las Vegas poker chip," he says. "In a casino, instead of gambling with your real money, you use little colored plastic disks, so it seems OK. This huge cart is something like that: it's so roomy you don't feel you're buying too much. Marketers fooled around with the size of these carts, getting them just right."

Twitchell loves this stuff. He loves it so much that he has switched from teaching and writing solely about Romantic-era poetry to buzzier issues, such as adolescents wearing dungarees slung low to reveal their Joe Boxers, and whether the Jolly Green Giant is an avatar of Zeus. And now, reveling in all these bedspreads and CD players and croquet sets and yellow raincoats, Twitchell tells his friends that one reason he began studying such fine points of mass marketing is that his parents, long ago, denied him Wonder Bread.

4   Twitchell's father, a Vermont physician, dismissed Wonder Bread as "air and water." His mother warned that Coca-Cola was sugar water that would "rot your teeth." Now he keeps a cellophane-wrapped loaf of Wonder Bread and an aluminum can of Coke—icons among American consumables—atop his computer monitor. In one of Twitchell's recent books, *Lead Us Into Temptation: The Triumph of American Materialism,* he wrote that everything he loved as a youth was from the forbidden mass culture: "It was mass produced, mass marketed and consumed en masse." And if he

wanted to savor Pepsi and Whoppers and Dairy Queen sundaes, he had to do it on the sly, "for we would not countenance them inside the family circle."

Twitchell—who is now in his 50s, trim and urbane—says his study of mass culture, especially advertising, began 15 years ago, when he was teaching a class on the Romantic poets. "I suddenly realized my students had no interest in what I had to say." He asked them to complete a line from Wordsworth: "My heart leaps up when I behold a ——— in the sky." Nobody could supply the missing "rainbow," but his students could flawlessly recite the contents of a Big Mac: two all-beef patties, special sauce, lettuce, cheese, pickles and onions on a sesame-seed bun.

"It was an epiphany," he says.

At the time, the much-discussed book by E. D. Hirsch, et al., *Cultural Literacy: What Every American Needs To Know,* argued that cultures need the glue of shared knowledge, like who Napoleon was or where Beirut is. "I realized he was right, we do need a body of information," explains Twitchell. "But he was wrong about what body of information we share, because it isn't from high culture—it's from pop culture, the world my students knew so well." His students knew little about Dickens or Keats. "But they could recite the 'Mmm, mmm good' Campbell's Soup jingle," he says. "They didn't know Rembrandt, but they could tell you Ben's and Jerry's last names." Twitchell was stunned. "I wanted to know why the stuff they knew was so powerful it pushed my stuff out of the way."

8   Since then, he has been observing himself, his law professor wife, his two daughters, now grown, his colleagues, students, neighbors. He has invited himself into advertising agencies as an academic gadfly on the wall. He has explored advertising's history. And he has learned the average adult now encounters some 3,000 advertisements every day, from bus flanks to messages over the telephone as the caller waits on hold. He has probed the impact of all that mass marketing in such works as *ADCULTUSA* and his latest book, *Twenty Ads That Shook the World.*

Academics usually excoriate modern materialism as spiritually deadening and socially corrupting, he observes. "My own take is that humans love things, and we've always been materialistic, but until the Industrial Revolution only the wealthy had things—now the rest of us are having a go at arranging our lives around things." Especially in the past 20 years, young people have had lots more money to spend. "Now they're driving the market for mass-produced objects." And especially for youths, Twitchell maintains, advertising has become our social studies text. "Ask 18-year-olds what freedom means, and they'll tell you, 'It means being able to buy whatever I want!'"

But advertising's job is not just urging, "Buy this!" Twitchell cites 1950s ad ace Rosser Reeves, who created a television commercial in which a hammer clangs an anvil to remind viewers how a headache feels (or maybe to induce one) while reporting good news: Anacin is "for fast, Fast, FAST relief. . . ." Reeves would hold up two quarters. It was advertising's task, he said, to make you believe those two quarters were different. Even more important, the ad had to persuade you that one of those quarters was worth more.

To illustrate the process, Twitchell points to 1930s ads claiming Schlitz steam-cleaned its beer bottles. What the ads omitted was that all brewers steam-cleaned their bottles. Thus, through advertising, the company achieved "ownership" of product purity—it created for itself what the ad industry calls a USP (Unique Selling Proposition).

12   According to Twitchell, it was in the Victorian era that mass culture reared up, driven by the steam-powered printing press, which spewed out text and images and notions for the "mob." Victorians invented the word "mob," he says, by shortening the Latin *mobile vulgus,* "rabble on the move." Victorian education strove to differentiate literature from pulp novels, to show classical music's superiority to dance-hall tunes, to instill "art appreciation." But with the machine age churning out cheap goods, consumerism was erupting all over, and so was advertising.

Thomas J. Barratt, the 19th-century manufacturer of Pears' Soap, noted: "Any fool can make soap. It takes a clever man to sell it." And Barratt was just that man. "The manufacture of soap is a turning point in civilization," says Twitchell. Originally, farmers boiled animal fats with wood ashes and molded the result into soap balls, which soon stank. With the machine age came soap concocted from caustic soda and vegetable fats, pressed into bars that lasted forever. But one soap was much like another.

In 1881, at James Gamble's soap factory in Cincinnati, a worker forgot to turn off the mixing machinery, inadvertently producing a batch of soap so air-filled it floated. Gamble claimed his new soap, Ivory, floated because it was pure—in fact, 99 44/100 percent pure.

Earlier, England's Andrew Pears—the father-in-law of Thomas J. Barratt—had developed a translucent soap. It seemed a natural to appeal to the class-conscious Briton's desire for whiter skin, versus a laborer's weathered tan. Barratt got the message across in such ways as plastering his company's new slogan, an early version of Nike's "Just Do It," on walls all over the British Empire: "Good Morning! Have You Used Your Pears' Soap?"

16   But Barratt's greatest coup was co-opting Bubbles, a John Everett Millais painting of the artist's angelic grandson watching a just-blown soap bubble waft upward. Barratt sold Millais on the notion that, distributed as a free poster, his painting would reach thousands upon thousands of potential new art lovers, for their edification. For their further edification, Barratt had a cake of the soap lying in the painting's foreground, inscribed "Pears'."

Branding made advertising possible. In the early 1800s, soap was just soap. Like biscuits or nails, it came in barrels, and to get some, you told the store clerk, "Two bars of soap, please." By the late 1800s—nudged by Barratt's advertising—you might specify Pears' Soap. Twitchell says Barratt's hijacking of art to sell soap "blurred, for the first time and forevermore, the bright line between art and advertising, between high culture and the vulgar, between pristine and corrupt." Today, art co-opted by advertising is so commonplace we do not blink at Michelangelo's David wearing Levi's cutoffs.

Back in the Wal-Mart, Twitchell veers toward a barrel displaying kitchen floor mats. "Two for five dollars!" he says, reading a sign. It is clearly tempting. Two floor mats, one price. But he pulls himself away from the alluring floor mats to ruminate about literature. "I'm supposed to teach English Romantic poetry," he says. "That period, the beginning of the 19th century, is where many of our views on materialism came from, because that was when the Industrial Revolution began producing the surfeit of things that will cause the trouble."

Surpluses produced by the new technologies, like steam power, were particularly apt to pile up after wars, and that was especially true in the aftermath of the Civil War. "What it takes to win a war is the ability to produce more war materials than your opponent, but when the war ends you have too many blankets, boots, rifles, and too much patent medicine—which was the subject of the first real advertising," he explains. "In the 1870s we had the rise of advertising, along with the rise of newspapers, and now we start talking about two nostrums or two pairs of boots as if they were different, when we know they are the same."

20   Modern advertising, Twitchell insists, learned its stuff from religion. "I grew up a Vermont Congregationalist. My father was a doctor in our town, and his father had been a doctor in our town, and my mother's family had lived around there since the Revolution." His was, except for Wonder Bread denial, a stable life. "In the world where I grew up, you knew who you were by a series of time-tested anchors—ancestry, land, religion, where you went to school, your accent, your job—but we've been rapidly losing those anchors," he argues. "One marriage out of two ends in divorce, the average person changes jobs seven or eight times during a lifetime." With the old determinants of social position shifting or gone, he says, "we're starting to build our identity around driving a Lexus or displaying Ralph Lauren's polo player on our shirt."

He notes that many of modern advertising's founders had religious backgrounds. A Baptist minister's son, Bruce Barton, cofounded the large ad agency Batten, Barton, Durstine & Osborne (which comedian Fred Allen suggested sounded like "a trunk falling downstairs"). Artemus Ward, who wrote psalms to Sapolio Soap, was the son of an Episcopal minister. John Wanamaker, whose marketing genius helped create the modern department store, once considered becoming a Presbyterian minister. Rosser Reeves, creator of the Anacin anvils, was the son of a Methodist minister.

Twitchell contends that these founders of modern advertising, and others like them, modeled their messages on parables they heard in church. He sketches a typical TV commercial in which someone is distressed. Perhaps it is a young woman, if the product is a dish detergent. Perhaps it is a middle-aged man, if the product is a cold remedy. The heroine or hero consults another person who gives witness: a certain product "works miracles." The product is tried. Relief! Ads create and then promise to absolve you of secular sins, such as halitosis or dandruff, or "ring around the collar" or "dishpan hands."

But Twitchell says that advertising also reaches back to paganism. Instead of Zeus in the clouds and dryads in trees, we have televisions that are inhabited by the Jolly Green Giant, the Michelin Man, the Man from Glad, Mother Nature, Aunt Jemima, the White Knight, the Energizer Bunny and Speedy Alka-Seltzer with his magical chant: "Plop, plop, fizz, fizz. . . ."

24   Commercial culture is so potent, Twitchell believes, that it has "colonized" society. For instance, Christmas was low-key until the 1800s, when stores reinvented the holiday to sell off their surpluses. On December 24, 1867, R. H. Macy kept his

Manhattan store open until midnight, setting a one-day sales record of more than $6,000.

Santa started as "a weird conflation of St. Nicholas (a down-on-his-luck noble-man who helped young women turn away from prostitution) and Kriss Kringle (per-haps a corruption of the German Christkindl, a gift giver)." Today's familiar Santa, Twitchell continues, originated in the 1930s, because Coca-Cola's sales slumped in winter. Ads began showing Santa—in his modern persona—relaxing in a living room after toy delivery, quaffing a Coke apparently left for him by the home's children. "Coke's Santa was elbowing aside other Santas—Coke's Santa was starting to own Christmas." Rudolph the Red-Nosed Reindeer was a 1930s creation of a Montgomery Ward copywriter. And Twitchell says Kodak ads universalized the tradition of blow-ing out birthday-cake candles and other "Kodak Moments" to "show what you can do with fast Kodak film and the Kodak Flashmatic attachment on your Kodak camera."

Ads have even changed our attitude toward debt, which once could lead to prison. "Think only of how consumer debt was merchandised until it became an ac-cepted habit, not an abhorred practice," observes Twitchell. "Think only of how the concept of shine and 'new and improved' replaced the previous value of patina and heirloom." Twitchell says politics hit its modern ad-driven stride starting with the 1952 "Eisenhower Answers America" Presidential campaign, designed by Rosser Reeves. Regarding his own ads, Ike said ruefully: "To think an old soldier should come to this."

Athletes have become logo-bedecked living billboards. But Twitchell argues that commercial culture has affected us all. Cereal, for example, is now synonymous with breakfast. "Before Messrs. Post and Kellogg, this meal consisted of breaking fast by finishing last night's dinner," he says, adding that leftovers went to the family dog. Dog food was a creation of Ralston Purina's ad agency. Twitchell says that some mar-keting ploys fizzled, of course, citing an old ad headlined: "Sunday is Puffed Grain Day."

28   Mother's Day began in the early 1900s when Philadelphia merchandiser John Wanamaker elevated to stardom a local woman mourning for her mother. He ran fullpage ads in the *Philadelphia Inquirer*. Soon only a blackguard would fail to buy Mom a present on her newly special day. Wanamaker reportedly gloated that he would rather be the founder of Mother's Day than the king of England.

Twitchell is no longer amazed that his students, inundated with commercial messages, display their status with manufacturers' logos on their shirt pockets or on their sunglasses. "At a Palm Beach store a woman explained to me that the more ex-pensive the sunglasses, the smaller the logo, so that with Cartier you can barely see the Cy." His students derogatorily refer to certain classmates as "Gaps," after the re-tail chain where they buy their clothes. In the 19th century, people learned manners from novels and magazines; in the 20th from sitcoms and ads. When his daughter was a teenager, he heard her telling friends, after watching a teen TV show, *90210*, "Can you believe how cool Kelly looked in Dylan's Porsche!" Twitchell shrugs: "That's all they have for Trollope."

Economist Thorstein Veblen coined the term "conspicuous consumption": dis-playing possessions to impress others. "Between ages 15 and 25, we males consume the most as a percentage of our disposable income because we're displaying our feathers to potential mates," says Twitchell. "Now it's more complicated because females are working and they can display too." But the urge wanes. "After about age 45, many people start moving away from acquisition. Thus, ads, TV shows, and movies, which are studded with paid-for product placements, concentrate ferociously on youths, who seem to get the message.

But not all analysts agree with Madison Avenue's youth fixation. In fact, according to Beth Barnes, an associate professor at Syracuse University and chair of the advertising department at the S. I. Newhouse School of Public Communications, advertisers are increasingly recognizing that the over-45 age-group is growing fast. And older Americans often have the magic ingredient: disposable income. "I think the change is slow, but inevitable," Barnes says. For one thing, she notes, advertising is increasingly segmented, exploiting today's highly segmented media to aim fine-tuned messages at specific subcultures, including age-groups. "Advertising for soft drinks may stay aimed at youth," she says. "But the trick is to go after older people with products in which they are not set in their ways—computers, for instance, or travel and tourism, or financial services, or new products, like Chrysler's PT Cruiser."

32   About a year ago, marketing circles buzzed over the surprising number of over-45 online shoppers. "It makes sense. They're amazingly machine savvy—my mother just got a new computer because her old one was too slow." It is true, Barnes continues, that younger people may be less loyal to brands, and easier to woo away. But she adds: "There's a flip side to that—young people are lot more skeptical too!"

Perhaps. "Why," asks James Twitchell, "are my daughters willing to buy a bottle of water worth two cents and pay $1.50?" They aren't buying the product itself; they're buying the values that advertising has attached to the product, such as being hip. He cites a Madison Avenue adage: "You don't drink the beer; you drink the advertising."

Many of today's ads leave the average reader or viewer totally confused about what is being sold. For instance, in one current TV commercial, a cool young couple is driving down a city street, their car's windshield wipers clacking. They are so tuned in, they notice that the passing scene is rife with tempos, such as a boy bouncing a basketball, all in perfect sync with the rhythmic clack of their windshield wipers. What is going on?

"Often advertising is not about keeping up with the Joneses, but about separating you from them," Twitchell points out. "That's especially true of advertising directed at a particular group, such as adolescents or young-adult males—it's called 'dog-whistle' advertising because it goes out at frequencies only dogs can hear." In this case, the "dogs" are the commercial's target group of young adults. The young couple is hip enough to be driving their model of Volkswagen. "The idea is, your parents can't understand this, but you can." He cites a recent advertisement for a new sport utility vehicle that actually has the headline: "Ditch the Joneses!"

36   The most egregious example of this oblique marketing ploy was, of course, Benetton's spate of ads that employed the force of shock in order to create product recognition. The image of a nun and a priest, locked in a passionate kiss, was offensive to many people. But the pieces de resistance were Benetton's portraits of 25 death row inmates in America's prisons. This ad campaign cost Benetton its lucrative

contract with Sears, Roebuck & Company and ended Oliviero Toscani's 18-year career as Benetton's creative director.

Such an ad may look senseless to a 50-year-old, Twitchell says, "but it's being properly decoded by a 23-year-old." It works. Today's average American consumes twice as many goods and services as in 1950, and the average home is twice as large as a post–World War II average home. A decade ago, most grocery stores stocked about 9,000 items; today's stores carry some 24,000.

Twitchell says he does not believe for a minute that our commercial society is a better world. "But it might be a safer world, oddly enough, if we value machine-made objects about which lies are told, rather than feuding over how to save souls," he says. "And we may be moving into a quieter world as people who were never able to consume before begin getting and spending."

He points upward, to the Wal-Mart's ceiling, with its exposed girders, pipes, wires and ducts, painted industrial gray. "That's to give you the illusion that you're buying stuff as close to the factory as possible," he says. His eyes fix upon Kraft Macaroni & Cheese boxes, each inscribed "The Cheesiest." He says, "It looks like a cornucopia, and the message is, 'Take one!' And see, the stack still sits on its freight pallet, to give you the idea there aren't many middlemen between you and the factory price."

40   Everything in the store is a brand-name product. "See, a stack of Fedders' air conditioners in their boxes. It was Wal-Mart founder Sam Walton's great insight that if he sold only branded items and negotiated lower prices, the manufacturers would do all the advertising for him."

Twitchell wanders back to the alluring display of floor mats that had first attracted his eye. He stares, transfixed. "Two for five dollars! I came in here meaning to buy one. That idea of two seemingly for the price of one took hold in the 1940s, especially with Alka-Seltzer, which you originally took as only one tablet until they halved the dosage so you'd take two: 'Plop, plop. . . .' " A few steps farther, he eyes a display of bottled mineral water. "This one is made by Pepsi. When they studied its marketing in Wichita, they were astonished to find out that buyers of these lower-priced mineral waters didn't care if it came from underground springs or runoff from Alpine glaciers—they bought the water because they liked the name and the feel of the bottle in their hand."

He pauses at a rack of greeting cards. "It's how we exchange emotions now, the commercializing of expression. The most touching are the cards to send to kids, offering your sympathy because their parents just got divorced." Such cards perform a useful service. "They're facilitators of difficulty, and they help us handle emotionally fraught events quickly and efficiently."

As his friends prepare to leave the Wal-Mart, without the dish drainer they had sought, Twitchell stops. "I'm going to go buy those two floor mats, but after you leave, because I'm ashamed to be seen succumbing to that two-for-the-price-of-one deal," he says.

44   Even so, Twitchell—deprived as a boy of Wonder Bread and Coke—believes the stuff cramming our stores, which advertisements strain to get us to buy, is not necessarily invidious to our cultural health. "After all," he says, "we don't call them 'bads'— we call them 'goods!' "

PERSONAL RESPONSE

Wolkomir and Wolkomir mention James B. Twitchell's comments on students wearing manufacturers' logos (paragraph 30). Do you wear such logos with pride, or do you avoid wearing them? Explore your viewpoint on this very popular practice.

QUESTIONS FOR CLASS OR SMALL-GROUP DISCUSSION

1. Wolkomir and Wolkomir conducted their interview of James B. Twitchell in a Wal-Mart store. Discuss the appropriateness of that location as a site for the interview. What is your impression of Twitchell as a result of this interview?

2. What do you understand Twitchell to mean by this comment: "[E]specially for youths [. . .] advertising has become our social studies text" (paragraph 9). To what extent do you think he is correct?

3. In response to Thomas J. Barratt's observation, "Any fool can make soap. It takes a clever man to sell it" (paragraph 13), discuss current advertising campaigns that you think are particularly clever, like the Pears' Soap campaign that Wolkomir and Wolkomir describe.

4. State in your own words what advertisers do to sell their products, commenting on some of the techniques to which Wolkomir and Wolkomir refer. How does the placing of manufacturers' logos on their products help sell the products? Why do you think that young people especially like those products?

THE BIRTH OF HIP-HOP

Kevin O'Rourke

Kevin O'Rourke, long-time writer about marketing and consumer news for Beverage Aisle *magazine, is senior editor of* Beverage Aisle *online. The magazine's target audience is retail executives. This article appeared in the December 15, 2003, issue of* Beverage Aisle.

The first bottles of Crystal Champagne were made exclusively for Czar Alexander II of Russia in 1876 and it wasn't available to the general public until the Czar and his entire family were executed. Even now, a bottle of Crystal Rose sells for over $1,200 a bottle, and at least one bottle can be found in the private stock of every major hip-hop artist. If you don't believe me, watch MTV's Cribs sometime.

Whether they are guzzling the Crystal or pouring it on the floor to make a point about their status, hip-hop artists have done more to solidify the status of Crystal as an icon of the good life than Alexander II ever did.

Influencing the public's perception of $1,200 champagne is just a hint of the power the hip-hop community can have on a brand. Marketers have been hip to the power of the hip-hop world for a couple of years, and it's time retailers began to take note.

4   Once upon a time retailers sold hip-hop artists' CDs. Now they are selling those artists' DVDs, clothing lines, sneakers, video games, and yes, beverages.

Hip-Hop Is Everywhere

On any given week, *Billboard*'s Hot Rap Tracks chart is filled with songs that serve as lyrical consumer reports for what are, or will be, the trendiest fashion, automobile, and even beverage brands.

"We are the best brand-building community in the world," says Russell Simmons, often called the "godfather of hip-hop." He founded a multi-million-dollar record company, Def Jam Records, and jump-started the careers of some of the recording industry's biggest artists. Simmons recently introduced DefCon3—what he calls "energy soda"—and Dallas-based convenience store giant 7-Eleven signed up as a distribution partner launching the product at all 5,000 of its US chain stores.

"The hip-hop community is important for the same reason that any consumer dynamic that is growing is important," explains Debbie Wildrick, 7-Eleven's category manager for non-carbonated beverages. "Another growing sector is the Hispanic consumer base. It is becoming one of the biggest growth segments. Any time there is some segment of society that is showing more growth and a move toward the consumer mainstream it is important to us.

8   "This consumer has been coming into our stores," continues Wildrick. "Convenience probably has a heavier base of this consumer than other outlets. Retailers have got to continue to try to understand what the taste profiles are and stock what people are looking for."

For 7-Eleven, DefCon3 is a unique product that offers added value by appealing, in name, taste and package perspective, to the hip-hop consumer. "Russell Simmons is what really attracted us to DefCon3," admits Wildrick. "[When] DefCon3 came to me it came with Russell Simmons. He has a strong voice in the hip-hop community and has become mainstream."

Simmons is sure that DefCon3 will be accepted by the public. "If we [the hip-hop community] decide that Tommy Hilfiger is hot, he gets hot," says Simmons. "If we decide to walk away from Tommy, he gets ice cold."

"There hasn't been any beverage that has really developed an organic, true, emotional relationship with the hip-hop community," says Jennifer Louie, marketing vice president at Russell Simmons Beverage Co. To separate his product from the competition, Simmons uses a best-of-both-worlds approach. He developed the concept of the "smart" energy soda, a combination of energy drink and soda.

12   Like many of Simmons' commercial endeavors, DefCon3 aims to give back to those who purchase it. "I made a commitment the first $5 million we earn will be put back into the community," says the hip-hop impresario, "and then 30 percent of our profits from then on forever. It makes it important and relevant that we have a product that helps support the community."

Straight Pimpin'

If there is one group that understands the power of hip-hop to sell, it is the artists themselves. And these savvy marketers have turned their considerable entrepreneurial skills to the beverage aisle. Along with Simmons, rapper/actor Ice-T has introduced Liquid Ice, rapper Nelly has introduced PimpJuice, and Jay-Z and his business partner/ producer Dame Dash have purchased the distribution rights to Armadale Vodka.

Ice-T launched Liquid Ice with his partner, Multimedia Inc., in August. Featuring two flavors—Electric Blue and Frosted Chrome—Liquid Ice is available in 8.3-ounce cans. "I believe I can make anything better than anyone," says Ice-T. Ice-T's follow-up to the release of Liquid Ice is Royal Ice malt liquor.

Meanwhile Nelly's PimpJuice has run into some controversy, thanks to its less-than-wholesome name, which comes from one of the rapper's songs. According to MTV News, many urban groups, including Project Islamic Hope, the National Alliance for Positive Action and the National Black Anti-Defamation League, have united to keep PimpJuice off store shelves in Los Angeles. Basically, "Pimp juice is anything that attracts the opposite sex," says Nelly, a St. Louis native. "It could be money, fame, or straight intellect."

16   While energy drinks are often mixed with vodka, Jay-Z and fellow Roc-A-Fella Record Co. execs Dash and Kareem "Biggs" Burke, have purchased a vodka company, Armadale. According to a recent report on BET.com, Roc-A-Fella, better known for its music label and fashion line, decided to venture into the beverage business because, "in songs, they often mentioned other brands, but were not getting compensation."

"You always hear about us talking about the [vodka] in the song so, like with the clothing and the music industry, we were like, 'Why are we still making money for everyone else?' We just acquired the company and said, 'Let's do it ourselves,' " said Burke.

The Takeover

Jay-Z has done more than just rap about the brands he loves—he has gotten paid by them. Heineken acknowledged the power of hip-hop when it turned to the Brooklyn-born rapper to star in a commercial last year.

"Hip-hop is pop culture today," explains Scott Hunter Smith, marketing manager for White Plains, NY–based Heineken USA. "It's a matter of relevance. Seventy percent of hip-hop music is bought by white Americans. It's the Beatles music of today, so to speak. It's what's hot, what's relevant. This is what kids are listening to— it's a lifestyle more than just music. Hip-hop is the dress, the clothes, the fashion and so forth."

20   Of course, it's one thing for rappers to extol the virtues of their favorite brands in their music, but another thing entirely for established brands to enlist the help of artists to pitch their brands. Hip-hop is a cultural phenomenon that came from the streets—and we're not talking Wall Street here.

"It is true that some of the producers and performers come from struggle and poverty," says Simmons. "They are purveyors of the coolest part of American culture, as were those that performed blues, jazz and rock 'n' roll."

Often, artists must struggle just to show that they haven't forgotten where they've come from. They must maintain their "street credibility." But street credibility can be a double-edged sword.

"You have to be careful of which artist you associate yourself with, because gaining street credibility can hurt you," cautions Hunter Smith. "But it is important for the artist, because he doesn't want to be seen as selling out. Jay-Z is probably one of the most credible artists and businessmen in hip hop culture today. He will only endorse certain products that he feels are right; he won't do a commercial unless he felt it's right."

24   One example of pushing the street envelope is the well-publicized split between Pepsi and Def Jam Records recording artist Ludacris. Pepsi took flack from parent groups that were offended by some of Ludacris' lyrics. As a result, Pepsi met with a number of members of the hip-hop community, and according to Pepsi spokesperson Nicole Bradley, agreed toward a common goal.

Together with members of the hip-hop community Pepsi formed the Pepsi-Cola/Hip-Hop Summit Partnership. "The goal of the organization is to create a community-based marketing and philanthropy initiative for the benefit of urban youth. We hope to encourage, educate and motivate young people to express themselves through visual and performing arts, including hip-hop," says Bradley.

Heineken involved Jay-Z in the making of The Takeover commercial early on. "He told us that if the commercial is not right, the deal is off," explains Hunter Smith. "It's about creating the right image with the right brand because it says something about him as well. It has to be credible. Consumers can smell a rat when it's a rat. Consumers see truth when it's truth. Jay-Z and Heineken make sense."

Heineken isn't the only major beverage company to look to hip-hop artists to help move a few extra cases. Pepsi signed Beyonce Knowles to appear in television spots, Coca-Cola looked to Missy Elliot when it introduced Vanilla Coke, and Coors Light has a commercial featuring Dr. Dre.

28   Also, this summer, the Silver Bullet celebrated its silver anniversary with a tribute to hip-hop. Coors Light hit the shelves with one-of-a-kind collectors' cans and title sponsorship of Nelly's summer tour. "Many of today's artists have been influenced by the hip-hop movement, which has never been more popular than it is now," notes Tom Dixon, assistant brand manager for Coors Light. "Coors Light not only wants to recognize hip-hop's widespread popularity, but also aims to celebrate the freedom of expression that it stands for—and has stood for—during the past 25 years."

Dr Pepper has looked to musical artists from different genres to tell their story of uniqueness in a cola-driven world. The whole point of Dr Pepper's ad campaign, which began 2002, is uniqueness. The tagline is "Be You" and the spots talk about originality and being an individual.

"We believe that hip-hop has entered the mainstream of music," says John Clark, chief advertising officer with Dr Pepper/Seven Up [DPSU]. "It is much more broadly based, and it has a particular skew towards the younger demographic and that is prime soft drink territory. However, as a subset of that, it is highly populated with African-Americans, who represent an important and growing segment of consumer products in general."

According to Clark, Dr Pepper tries to find artists that are originals, i.e., those who have accomplished something a little different, to set them apart from others in their genre. For the hip-hop community, DPSU enlisted two major names in RUN-DMC and LL Cool J.

32   "In that commercial, we look at RUN-DMC as one of the pioneers of hip-hop music," explains Clark. "They are really the focal point of celebration. We brought in LL Cool J, as a more contemporary artist to pay tribute to RUN-DMC as originals in their field of music. "The structure of our commercial is more than a rap artist singing a jingle. We hope that each of the commercial executions we put together will have broad appeal. That is, we hope it will appeal to the entire demographic."

Smaller beverage companies are also looking to hip-hop artists for support. James Robinson, co-CEO of Pacoima, CA–based Hip Hop Beverage Corp., maker of Pit Bull energy drink, is close to signing rapper DMX as a spokesman. "Hip-hop is all about the truth and the official conscious of the generation, and DMX is the pit bull of hip-hop," says Robinson.

No Sell-Out

Marketers have become adept at capitalizing on the exposure their products get via usage by high-visibility members of the hip-hop community. Some have implemented marketing executions to strengthen the connection with their consumers. Allied Domecq successfully refurbished the staid image of Courvoisier with a campaign that included ads in urban magazines like *Essence* and *Vibe*.

According to S. Madison Bedard, brand manager for Courvoisier, "Courvoisier is successful, in large part, because we have been embraced by hip-hop culture. About four years ago, we developed a strategy based on the proposition that hip-hop influences—and is influenced by—fashion trends. So what we did was position Courvoisier as a fashion accessory."

36   Allied Domecq also got hooked up with a free "phat" marketing coup after rapper Busta Rhymes released his song Pass the Courvoisier in tribute to the cognac. Allied Domecq insists that Rhymes isn't on the payroll, but admits the song has certainly helped Courvoisier gain momentum throughout hip-hop nation.

"Busta Rhymes embraced us because we established that credibility through our strategy," says Bedard. "That the product is a relevant part of his lifestyle—it is not different from the way other artists have embraced other brands. It's about whether it's credible, and whether it's relevant. And whether it's done in a way that doesn't patronize the community."

Other new brands that are courting urban consumers include Raw Dawg energy drink, which contains horny goat weed, as well as liquors such as ENVY, a sophisticated liqueur that combines cognac and vodka with passionfruit and guava. And just try watching BET without hearing a shout out to Hpnotiq Liqueur, another blend of French vodka, cognac and tropical fruit juices.

Transcending Ethnicity

OK, so hip-hop is here to stay and it is spreading like wildfire, but how can retailers be ready when hip-hop nation gets thirsty and goes shopping?

40   "The whole hip-hop craze is so new to most of us in retail," says 7-Eleven's Wildrick, "and we can learn more from the consumer who is using these products. As a retailer, I would like to do some focus groups to better understand this group of consumers specifically, because we don't know them as well as we should. We know that the consumer demographic is young, so hip-hop is going to cross over different taste profiles, and that younger demographic likes new, innovative, and sweeter beverages."

"Retailers must understand that hip-hop is not black, not Hispanic; often it is white," explains Heineken's Hunter Smith. "Embrace the culture. First, marketers must create the right merchandising and POS [point of sale] so that retailers can make them inclusive, rather than as a separate section. Then, retailers must display those products which will appeal to the hip-hop community in a way that consumers will know that this is a store that speaks to them."

Hip Hop Beverage Corp.'s Robinson suggests that retailers wake up and smell the coffee. "They must attract new, younger consumers into their stores," he explains. "Kmart's whole new apparel line was developed to attract the urban hip-hop consumer, because they understand that they need that new consumer. Retailers must understand what products will attract the hip hop audience to their stores, because the hip hop audience will spend money."

"Hip-hop consumers are going to respond to a person who they've actually seen drinking that product," offers Wildrick. "One of the things that attracted me to DefCon3 was their ability to get the product into the hands of those urban tastemakers so that consumers would see them using it."

44   Simmons compares today's hip-hop artists to Shakespeare. "Just as it was with Shakespeare and the poets and playwrights before him, today's artists are the voice of the people," says Simmons. "He spoke to the people, and the people spoke through him. Young people don't want to be part of the mainstream. An alternative voice often rises from struggle and that voice is hip-hop.

"Retailers have to listen to the community. New generations have new voices and retailers have to listen to those voices."

PERSONAL RESPONSE

Are you influenced by hip-hip groups to buy particular brands of products? If not, are you influenced by any musical groups or celebrities?

QUESTIONS FOR CLASS OR SMALL-GROUP DISCUSSION

1. What is the purpose of the opening anecdote about champagne and Czar Alexander II? How is it relevant to O'Rourke's central purpose?

2. How well does O'Rourke explain the impact of hip-hop groups on consumers?

3. What marketing techniques does O'Rourke mention? Are you familiar with those techniques?

4. What aspects of O'Rourke's writing style make it apparent that his audience is retail executives? How informative do you think they would find this article?

SHOPPING AND OTHER SPIRITUAL ADVENTURES IN AMERICA TODAY

Phyllis Rose

Phyllis Rose is the author of the following books: Woman of Letters: A Life of Virginia Woolf *(1978),* Parallel Lives: Five Victorian Marriages *(1983),* Jazz Cleopatra: Josephine Baker in Her Time *(1989),* The Norton Book of Women's Lives *(1993),* The Year of Reading Proust: A Memoir in Real Time *(1999), and* Never Say Good-Bye: Essays *(1991), from which this essay is taken.*

Last year a new Waldbaum's Food Mart opened in the shopping mall on Route 66. It belongs to the new generation of super-duper markets open twenty-four hours that have computerized checkout. I went to see the place as soon as it opened and I was impressed. There was trail mix in Lucite bins. There was freshly made pasta. There were coffee beans, four kinds of tahini, ten kinds of herb teas, raw shrimp in shells and cooked shelled shrimp, fresh-squeezed orange juice. Every sophistication known to the big city, even goat's cheese covered with ash, was now available in Middletown, Conn. People raced from the warehouse aisle to the bagel bin to the coffee beans to the fresh fish market, exclaiming at all the new things. Many of us felt elevated, graced, complimented by the presence of this food palace in our town.

This is the wonderful egalitarianism of American business. Was it Andy Warhol who said that the nice thing about Coke is, no can is any better or worse than any other? Some people may find it dull to cross the country and find the same chain stores with the same merchandise from coast to coast, but it means that my town is as good as yours, my shopping mall as important as yours, equally filled with wonders.

Imagine what people ate during the winter as little as seventy-five years ago. They ate food that was local, long-lasting, and dull, like acorn squash, turnips, and cabbage. Walk into an American supermarket in February and the world lies before you: grapes, melons, artichokes, fennel, lettuce, peppers, pistachios, dates, even strawberries, to say nothing of ice cream. Have you ever considered what a triumph of civilization it is to be able to buy a pound of chicken livers? If you lived on a farm and had to kill a chicken when you wanted to eat one, you wouldn't ever accumulate a pound of chicken livers.

4   Another wonder of Middletown is Caldor, the discount department store. Here is man's plenty: tennis racquets, panty hose, luggage, glassware, records, toothpaste. Timex watches, Cadbury's chocolate, corn poppers, hair dryers, warm-up suits, car wax, light bulbs, television sets. All good quality at low prices with exchanges

cheerfully made on defective goods. There are worse rules to live by. I feel good about America whenever I walk into this store, which is almost every midwinter Sunday afternoon, when life elsewhere has closed down. I go to Caldor the way English people go to pubs: out of sociability. To get away from my house. To widen my horizons. For culture's sake. Caldor provides me too with a welcome sense of seasonal change. When the first outdoor grills and lawn furniture appear there, it's as exciting a sign of spring as the first crocus or robin.

Someone told me about a Soviet émigré who practices English by declaiming, at random, sentences that catch his fancy. One of his favorites is, "Fifty percent off all items today only." Refugees from Communist countries appreciate our supermarkets and discount department stores for the wonders they are. An Eastern European scientist visiting Middletown wept when she first saw the meat counter at Waldbaum's. On the other hand, before her year in America was up, her pleasure turned sour. She wanted everything she saw. Her approach to consumer goods was insufficiently abstract, too materialistic. We Americans are beyond a simple, possessive materialism. We're used to abundance and the possibility of possessing things. The things, and the possibility of possessing them, will still be there next week, next year. So today we can walk the aisles calmly.

It is a misunderstanding of the American retail store to think we go there necessarily to buy. Some of us shop. There's a difference. Shopping has many purposes, the least interesting of which is to acquire new articles. We shop to cheer ourselves up. We shop to practice decision making. We shop to be useful and productive members of our class and society. We shop to remind ourselves how much is available to us. We shop to remind ourselves how much is to be striven for. We shop to assert our superiority to the material objects that spread themselves before us.

Shopping's function as a form of therapy is widely appreciated. You don't really need, let's say, another sweater. You need the feeling of power that comes with buying or not buying it. You need the feeling that someone wants something you have— even if it's just your money. To get the benefit of shopping, you needn't actually purchase the sweater, any more than you have to marry every man you flirt with. In fact, window-shopping, like flirting, can be more rewarding, the same high without the distressing commitment, the material encumbrance. The purest form of shopping is provided by garage sales. A connoisseur goes out with no goal in mind, open to whatever may come his or her way, secure that it will cost very little. Minimum expense, maximum experience. Perfect shopping.

8   I try to think of the opposite, a kind of shopping in which the object is all important, the pleasure of shopping at a minimum. For example, the purchase of blue jeans. I buy new blue jeans as seldom as possible because the experience is so humiliating. For every pair that looks good on me, fifteen look grotesque. But even shopping for blue jeans at Bob's Surplus on Main Street—no frills, bare-bones shopping—is an event in the life of the spirit. Once again I have to come to terms with the fact that I will never look good in Levi's. Much as I want to be mainstream, I never will be.

In fact, I'm doubly an oddball, neither Misses nor Junior, but Misses Petite. I look in the mirror, I acknowledge the disparity between myself and the ideal, I resign myself to making the best of it: I will buy the Lee's Misses Petite. Shopping is a time of reflection, assessment, spiritual self-discipline.

It is appropriate, I think, that Bob's Surplus has a communal dressing room. I used to shop only in places where I could count on a private dressing room with a mirror inside. My impulse then was to hide my weaknesses. Now I believe in sharing them. There are other women in the dressing room at Bob's Surplus trying on blue jeans who look as bad as I do. We take comfort from one another. Sometimes a woman will ask me which of two items looks better. I always give a definite answer. It's the least I can do. I figure we are all in this together, and I emerge from the dressing room not only with a new pair of jeans but with a renewed sense of belonging to a human community.

When a Solzhenitsyn rants about American materialism, I have to look at my digital Timex and check what year this is. Materialism? Like conformism, a hot moral issue of the fifties, but not now. How to spread the goods, maybe. Whether the goods are the Good, no. Solzhenitsyn, like the visiting scientist who wept at the beauty of Waldbaum's meat counter but came to covet everything she saw, takes American materialism too materialistically. He doesn't see its spiritual side. Caldor, Waldbaum's, Bob's Surplus—these, perhaps, are our cathedrals.

PERSONAL RESPONSE

Explain your attitude toward shopping. Do you go to discount stores or malls to shop or to buy? Does shopping give you the pleasure that Rose says it gives most Americans?

QUESTIONS FOR CLASS OR SMALL-GROUP DISCUSSION

1. How does the list of foods that Rose mentions in paragraph one relate to her central point? What function do the references to the Soviet émigré and the Eastern European scientist in paragraph 5 serve?

2. Discuss whether you get the pleasure from shopping in American discount stores and supermarkets that Rose describes in her essay. Consider, for instance, Rose's comment in paragraph 9 that "shopping is a time of reflection, assessment, spiritual self-discipline."

3. What criticisms of American consumerism does Rose imply in her ironic descriptions of shopping as a spiritual adventure and department stores as America's cathedrals?

4. In paragraph 10, Rose describes trying on jeans in a communal dressing room and of taking comfort from other women there. Do men experience the same kind of camaraderie when shopping that women often do? To what extent do you think there are differences between the way men and women view shopping in general?

○ PERSPECTIVES ON MARKETING AND THE AMERICAN CONSUMER ○
Suggested Writing Topics

1. Drawing on at least two readings in the chapter, write an essay on the importance of young consumers for the American economy.

2. Drawing on at least two of the readings in this chapter, explain the pressures you think America's high-consumption society puts on young people and the effects of those pressures.

3. Drawing on the comments of at least two writers in this chapter, write an essay on the image you think that American consumerism presents to the rest of the world and whether you think that image is a good or a bad one.

4. Phyllis Rose suggests in "Shopping and Other Spiritual Adventures in America Today" that malls, discount stores, and supermarkets are America's cathedrals, while James B. Twitchell, in "In Praise of Consumerism," asserts that consumerism has displaced religion. Write an essay explaining the extent to which you agree with these writers. Can you name other structures that would be more appropriate symbols of America's spiritual center? Is consumerism America's main religion?

5. In "Shopping and Other Spiritual Adventures in America Today," Phyllis Rose refers to the "wonderful egalitarianism of American business" (paragraph 2), and in James Twitchell's "In Praise of Consumerism," he notes that consumerism makes for a "more egalitarian world" (paragraph 25). Using those comments as a starting point, write an essay on American consumerism as a social equalizer.

6. Explain why you agree or disagree with the following remark by James B. Twitchell in Richard Wolkomir and Joyce Wolkomir's "You Are What You Buy." Referring to his daughters' willingness to spend $1.50 on a bottle of water worth two cents, Twitchell says, " 'They aren't buying the product itself; they're buying the values that advertising has attached to the product' " (paragraph 35).

7. Imagine that you are marketing a product that has traditionally been sold to one particular segment of the market, such as white, middle-class males. Now you want to increase your sales by targeting other groups. Select a particular group and create a sales campaign aimed at that group.

8. Using examples of people you know, either support or refute James B. Twitchell's contention in "In Praise of Consumerism" that Americans are committed to consumerism because "We like having stuff" (paragraph 8).

9. Explain the effects on you or someone you know of a change in income, suddenly coming into money, or acquiring some coveted material possession.

10. Analyze the positive and negative effects of America's emphasis on consumerism on one particular group of people, such as young people, the elderly, working-class people, the wealthy, or those living in poverty.

11. Explain what you think shopping malls, discount stores, and overstocked supermarkets suggest about Americans' values. For instance, what impression do you think that foreign visitors get of America when they see the sizes of and selections in those marketplaces?

Research Topics

1. Research the marketing strategies of a major business, perhaps one mentioned in this chapter. Assess what you see as its successes and/or failures in promoting its products.

2. Select a particular product (such as automobiles, cosmetics, clothing, or beer) or a particular target population (such as children, African-American women, or the elderly) and research the market strategies used by major companies for that particular product or group.

3. Research the recent advertising campaign of a major corporation whose product poses a threat to the environment or to human health and well-being.

4. Research the subject of American consumerism and arrive at your own conclusion about its effects on Americans and American values. This is a broad subject, so look for ways to narrow your focus as quickly as you can.

5. Research the impact of suburban malls on city-center or small "Mom and Pop," neighborhood businesses.

RESPONDING TO VISUALS

Shoppers carrying merchandise bags walk in front of a Gap® display ad on Fifth Avenue, New York City, November 20, 2000. Source: Chris Hondros/Newsmakers/Getty Images

1. How does the image capture the connection between young people and name brands?
2. How do the teenage girls contrast with the pictures of models in the store window?
3. Why did the photographer choose this moment to take the picture?
4. What is the effect of the girls walking with their purchases in front of the Gap® window?

RESPONDING TO VISUALS

Shoppers pass through the checkout counters of the Wal-Mart® Supercenter in Reno, Nevada, July 7, 2003. Source: AP Photo/Scott Sady

1. What is your first impression of this picture? Which details contribute to that impression?
2. What impressions of Wal-Mart® are conveyed by viewing the store from this perspective?
3. Find details in the photograph that indicate this is a "supercenter."

CHAPTER

24

THE WORKPLACE

The workplace can have enormous influence on people's lives. Most Americans work outside the home, either full-time or part-time, spending significant portions of their time on the job. The physical atmosphere of the workplace, the friendliness of co-workers, and the attitudes of supervisors or bosses play pivotal roles not only in the way workers perform but also in the way they feel about themselves. Tension, anxiety, and stress in the workplace can lower production for the company and produce actual illnesses in workers, whereas a pleasant atmosphere, good benefits, and relatively low stress can boost production and make employees look forward to going to work. The quality of life in the workplace has a direct effect on the quality of work employees do and on their general well being.

The essays in this chapter examine some of the issues related to the subject of the workplace. In "For Love or Money," Jay Matthews explains the debate over what motivates employees to do their best. Some research suggests that extrinsic rewards such as financial or other material bonuses do not necessarily result in better work or increased productivity. Rather, intrinsic rewards such as a sense of accomplishment or a feeling of contributing to the good of the company may prove to be more powerful incentives in the long run. What motivates you to do well at something? Do you respond to a promise of something tangible or material, such as a high grade, a gift, or money, or do you pursue the inner reward of knowing you have done your best work and that you are satisfied with your performance? Think about these questions as you read Matthews's review of the complex and multifaceted subject of what motivates human behavior.

Related to Matthews's piece is Matthew Boyle's "Beware the Killjoy," which discusses workplace fun, reports on low rates of job satisfaction, and suggests that corporations should find a balance between the worker-friendly culture of dot-coms and the traditional business model. If, like most college students, you have had a job or are currently working, think about the atmosphere at your work place. Do you feel a sense of community there? Is your work fun?

Next, Terry Golway's "Rewriting the Old Rules" suggests that, despite women's advancement in the corporate world, too often women have had to adopt male values. As you read his discussion about the demands that some professions place on their employees, think about your own employment future. Are you willing to follow what he calls the traditional business model? Is your college education preparing you for the kind of work life that Golway and other authors in this chapter say men and women must accept in order to succeed?

Finally, Barbara Ehrenreich's "Warning: This is a Rights-Free Workplace" treats the subject of the violation of basic rights that is routine in America's work places. Workers are forbidden the right to assemble, prohibited from going to the bathroom without permission, and denied many privacy rights. But, of all the invasions that workers experience, she writes, "the most ubiquitous invasion of privacy is drug testing." As you read her essay, ask yourself if your own job experience has been similar to those that she describes.

FOR LOVE OR MONEY

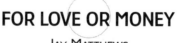

JAY MATTHEWS

Jay Matthews is a journalist who wrote this article for the December, 1993, issue of the Washington Post National Weekly Edition. *In it,*

*Matthews reviews some theories of behaviorists on what makes employ-
ees do their best work.*

In the early 1960s, two graduate students working independently on the ancient
problem of coaxing the best from human beings stumbled across results they did not
understand. Louise Brightwell Miller at the University of Kentucky discovered that
nine-year-old boys were less likely to solve a simple identification test when they were
paid for right answers than when they worked for free. Sam Glucksberg at New York
University found the same result for adults given a household engineering problem.

Among the behaviorists who have dominated much of American psychology
and motivational research since World War II, the notion that people would do better without a material incentive was, as Miller and her adviser said in their report, "an
unexpected result, unaccountable for by theory and/or previous empirical evidence."
Thirty years later, the Miller and Glucksberg experiments have become intriguing
parts of an intense academic debate over the roots of human motivation and have
raised doubts about the methods that American businesses have used for decades to
improve employee performance.

In books such as *Punished by Rewards: The Trouble with Gold Stars, Incentive
Plans, A's, Praise, and Other Bribes* by Alfie Kohn, who cites Miller and Glucksberg,
and *Second to None: How Our Smartest Companies Put People First* by Charles Garfield,
anti-behaviorist psychologists are arguing that money not only does not buy happiness, it can also, if misapplied, kill a worker's desire to do his or her best.

4   "When you do something for a reward you tend to become less interested in
what you're doing," says Kohn, a writer and lecturer on human behavior who cites the
work of dozens of social scientists. "It comes to seem like a chore, something you have
to get through in order to pick up the dollar or the A or the extra dessert. What this
means is that millions of well-meaning teachers and parents and managers are killing
off creativity and curiosity in their attempt to bribe people to do a good job."

To a certain extent, Kohn and Garfield and several other thinkers who take this
stand are reviving an old and much-ignored argument just as the anti-reward school
was having its greatest impact on Corporate America.

"We are involved in a major change in our culture," says Jim Schmitt, corporate
communications director for Westinghouse Electric Corp., speaking of the redesign
of jobs and work structures going on in many industries. "We have seen a culture
emerging where people are more involved in the decision making regardless of their
position in the organization."

But to those who want to encourage this trend, the day is still far off when everyone will leap out of bed eager for a day of intrinsically motivated work at the office.

8   "There are companies that are attempting to understand what truly motivates
human beings and then there are others, and I am afraid they are the majority, that
have this peculiar affection for pop psychology," including the latest ideas on how to
create desire with cash, says Garfield, an associate clinical professor at the University
of California at San Francisco.

Raises, promotions, stock options, performance bonuses, merit increases, trips to
Disney World, and even new cars are still the prime motivators in American business.
Many psychologists see nothing wrong with that. "I have worked with many people

for whom a kind word doesn't mean a thing," says E. Scott Geller, professor of psychology at Virginia Polytechnic Institute and State University, "but money can mean many things to many people."

Critics of monetary rewards begin by making sure everyone understands they are not advocating a return to slavery. They say people should be paid well enough so that they are no longer distracted by worries that they are underpaid. "Managers need to divorce the task from the compensation as best they can by paying people well and then doing everything possible to help them put money out of their minds," Kohn says.

A material reward might work in the short term, the anti-behaviorists argue. Who wouldn't get excited about a trip to Paris for the sales agent who unloads the most Pismo Beach condominiums? But over time, the theory says, the most successful salespeople will grow tired of trips to Paris and require a motive closer to their sense of themselves or lose their spark altogether.

12   Kohn even cites studies by his behaviorist critics to buttress his point. In 1987 Geller and several associates reviewed the effects of twenty-eight seat-belt use programs at nine different companies. The results, Geller and his group admitted in their research paper, were "inconsistent with basic reinforcement theory." Programs that did not offer cash or prizes for buckling up reported an average 152 percent increase in seat-belt use over periods up to a year, while the long-term gain for programs with rewards was no higher than 62 percent.

Several business surveys add to the impression of money as a comfort rather than a goal. A 1978 survey of more than fifty thousand utility company applicants found pay ranked sixth out of ten job factors. (The same applicants thought others would put money first.) A 1991 poll showed that even among allegedly money-fixated salespeople, increased compensation was the least commonly cited reason for changing jobs.

But the core of Kohn's book, and its most controversial aspect, is a long appreciation of the research of Edward Deci at the University of Rochester and Mark Lepper at Stanford. The two men insist material rewards do not motivate well, and actually poison natural motivators such as curiosity and self-esteem.

Lepper watched children in Head Start classrooms react to an experiment with Magic Markers. Some were told that if they used the markers they would be given a special certificate. Some were given the markers with no anticipated reward. After a week, the children who were told they would get a certificate were using the markers not only less frequently than the unrewarded children, but also less frequently than they themselves had used the markers before they were told of the reward.

16   Deci put college students in a room and asked each to work a puzzle. Half were promised money; half were not. He then announced a pause before "the next phase of the study began" and watched what they did in those idle moments. Those who had been promised money spent less time playing with the puzzle than those who had not anticipated reward.

Deci concluded that "money may work to 'buy off' one's intrinsic motivation for an activity." Deci and Lepper speculated that people thought they were being manipulated when offered a reward. Although they might do what was necessary to receive their prize, it left a bad taste that tainted what had once been an enjoyable activity for them.

Geller says the Deci–Lepper research is flawed. "People say, 'Well, yeah, once I started playing cards for money, I didn't enjoy playing just for fun any more,' " Geller says. "It has an intuitive feel." But the experiment overlooks what Geller calls "the contrast effect"—the sudden disappointment when the reward is no longer available. If the experimenter continued to watch a card player for several months after he swore off gambling, "you might find he would again eventually want to play cards for free."

20   Kohn says studies show that the harm to intrinsic motivation is enduring.

Some psychologists complain that human motivation and its impact on productivity is just too complex a subject to reduce to debates over extrinsic or intrinsic rewards. J. William Townsend, an industrial organizational psychologist and consultant in Memphis, says he accepts much of the anti-reward research but also knows that some employees will always be motivated by money and little else.

Another factor often overlooked in the debate is talent. "People cannot outperform their abilities," Townsend says. "I don't care how much you motivate me, I'm not going to play basketball better than Michael Jordan."

The anti-behaviorists nod at this and say, fine, what we are doing is giving each person the chance to do his best with the greatest joy in the effort, and without being distracted by money. Kohn offers three ways to stimulate workers' natural desire to do well: Find ways for them to work in teams; give them variety and a sense of worthwhile work; and give them as much choice as possible of what they do and how they do it.

"Choice is very important," says Marion Gindes, a psychologist and president of Marion Gindes & Associates in Larchmont, N.Y. "In one very old experiment with monkeys, some were able to control to some extent when they received an electric shock and some were not. Those that had some choice ended up in better shape." Many human studies have reached the same conclusion.

24   Once a worker has a comfortable salary, Garfield says, "you are looking at other motivators like autonomy, the opportunity to be creative in one's work."

Human resources executives began to play with different motivational formulas in the 1970s, says Neil Lewis, management psychologist in Atlanta, "but then we got into the eighties and everybody lost sight of these things. A monkey could have made money in the eighties. We didn't have to worry about all this employee motivation stuff."

Now that corporate downsizing and restructuring have revived the interest in such research, experts warn that there is still little verifiable data to guide executives who have to decide how to get better results from fewer people. Edward Lazear, a Stanford Business School economist and senior fellow at the Hoover Institution, says some initial studies—admittedly in factories with many complicating problems—are disappointing. Even when the new techniques seem to work, he says, they appear to be tied to other motivators that include money.

The motives of the critics of motivational methods are often as complex as those of the workers they study. Graef S. Crystal, editor of the Crystal Report and a passionate advocate of tying executive pay to corporate financial performance, admits that more or less money probably would not motivate million-dollar executives very much. So why argue so hard for linking their compensation to the stock price?

28   "Because," Crystal says, indulging his love for exaggerated metaphor, "even if none of this motivates the person, it still gives the shareholders the pleasure of sitting in the stands when the stock is plummeting and seeing the executives ripped to shreds by wild animals."

The long history of the debate between behaviorists, devotees of psychologists such as B. F. Skinner, and anti-behaviorists, who prefer the work of thinkers such as Frederick Herzberg, has made many business executives skeptical of both sides.

University of Chicago psychologist Mihaly Csikszentmihalyi says it is useful to remember that different situations produce different motivational needs. "Under the right conditions, material incentives can add to the intrinsic reward," he says, "but sometimes they don't make a difference and sometimes they detract from the intrinsic rewards."

Crystal says that although he accepts that money can be a poor motivator, he could not resist a chance years ago to tease Herzberg when the famous anti-behaviorist haggled with him over a fee for a lecture Herzberg was to give on why money doesn't motivate.

32   "Money in fact doesn't motivate me," Herzberg told Crystal without embarrassment, "but it sure as hell helps me sort out my priorities."

PERSONAL RESPONSE

Do you find that rewards—grades, money, prizes—motivate you to try harder or do better work than does a sense of satisfaction for having done a good job?

QUESTIONS FOR CLASS OR SMALL-GROUP DISCUSSION

1. How well does Matthews integrate the words of others with his own observations on his subject? Do you find his integration of sources well handled?

2. What do you think of the idea that people should be paid so well that they are not distracted by money worries (paragraph 10)? Would such a plan be possible in all work places? Might employers see the proposal differently from the way employees see it?

3. Matthews quotes Alfie Kohn, author of *Punished by Rewards: The Trouble with Gold Stars, Incentive Plans, A's, Praise, and Other Bribes,* as saying that " 'millions of well-meaning teachers and parents and managers are killing off creativity and curiosity in their attempt to bribe people to do a good job' " (paragraph 5). Has that been your own experience? In what ways have teachers tried to "bribe" you to do well in class? Do you think you would have done just as well or better without the extra incentives?

4. Discuss the three ways to stimulate workers' natural desire to do well that Kohn suggests in paragraph 22. Do you think they would motivate workers more than the incentives of money, trips, or prizes?

BEWARE THE KILLJOY

MATTHEW BOYLE

Matthew Boyle writes for Fortune *magazine. This article appeared in the July 23, 2001, issue of* Fortune.

All work and no play has made Jon a dull boy. A former dot-commer now at a multinational telecom, Jon (he'd rather we not use his last name) pines for the days of yore. "The bright, translucent plastics, the kooky flashing lights, the scooters—it's all gone," he sighs. An information architect, Jon says his managers "would keel over at the thought of color" and doubts that traditional firms will take any further steps toward emulating the footloose environments of the dot-com phenomenon. "Who cares about job happiness? That's not a measurable benefit," he grumbles. "The closest I get to job satisfaction is a 30-minute nap in my car after lunch."

Jon may just be a disgruntled dot-communist, but his bitterness echoes throughout the American workplace. Three out of four Americans are dissatisfied with or fundamentally disconnected from their jobs, according to a recent Gallup Management Journal survey. Granted, workers have been miserable for centuries—but now that the dot-com boom, which spawned a host of worker-friendly initiatives, has ended, is the joy gone for good?

Not by a long shot. The demise of Kozmo, Pets.com, and their ilk didn't kill workplace fun any more than their arrival created it. Rather, the dot-coms accelerated and took mainstream a trend that began well before anyone had heard of Yahoo. Traditional companies scrambled to provide a more fun atmosphere, as they figured the best way to keep their staff from joining the gold rush was to emulate the Silicon Valley culture. "The dot-coms caused a lot of fury around keeping people engaged," says Sherry Perley, senior VP of human resources at Snapple.

The slowdown, of course, has been quite a killjoy. "We're seeing a snap back now," says Orton Varona, team leader of corporate employment and technical recruiting at Southwest Airlines. "Organizations are reeling in some of the perks that they were so liberal with in the past." When companies snap back, workers feel the sting. A survey by the Society for Human Resource Management found that only 27% of companies offered a subsidized cafeteria, compared with 37% in 1999. Company-sponsored sports teams and concierge services are also on the decline.

What's worse, a worker-friendly culture stands accused of precipitating the failure of many dot-coms. "The stuffier side of establishment America is now backlashing and making fun of what was occurring in these dot-com environments," says Nigel Morris, president and CEO of credit card giant Capital One (which itself is still committed to fun—see following box). The dot-com culture as well as the business model is under indictment.

Rather than replace one extreme (emulation) with another (rejection), a better approach is to blend what worked in dot-com land with your existing culture. Casual dress, flextime, and telecommuting are three examples. All existed before the Internet craze (Levi's began its casual-dress crusade in 1992, and Hewlett-Packard rolled

AT THESE COMPANIES, THE FUN NEVER STOPS

- Capital One. A "fun budget" of $80 per employee per quarter to spend on activities such as white-water rafting.
- CDW Computer Centers. Krispy Kreme doughnuts once a month and free Dairy Queen every summer Wednesday. If the company meets sales goals, CDW offers an "old-timer" benefit for anyone with three years' service: a free trip for you and your family anywhere in the continental U.S. (awarded every other year).
- Southwest Airlines. Spirit parties, gate- and cake-decorating contests, barbecues, and chili cookoffs are just some of the events planned by local "culture committees."
- Snapple. Theme Fridays during the summer (tie-dye day, silly-hat day), and last year the company built a makeshift miniature golf course inside its corporate headquarters, with each department constructing a hole from materials they use during the course of the day.

out flextime way back in 1973). "Our prognostication is that we'll see blended cultures going forward," says Joan Caruso, managing director of organizational effectiveness at the Ayers Group. Indeed, in a recent survey of B-school students by academic consulting firm Universum, most respondents said they desired an informal work environment but at an established organization.

What you should avoid is segmenting fun. "There are companies that will try this as a program—like 'Send an e-mail out that we're all having fun today,' " says Art Friedson, VP of co-worker services at CDW Computer Centers. Adds Leslie Yerkes, change-management consultant and author of Fun Works: "This is a piece of your cultural fabric; don't create a department to do this." To get superiors to green-light fun, Dana Ardi, human capital partner at J. P. Morgan Partners, has a creative solution. "Call it an opportunity to be more creative in teams," she says. "Then corporations will admire it."

In the current climate, fun certainly isn't tops on management's list. But if you kill the fun now and ignore the lessons of the Gen X dot-commers, good luck getting Gen Y to work for you. Three out of four high school kids surveyed by the Families and Life Institute last year said having a fun job was a must—more important than making lots of money or doing challenging work. Think about that before you cut the company softball team.

PERSONAL RESPONSE

Describe the workplace environment at any of the jobs you have held. Was it "fun"? If so, what made it fun; if not, why was it not fun? If you have never had a job, describe your image of the ideal work place.

QUESTIONS FOR CLASS OR SMALL-GROUP DISCUSSION

8

1. How effective do you find Boyle's opening sentence? Does it work well to introduce his subject?

2. Boyle refers to "worker-friendly initiatives" of the dot-com companies (paragraph 2). What do you gather those initiatives are or were? Can you think of others that he does not mention?

3. Comment on the suggestion Boyle makes that employers would do well to adopt a balance between "an informal work environment" and the traditional ways of working at "an established organization" (paragraph 6). How do you envision such a work place? What informalities and more traditional practices would there be?

4. Boyle reports: "Three out of four high school kids surveyed [. . .] said having a fun job was a must—more important than making lots of money or doing challenging work" (paragraph 8). Does that statement surprise you? How would you answer such a survey? Is having fun more important to you than making money or doing challenging work?

REWRITING THE OLD RULES

Terry Golway

Terry Golway, city editor of the New York Observer *and a frequent columnist for* America *magazine, is author of* Irish Rebel: John Devoy and America's Fight for Ireland's Freedom *(1998),* For the Cause of Liberty: The Story of Ireland's Heroes *(2000),* Full of Grace: An Oral Biography of John Cardinal O'Connor *(2001), and* So Others Might Live: A History of New York's Bravest: The FDNY from 1700 to the Present *(2002). This essay was originally published in the April 23, 2001, issue of* America.

Women are about to outnumber men in the nation's law schools, a development heralding yet another milestone for women and a foreshadowing of great cultural change in the way law is practiced in this country.

There can be no doubt about the former. The latter may not be so easy.

Women have been breaking through glass ceilings in the workplace for more than 30 years, and with each new achievement (the first woman to run for national office, to pilot the space shuttle, to serve as attorney general), society has changed for the better. Young girls now have role models in fields ranging from politics to the sciences to professional sports. Can there be any doubt that historians will one day agree that the civil rights movement and the women's movement were among the transforming events of the 20th century?

What these historians will say about the impact of women in the workforce, however, remains to be seen. At the moment, it would be fair to argue that women have not changed the American workplace as much as the workplace has changed women.

Take law, for example. Even with women pouring into law firms across the country, the macho culture of the partner track remains undisturbed. Young men and women still are obliged to perform high-end penal servitude if they wish to become partners at a white-shoe, big-city law firm. Yes, they get paid startling amounts of money—first-year associates in New York during the recently departed boom were commanding salaries approaching six figures—but they are expected to work absurd hours. It is the law culture's equivalent of boot camp, except that the military puts its new recruits through only a few months of terror, while the fresh-faced associate can expect to spend his or her 20's living and breathing for the firm and the firm alone. At the end, of course, there are no guarantees. Those long hours and work-filled weekends may be for naught, at which time an associate had best look for work elsewhere.

4   Not to make any sweeping generalizations, but only a man could have come up with so ruthless a scheme.

We can be grateful that some law firms have begun to concede that their associates are entitled to a life outside the office and, under pressure from women, have adopted measures like flex-time and part-time work. For the most part, however, the remorseless, endless paper chase remains a signature part of big-time law's partner-track culture.

It isn't only law, however, that remains in the thrall of the otherwise discredited macho ethic. In fact, in nearly every profession, in every factory, workers are expected to think of their lives and their jobs as one, to the detriment of family, friends, outside interests and other small pleasures.

Despite the historic entry of millions of women into the workforce, the workplace rules and traditions that men enforce and celebrate have not been repealed. The hoary custom of measuring one's dedication, value and, yes, toughness by the number of hours logged per week hasn't changed. And managers still shake their heads disapprovingly when, in the phrase of one former colleague, a "clockwatcher" begins packing up at 5 P.M. The clockwatcher might have children who need help with homework, or an aged parent to care for, or an anniversary to celebrate. Under the rules of the macho workplace, however, those who let such considerations get in the way of all work, all the time, are considered slackers.

The global marketplace and the technological revolution have made matters worse for those trying to balance their work lives with real life. For millions of workers, there is no escape from professional obligations. I know men and women who feel

8   obliged to bring along their laptop computers when they are on "vacation"—a concept, incidentally, that is beginning to be thought of as yet another outdated ritual from the industrial age. I've been out to dinner with men and women who keep their cell phones ready on the table, just in case the boss (and the boss is not always a male) wants to reach them.

Recent data indicate that the culture of overwork is pervasive in American society. A survey conducted by the National Sleep Association found that 40 percent of the 1,004 adults polled said they worked longer hours than they did five years ago. The average work-week, according to the poll, was 46 hours, but 38 percent said they worked 50 hours or more a week. And then there are those, like the well-dressed fellow who sat next to me on the commuter train the other day, who keep working even when they're home. My seatmate put aside his work-related reading material to call his wife (from his cell phone) to make sure everybody at home knew he needed to use the family computer after dinner. Something to do with developments in the Asian markets.

Is it sexist to suggest that women—at least most women I know—have a far saner perspective on the balance between work and life? I hope not. I certainly believe it's true.

For the time being, women probably have little choice but to adhere to the old rules written by corporate America's macho men. But as more women gain power in corporate America, they will have a chance to rewrite the old rules and abolish the macho-overwork ethic for good.

Or so this macho-challenged male hopes.

PERSONAL RESPONSE

Does it surprise you that a man wrote this essay? Do you think your response to the essay would be any different were the author a woman?

QUESTIONS FOR CLASS OR SMALL-GROUP DISCUSSION

12

1. Explain your understanding of what Golway means when he refers to "the workplace rules and traditions that men enforce and celebrate" (paragraph 9); that is, what he calls "the macho culture" (paragraph 5).

2. Golway writes that women "have a far saner perspective on the balance between work and life" (paragraph 12). What do you think he means? In what ways might women have "a saner perspective" than men?

3. Golway refers to women's "breaking through glass ceilings" (paragraph 3). Does he explain that phrase clearly? What examples, other than the ones he mentions, can you give to illustrate it?

4. How effective do you think Golway's final paragraphs and especially his final sentence are? Do they bring the piece to a satisfying conclusion?

WARNING: THIS IS A RIGHTS-FREE WORKPLACE

Barbara Ehrenreich

Barbara Ehrenreich's articles appear in a variety of popular magazines and newspapers, including Time, The Progressive, Ms., *and the* New York Times, *among many others. Her books include* Witches,

Midwives, and Nurses: A History of Women Healers *(with Deirdre English) (1973)*, Hearts of Men: American Dreams and the Flight from Commitment *(1984)*, For Her Own Good: 150 Years of the Experts' Advice to Women *(with Deirdre English) (1989)*, Blood Rites: Origins and History of the Passions of War *(1997)*, Fear of Falling: The Inner Life of the Middle Class *(2000)*, Nickel and Dimed: On (Not) Getting by in America *(2001), and* Global Woman, *a collection of essays co-edited with Arlie Russell Hochschild (2002). This article appeared in the March 5, 2000, issue of the* New York Times.

If the laws of economics were enforced as strictly as the laws of physics, America would be a workers' paradise. The supply of most kinds of labor is low, relative to the demand, so each worker should be treated as a cherished asset, right? But there have been only grudging gains in wages over the last few years, and in the realm of dignity and autonomy, a palpable decline.

In the latest phase of America's one-sided class war, employers have taken to monitoring employees' workplace behavior right down to a single computer keystroke or bathroom break, even probing into their personal concerns and leisure activities. Sure, there's a job out there for anyone who can get to an interview sober and standing upright. The price, though, may be one's basic civil rights and—what boils down to the same thing—self-respect.

Not that the Bill of Rights ever extended to the American workplace. In 1996, I was surprised to read about a grocery store worker in Dallas who was fired for wearing a Green Bay Packers T-shirt to work on the day before a Cowboys-Packers game. All right, this was insensitive of him, but it certainly couldn't have influenced his ability to keep the shelves stocked with Doritos. A few phone calls though, revealed that his firing was entirely legal. Employees have the right to express their religious preferences at work, by wearing a cross or a Star of David, for example. But most other forms of "self-expression" are not protected, and strangely enough, Green Bay Packer fandom has not yet been recognized as a legitimate religion.

Freedom of assembly is another right that never found its way into the workplace. On a recent journalistic foray into a series of low-wage jobs, I was surprised to discover that management often regarded the most innocent conversation between employees as potentially seditious. A poster in the break room at one restaurant where I worked as a waitress prohibited "gossip," and a manager would hastily disperse any gathering of two or more employees. At the same time, management everywhere enjoys the right to assemble employees for lengthy anti-union harangues.

Then there is the more elemental and biological right—and surely it should be one—to respond to nature's calls. Federal regulations forbid employers to "impose unreasonable restrictions on employee use of the facilities." But according to Marc Linder and Ingrid Nygaard, co-authors of "Void Where Prohibited: Rest Breaks and the Right to Urinate on Company Time," this regulation is only halfheartedly enforced. Professionals and, of course, waitresses can usually dart away and relieve themselves as they please. Not so for many cashiers and assembly-line workers, some of whom, Linder says, have taken to wearing adult diapers to work.

In the area of privacy rights, workers have actually lost ground in recent years.
4 Here, too, the base line is not impressive—no comprehensive right to personal privacy on the job has ever been established. I learned this on my first day as a waitress, when my fellow workers warned me that my purse could be searched by management at any time. I wasn't carrying stolen salt shakers or anything else of a compromising nature, but there's something about the prospect of a purse search that makes a woman feel a few buttons short of fully dressed. After work, I called around and found that this, too, is generally legal, at least if the boss has reasonable cause and has given prior notification of the company's search policies.

Purse searches, though, are relatively innocuous compared with the sophisticated chemical and electronic forms of snooping adopted by many companies in the 90's. The American Management Association reports that in 1999 a record two-thirds of major American companies monitored their employees electronically: videotaping them; reviewing their e-mail and voice-mail messages; and, most recently, according to Lewis Maltby, president of the Princeton-based National Workrights Institute, monitoring any Web sites they may visit on their lunch breaks. Nor can you count on keeping anything hidden in your genes; a growing number of employers now use genetic testing to screen out job applicants who carry genes for expensive ailments like Huntington's disease.

But the most ubiquitous invasion of privacy is drug testing, usually of urine, more rarely of hair or blood. With 81 percent of large companies now requiring some form of drug testing—up from 21 percent in 1987—job applicants take it for granted that they'll have to provide a urine sample as well as a résumé. This is not restricted to "for cause" testing—of people who, say, nod or space out on the job. Nor is it restricted to employees in "safety-sensitive occupations," like airline pilots and school-bus drivers. Workers who stack boxes of Cheerios in my local supermarkets get tested, as do the editorial employees of this magazine, although there is no evidence that a weekend joint has any more effect on Monday-morning performance than a Saturday-night beer.

Civil libertarians see drug testing as a violation of our Fourth Amendment protection from "unreasonable search," while most jobholders and applicants find it simply embarrassing. In some testing protocols, the employee has to strip to her underwear and urinate into a cup in the presence of an aide or technician, who will also want to know what prescription drugs she takes, since these can influence the test results.

According to a recent report from the American Civil Liberties Union, drug
8 testing has not been proven to achieve its advertised effects, like reducing absenteeism and improving productivity. But it does reveal who's on antidepressants or suffering with an ailment that's expensive to treat, and it is undeniably effective at weeding out those potential "troublemakers" who are too independent-minded to strip and empty their bladders on command.

Maybe the prevailing trade-off between jobs and freedom would make sense, in the narrowest cost-benefit terms, if it contributed to a more vibrant economy. But this is hardly the case. In fact, a 1998 study of 63 computer-equipment and data-processing firms found that companies that performed both pre-employment and random drug testing actually "reduced rather than enhanced productivity"—by an eye-popping 29 percent, presumably because of its dampening effect on morale.

Why, then, do so many employers insist on treating their workers as a kind of fifth column within the firm? Certainly the government has played a role with its misguided anti-drug crusade, as has the sheer availability of new technologies of snooping. But workplace repression signals a deeper shift away from the postwar social contract in which a job meant a straightforward exchange of work for wages.

Economists trace the change to the 1970's, when, faced with falling profits and rising foreign competition, America's capitalists launched an offensive to squeeze more out of their workers. Supervision tightened, management expanded and union-busting became a growth industry. And once in motion, the dynamic of distrust is hard to stop. Workers who are routinely treated like criminals and slackers may well bear close watching.

The mystery is why American workers, the political descendants of proud revolutionaries, have so meekly surrendered their rights. Sure, individual workers find ways to cheat on their drug tests, outwit the electronic surveillance and sneak in a bit of "gossip" here and there. But these petty acts of defiance seldom add up to concerted resistance, in part because of the weakness of American unions. The A.F.L.-C.I.O. is currently conducting a nationwide drive to ensure the right to organize, and the downtrodden workers of the world can only wish the union well. But what about all the other rights missing in so many American workplaces? It's not easy to organize your fellow workers if you can't communicate freely with them on the job and don't dare carry union literature in your pocketbook.

In a tight labor market, workers have another option, of course. They can walk. The alarming levels of turnover in low-wage jobs attest to the popularity of this tactic, and if unemployment remains low, employers may eventually decide to cut their workers some slack. Already, companies in particularly labor-starved industries like ski resorts and software are dropping drug testing rather than lose or repel employees. But in the short run, the mobility of workers, combined with the weakness of unions, means that there is little or no sustained on-site challenge to overbearing authority.

What we need is nothing less than a new civil rights movement—this time, for American workers. Who will provide the leadership remains to be seen, but clearly the stakes go way beyond "labor issues," as these are conventionally defined. We can hardly call ourselves the world's pre-eminent democracy if large numbers of citizens spend half of their waking hours in what amounts, in plain terms, to a dictatorship.

PERSONAL RESPONSE

Describe any personal experiences you have had with an employer's restricting your rights.

QUESTIONS FOR CLASS OR SMALL-GROUP DISCUSSION

1. Summarize the central issue of Ehrenreich's essay and the position she has taken on that issue. How persuasive do you find her reasoning process?

2. Do Ehrenreich's examples of violated rights in the work place fully support her argument?
3. Ehrenreich says that it is a mystery why "American workers . . . have so meekly surrendered their rights" (paragraph 15), but then she suggests reasons that explain their behavior. Can you add other reasons to explain why American workers do not complain in large numbers about their treatment in the work place? Would you support the "new civil rights movement . . . for American workers" that she proposes in her final paragraph?

○ PERSPECTIVES ON THE WORKPLACE ○
Suggested Writing Topics

1. Drawing on at least one of the essays in this chapter, describe what you see as the ideal job or ideal working conditions.
2. Argue in support of or against this statement by Alfie Kohn, author of *Punished by Rewards: The Trouble with Gold Stars, Incentive Plans, A's, Praise, and Other Bribes:* " 'Millions of well-meaning teachers and parents and managers are killing off creativity and curiosity in their attempt to bribe people to do a good job' " (paragraph 5, Jay Matthews's "For Love or Money").
3. Matthew Boyle reports on a survey conducted by the Families and Life Institute (paragraph 8, "Beware the Killjoy") in which workers were asked what they value most in a job, such as having fun, making lots of money, or having a challenging job. Write a paper explaining which you value most and why. Or conduct your own informal interview on the subject of expectations for a job and report your results.
4. Describe your work experiences and the extent to which self-satisfaction or self-motivation contributes to your performance.
5. Argue in support of or against Barbara Ehrenreich's accusation in "Warning: This is a Rights-Free Workplace" that employers unfairly violate the basic rights of workers.
6. Read *Void Where Prohibited: Rest Breaks and the Right to Urinate on Company Time* by Marc Linder and Ingrid Nygaard and write a critique of it.
7. Argue in support of or against drug testing in the workplace.
8. Write an essay explaining whether you believe this statement by Terry Golway in "Rewriting the Old Rules" to be true: "Women have been breaking through glass ceilings in the workplace [. . .] and with each new achievement [. . .] society has changed for the better" (paragraph 3).

Research Topics

1. Combine library research and personal interviews with area employers for a paper on ways to motivate employees. As Jay Matthews points out in "For

Love or Money," the subject is open to debate, so you will need to take a position on which works better, extrinsic or intrinsic incentives.

2. Terry Golway in "Rewriting the Old Rules" suggests that women's ways of doing things are "saner" than men's ways. Research this topic, including interviews, if possible.

3. Research the topic of the effect of work place environment on employee productivity and morale.

4. Research the subject of the right to free speech or the right to privacy in the work place.

5. Research workers' perceptions of their work places. If possible, interview people who work full-time about their work place experiences and combine the results of your interview(s) with your other sources.

RESPONDING TO VISUALS

A waitress carries plates of food from the kitchen at Jimmy's Grille in Bridgeville, Delaware. Source: Kevin Fleming/CORBIS

1. How does the photographer give the impression of movement?
2. How does the photographer convey the stress of the woman's job?
3. What emotions does the server's face reveal?

RESPONDING TO VISUALS

A sign warns workers at a construction site about drug testing. Source: Michael Newman/Photo Edit

1. What is the impact of the chain-link fence in combination with the sign behind it?
2. What does the fence symbolize?
3. What message does the picture give to someone looking for work?

CHAPTER

25

THE ECONOMIC IMPACT OF OUTSOURCING

Throughout the 20th century, American wholesalers and retailers imported goods that were made abroad. American consumers were used to seeing the words "made in China" or "made in Taiwan," for instance, on the products that they purchased. Then, it became popular in the last decades of the century for American manufacturers to either outsource the labor to make their products in a foreign country or physically to move abroad. Workers in other countries could be hired to make parts and/or assemble products at wages considerably less than what manufacturers would have to pay workers in the United States, and many American manufacturers found it just as cost-effective to relocate their factories. Central and South America were particularly appealing for such moves because transportation of the products into the United States was fairly easy.

Now, with the development of high-tech telecommunications and the globalization of the economy, many businesses are outsourcing their work to countries all over the world, or they are offshoring completely. Now not only Central and South America, but also India, Eastern Europe, North and South Africa, Asia Pacific, and New Zealand have all become outsourcing centers for American businesses.

The practice of outsourcing—that is, hiring people outside one's own company to do work previously done on-site, or offshoring, physically relocating to another country—has always been subject to criticism from American workers and consumers. These critics charge that it is unethical, unfair, and damaging to the U. S. economy. Its defenders point out that such a practice is highly beneficial to the company's economic health. The articles in this chapter look at both sides of the issue and explore some of the economic benefits and drawbacks of offshore outsourcing.

First, N. Venkat Venkatraman's "Offshoring Without Guilt" defends the practice of offshoring and outsourcing by looking at the issue as a practical step and good business sense. He suggests that the debate on the ethics of offshoring misses the point: offshoring is the inevitable next generation of business practice. Next, "The Wal-Mart You Don't Know" by Charles Fishman looks at the world's largest retailer in terms of what being able to offer products at low cost actually costs Wal-Mart's suppliers and the people who work for them. Wal-Mart exerts enormous pressure on its suppliers to outsource in order to sell at low wholesale prices to Wal-Mart. Fishman wonders, Are we shopping our way straight to the unemployment line?

Then, Thomas L. Friedman in "30 Little Turtles" reports on his visit to a training center in India where young Indians are being trained to speak with a Canadian accent for their telephone service jobs. Friedman describes it as "an uplifting experience" and explains why he believes there is more to outsourcing than economics: "There's also geopolitics." Finally, Richard Appelbaum and Peter Dreier describe the brief history of a noble attempt to produce garments in the U. S. made by workers who are paid a fair wage, have health benefits, and are unionized. "SweatX Closes Up Shop" explains what the company's goals were and analyzes why it failed.

OFFSHORING WITHOUT GUILT

N. Venkat Venkatraman

N. Venkat Venkatraman is chairman of the Information Systems Department and Professor of Management at the Boston University School of Management. "Offshoring Without Guilt" was published in the Spring, 2004, issue of MIT's Sloan Management Review, *a peer-reviewed quarterly covering all management disciplines.*

The new hot topic being debated in boardrooms, at meetings and in Internet discussion groups is "offshoring," the practice among U.S. and European companies of migrating business processes overseas to India, the Philippines, Ireland, China and elsewhere to lower costs without significantly sacrificing quality. At first blush this would seem like nothing new, but the development of a powerful communication infrastructure is making offshoring an increasingly viable and commonly taken option: Nearly two out of three software companies are already involved, and in a number of industries, IT-enabled back-office business processes are prime candidates for such a shift.

At the heart of the debate is the issue of jobs and wages. As networking technologies have enabled companies to tap into the global marketplace for talent more easily, offshoring has put downward pressure on domestic salaries. What's more, we seem to be emerging from the current recession with no net increase in professional, higher-wage jobs, because many of these have migrated overseas. Unlike layoffs triggered by poor performance, these job shifts are mainly due to the availability of comparable talent elsewhere at lower cost. The public outcry about this practice has engendered so much corporate guilt that very few companies are keen to go on record publicly in this arena. This guilt, however, is misguided. Offshoring should be seen for what it is—a key element of the next-generation business model.

The Third Wave

The shifting geography of business processes is, in fact, the third wave of geography-related change in the design and operation of corporations. During the first wave, the improving transportation infrastructure of the 20th century enabled corporations to seek effective production capabilities in increasingly far-flung locations that provided access to new markets and tangible resources—land, local factories, mines and production workers. During the second wave, as capital markets became global and interconnected in the latter half of the 20th century, corporations began to capitalize on vibrant global financial markets for both debt and equity.

4   Now we are in the midst of the third wave—in which digitized business processes like order processing, billing, customer service, accounts and payroll processing, and design and development can be carried out without regard to physical location. As with the first two waves, the only relevant question for companies now is how to deliver maximum value to customers and shareholders.

Global realignment of jobs across different skill levels is continuous and dynamic. We have recently seen a major shift in the employment patterns of skilled white-collar jobs. In the early 1990s, middle-management jobs were restructured to take advantage of the increased power of computer and communication technologies. Jobs lost due to reengineering in large corporations were compensated for by job creation due to the Internet revolution and supported by venture-capital inflow. Indeed, the feeling at that time was that we needed to import high-skill labor to cope with the shortage. The rallying cry then was the "war for talent," yet just a few years later we are crying about the need to protect jobs. The challenge at hand is not to protect domestic jobs through tariffs or quotas but to recognize and exploit the emergent global network of such competencies.

When this question is framed as "offshoring," it misses the larger point. Despite the public relations backlash, offshoring is not synonymous with the use of sweatshop labor or the flouting of environmental laws. It is the creative and careful leveraging of new and available pools of skilled labor and exploiting the power of communication technologies to create new sources of competitive advantage. The true power of the Internet will be to alter the global footprint of business operations, blurring national and physical boundaries.

Leading the Shift

Within the next few years, this single issue has the potential to change the competitive cost structure in many settings for companies of all sizes. For example, for some time now managers have been asked to focus on their core competencies. Dell Inc. and Cisco Systems Inc. are just two of many companies that have begun to address successfully whether there are activities inside the firm that would best be carried out by someone else (outsourcing) or somewhere else (offshoring). Each company orchestrates a global supply chain for product delivery comprising many different companies and competencies—partnering, for example, with two electronic manufacturing services companies, Solectron Corp. (based in Milpitas, California) and Flextronics Corp. (headquartered in Singapore) for assembly, as well as FedEx Corp. and United Parcel Service Inc. for shipping.

8 Beyond the question of what is core, many companies are simply asking themselves which of their processes are location-independent and where those processes would best be located. HSBC, for instance, carries out credit card and loan processing from India and both Allstate Corp. and Prudential Property & Casualty Insurance Co. have application designers and call-center personnel working out of Ireland. General Electric Co.—arguably one of the pioneers in understanding this shift—has over 15,000 people in India alone carrying out a variety of knowledge-work business processes.

Once companies have decided, on the basis of core competencies and optimal location, on their offshoring strategy, the question of optimal governance of these processes arises. GE, Intel, J.P. Morgan Chase and Motorola all have opted for internal governance. They use their global reputation to attract talented professionals to work for them. Internal governance ensures that their offshore components strictly adhere to corporate worldwide procedures and rules. For other companies it is more attractive to contract with local service providers in India, Ireland, Malaysia and elsewhere. BP Plc, for example, has formed relationships in different parts of the world to take advantage of the vibrant competition among the service providers. The main advantages of this approach are flexibility and scale of operations. But this flexibility creates the need for investments in relationship management. (BP, for instance, has developed a set of web-enabled tools for effective governance, including performance dashboards and stakeholder maps for managing relationships.)

Regardless of which form of governance is chosen, thinking through how work will be both distributed and integrated is essential to assessing the benefits and costs of offshoring. For most companies, coordinating a far-flung network of business processes presents new challenges and they need to design management processes that will capture value on a sustained basis.

A New Frame of Reference

The location of factories, the physical machinery of production and the percentage of local content in products were all considerations that shaped industrial-age thinking, when companies were seen primarily as portfolios of product offerings. In the current age, however, when companies are best seen as portfolios of capabilities and relationships positioned within a global network of business processes, it is those processes and the dynamic creation of value within the entire network that frames our thinking. In that context, offshoring is but one of the critical challenges companies face. Job shifts and relocated operations are but aspects of the larger challenge to design the next-generation organization. This is not an issue merely for CIOs. It is a business strategy issue and managers would do well to think rationally—not emotionally—about it.

PERSONAL RESPONSE

In his concluding statement, Venkatraman advises managers to "think rationally—not emotionally—about" the business strategy of offshoring. Do you agree that the subject should be treated without emotion?

QUESTIONS FOR CLASS OR SMALL-GROUP DISCUSSION

1. Where does Venkatraman state his thesis? What evidence does he provide to support it?
2. Venkatraman says that "the only relevant question for companies now is how to deliver maximum value to customers and shareholders." Are you persuaded that that is the only relevant question when it comes to sending jobs overseas?
3. Look at the way that Venkatraman defines "offshoring" in paragraph 6 and explain whether you think his definition is accurate.

THE WAL-MART YOU DON'T KNOW
CHARLES FISHMAN

Charles Fishman began his writing career at the Washington Post *and held positions on the* Orlando Sentinel *and* Raleigh News & Observer *before joining the staff of* Fast Company, *where he is a senior writer. Andrew Moesel provided research assistance for this story, which appeared in the December, 2003, issue of* Fast Company.

A gallon-sized jar of whole pickles is something to behold. The jar is the size of a small aquarium. The fat green pickles, floating in swampy juice, look reptilian, their shapes exaggerated by the glass. It weighs 12 pounds, too big to carry with one hand. The gallon jar of pickles is a display of abundance and excess; it is entrancing, and also vaguely unsettling. This is the product that Wal-Mart fell in love with: Vlasic's gallon jar of pickles.

Wal-Mart priced it at $2.97—a year's supply of pickles for less than $3! "They were using it as a 'statement' item," says Pat Hunn, who calls himself the "mad scientist" of Vlasic's gallon jar. "Wal-Mart was putting it before consumers, saying, This represents what Wal-Mart's about. You can buy a stinkin' gallon of pickles for $2.97. And it's the nation's number-one brand."

Therein lies the basic conundrum of doing business with the world's largest retailer. By selling a gallon of kosher dills for less than most grocers sell a quart, Wal-Mart may have provided a service for its customers. But what did it do for Vlasic? The pickle maker had spent decades convincing customers that they should pay a premium for its brand. Now Wal-Mart was practically giving them away. And the fevered buying spree that resulted distorted every aspect of Vlasic's operations, from farm field to factory to financial statement.

4   Indeed, as Vlasic discovered, the real story of Wal-Mart, the story that never gets told, is the story of the pressure the biggest retailer relentlessly applies to its suppliers in the name of bringing us "every day low prices." It's the story of what that pressure does to the companies Wal-Mart does business with, to U.S. manufacturing, and to the economy as a whole. That story can be found floating in a gallon jar of pickles at Wal-Mart.

Wal-Mart is not just the world's largest retailer. It's the world's largest company—bigger than ExxonMobil, General Motors, and General Electric. The scale can be hard to absorb. Wal-Mart sold $244.5 billion worth of goods last year. It sells in three months what number-two retailer Home Depot sells in a year. And in its own category of general merchandise and groceries, Wal-Mart no longer has any real rivals. It does more business than Target, Sears, Kmart, J.C. Penney, Safeway, and Kroger combined. "Clearly," says Edward Fox, head of Southern Methodist University's J.C. Penney Center for Retailing Excellence, "Wal-Mart is more powerful than any retailer has ever been." It is, in fact, so big and so furtively powerful as to have become an entirely different order of corporate being.

Wal-Mart wields its power for just one purpose: to bring the lowest possible prices to its customers. At Wal-Mart, that goal is never reached. The retailer has a clear policy for suppliers: On basic products that don't change, the price Wal-Mart will pay, and will charge shoppers, must drop year after year. But what almost no one outside the world of Wal-Mart and its 21,000 suppliers knows is the high cost of those low prices. Wal-Mart has the power to squeeze profit-killing concessions from vendors. To survive in the face of its pricing demands, makers of everything from bras to bicycles to blue jeans have had to lay off employees and close U.S. plants in favor of outsourcing products from overseas.

Of course, U.S. companies have been moving jobs offshore for decades, long before Wal-Mart was a retailing power. But there is no question that the chain is helping accelerate the loss of American jobs to low-wage countries such as China. Wal-Mart, which in the late 1980s and early 1990s trumpeted its claim to "Buy American," has doubled its imports from China in the past five years alone, buying some $12 billion in merchandise in 2002. That's nearly 10% of all Chinese exports to the United States.

8   One way to think of Wal-Mart is as a vast pipeline that gives non-U.S. companies direct access to the American market. "One of the things that limits or slows the growth of imports is the cost of establishing connections and networks," says Paul Krugman, the Princeton University economist. "Wal-Mart is so big and so centralized that it can all at once hook Chinese and other suppliers into its digital system. So—wham!—you have a large switch to overseas sourcing in a period quicker than under the old rules of retailing."

Steve Dobbins has been bearing the brunt of that switch. He's president and CEO of Carolina Mills, a 75-year-old North Carolina company that supplies thread, yarn, and textile finishing to apparel makers—half of which supply Wal-Mart. Carolina Mills grew steadily until 2000. But in the past three years, as its customers have gone either overseas or out of business, it has shrunk from 17 factories to 7, and from 2,600 employees to 1,200. Dobbins's customers have begun to face imported clothing sold so cheaply to Wal-Mart that they could not compete even if they paid their workers nothing.

"People ask, 'How can it be bad for things to come into the U.S. cheaply? How can it be bad to have a bargain at Wal-Mart?' Sure, it's held inflation down, and it's great to have bargains," says Dobbins. "But you can't buy anything if you're not employed. We are shopping ourselves out of jobs."

The gallon jar of pickles at Wal-Mart became a devastating success, giving Vlasic strong sales and growth numbers—but slashing its profits by millions of dollars.

12   There is no question that Wal-Mart's relentless drive to squeeze out costs has benefited consumers. The giant retailer is at least partly responsible for the low rate of U.S. inflation, and a McKinsey & Co. study concluded that about 12% of the economy's productivity gains in the second half of the 1990s could be traced to Wal-Mart alone.

There is also no question that doing business with Wal-Mart can give a supplier a fast, heady jolt of sales and market share. But that fix can come with long-term consequences for the health of a brand and a business. Vlasic, for example, wasn't looking to build its brand on a gallon of whole pickles. Pickle companies make money on "the cut," slicing cucumbers into spears and hamburger chips. "Cucumbers in the jar, you don't make a whole lot of money there," says Steve Young, a former vice president of grocery marketing for pickles at Vlasic, who has since left the company.

At some point in the late 1990s, a Wal-Mart buyer saw Vlasic's gallon jar and started talking to Pat Hunn about it. Hunn, who has also since left Vlasic, was then head of Vlasic's Wal-Mart sales team, based in Dallas. The gallon intrigued the buyer. In sales tests, priced somewhere over $3, "the gallon sold like crazy," says Hunn, "surprising us all." The Wal-Mart buyer had a brainstorm: What would happen to the gallon if they offered it nationwide and got it below $3? Hunn was skeptical, but his job was to look for ways to sell pickles at Wal-Mart. Why not?

And so Vlasic's gallon jar of pickles went into every Wal-Mart, some 3,000 stores, at $2.97, a price so low that Vlasic and Wal-Mart were making only a penny or two on a jar, if that. It was showcased on big pallets near the front of stores. It was an abundance of abundance. "It was selling 80 jars a week, on average, in every store," says Young. Doesn't sound like much, until you do the math: That's 240,000 gallons of pickles, just in gallon jars, just at Wal-Mart, every week. Whole fields of cucumbers were heading out the door.

16   For Vlasic, the gallon jar of pickles became what might be called a devastating success. "Quickly, it started cannibalizing our non-Wal-Mart business," says Young. "We saw consumers who used to buy the spears and the chips in supermarkets buying the Wal-Mart gallons. They'd eat a quarter of a jar and throw the thing away when they got moldy. A family can't eat them fast enough."

The gallon jar reshaped Vlasic's pickle business: It chewed up the profit margin of the business with Wal-Mart, and of pickles generally. Procurement had to scramble to find enough pickles to fill the gallons, but the volume gave Vlasic strong sales numbers, strong growth numbers, and a powerful place in the world of pickles at Wal-Mart. Which accounted for 30% of Vlasic's business. But the company's profits from pickles had shriveled 25% or more, Young says—millions of dollars.

The gallon was hoisting Vlasic and hurting it at the same time.

Young remembers begging Wal-Mart for relief. "They said, 'No way,'" says Young. "We said we'll increase the price"—even $3.49 would have helped tremendously—"and they said, 'If you do that, all the other products of yours we buy, we'll stop buying.' It was a clear threat." Hunn recalls things a little differently, if just as ominously: "They said, 'We want the $2.97 gallon of pickles. If you don't do it, we'll see if someone else might.' I knew our competitors were saying to Wal-Mart, 'We'll do the $2.97 gallons if you give us your other business.'" Wal-Mart's business was so indispensable to Vlasic, and the gallon so central to the Wal-Mart relationship, that decisions about the future of the gallon were made at the CEO level.

20   Finally, Wal-Mart let Vlasic up for air. "The Wal-Mart guy's response was classic," Young recalls. "He said, 'Well, we've done to pickles what we did to orange juice. We've killed it. We can back off.'" Vlasic got to take it down to just over half a gallon of pickles, for $2.79. Not long after that, in January 2001, Vlasic filed for bankruptcy—although the gallon jar of pickles, everyone agrees, wasn't a critical factor.

By now, it is accepted wisdom that Wal-Mart makes the companies it does business with more efficient and focused, leaner and faster. Wal-Mart itself is known for continuous improvement in its ability to handle, move, and track merchandise. It expects the same of its suppliers. But the ability to operate at peak efficiency only gets you in the door at Wal-Mart. Then the real demands start. The public image Wal-Mart projects may be as cheery as its yellow smiley-face mascot, but there is nothing genial about the process by which Wal-Mart gets its suppliers to provide tires and contact lenses, guns and underarm deodorant at every day low prices. Wal-Mart is legendary for forcing its suppliers to redesign everything from their packaging to their computer systems. It is also legendary for quite straightforwardly telling them what it will pay for their goods.

John Fitzgerald, a former vice president of Nabisco, remembers Wal-Mart's reaction to his company's plan to offer a 25-cent newspaper coupon for a large bag of Lifesavers in advance of Halloween. Wal-Mart told Nabisco to add up what it would spend on the promotion—for the newspaper ads, the coupons, and handling—and then just take that amount off the price instead. "That isn't necessarily good for the manufacturer," Fitzgerald says. "They need things that draw attention."

It also is not unheard of for Wal-Mart to demand to examine the private financial records of a supplier, and to insist that its margins are too high and must be cut. And the smaller the supplier, one academic study shows, the greater the likelihood that it will be forced into damaging concessions. Melissa Berryhill, a Wal-Mart spokeswoman, disagrees: "The fact is Wal-Mart, perhaps like no other retailer, seeks to establish collaborative and mutually beneficial relationships with our suppliers."

24   For many suppliers, though, the only thing worse than doing business with Wal-Mart may be not doing business with Wal-Mart. Last year, 7.5 cents of every dollar spent in any store in the United States (other than auto-parts stores) went to the retailer. That means a contract with Wal-Mart can be critical even for the largest consumer-goods companies. Dial Corp., for example, does 28% of its business with Wal-Mart. If Dial lost that one account, it would have to double its sales to its next nine customers just to stay even. "Wal-Mart is the essential retailer, in a way no other retailer is," says Gib Carey, a partner at Bain & Co., who is leading a yearlong study of how to do business with Wal-Mart. "Our clients cannot grow without finding a way to be successful with Wal-Mart."

Many companies and their executives frankly admit that supplying Wal-Mart is like getting into the company version of basic training with an implacable Army drill sergeant. The process may be unpleasant. But there can be some positive results.

"Everyone from the forklift driver on up to me, the CEO, knew we had to deliver [to Wal-Mart] on time. Not 10 minutes late. And not 45 minutes early, either," says Robin Prever, who was CEO of Saratoga Beverage Group from 1992 to 2000, and made private-label water sold at Wal-Mart. "The message came through clearly: You have this 30-second delivery window. Either you're there, or you're out. With a customer like that, it changes your organization. For the better. It wakes everybody up. And all our customers benefited. We changed our whole approach to doing business."

But you won't hear evenhanded stories like that from Wal-Mart, or from its current suppliers. Despite being a publicly traded company, Wal-Mart is intensely private. It declined to talk in detail about its relationships with its suppliers for this story. More strikingly, dozens of companies contacted declined to talk about even the basics of their business with Wal-Mart.

28   Here, for example, is an executive at Dial: "We are one of Wal-Mart's biggest suppliers, and they are our biggest customer by far. We have a great relationship. That's all I can say. Are we done now?" Goaded a bit, the executive responds with an

almost hysterical edge: "Are you meshuga? Why in the world would we talk about Wal-Mart? Ask me about anything else, we'll talk. But not Wal-Mart."

No one wants to end up in what is known among Wal-Mart vendors as the "penalty box"—punished, or even excluded from the store shelves, for saying something that makes Wal-Mart unhappy. (The penalty box is normally reserved for vendors who don't meet performance benchmarks, not for those who talk to the press.)

"You won't hear anything negative from most people," says Paul Kelly, founder of Silvermine Consulting Group, a company that helps businesses work more effectively with retailers. "It would be committing suicide. If Wal-Mart takes something the wrong way, it's like Saddam Hussein. You just don't want to piss them off."

As a result, this story was reported in an unusual way: by speaking with dozens of people who have spent years selling to Wal-Mart, or consulting to companies that sell to Wal-Mart, but who no longer work for companies that do business with Wal-Mart. Unless otherwise noted, the companies involved in the events they described refused even to confirm or deny the basics of the events.

32   To a person, all those interviewed credit Wal-Mart with a fundamental integrity in its dealings that's unusual in the world of consumer goods, retailing, and groceries. Wal-Mart does not cheat suppliers, it keeps its word, it pays its bills briskly. "They are tough people but very honest; they treat you honestly," says Peter Campanella, who ran the business that sold Corning kitchenware products, both at Corning and then at World Kitchen. "It was a joke to do business with most of their competitors. A fiasco."

But Wal-Mart also clearly does not hesitate to use its power, magnifying the Darwinian forces already at work in modern global capitalism. What does the squeeze look like at Wal-Mart? It is usually thoroughly rational, sometimes devastatingly so.

John Mariotti is a veteran of the consumer-products world—he spent nine years as president of Huffy Bicycle Co., a division of Huffy Corp., and is now chairman of World Kitchen, the company that sells Oxo, Revere, Corning, and Ekco brand housewares.

He could not be clearer on his opinion about Wal-Mart: It's a great company, and a great company to do business with. "Wal-Mart has done more good for America by several thousand orders of magnitude than they've done bad," Mariotti says. "They have raised the bar, and raised the bar for everybody."

36   Mariotti describes one episode from Huffy's relationship with Wal-Mart. It's a tale he tells to illustrate an admiring point he makes about the retailer. "They demand you do what you say you are going to do." But it's also a classic example of the damned-if-you-do, damned-if-you-don't Wal-Mart squeeze. When Mariotti was at Huffy throughout the 1980s, the company sold a range of bikes to Wal-Mart, 20 or so models, in a spread of prices and profitability. It was a leading manufacturer of bikes in the United States, in places like Ponca City, Oklahoma; Celina, Ohio; and Farmington, Missouri.

One year, Huffy had committed to supply Wal-Mart with an entry-level, thin-margin bike—as many as Wal-Mart needed. Sales of the low-end bike took off. "I woke up May 1"—the heart of the bike production cycle for the summer—"and I needed 900,000 bikes," he says. "My factories could only run 450,000." As it happened, that same year, Huffy's fancier, more-profitable bikes were doing well, too, at Wal-Mart and other places. Huffy found itself in a bind.

With other retailers, perhaps, Mariotti might have sat down, renegotiated, tried to talk his way out of the corner. Not with Wal-Mart. "I made the deal up front with them," he says. "I knew how high was up. I was duty-bound to supply my customer." So he did something extraordinary. To free up production in order to make Wal-Mart's cheap bikes, he gave the designs for four of his higher-end, higher-margin products to rival manufacturers. "I conceded business to my competitors, because I just ran out of capacity," he says. Huffy didn't just relinquish profits to keep Wal-Mart happy—it handed those profits to its competition. "Wal-Mart didn't tell me what to do," Mariotti says. "They didn't have to." The retailer, he adds, "is tough as nails. But they give you a chance to compete. If you can't compete, that's your problem."

In the years since Mariotti left Huffy, the bike maker's relationship with Wal-Mart has been vital (though Huffy Corp. has lost money in three out of the last five years). It is the number-three seller of bikes in the United States. And Wal-Mart is the number-one retailer of bikes. But here's one last statistic about bicycles: Roughly 98% are now imported from places such as China, Mexico, and Taiwan. Huffy made its last bike in the United States in 1999.

40   As Mariotti says, Wal-Mart is tough as nails. But not every supplier agrees that the toughness is always accompanied by fairness. The Lovable Company was founded in 1926 by the grandfather of Frank Garson II, who was Lovable's last president. It did business with Wal-Mart, Garson says, from the earliest days of founder Sam Walton's first store in Bentonville, Arkansas. Lovable made bras and lingerie, supplying retailers that also included Sears and Victoria's Secret. At one point, it was the sixth-largest maker of intimate apparel in the United States, with 700 employees in this country and another 2,000 at eight factories in Central America.

Eventually Wal-Mart became Lovable's biggest customer. "Wal-Mart has a big pencil," says Garson. "They have such awesome purchasing power that they write their own ticket. If they don't like your prices, they'll go vertical and do it themselves—or they'll find someone that will meet their terms."

In the summer of 1995, Garson asserts, Wal-Mart did just that. "They had awarded us a contract, and in their wisdom, they changed the terms so dramatically that they really reneged." Garson, still worried about litigation, won't provide details. "But when you lose a customer that size, they are irreplaceable."

Lovable was already feeling intense cost pressure. Less than three years after Wal-Mart pulled its business, in its 72nd year, Lovable closed. "They leave a lot to be desired in the way they treat people," says Garson. "Their actions to pulverize people are unnecessary. Wal-Mart chewed us up and spit us out."

44   Believe it or not, American business has been through this before. The Great Atlantic & Pacific Tea Co., the grocery-store chain, stood astride the U.S. market in the 1920s and 1930s with a dominance that has likely never been duplicated. At its peak, A&P had five times the number of stores Wal-Mart has now (although much smaller ones), and at one point, it owned 80% of the supermarket business. Some of the antipredatory-pricing laws in use today were inspired by A&P's attempts to muscle its suppliers.

There is very little academic and statistical study of Wal-Mart's impact on the health of its suppliers and virtually nothing in the last decade, when Wal-Mart's size has increased by a factor of five. This while the retail industry has become much more concentrated. In large part, that's because it's nearly impossible to get meaningful data that would allow researchers to track the influence of Wal-Mart's business on companies over time. You'd need cooperation from the vendor companies or Wal-Mart or both—and neither Wal-Mart nor its suppliers are interested in sharing such intimate detail.

Bain & Co., the global management consulting firm, is in the midst of a project that asks, How does a company have a healthy relationship with Wal-Mart? How do you avoid being sucked into the vortex? How do you maintain some standing, some leverage of your own?

Bain's first insights are obvious, if not easy. "Year after year," Carey, a partner at Bain & Co., says, "for any product that is the same as what you sold them last year, Wal-Mart will say, 'Here's the price you gave me last year. Here's what I can get a competitor's product for. Here's what I can get a private-label version for. I want to see a better value that I can bring to my shopper this year. Or else I'm going to use that shelf space differently.' "

48   Carey has a friend in the umbrella business who learned that. One year, because of costs, he went to Wal-Mart and asked for a 5% price increase. "Wal-Mart said, 'We were expecting a 5% decrease. We're off by 10%. Go back and sharpen your pencil.' " The umbrella man scrimped and came back with a 2% increase. "They said, 'We'll go with a Chinese manufacturer'—and he was out entirely."

The Wal-Mart squeeze means vendors have to be as relentless and as microscopic as Wal-Mart is at managing their own costs. They need, in fact, to turn themselves into shadow versions of Wal-Mart itself. "Wal-Mart won't necessarily say you have to reconfigure your distribution system," says Carey. "But companies recognize they are not going to maintain margins with growth in their Wal-Mart business without doing it."

The way to avoid being trapped in a spiral of growing business and shrinking profits, says Carey, is to innovate. "You need to bring Wal-Mart new products—products consumers need. Because with those, Wal-Mart doesn't have benchmarks to drive you down in price. They don't have historical data, you don't have competitors, they haven't bid the products out to private-label makers. That's how you can have higher prices and higher margins."

Reasonable advice, but not universally useful. There has been an explosion of "innovation" in toothbrushes and toothpastes in the past five years, for instance; but a pickle is a pickle is a pickle.

52   Bain's other critical discovery is that consumers are often more loyal to product companies than to Wal-Mart. With strongly branded items people develop a preference for—things like toothpaste or laundry detergent—Wal-Mart rarely forces shoppers to switch to a second choice. It would simply punish itself by seeing sales fall, and it won't put up with that for long.

But as Wal-Mart has grown in market reach and clout, even manufacturers known for nurturing premium brands may find themselves overpowered. This July, in a mating that had the relieved air of lovers who had too long resisted embracing, Levi

Strauss rolled blue jeans into every Wal-Mart doorway in the United States: 2,864 stores. Wal-Mart, seeking to expand its clothing business with more fashionable brands, promoted the clothes on its in-store TV network and with banners slipped over the security-tag detectors at exit doors.

Levi's launch into Wal-Mart came the same summer the clothes maker celebrated its 150th birthday. For a century and a half, one of the most recognizable names in American commerce had survived without Wal-Mart. But in October 2002, when Levi Strauss and Wal-Mart announced their engagement, Levi was shrinking rapidly. The pressure on Levi goes back 25 years—well before Wal-Mart was an influence. Between 1981 and 1990, Levi closed 58 U.S. manufacturing plants, sending 25% of its sewing overseas.

Sales for Levi peaked in 1996 at $7.1 billion. By last year, they had spiraled down six years in a row, to $4.1 billion; through the first six months of 2003, sales dropped another 3%. This one account—selling jeans to Wal-Mart—could almost instantly revive Levi.

56 Last year, Wal-Mart sold more clothing than any other retailer in the country. It also sold more pairs of jeans than any other store. Wal-Mart's own inexpensive house brand of jeans, Faded Glory, is estimated to do $3 billion in sales a year, a house brand nearly the size of Levi Strauss. Perhaps most revealing in terms of Levi's strategic blunders: In 2002, half the jeans sold in the United States cost less than $20 a pair. That same year, Levi didn't offer jeans for less than $30.

For much of the last decade, Levi couldn't have qualified to sell to Wal-Mart. Its computer systems were antiquated, and it was notorious for delivering clothes late to retailers. Levi admitted its on-time delivery rate was 65%. When it announced the deal with Wal-Mart last year, one fashion-industry analyst bluntly predicted Levi would simply fail to deliver the jeans.

But Levi Strauss has taken to the Wal-Mart Way with the intensity of a near-death religious conversion—and Levi's executives were happy to talk about their experience getting ready to sell at Wal-Mart. One hundred people at Levi's headquarters are devoted to the new business; another 12 have set up in an office in Bentonville, near Wal-Mart's headquarters, where the company has hired a respected veteran Wal-Mart sales account manager.

Getting ready for Wal-Mart has been like putting Levi on the Atkins diet. It has helped everything—customer focus, inventory management, speed to market. It has even helped other retailers that buy Levis, because Wal-Mart has forced the company to replenish stores within two days instead of Levi's previous five-day cycle.

60 And so, Wal-Mart might rescue Levi Strauss. Except for one thing.

Levi didn't actually have any clothes it could sell at Wal-Mart. Everything was too expensive. It had to develop a fresh line for mass retailers: the Levi Strauss Signature brand, featuring Levi Strauss's name on the back of the jeans.

Two months after the launch, Levi basked in the honeymoon glow. Overall sales, after falling for the first six months of 2003, rose 6% in the third quarter; profits in the summer quarter nearly doubled. All, Levi's CEO said, because of Signature.

But the low-end business isn't a business Levi is known for, or one it had been particularly interested in. It's also a business in which Levi will find itself competing with lean, experienced players such as VF and Faded Glory. Levi's makeover might so improve its performance with its non-Wal-Mart suppliers that its established business will thrive, too. It is just as likely that any gains will be offset by the competitive pressures already dissolving Levi's premium brands, and by the cannibalization of its own sales. "It's hard to see how this relationship will boost Levi's higher-end business," says Paul Farris, a professor at the University of Virginia's Darden Graduate School of Business Administration. "It's easy to see how this will hurt the higher-end business."

64   If Levi clothing is a runaway hit at Wal-Mart, that may indeed rescue Levi as a business. But what will have been rescued? The Signature line—it includes clothing for girls, boys, men, and women—is an odd departure for a company whose brand has long been an American icon. Some of the jeans have the look, the fingertip feel, of pricier Levis. But much of the clothing has the look and feel it must have, given its price (around $23 for adult pants): cheap. Cheap and disappointing to find labeled with Levi Strauss's name. And just five days before the cheery profit news, Levi had another announcement: It is closing its last two U.S. factories, both in San Antonio, and laying off more than 2,500 workers, or 21% of its workforce. A company that 22 years ago had 60 clothing plants in the United States—and that was known as one of the most socially reponsible corporations on the planet—will, by 2004, not make any clothes at all. It will just import them.

In the end, of course, it is we as shoppers who have the power, and who have given that power to Wal-Mart. Part of Wal-Mart's dominance, part of its insight, and part of its arrogance, is that it presumes to speak for American shoppers.

If Wal-Mart doesn't like the pricing on something, says Andrew Whitman, who helped service Wal-Mart for years when he worked at General Foods and Kraft, they simply say, "At that price we no longer think it's a good value to our shopper. Therefore, we don't think we should carry it."

Wal-Mart has also lulled shoppers into ignoring the difference between the price of something and the cost. Its unending focus on price underscores something that Americans are only starting to realize about globalization: Ever-cheaper prices have consequences. Says Steve Dobbins, president of thread maker Carolina Mills: "We want clean air, clear water, good living conditions, the best health care in the world—yet we aren't willing to pay for anything manufactured under those restrictions."

68   Randall Larrimore, a former CEO of MasterBrand Industries, the parent company of Master Lock, understands that contradiction too well. For years, he says, as manufacturing costs in the United States rose, Master Lock was able to pass them along. But at some point in the 1990s, Asian manufacturers started producing locks for much less. "When the difference is $1, retailers like Wal-Mart would prefer to have the brand-name padlock or faucet or hammer," Larrimore says. "But as the spread becomes greater, when our padlock was $9, and the import was $6, then they can offer the consumer a real discount by carrying two lines. Ultimately, they may only carry one line."

In January 1997, Master Lock announced that, after 75 years making locks in Milwaukee, it would begin importing more products from Asia. Not too long after, Master Lock opened a factory of its own in Nogales, Mexico. Today, it makes just 10% to 15% of its locks in Milwaukee—its 300 employees there mostly make parts that are sent to Nogales, where there are now 800 factory workers.

Larrimore did the first manufacturing layoffs at Master Lock. He negotiated with Master Lock's unions himself. He went to Bentonville. "I loved dealing with Wal-Mart, with Home Depot," he says. "They are all very rational people. There wasn't a whole lot of room for negotiation. And they had a good point. Everyone was willing to pay more for a Master Lock. But how much more can they justify? If they can buy a lock that has arguably similar quality, at a cheaper price, well, they can get their consumers a deal."

It's Wal-Mart in the role of Adam Smith's invisible hand. And the Milwaukee employees of Master Lock who shopped at Wal-Mart to save money helped that hand shove their own jobs right to Nogales. Not consciously, not directly, but inevitably. "Do we as consumers appreciate what we're doing?" Larrimore asks. "I don't think so. But even if we do, I think we say, Here's a Master Lock for $9, here's another lock for $6—let the other guy pay $9."

PERSONAL RESPONSE

Do you shop at Wal-Mart? Has this article changed in any way your view of Wal-Mart?

QUESTIONS FOR CLASS OR SMALL-GROUP DISCUSSION

1. Comment on the effectiveness as a rhetorical strategy of Fishman's references to the gallon-sized jar of whole pickles throughout the essay.

2. What is "the real story of Wal-Mart, the story that never gets told" (paragraph 4)?

3. Comment on Fishman's use of examples. How do they work to illustrate his major points? Which do you think are the most effective or most dramatic examples?

4. Fishman reveals that he had trouble finding sources to corroborate his findings (paragraph 31). Does that weaken his article? Does he provide enough evidence to outweigh the drawbacks of uncooperative sources?

30 LITTLE TURTLES

Thomas L. Friedman

Thomas L. Friedman has written for the New York Times *since 1981. In 1995, he became the paper's foreign affairs columnist. Friedman was awarded the 1983 Pulitzer Prize for international reporting (from Lebanon) and the 1988 Pulitzer Prize for international reporting (from Israel). In 2002, he won the Pulitzer Prize for commentary. His book* From Beirut to Jerusalem *(1989) won the National Book Award for non-fiction in 1989.* The Lexus and the Olive Tree: Understanding Globalization *(2000) won the 2000 Overseas Press Club award for best non-fiction book on foreign policy and has been published in 20 languages. He is also author of* Longitudes and Attitudes: Exploring the World after September 11 *(2002) and* The World is Flat: A Brief History of the Twenty-first Century *(2005). This Op-Ed column was published in the February 29, 2004, issue of the* New York Times.

Indians are so hospitable. I got an ovation the other day from a roomful of Indian 20-year-olds just for reading perfectly the following paragraph: "A bottle of bottled water held 30 little turtles. It didn't matter that each turtle had to rattle a metal ladle in order to get a little bit of noodles, a total turtle delicacy. The problem was that there were many turtle battles for less than oodles of noodles."

I was sitting in on an "accent neutralization" class at the Indian call center 24/7 Customer. The instructor was teaching the would-be Indian call center operators to suppress their native Indian accents and speak with a Canadian one—she teaches British and U.S. accents as well, but these youths will be serving the Canadian market. Since I'm originally from Minnesota, near Canada, and still speak like someone out of the movie "Fargo," I gave these young Indians an authentic rendition of "30 Little Turtles," which is designed to teach them the proper Canadian pronunciations. Hence the rousing applause.

Watching these incredibly enthusiastic young Indians preparing for their call center jobs—earnestly trying to soften their t's and roll their r's—is an uplifting experience, especially when you hear from their friends already working these jobs how they have transformed their lives. Most of them still live at home and turn over part of their salaries to their parents, so the whole family benefits. Many have credit cards and have become real consumers, including of U.S. goods, for the first time. All of them seem to have gained self-confidence and self-worth.

4   A lot of these Indian young men and women have college degrees, but would never get a local job that starts at $200 to $300 a month were it not for the call centers. Some do "outbound" calls, selling things from credit cards to phone services to Americans and Europeans. Others deal with "inbound" calls—everything from tracing lost luggage for U.S. airline passengers to solving computer problems for U.S. customers. The calls are transferred here by satellite or fiber optic cable.

I was most taken by a young Indian engineer doing tech support for a U.S. software giant, who spoke with pride about how cool it is to tell his friends that he just spent the day helping Americans navigate their software. A majority of these call center workers are young women, who not only have been liberated by earning a decent local wage (and therefore have more choice in whom they marry), but are using the job to get M.B.A.'s and other degrees on the side.

I gathered a group together, and here's what they sound like: M. Dinesh, who does tech support, says his day is made when some American calls in with a problem and is actually happy to hear an Indian voice: "They say you people are really good at what you do. I am glad I reached an Indian." Kiran Menon, when asked who his role model was, shot back: "Bill Gates—I dream of starting my own company and making it that big." I asked C. M. Meghna what she got most out of the work:

"Self-confidence," she said, "a lot of self-confidence, when people come to you with a problem and you can solve it—and having a lot of independence." Because the call center teams work through India's night—which corresponds to America's day— "your biological clock goes haywire," she added. "Besides that, it's great."

There is nothing more positive than the self-confidence, dignity and optimism that comes from a society knowing it is producing wealth by tapping its own brains— men's and women's—as opposed to one just tapping its own oil, let alone one that is so lost it can find dignity only through suicide and "martyrdom."

8

Indeed, listening to these Indian young people, I had a déjà vu. Five months ago, I was in Ramallah, on the West Bank, talking to three young Palestinian men, also in their 20's, one of whom was studying engineering. Their hero was Yasir Arafat. They talked about having no hope, no jobs and no dignity, and they each nodded when one of them said they were all "suicide bombers in waiting."

What am I saying here? That it's more important for young Indians to have jobs than Americans? Never. But I am saying that there is more to outsourcing than just economics. There's also geopolitics. It is inevitable in a networked world that our economy is going to shed certain low-wage, low-prestige jobs. To the extent that they go to places like India or Pakistan—where they are viewed as high-wage, high-prestige jobs—we make not only a more prosperous world, but a safer world for our own 20-year-olds.

PERSONAL RESPONSE

Are you sympathetic with Friedman's view of the young Indians that he describes in his essay?

QUESTIONS FOR CLASS OR SMALL-GROUP DISCUSSION

1. Do you think that Friedman anticipated an audience who would be supportive or critical of him? How can you tell?
2. Do you find the title effective? How does it relate to the essay?
3. How well do Friedman's examples of individual Indians help convey his view that being with them was an "uplifting experience" (paragraph 2)?
4. How adequately does Friedman make his case that "there is more to outsourcing than just economics" (paragraph 8)? Are you convinced?

SWEATX CLOSES UP SHOP

Richard Appelbaum and Peter Dreier

Richard Appelbaum, co-author of Behind the Label: Inequality in the Los Angeles Apparel Industry *(2000), teaches sociology and global and international studies at the University of California, Santa*

Barbara. Peter Dreier, the E.P. Clapp Distinguished Professor of Politics at Occidental College in Los Angeles, is co-author of Place Matters: Metropolitics for the 21st Century *(2001) and* The Next Los Angeles: The Struggle for a Livable City *(2004). This article is from the July 19, 2004 issue of* The Nation.

The pilot manufacturing factory for SweatX, the noble anti-sweatshop brand that aspired to prove that fully unionized and even worker-owned garment factories can thrive in a sea of sweatshops, quietly closed its doors in May. The small Los Angeles plant, launched by the Hot Fudge venture capital fund run by Ben Cohen (co-founder of Ben & Jerry's), had struggled during its two years of operation.

"The reason why the thing failed," explains Cohen, "was some pretty serious mismanagement." Still, Cohen remains enthusiastic. "We discovered that it certainly is possible to cut and sew clothing in this country, pay workers a livable wage and decent benefits under good working conditions and still put out a product that is competitively priced."

The basic concept was simple: Hire experienced, motivated garment workers (hardly a problem in Los Angeles, where 120,000 workers toil in thousands of tiny factories that routinely violate federal minimum-wage, health and safety laws), install them in a new plant, pay them a living wage with full health benefits, sign them up with UNITE (the garment workers' union) and educate them in the virtues of cooperative ownership. Once the plant was up and running, the operation would be sold to its workers and managers, who would run it together. And once it had reached its initial market of socially aware consumers, liberal churches, unions, environmental and other social justice groups who would buy large wholesale orders for their organizations, it would branch out into mainstream department stores and retail outlets. The SweatX label would eventually become the socially conscious counterpart to Nike's swoosh.

4   SweatX's proponents believed it would provide a model that would give anti-sweatshop activists evidence to push major labels like Gap and Nike—whose products are made primarily in Asian and Latin American sweatshops—to raise their workplace standards. As Los Angeles mayor James Hahn said at the factory's well-publicized opening in April 2002, "Your decision to locate the factory [in LA] is going to change the world."

At the time, that claim did not seem far-fetched. Labor costs are only 6 percent of the retail price of garments made in the United States—60 cents for a $10 T-shirt. The increased cost required to compensate workers decently would hardly matter when consumers realized that they had an alternative to buying clothing made in sweatshops.

Unfortunately, SweatX suffered the same fate as many start-up apparel companies. Its problems included uneven quality, insufficient capacity and missed delivery deadlines. Cohen and his advisers installed an initial management team that lacked experience in the highly competitive garment industry. They leased an expensive building and purchased too much equipment. Too many managers added to costs, despite a "solidarity ratio" that limited them to earning no more than eight times what a worker earned.

In its two years of operation, the major customers for SweatX's T-shirts and polo shirts were unions, a few colleges that, under pressure from student activists, created "sweat-free zones" in campus bookstores and rock bands like the Grammy-winning Foo Fighters, who sold SweatX shirts at their concerts. But SweatX never penetrated the largest universities, social justice groups or religious organizations. The SweatX management team learned too late that it could not profitably sell its products directly from the factory to individual customers or even large nonprofit organizations. The clothing market is dominated by a layer of large intermediary supply houses from whose catalogues nonprofit organizations, silk-screeners and many chain stores purchase their inventory. SweatX was negotiating with one such supplier when it ran out of cash. "They were learning on the job," says Cristina Vázquez, UNITE's western regional director.

8   By the time it had assembled an appropriately experienced management team— its fifth (and last) CEO was Rick Roth, who runs Mirror Image, a successful, and unionized, silk-screen printing company—it was too late. "The candy store failed because it was run poorly," says Roth, "not because customers don't like candy."

There is, in fact, a growing market for clothing and other goods made to satisfy consumers' social conscience. Global Exchange, a Bay Area-based human rights group, has opened three "fair trade" stores that sell clothing, crafts, house fixtures, chocolate, tea and coffee made by worker-owned cooperatives and firms that pay fair wages in various countries. Last year these retail outlets, along with its online business, had revenues of $1.2 million. Its No Sweat brand sneakers—produced by union workers and found on a website of union-made apparel called No Sweat (www.nosweatapparel.com)—are one of its bestselling items. Starbucks, Peet's and Millstone are marketing a fair-trade coffee blend produced by worker cooperatives and certified by TransFair USA (www.transfairusa.org), a nonprofit monitoring agency. Across the country, consumers buy Newman's Own salad dressings and other foods, Patagonia clothing and Body Shop skin- and hair-care products because of their reputation as socially conscious companies.

Reputations don't always conform to reality. For example, American Apparel— which employs more than 1,000 workers in its LA T-shirt factory—aggressively promotes itself as a socially responsible "sweatshop free" employer. But last year, when its workers waged a union organizing campaign, the company initiated such a vicious intimidation effort that the National Labor Relations Board required it to sign a settlement agreement to refrain from antiunion practices in the future. And, as the *Wall Street Journal* noted recently, some retailers put big markups on their fair-trade products, which benefits them, not the producers.

SweatX's proponents argue that only an independent, democratic labor union can guarantee that a sewing factory is sweat-free, whether in the United States or overseas. But consumers need a way to verify that clothing is made under sweat-free conditions. Various groups, like the Worker Rights Consortium (www.workersrights.org), now play that role. Three years ago, for example, the WRC helped pressure Nike to require Kukdong, one of its huge contractors in Mexico, to allow workers to form an independent union.

12   Most of SweatX's thirty-five production workers have found other jobs, typically with harsher conditions and lower pay. But the company's most recent management

team wants to keep the label alive under a new, presumably wiser, company. They hope to convince some of the remaining union clothing factories around the United States to produce items under the SweatX label. SweatX would focus on the marketing and sales side of the business, which these mostly small-scale operations can't afford, and give union-made clothing much greater visibility.

SweatX could also link with human rights and labor groups like United Students Against Sweatshops (www.studentsagainstsweatshops.org) and the National Labor Committee (www.nlcnet.org), which have spent the past decade exposing sweatshop abuses and supporting workers' struggles to unionize around the world. SweatX could help create a US market for union goods made in poor countries by selling them under a highly visible brand name that can compete with Nike, Gap and others. For example, a union shop in El Salvador, Just Garments, had expressed interest in becoming a partner of SweatX just before the factory closed.

"I have no regrets," says Alfredo Guerra, a 40-year-old cutter from Guatemala who was one of SweatX's first production workers. "We know what went wrong. We know what to do differently. I think we could make it succeed."

PERSONAL RESPONSE

Does whether a company is socially conscious or not enter into your decision to purchase an article of its clothing? Explain why or why not.

QUESTIONS FOR CLASS OR SMALL-GROUP DISCUSSION

1. How well do Appelbaum and Dreier explain the concept behind SweatX?
2. How were the goals of SweatX related to the question of outsourcing?
3. Do Appelbaum and Dreier clearly explain what they mean by the statement "Reputations don't always conform to reality" (paragraph 10)? What examples do they give to illustrate that point?
4. What led to the failure of SweatX?

○ PERSPECTIVES ON THE ECONOMIC IMPACT OF OUTSOURCING ○
Suggested Writing Topics

1. Write a response to N. Venkat Venkatraman's "Offshoring Without Guilt" by explaining whether you agree with him that offshoring should be viewed as a wise business move without regard for anything else.
2. In response to Charles Fishman's "The Wal-Mart You Don't Know," defend Wal-Mart's business practices.
3. Write a critique of Thomas L. Friedman's "30 Little Turtles."
4. Describe your own buying habits in terms of whether you are socially conscious or not. Do you consciously buy only "fair trade" products, for instance? Do you boycott products of companies that employ sweatshop labor?

5. Select a statement from any of the essays in this chapter that you would like to respond to, elaborate on, or argue for or against.

6. Drawing on the readings in this chapter, compare and contrast the benefits of offshore outsourcing.

7. If you know someone who has lost a job because the company moved off-shore, narrate that person's experience.

Research Topics

1. Research Wal-Mart's business practices that make it a model of success.

2. Research one of the companies that supplies products to Wal-Mart, as mentioned in Charles Fishman's "The Wal-Mart You Don't Know," and chart its progress or decline.

3. Research the economic impact of outsourcing by focusing on one particular type of business.

4. Research the subject of sweatshops in Asian or Latin American countries that supply one of the major clothing labels in the United States.

5. Research and explain the work done by one of the human rights or labor groups mentioned by Richard Appelbaum and Peter Dreier in "SweatX Closes Up Shop."

RESPONDING TO VISUALS

Indian employees work at a call center in Bangalore, India, June 23, 2003.
Source: Jagadeesh/Reuters/CORBIS

1. What details contribute to your first impression of this picture?
2. How does the photographer use symmetry in the composition of the photograph?
3. Why does the photographer shoot the picture from this angle, when about half of the workers have their back to the camera?
4. What do the facial expressions and body language of those facing the camera suggest about their work experience?

RESPONDING TO VISUALS

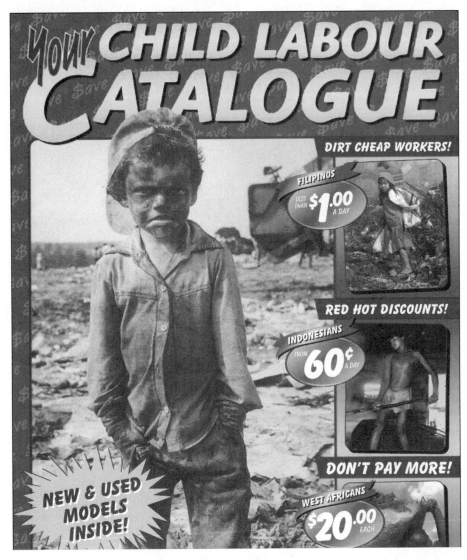

Hard working five-year-old. Source: UNICEF

1. What do the boy's facial expression and body language suggest about his feelings toward being photographed and the purpose for which the photo is being taken?
2. Does the image give an impression of a "hard-working five-year-old"? Does he look willing to "do anything"?
3. What is your emotional response to all of the images pictured here?

CHAPTER 26

THE GLOBAL MARKETPLACE

If we live in a "global village," we also buy and sell in a "global marketplace." Manufacturers that once exported goods to other nations now build plants and sell goods directly in those countries. American businesses that once limited themselves to the domestic market are now expanding operations beyond the United States as they compete in foreign markets. Indeed, most trade analysts predict that the twenty-first century will see enormous growth in global prosperity as businesses compete for foreign trade and increase their expansion in the global marketplace. Certainly, the ease of international travel makes the process of conducting business with other countries not much more difficult than travel from state to state was in former days, and the fax machine and Internet capabilities have had enormous impacts on business communication. Combine those factors with the rise in market economies in previously communist countries, and you have some compelling reasons to account for optimistic forecasts for the global economy in the twenty-first century.

The essays in this chapter focus on the issue of globalization and the place of the United States in the global market. First, UN Secretary-General Kofi Annan, in "Development without Borders," comments on the issue of globalization, including its benefits, how to get the most out of it, and how to expand opportunities for all nations, including underdeveloped ones. Next, Vito Tanzi, in "Globalization without a Net," reports that the process of global economic integration will require a fundamental overhaul of the role the state plays in pursuing social protection policies targeted toward specific groups. He argues that globalization undermines social protection and conjectures on the likely impact of the increasing harmonization of tax policy across countries. He ends by suggesting three main policy instruments to build the modern welfare state.

In "Mixing '60s Activism and Anti-Globalization," Robert Borosage reports on the increased activism of today's college students in their efforts to oppose what they see as the exploitative aspects of globalization. Taking on the global corporation might have seemed an impossible goal, but students influenced major American corporations to make changes in the way they conduct their manufacturing abroad. Borosage writes: "Already, even pundits who disparage the demonstrators have begun to accept that worker rights and the environment, food and workplace safety can no longer be ignored in the global market."

Finally, in defense of globalization, Murray Weidenbaum's speech, "Dispelling the Myths about the Global Economy," addresses ten myths or misunderstandings that he says people have about the global economy and its impact on the American business system. Taking each one in turn, he explains why the belief is a myth and what the reality is. As you read his responses to the attacks of student groups, environmentalists, unionists, and human-rights groups, among others, against globalization, consider the extent to which you agree with him. Can you offer counterarguments to his assertions? Indeed, as you read all of the readings in this chapter, consider what implications America's place in the global market has for your own future.

DEVELOPMENT WITHOUT BORDERS
KOFI ANNAN

Kofi Annan of Ghana is the seventh Secretary-General of the United Nations, the first to be elected from the ranks of the United Nations staff. He joined the United Nations in the early 1970s and has held many positions, including Assistant Secretary-General for Program Planning, Budget and Finance; head of human resources; director of the budget; chief of personnel for the High Commissioner for Refugees; administrative officer for the Economic Commission for Africa; and Under-Secretary-General for Peacekeeping Operations. Kofi Annan and the United Nations were awarded the 2001 Nobel Peace Prize. This paper was published in the Summer, 2001, issue of the Harvard International Review.

What is globalization? More than ever before, groups and individuals are interacting directly across borders without involving the state. This happens partly due to new technology and partly because states have found that prosperity is better secured by releasing the creative energies of their people than by restricting them.

The benefits of globalization are obvious: faster growth, higher standards of living, and new opportunities. However, globalization's benefits are very unequally distributed; the global market is not yet underpinned by shared social objectives, and if all of today's poor follow the same path that brought the rich to prosperity, the earth's resources will soon be exhausted. The challenge we face is to ensure that globalization becomes a positive force for all people instead of leaving billions in squalor.

If we are to get the most out of globalization, we must learn how to provide better governance at the local, national, and international levels. We must think afresh about how we manage our joint activities and our shared interests, since so many challenges that we confront today are beyond the reach of any state acting on its own.

4   This should not be seen as a future of world government or the eclipse of nation states. On the contrary, states will draw strength from each other by acting together within the framework of common institutions based on shared rules and values. Governments must work together to make these changes possible, but governments alone cannot make them happen. Much of the heavy lifting will be done by private investment and charitable foundations.

The best ideas, however, will come from nongovernmental sources: from academic researchers, nonprofit organizations, business, the media, and the arts. These elements compose civil society, and they have a vital role to play.

At the UN Millennium Summit in September 2000, world leaders resolved to halve three figures: the number of people whose income is less than one US dollar a day, the proportion of people who suffer from hunger, and the proportion of people who are unable to reach or afford safe drinking water. They resolved to accomplish these goals by 2015. History will judge this generation by what it did to fulfill that pledge.

Success in achieving sustained growth depends on expanding access to the opportunities of globalization. That in turn depends in large measure on the quality of governance a country enjoys. Countries can only compete in the global market if their people benefit from the rule of law, effective state institutions, transparency and accountability in the management of public affairs, and respect for human rights. Their people must have a say in the decisions that affect their lives.

8   If developing countries succeed in creating the right economic and social environment, new technology can put many opportunities within their reach. That is especially true of information technology, which does not require vast amounts of hardware, financial capital, or even energy, and which is relatively environment-friendly. What information technology does require is brain power—the one commodity that is equally distributed among the peoples of the world. So for a relatively small investment—for example, an investment in basic education—we can bring all kinds of knowledge within reach of the world's poor and enable poor countries to leapfrog some of the long and painful stages of development that other nations had to go through.

In short, there is much that poor countries can do to help themselves. But rich countries have an indispensable role to play. For wealthy nations to preach the virtues of open markets to developing countries is mere hypocrisy if they do not open their own markets to those countries' products or stem the flooding of the world market with subsidized food exports that make it impossible for farmers in developing countries to compete. Nor can they expect developing countries to protect the global environment, unless they are ready to alter their own irresponsible patterns of production and consumption.

Developing countries must be helped to export their way to prosperity. Everyone now agrees that the burden of debt must be lifted from the poorest countries, but developed countries have not yet come forward with sufficient resources to alleviate this burden. Nations, whether in debt or not, need help to reach the stage where they can produce goods and services that the rest of the world wants to buy. Many also need help in resolving destructive conflicts and rebuilding a peaceful, productive society.

Long ago, all members of the Organization for Economic Cooperation and Development committed 0.7 percent of their gross domestic product to development aid. Very few made good on that commitment. Private companies, as well as governments, have an obligation to consider the interests of the poor when making investment choices and when pricing their products. Companies are the largest beneficiaries of globalization; it is in their interest to make this trend sustainable, by helping it work for all.

12   Only when the lives of ordinary men, women, and children in cities and villages around the world are made better will we know that globalization is becoming inclusive, allowing everyone to share in its opportunities. This is the key to eliminating world poverty.

PERSONAL RESPONSE

Do you agree with Annan that rich countries have an obligation to help developing countries?

QUESTIONS FOR CLASS OR SMALL-GROUP DISCUSSION

1. How well does Annan support his statement that "the benefits of globalization are obvious" but that they "are very unequally distributed" (paragraph 2)?

2. Do you think it possible for world leaders to achieve the goals resolved upon at the UN Millennium summit (paragraph 6)? What do you think they will have to do to accomplish these goals?

3. Discuss ways in which rich or strong nations could help poor or developing countries enhance their brain power (paragraph 8).

4. Explain the extent to which you agree with this statement: "Private companies, as well as governments, have an obligation to consider the interests of the poor when making investment choices and when pricing their products" (paragraph 11).

GLOBALIZATION WITHOUT A NET

Vito Tanzi

Vito Tanzi has served as director of the Fiscal Affairs Department of the International Monetary Fund since 1981. He is author or editor of over a dozen books, including Taxation in an Integrating World (Integrating National Economies: Promise and Pitfalls) *(1995),* Income Distribution and High-Quality Growth *(1997),* Public Spending in the Twentieth Century: A Global Perspective *(2000), and* Policies, Institutions, and the Dark Side of Economics *(2000). This essay appeared in the July/August, 2001, issue of* Foreign Policy.

Today's fractious debates over economic and financial globalization often turn on how best to care for the people most vulnerable to sudden changes wrought by new technologies, foreign competition, or industrial relocation. On this question, however, a new consensus is emerging around a simple, compelling proposition: Countries can harness the many benefits of global integration as long as they provide strong social protection programs that mitigate the fallout on society's weakest members. As World Trade Organization Director-General Michael Moore expressed in October 2000: "Of course, some people do lose in the short run from trade liberalization. . . . But the right way to alleviate the hardship of the unlucky few is through social safety nets and job retraining rather than by abandoning reforms that benefit the many."

This call for strengthened social protection evokes similar efforts in the aftermath of World War II when many nations, particularly in Western Europe, erected formal, state-financed social protection systems to safeguard citizens from the risks linked to old age, illness, unemployment, and poverty. Governments deployed three main policy instruments to build the modern welfare state: first, direct public spending on social programs such as healthcare, pension benefits, and unemployment compensation; second, tax deductions for "socially desirable" spending by individuals, such as interest payments on home mortgages and medical and educational expenses; and third, regulations that protect workers or other special groups, including minimum-wage laws, rent controls, subsidized student loans, and reduced rates on public utilities.

Today, however, the growing integration of economies and the free movement of capital across borders threaten to undermine the effectiveness of these policy tools. Even as the forces of globalization boost the demand for strong social safety nets to protect the poor, these forces also erode the ability of governments to finance and implement large-scale social welfare policies.

4   Consider the tax revenue needed to finance social spending. Although many industrialized economies have their fiscal houses in order, with tax revenues near historical highs, several "fiscal termites" linked to globalization are nevertheless gnawing at their foundations. These termites include increased travel by individuals, which allows them to purchase expensive and easily transportable items in countries or regions with low sales taxes, thus encouraging small nations to reduce taxes on luxury products to attract foreign buyers. Similarly, the growth of global e-commerce represents a nightmare for tax authorities, since paperless, electronic transactions leave few footprints. Even if governments try to implement origin-based taxation of e-commerce, stores and other sales establishments will simply relocate to places with few or no sales taxes. And as products formerly sold only in shops and offices—everything from music, movies, and books to financial advice, engineering plans, and educational services—increasingly become digital products sold over the Internet, the very concept of a tax jurisdiction will seem a quaint anachronism.

The growing use of offshore tax havens as conduits for financial investments likewise weakens national tax collection since individuals or corporations holding such assets—recently estimated at $5 trillion worldwide—are unlikely to report the income they earn to the revenue authorities in their home countries. The rise of unregulated hedge funds and new financial instruments, including derivatives, also pose enormous challenges for tax authorities seeking to identify individuals, transactions, and incomes. Finally, the growth of international trade among subsidiaries of the same multinational corporation further complicates tax collection, since companies can easily manipulate internal prices to keep profits in low-tax jurisdictions—so-called transfer pricing. For example, some analysts have questioned the high profits that multinational firms record as originating in Ireland (a country that happens to offer particularly low tax rates for corporations). Put together, these elements will keep governments from maintaining current tax revenues; thus, policymakers will have little choice but to cut spending on social protection programs.

The increasing harmonization of tax policy across countries—resulting from tax competition to attract investment—will place downward pressure on tax rates and further restrict governments' ability to use tax policy for social protection. A survey of corporate tax rates in 14 major industrialized countries already shows a precipitous decline in recent years, from an average of about 46 percent in 1985 to 33 percent in 1999. Similar reductions have occurred with tax rates on individuals.

Finally, globalization undermines social protection by introducing deregulatory pressures. In an attempt to make local companies more efficient and more competitive internationally, for instance, governments may further privatize additional public enterprises and liberalize national labor and credit markets, curtailing or eliminating laws that make it difficult to fire workers or that give credit preferences to vulnerable groups.

8   Of course, the competitive pressures of globalization, as well as the need to comply with new international agreements, may push policymakers to increase spending on education, training, research and development, the environment, and on reforming government institutions. Such initiatives likely would offer broad benefits to society as a whole. Ultimately, however, the process of global economic integration will require a fundamental overhaul of the role the state plays in pursuing social protection policies targeted toward specific groups—including those adversely affected by the downsides of globalization.

PERSONAL RESPONSE

Are you convinced by Tanzi's argument that participation in the global economy will make it increasingly impossible to protect vulnerable populations?

QUESTIONS FOR CLASS OR SMALL-GROUP DISCUSSION

1. Summarize the risks that Tanzi implies are likely to befall "the people most vulnerable to sudden changes wrought by new technologies, foreign competition, or industrial relocation" (paragraph 1).

2. How convincing is Tanzi's argument that "even as the forces of globalization boost the demand for strong social safety nets to protect the poor, these forces also erode the ability of governments to finance and implement large-scale social welfare policies" (paragraph 3)?

3. Tanzi writes: "Ultimately, however, the process of global economic integration will require a fundamental overhaul of the role the state plays in pursuing social protection policies targeted toward specific groups" (paragraph 8). How would you envision such a change taking place?

MIXING '60S ACTIVISM AND ANTI-GLOBALIZATION
ROBERT BOROSAGE

Robert Borosage, professor of law at American University, is a co-founder, with Roger Hickey, of the Campaign for America's Future. He has written on political, economic, and national security issues for publications including the New York Times *and* The Nation. *He is co-editor of* The Next Agenda: Blueprint for a New Progressive

Movement *(2000). This article appeared in the April 23, 2000, issue of the* Los Angeles Times.

Kids today can't get any respect. First, their generation was described as apathetic, stirred only by dreams of dot-com fortunes. Then, when students stunned the world by joining turtle lovers and Teamsters to shut down the World Trade Organization meeting in Seattle last December, they were disparaged as "flat-Earth advocates." Last week, when they rallied against the World Bank and International Monetary Fund in Washington and 1,300 were arrested in nonviolent protest, they were labeled "imitation activists," filling the time between "spring break and summer vacation, and between the last body-piercing and the first IPO." At least Washington and Seattle captured headlines. For the most vibrant student movement in years is roiling America's university campuses in relative obscurity.

Here's the reality so many can't see. Activist, idealistic students are in motion once again, seized of a morally compelling cause. Their target, amazingly, is nothing less than the global corporation. They are challenging the conservative free-trade agenda that dominates both major political parties. Already, they are forcing global companies such as Nike to scramble for cover. They've only just begun.

The most vital part of this growing movement is, perhaps, the least noticed. On more than 175 campuses, students are calling global corporations to account for their exploitation of workers abroad. They are mounting demonstrations, going on hunger strikes, seizing administration buildings, confronting university trustees and administrators, and getting arrested by the dozens in nonviolent protests. The two-person staff of the coordinating group, United Students Against Sweatshops, can't keep up with the e-mail from students seeking to get involved both here and abroad.

4   This movement is less than four years old. Its roots trace back to 1996, when human-rights advocate Charles Kernaghan focused national attention on Honduran sweatshops in which young women worked at poverty wages, surrounded by barbed wire and armed guards, to sew clothes for a Kathie Lee Gifford fashion line. That summer, hundreds of university students joined worker struggles in this country as part of the AFL-CIO's Union Summer. Since then, groups of students have visited Central America to witness how women their own age work and live.

The students had a compelling moral argument: Let's not support companies that profit from exploiting workers abroad—and they acted on it. They targeted university apparel shops that buy logo clothing from global corporations with factories in Honduras, Indonesia and China, where worker rights are trampled. The $2.5-billion collegiate retail-apparel industry represents just 1% of the U.S. apparel market but is key to the youth market. So students started calling for their universities to enforce a code of conduct on suppliers.

University administrators didn't need the hassle but had no ready response for the students. The companies realized they were in trouble. Nike's swoosh symbol started being associated less with Michael Jordan than with impoverished young women abroad. Nike and others circled the wagons, enlisting a few human-rights groups to form the Fair Labor Assn., establishing their own code of conduct with the companies in control. Company-paid consultants did inspections, with factories notified ahead of time. Reports were kept private while the company "remedied" any problem. The Clinton administration pumped money into the operation. Relieved university administrators signed up.

But the students weren't buying. As Marikah Mancini, a graduate student at Purdue, said, "The basic question was whether you were empowering the companies or the workers." The result of the FLA, Sarah Jacobson of the University of Oregon argued, "would be to hide, not expose sweatshop conditions." The students insisted that any code of conduct include protections for the rights of women and workers, require a living wage and ban production from countries where workers had no right to organize. Most important, the students demanded that companies disclose the location of all factories. This would allow local church and human-rights groups to do independent monitoring. Nike and others refused.

8   So the students organized a Worker Rights Consortium to monitor company practices, financed by 1% of the revenues produced by university garment sales. It would sponsor independent monitoring by local human-rights groups and make findings public.

When university administrators resisted, the students upped the ante. At the University of Pennsylvania, the University of Wisconsin and elsewhere, students took over administration buildings. At Purdue, students camped out on the square, with several risking an 11-day hunger strike. At the University of Wisconsin, Eric Brakken was told he didn't have the student body's support. So he ran for student-government chairman on a no-sweatshops platform and won. Even at the University of Oregon, next door to Nike's corporate headquarters, students took over the president's office until he agreed to join the WRC.

Last year, facing suspension of contracts with Duke and other universities, Nike blinked and disclosed its factory locations. The other companies soon followed suit. Forty-four universities have now joined the WRC, including six Big 10 universities, Brown, Columbia and Georgetown. Two weeks ago, the entire University of California system signed up, issuing a code of conduct that demands a living wage of all contractors.

The students have identified an issue—the spread of sweatshop labor—that cuts through the cant about free trade. They have found the leverage to move not just their campuses, but global corporations—and maybe even the entire debate about globalization. They are directly challenging the laissez-faire assumptions of the last quarter-century, demanding corporations be held to some basic moral standards of conduct. Their focus on global corporations enlists the energies of many student passions, from the environmentalists to pro-Tibetan activists. And unlike the antiwar movement in the 1960s that was confronted by "hard hats," the SAS is forging links between students and workers, and between the environment and worker rights.

12   As President Bill Clinton and anyone active in the 1960s understands, when students are aroused about a moral issue, they can change the direction of the country. Already, even pundits who disparage the demonstrators have begun to accept that worker rights and the environment, food and workplace safety can no longer be ignored in the global market.

But the students are making the larger connections. Last week, SAS activists gathered in Washington for the march against the World Bank and IMF, arguing that their "structural adjustment programs," in the words of Erica Hiegelke, Smith College freshman, "press governments to attract Western investment by denying workers fundamental, internationally recognized rights."

These are not Neanderthal protectionists, nor bored kids looking for something to do. This student movement is internationalist, passionate and on the rise. And it is raising questions that might well mark the end of the conservative era of the last quarter-century.

PERSONAL RESPONSE

Write for a few minutes about your opinion of the kind of student activism Borosage describes. Are you personally involved in the anti-globalization movement? If not, would you like to become involved or would you rather not? Explain your reasons for being involved, wanting to become involved, or avoiding such involvement.

QUESTIONS FOR CLASS OR SMALL-GROUP DISCUSSION

1. How effective do you find Borosage's opening and closing paragraphs?
2. To what extent do you agree with students who argue that we should "not support companies that profit from exploiting workers abroad" (paragraph 5)? In what ways, according to this article, do companies exploit workers abroad? Can you give other examples of such exploitation?
3. Borosage writes: "[Students] are directly challenging the laissez-faire assumptions of the last quarter-century, demanding corporations be held to some basic moral standards of conduct" (paragraph 11). What do you understand by the term *laissez-faire assumptions?* What examples of those assumptions does Borosage provide? How do "basic moral standards of conduct" apply to those examples?
4. Discuss your opinion of the student movement Borosage describes. Do you admire the students who are involved in the organizations he mentions, or not?

DISPELLING THE MYTHS ABOUT THE GLOBAL ECONOMY

Murray Weidenbaum

Murray Weidenbaum is honorary chairman of the Weidenbaum Center on the Economy, Government, and Public Policy at Washington University in St. Louis. He has written and edited a number of books on business and the economy, including An Agnostic Examination of the Case for Action Against Global Warming *(1998) and the textbook* Business and Government in the Global Marketplace, *now in its seventh edition (2003). This speech was presented to the Economic Club of Detroit on January 22, 2001.*

Today I want to deal with a perplexing conundrum facing the United States: this is a time when the American business system is producing unparalleled levels of prosperity, yet private enterprise is under increasing attack. The critics are an unusual alliance of unions, environmentalists, and human rights groups and they are focusing on the overseas activities of business. In many circles, globalization has become a dirty word.

How can we respond in a constructive way? In my interaction with these interest groups, I find that very often their views arise from basic misunderstandings of the real world of competitive enterprise. I have identified ten myths about the global economy—dangerous myths—which need to be dispelled. Here they are:

1. Globalization costs jobs.
2. The United States is an island of free trade in a world of protectionism.
3. Americans are hurt by imports.
4. U.S. companies are running away, especially to low-cost areas overseas.
5. American companies doing business overseas take advantage of local people, especially in poor countries. They also pollute their environments.
6. The trade deficit is hurting our economy and we should eliminate it.
7. It's not fair to run such large trade deficits with China or Japan.
8. Sanctions work. So do export controls.
9. Trade agreements should be used to raise environmental and labor standards around the world.
10. America's manufacturing base is eroding in the face of unfair global competition.

That's an impressive array of frequently heard charges and they are polluting our political environment. Worse yet, these widely held myths fly in the face of the facts. I'd like to take up each of them and knock them down.

1. Globalization Costs Jobs

This is a time when the American job miracle is the envy of the rest of the world, so it is hard to take that charge seriously. Yet some people do fall for it. The facts are clear: U.S. employment is at a record high and unemployment is at a 30-year low. Moreover, the United States created more than 20 million new jobs between 1993 and 2000, far more than Western Europe and Japan combined. Contrary to a widely held view, most of those new jobs pay well, often better than the average for existing jobs.

4   Of course, in the best of times, some people lose their jobs or their businesses fail, and that happens today. However, most researchers who have studied this question conclude that, in the typical case, technological progress—not international trade—is the main reason for making old jobs obsolete. Of course, at the same time, far more new jobs are created to take their place.

2. The United States Is an Island of Free Trade in a World of Protectionism

Do other nations erect trade barriers? Of course they do—although the trend has been to cut back these obstacles to commerce. But our hands are not as clean as we like to think. There is no shortage of restrictions on importers trying to ship their products into this country. These exceptions to free trade come in all shapes, sizes, and varieties. They are imposed by federal, state, and local government. U.S. import barriers include the following and more:

- Buy-American laws give preference in government procurement to domestic producers. Many states and localities show similar favoritism. Here in Michigan, preference is given to in-state printing firms;
- The Jones Act prohibits foreign ships from engaging in waterborne commerce between U.S. ports; many statutes limit the import of specific agricultural and manufactured products, ranging from sugar to pillowcases;
- We impose selective high tariffs on specific items, notably textiles; and many state and local regulatory barriers such as building codes, are aimed at protecting domestic producers.

It's strange that consumer groups and consumer activists are mute on this subject. After all, it is the American customer who has to pay higher prices as a result of all of this special interest legislation. But these barriers to trade ultimately are disappointing. Nations open to trade grow faster than those that are closed.

3. Americans Are Hurt by Imports

The myth that imports are bad will be quickly recognized by students of economics as the mercantilist approach discredited by Adam Smith over two centuries ago. The fact is that we benefit from imports in many ways. Consumers get access to a wider array of goods and services. Domestic companies obtain lower cost components and thus are more competitive. We get access to vital metals and minerals that are just not found in the United States. Also, imports prod our own producers to improve productivity and invest in developing new technology.

I'll present a painful example. By the way, I have never bought a foreign car. But we all know how the quality of our domestic autos has improved because of foreign competition. More recently, we had a striking example of the broader benefits of imports. In 1997–98, the expanded flow of lower-cost products from Asia kept inflation low here at a time when otherwise the Fed would have been raising interest rates to fight inflation. The result would have been a weaker economy. Moreover, in a full employment economy, imports enable the American people to enjoy a higher living standard than would be possible if sales were limited to domestic production.

8   In our interconnected economy, the fact is that the jobs "lost" from imports are quickly replaced by jobs elsewhere in the economy—either in export industries or in companies selling domestically. The facts are fascinating: the sharp run-up in U.S. imports in recent years paralleled the rapid growth in total U.S. employment. Both trends, of course, reflected the underlying health of our business economy.

The special importance of imports was recently highlighted by the director of the Washington State Council on International Trade. "The people who benefit most critically are families at the lower end of the wage scale who have school-age children and those elderly who must live frugally." She goes on to conclude: "It is a cruel deception that an open system of free trade is not good for working people."

4.   U.S. Companies Are Running Away, Especially to Low-Cost Areas Overseas

Right off the bat, the critics have the direction wrong. The flow of money to buy and operate factories and other businesses is overwhelmingly into the United States. We haven't had a net outflow of investment since the 1960s. That's the flip side of our trade deficit. Financing large trade deficits means that far more investment capital comes into this country than is leaving.

But let us examine the overseas investments by American companies. The largest proportion goes not to poor countries, but to the most developed nations, those with high labor costs and also high environmental standards. The primary motive is to gain access to markets. That's not too surprising when we consider that the people in the most industrially advanced nations are the best customers for sophisticated American products. By the way, only one-third of the exports by the foreign branches of U.S. companies goes to the United States. About 70 percent goes to other markets, primarily to the industrialized nations.

12   Turning to American investments in Mexico, China, and other developing countries, the result often is to enhance U.S. domestic competitiveness and job opportunities. This is so because many of these overseas factories provide low-cost components and material to U.S.-based producers who are thus able to improve their international competitiveness.

In some cases, notably the pharmaceutical industry, the overseas investments are made in countries with more enlightened regulatory regimes, such as the Netherlands. "More enlightened" is not a euphemism for lower standards. The Dutch maintain a strong but more modern regulatory system than we do.

5.   American Companies Doing Business Overseas Take Advantage of Local People and Pollute Their Environments

There are always exceptions. But by and large, American-owned and managed factories in foreign countries are top-of-the-line—in terms of both better working conditions and higher environmental standards than locally-owned firms. This is why so many developing countries compete enthusiastically for the overseas location of U.S. business activities—and why so many local workers seek jobs at the American factories. After all, American companies manufacturing overseas frequently follow the same high operating standards that they do here at home. I serve on a panel of Americans who investigate the conditions in some factories in China. I wish the critics could see for themselves the differences between the factories that produce for an American company under its worldwide standards and those that are not subject to our truly enlightened sense of social responsibility.

I'll give you a very personal example of the second category of facilities. While making an inspection tour, I tore my pants on an unguarded piece of equipment in one of those poorly-lit factories. An inch closer and that protruding part would have dug into my thigh. I also had to leave the factory floor every hour or so to breathe some fresh air. When I said that, in contrast, the American-owned factories were top-of-the-line, that wasn't poetry.

16   Yes, foreign investment is essential to the economic development of poor countries. By definition, they lack the capability to finance growth. The critics do those poor countries no favor when they try to discourage American firms from investing there. The critics forget that, during much of the nineteenth century, European investors financed many of our canals, railroads, steel mills, and other essentials for becoming an industrialized nation. It is sad to think where the United States would be today if Europe in the nineteenth century had had an array of powerful interest groups that were so suspicious of economic progress.

6. The Trade Deficit Is Hurting Our Economy and We Should Eliminate It

Yes, the U.S. trade deficit is at a record high. But it is part of a "virtuous circle" in our economy. The trade deficit mainly reflects the widespread prosperity in the United States, which is substantially greater than in most of the countries we trade with. After all, a strong economy such as ours—operating so close to full employment and full capacity—depends on a substantial amount of imports to satisfy our demands for goods and services. Our exports are lower primarily because the demand for imports by other nations is much weaker.

The acid test is that our trade deficit quickly declines in the years when our economy slows down and that deficit rises again when the economy picks up. Serious studies show that, if the United States had deliberately tried to curb the trade deficit in the 1990s, the result would have been a weak economy with high inflation and fewer jobs. The trade deficit is a byproduct of economic performance. It should not become a goal of economic policy.

There is a constructive way of reducing the trade deficit. To most economists, the persistence of our trade imbalance (and especially of the related and more comprehensive current account deficit) is due to the fact that we do not generate enough domestic saving to finance domestic investment. The gap between such saving and investment is equal to the current account deficit.

20   Nobel laureate Milton Friedman summed up this point very clearly: "The remarkable performance of the United States economy in the past few years would have been impossible without the inflow of foreign capital, which is a mirror image of large balance of payments deficits."

The positive solution is clear: increase the amount that Americans save. Easier said than done, of course. The shift from budget deficits (dissaving) to budget surpluses (government saving) helps. A further shift to a tax system that does not hit saving as hard as ours does would also help. The United States taxes saving more heavily than any other advanced industrialized nation. Replacing the income tax with a consumption tax, even a progressive one, would surely be in order—but that deserves to be the subject of another talk.

7. It's Not Fair to Run Such Large Trade Deficits with China or Japan

Putting the scary rhetoric aside, there really is no good reason for any two countries to have balanced trade between them. We don't have to search for sinister causes for our trade deficits with China or Japan. Bilateral trade imbalances exist for many benign reasons, such as differences in per capita incomes and in the relative size of the two economies. One of the best kept secrets of international trade is that the average Japanese buys more U.S. goods than the average American buys Japanese goods, Yes, Japan's per capita imports from the United States are larger than our per capita imports from Japan ($539 versus $432 in 1996). We have a large trade deficit with them because we have more "capita" (population).

8. Sanctions Work, So Do Export Controls

It is ironic that so many people who worry about the trade deficit simultaneously support sanctions and export controls. There is practically no evidence that unilateral sanctions are effective in getting other nations to change their policies or actions. Those restrictions on trade do, however, have an impact: they backfire. U.S. business, labor, and agriculture are harmed. We lose an overseas market for what is merely a symbolic gesture. Sanctions often are evaded. Shipping goods through third countries can disguise the ultimate recipient in the nation on which the sanctions are imposed. On balance, these sanctions reduced American exports in 1995 by an estimated $15–20 billion.

24   As for export controls, where American producers do not have a monopoly on a particular technology—which is frequent—producers in other nations can deliver the same technology or product without the handicap imposed on U.S. companies. A recent report at the Center for the Study of American Business showed that many business executives believe that sanctions and export controls are major obstacles to the expansion of U.S. foreign trade.

9. Trade Agreements Should Be Used to Raise Environmental and Labor Standards around the World

At first blush, this sounds like such a nice and high-minded way of doing good. But, as a practical matter, it is counterproductive to try to impose such costly social regulations on developing countries as a requirement for doing business with them. The acid test is that most developing nations oppose these trade restrictions. They see them for what they really are—a disguised form of protectionism designed to keep their relatively low-priced goods out of the markets of the more advanced, developed nations. All that feeds the developing nations' sense of cynicism toward us.

In the case of labor standards, there is an existing organization, the International Labor Organization, which has been set up to deal specifically with these matters. Of all the international organizations, the ILO is unique in having equal representation from business, labor, and government. The United States and most other nations are members. The ILO is where issues of labor standards should be handled. To be taken more seriously, the United States should support the ILO more vigorously than it has.

As for environmental matters, we saw at the unsuccessful meetings on climate change at the Hague late last year how difficult it is to get broad international agreement on environmental issues even in sympathetic meetings of an international environmental agency. To attempt to tie such controversial environmental matters to trade agreements arouses my suspicions about the intent of the sponsors. It is hard to avoid jumping to the conclusion that the basic motivation is to prevent progress on the trade front.

28   I still recall the signs carried by one of the protesters in Seattle, "Food is for people, not for export." Frankly, it's hard to deal with such an irrational position. After all, if the United States did not export a major part of its abundant farm output, millions of people overseas would be starving or malnourished. Also, thousands of our farmers would go broke.

The most effective way to help developing countries improve their working conditions and environmental protection is to trade with and invest in them. As for the charge that companies invest in poor, developing nations in order to minimize their environmental costs, studies of the issue show that environmental factors are not important influences in business location decisions. As I pointed out earlier, most U.S. overseas direct investment goes to developed nations with high labor costs and also high environmental standards.

10.   America's Manufacturing Base Is Eroding in the Face of Unfair Global Competition

Unfortunately, some of our fellow citizens seem to feel that the only fair form of foreign competition is the kind that does not succeed in landing any of their goods on our shores. But to get to the heart of the issue, there is no factual basis for the charge that our manufacturing base is eroding—or even stagnant. The official statistics are reporting record highs in output year after year. Total industrial production in the United States today is 45 percent higher than in 1992—that's not in dollars, but in terms of real output.

Of course, not all industries or companies go up—or down—in unison. Some specific industries, especially low-tech, have had to cut back. But, simultaneously, other industries, mainly high-tech, have been expanding rapidly. Such changes are natural and to be expected in an open, dynamic economy. By the way, the United States regularly runs a trade surplus in high-tech products.

32   It's important to understand the process at work here. Technological progress generates improved industrial productivity. In the United States, that means to some degree fewer blue-collar jobs and more white-collar jobs. That is hardly a recent development. The shift from physical labor to knowledge workers has been the trend since the beginning of the 20th century. On balance, as I noted earlier, total U.S. employment is at an all-time high.

If you have any doubt about the importance of rising productivity to our society, just consider where we would be if over the past century agriculture had not enjoyed rising productivity (that is, more output per worker/hour). Most of us would still be farmers.

It is vital that we correct the erroneous views of the anti-globalists. Contrary to their claims, our open economy has raised living standards and helped to contain inflation. International commerce is more important to our economy today than at any time in the past. By dollar value and volume, the United States is the world's largest trading nation. We are the largest importer, exporter, foreign investor, and host to foreign investment. Trying to stop the global economy is futile and contrary to America's self-interest.

Nevertheless, we must recognize that globalization, like any other major change, generates costs as well as benefits. It is essential to address these consequences. Otherwise, we will not be able to maintain a national consensus that responds to the challenges of the world marketplace by focusing on opening markets instead of closing them. The challenge to all of us is to urge courses of action that help those who are hurt without doing far more harm to the much larger number who benefit from the international marketplace.

36 We need to focus more attention on those who don't share the benefits of the rapid pace of economic change. Both private and public efforts should be increased to provide more effective adjustment assistance to those who lose their jobs. The focus of adjustment policy should not be on providing relief from economic change, but on positive approaches that help more of our people participate in economic prosperity.

As you may know, I recently chaired a bipartisan commission established by Congress to deal with the trade deficit. Our commission included leaders of business and labor, former senior government officials, and academics. We could not agree on all the issues that we dealt with. But we were unanimous in concluding that the most fundamental part of an effective long-run trade adjustment policy is to do a much better job of educating and training. More Americans should be given the opportunity to become productive and high-wage members of the nation's workforce.

No, I'm not building up to a plea to donate to the college of your choice, although that's a pretty good idea.

Even though I teach at major research universities—and strongly believe in their vital mission—let me make a plea for greater attention to our junior colleges. They are an overlooked part of the educational system. Junior colleges have a key role to play. Many of these community-oriented institutions of learning are now organized to specially meet the needs of displaced workers, including those who need to brush up on their basic language and math skills. In some cases, these community colleges help people launch new businesses, especially in areas where traditional manufacturing is declining. A better trained and more productive workforce is the key to our long-term international competitiveness. That is the most effective way of resisting the calls for economic isolationism.

40 Let me leave you with a final thought. The most powerful benefit of the global economy is not economic at all, even though it involves important economic and business activities. By enabling more people to use modern technology to communicate across traditional national boundaries, the international marketplace makes possible more than an accelerated flow of data. The worldwide marketplace encourages a far greater exchange of the most powerful of all factors of production—new ideas. That process enriches and empowers the individual in ways never before possible.

As an educator, I take this as a challenge to educate the anti-globalists to the great harm that could result from a turn to economic isolationism. For the twenty-first century, the global flow of information is the endless frontier.

PERSONAL RESPONSE

To what extent are you convinced that the "myths" Weidenbaum discusses are truly "myths"?

QUESTIONS FOR CLASS OR SMALL-GROUP DISCUSSION

1. Weidenbaum says that there are "ten myths about the global economy—dangerous myths—which need to be dispelled" (paragraph 2). Discuss each of the "myths" in turn, examining his rationale for why they are not myths and explaining the extent to which you are convinced by his argument.

2. What do you think Weidenbaum means when he says, "Trying to stop the global economy is futile and contrary to America's self-interest" (paragraph 34)?

3. Weidenbaum suggests: "More Americans should be given the opportunity to become productive and high-wage members of the nation's workforce" (paragraph 37). Does he adequately explain how those goals can be accomplished? Do you agree that both of those goals are achievable?

○ PERSPECTIVES ON THE GLOBAL MARKETPLACE ○
Suggested Writing Topics

1. Compare and/or contrast the positions of any two of the writers in this chapter on the subject of globalization of the economy.

2. Drawing on at least two of the essays in this chapter, discuss possible solutions to the problem of how to moderate the desire of corporations to make money in the global marketplace with the altruistic goal of providing adequate attention to the needs of poor or developing countries.

3. Kofi Annan writes in "Development without Borders": "In short, there is much that poor countries can do to help themselves. But rich countries have an indispensable role to play." Drawing on Annan's article, write an essay explaining what poor countries can do and how rich countries can help them.

4. Discuss the implications for both American consumers and American businesses of the rapid expansion of the global marketplace.

5. Write an essay explaining how you see changes in the global economy affecting you personally, both as a consumer and as a (perhaps future) member of the workforce.

6. Assess the impact of foreign products on a typical day in your life. Which imported items are important to your daily life?

7. Write an essay elaborating on this statement from Vito Tanzi's "Globalization without a Net": "Countries can harness the many benefits of global integration as long as they provide strong social protection programs that mitigate the fallout on society's weakest members" (paragraph 1).

8. Interview a specialist in international marketing or economics about the global market and its importance for the American economy in the twenty-first century. Then write an essay on America's future in the global economy in which you include both the specialist's remarks and those of any of the authors in this chapter.

9. Write an essay from the point of view of a market researcher for a new corporation looking for rapid growth through global marketing. Make up a product and a corporation name; then prepare a report for the board of directors of your company in which you recommend expanding efforts in one of the world's newest market areas.

10. Select a statement from any of the readings in this chapter and write a response in support of or against it.

Research Topics

1. Research the economic changes in the past decade in any of these geographic areas: Asia, Asia Pacific, Latin America, Eastern Europe, or sub-Saharan Africa. Read about developments in the area and projections for the future, and then report your findings and conclusions.

2. Research the global investment strategies of any major American corporation. Draw some conclusions about the effectiveness of such strategies in your paper.

3. Analyze the connections between the information revolution and the global spread of market economies. How do they affect or influence one another?

4. Select an area such as politics, technology, or economics. Then conduct library research to determine both the positive and negative implications of the enormous global changes in that area, including a prediction of the effects of these changes on the American economy in the next decade.

5. Research and assess the effectiveness of any of the following: the UN Millennium Summit of September, 2000, or the Organization for Economic Cooperation and Development (Kofi Annan's "Development without Borders"); the United Students Against Sweatshops, the Fair Labor Association, or the Worker Rights Consortium (Robort Borosage's "Mixing '60s Activism and Anti-Globalization").

RESPONDING TO VISUALS

International commerce. Source: Images.com/CORBIS

1. What comment on international commerce does this image make?
2. What do the dollar bills represent? What is the significance of the holes in Europe and South America?
3. Why does the U.S. man have a briefcase in his hand and the others do not?
4. What is the significance of the U.S. man's head being in a cloud?

RESPONDING TO VISUALS

A protestor against the World Trade Organization holds a sign outside the Washington State Convention Center, November 29, 1999. Source: Reuters/CORBIS

1. How has the photographer arranged details of the picture for the best effect?
2. What is the meaning of the sign that the man is carrying?
3. What generalizations can you draw about the man with the sign on the basis of the clothes he is wearing, his facial expression, and other details of the picture?

E-Readings Online for Part Five
InfoTrac College Edition

http://www.infotrac-college.com
(Search for each article by author or title after entering your Infotrac College Edition password.)

Chapter 23 Marketing and American Consumer

Children are an important target population for marketers. As consumers, they can have an enormous influence on their parents and other adults by pressuring them to buy toys, favorite food products, and specific brands of clothes; they also influence parents on such important purchasing decisions as what kind of car to buy, where to travel for vacations, and what restaurants to eat at. Furthermore, as a group, they have a considerable amount of their own money to spend. Children get most of their information about products from television, but billboards, print advertisements, and other marketing media reach them as well. A phenomenon known as tweening or age compression is the latest trend in marketing to children, where products originally made for older children are marketed to very young children. Thus, sexually revealing clothing, make-up, and jewelry are being pitched to girls as young as five and six, while violent games and other toys are made attractive to very young boys. These articles look at the issues associated with the marketing of age-inappropriate products to young children.

○

DAVID BENADY

Deflowering Innocence?

Explores the controversy over using sex to market products to young girls.

○

AMY BLOOM

Sex and the 6-year-old girl: Low-riders. Belly-button-baring Halters. High Heels. Fake Nails. Why are Today's Parents Permitting their Little Girls to Dress like Glitzy Streetwalkers?

Laments that marketers sell sex and glamour to little girls, robbing them of their childhoods.

○

KATY KELLY AND LINDA KULMAN

Kid Power

Looks at viewpoints of both parents and advertisers on the subject of advertising aimed at child consumers.

QUESTIONS FOR DISCUSSION OR WRITING

1. Should more limits be placed on advertising to children? If so, what form should the limits take?
2. Do you think that advertising directed at children is exploitative or just good business?
3. How would you answer the question that Amy Bloom poses in the subtitle to her article? Is some advertising putting pressure on kids to grow up too quickly?

Chapter 24 The Workplace

The work place is an important part of many people's lives, but a number of factors determine whether going to work is a positive or a negative experience. A host of issues can make the work place difficult: a co-worker may create an atmosphere of unease or hostility, an employer may be inflexible or unfriendly, the job itself may be stressful, or the work place environment may be unhealthy. One factor contributing to the way workers rate their job satisfaction is the degree to which they feel free to exercise their basic civil rights in the work place. Many employees feel that those rights are being violated. Company policy may require drug tests, for instance, which some workers feel is a violation of their right to privacy. Many employers monitor Internet use, dress, language, length of break time, and use of the telephone for personal calls. Off-site, Global Positioning System (GPS) makes it possible for employers to track company vehicles and cell phones. These articles look at this issue of employee rights in the work place from the perspectives of both employers and employees.

○

MATTHEW W. FINKIN

Void Where Prohibited: Rest Breaks and the Right to Urinate on Company Time

Reviews a book about restrictions that employers impose on their workers.

SANDY SMITH

What Every Employer should Know about Drug Testing in the Workplace: Think You Don't Have a Problem with Drugs in the Workplace? Think Again.

Provides guidelines for employers to put an effective drug-testing policy in place.

LUCAS CONLEY

The Privacy Arms Race

Warns that using high-tech tools to monitor workers is an invasion of privacy that leads to low morale and decreased productivity.

QUESTIONS FOR DISCUSSION OR WRITING

1. What do these articles tell you about the factors that affect job satisfaction and performance?
2. Are you sympathetic with employers' need to monitor employee activities?
3. How can the work place be a positive environment in light of the restrictions placed on employee activity? What can both employees and employers do to keep the work experience positive?

Chapter 25 The Economic Impact of Outsourcing

The issue of outsourcing abroad has been heavily debated, with many people agreeing that offshore outsourcing is good for companies in terms of costs saved and increased profits. However, some analysts feel that the debates have ignored some very important issues. A number of writers have therefore focused on questions that have not been asked or, if asked, have not been answered satisfactorily. These include questions such as the following: What are the moral, ethical, and economic issues associated with offshore outsourcing? What is the effect of outsourcing on United States employment? Is the United States prepared to compete in a globalized market? What does the United States need to invest in now to counterbalance the negative effects of outsourcing on American workers? These readings give an overview of the questions that experts feel are not being asked or answered fully and suggest that the long-range effects of outsourcing have not been fully anticipated.

○

JOHN CASSIDY

Winners and Losers

Argues that the United States must invest in its human, social, and cultural capital if it wants to meet capably the challenges of a global economy.

○

TIME MAGAZINE'S BOARD OF ECONOMISTS

Think Globally, Act Locally

Time's board of economists says that the outsourcing debate has been ignoring a larger question.

○

MATERIAL HANDLING MANAGEMENT, AUGUST 2004:16

It's a Small World After All

Suggests that outsourcing could cost United States businesses more than they think.

QUESTIONS FOR DISCUSSION OR WRITING

1. What issues associated with outsourcing are not being addressed fully, according to the writers of these articles?
2. John Cassidy in "Winners and Losers" suggests that the United States is not willing to invest in what it needs to ensure the prosperity of the country. Are you convinced by his argument?
3. What issues about offshore outsourcing do you think are the most important to explore when weighing its benefits and drawbacks?

Chapter 26 The Global Marketplace

Does the United States, which has a robust presence in the global marketplace, have an obligation to help weaker nations become economically stronger? Many American manufacturers are profiting from their position in the global marketplace. Should such businesses bear the responsibility of helping to strengthen the economic stability of weaker developing countries? What part, if any, should American businesses play in helping developing countries overcome the conditions that keep its economy weak? And if they should play a role, what form should that role take? These questions are being asked by economists, foreign policy analysts, heads of businesses, and others concerned about the health of poor nations in contrast to that of wealthy nations enjoying a robust global economy. Poor nations not only have weak economies, with a high rate of poverty, but they also have high levels of disease, illiteracy, and starvation. These articles treat the subject of what healthy nations vigorously active in the global marketplace ought to do to help weaker ones.

○

MICHAEL SMITH AND JOHN BOND

Businesses Urged to Close the World's Poverty Gaps

Suggests ways that business can make a difference in countries with emerging economies.

○

MOIN SIDDIQI

No Real Will to Attack Global Poverty

Argues that there is little or no real commitment to help solve the problems of the developing world.

○

BARBARA FRASER AND PAUL JEFFREY

A Call for Economic Change: Latin America Today

Focuses on Latin America's search for a future and the role other nations can play in helping them reach that goal.

QUESTIONS FOR DISCUSSION OR WRITING

1. What factors account for the widening economic gap between rich countries and poor?
2. What do these readings suggest must or ought to be done to help developing countries achieve equality in the global community?
3. What do you consider the key issues in the question of what, if anything, American businesses should do to help developing countries improve their economy?

APPENDIX

1

DEFINITIONS OF TERMS USED IN DISCUSSION QUESTIONS AND WRITING TOPICS

Abstract. A summary of the essential points of a text. It is usually quite short, no more than a paragraph.

Analysis. Dividing a subject into its separate parts for individual study.

Argument/persuasion. An argument is an attempt to prove the validity of a position by offering supporting proof. Persuasion takes argument one step further by convincing an audience to adopt a viewpoint or take action.

Book review. A report that summarizes only the main ideas of a book and provides critical commentary on it. Usually in a book review, you will also be asked to give your personal response to the book, including both your opinion of the ideas it presents and an evaluation of its worth or credibility.

Case study. A situation or profile of a person or persons, for which you provide a context and background information.

Citation. A reference that provides supporting illustrations or examples for your own ideas; the authority or source of that information is identified.

Comparison. A likeness or strong similarity between two things.

Contrast. A difference or strong dissimilarity between two things.

Debate. A discussion involving opposing points in an argument. In formal debate, opposing teams defend and attack a specific proposition.

Description. A conveyance through words of the essential nature of a thing.

Diction. A writer's word choice and level of usage, which varies in informal and formal language; slang, regional, nonstandard, and colloquial language; and jargon.

Evaluation. A judgment about worth, quality, or credibility.

Forum. An open discussion or exchange of ideas among many people.

Freewriting. The act of writing down every idea that occurs to you about your topic without stopping to examine what you are writing.

Hypothesis. A tentative explanation to account for some phenomenon or set of facts. It is in essence a theory or an assumption that can be tested by further investigation and is assumed to be true for the purpose of argument or investigation.

Illustration. An explanation or clarification, usually using example or comparison.

Journal. A personal record of experiences, thoughts, or responses to something, usually kept separate from other writings, as in a diary or notebook.

Literature search. A process of locating titles of articles, books, and other material on a specific subject.

Narration. Telling a story.

Panel discussion. A small group of people (usually between three and six) gathered to discuss a topic. Often each member of a panel is prepared to represent a certain position or point of view on the subject of discussion, with time left after the presentations for questions from audience members.

Paraphrase. A restatement of a passage in your own words. A paraphrase is somewhat shorter than the original but retains its essential meaning.

Position paper. A detailed report that explains, justifies, or recommends a particular course of action.

Proposition. A statement of a position on a subject, a course of action, or a topic for discussion or debate.

Reflective writing. A process of drawing on personal experience to offer your own response to something. For this kind of writing, use the first person.

Report. A detailed account of something.

Subject. A general or broad area of interest.

Summary. A shortened version of a passage, stated in your own words. A summary resembles a paraphrase, in that you are conveying the essence of the original, but it is shorter than a paraphrase.

Synthesis. Combining the ideas of two or more authors and integrating those ideas into your own discussion.

Thesis. A statement of the specific purpose of a paper. A thesis is essentially a one-sentence summary of what you will argue, explain, illustrate, define, describe, or otherwise develop in the rest of the paper. It usually comes very early in a paper.

Tone. A writer's attitude toward the subject and the audience, conveyed through word choice and diction.

Topic. A specific, focused, and clearly defined area of interest. A topic is a narrow aspect of a subject.

Workshop. Similar in intent to a forum, a workshop is characterized by exchanges of information, ideas, and opinions, usually among a small group of people. Both workshops and forums involve interaction and exchange of ideas more than panel discussions, which typically allot more time to panel members than to audience participants.

FORMATTING GUIDELINES FOR COURSE PAPERS

Your instructor may give you formatting guidelines for your papers, but if not, the following guidelines should serve you well in most cases.

MARGINS, SPACING, AND PAGE NUMBERS

Leave a one-inch margin on both sides and at the top and bottom of each page, except for the page number. Double space everything throughout the paper. Number pages consecutively throughout the paper except for the first page, which you need not number. Place page numbers on the right-hand side, one-half inch from the top of the paper, flush with the right margin. Some instructors request that you include your last name with each page number after the first.

HEADING AND TITLE ON FIRST PAGE

If your instructor tells you to put the endorsement on the first page of your paper rather than on a separate title page, drop down one inch from the top of the first page and write all the information your instructor requires flush with the left margin. Then write your title, centered on the page. Double space between all lines, including between the date and the title and between the title and the first line of the paper. Do not underline your own title or put it in quotation marks.

Elizabeth Konrad
Professor Lee
English 102
November 28, 2005

The Place of Spirituality in the College Curriculum

Education today is more complicated than ever before. The rapid rate at which knowledge increases and the almost constantly changing nature of our society and the jobs required to sustain it put great pressure on institutions of higher education and students alike.

TITLE PAGE

If your instructor requires a title page, center your title about half way down the page. Do not underline your title or use quotation marks around it. Underneath the title, write your name. Then drop down the page and put your instructor's name, the course, and the date.

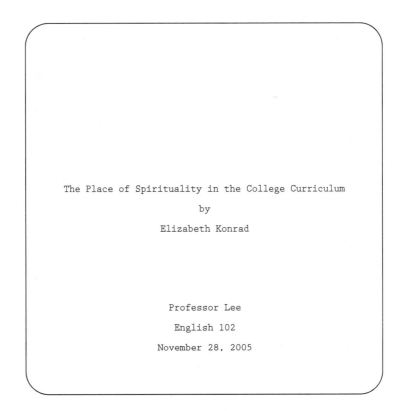

CREDITS

American Spectator commentary. "The Galileo of Global Warming," May 2001. Reprinted by permission of *American Spectator*.

Annan, Kofi. "Development Without Borders." *Harvard International Review*, 23.2 (Summer 2001): 84. Reprinted by permission.

Applebaum, Richard, and Peter Dreier. "SweatX Closes Up Shop." Reprinted with permission from the July 19, 2004, issue of *The Nation*. For subscription information, call 1-800-333-8536. Portions of each week's Nation magazine can be accessed at http://www.thenation.com.

Ash, Timothy Garton. "Fortress America." Reprinted by permission of the author.

Bacon, Perry. "How Much Diversity Do You Want from Me?" © 2003 TIME Inc. Reprinted by permission.

Baron, Lee Ann Fisher. "The Influence of 'Junk Science' and the Role of Science Education." Copyright © 2001. Reprinted by permission from *IMPRIMIS*, the monthly journal of Hillsdale College.

Barrett, Wayne M. and Bernard Rowe. "What's Wrong with America and Can Anything Be Done About It?" Reprinted from *USA Today Magazine*, November 1994, Copyright © 1994 by the Society for the Advancement of Education.

Berdik, Chris. "Voices from Abroad." *The Boston Globe*, June 27, 2004. Reprinted with permission.

Bernikow, Louise. "Cinderella at the Movies," pp. 17–37 of *Among Women* by Louise Bernikow. Reprinted by permission of the author.

Bok, Sissela. "Aggression: The Impact of Media Violence." From *Mayhem: Violence as Public Entertainment by Sissela Bok*. Copyright © 1998 by Sissela Bok. Reprinted by permission of Perseus Books PLC, a member of Perseus Books, L.L.C.

Booth, William. "One Nation, Indivisible: Is It History?" Copyright © 1998. The Washington Post. Reprinted with permission.

Borosage, Robert. "Mixing '60s Activisim and Anti-Globalization." *Los Angeles Times*, April 23, 2000. Reproduced by permission of the publisher via Copyright Clearance Center, Inc.

Boyle, Matthew. "Beware the Killjoy," from the 7/23/2001 issue of *Fortune*. Copyright © 2001 Time Inc. All rights reserved. Reprinted with permission.

Bronowski, Jacob. "The Reach of the Imagination." Delivered as the Blashfield Address, May 1966. Reprinted by permission from the *Proceedings* of the American Academy of Arts and Letters and the National Institute of Arts and Letters, second series, no. 17, 1967, and by the Estate of Jacob Bronowski.

Jennings, Marianne M. "The Real Generation Gap," from the August 1998 issue of *IMPRIMIS.* Reprinted by permission from *IMPRIMIS,* the monthly journal of Hillsdale College.

Kilbourne, Jean. "Advertising's Influence on Media Content." Reprinted with the permission of The Free Press, a Division of Simon & Schuster, Inc., from *Can't Buy My Love: How Advertising Changes the Way We Think and Feel* (originally published as *Deadly Persuasion*) by Jean Kilbourne. Copyright © 1999 by Jean Kilbourne. All rights reserved.

Kingsolver, Barbara. "A Pure, High Note of Anguish." Copyright © 2001, Los Angeles Times. Reprinted with permission.

Kleck, Gary. "There Are No Lessons to Be Learned from Littleton." Reprinted by permission of The Institute for Criminal Justice Ethics, 555 West 57th Street, Suite 601, New York, NY 10019-1029.

Kohn, Alfie. ""The Dangerous Myth of Grade Inflation." Copyright © 2002 by Alfie Kohn. Reprinted from the *Chronicle of Higher Education* with the author's permission.

Kotlowitz, Alex. "Colorblind." Copyright © 1998 by The New York Times Co. Reprinted by permission.

Krauthammer, Charles. "Smallpox Shots: Make them Mandatory," copyright © 2002 by Time, Inc. Reprinted by permission.

Lamson, Susan R. "TV Violence: Does it Cause Real-life Mayhem?" Reprinted with permission of the National Rifle Association of America.

Lee, Linda. "Who Needs College?" Reprinted with the permission of *Family Circle* magazine.

Leo, John. "Liberal media? I'm shocked!" Copyright © 2004 U. S. News & World Report, L. P. Reprinted with permission.

Levy, Steven. *"The Day I Got Napsterized."* From *Newsweek,* 5/28/01. Copyright © 2001 Newsweek, Inc. All rights reserved. Reprinted by permission.

Leymarie, Isabelle. "Rock 'n' Revolt," from reprinted from *The UNESCO Courier,* February 1993.

Lyon, Jeff. "Playing God: Has Science Gone Too Far?" Reprinted with permission from *Family Circle* magazine.

Males, Mike. "Stop Blaming Kids and TV." Reprinted by permission from The Progressive, 409 East Main Street, Madison, WI 53703.

Mansfield, Harvey C. "Grade Inflation: It's Time to Face the Facts." Copyright © 2001 by Harvey C. Mansfield. Reprinted from the *Chronicle of Higher Education* with the author's permission.

Matthews, Jay. "For Love or Money." Copyright © 1993, The Washington Post. Reprinted with permission.

McCullough, David. "No Time to Read?" Reprinted with the permission of *Family Circle* magazine.

McGeary, Johanna. "Death Stalks a Continent." Copyright © 2001 by Time, Inc. Reprinted by permission.

McWhorter, John. "Up from Hip-Hop." Reprinted from COMMENTARY, March 2003, by permission; all rights reserved.

Mitchell, Whitney. "Deconstructing Gender, Sex, and Sexuality as Applied to Identity." Reprinted with permission of *The Humanist.*

Moody, Howard. "Sacred Rite or Civil Right?" Reprinted with permission from the June 5, 2004, issue of *The Nation.* For subscription information, call 1-800-333-8536. Portions of each week's *Nation* magazine can be accessed at <http://www.thenation.com>.

Sullivan, John. "Deadly Stakes: The Debate over Capital Punishment." Reprinted by permission of the author.

Tanzi, Vito. "Globalization Without a Net." Reprinted with permission from *Foreign Policy* #125 (July/August 2002). Copyright © 2002 by the Carnegie Endowment for International Peace.

Tierney, John. "Here Come the Alpha Pups." Copyright © 2001 The New York Times Co. Reprinted with permission.

Twitchell, James B. "In Praise of Consumerism." From *Lead Us into Temptation* by James Twitchell. Copyright © 1999. Reprinted by permission of Columbia University Press.

Venkatraman, N. Venkat. "Offshoring Without Guilt." Reprinted from *MIT Sloan Management Review* Spring 2004: 14+, by permission of publisher. Copyright © 2004 by Massachusetts Institute of Technology. All rights reserved.

Watson, James D. "All for the Good." Copyright © 1999 by Time, Inc. Reprinted by permission.

Weidenbaum, Murray. "Dispelling the Myths about the Global Economy." Reprinted by permission of the author.

Williams, Harold M. "Don't Ignore the Arts." Reprinted from *USA Today Magazine,* September 1995, Copyright © 1995 by the Society for the Advancement of Education.

Wilmut, Ian. "Dolly's False Legacy," *Time* magazine, January 11, 1999. Reprinted by permission of the author.

Wolkomir, Joyce, and Richard Wolkomir. "You Are What You Buy." Reprinted with permission from the October 2000 *Smithsonian.* Copyright © 2000 by Richard and Joyce Wokomir.

PHOTO/REALIA CREDITS

INDEX